OXFORD STUDIES IN EUROPEAN LAW

General Editors: PAUL CRAIG AND GRÁINNE DE BÚRCA

The Foundations of European Union Competition Law

Competition Law

The Objective and Principles of Article 102

The Foundations
of European Union
Competition Law

The Objective and Principles of Article 102

RENATO NAZZINI

OXFORD
UNIVERSITY PRESS

OXFORD
UNIVERSITY PRESS

Great Clarendon Street, Oxford, OX2 6DP,
United Kingdom

Oxford University Press is a department of the University of Oxford.
It furthers the University's objective of excellence in research, scholarship,
and education by publishing worldwide. Oxford is a registered trade mark of
Oxford University Press in the UK and in certain other countries

Published in the United States of America by Oxford University Press
198 Madison Avenue, New York, NY 10016, United States of America

British Library Cataloguing in Publication Data
Data available

Library of Congress Control Number: 2011939865

ISBN 978–0–19–922615–3

To the memory of Professor Avv. Vincenzo Cavallo

Preface

In this book I have endeavoured to develop a coherent analytical framework for the application of Article 102 of the Treaty on the Functioning of the European Union (TFEU) that is faithful to the normative and legal foundations of EU competition law. The task has taken much longer than I expected. When I conceived this book, I had in mind a short monograph explaining how Article 102 should be applied in the light of its welfare objective, which at the time I believed to be the welfare of consumers. Over the years, and with the benefit of short but intense periods of research in almost total seclusion, my thinking has changed significantly. It soon became apparent to me that consumer welfare was not—and could not be—the objective of EU competition law. It took me longer to understand what the objective of EU competition law is, not least because, as time went by, this question became intertwined with the more general problem of the purpose of competition law from a normative point of view. In the end, I have come to the conclusion that competition law should aim at maximizing the long-term welfare of society as a whole and that it is possible to understand social welfare not simply as a monetary measure of industry surplus but as the reflection of the values of society as enshrined in its legal order at a given time in history. This normatively optimal objective was also the objective that the Treaty of Rome of 1957 assigned to the competition rules of the European Economic Community and is still the objective of the competition rules of the TFEU. Free trade, economic freedom, and fairness and equality of opportunities are not necessarily inconsistent with it. On the contrary, properly understood, these concepts can function as operational norms ensuring the full effectiveness of the long-term social welfare objective of competition law.

Having thus clarified the normative and legal foundations of EU competition law, I set out to develop a systematic approach to the assessment of conduct that may be abusive under Article 102 TFEU, including not only exclusionary but also exploitative and discriminatory abuses. To the best of my knowledge, this task has not been undertaken so far in a book with the same coverage and methodology as this one. At this point I should, however, stop. It is not the purpose of a Preface to explain the structure and the method of the prefaced work and to demonstrate what the author believes to be its strengths and originality. This is the task of the Introduction, to which I would refer the readers who have been so patient as to read as far as here and would like to learn more. In this Preface, I simply wanted to give a retrospective account of the evolution of my thinking on the objective of competition law that lies at the heart of this book, but that may not be apparent in the book itself. And I hope that my students, my friends, and my publisher will one day forgive me if this reflection has taken so long. But so that I shall not soon be in the position to beg for forgiveness also for the excessive length of the Preface, I must now turn without hesitation to its more important part.

Many institutions and individuals have deserved the acknowledgment of my gratitude for contributing, directly or indirectly, to the strengths of this book, while I remain solely responsible for its weaknesses. Among my academic colleagues, I am particularly grateful to the Head of the Law School of the University of Southampton, Professor Natalie Lee, who understands the challenges and demands of academic research (something not to be taken for granted); to Dr Okeoghene Odudu, for agreeing to read a much longer version of this work in the autumn of 2010; to Professor Richard Whish, who, with his usual generosity, helped me recruit one of my research assistants; and to Professors Silvia Ferreri, Gianmaria Ajani, Raffaele Caterina, and Michele Graziadei, for their support during my Visiting Professorship at the University of Turin, when I wrote key parts of what are now Chapters 6 and 7. In addition, I would like to thank those who greatly facilitated the writing of this book by exceeding any expectation of high professional standards, and in particular the staff of the Central Archives of the Council of the European Union, Joy Caisley, Law and Official Publications Librarian at the University of Southampton, and the Oxford University Press teams who have been involved in the different stages of the publication process. Above all, I would like to acknowledge the invaluable help provided by my research assistants Baskaran Balasingham, Scott Spearman, and Gillian Waugh, and also by my PhD student Valerio Torti. Gillian was especially helpful in providing much needed discipline during the long months when the first draft of this book was completed. Some discipline—but not too much—was also provided, during the two long Italian summers of 2008 and 2009, by Anna Rossini, with whom I held long and unconventional conversations on many of the issues which are dealt with in Chapters 6 to 8.

This book is dedicated to the memory of my grandfather, for the example he set for me as a scholar and for his work on the relationship between human freedom and the concept of legal liability,[1] which inspired my reflection on the concept of freedom underpinning the treatment of this topic in Chapters 2 and 4.

Renato Nazzini
Maenam

August 2011

---

[1] This theme occupied him from the beginning of his career. Indeed, it was his very first monograph which laid the foundations for his future work in this area: see V Cavallo, *La Libertà Umana Nella Filosofia Contemporanea* (Napoli-Città di Castello, F Perrella 1933).

Contents

II LEGAL FOUNDATIONS

III TESTS OF ABUSE

List of Figures

List of Abbreviations

General

AAC	average avoidable cost(s)
AC	average costs(s)
AFC	average fixed costs
AR	average revenue
ATC	average total costs(s)
AVC	average variable cost(s)
CAT	Competition Appeal Tribunal (UK)
CCAT	Competition Commission Appeal Tribunal
CSR	corporate social responsibility
DoJ	Department of Justice (US)
DRAM	dynamic random access memory
DTI	Department of Trade and Industry
ECHR	European Convention on Human Rights (in full, Convention for the Protection of Human Rights and Fundamental Freedoms)
ECSC	European Coal and Steel Community
Euratom	European Atomic Energy Community
FTC	Federal Trade Commission (US)
ICN	International Competition Network
LRAIC	long-run average incremental cost(s)
LRATC	long-run average total cost(s)
MC	marginal cost(s)
MR	marginal revenue
OECD	Organisation for Economic Co-operation and Development
OFT	Office of Fair Trading (UK)
SMEs	small and medium-sized enterprises
SRATC	short-run average total cost(s)
TC	total cost(s)
TEU	Treaty on European Union
TFEU	Treaty on the Functioning of the European Union

Publications

CLJ	Cambridge Law Journal
CLP	Current Legal Problems

CML Rev	Common Market Law Review
Comp Law	Competition Law Journal
EBOR	European Business Organization Law Review
ECC	European Commercial Cases
ECLR	European Competition Law Review
EIPR	European Intellectual Property Review
EL Rev	European Law Review
ELJ	European Law Journal
ICLQ	International and Comparative Law Quarterly
Ind Org Rev	Industrial Organization Review
Intl J Ind Org	International Journal of Industrial Organization
Intl Rev IP & Comp L	International Review of Intellectual Property and Competition Law
J Comp L & Econ	Journal of Competition Law and Economics
JL Econ & Org	Journal of Law, Economics and Organization
LIEI	Legal Issues of Economic Integration
Mich L Rev	Michigan Law Review
NYU L Rev	New York University Law Review
OJLS	Oxford Journal of Legal Studies
Rev Econ Stud	Review of Economic Studies
Rev Econ & Stat	Review of Economics and Statistics
Rev Ind Org	Review of Industrial Organization
SMU L Rev	Southern Methodist University Law Review
Stan L Rev	Stanford Law Review
U Chi L Rev	University of Chicago Law Review
Minn L Rev	Minnesota Law Review
YEL	Yearbook of European Law

Table of Cases

GENERAL COURT/COURT OF FIRST INSTANCE

Alphabetical

Numerical

EUROPEAN COMMISSION

EUROPEAN COURT OF HUMAN RIGHTS CASES

NATIONAL CASES

France

United Kingdom

General

Office of Fair Trading

Competition Commission

United States

Table of Treaties and Conventions

Table of European Union Legislation

Table of National Legislation

1

Introduction

A. The problem

Article 102 prohibits any abuse by one or more undertakings of a dominant position within the internal market. It is a fundamental element of the economic law of the European Union. However, its objective and scope are undefined. Therefore, since the very first cases that it had to decide, the Court of Justice has had to adopt a teleological approach to its interpretation.[1] A teleological interpretation of Article 102 is the only way to give substantive content to the provision by turning the open-textured concept of abuse into operational tests that are neither arbitrary nor the expression of discretionary policy choices but the outcome of an hermeneutic process solidly anchored to the rule of law. However, the determination of the objective of Article 102 within the wider context of the Treaty or Treaties as in force at the relevant time has always been a legally complex and politically difficult exercise. The EU courts have often shied away from a robust analytical approach to identifying the goals of EU competition law by hiding themselves behind formulas derived from the text of the Treaties. Following the structure of the Treaties, Article 102 has, therefore, been construed as a provision aimed at ensuring that competition is not distorted. Undistorted competition has in turn been understood as aiming to achieve the general objectives of the Union.[2] While this interpretive process is correct, the case law has done little more than quote extracts from the Treaties without exploring the rationale for its conclusions.[3] As a result, the objective of EU competition law, and of Article 102 in particular, has been left obscure. This has led to the development of principles and tests under Article 102 that may appear to lack a coherent analytical underpinning and adopt formalistic approaches to different types of conduct that are potentially anti-competitive. Since the mid-1990s, the case law on EU competition law has come under increasing criticism by those who argued that competition law, and, therefore, also Article 102, should be concerned with economic welfare or efficiency and not with the protection of competition defined as

---

[1] eg Case 6/72 *Europemballage Corp and Continental Can Co Inc v Commission* [1973] ECR 215 (*Continental Can*), paras 24–29.

[2] eg Case C-52/09 *Konkurrensverket v TeliaSonera Sverige AB* (17 February 2011) (*TeliaSonera*), paras 20–22.

[3] ibid. See also the case law on dominance, eg Case 27/76 *United Brands Co and United Brands Continentaal BV v Commission* [1978] ECR 207, paras 63–65.

a pluralistic market structure. The European Commission went along with this view. In a number of guidelines, the guardian of the Treaties appears to have made a conscious policy decision to interpret Article 101 as a provision mainly concerned with the protection of consumer welfare.[4] The Court of First Instance was sympathetic to this approach[5] but was rebuked by the Court of Justice.[6] This state of affairs has had significant implications for the prevailing discourse on the law on Article 102, especially in the English-language literature and economic circles. Commentators have focused on the need to interpret Article 102 as protecting consumer welfare and have reproached the EU courts for continuing to adopt a formalistic, structuralist, or 'ordoliberal' approach to abuse of dominance.[7] To respond to these criticisms, the Commission attempted a process of 'modernization' of Article 102. In 2005, it published a Discussion Paper on exclusionary abuses.[8] While this was never the stated policy position, the natural outcome of such an exercise would have been the publication of guidelines inspired by the same principles as those on Article 101. Instead, after a considerable amount of time had passed, the Commission issued a Guidance on Article 102, which is limited to setting the Commission's enforcement priorities in relation to exclusionary abuses and does not purport to be a statement of the law on Article 102.[9] The Guidance adopts a consumer welfare approach which appears to be broadly consistent with the policy on Article 101 and mergers. However, because it is neither based on a teleological interpretation of Article 102 nor does it follow the case law, such an approach raises more problems that it solves. Given that the Commission appears to have made a choice, it becomes even more important to understand the objective of Article 102. Only once the objective has been identified, can the legal tests for dominance and abuse be understood and developed consistently with the teleological hermeneutics that the case law mandates. That is the aim of this book.

[4] eg Commission Notice—Guidelines on Vertical Restraints [2000] OJ C291/1, now replaced by the Guidelines on Vertical Restraints [2010] OJ C130/1; Communication from the Commission—Notice—Guidelines on the application of Article 81(3) of the Treaty [2004] OJ C101/97 (Guidelines on Art 101(3)).

[5] Case T-168/01 *GlaxoSmithKline Services Unlimited v Commission* [2006] ECR II-2969.

[6] Joined Cases C-501/06 P, C-513/06 P, C-515/06 P, and C-519/06 P *GlaxoSmithKline Services Unlimited v Commission* [2009] ECR I-9291.

[7] It would be pointless to cite here the vast literature on this topic, which is discussed throughout this book. See, as illustrative of the trends highlighted in the text, C Ahlborn, DS Evans, and JA Padilla, 'The Antitrust Economics of Tying: A Farewell to Per Se Illegality' (2004) 49 Antitrust Bull 297; J Kallaugher and B Sher, 'Rebates Revisited: Anti-Competitive Effects and Exclusionary Abuse under Article 82' (2004) 25 ECLR 263; M Motta and A de Streel, 'Excessive Pricing and Price Squeeze under EU Law' in CD Ehlermann and I Atanasiu (eds), *European Competition Law Annual 2003: What Is an Abuse of a Dominant Position?* (Oxford, Hart Publishing 2006) 91.

[8] European Commission, DG Comp, 'DG Competition discussion paper on the application of Article 82 of the Treaty to exclusionary abuses' (Brussels, December 2005) (the 'DG Comp Discussion Paper on Art 102').

[9] Communication from the Commission—Guidance on the Commission's enforcement priorities in applying Article 82 of the EC Treaty to abusive exclusionary conduct by dominant undertakings ('Guidance on Art 102') [2009] OJ C45/7.

B. The method

The analysis in this book is carried out in a way which is different from the current approaches to Article 102 in at least three ways.

First, this book adopts an integrated and holistic approach to the analysis of the objective and the tests of Article 102. To understand Article 102, it is necessary to study its objective and the dominance and abuse tests across the whole spectrum of exclusion, exploitation, and discrimination. Any results arrived at by focusing only on exclusionary abuses would be inherently suspect because they would lack the benefit of the understanding of important areas of application of Article 102. In this holistic approach to Article 102, the EU courts and the Commission have not been sufficiently supported by the literature. There are a myriad articles and book chapters on individual aspects of Article 102 but, by their very nature, such contributions cannot provide the integrated analysis of the objective and tests that a holistic approach requires. The few, very valuable, English-language monographs on the subject are also limited in scope. They have either not provided a thorough normative and legal analysis of the objective of Article 102[10] or have focused on exclusionary abuses only.[11] As a consequence, their conclusions lack the foundation of either a solid teleological interpretation of Article 102 or a holistic approach to exclusion, exploitation, and discrimination seen as different aspects of the same objective and analytical foundations. Also different from this book are contributions with a stronger focus on the objective but without an integrated analysis of the full implications of the identification of the objective of Article 102 for the development of the legal tests of anti-competitive exclusion, exploitation, and discrimination.[12] This book rests on the methodological premise that in order to reach robust conclusions on how Article 102 should be applied, it is necessary to accomplish both tasks: that is, to identify, on the basis of a thorough normative and legal analysis, the objective of Article 102 and to study the tests that apply to all types of abuses in the light of the objective in question. In carrying out both tasks, the method is both deductive and inductive. Certain principles, for instance that less efficient competitors must not be protected under Article 102, can be derived directly from its objective. Other principles, for instance those that apply to determining whether below-cost prices are abusive, must be understood by reviewing the case law in the light of the objective of Article 102. This method produces interesting results, above all the conclusion that the case law of the EU courts is not at all out of line with the

---

[10] E Rousseva, *Rethinking Exclusionary Abuses in EU Competition Law* (Oxford, Hart Publishing 2010) and R O'Donoghue and AJ Padilla, *The Law and Economics of Article 82 EC* (Oxford, Hart Publishing 2006).

[11] Rousseva, *Rethinking Exclusionary Abuses in EU Competition Law*; LL Gormsen, *A Principled Approach to Abuse of Dominance in European Competition Law* (Cambridge, CUP 2010) 113–149.

[12] Gormsen, *A Principled Approach to Abuse of Dominance in European Competition Law*.

objective of Article 102. On the contrary, the EU courts have developed a coherent framework of principles and tests that form a solid fabric on which to build a predictable and effective abuse of dominance regime. This is not to say that the case law is perfect as it is. This book will recommend significant changes in vast and hugely important areas of the law such as conditional above-cost rebates, tying, market-distorting discrimination, and exploitation. But these changes are incremental and not revolutionary because they represent developments, often radical and controversial, but developments nevertheless: not an abandonment of the fundamental values and principles that the EU courts have correctly indentified as underpinning Article 102.

Secondly, this book examines the objective and principles of Article 102 within the framework of the Treaties. The point may seem obvious but the analysis of the objective of the EU competition rules is all too often driven by policy considerations and not by the values which the Member States have enshrined in the Treaties as the foundations of the European polity. In the development of the competition tests, there is often an undisclosed assumption that the competition rules are special and insensitive to the overall system of EU law. However, nothing could be more wrong. The competition rules are explicitly linked to the objectives of the European Union, and the EU courts approach competition issues in much the same way as they would approach other issues, for instance in the area of the free movement of goods and services. This way of understanding Article 102 produces significant results, perhaps the most important of which is that the TFEU competition rules, and Article 102 in particular, do not have the objective of promoting or protecting consumer welfare, not even as one of several objectives. Article 102 has one overarching objective: to maximize long-term social welfare, this being understood as the sum of producer and consumer surplus incorporating the values and the positive and negative preferences of society. But the relevance of the contextualization of EU competition law goes beyond the debate on its objective. It reveals, for instance, that the general framework of Article 102 is based on the principle of proportionality, which has implications for the distinction between prima facie tests and defences, for the varying intensity of anti-competitive effect required under different abuse tests, and for the way in which objective justification defences are examined.

Thirdly, this book analyses Article 102 not only from a legal perspective but also under the lense of economics. It does so, however, in a way which is different from many studies in this field. The aim of the interdisciplinary approach in this book is not to assess the law against the yardstick of given economic theories or models; neither is it to understand whether the law reflects one given economic school of thought or another, or perhaps a combination of several, and in what proportion. These are relevant aspects of the analysis but not the most important ones. Instead, the adopted methodology reverses the relationship between law and economics on the assumption that a society based on the rule of law has chosen its economic values by creating a given legal framework. As a result, economics serves two purposes, one external and one internal to the legal process. In its external role, economics verifies whether the law is fit to achieve its intended objective. In its internal role, economics contributes to shaping legal tests in order to enable them to achieve their intended purposes. These two roles of economics mean that it is necessary to make value choices from among economic theories on the basis of the model of society that the competition rules enact or reflect. On this basis, economics provides key insights to understanding the law on predation, tying, conditional rebates, and discrimination, albeit this approach does not necessarily lead to the conclusions that the proponents of the 'more economic' or 'effects-based' approach to Article 102 would expect. To give only a few examples, this book concludes that the current law on predation is correct and recoupment should not be a necessary element of the test, and that tying should be examined under an intent test.

C. The structure of the inquiry

This book is divided into five Parts. The first is devoted to a purely normative analysis of the objective of competition law and the tests for abuse of dominance. The analysis is based on economics, political economy, and modern philosophy. This separation of the normative analysis from the legal hermeneutics has three advantages. First, it avoids the contamination of the legal interpretation with normative values or choices. If the legal interpretation yields results that are inconsistent with the optimal normative standards, the solution is to change the law not to distort its interpretation. Secondly, it allows the normative analysis to perform its external role in a transparent way: the results of the legal analysis can be compared with the results of the normative analysis simply by juxtaposing the results in Part I and the results in Parts II and III. Thirdly, it allows the normative analysis to perform its internal function effectively: assuming the objective of the law is consistent with the normatively optimal objective, the legal tests may be developed by importing principles from Part I into Parts II and III.

Part II sets out the legal analysis of the objective and the general framework of Article 102. Chapter 4 identifies the objective of EU competition law and Article 102 in particular, coming to the conclusion that consumer welfare is not a relevant objective of EU competition law. Instead, the Treaties establish that long-term social welfare is the objective of the competition rules. The Court of Justice has clearly recognized this.[13] Market integration, economic freedom, and fairness or equality of opportunities are legal norms that must be understood in the light of this objective. But how does Article 102 give effect to the long-term social welfare objective? Chapter 5 sets out the conceptual and contextual premises of the tests under Article 102. These are the development of proportionality as an analytical

---

[13] Case C-52/09 *TeliaSonera* paras 20–21; Case C-94/00 *Roquette Frères SA v Directeur général de la concurrence, de la consommation et de la répression des fraudes* [2002] ECR I-9011, para 42; Joined Cases 46/87 and 227/88 *Hoechst AG v Commission* [1989] ECR 2859, para 25.

structure and the application of the principle of proportionality in EU law in general and under Article 101 in particular. The chapter goes on to analyse the proportionality test under Article 102 and the key principles that shape the concept of abuse, namely the definition of abuse in the case law, the meaning of effective competition, and the 'doctrine' of the special responsibility of the dominant undertaking. Finally, the chapter examines the causal link between dominance, conduct, and effect. Part III develops the tests for the assessment of potential abusive conduct. Chapters 6 to 8 examine the three tests that the EU courts have applied to determine whether conduct is prima facie abusive under Article 102: the intent test (or tests), the as efficient competitor test, and the consumer harm test. The analysis is carried out by test and not, as is normally done, by abuse. This approach allows for the detection of the main themes in the complex case law of the EU courts and for parallels to be drawn between the principles relevant to abuses that have traditionally been seen as different, such as, for instance, predation and tying or margin squeeze and conditional rebates. Overall, these chapters demonstrate that the case law of the EU courts relies on a set of values and assumptions that are consistent with both the objective of Article 102 and the normative standards identified in Part I. The main problem with the case law is that it fails to articulate clear narratives capable of giving the law the required level of legitimacy, coherence, and predictability. These chapters also identify the main areas where the case law is in need of being reviewed because it is not consistent with the objective of Article 102. Chapter 9 analyses the often neglected topic of defences. Here, too, an abuse-by-abuse approach is rejected. After a discussion of the burden of proof and the standard of anti-competitive effects, Chapter 9 deals with two types of defence: proportionality defences and objective justification. Objective justification is understood to comprise an efficiency defence and a social welfare defence. This new taxonomy provides a more robust basis for a balancing of the benefits of potentially anti-competitive conduct against the harm it causes. Currently, the scales lean too heavily in favour of finding an infringement and against the consideration of the long-term benefits of conduct by dominant undertakings. The Guidance on Article 102 reinforces this trend. This approach is, however, inconsistent with the objective of Article 102 and should be restored to a more balanced position.

Part IV examines dominance. In the standard treatment of Article 102, dominance is discussed before the abuse. This is also what happens in practice, for reasons of expediency and judicial economy: an undertaking which is not dominant, cannot commit an abuse. However, the analytic of the concept of dominance logically follows the definition of abuse. Only if it is clear what abuse means, is it possible to understand why an abuse can only be committed only by certain undertakings that Article 102 considers to be dominant. Dominance itself is a complex concept. Article 102 and the case law would appear to suggest that there is a unitary concept of dominance. Instead, there are three: single dominance, which is discussed in Chapter 10, and non-oligopolistic and oligopolistic collective dominance, which are both discussed in Chapter 11.

Part V brings together the different strands of the analysis developed throughout the book. Chapter 12 sets out the main conclusions. It does so in three ways: (a) by setting out the main reasoning of the book, from the identification of the normative objective of competition law to the development of the tests; (b) by setting out the main principles and tests developed in the analysis so as to present a coherent analytical framework for the assessment of abuse under Article 102; and (c) by pointing out the main areas in the case law of the EU courts and in the enforcement practice of the Commission that need to be reviewed in order to bring the current application of the law into line with the purpose and principles of Article 102.

PART I

NORMATIVE FOUNDATIONS

2

Normative Theory of Competition Law

A. Introduction

This chapter discusses why competition law is beneficial and which objectives it should pursue from a theoretical and normative perspective. The concept of 'competition' is, in and of itself, indeterminate. Moreover, competition rules rely on concepts such as 'prevention, restriction or distortion of competition'[1] or 'abuse...of a dominant position'.[2] These concepts may themselves have different meanings depending on factors such as the political environment, prevailing market conditions, or economic and political theories. As a result, competition law may be used to pursue different objectives. This does not mean, however, that the competition rules of the Treaty on the Functioning of the European Union (TFEU) can be construed differently, depending on which political objectives or economic or political theories are most popular at the time. The TFEU competition provisions are not a mere declaration of intent or a programme to be implemented through a political process; they are rules that have legal effect for Member States and for individuals. Those rules have a prescriptive content ascertainable through a process of interpretation, however complex it may be. Thus, to put it simply, it cannot be the case that an ordoliberal interpretation of Articles 101 and 102 was right up to a point in time, but now a consumer welfare-based interpretation is correct. Either both interpretations coexist as a matter of law, or one must be wrong and the other right. The answer to this alternative does not depend on a theoretical or empirical analysis of which interpretation is preferable, given a normative objective selected regardless of the legal framework of the Treaties. The answer depends on the correct interpretation of the rules given their literal, contextual, and teleological dimension.

These observations are not as obvious as they should be. Much of the debate on the objectives and content of the EU competition rules has centred on the desirability of a consumer welfare objective over an allegedly ordoliberal one, in an astonishing disregard for the interpretation of the rules based on the canons of the legal hermeneutics of EU law. To identify the objectives of EU competition law, a different approach is needed. It is still necessary to discuss the objectives of competition law from a normative perspective but in order to inform the analysis of the competition rules, their legal content, and their function within the framework

---

[1] Art 101(1) TFEU.   [2] Art 102 TFEU.

of the Treaties. In this analysis, economic and political theories of competition are relevant in three ways: first, as the background to understanding the drafting of the Treaties and their subsequent amendments; secondly, as an aid to clarifying the meaning, or at least the possible meanings, of undetermined concepts and phrases; and, thirdly, as normative standards to assess the appropriateness and desirability of the objective of the EU competition rules and the suitability of such rules to achieving their objective. This approach, however, must not be reduced to an *ex post* rationalization or justification of EU competition law. It may well be that, at the end of the inquiry, the EU competition rules are found to be flawed because they pursue the wrong objectives or because the drafters of the Treaties have failed to design rules suitable to achieving their objectives, however desirable and appropriate those objectives would be. Faced with such outcomes, however, an intellectually rigorous analysis founded upon respect for the rule of law would not go on to argue that the EU competition rules should therefore pursue some other objectives, which are considered appropriate and desirable, and be given a different content in order to satisfy these objectives. Rather, it would call for a reform of the Treaties because, however unrealistic this may appear in practice, legal reform would be the only way to achieve the desired normative goal of a competition policy that pursues appropriate and desirable objectives that are not currently reflected in the legal framework. Not only is this the only legally practicable solution, it is also the only politically legitimate one. If the Member States have assigned certain objectives and a given content to the EU competition rules, it is for the Member States alone to change those objectives and that content, and not for bureaucrats or judges backed up by the vocal support of certain quarters of private practice, business, and academia.

However unprincipled and arbitrary the current debate appears to be, this state of affairs is not without its reasons. The Treaties do not make clear which objective or objectives must be ascribed to the EU competition rules. Nor is there a consensus on which objectives competition law should pursue from a normative point of view. Turning to abuse of dominance in particular, a 2007 ICN Report on the Objectives of Unilateral Conduct Laws identified no fewer than ten objectives of unilateral conduct rules: ensuring an effective competitive process,[3] promoting consumer welfare,[4] maximizing efficiency, ensuring economic freedom, ensuring a level playing field for small and medium-sized enterprises (SMEs), promoting fairness and equality, promoting consumer choice, achieving market integration, facilitating privatization and market liberalization, and promoting

---

[3] 'Effective' is a key term in the definition of the competitive process or the market structure which competition law aims at protecting. 'Effective' refers to a relational concept and denotes a competitive process or a competitive market structure which is such as to achieve its intended or desired objectives. A full understanding of the term 'effective' requires, therefore, a definition of the objectives of the competitive process or a competitive market structure. On the meaning of 'effective' in EU Competition Law, see below 172–174.

[4] Consumer welfare or surplus is a consumer's valuation of a product minus the price he paid for it. Consumer welfare or surplus in an industry is the aggregate surplus of all consumers in that industry.

competitiveness in international markets.[5] But even this long catalogue is not complete. At least two further objectives that were not explicitly addressed by the respondents to the ICN questionnaire must be added to this list: increasing productivity[6] and promoting social welfare.[7]

Not only are different objectives of competition law adopted in different jurisdictions but even a single jurisdiction often adopts, in its statutory framework or through evolving court jurisprudence and enforcement practice, more than one objective.[8] It may be tempting to argue that different existing or desirable objectives of competition law may be reconciled and all pursued at the same time. In this way, competition law within a given jurisdiction and the competition laws of different jurisdictions pursuing apparently different objectives would all ensure at the same time an efficient allocation of resources, maximize consumer and social welfare, protect small and medium-sized enterprises, and achieve a level playing field in which all firms and consumers are treated fairly and granted the economic freedom to which they are entitled. However, different objectives of competition law cannot always be reconciled. A simple example illustrates the tension between productive efficiency and consumer welfare. If a higher-cost undertaking enters the market, the dominant undertaking may exclude it by lowering its price below the cost of the entrant but still above its own costs. A consumer welfare-based competition law would protect the entrant in these circumstances because the entrant will increase market output and cause market prices to fall on a lasting basis. An efficiency-based competition law would balance the increase in allocative efficiency resulting from lower prices against the decrease in productive efficiency resulting from the entrant capturing some of the sales of the incumbent. Intervention to protect the less efficient entrant is not as obvious as it would be under a consumer welfare objective.

The trade-offs between different objectives also crucially depend on how each objective is defined. Much of the current confusion stems not only from the

---

[5] International Competition Network (ICN), 'Objectives of Unilateral Conduct Laws, Assessment of Dominance/Substantial Market Power, and State-Created Monopolies', ICN Report (2007) (the '2007 ICN Report'). The Report is based on questionnaires submitted by 35 ICN members. A number of ICN members emphasized that the objectives of unilateral conduct rules are the same as the objectives of competition law more generally (ibid 6–8) and, therefore, this overview may be used as a starting point for a catalogue of the possible objectives of competition law.

[6] ME Porter, *The Competitive Advantage of Nations* (New York, The Free Press 1990) 6–7.

[7] M Taylor, *International Competition Law: A New Dimension for the WTO* (Cambridge, CUP 2009) 8–12; H Bork, *The Antitrust Paradox* (New York, Free Press 1993) 107–110 (somewhat misleadingly using the phrase 'consumer welfare' to denote social welfare). Social welfare is the sum of the surplus of producers and consumers in an industry. Producer surplus is the price of a product minus the opportunity cost of producing it. In this book, the phrase 'social welfare' will be used instead of 'total welfare' to emphasize that the maximization of the sum of the surplus of producers and consumers benefits society as a whole.

[8] An interesting example is the Canadian Competition Act (RS, 1985, c C-34), s 1(1), which reads as follows: 'The purpose of this Act is to maintain and encourage competition in Canada in order to promote the efficiency and adaptability of the Canadian economy, in order to expand opportunities for Canadian participation in world markets while at the same time recognizing the role of foreign competition in Canada, in order to ensure that small and medium-sized enterprises have an equitable opportunity to participate in the Canadian economy and in order to provide consumers with competitive prices and product choices.'

uncertainty as to what the objective competition law does, or should, pursue but also from the lack of clarity and precision as to the what is meant by each objective. This is particularly true of the objectives of a more political or legal nature, such as the protection of competition as an institution or the protection of economic freedom, but also of economic concepts, such as efficiency or productivity. Economic objectives are capable of being defined with a significant degree of precision in theory, but are often used in a general and unprincipled way in practice. A clear definition of these objectives, however, is important to provide the background for understanding the choices that the Member States have made in the Treaties and to interpret the EU competition rules in the light of the relevant objective.

This chapter examines potential objectives of competition law. It discusses the non-welfare objectives that have been assigned to competition law in the literature and in the law and argues that none of them is capable of being an objective of competition law by itself. From this analysis, the need for a welfare objective emerges. The various concepts of efficiency are relative to the achievement of a given measure of welfare and, while relevant, cannot be objectives of competition law in themselves. Social or consumer welfare are then discussed and the superiority of long-term social welfare over consumer welfare is demonstrated. The relevance of consumer welfare is that consumer harm can, in certain circumstances, be a test for anti-competitive behaviour which achieves the objective of maximizing long-term social welfare. The concepts of economic freedom and fairness can also be properly understood only in the light of this objective.

B. Non-welfare objectives

(1) The competitive process and a competitive market structure

A possible objective of competition law is the protection of the competitive process as such. Advocate General Kokott in *British Airways* expressed this objective as being the protection of the structure of the market and thus competition 'as an institution'.[9] This analysis was, at least indirectly, endorsed by the Court of Justice in the same case. The Court, relying on *Continental Can*,[10] reiterated that Article 102 TFEU is aimed not only at practices that may cause prejudice to consumers directly, but also at those which are detrimental to them through their impact on an effective competition structure.[11]

---

[9] Case C-95/04 P *British Airways plc v Commission* [2007] ECR I-2331 (*British Airways*), Opinion of AG Kokott, 23 February 2006, para 68. The AG relied on Art 3(1)(g) EC, which provided that the activities of the European Community included the establishment and maintenance of a system ensuring that competition in the internal market was not distorted. The absence of an equivalent provision in the TEU or TFEU does not have a material impact on the interpretation of Arts 101 and 102 as having the immediate objective of ensuring that competition in the internal market is not distorted: see 113–121 below.

[10] Case 6/72 *Europemballage Corporation and Continental Can Company Inc v Commission* [1973] ECR 215 (*Continental Can*), para 26.

[11] Case C-95/04 P *British Airways*, paras 103–108.

The use of 'competitive market structure' and 'competitive process' terminology requires further clarification. 'Competitive process' relates to the dynamic interaction of firms over a specified time frame, whereas 'market structure' denotes a static state of the market at a specific point in time. 'Market structure' is a neutral term that describes the subject-matter of any competition analysis rather than an objective of competition law. However, competition law is concerned with the impact of behaviour on markets and so the application of competition rules almost invariably requires the observation of the market over a certain period of time, not at a specific point in time.[12] When an effect on market structure is required, the subject-matter of the analysis is the outcome of market behaviour, which materializes over time, and not the market structure itself. In a similar vein, the preservation of a competitive market structure requires, at the very least, a comparison between two states of affairs, one in which the conduct under review is likely to have a certain impact on the market and one in which such conduct is absent. This can only be appraised by examining the competitive process. Therefore, the term 'market structure' is equivalent, in all respects, to 'competitive process'; the two terms can be used interchangeably.

This is different from the idea that certain market structures should be preserved because of their inherent benefits while other market structures should be looked at with suspicion because they are inherently harmful or are conducive to anticompetitive behaviour. The classic example of such an approach is the structure-conduct-performance paradigm of the Harvard School.[13] Even in this sense, however, the protection of a 'competitive market structure' cannot be an objective of competition law in itself. What is a competitive market structure? Why is an oligopoly more competitive than a monopoly? Unless it is assumed that the more

---

[12] The only exceptions being *per se* violations of competition law, a concept that denotes the prohibition of certain forms of conduct regardless of any market analysis. The origin of the *per se* rule can be traced back to the US case *Drystone Pipe & Steel Co v US* 175 US 211 (1899). For a discussion of the meaning of *per se* rules see O Black, 'Per Se Rules and the Rule of Reason: What Are They?' (1997) 18 ECLR 145.

[13] ES Mason, 'Monopoly in Law and Economics' (1937) 47 Yale LJ 34; ES Mason, 'Price and Production Policies of Large-Scale Enterprise' [1939] American Economic Rev 61–74; G Rosenbluth, 'Measures of Concentration' in National Bureau of Economic Research, *Business Concentration and Price Policy* (Princeton New Jersey, Princeton University Press 1955) 69; S Bain, *Industrial Organization* (2nd edn New York, John Wiley and Sons 1968); A Phillips, 'A Critique of Empirical Studies of Relations between Market Structure and Profitability' (1976) 24 Journal of Industrial Economics 241; JH Agnew, *Competition Law* (London, Allen & Unwin 1985) 35; WG Sheperd, *The Economics of Industrial Organization* (2nd edn New Jersey, Prentice-Hall 1985) 1, 2, 53; WG Sheperd, 'The Twilight of Antitrust' (1986) 18 Antitrust Law and Economics Rev 21; WL Baldwin, *Market Power, Competition and Antitrust Policy* (Homewood Illinois, Irwin 1987) 108, 304, 306; BE Hawk, *United States Common Market and International Antitrust, Volume II* (2nd edn New Jersey, Prentice Hall Law & Business 1990) 7; I Schmidt, *Wettbewerbspolitik und Kartellrect: Eine Einführung* (4th rev edn New Jersey, G Fischer 1993) 24; S Martin, *Industrial Economics: Economic Analysis and Public Policy* (2nd edn New York, Macmillan 1994) 7–8; EJ Mestmäcker, 'Meinungsfreiheit und Medienwettbewerb' (1994) 28 Sandai L Rev 293, 298–302; K Aiginger, D Mueller, and C Weiss, 'Objectives, Topics and Methods in Industrial Organization during the Nineties: Results from a Survey' (1998) 16 Intl J Ind Org 799; D Hildebrand, *The Role of Economic Analysis in the EC Competition Rules* (3rd edn Alphen aan den Rijn, Kluwer Law International 2009) 120–130.

firms there are, the more competitive the market, a proposition nobody would sub-scribe to at this level of generality, a further objective must be identified to explain what a competitive market structure is. For instance, an oligopoly is more com-petitive than a monopoly because the price is lower. But this already assumes a consumer or social welfare objective. Or, an oligopoly is more competitive than a monopoly because more firms have the opportunity to participate in the market. This already assumes that pluralistic and non-concentrated market structures are preferable for a given reason, for instance because of distributional concerns—in-dustry profits are shared among more firms—or political ones—market power[14] is diffused so that it cannot be leveraged into political power and lead to undemo-cratic political outcomes.[15]

The problem of elevating the protection of a 'competitive market structure' or the 'competitive process' to the ultimate objective of competition law is that such an objective would be, in itself, indeterminate. It is not possible to define what 'competitive process' means in a market context without reference to a further objective.[16] Even a definition of the 'competitive process' as a process of rivalry among firms on a given market would not take the matter much further because it would fail to provide a standard for distinguishing anti-competitive behaviour from normal market conduct. Rivalry may be defined as a process in which, if A and B both desire x, A obtaining x is incompatible with B also obtaining it. This, however, does not provide any clue as to the circumstances in which the process of rivalry between A and B may be restricted except, perhaps, if A and B agree not to compete. If, by its unilateral conduct, A obtains x and excludes B, when is the behaviour in question a restriction of competition and when is it competition in action? By focusing on the 'competitive process', it is impossible to answer such a

---

[14] There is no legal definition of market power. Nor is there a definition of market power in EU competition law. Market power may be defined as the ability of a firm to affect market price. Alternatively, and more precisely, market power may be defined as the ability of a firm profitably to set a price above marginal cost (MC) or, which is the same, the ability of a firm to earn a supra-competitive profit. There are subtle differences between these definitions. For instance, a firm may be able to price discriminate by setting some of its prices above MC but without earning an economic profit overall, ie across all markets. In this book, references to market power in an economic sense will be to the definition of market power as a firm's ability to earn an economic profit, ie as a firm's ability to set the price above MC and to generate a revenue that exceeds the opportunity cost of capi-tal. This does not mean that EU competition law, and even less Art 102, are concerned with market power as such. In particular, Art 102 applies to firms having the ability and incentive to harm social welfare in the long term, which requires the possession of substantial and durable market power: see Ch 10 below.

[15] A major concern of the first generation of ordoliberals: F Böhm, 'Das Problem der privaten Macht: Ein Beitrag zur Monopolfrage' (1928) 3 Die Justiz 324 and W Eucken, *Die Grundlagen der Nationalökonomie* (9th edn Berlin, Springer 1989) 169–204. Thus, according to ordoliberalists, private economic power had to be prevented: W Eucken, *Grundsätze der Wirtschaftspolitik* (6th edn Tübingen, JCB Mohr 1990) 334: 'Erster Grundsatz: Die Politik des Staates sollte darauf gerichtet sein, wirtschaftliche Machtgruppen aufzulösen oder ihre Funktionen zu begrenzen.' Competition policy had a political as well as an economic dimension as an essential instrument for the diffusion and fragmentation of political power: F Böhm, 'Freiheit und Ordnung in der Marktwirtschaft' (1971) 22 ORDO 11, 20: 'Daher die große Bedeutung, die dem Wettbewerb zukommt, der keineswegs nur ein Leistungsansporn, sondern vor allem auch ein *Entmachtungsinstrument* ist.'

[16] R Nazzini, 'Welfare Objective and Enforcement Standard in Competition Law' in U Bernitz and A Ezrachi (eds), *Private Labels, Brands and Competition Policy* (Oxford, OUP 2009) 379, 387–388.

simple question. Even those who argue that competition law has the objective of protecting the 'competitive process' would agree that it is necessary to introduce a further normative standard in order to establish whether a dominant undertaking's unilateral conduct is anti-competitive. Such a normative standard cannot be the 'competitive process' itself, because this would not take the analysis any further. Consider a price cut by a dominant undertaking that excludes a competitor from the market. Focusing simply on rivalry, namely the interaction between the firms, it is impossible to say whether the price cut is anti-competitive. The simplest answer is to consider a price cut below cost anti-competitive. But why should this make a difference? Because—it may be thought—a below-cost price cut generates a loss. A large firm may offset the loss against profitable sales to other customers but a small firm may be unable to absorb the loss and, therefore, it could not survive on the market for long. This simplistic reasoning has already introduced a further objective to determine what amounts to a restriction of the competitive process, namely fairness as between large and small firms. Economic explanations would distinguish between above-cost and below-cost price cuts based on the ability and incentive of a dominant firm to exclude competitors in order to protect or obtain market power rents and this, again, introduces further objectives in the analysis, namely consumer or social welfare.

This analysis demonstrates that, as a matter of logic, the protection of the competitive process, competitors, or a competitive market structure cannot be the objectives of competition law. These objectives are incapable of a workable definition and, if adopted, they would result in random enforcement and arbitrary decisions. This does not mean, however, that the competitive process, which necessarily includes the appraisal of the position of competitors and market structures, is unimportant in competition law. On the contrary, market structure and the competitive process are the subject-matter of competition law analysis even if they are not the ultimate objective of protection. This can be illustrated by a straightforward example. Assuming, for the sake of the argument, that long-term social welfare is the ultimate objective of competition law, only conduct that is detrimental to long-term social welfare through a restriction, prevention, or distortion of the competitive process is prohibited by competition law. Conduct that is so detrimental without interfering with the competitive process is irrelevant under competition law. Nobody would dream of applying competition law to gender discrimination in the workplace even if such discrimination was highly detrimental to long-term social welfare. As a result, when a given objective of competition law has been identified, the legal question becomes which effects on the competitive process are detrimental to the objective, and, therefore, prohibited, and which are not so detrimental, and, therefore, allowed. The issue in resolving this question is how to define the competitive process in the light of the objectives. It is then perfectly legitimate to say that competition law protects the competitive process, provided that competitive process is defined in the light of a normative standard, which itself derives from the objective that, in the eyes of the law, makes the competitive process worthy of protection. On this basis, and on this basis only, the protection of the competitive process may legitimately be said to be an objective of competition law.

(2) Economic freedom

'La liberté est un mystère'.[17] Freedom is a mystery. That the very concept of free-dom is complex and difficult to understand is not new in western philosophy, theology, and legal thinking. The problem comes from the idea that freedom is unfettered exercise of choice, unconstrained potentiality for being, unencumbered determination of one's course of action. But in a world governed by the law of caus-ality, there is no room for freedom. The paradox of freedom becomes particularly clear when competition law is recast through the lens of neoclassic economics. Neoclassic economics postulates that firms and consumers act rationally. The pos-tulate of rationality is simply a way of expressing the law of causality. In a given set of circumstances, certain actions are rational while others are not. Even when a firm or a consumer appears to have more than one rational option, the exercise of choice is not 'freedom'. The choice can always be explained rationally and, unless two options are perfectly equivalent, there will be *only* one rational choice. Even when several actions are absolutely equivalent, the choice will not be an expression of freedom but of indifference. To give a concrete example, a consumer of a homo-geneous product does not have a choice as to whether to buy the product from undertaking A at price x or from undertaking B at price x + y. His only rational choice is to buy the product at the lower price. If A and B offered differentiated products with B offering a higher quality product, the analysis would be no dif-ferent. The consumer may decide to buy the product from B. But he will only do so if its price does not exceed his willingness to pay for it, which is a reflection of the product's higher quality. Even if, in normal parlance, it may be possible to say here that the consumer is free to buy the lower or higher priced product depending on their relative qualities and prices, given his preferences, the consumer will only have one rational choice. And his choice is governed by the law of causality, not by the exercise of freedom.

   Would the presence of a restriction of competition, however defined, make any difference to this analysis? If firm A is dominant and imposes on the consumer a cost for switching to firm B, which outweighs any increased utility the con-sumer would derive from buying from B, and which could not be compensated by B because to do so would result in B's long-run incremental cost (LRAIC) being above its long-run incremental revenue, the consumer has, again, only one rational choice, which is to buy from firm A. Has his freedom being restricted compared to the previous scenarios in which there was no restriction of com-petition? As a matter of logic, the answer must be no because he was not free to choose in the counterfactual scenarios. Since there was no freedom in the first place, no restriction of freedom can occur. But let it be assumed, for the sake of argument, that in the counterfactuals the consumer was free. In the presence of the switching cost imposed by A, the consumer still has only one rational choice.

---

[17] A Schopenhauer, *The World as Will and Representation*, vol 1 (J Norman, A Welchman, and C Janaway eds and trs, Cambridge, CUP 2010) 431 (the quotation is wrongly attributed by Schopenhauer to Nicolas de Malebrache).

His choice is dictated by the same determinants, namely the price of the product and his willingness to pay for it. Why then would it be possible to say that the consumer's freedom has been restricted when undertaking A imposes on him a switching cost which is designed to exclude undertaking B? There are three possibilities.

The first is a commutative justice rationale that requires fairness in dealings between parties, in this example the transaction between A and the consumer.[18] However, the switching cost imposed by A on the consumer does not correspond to any element of the transaction between undertaking A and the consumer. It is designed to exclude undertaking B from the market. It may well be that a commutative justice rationale underpins certain judgments that equate a restriction of freedom to a restriction of competition.[19] However, the protection of freedom based on commutative justice is incapable of being generalized as an objective of competition law because not all restrictions of competition result in a prejudice to the other party in a given transaction. In predation, for instance, the consumer benefits from the transaction. Even when recoupment is part of the test, the consumer charged a higher price is not necessarily the same consumer who benefited from a lower price. Furthermore, it is difficult to argue that the post-exclusion transaction between the dominant firm and the consumer does not conform to the canons of commutative justice because the higher price is the result of exclusion. If the competitor had exited the market because of his bad business strategy, the same post-exclusion price would not be anti-competitive. Clearly, the answer is that the recoupment price is anti-competitive because it is the result of predatory conduct but the argument shifts the focus from the transaction between the dominant firm and the consumer to the behaviour of the dominant firm vis-à-vis a competitor. Thus, commutative justice is incapable of explaining why exclusionary conduct is anti-competitive.

The second is that undertaking A's behaviour restricts the freedom of undertaking B to compete. But this simply shifts the problem from the transaction between undertaking A and the consumer to the competitive relationship between undertaking A and undertaking B. A commutative justice argument cannot be easily made with regard to this competitive relationship because A and B are not transacting with each other. Nor is it possible to find any way to explain when

---

[18] R Coke, *Treatises of the Nature of Man* (London, J Cotteral & F Collins 1696); JO Wilson, 'The "Junk Bond King" of Wall Street: A Discourse on Business Ethics' in RM Coughlin (ed), *Morality and Efficiency: New Perspectives on Socio-Economics* (New York, ME Sharpe 1991) 204–205; JO Wilson, 'Economy, Society and Ethics' in P Ekins and MA Max-Neef (eds), *Real Life Economics: Understanding Wealth Creation* (London and New York, Routledge 1992) 54–58; L Armour, 'Is Economic Justice Possible' (1994) 21(10) International Journal of Social Economics 32; EK Brown-Collier, 'Self-Interest, Economic Efficiency and the General Welfare' in EJ O'Boyle (ed), *Social Economics: Premises, Findings and Policies* (London, Routledge 1996) 89–96.

[19] Even the reference in Case 85/76 *Hoffmann-La Roche & Co AG v Commission* [1979] ECR 461, para 91, to 'normal competition in products or services on the basis of the transactions of commercial operators' is reminiscent of a commutative justice language. The same can be said of certain case law on rebates, which considers relevant whether the rebate confers 'an advantage not based on any economic service justifying it': eg Case 322/81 *NV Nederlandsche Banden-Industrie Michelin v Commission* [1983] ECR 3461 (*Michelin I*), para 73.

harm to firm B is anti-competitive and when it is the result of effective competition relying exclusively on an abstract idea of economic freedom. This impasse points to the need for a definition of economic freedom, which is based on a value other than freedom itself.

The third is to recognize the obvious, namely that it is the restriction of competition which makes the difference but then to accept the only logical consequence of this proposition, which is that the restriction of competition, and, in particular, the concept of competition, must be defined independently of the concept of economic freedom. This issue arises in a similar way as regards other 'freedoms'. For instance, freedom of thought, conscience, and religion in Article 9 of the European Convention on Human Rights (ECHR) presupposes an understanding of 'thought', 'conscience', and 'religion', which cannot be derived from the concept of 'freedom'. The difference may be that concepts such as 'thought', 'conscience', and 'religion' are, at least intuitively, easier to grasp as they relate to the existence of the individual, which each human being perceives as part of his being or existential experience. The concept of 'competition', instead, is a purely social construct; it requires a process of learning, reasoning, and analysis even to grasp the idea in its most basic form. Therefore, there may be a mistaken perception that freedom of thought, conscience, and religion is immediately comprehensible as freedom while economic freedom is not. In reality all of these freedoms require a further concept to be accurately comprehended and to become operational. This process is simply superficially less intuitive as regards economic freedom than more basic freedoms relating to the existence of the individual.

These observations should already make clear that the concept of economic freedom, while not free-standing, is not redundant in competition law. The legal concept of freedom is generally associated with the ideas of freedom from certain types of external interference with one's own sphere of action (negative freedom) and freedom to develop one's own potentiality for being (positive freedom). Both ideas are perfectly apt to explain the individualized dimension of competition law.[20] Once competition has been defined, it is perfectly possible to define the economic freedom of undertakings and consumers as the freedom not to be limited in their economic activity by anti-competitive behaviour. In the previous examples, the consumer is always constrained in his economic behaviour but, when he is constrained by the forces of the free market, by which is meant a market with no anti-competitive restrictions, his economic freedom is not restricted. His freedom is only restricted when his economic behaviour is constrained by anti-competitive conduct. However, economic freedom is not a constituent element of the definition of competition. On the contrary, competition is a constituent element of the definition of economic freedom. The same applies to the economic freedom of firm B. Its freedom is restricted by the anti-competitive practice of firm A but not by A charging a lower price for its product thanks to its lower

---

[20] A-L Sibony, *Le Juge et le raisonnement économique en droit de la concurrence* (Paris, LGDJ 2008) 394, relying on the classic analysis of H Motulsky, *Principes d'une réalisation méthodique du droit privé : la théorie des eléments générateurs des droits subjectifs* (reprinted Paris, Dalloz 2002).

costs, although the effect, in both cases, is the same: firm B may be unable to compete and may have to leave the market. Economic freedom is, therefore, in the first place the right not to suffer any limitation of market opportunities resulting from anti-competitive behaviour. But freedom is also, in its positive dimension, the right to participate in the market, as a consumer or as a competitor, and develop one's own potential in a free market environment. This definition is simply a different way of expressing the previous concept of negative freedom. But it is important because it emphasizes the right of each market participant to seek to increase his own welfare and contribute to society in a positive way. Indeed, this positive, or assertive, concept of freedom is the foundation of its negative counterpart. Negative freedom is the way in which the legal system protects the positive freedom to participate in the market.

In this perspective, the concept of free market is simply a description of a market where the economic freedom of market participants is recognized and protected in much the same way as a free society is a society in which the freedom of the individual is safeguarded and guaranteed. Free market is not synonymous with competitive market. A highly concentrated oligopolistic market with substantial non-behavioural entry barriers is not a competitive market. Prices may be higher than in a competitive market and innovation lower; but in the absence of private or State restrictions of competition,[21] the market would be described as a free market, although perhaps as a failed one.

(3) Fairness

Fairness is a concept as difficult to pin down as freedom.[22] It is, however, a concept familiar to lawyers for having different meanings in different contexts.

---

[21] There are clear parallels between private restrictions of competition and state measures restricting competition. The State aid provisions of the TFEU are in the same Chapter as the competition provisions applicable to undertakings. Chapter I of Title VII of the TFEU is entitled 'Rules on competition', thus making it clear that competition may be restricted either by firms or by the State. However, there are significant differences between restrictions of competition by firms and restrictions of competition by the State, particularly as regards the incentives, motives, and objectives of the restrictions (profit for firms and other policy objectives for the State) and the ways in which a restriction manifests itself (private conduct for firms and State measures for the State). Therefore, the present analysis focuses on the rules applicable to undertakings unless a comparison with the rules on State aid is necessary or useful in a particular context. On State aid generally, see: A Biondi, P Eeckhout, and J Flynn, *The Law of State Aid in the European Union* (Oxford, OUP 2004); L Hancher, T Ottervanger, and PJ Slot, *EC State Aids* (3rd edn London, Sweet & Maxwell 2006); JD Braun and J Kuhling, 'Article 87 EC and the Community Courts: From Revolution to Evolution' (2008) 45 CML Rev 465; K Bacon, *European Community Law of State Aid* (Oxford, OUP 2009); C Quigley, *European State Aid Law and Policy* (2nd edn Oxford, Hart Publishing 2009).

[22] For a critique of the role of fairness in what the authors call 'social decisionmaking' see L Kaplow and S Shavell, *Fairness versus Welfare* (Cambridge, Mass and London, England, Harvard University Press 2002). Their key argument is that fairness as an independent evaluative principle can make individuals worse off and will inevitably make individuals worse off whenever the outcome under fairness as an independent evaluative principle diverges from the outcome that would be achieved under economic welfare as an independent evaluative principle: ibid 52–58. The argument developed in the text is closer to Kaplow and Shavell's other argument against notions of fairness, namely that their rationale is indeterminate: ibid 59–62.

Fairness in the context of consumer law[23] is not the same as fairness in Article 6 of the ECHR.[24]

To determine the meaning of fairness in competition law, it is helpful to start from first principles. It is possible to distinguish formal fairness from substantive fairness. Formal fairness denotes the absence of bias or discrimination in the application of rules or the allocation of resources. Its meaning denotes a process in which all participants are given equal opportunities. What must be fair is the process not the outcome.[25] Substantive fairness is an attribute of the outcome of an allocation of resources.[26] It means that total surplus on a given market must be allocated between all producers and consumers in a way that is 'fair'. This is, essentially, a distributional question. Therefore, if the objective of competition law were to achieve substantive fairness, the competition rules would prohibit or reverse any allocation of resources that was not socially desirable. Competition law would become a mechanism to correct market outcomes that are not fair in distributional terms. This *ex post* distributional function is, however, alien to competition law. Competition law protects the market from restrictions of competition because the allocation of resources, which results from the competitive dynamics of the market, is considered, at least prima facie, fair. If such an allocation is not fair for whatever reason, other instruments, such as social policy or taxation, are used to address the distributional issue. Competition law is concerned with competition. Competition, as the struggle of one economic agent against another, is a process rather than an outcome. The reason why the competitive process is considered beneficial may well be because of its outcome but competition law does not directly mandate an outcome. It protects a process as a way of achieving a desired outcome. The concept of fairness that applies to competition law is, therefore, procedural. Competition law is not concerned with the fairness of the ultimate allocation of resources but with the protection of fairness on the market as the mechanism to allocate scarce resources. Fairness requires that the market mechanism not be distorted in favour of one economic agent to the prejudice of another.

The proof of the proposition that competition law is concerned with procedural fairness is that, if fairness were concerned with the substantive allocation of surplus rather than the process of its allocation, competition law would be superfluous.

---

[23] N Reich, 'Some Reflections on Rethinking Community Consumer Law' in JS Ziegler (ed), *New Developments in International Commercial and Consumer Law: Proceedings of the Biennial Conference of the International Academy of Commercial and Consumer Law* (Oxford, Hart Publishing 1998) 431, 446–448; HG Beale, W Bishop, and MP Furmston, *Contract: Cases and Materials* (5th edn Oxford, OUP 2008) 819–837.

[24] DL Jones, 'Article 6 ECHR and Immunities Arising in Public International Law' (2003) 52 ICLQ 463; JF McEldowney, *Public Law* (3rd edn London, Sweet & Maxwell 2002) 452–453 and 471–472; HWR Wade and CF Forsyth, *Administrative Law* (10th edn Oxford, OUP 2009) 476–480; P Mahoney, 'Right to a Fair Trial in Criminal Matters under Article 6 E.C.H.R.' (2004) 4 Judicial Studies Institute Journal 107; H Fenwick, *Civil Liberties and Human Rights* (4th edn New York, Routledge-Cavendish 2007) 1277–1278; A Mowbray, *Cases and Materials on the European Convention on Human Rights* (2nd edn Oxford, OUP 2007) 341–467.

[25] eg R Nozick, *Anarchy, State, and Utopia* (New York, Basic Books 1974).

[26] See eg, in the utilitarian tradition, J Rawls, *A Theory of Justice* (rev edn Harvard, Harvard University Press 1999).

The law could more straightforwardly provide for a tax on profits or on consumption when the surplus of the economic agents exceeded the amount the law considered fair. A normative standard other than the competitive process, excluded by definition under a purely substantive analysis, would apply to determine what a fair distribution of wealth was. But this would have nothing to do with competition law. Other instruments are better suited to achieving distributional objectives. For example, taxation on profits and consumption with distributional objectives is commonly applied.[27] It is not, however, part of competition policy.

If competition law is concerned with a purely procedural concept of fairness, it is necessary to specify the criteria that determine when one economic agent is unfairly favoured or prejudiced. Since competition law is concerned with the anti-competitive behaviour of firms, an economic agent cannot be unfairly prejudiced within the meaning of competition law if he is at a disadvantage as a result of objective factors inherent in the structure of the market. If the market is characterized by economies of scale, undertakings operating at higher cost because, given the capacity constraint of their plants, they cannot achieve a minimum efficient scale of production, cannot be said to be unfairly prejudiced. So if an incumbent applies a lower price because it is able to produce more efficiently, less efficient undertakings are, again, not unfairly prejudiced. But what if the incumbent applies a price that makes it difficult or impossible for an entrant to achieve the minimum efficient scale of production? Clearly, not any price which harms the entrant is banned. Fairness cannot be protection of one party against the other regardless of a criterion that, at the very least, defines who should be protected and when. Otherwise, the choice between protecting the incumbent or protecting the entrant would be simply arbitrary. The answer cannot be that an undertaking with a smaller market share or higher costs should always be protected. Such a policy would be unfair to the incumbent whenever the latter is more efficient than the entrant. Part of the answer is that fairness does not dictate that parties must be placed in the same position in a given transaction but that they must have equal opportunities to participate in the market. In competition law, one way of expressing this idea is the as efficient competitor principle,[28] which appears well suited to accommodating the concept of equality of opportunities inherent in the idea of fairness. However, the idea of equality of opportunities may also be applied to protect a less efficient competitor. This may be appropriate, for instance, when an entrant cannot match the efficiency of the dominant undertaking or, at least, not for a period of time.[29] Is it fair to the incumbent to prevent him from exploiting his superior efficiency, which he may have achieved through investment and wise business decisions? Or is it unfair to the entrant to allow the incumbent to rely on its superior efficiency because the entrant cannot immediately be as efficient as

---

[27] eg J Tiley, *Revenue Law* (5th edn Oxford, Hart Publishing 2005) 3–4, 809.

[28] The principle would condemn as prima facie abusive conduct that is capable of excluding a competitor who is as efficient as the dominant firm. On this principle, see Ch 7 below.

[29] Communication from the Commission—Guidance on the Commission's enforcement priorities in applying Article 82 of the EC Treaty to abusive exclusionary conduct by dominant undertakings [2009] OJ C45/7 ('Guidance on Art 102') para 24.

the incumbent? Fairness and equality of opportunities cannot provide an answer. Rather, the solution depends on the application of further criteria, for instance, how much productive efficiency is valued over lower prices. Furthermore, fairness and equality of opportunities do not account for all forms of anti-competitive conduct. Consider a cartel that does not exclude new members. All undertakings may be said to have equal opportunities. Consumers, of course, suffer. But, if the cartel applies to the entire market, they also enjoy equal opportunities. And yet there is little doubt that a cartel is, almost always, anti-competitive even if it is difficult to say that any economic agent has been denied equal opportunities to participate in the market. The answer to this problem is two-fold. First, the market is not free. As explained in the previous section, there is on this market a restriction of competition. But, as explained above, the concept of freedom does not provide a definition of what a restriction of competition is. Secondly, it is possible, in fact intuitive, to say that the market is not fair because the consumers are paying a higher price than they would in the absence of the cartel. However, it is not the absolute level of prices and profits which count but the fact that the higher prices and profits are the result of the cartel. The cartel is a restriction of competition. Yet again, the key to understanding fairness must lie in the definition of restriction of competition, which must be independent of the concept of fairness.

In conclusion, the concepts of fair competition and fair market denote a market process in which all economic agents have equal opportunities to benefit from the market, both as sellers and as consumers. If there is no equality of opportunities, there is no fair competition and, therefore, it is possible to say that competition is restricted. However, fairness is not capable of being accurately defined and applied in practice without resorting to further criteria. Therefore, it cannot be the ultimate objective of competition law. An economic agent is unfairly prejudiced when he is harmed by anti-competitive behaviour. But anti-competitive behaviour cannot be entirely defined in the light of a free-standing concept of fairness.

(4) Protection of competitors and small and medium-sized enterprises

It is often said that competition law should protect competition and not competitors.[30] The objective of protecting the 'market structure' or the 'competitive process' has often been criticized on the ground that it disguises the real aim of protecting competitors.[31] The slogan that competition law should protect competition and

---

[30] P Jebsen and R Stevens, 'Assumptions, Goals and Dominant Undertakings: The Regulation of Competition under Article 86 of the European Union' (1996) 64 Antitrust Law Journal 443, 488; EM Fox, 'We Protect Competition, You Protect Competitors' (2003) 26 World Competition 149, 155; M Motta, *Competition Policy: Theory and Practice* (Cambridge, CUP 2004) 22; IS Forrester, 'Article 82: Remedies in Search of Theories?' (2005) 28 Fordham Intl LJ 919, 926; JS Venit, 'Article 82: The Last Frontier—Fighting Fire With Fire?' (2005) 28 Fordham Intl LJ 1157; E Rousseva, 'Modernizing by Eradicating: How the Commission's New Approach to Article 81 EC Dispenses With the Need to Apply Article 82 EC to Vertical Restraints' (2005) 42 CML Rev 587, 592. See, however, critically H Schweitzer, 'The History, Interpretation and Underlying Principles of Section 2 Sherman Act and Article 82 EC' in C-D Ehlermann and M Marquis (eds), *European Competition Law Annual 2007: A Reformed Approach to Article 82 EC* (Oxford, Hart Publishing 2008) 119, 161.

[31] EM Fox, 'What is Harm to Competition? Exclusionary Practices and Anti-competitive Effect' (2002) 70 Antitrust LJ 371, 392; Forrester, 'Article 82: Remedies in Search of Theories?'

not competitors is given such force, almost that of an ontological truth, that it is sometimes used as if it were a legal principle in itself. However, this conclusory slogan is only true if the protection of competitors is intended as protection of a given firm regardless of any further criterion determining when a firm is entitled to protection. But this way of undertaking the protection of competitors is absurd and has never been advocated in competition policy. It is uncontroversial that the mere fact that a firm is excluded from a market or is otherwise harmed as a result of the conduct of another firm or other firms cannot amount to a breach of competition law. Unless protection of competitors meant that competition law should be concerned with preserving or increasing the number of undertakings on the market, which cannot be seriously argued,[32] it is impossible to say what the rationale of the protection of competitors would be and what legal principles and tests should be derived from it. To argue that the objective of competition law is to protect competitors would be the same as saying that the objective of company law is to protect the shareholders. In both cases, there are clearly other stakeholders who are protected: consumers in competition law, creditors in company law. More importantly, competitors in competition law, as shareholders in company law, are only protected against certain conduct and in certain circumstances. Shareholders are not protected if the market value of their shares falls because other companies perform better due to a superior human resource strategy. But minority shareholders may be protected against certain forms of appropriation of the company's assets by the majority shareholders. In the same vein, competition law does not protect competitors against the forces of a competitive market but does protect them against anti-competitive behaviour. The UK Competition Appeal Tribunal (CAT) expressed this very clearly in *Burgess v Office of Fair Trading*,[33] a case in which the Office of Fair Trading (OFT) was defending a non-infringement decision under the Chapter II prohibition of the Competition Act 1998, the national equivalent of Article 102.[34] The OFT relied on the argument that competition law should protect competition, and not competitors. The CAT agreed with the OFT that Article 102 and the Chapter II prohibition were not intended to protect competitors *per se*.[35] The CAT went on to say:[36]

We accept therefore that the OFT is correct, up to a point, in submitting that the aim of the Chapter II prohibition is not to protect competitors, but to protect competition. On the other hand, where effective competition is already weak through the presence of a dominant firm, there are circumstances in which competition can be protected and fostered only by imposing on the dominant firm a special responsibility under the Chapter II

919; V Korah, *An Introductory Guide to EC Competition Law and Practice* (9th edn Oxford, Hart Publishing 2007) 14.

[32] Motta, *Competition Policy*, 22–23 argues that there is no proved correlation between the number of firms on the market and social or consumer welfare. As a general proposition, this is very likely to be correct.

[33] *ME Burgess, JJ Burgess and SJ Burgess (trading as JJ Burgess & Sons) v The Office of Fair Trading* [2005] CAT 25, [2005] Comp AR 1151, paras 166–245.

[34] Decision of the Office of Fair Trading No CA98/06/2004 *Refusal to supply JJ Burgess & Sons Limited with access to Harwood Park Crematorium*, 29 June 2004 (Case CP/0055/02) (*Harwood Park Crematorium*).

[35] *Burgess v OFT*, para 332.   [36] ibid para 333.

prohibition not to behave in certain ways vis-à-vis its remaining competitors, particularly where barriers to entry are high. In such circumstances the enforcement of the Chapter II prohibition may in a sense 'protect' a competitor, by shielding the competitor from the otherwise abusive conduct of the dominant firm. However, that is the necessary consequence of taking action in order to protect effective competition... While Burgess is not entitled to be protected against normal market forces, it is in our view entitled under the Act not to be eliminated as an efficient operator in the market by the abusive practices of a dominant firm.

The same principle applies to the protection of SMEs, which is sometimes believed to be an objective of competition law.[37] It is difficult to accept that competition law protects SMEs *per se*. The reason for this is the same as that applying to the protection of competitors, ie it would be too narrow and too indeterminate an objective. Competition law applies even when no SME, however defined, is harmed. On the other hand, the protection of SMEs in itself would not be a meaningful objective. Should competition law intervene each time a SME is harmed by the conduct of a dominant undertaking or by an agreement by two or more other undertakings? Clearly not. What does the protection of SMEs then mean? It can only mean that SMEs are entitled, as are all other undertakings, to be protected against anti-competitive behaviour but not against disadvantages resulting from competitive market forces. The key issue is, yet again, the definition of 'restriction of competition'.

(5) Market integration

Market integration is another possible objective of competition law. It has prominence, especially within the European Union,[38] but also in other jurisdictions such as the Russian Federation[39] and New Zealand.[40] The economically oriented literature points out that this objective is not necessarily compatible with a social or consumer welfare objective.[41] The classic example is price discrimination across different countries based on the different willingness to pay of consumers in those countries. There seems to be a consensus in economic literature that a *per se* rule

---

[37] 2007 ICN Report, 17.

[38] BE Hawk, 'The American (Anti-trust) Revolution—Lessons for the EEC?' (1988) 9 ECLR 53, 54; BE Hawk, 'Antitrust in the EEC—The First Decade' (1992) 41 Fordham L Rev 229, 231; DJ Gerber, *Law and Competition in Twentieth Century Europe* (Oxford, OUP 1998) 347–348; G Monti, *EC Competition Law* (Cambridge, CUP 2007) 39–44; R Whish, *Competition Law* (6th edn Oxford, OUP 2008) 22–23; A Tryfonidou, 'Further Steps on the Road to Convergence among the Market Freedoms' (2010) 35 EL Rev 36; Hildebrand, *The Role of Economic Analysis in the EC Competition Rules*, 3; Joined Cases 56/64 and 58/64 *Etablissements Consten SàRL and Grundig-Verkaufs-GmbH v Commission* [1966] ECR 299 (*Consten and Grundig*); Case 226/84 *British Leyland plc v Commission* [1986] ECR 3263; *Volkswagen* [1998] OJ L124/60, upheld in Case T-62/98 *Volkswagen v Commission* [2000] ECR II-2707, appeal dismissed in Case C-338/00 P *Volkswagen v Commission* [2003] ECR I-9189; Case T-13/03 *Nintendo Co Ltd and Nintendo of Europe GmbH v Commission* [2009] ECR II-947.

[39] 2007 ICN Report.   [40] ibid.

[41] V Korah, 'EEC Competition Policy—Legal Form or Economic Efficiency' (1986) 39 CLP 85, 91; R Wesseling, *The Modernisation of EC Antitrust Law* (Oxford, Hart Publishing 2000) 88; Korah, *An Introductory Guide to EC Competition Law and Practice*, 14.

prohibiting price discrimination across different countries or restrictions on parallel imports, which are necessary for price discrimination to work, is not justified
on social or consumer welfare grounds.[42] A *per se* prohibition could even induce a
monopolist not to sell at all in countries where it would sell if price discrimination
were allowed.[43]

The perception of a clash between the market integration goal and welfare
objectives of competition law may be explained in the light of certain case law[44]
and enforcement practice in the European Union[45] but, from a theoretical perspective, it is totally unjustified. Since the times of Smith[46] and Ricardo,[47] it has
become well established that freedom of trade is an indispensable condition of economic growth and increased social and consumer welfare.[48] If private economic
agents were able to erect, in their self-interest, barriers to trade through cartels,
vertical distributional practices, and unilateral conduct by dominant firms, a large
part of the benefits resulting from comparative advantage, specialization, and
increased productivity would be lost.[49] This would have negative effects on both
social and consumer welfare as well as on economic growth and, ultimately, the
well-being of the nation.

It is important, however, to distinguish those restrictions of trade resulting from
State measures and those resulting from private conduct. Historically, the principle of free trade has been applied first to remove protectionist measures enacted
by the State. The effect of anti-protectionist interventions is to increase all firms'
ability to trade. Even when a State measure which simultaneously restricts trade
and benefits certain firms is removed, it is reasonably uncontroversial that, at least
in the general case and in the long term, the harm to the firms favoured by the
protectionist measure is far outweighed by the benefits of trade for the society as a

---

[42] Motta, *Competition Policy*, 23; R O'Donoghue and AJ Padilla, *The Law and Economics of
Article 82 EC* (Oxford, Hart Publishing 2006) 555 and 558–562.

[43] Motta, *Competition Policy*, 23.

[44] eg Case T-368/00 *General Motors Nederland BV and Opel Nederland BV v Commission* [2003]
ECR II-4491; Case T-67/01 *JCB Service v Commission* [2004] ECR II-49; Joined Cases C-468/06 P to
478/06 P *Sot Lélos kai Sia EE v GlaxoSmithKline AEVE Farmakeftikon Proionton* [2008] *ECR* I-7139;
Joined Cases C-501/06 P, 513/06 P, 515/06 P, and 519/06 P *GlaxoSmithKline Services Unlimited v
Commission* [2009] ECR I-9291.

[45] eg *Bayer AG/Adalat* [1996] OJ L201/1, annulled in Case T-41/96 *Bayer AG v Commission*
[2000] ECR II-3383, appeal dismissed in Joined Cases C-2/01 P and C-3/01 P *Bundesverband der
Arzneimittel-Importeure eV v Commission* [2004] ECR I-23.

[46] A Smith, *An Inquiry into the Nature and Causes of Wealth of Nations* 2 Vols (reprint London,
Methuen 1904).

[47] D Ricardo, *On the Principles of Political Economy and Taxation* (reprint London, Empiricus
Books 2002).

[48] Arguments in favour of the benefits of trade can be traced back to the 17th century: H Parker
Esq, *Of a Free Trade* (London, Fr Neile for Robert Bostock dwelling in Pauls Church-yard at the Signe
of the King's Head 1648). For the contemporary view, see: M Friedman, *Free to Choose: A Personal
Statement* (London, Pan 1990); DTI, 'Liberalisation and Globalisation: Maximising the Benefits of
International Trade and Investment' Department of Trade and Industry (DTI) Economics Paper
No 10 (July 2004); WTO, '10 Benefits of the WTO Trading System' The World Trade Organization
(WTO) Pamphlets (2008).

[49] On the idea that trade increases productivity by allowing firms to specialize in the activity in
which they enjoy a comparative advantage, see M Parkin, M Powell, and K Matthews, *Economics*
(5th edn Harlow, Pearson Education Ltd 2003) 29–32.

whole. Furthermore, after the restriction is lifted, all firms have equal opportunities to trade, including those who were previously favoured.

Private restrictions to trade are more problematic. When the law forbids private conduct which restricts trade, there are two opposing effects. On the one hand, they increase the trading ability of the firms that were prejudiced by the restriction. On the other hand, they also limit the ability of the firms that imposed the restriction to determine their own commercial strategy, which may have negative effects on their incentives to trade and to invest. For example, if a supplier is prevented from entering into a distribution agreement on terms that guarantee absolute territorial protection to the distributor,[50] the effect of the prohibition is not obviously positive. If passive sales are significant, competition among distributors may give rise to a free-rider problem, which reduces the distributors' incentives to invest in promoting the product. In the same vein, a dominant undertaking's duty to supply a rival with an indispensable input may increase trade in the output market, but may lower the dominant undertaking's incentives to invest in upgrading the input. An indiscriminate prohibition on all privately created trade restrictions, defined as all practices that have a negative effect on the flow of goods and services across distinct geographic markets, is not necessarily beneficial to trade and may ultimately do harm to the economic goals which trade aims to achieve.

A strong protection of freedom of trade may also be justified on the ground that trade does not only have economic objectives but also social and political goals. Closer economic links between regions and nations contribute to social cohesion, cultural exchanges, and stability in international relations. The European Economic Community's real purpose was to foster economic ties among the European nations so that war would become unlikely in western Europe. But these objectives, which may well be more important than economic growth and increased social welfare, presuppose a market integration that achieves its immediate economic goals. It would be difficult to say that market integration has the objective of fostering social cohesion within the European Union if it resulted in lower economic growth and reduced social welfare. In fact, opposition to European integration often surfaces when there is a perception that the integration process has a negative effect on wages, wealth, and the standard of living of a region or nation. The economic benefits of trade are a condition for the achievement of its social and political objectives. Competition law, as an element of economic policy, achieves the goals of social cohesion, cultural enrichment, and political stability through the increase in social welfare which trade brings about in the first place.

In conclusion, market integration is a legitimate objective of competition law that is not only perfectly compatible with economic objectives such as social welfare, economic growth, and productivity but is also a necessary condition for the attainment of those economic objectives. However, because competition law applies the principle of market integration to private restrictions on trade, it is not possible to say that all conduct that has the effect of a quantitative restriction on

---

[50] Commission Regulation (EC) 330/2010 of 20 April 2010 on the application of Article 101(3) of the Treaty on the Functioning of the European Union to categories of vertical agreements and concerted practices [2010] OJ L102/1, Art 4(1)(b)(i).

trade is anti-competitive. When a practice has the sole or overwhelmingly predominant purpose of impeding trade, a presumption that the practice is anti-competitive may perhaps be justified because trade is a necessary condition of social welfare increasing as a result of specialization and comparative advantage. But the presumption must always be rebuttable because a restriction on the freedom of an undertaking to determine its own business strategy may also have negative effects on its incentives to trade and to invest. Furthermore, when a practice does not have the impediment of trade as its sole or overwhelmingly predominant purpose, but nevertheless has the effect of restricting trade, a balance must be struck between two opposing principles. On the one hand, market integration is essential to the achievement of the economic benefits of trade. On the other hand, restricting the freedom of an undertaking to devise its business strategy may have negative effects on its incentives to trade and to invest. In other words, not all restrictions on the freedom to trade are restrictions on competition. Which restrictions of trade are restrictions of competition must be determined in the light of the economic objectives of market integration and the concept of 'restriction of competition'.

(6) Market liberalization

Market liberalization is also occasionally cited as an objective of competition law in its own right.[51] However, the better view appears to be that market liberalization is not an objective of competition law. Rather, competition law is an essential element of any liberalized market. The benefits of liberalization in terms of enhanced efficiency and social welfare would be thwarted if incumbent undertakings were allowed to behave anti-competitively in order to protect the market power which they inherited from former State monopolies.

A different question is whether competition law should be used to facilitate the liberalization process in certain industries. Recently liberalized industries are often heavily concentrated and incumbent undertakings may possess significant market power, which they acquired not as a result of superior market performance but thanks to State intervention. Furthermore, certain liberalized industries are associated with essential infrastructures that it would be inefficient to replicate, or with services that have a significant social dimension. In these industries, there may be a case for imposing stricter rules on incumbents and giving entrants extra protection. There are two ways of approaching this question. On the one hand, the features of a newly liberalized market may be considered as relevant elements of the factual matrix to which competition law applies. An above-cost rebate system established by a newly privatized telecommunications operator with a 95 per cent market share may be seen as more seriously anti-competitive than the same practice adopted by a dominant firm with a 50 per cent market share in a consumer goods market that has never been affected by regulatory barriers to entry. The reason is that in a newly

---

[51] 2007 ICN Report, 20.

liberalized market the contestable share of demand[52] may be very small, while in a consumer goods market with a dominant undertaking having a 50 per cent market share the contestable share of demand may be large, possibly well above 50 per cent,[53] so that above-cost rebates may hardly have an anti-competitive effect. On this analysis, the same competition rules apply to newly liberalized markets as to all other markets, but different facts may lead to different outcomes.[54] On the other hand, competition law may be used to foster the liberalization process. For instance, a lower threshold for refusal to supply could apply in newly liberalized markets because of the policy objective of opening up the market to competition and the belief that mandating access would not have a negative effect on the incumbent's investment incentives, given that the investment in the infrastructure was financed by the State.[55] Using competition law to facilitate liberalization processes would result in the introduction of different sets of competition rules to suit the requirements of specific liberalized industries. Not only would each market have its own rules, so that competition law in the energy sector would differ from competition law in the telecoms sector, but it would also be difficult to determine when a market should be considered sufficiently competitive and thus no longer deserving special treatment. This would be at odds with the general nature and scope of the competition rules. It would also introduce an unacceptable degree of discretion in their application because conflicting regulatory and competition objectives might have to be reconciled, entailing a 'political' balancing of interests, which would not be appropriate to the structure of legal rules but would be better suited to regulatory intervention. In markets where newly liberalized industries require extra intervention either until the liberalization process is completed or on a permanent basis, an appropriate regulatory framework should be put in place alongside competition law but competition law should not be distorted or used to pursue sector-specific policy objectives.

(7) Consumer choice

Consumer choice features prominently in policy statements[56] and competition cases.[57] Generally, consumer choice is discussed in the context of the consumer

---

[52] The contestable share of demand is the portion of demand that customers are prepared to source from competitors of a dominant firm within a given time frame. On this concept see further 236–237 below.

[53] There will be a point at which a large contestable share is incompatible with the market leader being dominant: on the concept of dominance, see Chs 10 and 11 below.

[54] An example of this approach is Case T-271/03 *Deutsche Telekom AG v Commission* [2008] ECR II-477, upheld in Case C-280/08 P *Deutsche Telekom AG v Commission* [2010] OJ C346/4, where the European courts applied the margin squeeze test in a way which was sensitive to the fact that the market had recently been liberalized and new undertakings were for the first time entering the industry and trying to grow.

[55] For this approach see Guidance on Art 102, para 82.

[56] N Kroes, 'Delivering Better Markets and Better Choices' Speech at the European Consumer and Competition Day, London SPEECH/05/512 (15 September 2005); European Commission, 'Antitrust: Commission Accepts Microsoft Commitments to Give Users Browser Choice' Press Release IP/09/1941 (16 December 2009).

[57] Joined Cases C-241/91 P and C-242/91 P *Radio Telefís Eireann (RTE) and Independent Television Publications Ltd (ITP) v Commission* [1995] ECR I-743 (*Magill*), para 54; Case C-481/01 *IMS Health*

welfare objective. However, it is sometimes viewed as an objective in its own right. In both cases, consumer choice *per se* is wholly inappropriate as an objective of competition law. While, generally, effective competition enhances consumer surplus, it is difficult to determine how much choice maximizes consumer surplus, all other things being equal. Excessive product differentiation may increase transaction costs for consumers and raise costs for undertakings trying to gain market share through inefficient advertising and other wasteful strategies.[58] Even if a consumer welfare objective is preferred, the better approach would be to focus on price and output only, rather than on 'choice'. Furthermore, an emphasis on choice may lead to competition authorities and courts making qualitative judgments as to how many different products should be on the market. This would almost inevitably lead to a very high risk of false positive errors.[59] When consumer choice is seen as an objective in its own right, it may become a disguised form of competitor protection: a competitor deserves to be protected solely on the basis that it offers a differentiated product. As explained above, protection of a competitor from any prejudice caused to him by the market behaviour of other undertakings is not a workable competition law standard and should be rejected. As a general principle, whether or not the competitor offers a differentiated product should not make any difference.

This analysis does not mean that consumer choice is not important in competition law. On the contrary, an efficient level of product differentiation and consumer choice results from an effective competitive process. Effective competition determines how many products are on the market and how differentiated they are. Excessive differentiation that customers do not value will result in market exit. On

---

GmbH & Co OHG v NDC Health GmbH & Co KG [2004] ECR I-5039, para 38; Case T-201/04 *Microsoft Corp v Commission* [2007] ECR II-3601 (*Microsoft I*), paras 643–665; *Intel* [2009] OJ C227/13.

[58] FM Scherer and D Ross, *Industrial Market Structure and Economic Performance* (3rd edn Boston, Houghton Mifflin 1990) 601; J Church and R Ware, *Industrial Organization: A Strategic Approach* (Boston, McGraw-Hill 2000) 373–374; DW Carlton and JM Perloff, *Modern Industrial Organization* (4th edn Boston, Pearson/Addison Wesley 2005) 201; B Schwartz, *The Paradox of Choice: Why More is Less* (New York, HarperCollins 2005) 86; NW Averitt and RH Lande, 'Using the "Consumer Choice" Approach to Antitrust Law' (2007) 74 Antitrust LJ 175, 192.

[59] A false positive error occurs when, in an individual case, conduct is prohibited that, under the relevant rule, should not have been prohibited. A false negative error occurs in the opposite scenario in which unlawful conduct escapes prohibition under the relevant rule. The principle that legal tests in competition law should reflect the balance between the risks and costs of false convictions and false acquittals, over-deterrence and under-deterrence is well established: F Easterbrook, 'The Limits of Antitrust' (1984) 63 Texas L Rev 1; AM Polinsky and S Shavell, 'Legal Error, Litigation, and the Incentive to Obey the Law' (1989) JL Econ & Org 99; D Besanko and DF Spulber, 'Antitrust Enforcement Under Asymmetric Information' (1989) 99 Economic Journal 408; CF Beckner III and SC Salop, 'Decision Theory and Antitrust Rules' (1999) 67 Antitrust LJ 41; SC Salop and RC Romaine, 'Preserving Monopoly: Economic Analysis, Legal Standards, and Microsoft' (1999) 7 Geo Mason L Rev 617, 659–665; R Cass and K Hylton, 'Preserving Competition: Economic Analysis, Legal Standards and Microsoft' (1999) 8 Geo Mason L Rev 1, 33–38; KN Hylton and M Salinger, 'Tying Law and Policy: A Decision-Theoretic Approach' (2001) 69 Antitrust LJ 469, 498–502; DS Evans and AJ Padilla, 'Excessive Prices: Using Economics to Define Administrable Legal Rules' (2005) 1 J Comp L & Econ 97, 114–118; A Christiansen and W Kerber, 'Competition Policy with Optimally Differentiated Rules Instead of "Per Se Rules v Rules of Reason"' (2006) 2 J Comp L & Econ 215, 225–235; WH Page, 'Microsoft and the Limits of Antitrust' (2010) 6 J Comp L & Econ 33, 35; GA Manne and JD Wright, 'Innovation and the Limits of Antitrust' (2010) 6 J Comp L & Econ 153, 158–168.

the other hand, unsatisfied demand for new product characteristics will be met by new entrants, provided that the cost of entry does not exceed the profits from the new differentiated product, given post-entry prices. The efficient level of differentiation in an industry is thus an important element of the welfare of the society. This also means that the analysis of product differentiation on the market, or the lack thereof, can provide evidence of anti-competitive behaviour. For instance, unmet demand or lack of product innovation may be evidence that conduct which excludes competitors is anti-competitive.[60] However, increasing or preserving consumer choice as such is not an objective of competition law.

C. Social welfare

(1) The search for the economic purpose of the law

As explained above, an effective competitive process, economic freedom, fairness, and market integration are all legitimate objectives of competition but are not, each on its own or in combination with the others, sufficient to define what a restriction of competition is. In order to answer this question, a further objective must be identified. It is logical to assume that competition, as with all other economic arrangements that a society considers beneficial, is protected because it increases the welfare of the society. And, since competition law is concerned with the economic processes in the society, it is also logical to infer that competition is beneficial to the economic welfare of the society.[61] This does not mean that fairness and freedom are irrelevant, or even inimical, as certain literature suggests, to competition law.[62] On the contrary, they are fundamental building blocks of the concept of competition. However, they are not sufficient on their own to account for what is prohibited and what is allowed under competition law. In order to move from abstract concepts of freedom and fairness to workable and operational conceptions of freedom and fairness in competition law, there is no alternative but to determine the economic objective of the law. Such an objective cannot be other than the long-term economic welfare of the society or

---

[60] See 269–272 and 279–280 below.

[61] Economists and, increasingly, a number of jurisdictions around the world in their enforcement practice and jurisprudence support a welfare objective as the goal of competition law: Motta, *Competition Policy*, 17–22; RJ Van den Bergh and PD Camesasca, *European Competition Law and Economics: A Comparative Perspective* (2nd edn Sweet & Maxwell, London 2006) 18–19; O'Donoghue and Padilla, *The Law and Economics of Article 82 EC*, 4; S Bishop and M Walker, *The Economics of EC Competition Law* (3rd edn London, Sweet & Maxwell 2010) 29–32.

[62] J Basedow, *Von der deutschen zur europäischen Wirtschaftsverfassung* (Tübingen, JCB Mohr 1992) 24; C Ahlborn and AJ Padilla, 'From Fairness to Welfare: Implications for the Assessment of Unilateral Conduct under EC Competition Law' in C Ehlermann and M Marquis (eds), *European Competition Law Annual 2007: A Reformed Approach to Article 82 EC* (Oxford, Hart Publishing 2008) 55; W Wurmnest, *Marktmacht unter Verdrängungsmissbrauch: Eine rechtsvergleichende Neubestimmung des Verhältnisses von Recht und Ökonomik in der Missbrauchsaufsicht über marktbeherrschende Unternehmen* (Tübingen, Mohr Siebeck 2010) 100.

social (or total) welfare. This does not make competition law a purely utilitarian, value-free economic tool. Competition law enshrines the fundamental values of a market economy in which all economic agents must be free to participate in the process of the creation of economic wealth on the basis of equal opportunities. However, freedom, fairness, and the pluralistic structure of the market would be meaningless and unworkable concepts without the guide and the limiting force of an economic objective. This economic objective is the maximization of the wealth of the society. Nor is this objective, as some may argue,[63] purely monetary, and, therefore, valueless. To show why, it is sufficient to consider the concept of willingness to pay, which is key to the measure of social welfare, as it is one of the determinants of market price. Willingness to pay depends on the consumers' valuation of a product. In a society that places a high value on a green and unpolluted environment, the willingness to pay for environmentally friendly products is higher. All other things being equal, production focuses on environmentally friendly products because they command a higher price. So while it is true that social welfare is expressed as a monetary value, this is only a way of representing social welfare analytically. In reality, social welfare reflects the values that human beings place on their being in the world.

(2) Social welfare, consumer welfare, and economic efficiency

Social welfare is the sum of the surplus of producers and consumers in a given industry. Producer surplus (or welfare) is the sum of the profits of the producers. Consumer surplus (or welfare) is the difference between the sum of the consumers' willingness to pay for a product and the sum of what they actually paid for it.[64]

It is important to determine the relationship between social welfare and the different concepts of economic efficiency. Efficiency is not a stand-alone concept. Efficiency is relative to a given objective. Economic efficiency is relative to the maximization of wealth understood as social welfare. Allocative efficiency relates to the efficient use of resources in that resources are used to produce what society values most highly and production cannot be increased without forgoing production of a more valued product. Allocative efficiency is maximized when price equals marginal cost (MC). Figure 2.1 below illustrates the allocative efficiency of perfect competition. At the equilibrium point, E, the consumer surplus is the striped area and the producer surplus is the dotted area. At the competitive output, Q_0, the sum of the consumer and producer surpluses is maximized. Reducing the quantity produced by the market to Q_1 would reduce the consumer surplus and the producer surplus by the areas A and B respectively. Similarly, forcing the producers to produce Q_2 and sell it to consumers at the price P_2 would increase the consumer surplus by area P_0P_2SE, but

---

[63] Sibony, *Le Juge et le raisonnement économique en droit de la concurrence*, 94; D Hausman, *The Inexact and Separate Science of Economics* (Cambridge, CUP 1992) 66–67.

[64] eg Motta, *Competition Policy*, 17–22.

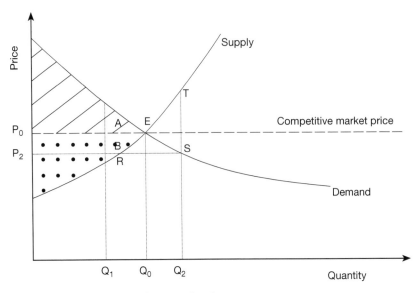

Figure 2.1 The allocative efficiency of perfect competition

the producer surplus would reduce by area P_0P_2RE. In turn, whilst it appears we have gained ERS, there is also a loss of social welfare equal to EST. This demonstrates the allocative efficiency of perfect competition at the equilibrium point.

On the other hand, as shown in Figure 2.2 below, a monopolist will choose to produce at the output where MC equals marginal revenue (MR) and charge

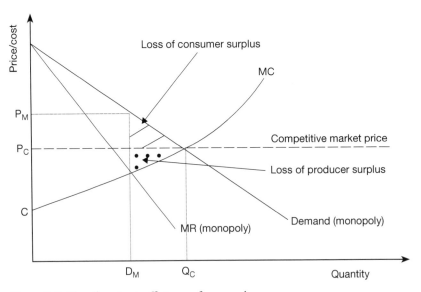

Figure 2.2 The allocative inefficiency of monopoly

consumers a price P_M in order to maximize his profits. This results in a loss of consumer and producer surpluses, indicated by the striped and dotted areas respectively. This is known as the deadweight loss under monopoly and illustrates that, in terms of allocative efficiency, a monopoly is less efficient than the same industry under perfect competition.

Productive efficiency relates to efficiency in production. Production is efficient when a given output is produced at the lowest possible cost given the current technology. Productive efficiency clearly increases social welfare, although it may have a different impact on producer or consumer surplus depending on whether the benefits of lower production costs are passed on to consumers or accrue to producers. Whether lower production costs are passed on to consumers depends, in turn, on the effect of the cost reduction on MC and the competitive structure of the market. The two graphs which make up Figure 2.3 below indicate that a monopoly

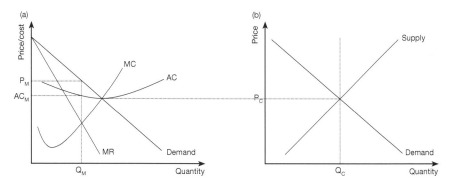

Figure 2.3 Productive efficiency under monopoly and perfect competition

is also productively inefficient. This can be seen by the fact that the monopolist chooses not to produce at the lowest point on the average cost curve. The industry in perfect competition would see costs reduced to the minimum point on the average cost curve. Assuming that no new technology existed to reduce costs, then production would be efficient under the perfect competition scenario shown in the second of the two charts.

Figure 2.4 below shows that monopolies may also be X inefficient, since they have less incentive to lower their costs. This means that the cost curves, AC and MC, may be shifted up and to the left of their optimal position as below with AC' and MC'.

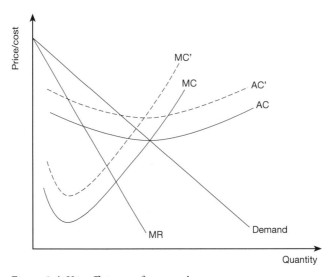

Figure 2.4 X inefficiency of monopoly

Figure 2.5 below illustrates the importance of productive efficiency. The left-hand side of the graph illustrates a situation in which production is inefficient across the industry. If the industry could reduce costs of production to the lowest possible cost given the current technology then we would see the supply curve shift as shown in the diagram, the equilibrium price fall, and a greater output being achieved. We also see that this increase in productive efficiency leads to greater consumer and producer surpluses; the areas ABPe and CBPe are both larger than the areas CDPi and EDPi.

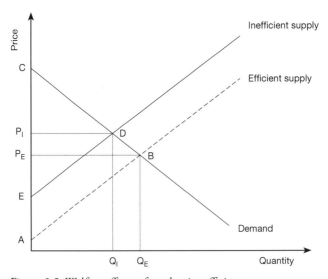

Figure 2.5 Welfare effects of productive efficiency

Dynamic efficiency relates to the introduction of new production technologies or product developments. The introduction of a new production technology increases productive efficiency. Product development increases demand and, therefore, the price that consumers are willing to pay for the product. The effect of dynamic efficiency may be described as innovation. Figure 2.6 illustrates the effects of an improvement in dynamic efficiency in an industry. When a more efficient manufacturing process is introduced across the industry, then the supply curve shifts from S to S', meaning more can be produced at each price level. If demand stays constant at D, the equilibrium price falls. However, improvements in dynamic efficiency could also mean the production of a better product that consumers value more, thus meaning they will purchase more at each price, resulting in a shift of the demand curve from D to D'. If the increase in demand is greater than the increase in supply, as shown in the graph, then the equilibrium price will be raised from P to P'. Crucially, both the producer and consumer surpluses will increase. To see this increase in social welfare, compare the size of the areas PCE and PCF with P'BA and P'BG.

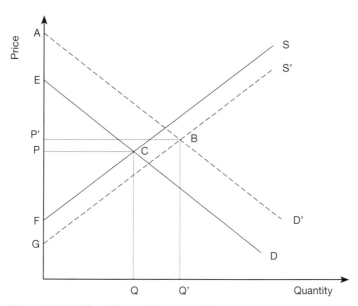

Figure 2.6 Welfare effects of dynamic efficiency

A concept strongly related to productive and dynamic efficiency is productivity, defined as the value of output produced by a unit of labour or capital. The value of the output is determined by price and, therefore, the quality of the products. The value of a unit of labour or capital is determined by productive efficiency and the introduction of new technologies.

All measures of economic efficiency and productivity are not ends in themselves but result in increased social wealth. Allocative efficiency results in the satisfaction of consumption at the lowest cost to society. From a static perspective, it maximizes social welfare although it allocates all surplus to consumers. Productive efficiency results in higher profits or lower prices or both and, therefore, increases social welfare with ambiguous effect on the allocation of the increased surplus between producers and consumers. Dynamic efficiency results in higher profits and the satisfaction of previously unmet consumption needs. It increases profits and, generally but not necessarily, consumer surplus.[65] Productivity is a measure of the quality and quantity of output and efficiency in production, but also determines the level of wages and the return on capital.

Allocative efficiency, productive efficiency, dynamic efficiency, and productivity cannot, in themselves, be objectives of competition law. They are, rather, measures of how an objective, ie the maximization of wealth, is pursued.[66] However, they are essential elements of competition analysis because the maximization of wealth is achieved through improvements in economic efficiency. It is, therefore, often said that certain behaviour is anti-competitive because it harms allocative efficiency by raising prices or dynamic efficiency by eliminating investment incentives. What is meant, however, is that social welfare is reduced because of the negative impact of the conduct under review on the relevant measure of efficiency.

The economic objective of competition law must be, therefore, a certain measure of welfare. Nobody seriously argues that producer surplus should be the objective of competition law. Often egregious anti-competitive conduct, for instance a market-wide cartel, does increase producer surplus and is, in fact, implemented precisely because it has this effect. This means that the problem is whether the economic objective of competition law should be social or consumer welfare.

A choice is required because, while social and consumer welfare may be reconcilable objectives in certain cases, a conflict may arise. It is, of course, not always so. An increase in market power generally increases the profits of the undertakings in question less than it decreases consumer surplus. Therefore, all other things being equal, if market power increases, short-term social and consumer welfare decrease. However, social welfare and consumer welfare do not necessarily change in the same direction. A merger that substantially reduces the merging undertakings' fixed costs but substantially increases their market power is likely to reduce consumer welfare but may increase social welfare if producer surplus increases more than consumer surplus decreases. Prima facie, such a merger would be allowed under a social welfare objective and prohibited under a consumer welfare objective. Therefore, it is necessary to determine whether social or consumer welfare is the objective of competition law.

---

[65] Consider, for instance, the case of a new technology that results in lower fixed costs which are not passed on to consumers: M Spence, 'Product Selection, Fixed Costs, and Monopolistic Competition' (1976) 43 Rev Econ Stud 217; JF Brodley, 'The Economic Goals of Antitrust: Efficiency, Consumer Welfare and Technological Progress' (1987) 63 NYU L Rev 1020; J Farrell and C Shapiro, 'Dynamic Competition with Switching Costs' (1988) 19 RAND Journal of Economics 123.

[66] Sibony, *Le Juge et le raisonnement économique en droit de la concurrence*, 91.

(3) Theoretical and normative superiority of the long-term social welfare objective

On an orthodox view, competition is beneficial because it maximizes social welfare.[67] A static, short-term[68] version of the social welfare objective is as follows. In conditions of perfect competition, social welfare is maximized and production and consumption are efficient. No possible rearrangement of resources can increase the output of one product without reducing the output of at least one other product. Buyers place, on consuming the product, a value equal to its MC of production, and no rearrangement of products among consumers can benefit a consumer without harming at least one other consumer.[69]

The social welfare objective, however, if applied in a short-term, static framework, may lead to welfare loss in the long term. If undertakings are allowed to increase their market power, provided that their increased profits offset the sum of the decrease in consumer surplus and the deadweight loss in the short term, this may significantly reduce or even eliminate the firms' incentives to behave efficiently,[70] thus reducing social welfare in the long term. A simple example can illustrate this point. Let us assume that a merger to monopoly leads to a fixed cost saving that outweighs the reduction in consumer surplus and the increase in the deadweight loss from duopoly to monopoly. The market is characterized by high barriers to entry. Should a competition authority clear such a merger? Under a short-term social welfare standard, the answer would be yes. However, the problem with clearing a merger to monopoly in a market with high entry barriers is that to allow further concentration in the industry does not take into account the long-term benefits of competitive pressure for efficiency and economic growth and, thus, for long-term social welfare. In a merger to monopoly in a market with high entry barriers, a short-term increase in social welfare is likely to be outweighed by the long-term inefficiency of the monopoly. High prices, rent seeking, X-inefficiencies, and lack of innovation are likely to characterize a monopoly that does not face any credible competitive pressure in the long term.[71] To avoid

---

[67]   Taylor, *International Competition Law*, 8–12; Bork, *The Antitrust Paradox*, 107–110.

[68]   In the short-term, all factors of production are fixed.

[69]   This concept of social welfare is also called Pareto efficiency, the criterion being that no other reallocation of resources could make at least one person better off without making anybody else worse off. An alternative way of measuring social welfare maximization or improvements is to determine whether, given a wealth transfer, the winners would hypothetically compensate the losers and still be better off. This criterion is named Kaldor-Hicks after the economists who first introduced it: see JR Hicks, 'The Foundations of Welfare Economics' (1939) 49 Economic Journal 696 and N Kaldor, 'Welfare Propositions In Economics and Inter-Personal Comparisons Of Utility' (1939) 49 Economic Journal 549.

[70]   In the long term, all factors of production may change. In economics, the medium term is the period in which some but not all factors of production may be varied. For the sake of textual simplification, in this book long-term will also denote a period over which not all but only some of the factors of production may be varied, unless the context clearly and unequivocally requires otherwise.

[71]   Carlton and Perloff, *Modern Industrial Organization*, 94–97 and Motta, *Competition Policy*, 40–64. A monopoly, of course, is not necessarily harmful to long-term social welfare: see eg the classic contribution by H Demesetz, 'Two Systems of Belief About Monopoly' in H Goldschmidt et al (eds), *Industrial Concentration: The New Learning* (Boston, Little Brown 1974) 164.

this undesirable outcome, it is necessary to introduce a temporal framework in the analysis to determine whether any short-term increase in social welfare is sustainable. The sustainability of welfare increases in the long term depends on firms continuing to have sufficient incentives to behave efficiently. The incentives that competition law intends to protect are those that result from effective competitive pressure on the market. It follows from this analysis that the social welfare that competition law intends to promote is long-term social welfare that results from effective competition.

In its long-term dimension, social welfare is theoretically superior to consumer welfare as the objective of competition law because it relies on formal equality among all economic agents. The welfare of all economic agents is valued the same. Furthermore, social welfare ensures that the welfare of the society as a whole is maximized. Under the consumer welfare objective, conduct which increases the welfare of the society as a whole is prohibited if it reduces the welfare of consumers. Prima facie, this is undesirable unless it is shown that the welfare of consumers must be given more weight than the welfare of producers.

(4) Consumer welfare

(a) Definition of the long-term consumer welfare objective

As an alternative to total welfare, many commentators argue that the objective of competition law should be to prohibit behaviour that reduces consumer welfare.[72] A number of competition authorities also support this view.[73] Undertakings' behaviour that, through the exercise or acquisition of market power, results in higher prices or lower output reduces consumer surplus.[74] It also brings about allocative inefficiency, as the decreased consumer surplus is greater than the increased profits, due to the deadweight loss of market power.

A consumer welfare objective—in its static, short-term formulation—does not take into account dynamic efficiency. Undertakings' profits may be invested in the development of new technologies or new products.[75] Increased short-term

---

[72] D Neven, P Papandropoulos, and P Seabright, *Trawling for Minnows* (London, Centre for Economic Policy Research 1998) 12; RJ Van den Bergh, 'The Difficult Reception of Economic Analysis in European Competition Law' in P Cucinotta, R Pardolesi, and R Van den Bergh (eds), *Post-Chicago Developments in Antitrust Law* (Cheltenham, Edward Elgar 2002) 42; SC Salop, 'Question: What is the Real and Proper Antitrust Welfare Standard? Answer: The True Consumer Welfare Standard', Antitrust Modernization Commission (4 November 2005); C Townley, *Article 81 and Public Policy* (Oxford, Hart Publishing 2009) 177–181; Bishop and Walker, *The Economics of EC Competition Law*, 24; N Kroes, 'Preliminary Thoughts on Policy Review of Article 82' Speech at the Fordham Corporate Law Institute, SPEECH/05/537 (New York, 23 September 2005); N Kroes, Opening address at conference 'Competition and Consumers in the 21st Century', SPEECH/09/486 (Brussels, 21 October 2009).

[73] 2007 ICN Report.

[74] Consumer welfare can be understood as a social welfare objective where the welfare of the producers is given no weight. However, in this book social welfare will refer to the welfare of the society as a whole, which includes producers and consumers, while consumer welfare will denote the welfare of consumers.

[75] JA Schumpeter, *Capitalism, Socialism and Democracy* (6th edn London, Allen & Unwin 1943); MI Kamien and NL Schwartz, 'Potential Rivalry, Monopoly Profits and the Pace of Inventive Activity' (1978) 45 Rev Econ Stud 547; D Hildebrand, 'The European School in EC Competition

producer surplus resulting from a short-term reduction in consumer surplus may be used to lower the cost of production in the long term by introducing a new technology, thus resulting in lower prices and larger output that may offset or even overcome any short-term reduction in consumer surplus. The same can be said as regards dynamic efficiencies resulting in the introduction of new products. New products may expand output in a given industry by satisfying an as yet unmet demand. But to develop new products firms may need to earn supra-competitive profits in the short term.[76] Therefore, a long-term consumer welfare objective does not disregard producer surplus. However, it takes it into account only insofar as it is passed on to consumers in the form of lower prices, larger output, or new products. The question is why the surplus of consumers must be valued more than the surplus of producers to the extent that the society attaches no value whatsoever to the latter unless it is passed on to consumers.

(b) Redistribution of wealth

The most straightforward argument favouring consumer welfare instead of social welfare is based the desirability of the redistribution of wealth. While a social welfare objective assumes that wealth transfers are neutral, some argue that wealth transfers from consumers to producers should not be seen as welfare neutral but as regressive.[77] The consumer welfare objective means that competition law would, on average, bring about a transfer of wealth from individuals with a lower marginal utility of income to individuals with a higher marginal utility of income.[78]

At the theoretical level, the desirability of distributional policies is a complex matter.[79] As regards the distributional objective of competition, however, it is not necessary to express a definite view on the circumstances in which redistribution of income is desirable and, if so, how this may be achieved. It is sufficient to show that, even if redistribution of income were a legitimate aim in a given society, competition law would be ill-suited to pursuing it.

Even if income redistribution was held to be desirable, a consumer welfare objective would not prevent regressive wealth transfers from lower income consumers to higher income firm owners. To achieve such an objective, competition authorities and courts would have to determine the levels of income of firm owners and consumers in individual cases and make a judgment on the distributional

Law' (2002) 25 World Competition 3, 3–9. But see, for a different view, KJ Arrow, 'Economic Welfare and the Allocation of Resources for Invention' in The National Bureau of Economic Research, *The Rate and Direction of Inventive Activity: Economic and Social Factors* (Princeton, Princeton University Press 1962, reprint 1975) 609.

[76] A case in point may be the pharmaceutical industry, where supra-competitive profits from patented medicines are needed to continue to research and develop new drugs.

[77] R Pittman, 'Consumer Surplus as the Appropriate Standard for Antitrust Enforcement' [2007] Competition Policy International 205, 207–215.

[78] ibid 208.

[79] See also, for further references, AB Atkinson and D Bourguignon, *Handbook of Income Distribution* (Amsterdam, Elsevier 2000); F Campano and D Salvatore, *Income Distribution* (Oxford, OUP 2006); G Bertola, R Foellmi, and J Zweimüller, *Income Distribution in Macroeconomic Models* (Princeton, Princeton University Press 2005); EN Wolff, *Poverty and Income Distribution* (2nd edn Hoboken, Wiley-Blackwell 2009).

effects of the transfer. This would lead to outcomes that have little to do with competition law as it is currently understood and would be unfeasible in the framework of competition analysis. However, it may be that distributional issues should not be considered on a case-by-case basis. Redistribution is the rationale for choosing consumer welfare as the objective of competition law.[80] Once the objective has been determined, the case-by-case assessment of firms' conduct will be carried out against a consumer welfare standard without consideration of redistributive issues. However, if competition authorities and courts are not required to have regard to redistributive issues in individual cases, but only to determine whether the conduct under review reduces consumer surplus, all that can be said is that a transfer from consumers to owners of firms is prohibited. It is impossible to say whether the redistribution achieved by applying this standard is from higher income firm owners to lower income consumers or from lower income firm owners to higher income consumers, or indeed from one group of consumers to another. Consumers often own interests in firms, directly or indirectly, and increased profits result in higher equity yields.[81] The intended distributional outcome would depend on the structure of company ownership in any given industry and the income of the consumers of the product in question. For luxury goods produced by firms regularly distributing high dividends and owned by low income investors, a producer surplus rather than a consumer surplus standard would be appropriate to achieve distributional goals. Furthermore, a redistributive consumer welfare objective also disregards the observation that the salaries of the firms' employees are determined by their productivity, which is a function, among other things, of the value of production. Higher prices, therefore, not only translate into higher profits but may also translate into higher salaries, which may also be a redistributive effect from higher income to lower income individuals.

The above considerations already demonstrate that income redistribution is incapable of justifying the choice of consumer welfare over social welfare as the objective of competition law. However, let us assume, for the sake of argument, that competition law should prohibit wealth transfers from consumers to producers. Such redistribution would be random because it would occur only in industries where undertakings engage in anti-competitive behaviour. In an oligopolistic industry, firms may be able to earn supra-competitive profits on a lasting basis without breaching competition law by simply observing each other's prices. No redistributive concern would arise here. Now suppose that the same industry is less concentrated and firms can only earn supra-competitive profits if they form a cartel, which they do. In such an industry, the law would be concerned with the redistribution of income. But why would this be the case? If the objective of competition law were the redistribution of income, one would expect this objective to be relevant whenever there is a wealth transfer from consumers to producers. Instead, such wealth transfers become relevant only where there is a restriction of competition.

---

[80] In Pittman, 'Consumer Surplus as the Appropriate Standard for Antitrust Enforcement', 209–210.

[81] This argument is also discussed by J Farrell and ML Katz, 'The Economics of Welfare Standards in Antitrust', Competition Policy Center, Institute of Business and Economic Research, UC Berkeley (20 July 2006) 12.

But there does not seem to be a coherent link between anti-competitive behaviour and wealth transfers. Assuming that the redistribution of wealth is a desirable objective, there appears to be a strong argument for pursuing this objective across the society in a principled way and not randomly through competition law. Other policy frameworks, such as taxation or social policy, may take into account and weigh up the factors that are relevant to redistributive objectives more efficiently, transparently, and consistently than competition law may do.[82]

(c) Imperfections in corporate governance

Consumer welfare may be preferable to social welfare on the ground that, because of imperfections in corporate governance, part of the profits of firms is dissipated by management in their own interest.[83] The factual premise of this theory is questionable. Even in the presence of dissipation of profits, it is highly likely that part of the profits will also be distributed to shareholders or reinvested. Therefore, in order to account for managerial dissipation of profits, competition authorities and courts would have to undertake a case-by-case analysis of the managerial performance of the firms under investigation. Otherwise, a competition policy that weighed consumer surplus more than producer surplus because of managerial dissipation of profits would penalize efficient corporate governance structures and effective shareholder supervision. Firms whose managers do not dissipate profits because of the integrity of their managers, the efficiency of their corporate governance arrangements, and the active supervision of their shareholders would be penalized in competition law investigations. Their profits would not be taken into account in assessing whether their conduct is an infringement of competition law on the ground that in other firms profits are dissipated. Such a standard would discourage shareholders from investing optimally in the active supervision of the firm. The problem of managerial dissipation of profits is best addressed at the level of the company by designing an appropriate framework for corporate governance and managerial supervision. It has nothing to do with the objective of competition law.

(d) Enforcement, efficiency, and institutional capability

It is also argued that a consumer welfare standard is easier to administer and allows for simpler monitoring of the outcomes achieved through competition law intervention. The short-term impact of the conduct under review on price and output is easier to assess, both *ex ante* and *ex post*, than the impact on social welfare.[84] This argument is incorrectly posited. If a consumer surplus standard is thought

---

[82] Social policy-makers, whether the legislature or public officials, would be able to consider the specific features of the distributional issue to be addressed and tailor the policy to the need in question, which may change over time, even quite rapidly. Distributional choices, furthermore, require political judgments that competition authorities and courts should not be required to make because they lack democratic legitimacy and accountability.

[83] Farrell and Katz, 'The Economics of Welfare Standards in Antitrust', 12, raise and reject this argument.

[84] Salop, 'Question: What is the Real and Proper Antitrust Welfare Standard? Answer: The True Consumer Welfare Standard', 22–23.

to be desirable, this conclusion must be justified regardless of whether a consumer surplus test is easier to apply. To reason otherwise would lead to absurd results. For instance, a set of clear *per se* rules is the easiest standard to apply. One could conceive of a competition law system prohibiting all cartels and all other agreements between competitors with a combined market share of 40 per cent or above, all mergers resulting in a post-merger market share of more than 50 per cent, and so on. But this system would result in too many enforcement errors, both false convictions and false acquittals. The reality is that this argument addresses the question from the wrong end. What is required is to identify the appropriate objective of competition law and then, based on such an objective, design administrable legal tests. It is absurd to identify an administrable enforcement test first and then elevate it to the objective of competition law.

A variant of this argument may be based on the observation that any competition law standard must be such that competition authorities and courts are able to apply it (an institutional capability argument). This argument is powerful but cannot provide a solution to the problem of the objective of competition law. The objective of competition law should be determined in the light of the desirable social outcome to be pursued. The objective does not equal the legal test. The determination of the objective will have to be translated into administrable legal rules that minimize the risks of erroneous interventions and maximize the efficiency of the enforcement process. However, there should be no suggestion that legal rules should pursue the wrong objective, which could be harmful to society, because in this way they will be easy to administer and apply. In an extreme scenario, if, ultimately, it appears that it is impossible to design efficient legal rules that translate the desirable objective of competition law into an administrable system, the conclusion should be the abolition of competition law altogether rather than the choice of an inappropriate or even harmful objective. An appraisal based on the need for administrable tests that competition authorities and courts are capable of applying is properly directed at the design of legal rules and institutional structures rather than at the determination of the objective of competition law.

(e) *The misuse of the consumer welfare objective*

The previous sections have demonstrated that there is no theoretical justification for the choice of consumer welfare as the goal of competition law. In practice, however, consumer welfare has been advocated as the appropriate objective of competition law by academics, practitioners, business, and competition officials. Its popularity as the objective of competition law can be explained by three main reasons.

First, consumer welfare, as a test, is easier to apply than social welfare. It is more straightforward to argue—although not necessarily to prove—that as a result of the exclusion of a competitor or of an agreement between firms prices will be higher, than to explain why the aggregate producer and consumer surplus will be lower. This approach is affected by a double error. The first error is to assume that the objective of competition law necessarily corresponds to the rules and tests that apply to different types of conduct. As will be explained below, consumer harm may be, in certain circumstances, the appropriate test to achieve a social welfare objective, but a consumer harm test does not imply a consumer welfare objective. The other error is that the mere fact that a test is easy to apply does not make it a good test and even less does it make it the objective of the law.

Secondly, consumer welfare is a politically acceptable way of arguing for an economic approach to competition law. The very mention of the word 'consumer' evokes ideas of fairness, redistribution, and protection of the many and vulnerable, making this rhetoric attractive to politicians, policy-makers, and competition officials. On the other hand, the consumer welfare objective may be applied so that, in many circumstances, it leads to precisely the same consequences as a social welfare objective. Predation analysis does not differ significantly under these two objectives. The exclusion of an equally efficient competitor by a dominant undertaking is likely to harm both social and consumer welfare. The same can be said of a cartel. Consumer welfare can be used as a populist slogan to sell, to the public, an economic approach to competition law.

Thirdly, consumer welfare is a politically acceptable way to disguise a non-interventionist agenda. It would be more difficult politically to argue that a tying practice by a dominant undertaking should be allowed because it does not make any difference to the sum of industry profits and consumer surplus than to argue that it should be allowed because an integrated product is good for consumers.

In conclusion, not only is consumer welfare not an appropriate objective of competition law, it is also used, in practice, to disguise different objectives and ulterior purposes. The use of the consumer welfare slogan confuses the debate and creates the false impression of a consensus on the objective of competition law, when in reality the slogan is used to pursue and disguise different agendas.

(5) A different perspective: consumer harm as a test to achieve a social welfare objective

(a) *The problem*

The previous analysis suggests that the appropriate objective of competition law is the maximization of social welfare in the long term. However, this does not mean that the test that competition authorities and courts should apply is a social welfare test. The objective of the law must inform the construction of open-textured principles and concepts but is not the same as the content of the rules. It may be that, in certain circumstances, a focus on the short-term or long-term effect of a practice on consumers may provide a workable enforcement standard that ensures that social welfare is maximized in the long term.

The debate about the appropriate economic welfare test in competition policy has focused on the merits of attaching more weight to consumer surplus than to producer surplus. Arguments that are often cited in favour of a consumer welfare test are information asymmetry, self-selection, and biases in the decision-making process caused by lobbying by firms. These arguments do not rely on redistribution in order to set consumer surplus as the objective of competition law. Rather, under these models, it is accepted that the maximization of social welfare should be the ultimate objective of competition law. However, in certain circumstances, consumer surplus may be a better test to achieve the intended outcome of prohibiting and deterring conduct that reduces social welfare in the long term.

(b) Information asymmetry

Besanko and Spulber study a model in which the marginal cost post merger is the private information of the merging firms and the competition authority can only have beliefs about the cost savings resulting from the merger. The game has four stages. In the first stage, a social welfare standard is set. This standard plainly maximizes social welfare. In the second stage, firms decide whether to merge. In the third stage, the competition authority decides whether to challenge the merger. The authority's objective is to maximize expected welfare, taking into account the firms' decision to merge. Information asymmetry plays a key role at this stage. Once the firms have decided to merge, the standard that maximizes social welfare has exhausted its function as a self-selection device. The decision-maker has the incentive to minimize the risk of false positive errors and this is achieved by approving all mergers.[85]

The solution to the information asymmetry problem is to adopt a standard that gives relatively more weight to consumer surplus than to producer surplus. Such a standard introduces a bias in favour of false positive errors that counterbalances the bias in favour of the non-intervention that is inherent in the adoption of a social welfare standard.[86] This theory is open to criticism because it assumes that the decision-maker cannot commit to a given enforcement standard,[87] which seems rather implausible in a system based on the rule of law. Furthermore, it adopts a model in which the merger reduces MC but ignores the effect of increased market power.[88] It appears, therefore, that its conclusions are particularly difficult to generalize.

(c) Self-selection

Lyons argues that a social welfare standard of individual mergers is unlikely to maximize social welfare.[89] The reason for this is that competition authorities can only assess mergers that are proposed by firms, and firms will propose the most profitable private merger that would be approved. Under a social welfare standard, firms would propose less socially desirable mergers than under a consumer welfare standard. The basic assumption on which this argument relies is that economic conditions and market structures are such that there is a sufficient range of merger opportunities that allow comparable efficiencies to be realized with different market power outcomes. Under a consumer harm standard, firms will propose

[85] D Besanko and DF Spulber, 'Contested Mergers and Equilibrium in Antitrust Policy' (1993) JL Econ & Org 1.

[86] ibid 16–19.

[87] Farrell and Katz, 'The Economics of Welfare Standards in Antitrust', 22.   [88] ibid.

[89] B Lyons, 'Could Politicians Be More Right than Economists? A Theory of Merger Standards' Revised Centre for Competition and Regulation (CCR) Working Paper CCR 02-1 (European University Institute, 2003).

mergers that allow comparable efficiencies to be realized but with a lower market power increase. As a result, the merger proposed is socially better than the merger that would be proposed under a social welfare standard. Under a social welfare standard, firms are likely to propose mergers that increase (or do not affect) social welfare but with a higher market power increase and that are, therefore, inferior from a social welfare point of view. The analysis can be extended to other types of behaviour, such as collusion (short of a merger) and unilateral conduct as firms entering into potentially anti-competititve agreements or choosing their unilateral course of conduct also face a range of opportunities some of which may be more privately profitable but less socially desirable than others. Furthermore, firms entering into potentially anti-competitive agreements or choosing their unilateral course of conduct also have a self-selection advantage over a competition authority or court. Competition authorities and courts cannot impose a first-best solution[90] on firms but must review agreements or conduct that the firms have chosen among the opportunities open to them.

However, this model also has significant limitations. Farrell and Katz show that a consumer surplus standard may also lead to lower social welfare than a social welfare standard.[91] This is intuitive in circumstances in which the firms face merger opportunities that increase market power but realize significant productive efficiencies that are unlikely to be passed on to consumers in full. Firms may thus choose not to merge at all so that no efficiencies are realized, even if the merger would have increased profits more than it would have reduced consumer surplus. In the alternative, firms may choose a merger which does not reduce consumer surplus but which is the least profitable for the merging firms in circumstances in which very significant productive efficiencies could have been realized at the expense of some reduction in consumer surplus. Furthermore, it is difficult to draw general conclusions from a model that relies exclusively on the range of merger opportunities that the merging firms can select, as the opportunities open to firms depend, as Lyons explains, on the general economic conditions of the market. In large economies open to international markets, firms are more likely to face a range of merger opportunities, some of which are likely to be socially preferable but less privately profitable. The next step of the generalization process would be to say that in large economies, such as those of the United States or the European Union, a consumer surplus standard would perform better than a social welfare standard in achieving a social welfare objective. The objection to this generalization, however, is that the range of merger opportunities faced by a firm not only depends on the size of the economy as a whole, but on the size and structure of the industry. International mergers are more likely in certain industries than in others. Even in large open economies the range of merger opportunities faced by a firm may be

---

[90] A first-best solution is an allocation that can be achieved when the only constraints on the policy-maker are technology and resources. Such an allocation can be economically efficient. If the policy-maker faces constraints in addition to technology and resources—eg information asymmetry—only second-best solutions can be achieved.

[91] Farrell and Katz, 'The Economics of Welfare Standards in Antitrust', 18.

limited and a consumer surplus standard may prevent the most socially preferable merger.

(d) Lobbying

Farrel and Katz focus on a perspective that gives weight to biases that arise in the decision-making process leading up to a merger prohibition.[92] During the first stage, parties decide whether to merge and competitors or consumers may engage in lobbying. At the second stage, an agency decides whether to challenge a merger. At the third stage, the courts review the decision. If at any stage of the process there is a bias towards producer surplus, it makes sense to introduce a bias towards consumer surplus at another stage so as to move the ultimate outcome closer to the first-best.

Neven and Röller discuss the optimal standard in merger review in a model in which merging firms and competitors engage in lobbying, but consumers do not.[93] They find that neither a consumer welfare nor a social welfare standard performs better in all or even in most circumstances. However, their model tends to suggest that lobbying by firms introduces a potential bias in the decision-making process. If the decision-maker is subject to perfect monitoring, this eliminates the bias and the best standard would appear to be social welfare. If, however, monitoring is not perfect, the function of the decision-maker may lead to the first-best outcome if a consumer surplus bias is introduced. The size of mergers also plays a role, as firms are willing to invest more in lobbying in large and, thus, very profitable mergers. This would suggest that, in an environment in which the average size of mergers is large, a consumer welfare standard may perform better.[94]

The main thrust of these theories is that the appropriate standard must take account of the biases inherent in the decision-making process. The optimal standard then depends on the influence that stakeholders exercise in the process. The observation that firms engage in lobbying and consumers do not appears capable of being generalized. However, it only applies to final consumers. On intermediate markets customers may well be prepared to invest in lobbying as much as the parties to the merger or the allegedly anti-competitive conduct. Furthermore, lobbying by competitors of the merging firms should also be taken into account. Overall, these theories do not seem to provide a solid enough basis for choosing a consumer harm test to achieve a social welfare objective.

(e) Limited (not general) validity of consumer harm as a test

None of the models discussed above is capable of providing conclusive proof that a consumer harm test is optimal in achieving a social welfare objective in all or even in most circumstances. However, the fundamental idea that the optimal test to be applied by the decision-maker does not need to be the same as the ultimate

---

[92] ibid.
[93] DJ Neven and L-H Röller, 'Consumer Surplus vs. Welfare Standard in a Political Economy Model of Merger Control' (2005) 23 Intl J Ind Org 829.
[94] ibid 846–847.

objective of the law is correct. Furthermore, the observation that there are biases in the system induced by the firms' advantage in self-selecting their market conduct and asymmetric information is empirically and intuitively correct. Therefore, the models analysed in this section, while not conclusive, provide support for the proposition that a test biased towards consumer surplus may be suitable to achieve a social welfare objective, at least in certain circumstances.[95] Importantly, however, the consumer, under this framework, does not have to be the final consumer. A negative effect on the customer of a product is sufficient to infer that the conduct under review is likely to harm social welfare. The consumer harm test has nothing to do with the protection of the welfare of the final consumer.[96]

D. Conclusion

This chapter indentifies long-term social welfare as the ultimate objective of competition law. From a legal perspective, firms' behaviour that reduces market rivalry so as to harm long-term social welfare should be prohibited. This prohibition should be based on three pillars which give it substance and make it operational as a set of legal rules: the protection of the competitive process or a competitive market structure, economic freedom, and fairness. However, these concepts must be interpreted in the light of the long-term social welfare objective. The competitive process or a competitive market structure which competition law should protect is the dynamic rivalry of firms that, given the existing non-behavioural constraints in the industry, maximizes social welfare in the long term. However, this does not necessarily require an analysis of the impact of a change in market structure on long-term social welfare. In the eyes of the law, certain behaviour may be prohibited because it is likely, in the majority of cases, to reduce social welfare in the long term. Similarly, the economic freedom which competition law should protect is the freedom of economic agents not to be limited in their economic activity by anti-competitive behaviour defined as a reduction of rivalry resulting from the conduct of firms and harming long-term social welfare. This is the negative dimension of economic freedom, that is the freedom from external interference within one's economic sphere. Economic freedom, however, also has a positive dimension which sees freedom as the right to participate in the market, as a consumer or as a firm, and develop one's own potential in a free market environment. Thus, each market participant has the right to seek to increase his own welfare and contribute to maximizing the welfare of society in the long term. This positive, or assertive,

---

[95] EU competition law provides several examples of consumer harm tests: eg Art 101(3) TFEU and Art 102(b) TFEU.

[96] That in EU competition law 'consumer' means 'customer' is well established in practice: see Communication from the Commission—Notice—Guidelines on the application of Article 81(3) of the Treaty [2004] OJ C101/97 ('Guidelines on Art 101(3)'), para 84 and Guidance on Art 102, para 19, fn 15. This chapter demonstrates that the approach in EU law is theoretically correct because the consumer harm test has nothing to do with the protection of final consumers but is a way of verifying whether a restriction of rivalry on the supply side of the market is likely to harm social welfare in the long term.

concept of freedom is the foundation of its negative counterpart. Negative freedom is the way in which the legal system protects the positive freedom to participate in the market. Finally, fairness denotes the equality of opportunities for all market agents to participate in the economy and benefit from a free market which is not affected by behavioural reductions of rivalry likely to harm social welfare in the long term. A market agent is unfairly prejudiced when he is harmed by anticompetitive behaviour.

Long-term social welfare is theoretically superior to any other objective. In particular, there are no sound justifications for saying that consumer welfare is the objective of competition law. However, the ultimate objective of the law is not the same as the prescriptive content of the rules which pursue that objective. Thus, consumer harm can, in certain circumstances, be the appropriate operational test to achieve a long-term social welfare objective. More generally, rules aimed at prohibiting any conduct on the part of firms that reduces rivalry so as to harm social welfare in the long term do not have to be framed as 'any conduct by a firm or firms that reduces rivalry so as to harm social welfare in the long term is prohibited'.

Allocative, productive, and dynamic efficiency, and germane measures of efficiency such as productivity, are all relevant to the measure of social welfare in the long term. They are all, therefore, elements of a competition law analysis aimed at determining whether the conduct under review harms long-term social welfare. None of them is, however, an objective of competition law on its own.

3

The Design of the Optimal Abuse Tests

A. Introduction

The objective of competition law is to maximize long-term social welfare. However, an abuse test that required proof that the conduct under review reduces long-term social welfare would lack both the qualities that a legal test should possess: certainty and administrability. It is therefore necessary to frame a test, or several tests, that, by relying on elements other than direct proof that a reduction of competitive pressure on the dominant firm has a negative impact on long-term social welfare, are capable of distinguishing conduct that is harmful to competition from pro-competitive behaviour.

This chapter adopts the traditional taxonomy whereby abuses are distinguished as exclusionary, exploitative, or discriminatory. What distinguishes these three categories of abuse is not the ultimate negative effect that the law intends to avoid or the values that underpin the competition rules; the difference lies in the way in which long-term social welfare may be harmed by the unilateral conduct of firms. Thus, exclusionary abuses are abuses that harm long-term social welfare by excluding or marginalizing competitors of the dominant undertaking. Exploitative abuses are abuses that harm long-term social welfare by applying prices or trading conditions that are, respectively, higher or more onerous than those that would prevail under conditions of effective competition. And, finally, discriminatory abuses are abuses that harm long-term social welfare as a result of the charging of different prices or the application of different trading conditions to different customers, where the differences in price or trading terms are not justified by a difference in cost.

This chapter discusses the possible abuse tests applicable to exclusionary, exploitative, and discriminatory abuses. It starts by asking the fundamental question of whether, from a normative standpoint, there should be one abuse test. Then it goes on to examine the tests that have emerged in the literature or in the case law. First, it examines the tests for exclusionary abuses. The order in which the tests are discussed reflects a progression that goes from the most permissive to the strictest. One apparent oddity is that the most permissive tests are also those that may appear to require a competition authority or claimant to prove less. The intent test, for instance, is met if there is proof that the dominant firm intended to harm competition and implemented conduct reasonably capable of doing so. The burden on a competition authority of the claimant is lower than under the consumer harm test which requires proof that the net effect of the conduct is to increase prices and decrease output. But the intent test is also the most permissive because it would prohibit only the most egregiously anti-competitive behaviour. Most business practices that have pro-competitive and anti-competitive justifications would be allowed under the intent test. At the other end of the spectrum, the consumer harm test requires a competition authority or claimant to prove that the conduct has a net negative effect on price and output. This is a demanding test but it captures a much wider range of business behaviour than the intent test, including conduct implemented for the purpose of realizing efficiencies as long as such efficiencies are not passed on to consumers so as to offset the negative effects resulting from any increase of the dominant firm's market power. Therefore, whether a test is more or less permissive depends on the range of conduct that is prohibited assuming perfect information, and not on how difficult it is to prove an infringement in any individual case. Based on this methodology, the tests are discussed in the following order: intent, which also includes naked exclusion, naked exploitation, and naked discrimination; no economic sense; as efficient competitor, which also includes the test for abusive discrimination; and consumer harm, covering both exclusionary and exploitative abuses. The conclusion sets out the test that, from a normative point of view, should apply to exclusionary, exploitative, and discriminatory conduct.

B. The search for a single test

It is clear that no single abuse test could be suitable for application to all conceivable abusive practices by dominant firms. In particular, no single test could be applied to exclusionary, exploitative, and discriminatory abuses. However, it is less clear whether a single test could be appropriate for all exclusionary abuses.[1]

---

[1] The majority of authors suggest a single test for the assessment of abusive conduct, eg J Ordover and R Willig, 'An Economic Definition of Predation: Pricing and Product Innovation' (1981) 97 Yale LJ 8 (influential in developing the sacrifice test); AD Melamed, 'Exclusionary Conduct Under the Antitrust Laws: Balancing, Sacrifice, and Refusals to Deal' (2005) 20 Berkeley Technology LJ 1247 (no economic sense variant of sacrifice test); GJ Werden, 'Identifying Exclusionary Conduct Under Section 2: The "No Economic Sense" Test' (2006) 73 Antitrust LJ 413 (no economic sense variant of sacrifice test); RA Posner, *Antitrust Law: An Economic Perspective* (2nd edn Chicago, University of Chicago Press 2001) 194–195 (equally efficient competitor test); H Hovenkamp, 'Exclusion and the Sherman Act' (2005) 72 University of Chicago L Rev 147 ('disproportionality' of effects test); SC Salop, 'Exclusionary Conduct, Effect on Consumers, and the Flawed Profit Sacrifice Standard' (2006) 73 Antitrust LJ 311 (consumer welfare test); E Elhauge, 'Defining Better Monopolization Standards' (2003) 56 Stan L Rev 253 (an efficiency-based test which focuses on whether the alleged exclusionary abuse strengthens the dominant firm's position because it improves its own efficiency or only because it limits the competitor's production); R O'Donoghue and AJ Padilla, *The Law and Economics of Article 82 EC* (Oxford, Hart Publishing 2006) 191–194 (support for the consumer welfare test); D Hildebrand, *The Role of Economic Analysis in the EC Competition Rules* (3rd edn Alphen aan den Rijn, Kluwer Law International 2009) 366 (equally efficient competitor test). However, some authors suggest a multi-test approach (ie the application of different tests to various types of exclusionary conduct): R Hewitt Pate, 'The Common Law Approach and Improving Standards for Analyzing Single Firm Conduct', address before the Thirteenth Annual Conference on International Antitrust Law and Policy, Fordham Corp Law Institute (New York, 23 October 2003); AI Gavil, 'Exclusionary Distribution Strategies by Dominant Firms: Striking a Better Balance' (2004) 72 Antitrust LJ 3; J Vickers, 'Abuse of Market Power' (2005) 115 Economic Journal 244; M Lao, 'Defining Exclusionary

A single abuse test would appear desirable because the same anti-competitive effect may be caused by many different practices. A dominant firm can exclude a new entrant by exclusive purchasing obligations, predatory pricing, or rebate systems. It could be argued that the same test should apply to any practice which has the effect of excluding the new entrant because any such practice would cause the same competitive harm. Moreover, an approach that applied completely different tests to specific practices would increase the dominant firm's incentives to behave strategically by choosing the anti-competitive practice that is treated more leniently. However, what is important in assessing conduct that may be anti-competitive is not only the effect but also the means employed to achieve it. Different forms of conduct that, in the abstract, could all produce the same anti-competitive result may in reality be more or less likely to have an anti-competitive purpose and more or less likely to be competition on the merits. Unconditional above-cost discounts and prices lower than the average variable costs (AVC) of the dominant firm can both exclude a competitor, thereby harming social welfare in the long term. However, unconditional above-cost discounts are much less likely to do so and much more likely to be competition based on efficiency. Therefore, a different and more permissive test should apply to unconditional above-cost price cuts than to prices below AVC.[2] In framing a test, not just the type and magnitude but also the likelihood of anti-competitive effects should be taken into account. Therefore, practices should be treated differently if the likelihood of them having anti-competitive effects is different. This approach minimizes the risk of strategic behaviour by dominant undertakings.[3] Practices are treated more leniently

Conduct Under Section 2: The Case for Non-Universal Standards' in BE Hawk (ed), *International Antitrust Law & Policy: Fordham Competition Law 2006* (New York, Juris Publishing 2007) 433; MS Popofsky, 'Defining Exclusionary Conduct: Section 2, the Rule of Reason, and the Unifying Principle Underlying Antitrust Rules' (2006) 73 Antitrust LJ 435, 443.

[2] On the principle that the legal tests in competition law should reflect the balance between the risks and costs of false convictions and false acquittals, over-deterrence and under-deterrence, see the literature cited at 31, n 59 above. The importance of this approach to the design of the competition law tests does not mean that one type of enforcement error or cost must be seen, for ideological or theoretical reasons, as more serious or of a greater magnitude than another. Currently, the majority of the literature emphasises the need to avoid false convictions and over-deterrence as a paramount concern of competition law, particularly in the area of abuse of dominance: see, eg, KN Hylton and M Salinger, 'Tying Law and Policy: A Decision-Theoretic Approach' (2001) 69 Antitrust LJ 469; DS Evans and AJ Padilla, 'Excessive Prices: Using Economics to Define Administrable Legal Rules' (2005) 1 J Comp L & Econ 97; Werden, 'Identifying Exclusionary Conduct under Section 2: The "No Economic Sense" Test'. However, there is little or no empirical evidence or theoretical justification for this claim as a general proposition: see, convincingly, OFT, 'The Cost of Inappropriate Interventions/Non Interventions under Article 82' Economic Discussion Paper OFT864 (September 2006). The point made in this book is that different practices in different market contexts may be more likely to be anti-competitive or pro-competitive, their anti-competitive or pro-competitive effects may be easier or more difficult to prove, and the magnitude of the potential competitive harm associated with them may be greater or smaller. Therefore, the balance of the risks and costs of false convictions and over-deterrence and false acquittals and under-deterrence should not be carried out once and for all on the basis of theoretical assumptions or ideological beliefs but in relation to each type of conduct and in a way that leaves sufficient flexibility to take into account the specifics of the market context in which the conduct in question takes place.

[3] A risk identified by, among others, I Lianos, 'Categorical Thinking in Competition Law and the "Effects-based" Approach in Article 82 EC' in A Ezrachi (ed), *Article 82 EC: Reflections on Its Recent Evolution* (Oxford, Hart Publishing 2009) 19, 41–43.

because they have a lower potential for anti-competitive effects and, therefore, the risk of a dominant undertaking choosing such behaviour because it is treated more leniently is by definition lower.

A further argument in support of a single test is that such an approach would allow conduct which has not been examined before to be assessed in a principled way. The *AstraZeneca* case illustrates this point.[4] In that case, the Commission found that misleading representations made to patent offices with the objective of delaying new entry are an abuse.[5] This was a novel infringement. In its legal assessment, the Commission relied on the doctrine of the special responsibility of the dominant undertaking not to impair genuine undistorted competition in the internal market.[6] It further referred to the need for a dominant undertaking to ensure that its conduct is proportionate to the objectives it intends to achieve[7] and to the 'concept' of abuse set out in *Hoffmann-La Roche*.[8] The Commission was also able to rely on precedents holding that the use of legal procedures can amount to an abuse.[9] Furthermore, *Compagnie Maritime Belge*,[10] *Irish Sugar*,[11] and *Michelin II*[12] supported the proposition that proof of actual market effects was not required. However, the absence of a clearly established analytical structure for the assessment of abuse meant that the analysis of the case had to be based on vague concepts which offered little or no guidance on how to assess the conduct under review. This creates a double problem of legitimacy and legal certainty. On the one hand, to impose a heavy fine on a dominant firm based on indeterminate concepts such as the doctrine of special responsibility or the general concept of abuse gives rise to the impression that the Commission acted arbitrarily and outside the boundaries of predictable decision-making firmly anchored to rule of law. On the other hand, dominant firms have little guidance on which conduct may constitute an abuse beyond the categories clearly established in the case law. It could also be argued that the problem of legal certainty is particularly acute in the European

---

[4] *Generics/AstraZeneca* [2006] OJ L332/24, substantially upheld in Case T-321/05 *AstraZeneca AB v Commission* [2010] OJ C221/33, under appeal in Case C-457/10 P *AstraZeneca AB v Commission* [2010] OJ C301/18.

[5] *Generics/AstraZeneca*, recitals 324–328.

[6] ibid recital 325. See Case 322/81 *NV Nederlandsche Banden Industrie Michelin v Commission* [1983] ECR 3461 (*Michelin I*), para 57; Joined Cases C-395/96 P and C-396/96 P *Compagnie Maritime Belge Transports SA v Commission* [2000] ECR I-1365, para 85; Case T-83/91 *Tetra Pak International SA v Commission* [1994] ECR II-755 (*Tetra Pak II*), para 114.

[7] *Generics/AstraZeneca*, recital 327.   [8] ibid recital 324.

[9] Case C-395/96 P and C-396/96 P *Compagnie Maritime Belge*, paras 82–88; Case T-111/96 *ITT Promedia NV v Commission* [1998] ECR II-2937; *French-West African Shipowners' Committees* [1992] OJ L134/1.

[10] Joined Cases T-24/93 to T-26/93 and T-28/93 *Compagnie Maritime Belge SA v Commission* [1996] ECR II-01201, para 149.

[11] Case T-228/97 *Irish Sugar plc v Commission* [1999] ECR II-2969, para 191.

[12] Case T-203/01 *Manufacture Française des Pneumatiques Michelin v Commission* [2003] ECR II-4071 (*Michelin II*), paras 239 and 241.

Union in the context of modernization[13] and an increasing number of private actions.[14] National competition authorities or national courts may have to decide

---

[13] 'Modernisation' denotes the reforms of EU competition law proposed in: European Commission, White Paper on Modernisation of the Rules Implementing Articles 85 and 86 of the EC Treaty OJ [1999] C-132/1 and implemented in Council Regulation (EC) 1/2003 of 16 December 2002 on the implementation of the rules on competition laid down in Articles 81 and 82 of the Treaty [2003] OJ L1/1. On modernization, see C-D Ehlermann, 'The Modernization of EC Antitrust Policy: A Legal and Cultural Revolution' (2000) 37 CML Rev 537; J Rivas and M Horspool (eds), *Modernisation and Decentralisation of EC Competition Law* (The Hague, Kluwer Law International 2000); A Riley, 'EC Antitrust Modernisation: The Commission Does Very Nicely—Thank You! Part One: Regulation 1 and the Notification Burden' (2003) 24 ECLR 604; A Riley, 'EC Antitrust Modernisation: The Commission Does Very Nicely—Thank You! Part Two: Between the Idea and the Reality: Decentralisation under Regulation 1' (2003) 24 ECLR 657; D Samuels, 'Is Modernisation Working?' (2005) 8 Global Competition Rev 17; A Andreangeli, 'The Impact of the Modernisation Regulation on the Guarantees of Due Process in Competition Proceedings' (2006) 31 EL Rev 342; DJ Gerber and P Cassinis, 'The "Modernization" of European Community Competition Law: Achieving Consistency in Enforcement: Part 1' (2006) 27 ECLR 10; DJ Gerber and P Cassinis, 'The "Modernization" of European Community Competition Law: Achieving Consistency in Enforcement: Part 2' (2006) 27 ECLR 51; AP Komninos, 'Modernisation and Decentralisation: Retrospective and Prospective' in G Amato and C-D Ehlermann (eds), *EC Competition Law: A Critical Assessment* (Oxford, Hart Publishing 2007) 629; P Lowe, 'The Design of Competition Policy Institutions for the 21st Century—the Experience of the European Commission and DG Competition' (2008) 3 European Commission Competition Policy Newsletter 1.

[14] The evolution of the legal thinking on the right to damages for breach of EU competition law is reflected in J Temple Lang, 'Community Antitrust Law: Compliance and Enforcement' (1981) 18 CML Rev 335; F Jacobs, 'Damages for Breach of Article 86 EEC' (1983) 8 EL Rev 353; J Temple Lang, 'EEC Competition Actions in Member States: Claims for Damages, Declarations and Injunctions for Breach of Community Antitrust Law' in BE Hawk (ed), *Annual Proceedings of the Fordham Corporate Law Institute: Antitrust and Trade Policies of the European Economic Community* (New York, Matthew Bender 1984) 219; F Jacobs, 'Civil Enforcement of EEC Antitrust Law' (1984) 82 Mich L Rev 1364; JS Davidson, 'Actions for Damages in the English Courts for Breach of EEC Competition Law' (1985) 34 ICLQ 178; J Steiner, 'How to Make the Action Suit the Case: Domestic Remedies for Breach of EEC Law' (1987) 12 EL Rev 102; J Maitland-Walker, 'A Step Closer to a Definitive Ruling on a Right in Damages for Breach of EC Competition Rules' (1992) 13 ECLR 3; JHJ Bourgeois, 'EC Competition Law and Member State Courts' in BE Hawk (ed), *International Antitrust in a Global Economy: Fordham Corporate Law 1993* (New York, Kluwer Law and Taxation 1994) 20; R Whish, 'The Enforcement of EC Competition Law in the Domestic Courts of Member States' (1994) 15 ECLR 60; D Good 'Eurotort with Europrocedure?' in M Hutchings and M Andenas, *Competition Law Yearbook 2002* (London, British Institute of International and Comparative Law 2003) 345; D Waelbroeck, 'Private Enforcement of Competition Rules and its Limits' in M Hutchings and M Andenas, *Competition Law Yearbook 2002* (London, British Institute of International and Comparative Law 2003) 369; WPJ Wils, 'Should Private Enforcement Be Encouraged in Europe?' (2003) 26 World Competition 473; CA Jones, 'Private Antitrust Enforcement in Europe: A Policy Analysis and Reality Check' (2004) 27 World Competition 13; U Boge, 'Public and Private Enforcement: Harmony or Discord?' (2006) 5 Comp Law 114; M Debroux and E Tricot, 'Competition—EU Competition Law Enforcement: Towards a US Style Private Antitrust Action?' (2006) 27 BLR 256; J Pheasant, 'Damages Actions for Breach of the EC Antitrust Rules: the European Commission's Green Paper' (2006) 27 ECLR 365; A Andreangeli, 'The Enforcement of Article 81 EC Treaty Before National Courts After the House of Lords' Decision in Inntrepreneur Pub Co Ltd v Crehan' (2007) 32 EL Rev 260; S McMichael and B Kemp, 'Private Enforcement' (2007) 6 Competition Law Insight 14; M Hilgenfeld, 'Private Antitrust Enforcement: Towards a Harmonised European Model or a "Patchwork" of Various Member States' Rules?' (2008) 14 International Trade Law & Regulation 39; P Nebbia, 'Damages Actions for the Infringement of EC Competition Law: Compensation or Deterrence?' (2008) 33 EL Rev 23; M Danov, 'Awarding Exemplary (or Punitive) Antitrust Damages in EC Competition Cases with an International Element—the Rome II Regulation and the Commission's White Paper

whether certain conduct on which there is no clear EU law precedent constitutes an infringement of Article 102. In the absence of a single test, there is a heightened risk of inconsistency of approach. This could also lead to a greater number of references to the Court of Justice under Article 267 TFEU which would have the effect of prolonging national proceedings by years. This would not necessarily increase legal certainty if a practice-by-practice approach were to be retained because each time a new practice was examined, a new reference to the Court of Justice would be required. Legitimacy and legal certainty, however, do not necessarily require a single abuse test for exclusionary conduct. Novel conduct could be subsumed under one of several existing tests as long as it is clear when each test applies. Let us assume, for instance, that the law adopts two tests: conduct is prohibited either if it excludes competitors that are as efficient as the dominant firm or if it has the sole purpose of excluding competitors, has no cognizable efficiencies, and is capable of causing competitive harm. A novel infringement such as the one in *AstraZeneca* could have been assessed under either test. There is no need for each test to contemplate all forms of conduct that may fall within its scope. It is only necessary that all the elements of the test are present in the conduct under review and there is no material element distinguishing the conduct in question from that which the test contemplates. The conduct that a test contemplates is conduct that carries the same risk of competitive harm and has the same likelihood of being pro-competitive as the conduct that the test intends to prohibit.

In conclusion, not only is a single abuse test unthinkable as it could not apply to exclusionary, exploitative, and discriminatory abuses but even a single exclusionary abuse test may not be appropriate because different practices may carry different risks of competitive harm and have different probabilities of being pro-competitive. Nor is a single test absolutely required for the purposes of legitimacy and legal certainty. Predictable outcomes can equally be achieved by a set of tests, provided that their application to individual practices can be justified based on clear principles within a coherent analytical structure. The analysis below examines the tests applicable to exclusionary, exploitative, and discriminatory abuses. It demonstrates that no single test is suitable to the assessment of all types of conduct that may be abusive, not even all types of potentially exclusionary conduct. However, each test provides important insights to understanding when conduct by a dominant firm is

on Damages' (2008) 29 ECLR 430; A Ezrachi, 'From *Courage v Crehan* to the White Paper—the Changing Landscape of European Private Enforcement and the Possible Implications for Article 82 EC Litigation' in M-O Mackenrodt, B Conde Gallego, and S Enchelmaier (eds), *Abuse of Dominant Position: New Interpretation, New Enforcement Mechanisms?* (Berlin, Springer 2008) 117; HKS Schmidt, 'Private Enforcement—Is Article 82 EC Special?' in M Mackenrodt, B Conde Gallego, and S Enchelmaier (eds), *Abuse of Dominant Position: New Interpretation, New Enforcement Mechanisms?* (Berlin, Springer 2008) 137; AP Komninos, *EC Private Antitrust Enforcement: Decentralised Application of EC Competition Law by National Courts* (Oxford, Hart Publishing 2008); WPJ Wils, 'The Relationship between Public Antitrust Enforcement and Private Actions for Damages' (2009) 32 World Competition 3; KS Bernard, 'Private Antitrust Litigation in the European Union—Why Does the EC Want to Embrace What the US FTC is Trying to Avoid?' (2010) 3 Global Competition Litigation Rev 69; F Rizzuto, 'The Private Enforcement of European Union Competition Law: What Next?' (2010) 3 Global Competition Litigation Rev 57.

abusive and, either by itself or in combination with other elements, can be used in the design of the legal tests under Article 102.

C. Intent

(1) Origins of the test

Perhaps the most intuitive and earliest test used to distinguish anti-competitive conduct by dominant firms from harmless or pro-competitive behaviour is intent. There is no doubt, for instance, that under section 2 of the Sherman Act 'a defendant's state of mind or intent is an element of a criminal antitrust offense which must be established by evidence and inferences drawn therefrom and cannot be taken from the trier of fact through reliance on a legal presumption of wrongful intent from proof of an effect on prices'.[15] Specific intent is not required to establish a civil offence under the US antitrust laws[16] but this does not mean that courts do not apply an intent test in certain circumstances.[17] The EU courts explicitly apply a test of intent to determine whether a dominant undertaking's pricing strategy is abusive when prices are above AVC but below average total cost (ATC).[18]

(2) Defining intent

Before any analysis of the arguments for and against a test of intent in competition law, it is necessary to clarify the meaning of intent.

It is important to clarify, first of all, that a test of intent for abuse of dominance is distinct from the relevance of intent evidence to establish objective elements of a different test. If, for instance, a consumer harm test is adopted, evidence of the dominant firm's intent to raise its prices following the successful exclusion of a competitor may be indirect evidence of consumer harm. The relevance of the evidence, however, is not that it casts light on the firm's state of mind but that it provides information on the likely effect on the firm's conduct on the market.

Intent can be general or specific. General intent denotes the intent of carrying out the relevant conduct. Specific intent is the intent to cause the harm that the law

---

[15] *United States v United States Gypsum Co* 438 US 422, 435 (1978).

[16] eg *United States v Aluminum Co of America* 148 F 2d 416, 432 (2d Cir 1945), reasoning that to require specific intent for a civil infringement under s 2 of the Sherman Act 'makes nonsense of it, for no monopolist monopolizes unconscious of what he is doing'. Interestingly, proof of specific intent is dispensed with on the ground that the element will always be present and, therefore, proof thereof would be superfluous.

[17] *Aspen Skiing Co v Aspen Highlands Skiing Corp* 472 US 585 (1985) and *Eastman Kodak Co v Image Technical Services* 504 US 451 (1992).

[18] Case C-62/86 *AKZO Chemie BV v Commission* [1991] ECR I-3359; Case T-83/91 *Tetra Pak II*, upheld in Case C-333/94 P *International SA v Commission* [1996] ECR I-5951 (*Tetra Pak II*); Case T-340/03 *France Télécom SA v Commission* [2007] ECR II-107, upheld in Case C-202/07 P *France Télécom SA v Commission* [2009] ECR I-2369.

prohibits. In predatory pricing, general intent would be established if the dominant firm engaged in pricing below a relevant measure of cost voluntarily, and thus neither inadvertently nor by mistake. Specific intent would be established by proof that the dominant firm lowered its prices below cost in order to exclude a rival so as to protect or enhance its market power.

A further distinction is sometimes drawn between subjective and objective intent. Subjective intent denotes a person's state of mind accompanying an act. Objective intent would be 'a state of mind reasonably attributable to defendant in light of his conduct'.[19] However, it is not clear that this distinction is helpful in framing a test for abuse of dominance. Intent is a subjective state of mind. A test which looks at the objective tendency of the conduct of a dominant firm to achieve a certain purpose or effect is not a test of intent. It is a test of effect. In reality, the theory of 'objective' intent tries to conflate and solve two separate problems and it does so by creating an unnecessary legal concept. The first problem is that when a test of intent is applied, this does not mean that an abuse of a dominant position may be established based purely on evidence of subjective intent. As a minimum, the intent to cause competitive harm must be implemented in acts that are objectively capable of causing the harm in question. In modern legal systems, it is, or should be, uncontroversial that nobody can be punished purely because of his own thoughts and intentions, however evil they may be in the eyes of the society or the State. Furthermore, it is also reasonably clear that intent must be implemented in acts that are at least capable, in the context of empirically plausible chains of cause and effect, to achieve the intended harm.[20] Therefore, any subjective intent test is always also objective. It does not follow, however, that there is a category of objective intent as opposed to subjective intent. The second problem is evidential. Evidence of intent need not be subjective but may consist of objective elements from which it is possible to infer that the dominant firm intended the anti-competitive harm. This is in no way different from other areas of the law. The specific intent required for murder can be established by a confession. This is the only conceivable direct proof of subjective intent. But in most contested murder trials, proof of intent would be circumstantial and based on the motive or conduct of the defendant. There is no reason to say that when the defendant confesses to murder the test is subjective intent, while when the intention to kill a person is established based on circumstantial evidence the test is objective intent. The legal test is the same in both cases. The only difference is the evidence relied on to prove that the test is met.[21]

---

[19] RA Cass and KN Hylton, 'Antiturst Intent' Boston University School of Law, Working Paper Series, Law and Economics, Working Paper No 00-02 (Boston, 2000) 4.

[20] eg nobody would dream, it is hoped, of finding an abuse of dominance because the board of a dominant undertaking performed a voodoo ritual aimed at destroying a competitor in order to protect the undertaking's dominant position.

[21] See M Lao, 'Reclaiming a Role for Intent Evidence in Monopolization Analysis' (2004) 54 American University L Rev 151, 202–212, where she uses the terminology 'objective intent' and 'subjective intent' but she clearly means by 'objective intent' intent 'inferred from concrete acts taken by the defendant' (ibid 202).

In conclusion, a test of intent would ask whether the dominant undertaking intended to cause competitive harm, however defined, and implemented acts that, as a minimum, are reasonably capable of causing the intended harm.

(3) Naked abuse as a test of intent

Perhaps the most egregiously anti-competitive conduct is behaviour that has the sole or overwhelmingly predominant[22] purpose of harming competition,[23] has no conceivable redeeming virtue either by way of economic efficiencies or otherwise, and is reasonably capable of causing competitive harm. An example may be a dominant firm obtaining a patent that blocks the entry of rivals to the relevant market in circumstances in which the dominant firm is clearly not entitled to the patent and only obtains it by perpetrating fraud on the relevant patent office.[24] This conduct may be described as naked exclusion because it is obviously exclusionary on its face.

Different formulations have been suggested to describe nakedly exclusionary conduct. Some commentators have suggested that the hallmark of this type of behaviour is that it is not costly for the dominant firm.[25] However, while this can be empirically correct in most circumstances in the sense that the investment in naked exclusion is generally negligible compared to the potential gains, this feature is certainly not sufficient to define naked exclusion. In fact, naked exclusion has been defined as 'behaviour that unambiguously fails to enhance any party's efficiency, provides no benefits (short or long-term) to consumers, and in its economic effect produces only costs for the victims and wealth transfers to the firm's engaging in the conduct (apart from its contribution to market power)'.[26] According to a different formulation relating to deceitful and fraudulent practice, it should be a prima facie abuse for a monopolist to engage in a deceitful practice if the 'deceit reasonably appears capable of making a significant contribution to its attaining or maintaining monopoly power'.[27] Several examples of naked exclusion have been identified, including opportunistic behaviour in a private standard setting context,[28] tortious conduct such as

---

[22] The wording 'overwhelmingly predominant' is necessary to rule out instances in which other purposes are conceivable but clearly trivial.

[23] Competitive harm can take the form of exclusion of rivals, exploitation of a dominant position, or distortions of competition among customers and suppliers caused by discrimination. For ease of exposition, the text will refer to exclusionary abuses but the same principles apply to exploitation and discrimination.

[24] Similarly to the US case of *Walker Process Equipment, Inc v Food Machinery and Chemical Corp* 382 US 172 (1965).

[25] SA Creighton et al, 'Cheap Exclusion' (2005) 72 Antitrust LJ 975, 977.

[26] ibid 982.

[27] ME Stucke, 'How Do (and Should) Competition Authorities Treat a Dominant Firm's Deception?' (2010) 63 SMU L Rev 1069, 1113.

[28] Creighton et al, 'Cheap Exclusion', 987–989. This would be the case, for instance, if a dominant firm participating in a private standard-setting process fraudulently induced the standard setting body to adopt a standard that reinforced its dominant position on the market.

fraud or deception,[29] and the misuse 'of courts and governmental agencies' in order to create or reinforce barriers to entry or expansion.[30]

On a closer analysis, it is appropriate to frame the naked exclusion test as a test of intent. Because the conduct in question has no purpose other than to harm competition, nakedly exclusionary conduct is inconceivable unless the dominant undertaking implements the conduct with the intent to cause such harm. Harm to competition in this context relates to the harmful elements of the conduct, not necessarily to the ultimate harm that competition law aims to deter. Because, as discussed below, in nakedly exclusionary abuses the harmful elements of the conduct are harm to rivals, absence of efficiencies, and the preservation or increase of market power, specific intent must relate to these elements cumulatively. Simply the intention of harming rivals or the intention to increase market power would not be sufficient. Crucially, the dominant firm must not intend to generate efficiencies of any kind, whether in the form of lower prices and larger output, lower costs, or new production processes or products. This test of intent is consistent with the very nature of the type of behaviour under consideration. Fraud, deception, opportunistic behaviour, and rent seeking are practices that are implemented with a specific intent to cause harm. They are not, at least not in the general case, negligent or inadvertent 'accidents'. So defined, intent in this test plays a fundamental role in minimizing the risk of false convictions and over-deterrence, so that negligent or inadvertent mistakes are not interpreted as prima facie infringements of the competition rules without a thorough market inquiry. If no specific intent were required, the naked exclusion test would pose too high a risk of false convictions and over-deterrence, as it would condemn conduct without consideration of its economic effects on long-term social welfare other than an abridged test of capability to cause harm. However, because of the objective features of the conduct in question, intent is in principle suitable to be the sole test for abuse. Once it is proved that the conduct harms the competitive opportunities of rivals, has no cognizable efficiencies, and is reasonably capable of harming competition, and that it was implemented with the sole or overwhelmingly predominant intent of causing competitive harm, no more should be required to establish a prima facie abuse. It is then for the dominant firm to adduce evidence tending to invalidate the prima facie case of infringement.

While this test may appear to be the most intuitive, it has been the last to emerge in the literature. The reason for this is probably that section 2 of the Sherman Act and Article 102 TFEU, the archetypical unilateral conduct rules that have generated most of the literature on the subject, have been applied predominantly to business practices that may have an anti-competitive effect but could also conceivably

---

[29] ibid 989–990; see also generally on deceit Stucke, 'How Do (and Should) Competition Authorities Treat a Dominant Firm's Deception?' One example could be a dominant firm knowingly making false claims about the quality and functionality of a competitor's product.

[30] H Bork, *The Antitrust Paradox: A Policy at War with Itself* (New York, The Free Press 1993) 347–364; Creighton et al, 'Cheap Exclusion' 990–993. The classic example is a dominant firm obtaining a patent that constitutes an additional significant barrier to entry by perpetrating fraud on the relevant patent office. Another example could be a dominant firm inducing the government to erect or maintain regulatory barriers to entry, either by bribery or by deception.

be a form of competition based on efficiency. This initial and predominant focus of unilateral conduct rules can be explained by observing that nakedly exclusionary conduct is often prohibited by rules other than competition law. Conduct having the sole or overwhelming purpose of harming others and no conceivable socially desirable effects is likely to be prohibited by tort law, consumer protection law, contract law, or other specific rules governing the particular activity in question. The application of competition law to these practices may not have been a priority for the parties or for the competition authorities for a certain period of time. However, the growing complexity and globalization of the business environment has increased both the opportunities to engage in nakedly exclusionary practices and the competitive harm that they cause so that the application of competition law may be the only suitable way of addressing them effectively. To this end, the naked exclusion test is theoretically sound, provided that it is correctly defined and applied. Its major shortcoming is that, by penalizing conduct without a full appraisal of its economic effects, it may give rise to a very high risk of false convictions and over-deterrence. Its major advantage is that it minimizes enforcement costs. If it is really possible to identify conduct that, on its face, is unequivocally harmful, it would appear wasteful to engage in a thorough analysis relating, for instance, to the costs and revenues of the dominant firm or to the likely impact of the dominant firm's conduct on price and output. In fact, such inquiries may generate unnecessary risks of false acquittals and under-deterrence. A dominant firm that manages to maintain its monopoly by perpetrating fraud on the relevant patent office could escape liability because of lack of proof that the fraud resulted in lower market output. However, fraud is unequivocally harmful. Fraud perpetrated by a dominant firm as a result of which the latter acquires or maintains exclusive rights is reasonably capable of harming competition. And punishing and deterring fraud does not appear to give rise to significant enforcement costs even if competition law might occasionally punish and deter fraud that does not, on the facts of a particular case, decrease social welfare in the long term by reducing the intensity of competition on the market. In this way, the naked exclusion test gives rise to low enforcement risks while achieving significant enforcement cost gains.

While the naked exclusion test is a test of intent, mere intent is, of course, not sufficient to establish a prima facie case of abuse. First, the conduct must impair the competitive opportunities of rivals. It should not be necessary, however, to inquire whether the conduct is capable of excluding equally efficient rivals. Generally, nakedly exclusionary conduct is capable of excluding all rivals, including equally efficient ones. But proof of intent should dispense with proof of exclusion of equally efficient rivals. If the conduct was engaged in with the sole or overwhelmingly predominant purpose of excluding competitors, it is reasonable to infer that exclusion was both feasible and profitable. Secondly, the conduct must also be such that no efficiencies or other benefits are conceivable, at least prima facie. Fraud on governmental agencies or bribery of public officials clearly satisfies the test. It is important to note that the test applies to the conduct in the abstract not to its effect on the specific facts of the case. The circumstance that the excluded rival had higher costs than the dominant undertaking does not mean that the conduct increases productive efficiency. Fraud or bribery does not generate efficiencies. They are inherently incapable of doing so. Whether on the facts they happen to exclude a less efficient competitor is a mere accident that does not turn nakedly exclusionary conduct into competition based on efficiency. Finally, the conduct must be reasonably capable of causing competitive harm. Competitive harm is harm to social welfare in the long term by a reduction of market rivalry. However, harm to long-term social welfare can legitimately be inferred from other elements. In the case of naked exclusion, the conduct is reasonably capable of excluding or marginalizing competitors. The conduct is also such that no cognizable efficiencies are conceivable. The only other element that appears to be necessary for an inference of competitive harm to be drawn is that the conduct must be reasonably capable of preserving or increasing the market power of the dominant firm. A reduction of rivalry capable of preserving or maintaining market power as a result of conduct that has no conceivable efficiencies is plainly sufficient to raise a presumption that the conduct under review harms social welfare in the long term.

Notwithstanding the fact that it is possible to formulate a workable test of naked exclusion, there are still two problems of principle. The first problem is whether there is conduct that, by its very nature, is only capable of impairing the competitive opportunities of the rivals of a dominant firm and has no redeeming virtues. This is, of course, an empirical question but it appears that, at least in certain extreme cases of fraud and deception, this limb of the objective test of naked exclusion is capable of being met. It is of the utmost importance, however, not to broaden this category too much, particularly in the sphere of pricing behaviour and investment decisions. Pricing and investment decisions would appear to fall squarely into the category of conduct that, by its very nature, may be either pro-competitive or anti-competitive, depending on the circumstances. Only the strongest evidence of intent would be able to rebut this presumption and determine the application of the naked exclusion test. The second problem is whether competition should apply to punish and deter conduct that is also prohibited by other rules. Deceitful behaviour, for instance, may be a tort, may infringe consumer protection rules, or may constitute a crime if it involves the provision of false or misleading information to public authorities. On first principles, the answer is clearly that the same behaviour can be prohibited by different rules having different objectives and protecting different interests by providing for different remedies. Competition law generally does not, and should not in principle, have a residual application. The application of competition law should not be excluded by the fact that the conduct in question amounts to a breach of contract, a tort, or a crime under other relevant legal rules. This is because none of these branches of the law address the harm that competition law aims to prevent, namely the harm to long-term social welfare caused by firms' behaviour that reduces the intensity of market rivalry. However, this does not automatically make a breach of contract, a tort, or a crime committed by a dominant firm against a rival an infringement of competition law. The conduct must always satisfy the relevant competition test and an appropriately framed competition test would only prohibit conduct that causes the harm that competition law aims to deter. The objective dimension of the naked exclusion test must, therefore, always require an assessment of the capability of the conduct under review to cause competitive harm. That assessment may, however, be less demanding than for other types of conduct because of the prima facie absence of any socially desirable purpose or effect of the conduct and the proof that the only or overwhelming purpose of the conduct was to harm the competitive opportunities of rivals and to preserve or increase the dominant undertaking's market power.

(4) The test of intent beyond naked abuse and its limitations

A test of intent for abuse of dominance is clearly attractive. Economic tests requiring, for instance, proof of output restrictions or exclusion of competitors that are as efficient as the dominant undertaking, are difficult to apply and sometimes yield ambiguous results. Intent may be an alternative to proof of economic effects[31] or may complement the assessment of the effects of the conduct.[32] According to one view, intent may be a proxy for anti-competitive effects. If firms engage in certain conduct that could be harmful to competition with the intent to harm competition, it is reasonable to infer harm from intent.[33] According to another view, evidence of intent contributes to casting light on the strategic motives and incentives that led firms to engage in the conduct under review. The motives and incentives of firms play a key role in post-Chicago economics in distinguishing welfare-reducing exclusion from harmless or pro-competitive behaviour.[34] When evidence of economic effects is ambiguous, evidence of intent clarifies whether the conduct has an anti-competitive purpose or is competition on the merits.

Notwithstanding the above arguments, and, more generally, the intuitive appeal of intent as a legal test, intent has not fared well as a general test for abuse of dominance. A recurring objection is that it is not possible to distinguish anti-competitive intent from the intent to succeed on the market. The intent to eliminate a competitor is clearly not sufficient. A dominant firm can eliminate a competitor thanks to the dominant firm's superior efficiency or by deploying a predatory strategy that harms long-term social welfare. Even the intent to create or maintain monopoly power would not be sufficient because whether to do so is prohibited depends on the means employed. A monopoly can be created or defended competitively or anti-competitively.[35] This objection is only superficially valid.

---

[31] O Odudu, 'The Role of Specific Intent in Section 1 of the Sherman Act' (2002) 25 World Competition 463, 486–491.

[32] Lao, 'Reclaiming a Role for Intent Evidence in Monopolization Analysis', 192–199.

[33] Odudu, 'The Role of Specific Intent in Section 1 of the Sherman Act', 489–490.

[34] Lao, 'Reclaiming a Role for Intent Evidence in Monopolization Analysis', 196–199. Under this approach, intent is not a test but evidence of effects. However, the arguments that support this conclusion would equally support requiring proof of intent, at least in circumstances in which the evidence of anti-competitive effects is systematically ambiguous.

[35] H Hovenkamp, 'The Monopolization Offense' (2000) 61 Ohio State LJ 1035, 1039; Posner, *Antitrust Law*, 214–215. These views rest on the simplistic observation that 'competitive and exclusionary conduct look alike': see FH Easterbrook, 'When Is It Worthwhile to Use Courts to Search for Exclusionary Conduct?' (2003) Columbia Business L Rev 345.

The intent inquiry does not ask the simplistic question of whether the dominant firm intended to exclude a rival or to gain market share. Rather, a test of intent requires an understanding of the incentives of the dominant firm and the means employed to achieve the intended result.[36] Intent evidence that demonstrates the aim of increasing market share or overcoming a rival will be irrelevant. But intent evidence that reveals that the board of a dominant company had decided to incur significant losses in a pricing campaign believing that this would force a rival out of the market, as a result of which prices could be raised significantly above MC, would show a specific intent to harm competition.

The objection that intent evidence is unreliable because it is subjective and susceptible to being misunderstood[37] is even less convincing. This is an issue of the reliability and weight of the evidence. Any internal document setting out a strategy vis-à-vis a rival will have to be interpreted according to its meaning, its context, and the aim, background, and character of its authors. This is true of the evaluation of evidence more generally. There is no reason to believe that evidence of intent in competition matters is subject to such a high risk of error of assessment that it ought to be excluded altogether, with the consequence that intent cannot be a substantive test for abuse of dominance.[38] Ultimately, if the evidence is unreliable it will not be believed. But relevance and weight should guide the admissibility and assessment of the evidence, not purported 'exclusionary rules' that withhold relevant material from the tribunal of fact on the grounds either of inherent unreliability or the inability of competition authorities or courts to assess the evidence.

It is also easy to prove the weakness of the argument that the availability of intent evidence 'is often a function of luck and the defendant's legal sophistication'.[39] In response, it has been pointed out that the same applies to all disputes where specific intent is in issue.[40] More generally, the problem of the availability of evidence and the risk of fabrication or suppression of evidence relates not only to intent. Reliable cost data may not be available or may, to a certain extent, be manipulated by a dominant firm. Does this mean that cost tests must be banned from the realm of competition law? This argument also ignores the fact that intent evidence is always going to be assessed together with evidence of conduct. What matters is not the presence, or absence, of an 'embarrassing' document but whether it is possible, on the whole of the evidence, to infer that the dominant firm engaged in the conduct under review with the intention of causing competitive harm or for lawful or even pro-competitive reasons.

The most powerful objection to intent as a test for abuse is that competition law, by its very nature, requires the application of an objective standard. The aim of competition law is to prohibit any conduct by firms that may harm long-term social welfare by reducing market rivalry. When a restriction of

---

[36] Lao, 'Reclaiming a Role for Intent Evidence in Monopolization Analysis', 200–201.
[37] eg Posner, *Antitrust Law*, 214–215.
[38] Lao, 'Reclaiming a Role for Intent Evidence in Monopolization Analysis', 206–211.
[39] Posner, *Antitrust Law*, 214–216.
[40] Lao, 'Reclaiming a Role for Intent Evidence in Monopolization Analysis', 211–212.

competition harms long-term social welfare, the conduct must be prohibited. If conduct that apparently reduces the intensity of market rivalry does not reduce long-term social welfare, the conduct under review is perfectly lawful. Intent has no role to play in the assessment of the effect of conduct on the welfare of society. Harmful conduct should not be allowed because it is carried out with no specific intent to harm competition. Conversely, it would be absurd to prohibit and punish pro-competitive conduct because it was carried out with the intention or belief that it would cause competitive harm.[41] This proposition accords with the theory that competition law has the objective of maximizing long-term social welfare.[42] Therefore, it is certainly valid both as a general principle and as a default position as long as the basic assumption on which it rests holds true, namely that it is possible to determine whether the conduct under review causes the competitive harm that the law aims to deter. There are, however, cases in which evidence of conduct and effects is not capable of proving, by itself, that the practice under review causes the relevant anti-competitive harm. Obviously, in such cases the default position is non-intervention: an infringement is not established. However, if the law refuses to accept a systematic risk of false acquittals because a particular type of conduct whose effects are systematically ambiguous may well cause significant competitive harm, the intent test can be used to tilt the balance one way or another.[43] For instance, the law may provide that, when anti-competitive effects are plausible but not conclusively established, the conduct under review is prohibited only if there is also proof of specific intent.[44] Intent may also play a role as an additional element of a legal test that already requires proof of anti-competitive effects in order to guard against the risk of false convictions.[45] There may be cases, for instance, exclusionary above-cost price cuts, in which a restriction of competition may well cause competitive harm but the risk of a false conviction and over-deterrence is very high. The law may, therefore, require not only proof of competitive harm but also proof of specific intent. Since the conduct is prohibited only if it was carried out with the intent of harming competition, the risk of prohibiting or deterring efficient behaviour is significantly reduced.[46]

---

[41] For a version of this argument relating to a consumer welfare standard, see SC Salop and RG Romaine, 'Preserving Monopoly: Economic Analysis, Legal Standards, and Microsoft' (1999) 7 Geo Mason L Rev 617, 651–653.

[42] See Ch 2 above.

[43] Lao, 'Reclaiming a Role for Intent Evidence in Monopolization Analysis', 192–199, but discussing the relevance of evidence of intent, not intent as a legal test.

[44] In EU law, it is arguable that intent plays this role in predation cases when prices are above AVC but below ATC: see Case C-62/86 *AKZO*; Case T-83/91 *Tetra Pak II*, upheld in Case T-333/94 P *Tetra Pak II*; Case T-340/03 *France Télécom*, upheld in Case C-202/07 P *France Télécom*.

[45] Cass and Hylton, 'Antitrust Intent', 38–45. These authors suggest that proof of intent should always be required in addition to proof of anti-competitive effects. This seems excessive and would sway the law towards systematic false acquittals. Instead, intent should be an additional element of the test only where the risk and cost of false acquittals is particularly high.

[46] The EU courts have relied on proof of intent in addition to proof of anti-competitive effects to condemn unconditional above-cost price cuts: see Joined Cases C-395/96 P and C-396/96 P *Compagnie Maritime Belge*, paras 116–119.

D. The no economic sense test

The no economic sense test was first formulated as a profit sacrifice test, which is thought to have its origin in the case law on predation, particularly in the United States.[47] The profit sacrifice test asks whether the dominant firm sacrifices short-term profits that will be compensated by (increased) monopoly profits earned as a result of the exclusion of rivals.[48] The loss of short-term profits is only rational because of the tendency to exclude rivals and earn supra-competitive profits as a result of the exclusion.[49]

[47] BE Hawk, 'The Current Debate About Section 2 of the Sherman Act: Judicial Certainty Versus Rule of Reason', paper delivered at the II Lisbon Conference on Competition Law and Economics (15 and 16 November 2007) 10; M Lao, 'Defining Exclusionary Conduct Under Section 2: The Case for Non-Universal Standards', 440. In fact *Brooke Group Ltd v Brown & Williamson Tobacco Corp* 509 US 209 (1993) (*Brooke Group*), the leading US case on predatory pricing, does not adopt the profit sacrifice test. In that case, the US Supreme Court held that, in order to succeed on a predatory pricing claim, the plaintiff must prove that the prices complained of are below an appropriate measure of its rival's costs and that the dominant firm has a dangerous probability of recouping its investment in below-cost prices. The whole reasoning of the Court in *Brooke Group* focuses on two pillars: a) it is undesirable to allow as a matter of law a finding of liability for above-cost prices; b) proof of a reasonable prospect or a dangerous probability of recoupment is necessary because, in its absence, low prices benefit and do not harm consumers (ibid 223–224). The requirement to prove a dangerous probability of recoupment points in the direction of a consumer welfare test. The requirement that prices be below costs is based on the observation that any inquiry into the lawfulness of above-cost pricing would give rise to high risks of errors and over-deterrence of pro-competitive conduct (ibid 223: 'As a general rule, the exclusionary effect of prices above a relevant measure of cost either reflects the lower cost structure of the alleged predator, and so represents competition on the merits, or is beyond the practical ability of a judicial tribunal to control without courting intolerable risks of chilling legitimate price-cutting.') Some lower courts have, however, adopted the profit sacrifice test: see *MetroNet Servs Corp v Qwest Corp* 383 F3d 1124, 1134 (9th Cir 2004) 1134; *Covad Communications Co v Bell Atl Corp* 398 F3d 666, 676 (DC Cir 2005), rehearing denied 407 F3d 1220 (DC Cir 2005); *Stearns Airport Equipment Co Inc v FMC Corp* 170 F3d 518 (5th Cir 1999).

[48] Given that the test requires sacrifice of short-term profits in order to earn monopoly profits following exclusion, it appears that the profit sacrifice test was not adopted in *Aspen Skiing Co v Aspen Highlands Skiing Corp* 472 US 585 605 (1985), where the Court said that the dominant firm's refusal to supply a rival at current market prices supported 'an inference that Ski Co. was not motivated by efficiency concerns and that it was willing to sacrifice short-run benefits and consumer goodwill in exchange for a perceived long-run impact on its smaller rival'. This dictum is not a statement of the general test for anti-competitive exclusion under s 2 of the Sherman Act. Rather, the Court was examining an element of the test, which was whether the conduct had a legitimate business justification. Nor can *Verizon Communications Inc v Law Offices of Curtis V Trinko* LLP 540 US 398 (2004) (*Trinko*) 406 be construed as adopting the test. In *Trinko*, the Court distinguished the *Aspen Skiing* case saying that in the latter case 'the unilateral termination of a voluntary (and thus presumably profitable) course of dealing suggested a willingness to forsake short-term profits to achieve an anticompetitive end'. However, this statement only focused attention on the distinguishing factor that excluded the application of *Aspen Skiing* in *Trinko*. It was not a reference to the test for antitrust liability under s 2 of the Sherman Act.

[49] Bork, *The Antitrust Paradox*, 144: 'Predation may be defined, provisionally, as the firm's deliberate aggression against one or more rivals through the employment of business practices that would not be considered profit-maximizing except for the expectation either that (1) rivals will be driven from the market, leaving the predator with a market share sufficient to command monopoly profits, or (2) rivals will be chastened sufficiently to abandon competitive behaviour the predator finds inconvenient or threatening'; PH Areeda and DF Turner, 'Predatory Pricing and Related Practices under Section 2 of the Sherman Act' (1975) 88 Harv L Rev 697, 698: 'predation in any meaningful sense cannot exist unless there is a temporary sacrifice of net revenues in the expectation of greater

The profit sacrifice test is not suitable as a general test for abuse. Exclusionary conduct may not entail any short-term profit sacrifice. A number of pricing practices raising rivals' costs may not require the dominant undertaking to forgo profits in the short-term.[50] If a share of demand is not contestable,[51] the dominant undertaking may recoup any discount granted on additional units by charging a higher price for the non-contestable units. The average price may thus be the profit-maximizing supra-competitive price. Such a strategy would not require a short-term profit sacrifice.[52] The same can be said of mixed bundling, in certain circumstances.[53] Furthermore, in cases in which the dominant undertaking engages in exclusionary conduct in order to preserve its market power, there may be no increase in profits to compensate for the cost of the exclusionary conduct. It is difficult in such circumstances to discern whether the dominant firm is sacrificing profits or competing aggressively. The analysis would require the calculation of the benchmark price for recoupment, which is the price that would have prevailed but for the exclusion. The complexity of this task generates a significant risk of false acquittal.[54] Finally, conduct which sacrifices short-term profits in the expectation of supra-competitive prices is not necessarily anti-competitive. Investment in research and development may require the sacrifice of short-term profits to be compensated by the charging of supra-competitive prices if the project is successful. This conduct is not anti-competitive but would be condemned under a profit sacrifice test.[55] Therefore, because profit sacrifice is neither a necessary nor

future gains'; Posner, *Antitrust Law*, 28: 'an exclusionary practice is generally a method by which a firm (or firms) having or wanting monopoly position trades a part of its monopoly profits, at least temporarily, for a larger market share, by making it unprofitable for the other sellers to compete with it', but see Posner, *Antitrust Law*, 207–223, where the author appears to favour the as efficient competitor test; JA Ordover and RD Willig, 'An Economic Definition of Predation: Pricing and Product Innovation' 9–10: 'predatory behaviour is a response to a rival that sacrifices part of the profit that could be earned under competitive circumstances, were the rival to remain viable, in order to induce exit and gain consequent additional monopoly profit'. See also GJ Werden, 'Identifying Single-Firm Exclusionary Conduct: From Vague Concepts to Administrable Rules' in BE Hawk (ed), *International Antitrust Law & Policy: Fordham Competition Law 2006* (New York, Juris Publishing 2007) 509, 527–529, and Werden, 'Identifying Exclusionary Conduct under Section 2: The "No Economic Sense" Test', 422.

[50] Salop, 'Exclusionary Conduct, Effect on Consumers, and the Flawed Profit-Sacrifice Standard', 311, 358–359.

[51] A non-contestable share of demand is a share of the demand of customer or total market demand which is not open to competition. This may be the case because competitors of a dominant firm are capacity constrained or because the product of the dominant firm is a must-stock consumer good.

[52] Communication from the Commission—Guidance on the Commission's enforcement priorities in applying Article 82 of the EC Treaty to abusive exclusionary conduct by dominant undertakings [2009] OJ C45/7 ('Guidance on Art 102') paras 39–41.

[53] DA Crane, 'Mixed Bundling, Profit Sacrifice, and Consumer Welfare' (2006) 55 Emory LJ 423, 459–462; BJ Nalebuff, 'Bundling as a Way to Leverage Monopoly' 1 Yale School of Management Working Paper No ES-36 (1 September 2004); BJ Nalebuff, 'Exclusionary Bundling' 5–6 Yale Law School, Law, Economics & Organization Workshop (2004).

[54] Salop, 'Exclusionary Conduct, Effect on Consumers, and the Flawed Profit-Sacrifice Standard'.

[55] Werden, 'Identifying Exclusionary Conduct under Section 2: The "No Economic Sense" Test'; Elhauge, 'Defining Better Monopolization Standards', 271, 274–279.

a sufficient condition for anti-competitive exclusion,[56] the profit sacrifice test is subject to systematic false positive and false negative errors. It is both over-inclusive and under-inclusive.

The attempt has been made to generalize the intuition which lies at the heart of the profit sacrifice test in a way that addresses its systematic over- and under-inclusive nature. This reformulation of the profit sacrifice test is known as the no economic sense test.[57] This test asks whether conduct tends to restrict competition and would make no economic sense but for its effect of restricting competition and thus creating or maintaining monopoly power.[58] The claimed benefits of the

[56] Werden, 'Identifying Exclusionary Conduct under Section 2: The "No Economic Sense" Test'; Elhauge, 'Defining Better Monopolization Standards'.

[57] The US Department of Justice (DoJ) unsuccessfully argued for the adoption of the no economic sense test on several occasions. The brief for the United States and the Federal Trade Commission (FTC) in the *Trinko* case, concerning refusal by the incumbent owner of the local telephone network to allow access to the network to a competitive local exchange carrier, stated that the complaint failed to allege exclusionary conduct because it nowhere asserted 'that, by refusing to sell to competitors as a wholesaler at regulated rates, instead of serving customers itself as a retailer, petitioner undertook a sacrifice of short-term profits that would make sense only if it had the effect of impairing competition'. The test was summarized as follows: 'conduct is not exclusionary or predatory *unless* it would make no economic sense for the defendant but for its tendency to eliminate or lessen competition'. The argument was, however, explicitly limited to refusal to supply cases. See Brief for the United States and the FTC as amici curiae supporting petitioner 7–8 (No 02-682), *Verizon Communications Inc v Law Offices of Curtis V Trinko* LLP 540 US 398 (2004). In the *American Airlines* case, concerning an allegation of predatory conduct on four routes by adding additional money-losing capacity to respond to competition from low-cost rivals, the DoJ argued that 'providing money-losing capacity made no business sense except for the fact that American stood to gain much more in the long run by forestalling competition and keeping prices higher once competition was driven away'. The test was framed as follows: 'distinguishing legitimate competition from unlawful predation requires a common-sense business inquiry: whether the conduct would be profitable, apart from any exclusionary effects. Conduct that causes a firm "to forgo profits", but is nonetheless "rational" only because the conduct's ability to eliminate competition gives the firm "a reasonable expectation of recovering, in the form of later monopoly profits, more than the losses suffered", is predatory.' See Brief for the appellants United States of America (public redacted version) 5 (No 02-682), *United States of America v AMR Corp* 335 F3d 1109 (10th Cir 2003).

[58] There are several formulations of the test: Werden, 'Identifying Single-Firm Exclusionary Conduct: From Vague Concepts to Administrable Rules', 528: 'The conduct of a single competitor is unlawfully exclusionary if, and only if, the conduct (1) does not fall within any safe harbor or established exemption; (2a) appears reasonably capable of making a significant contribution to maintaining monopoly power, or (2b) gives rise to a dangerous probability of creating monopoly power and is specifically intended to do so; and (3) would make no economic sense but for its effect of eliminating competition and thus creating or maintaining monopoly power'; Werden, 'Identifying Exclusionary Conduct under Section 2: The "No Economic Sense" Test', 415: 'if conduct allegedly threatens to create a monopoly because of a tendency to exclude existing competitors, the test is whether the conduct likely would have been profitable if the existing competitors were not excluded and monopoly was not created. If the conduct allegedly maintains a monopoly because of a tendency to exclude nascent competition, the test is whether conduct likely would have been profitable if the nascent competition flourished and the monopoly was not maintained'; AD Melamed, 'Exclusive Dealing Agreements and Other Exclusionary Conduct—Are There Unifying Principles?' (2006) 73 Antitrust LJ 375, 389: 'conduct is anticompetitive if, but only if, it makes no business sense or is unprofitable for the defendant but for the exclusion of rivals and resulting supra-competitive recoupment'; Melamed, 'Exclusionary Conduct Under the Antitrust Laws: Balancing, Sacrifice, and Refusals to Deal', 1255: 'the sacrifice test asks whether the allegedly anticompetitive conduct would be profitable for the defendant and would make good business sense even if it did not exclude rivals and thereby create or preserve market power for the defendant. If so, the conduct is lawful. If not—if the conduct would be unprofitable but for the exclusion of rivals and the resulting market power—it is anticompetitive.'

no economic sense test would be that it provides clear and meaningful guidance to dominant undertakings, competition authorities, and courts.[59] The test would be simpler to apply than a consumer welfare test because it only requires an *ex ante* assessment of the effect of the conduct on the dominant undertaking,[60] rather than an assessment and weighing-up of the effects of the conduct on consumers. However, it is doubtful whether the no economic sense test fully addresses the shortcomings of the profit sacrifice test.[61] If a firm invests in innovation in the expectation that, if the innovation is successful, it will allow it to exclude rivals and reap monopoly profits, the conduct only makes economic sense because of the exclusion. It would be prohibited under the no economic sense test.[62] Proponents of the no economic sense test have responded by saying that 'investments in opportunities for future profits normally are not deemed exclusionary under the test both because they make economic sense apart from any tendency to eliminate competition and because they have no such tendency'.[63] Furthermore, the no economic sense test would not apply to the investment in innovation, but only to the terms on which the new product is commercialized because the test only applies to conduct that excludes rivals and what excludes rivals is not the investment but the commercialization of the new product.[64] These attempts at rationalizing the application of the tests are not entirely successful. Of course, investment in innovation is not to be prohibited by competition law, the reason being that it is normally beneficial to social welfare and productivity growth. However, it is not immediately apparent that it would not be caught by the no economic sense test. It is possible to say that investments in innovation that are only profitable if the innovator increases its market power as a result of excluding competitors, only make economic sense because they 'eliminate competition'. It is also possible to say that they have the 'tendency to eliminate competition' because they are capable of excluding rivals. Equally, it is unclear why the decision to invest in innovation and the commercialization of the product should be subject to two different tests, the former being outside the 'jurisdictional' reach of competition law. A decision by a monopolist to invest in additional capacity to deter prospective entrants or to invest in a new product that is incompatible with that of the rivals should in principle be subject

---

[59] Werden, 'Identifying Single-Firm Exclusionary Conduct: From Vague Concepts to Administrable Rules', 532–534; Melamed, 'Exclusive Dealing Agreements and Other Exclusionary Conduct—Are There Unifying Principles?', 392–393.

[60] Melamed, 'Exclusive Dealing Agreements and Other Exclusionary Conduct—Are There Unifying Principles?', 387

[61] Werden, 'Identifying Exclusionary Conduct under Section 2: The "No Economic Sense" Test', 420–422 ('advocating for the utility of the test but recognising that its application may be difficult in practice'); Salop, 'Exclusionary Conduct, Effect on Consumers, and the Flawed Profit-Sacrifice Standard', 357–363 (arguing that the difficulty in applying the test in cases of simultaneous recoupment and monopoly maintenance and the complexity of defining the benchmark output make the test conducive to both false positive and false negative errors).

[62] Elhauge, 'Defining Better Monopolization Standards', 274–279.

[63] Werden, 'Identifying Exclusionary Conduct under Section 2: The "No Economic Sense" Test', 424.

[64] Melamed, 'Exclusive Dealing Agreements and Other Exclusionary Conduct—Are There Unifying Principles?', 395–396.

to competition law. Intervention may be rare or even excluded altogether but this must follow from the application of the appropriate test and not be postulated, as an article of faith, as a carve-out from a test which would apply, and prohibit, the conduct in question.

A more serious difficulty associated with the no economic sense test is that the test requires a comparison between the profits which would have been earned in the absence of the exclusionary effect, and the profits which are (likely to be)[65] earned following the exclusion. Competition authorities and courts would have to reconstruct the market price that would have prevailed if the rivals had not been excluded and assess whether the conduct under review would have been profitable in that counterfactual. It is also possible that rivals have not been excluded from the market but allege either that they will exit after a certain time if the conduct under review is allowed to continue, or that they are simply forced to raise their prices and restrict output. If this is the case, competition authorities and courts will have to construct and predict two scenarios which may occur in the future: a market in which the rivals are not present or have raised their prices and restricted their output, and a market in which the rivals are present or have not raised their prices or restricted output. Only if the conduct under review would be profitable in the latter market situation, would it pass muster under the no economic sense test.

The above considerations already demonstrate that, because the no economic sense test requires the calculation or estimation of the price which would prevail following the exclusion of rivals, it is actually very close to a static consumer welfare test.[66] To assess the effect of the conduct on consumer welfare it is also necessary to estimate or calculate the market price that would prevail following the exclusion of rivals. Furthermore, both tests require an assessment of the efficiencies generated by the conduct and their magnitude. The difference between the two tests is that the consumer welfare test requires proof of two additional elements. First, because the consumer welfare test examines the likely or actual effects on consumers, it requires, at the very minimum, an assessment of the likelihood of exclusion.[67] The no economic sense test simply assumes exclusion and compares the cost and revenues in two scenarios, with and without exclusion. Secondly, the consumer welfare test asks whether the efficiencies 'outweigh' the harm to consumers. This element is expressed in many different ways as a 'reasonableness',[68]

---

[65] The profits earned after the exclusion of rivals will have to be estimated at some future time if the conduct is ongoing and the rivals have not yet been excluded.

[66] Melamed, 'Exclusive Dealing Agreements and Other Exclusionary Conduct—Are There Unifying Principles?', 399.

[67] eg Guidance on Art 102, paras 19–20.

[68] Case 27/76 *United Brands Co and United Brands Continentaal v Commission* [1978] ECR 207, para 189; Case C-62/86 *AKZO*; T-65/89 *BPB Industries plc and British Gypsum Ltd v Commission* [1993] ECR II-389 (*British Gypsum*), para 69; Joined Cases C-395/96 P and C-396/96 P *Compagnie Maritime Belge*, para 148; Joined Cases T-191/98, T-212/98, and T-214/98 *Atlantic Container Line v Commission* [2003] ECR II-3275, para 1114; Case T-340/04 *France Télécom*, para 185, upheld in Case C-202/07 P *France Télécom*, paras 46–48; Opinion of AG Jacobs in Case C-53/03 *Synetairismos Farmakopoion Aitolias & Akarnanias (Syfait) v GlaxoSmithKline AEVE* [2005] ECR I-4609, para 100.

'proportionality',[69] or 'balancing'[70] inquiry.[71] Compared to the consumer harm test, the no economic sense test is, therefore, under-inclusive. Conduct that generates insignificant efficiencies would be allowed even if it has a significant negative impact on competition and long-term social welfare. The reason is that the no economic sense test has no framework for assessing the nature and magnitude of the efficiencies generated by the exclusionary conduct and comparing them with the extent of the competitive harm it causes.

The most fundamental objection to the no economic sense test is that it is subject to both false negative and false positive errors. The main focus of this criticism is, however, on the under-inclusive nature of the test. Salop gives the example of the design of a new product that increases the value of the product for consumers by €5, but is incompatible with rivals' products so that the innovator obtains a monopoly. The monopoly price is €50. Consumer welfare and social welfare may both be reduced under these assumptions but provided that the investment does not cost more than €5, the conduct is allowed under the no economic sense test.[72] More generally, because the test focuses only on the effect of the conduct on the dominant undertaking and disregards the effects on competitors and consumers, it is clearly biased towards false negative errors both under a social welfare and under a consumer welfare standard. The proponents of the test recognize this bias but argue that the benefits in terms of legal certainty and avoidance of false positive errors outweigh the risk of false negatives,[73] because they believe that false positives are more harmful than false negatives.[74] This argument rests on the ideological assumption that the law should be biased in favour of non-intervention. However, the objective of optimal abuse of dominance tests should be to strike the right balance between the risk of false convictions and over-deterrence and false acquittals and under-deterrence. The no economic sense test fails to accomplish this.

The difficulties highlighted above demonstrate that the no economic sense test does not fare well as a unifying analytical structure to assess exclusionary conduct.

---

[69] H Hovenkamp, *The Antitrust Enterprise: Principle and Execution* (Cambridge Mass, Harvard University Press 2005) 154; P Areeda and H Hovenkamp, *Antitrust Law: An Analysis of Antitrust Principles and Their Application* (2nd edn New York, Aspen Law & Business 2010) 650a, 71; *United States of America v Microsoft Corp* 253 F3d 34 (DC Cir 2001) 107.

[70] C Townley, *Article 81 EC and Public Policy* (Oxford, Hart Publishing 2009) 111–197; C Desogus, 'Parallel Trade and Pharmaceutical R&D: The Pitfalls of the Rule of Reason' (2008) 29 ECLR 649, 656–665; M Motta, 'Michelin II—The Treatment of Rebates' in B Lyons (ed), *Cases in European Competition Policy: the Economic Analysis* (Cambridge, CUP 2009) 29, 42.

[71] It is worth noting that under the no economic sense test, the counterfactual is a market in which the rivals have not been excluded. Under the consumer welfare test, the counterfactual is a market in which the conduct under review has not been carried out.

[72] Salop, 'Exclusionary Conduct, Effect on Consumers, and the Flawed Profit-Sacrifice Standard', 345–346.

[73] Melamed, 'Exclusive Dealing Agreements and Other Exclusionary Conduct—Are There Unifying Principles?', 393–395.

[74] Werden, 'Identifying Single-Firm Exclusionary Conduct: From Vague Concepts to Administrable Rules', 518–519.

In its application to individual practices the test needs to be explained and reinterpreted in the light of the relevant welfare standard. In this way, it loses its attraction as a unifying test for anti-competitive exclusion. In particular, the no economic sense test should not be applied so as to rule out some form of assessment of the nature and magnitude of the efficiencies that the conduct under review is claimed to generate.[75] The only conceivable usefulness of the no economic sense test is that it may play a role in proving intent when conduct is exclusionary under another test. Assuming, for instance, that exclusionary conduct is defined as conduct that is capable of excluding a competitor that is as efficient as the dominant firm but that an objective test would, in certain circumstances, give rise to too high a risk of false convictions and over-deterrence, the no economic sense test could be applied as a test of intent[76] to guard against such a risk.

E. The as efficient competitor test

(1) Consistency of the as efficient competitor test with fundamental principles

The as efficient (or equally efficient) competitor test asks whether the conduct under review is likely to exclude a competitor that is at least as efficient as the dominant undertaking.[77] The test distinguishes harmful exclusion from exclusion that is the result of an undistorted competitive process based on the principle that

---

[75] This is done, under EU law, as part of the objective justification test: see Ch 9 below.

[76] On this role of the intent test, see 208–209 below.

[77] Posner, *Antitrust Law*, 194: 'the plaintiff must first prove that the defendant has monopoly power and second that the challenged practice is likely in the circumstances to exclude from the defendant's market an equally or more efficient competitor'. Hovenkamp, 'Exclusion and the Sherman Act' 153 claims that the test has had 'some traction' in US law. In *Barry Wright Corp v ITT Grinnell Corp* 724 F2d 227 (1st Cir 1983), a case concerned, *inter alia*, with allegedly exclusionary above-cost prices, the court noted that prices below incremental or avoidable costs may raise competition concerns because 'equally efficient competitors cannot permanently match this low price and stay in business' (ibid 232). In *Northeastern Telephone Co v AT & T* 651 F2d 76 (2nd Cir 1981), cert denied 455 US 943 (1982), the Second Circuit held that the appropriate cost benchmark for predatory pricing is marginal cost. When the price of a dominant firm's product equals or exceeds the product's marginal costs, only less efficient firms will suffer losses per unit of output. *Northeastern Telephone Co v AT & T* was relied on in *MCI Communications Corp v American Telephone and Telegraph Co* 708 F2d 1081 (7th Cir 1983). However, both courts were dealing with the narrower issue of the relevant cost benchmark for predatory pricing rather than with the broader issue of the test for exclusion under s 2 of the Sherman Act. In *Borden Inc v Federal Trade Commission* 674 F2d 498 (6th Cir 1982), vacated on other grounds, in *Borden Inc v Federal Trade Commission* 461 US 940 (1983), the Sixth Circuit, after reviewing direct evidence of Borden's intention to maintain its monopoly power, increase its market share, and stifle competition, concluded that when a monopolist, through brand identification or otherwise, manipulates prices in such a way as to exclude equally efficient competitors by requiring them to sell below their average variable costs, such price manipulation is an unreasonable use of power to maintain the monopolist's market position. The case was a petition to review an order of the FTC, finding that the petitioner violated s 5 of the Federal Trade Commission Act, 15 USC § 45. The decision and order of the Commission are reported at 92 FTC 669–833 (1978). Although s 5 of the Federal Trade Commission Act and ss 1 and 2 of the Sherman Act are not co-extensive, in the *Borden* case the FTC and the Court of Appeals restricted their analysis to grounds that would have been relevant also under s 2 of Sherman Act.

competition law should not protect inefficient competitors. Competition as a driver of long-term social welfare and productivity growth includes a strong productive efficiency component. Therefore, it is not sufficient for an abuse to be established that a rebate system, a bundle, or an unconditional price cut excludes a competitor. These practices are only abusive if they are capable of excluding from the market a firm that is as efficient as the dominant undertaking. As far as pricing behaviour, the test asks whether the dominant undertaking's prices are below an appropriate measure of the dominant undertaking's costs.

The test is consistent with the normative objective of competition law, which is to maximize long-term social welfare. Productive and dynamic efficiencies are key drivers of long-term social welfare and productivity growth. Suppose that a dominant undertaking is supplying product x at a cost of £10 and at a price of £18. Only one other undertaking is present on the market and is supplying the same product at a cost of £13 and at a price of £16 (the lower price is due to the dominant undertaking's strong brand premium or the rival's capacity constraint). A new competitor, with imperfect understanding of the incumbents' costs, enters the market and supplies the product at a cost of £13 and at a price of £15. At this point, the dominant undertaking responds by lowering its price to £12. Both competitors are excluded because they are less efficient than the dominant undertaking. The welfare effects of the conduct in the short-term are unambiguously beneficial. Both social welfare and consumer welfare increase. In the long-term the effects are less clear. Once both competitors have exited the market, the dominant undertaking has the ability and the incentive to set the price at monopoly level, higher than the previous duopoly price. However, all the units on the market are supplied at the most efficient cost of £10. The welfare effects depend on the trade-off between the increase in productive efficiency, the decrease in consumer welfare, and the increase in the deadweight loss. Therefore, intervention to prohibit the dominant undertaking's limit pricing is problematic. The short-term welfare effect of that conduct is positive. The long-term effects, on the other hand, are ambiguous and very difficult to assess in individual cases. Furthermore, prohibiting above-cost responses to entry carries a very high risk of over-deterrence. Dominant undertakings will be held to a price floor which is not their MC but the MC of the most inefficient competitor. This would dampen the incentives of actual and potential competitors to be productively efficient because they anticipate that the dominant firm will have to charge a price no lower than their MC and possibly higher if there are even less efficient rivals on the market. The incentives for dominant undertakings to become more efficient would also be affected because dominant undertakings would know that they would not be able to take full advantage of their lower costs to compete with less efficient rivals. The as efficient competitor test avoids these problems by adopting as a benchmark the efficiency of the dominant firm. On the one hand, actual and potential competitors will have a strong incentive to be more efficient than the dominant firm because they know that they can only succeed on the market by taking advantage of their superior efficiency. On the other hand, the dominant firm also retains the incentive to increase its efficiency because superior efficiency will provide a legitimate way of defending its commercial interests against competition from existing rivals or new entrants.

The as efficient competitor test is also consistent with the principle of fairness and equality of opportunities, which provides a strong normative foundation for allowing a dominant firm to take full advantage of its superior efficiency. This principle applies with equal force to permit the dominant firm to protect its commercial interests as it does to shield its competitors from anti-competitive behaviour. To prevent a dominant firm from exploiting, to the greatest possible extent, its superior efficiency would place it at a competitive disadvantage vis-à-vis its competitors.

Finally, the equally efficient competitor test provides sufficient guidance to the dominant firm *ex ante* by allowing it to carry out its self-assessment based on its own cost structure.[78] This self-assessment does not depend on a number of market factors external to the dominant undertaking, which is the case under a consumer welfare test. Under a consumer welfare test, the dominant undertaking is required to make predictions about the impact of its conduct on price and output and the degree to which any efficiencies are likely to be passed on to consumers. This depends on the reaction of competitors, their actual cost structures, and access to external financing, about which the dominant undertaking may have no or little knowledge.

(2) Under-inclusiveness of the as efficient competitor test

The main problem with the as efficient competitor test is that it is under-inclusive. For instance, it is striking that the as efficient competitor test as the sole abuse test would allow naked exclusionary practices. Providing misleading information to patent offices or making payments to suppliers on condition that they do not test a rival's product would not be prohibited unless they were capable of excluding equally efficient competitors. These practices, however, have no efficiency rationale. While in theory their impact on social welfare and productivity still depends on the relative efficiency of the foreclosed rivals, there appears to be a strong enforcement rationale for prohibiting this type of conduct because of its naked exclusionary purpose without any inquiry into its capability to exclude an equally efficient competitor.[79] This would already be sufficient to demonstrate that the as efficient competitor test should not be the only test for exclusionary abuses.

More fundamentally, competitive pressure from less efficient rivals may be beneficial not only under a consumer welfare standard but also under a long-term social welfare standard.[80] Suppose that a monopolist is supplying product x at

---

[78] Legal certainty is one of the reasons why EU courts have adopted the as efficient competitor test: Case T-271/03 *Deutsche Telekom AG v Commission* [2008] ECR II-477, upheld in Case C-280/08 P *Deutsche Telekom AG v Commission* [2010] OJ C346/4.

[79] Hovenkamp, 'Exclusion and the Sherman Act'; O'Donoghue and Padilla, *The Law and Economics of Article 82 EC*, 190.

[80] Salop, 'Exclusionary Conduct, Effect on Consumers, and the Flawed Profit-Sacrifice Standard', 328–329.

a cost of £10 and at a price of £18. If a new firm enters the market and supplies the same product at a cost of £13 and at a price of £16 with no capacity constraints, the dominant undertaking will have to lower its price to at least £16. In the post-entry scenario, consumer welfare clearly increases. However, consumer welfare is not the objective of competition law. What matters is the effect of entry on long-term social welfare. Social welfare may increase depending on whether the profits on the additional units sold (given the lower price) and the increased consumer surplus outweigh the profits lost due to the productive inefficiency of the new entrant. In the abstract, all that can be said is that it is quite possible that, if the increase in output is sufficiently large and the relative inefficiency of the entrant not too great, the post-entry duopoly increases social welfare. In the long-term, account should also be taken of the incentives of the firms to invest in new production processes and product development. In terms of long-term dynamic efficiency, a duopoly may be not much different from a monopoly if the duopolists choose not to compete vigorously. On the other hand, there is at least one more source of competitive pressure on the market; and long-term investment incentives may be higher in the duopoly than in the monopoly. In this example, the as efficient competitor test would allow the dominant undertaking to price at £12, thus excluding the new entrant and maintaining the potentially less socially desirable monopoly. Assuming that there are significant barriers to entry to the market (which is a condition for a finding of dominance),[81] if the new entrant benefited from favourable circumstances unlikely to be repeated in the foreseeable future, non-intervention may allow the dominant undertaking to defend a durable monopoly with a net long-term welfare and productivity loss. Whether this is the case is, however, a difficult question to answer in any given case. On the other hand, the as efficient competitor test, without any doubt, safeguards short-term productive efficiency and long-term incentives to produce at the lowest possible cost. Ultimately, whether the under-inclusion problem highlighted here is a fatal flaw of the as efficient competitor test depends on whether the benefits of competition law intervention to prevent exclusion of less efficient competitors outweigh its costs in terms of the complexity of the analysis and the consequent risk of false positive errors and over-deterrence. In the vast majority of cases, it would appear that the answer is in the negative.

A more powerful criticism of the test is that entry into a concentrated market almost invariably occurs on a relatively small scale. If there are economies of scale[82] or learning effects,[83] at the beginning the costs of the new entrant will be higher than those of the dominant firm until the scale economies or the learning effects are fully achieved. The question is whether the rival's efficiency should be assessed in a static sense, given its costs at the time of the allegedly exclusionary conduct, or whether the potential for the rival to achieve scale economies and learning

---

[81] See Ch 10 below.

[82] Economies of scale arise when average cost decreases as output is increased.

[83] Learning by doing or learning effects arise when average cost decreases as output increases as a result of the producer gaining experience in the market.

effects must be taken into account by constructing its long-term cost curve.[84] This task may be complex and, above all, will have to rely on a number of assumptions which are difficult to test with the degree of accuracy required in the legal process. This problem is particularly acute because dominant undertakings often have the incentive and the ability to exclude rivals precisely in order to deny them the opportunity to achieve their minimum efficient scale or reap the benefit of learning by doing.[85] Consider rebate systems which successfully foreclose 80 per cent of the market but do not result in an average price or an effective price below the costs of the dominant firm. If the minimum efficient scale of a competitor is 30 per cent, because of its higher costs, the competitor is forced to offer higher prices and is unable to gain market share so as to benefit from economies of scale. However, because the rival's costs are higher than the costs of the dominant undertaking, which takes full advantage of scale economies, the conduct in question would not be condemned under the as efficient competitor test. And yet, it is the rebate scheme and nothing else that prevents the rival from becoming as efficient as the dominant undertaking. There appear to be strong arguments, therefore, to protect competitors that may become as efficient as the dominant undertaking but are prevented from doing so by the very practice that is alleged to be abusive. Because the necessary condition for the application of this test is that the foreclosed competitor is prevented from becoming as efficient as the dominant firm by the latter's conduct, this approach is better understood as an extension of the as efficient competitor test rather than an exception to it.

(3) Over-inclusiveness of the as efficient competitor test

The as efficient competitor test can be criticized for being over-inclusive. The strongest argument is that the exclusion of an equally efficient competitor is not always welfare-reducing. If a dominant undertaking has monopoly power in the market for product x and also supplies the complementary product y in a market in which it also has market power, setting the price of x and y independently at the profit-maximizing level would reduce output. The supra-competitive price of product x lowers the sales of product y and vice versa. The dominant undertaking may expand output and maximize profits by charging a lower price to customers who buy both products. If the incremental price of product y is lower than the incremental cost of supplying it, an equally efficient competitor on the market for product y would be excluded. However, the practice could still be beneficial on balance if the increase in social welfare resulting from the elimination of double marginalization outweighs any deadweight loss resulting from the increased market power of the dominant undertaking in all or any of the affected markets.

---

[84] Melamed, 'Exclusive Dealing Agreements and Other Exclusionary Conduct—Are There Unifying Principles?', 388.
[85] Hovenkamp, 'Exclusion and the Sherman Act', 154–155.

To account for circumstances in which the exclusion of an as efficient competitor may be, on balance, pro-competitive, it seems reasonable to allow the dominant firm to show that the conduct is beneficial.[86] However, to allow for this balancing of anti-competitive and pro-competitive effects would make the test more difficult to apply. Therefore, the proponents of the consumer welfare test argue that benefits of the as efficient competitor test in terms of administrability may not be significant as compared with a consumer welfare test.[87] This, of course, is not necessarily a fatal flaw of the test. It is always possible, and indeed consistent with the objective of competition law, which is to maximize social welfare in the long term, to allow a dominant undertaking to adduce evidence tending to show that the conduct under review is, on balance, beneficial. This simply means that the as efficient competitor test must be integrated into a wider framework in which the harm resulting from the exclusion of an equally efficient competitor can be compared with the benefits of the conduct in question.

(4) The problem of multi-product firms

As well as being under- and over-inclusive, the as efficient competitor test may be difficult to apply in practice. The definition of an equally efficient competitor is particularly problematic beyond the case of single-product firms producing homogenous products.[88] For multi-product firms, the question arises of whether the hypothetical as efficient competitor should be a single-product firm or a firm supplying the same range of products as the dominant undertaking.[89] This difficulty in defining an as efficient competitor may be illustrated by the case of bundling. Is product diversification a form of efficiency or should efficiency be

---

[86] Posner, *Antitrust Law*, 194, explaining that the plaintiff can rebut a prima facie case of anti-competitive conduct 'by proving that although it is a monopolist and the challenged practice exclusionary, the practice is, on balance, efficient'.

[87] O'Donoghue and Padilla, *The Law and Economics of Article 82 EC*, 190.

[88] SC Salop 'The Controversy over the Proper Antitrust Standard for Anticompetitive Exclusionary Conduct' in BE Hawk (ed), *International Antitrust Law & Policy: Fordham Competition Law 2006* (New York, Juris Publishing 2007) 477, 488.

[89] Multi-product discount cases in the US have relied on the definition of an as efficient competitor as a competitor supplying only one product of the bundle. In *Ortho Diagnostic Systems Inc v Abbott Laboratories Inc* 920 F Supp 455 (SDNY 1996), the plaintiff complained that the defendant had unlawfully used its monopoly power in the markets for some of the five blood screening tests it supplied to gain an inappropriate advantage in the other markets. The defendant offered bundled rebates to customers buying five or four of the assays. None of the products were sold individually below their AVC. The Court held that, for the plaintiff to succeed, the defendant must have monopoly power on some of the products and it must either price the bundle below AVC or, by forcing the competitor to absorb the difference between the bundled and unbundled prices, must make it unprofitable for an equally efficient competitor producing only one product to continue to produce. In *LePage's Inc v 3M (Minnesota Mining and Manufacturing Co)* 324 F3d 141 (3rd Cir 2003) (en banc), cert denied, 124 S Ct 2932 (2004), the Court said that bundled rebates may make it impossible even for an equally efficient rival to compensate for lost discounts on products that it does not produce. The Court explained: 'The principal anticompetitive effect of bundled rebates as offered by 3M is that when offered by a monopolist they may foreclose portions of the market to a potential competitor who does not manufacture an equally diverse group of products and who therefore cannot make a comparable offer' (ibid 155).

assessed on a market-by-market basis?[90] If diversification is a form of efficiency, then the exclusionary effect of the bundle would be assessed by analysing the effects of the bundle on a multi-product rival. This, however, may not be realistic if entry can only occur by a single-product firm and competitors on all relevant markets cannot effectively coordinate their strategy by offering a bundle comparable to that of the dominant undertaking. The application of the as efficient competitor test would, therefore, require the reconstruction of a hypothetical undertaking supplying only one product each time but with the same cost structure as the dominant undertaking. According to one view,[91] whether product diversification is a form of efficiency depends on the welfare effects of the bundling. If the bundling is a way of achieving productive or transactional efficiencies, economies of scope,[92] or improved product interoperability, then diversification is a form of efficiency. If, however, the bundling is a way of enhancing brand loyalty or to price discriminate, the assessment of its welfare effects would be 'virtually unanswerable in litigation'.[93]

As a starting point, it would appear that product diversification is a legitimate competitive strategy. Clearly, producing more than one product allows the dominant firm to realize economies of scope, which may result in increased efficiency. It could be argued, therefore, that the equally efficient competitor should be a competitor who is able to realize the same economies of scope as the dominant firm. This approach is consistent with the principle of fairness and equality of opportunities requiring that a dominant undertaking be allowed to benefit from its superior efficiency. And, as long as the dominant undertaking's conduct reflects superior efficiency, such an approach is also consistent with the objectives of competition law to enhance social welfare in the long term.

The objection to this approach is that it may be unrealistic to assume that a new entrant in a multi-market setting should enter all the markets at the same time. Such a policy may deter entry to an excessive extent. It would be more reasonable to assume that a rival may challenge the dominant undertaking by entering only one or some markets but not necessarily all relevant markets at the same time.[94]

Which approach is preferable? In order to answer this question, it is necessary to go back to first principles. The objective of competition law is to maximize long-term social welfare. Long-term social welfare is best served when goods are produced at the minimum cost of production. Competition is essential to provide firms with the incentive to be as efficient as possible. There are a number of competitive strategies available to firms. One is to produce a product as cheaply as

---

[90] Crane, 'Mixed Bundling, Profit Sacrifice, and Consumer Welfare', 463.

[91] ibid 463–464.

[92] Economies of scope arise when the cost of supplying two or more products together is lower than the cost of supplying each of them separately.

[93] Crane, 'Mixed Bundling, Profit Sacrifice, and Consumer Welfare', 464, quoting Posner, *Antitrust Law*, 202–203.

[94] O'Donoghue and Padilla, *The Law and Economics of Article 82 EC*, 260, appear to accept this proposition when they note that an incremental cost approach to multi-product abuses 'could create a significant disadvantage for a rival firm that is only active in one market and therefore has to incur all the stand-alone costs of serving that market'.

possible. But this is not the only option. An important competitive strategy is to differentiate and create synergies among different lines of business. If a firm were then mandated to price all products on markets that may be related to each other at a price equal to or above their stand-alone cost, as soon as it becomes dominant on one such market, a fundamental incentive to diversify and realize economies of scope would be lost. So would the social welfare and productivity gains resulting from economies of scope. Instead of expanding through organic growth or merger, rivals of multi-product dominant firms could claim a share of the profits of the dominant firm by taking advantage of a price floor above the efficient cost of production of the product in question. Therefore, the definition of an equally efficient competitor that is consistent with the objective of competition law to maximize social welfare and productivity in the long term is a competitor who is able to realize the same economies of scope as the dominant firm. However, when entry to all related markets is either impossible or excessively difficult and the dominant firm is excluding a competitor who could become as efficient as the dominant firm but for the exclusionary conduct, competition law intervention is not inconsistent with the as efficient competitor test provided that effective rules can be framed based either on an extension of the as efficient competitor test itself or on another test, such as consumer harm or intent.

(5) Extension of the as efficient competitor test to abusive discrimination

(a) *The problem*

Price discrimination occurs when a supplier sells the same product to two consumers at different prices and the price difference does not reflect the different costs of supplying the product. The key criterion is the relationship between price and cost rather than a difference in price or a difference in cost.[95] Therefore, the same price charged to two different consumers may be discriminatory if the cost of supplying the product is different. For the same reason, two different prices for the same product are not discriminatory if the difference reflects the different costs of supply. The concept of discrimination may be broadened to non-price terms. Different conditions applied to different customers are discriminatory when the transactions entail the same cost for the dominant undertaking.

The economic concept of price discrimination may be relevant to a number of potentially abusive practices. Margin squeeze may be seen as a form of price discrimination between the downstream division of the vertically integrated dominant undertaking and other undertakings that need the upstream input to compete on the downstream market.[96] Tying may be a way of price-discriminating between low-quantity and high-quantity users of a product, which is used

---

[95] J Tirole, *The Theory of Industrial Organization* (Cambridge Mass, The MIT Press 1988) 133–134. Economists use marginal cost as the yardstick: see M Armstrong and J Vickers, 'Competitive Price Discrimination' (2001) 32 RAND Journal of Economics 579, 581.

[96] D Geradin and R O'Donoghue, 'The Concurrent Application of Competition Law and Regulation: The Case of Margin Squeeze Abuses in the Telecommunications Sector' (2005) 1 J Comp L & Econ 355, 358.

in conjunction with variable quantities of a complementary product.[97] Mixed bundling is a price-discrimination device which sorts customers based on their different but not otherwise directly observable valuations of the bundled products.[98] Predation and unconditional above-cost price cuts are very often targeted at a competitor's customer rather than applied across the board.[99] Rebates may result in different customers buying the same quantity of a product at different prices, which do not reflect the difference in the cost of supply.[100] A dominant undertaking may charge excessive prices or impose other unfair trading conditions in one segment of the market where it is shielded from competition while applying lower, or even predatory, prices in another market segment which is more open to competition.[101] Almost every abusive practice does or may entail some form of discrimination. This should not come as a surprise. The economic definition of price discrimination is very broad, essentially encompassing any non-cost-reflective price differential. However, whether or not a certain type of abuse can be characterized as a form of price discrimination may be of analytical interest but, strictly speaking, should be irrelevant as a matter of law. The legal problem of the test for abusive price discrimination is whether there is a form of price discrimination that is neither exclusionary of rivals nor exploitative of customers and yet should still be prohibited by competition law because it harms long-term social welfare through a reduction of competition. The analysis below demonstrates that discrimination may harm long-term social welfare when it harms the ability to compete of customers or suppliers of the dominant undertaking that would be as efficient as their competitors in the absence of the discrimination. The test for abusive discrimination is, therefore, a version of the as efficient competitor test, where the comparator is not the dominant undertaking but the latter's suppliers or customers that benefit from the discrimination.

(b) General welfare effects of discrimination

As discussed above, price discrimination occurs when a firm sells the same product to two consumers at different prices that do not exactly reflect the different costs of supplying the product.[102]

---

[97] Bork, *The Antitrust Paradox* 376–378; Posner, *Antitrust Law*, 199–200.

[98] K-U Kühn, R Stillman, and C Caffarra, 'Economic Theories of Bundling and Their Policy Implications in Abuse Cases: An Assessment in Light of the Microsoft Case' (2005) 1 European Competition Journal 85, 89–91.

[99] eg Case T-83/91 *Tetra Pak II*, paras 163–164.

[100] eg Case 85/76 *Hoffmann-La Roche & Co AG v Commission* [1979] ECR 461, para 90 and Case 322/81 *Michelin I*, para 73.

[101] Decision of the Director General of Fair Trading No CA98/2/2001 *Napp Pharmaceutical Holdings Ltd and Subsidiaries*, OFT (30 March 2001) (*Napp*) and, on appeal, *Napp Pharmaceutical Holdings Ltd v Director General of Fair Trading* [2002] CAT 1, [2002] Comp AR 13, [2002] ECC 13 (*Napp v DGFT*). For a comment on the price discrimination aspect of the case, see M Furse, 'Caught Napping: DGFT and Napp Pharmaceutical Holdings Ltd' (2001) 22 ECLR 477, 479.

[102] Other definitions are possible. For instance, Carlton and Perloff define 'nonuniform pricing' as 'charging customers different prices for the same product or charging a single customer a price that varies depending on how many units the customer buys'. They then define price discrimination as 'any nonuniform pricing policy used by a firm with market power to maximise its

Not all firms are able to price discriminate. The conditions that make price discrimination possible can be described as follows:

1. The supplier must be able to sort customers based on their willingness to pay. The different ways of sorting customers are the basis for the classic taxonomy of first-degree, second-degree, and third-degree price discrimination.[103] This taxonomy is important because the welfare effects of price discrimination depend, to a certain extent, on which type of price discrimination is being implemented. First-degree price discrimination occurs when an undertaking knows each individual customer's valuation of the product and is able to charge to each customer the maximum price that that customer is prepared to pay. First-degree price discrimination carried out by a monopolist maximizes social welfare by allowing all consumer surplus to be extracted by the supplier. Therefore, the whole surplus on the market is appropriated by the producer, there is no deadweight loss, and consumer surplus is zero.[104] Second-degree price discrimination occurs when the supplier knows that its customers have different valuations of the product but cannot observe the individual valuation of each customer. When this is the case, the supplier can still price discriminate by offering a menu of differently priced packages from which the customers can choose. Third-degree price discrimination occurs when the supplier cannot observe each individual consumer's willingness to pay but can sort consumers based on exogenous information such as the age, location, or occupation of the customer.

2. No arbitrage must be possible between customers. It is clear that if low-valuation customers can resell the product to high-valuation customers, any attempt at price discrimination will fail. Only low-valuation customers will buy from the supplier, and high-valuation customers will buy from low-valuation customers. Obstacles to arbitrage may relate to the nature of the product, as in the case of medical treatment, or to external factors, for instance transport costs exceeding the difference between the higher and the lower price. A specific competition law issue arises when obstacles to arbitrage are the result of contractual restraints or unilateral conduct by the supplier.[105]

3. A third condition is sometimes included but is highly controversial. Some argue that, in order to price discriminate, the supplier must have market power. The reasoning is simple. Market power is the power to set prices above MC. Since price discrimination must involve setting prices above MC at least to some customers, the supplier must have market power.[106] Others have sought to demonstrate that price discrimination may occur without market power in a number of circumstances. The model that perhaps more frequently resembles business

---

profits': DW Carlton and JM Perloff, *Modern Industrial Organization* (4th edn Boston, Pearson/Addison Wesley 2005) 290.

[103] AC Pigou, *The Economics of Welfare* (4th edn London, MacMillan 1932) 278–279.
[104] Carlton and Perloff, *Modern Industrial Organization*, 299–301.
[105] See 193–196 below.   [106] Carlton and Perloff, *Modern Industrial Organization*, 294.

reality is the recovery of common costs under competitive conditions. A supplier facing common costs has the incentive to recover those costs by charging different prices to different customers depending on their willingness to pay or, which is the same, depending on the slope of their demand curve. But all suppliers on the market will have the same incentive and will be competing for the same groups of customers. Total market output is at the competitive level because total revenue equals total costs.[107] It is not difficult to point to the airline industry as the most obvious example of this type of common cost recovery through price discrimination. Even on the most competitive routes, airlines will try to equal their total revenue to their total cost by second-degree and third-degree price discrimination, for example by discriminating between business and economy class passengers (second-degree price discrimination) or between passengers booking the flight in different locations (third-degree price discrimination). Airlines will fiercely compete against each other for different categories of customers but none of them will set a uniform price. And yet, it is quite possible that none of them will earn a monopoly profit.[108] The issue turns largely, albeit not exclusively, on the definition of market power. Clearly, if market power is defined as the ability to price above MC, then price discrimination presupposes market power. But if market power is defined as the ability to earn an economic profit, then price discrimination may occur in the absence of market power. As regards abuse of dominance, this debate is largely moot because dominance already requires the possession of substantial and durable market power defined as the ability to reduce market output and raise market prices, which is a condition for earning significant and persistent supra-competitive profits.[109] It follows that it is indisputable that undertakings that are not dominant may have the ability and incentive to price discriminate and that price discrimination in itself is not, and cannot be, evidence of dominance.

Economists are generally concerned with the short-term impact of price discrimination on social welfare. Unsurprisingly, such an effect depends on the cost and demand functions and their interdependence. It also depends on whether discrimination takes place vis-à-vis final consumers or intermediate purchasers. The reason for this is that in the latter case the analysis cannot be limited to the effect on seller and buyer surplus on the intermediate market. The implications for the downstream markets are also relevant, particularly as concerns the productive and

---

[107] ME Levine, 'Price Discrimination Without Market Power' (2002) 19 Yale Journal on Regulation 1, 13.

[108] ibid 21–25.

[109] On the concept of dominance, see Chs 10 and 11 below. For present purposes, suffice it to say that the concept of dominance must be derived from the objective of competition law and the content of unilateral conduct rules. Because the objective of competition law is to maximize long-term social welfare, and abuse of dominance prohibits unilateral conduct that runs counter to the objective of competition law, dominance must be the ability of a firm to harm long-term social welfare unilaterally. Only firms with substantial and durable market power have the ability to harm social welfare in the long term by acting alone and not in collusion with other firms because only substantial and durable market power gives a firm the ability to affect market output unilaterally to such a degree that competitive harm becomes reasonably probable and not just theoretically possible.

dynamic efficiency of the intermediate buyers and the surplus of the final purchasers.[110] Furthermore, on intermediate markets, buyers are interdependent.
Prices charged to one buyer affect the other buyer's demand.[111]

As regards the effects of price discrimination on the market where it takes place,
it is useful to distinguish first-, second-, and third-degree price discrimination.

Perfect price discrimination by a monopolist reduces consumer surplus to zero but
is allocatively efficient.[112] The proponents of the consumer welfare objective or test
should therefore at the very least ban perfect price discrimination. But, of course,
such a policy would be misconceived as it would outlaw an outcome that is more
efficient from the society's point of view than the uniform monopoly price. Under a
long-term social welfare objective, there is no case for prohibiting first-degree price
discrimination.

Second-degree price discrimination gives rise to the problem of comparing second best solutions. If the choice is between uniform prices and price discrimination, there are circumstances in which non-linear prices increase welfare and
circumstances in which welfare is reduced. Two-part tariffs may increase social
welfare because the marginal price is closer to the MC as the monopolist earns a
larger share of the rents through the fixed fee.[113] On the other hand, provided that
all customers continue to be served, second-degree price discrimination by tying
may lower social welfare because, in its absence, the tied product would be priced
at MC.[114] A more general point is that the effect of second-degree price discrimination depends on whether, under a uniform price, the monopolist would find it
profitable to forgo sales to more price-sensitive customers. If this is the case, a ban
on price discrimination reduces welfare.[115] The difficulty is that it cannot be readily assumed that, if price discrimination is forbidden, some consumers will not be
served at all. If the low value markets are large enough and consumers' willingness
to pay does not diverge dramatically across markets, a prohibition of price discrimination may well result in lower market prices and increased welfare.

Third-degree price discrimination allows the dominant undertaking to capture
more profits and, thus, *ceteris paribus*, to reduce the deadweight loss.[116] However,
it distorts the allocation of resources as between different customers. Customers
with a higher valuation may wish to buy from customers with a low valuation

---

[110] Y Yoshida, 'Third-Degree Price Discrimination in Input Markets: Output and Welfare'
(2000) 90 American Economic Rev 240.

[111] JA Ordover and JC Panzar, 'On the Nonlinear Pricing of Inputs' (1982) 23 Intl Economic
Rev 659.

[112] Even this reasonably well established proposition is not universally true. See eg, V Bhaskar
and T To, 'Is Perfect Price Discrimination Really Efficient? An Analysis of Free Entry' (2004) 35
RAND Journal of Economics 762, who demonstrate that perfect price discrimination may be inefficient if there is free entry because entry will be excessive as 'the marginal firm captures its marginal
contribution relative to an *inefficient* allocation rather than an efficient one'.

[113] Tirole, *The Theory of Industrial Organization*, 146.   [114] ibid 147.

[115] On the implications of second-degree price discrimination see R Chiang and CS Spatt,
'Imperfect Price Discrimination and Welfare' (1982) 49 Rev Econ Stud 155; KWS Roberts, 'Welfare
Considerations of Nonlinear Pricing' (1979) 89 Economic Journal 66; ML Katz 'Non-Uniform
Pricing, Output and Welfare under Monopoly' (1983) 50 Rev Econ Stud 37.

[116] Carlton and Perloff, *Modern Industrial Organization*, 301–303.

but are prevented from doing so because no arbitrage is possible. This distortion is created by price discrimination in addition to the distortions of monopoly.[117] Furthermore, customers may be encouraged to engage in wasteful behaviour in order to purchase the product. In order to price discriminate, the supplier may bundle the lower-price product with a commodity which consumers dislike, such as a strict cancellation policy for a hotel reservation.[118] In order to offset these negative effects, it is well established that a larger output is a necessary condition for welfare to improve under third-degree price discrimination.[119] Non-output-expanding price discrimination would be generally welfare reducing.

The above analysis demonstrates that a competition concern can only arise with second- and third-degree price-discrimination and that, generally, a necessary condition for price discrimination to be harmful is that it reduces output. The problem is that it is difficult to predict whether a ban on price discrimination will increase or decrease output. To illustrate this point, it may be instructive to consider why a supplier may wish to price discriminate and what happens if price discrimination is prohibited. As shown in Figure 3.1 below, if a monopolist faces two different markets, A and B, and is able to apply third-degree price discrimination, rational profit maximizing implies that the monopolist 'should charge more in markets with the lower elasticity of demand'.[120] If price discrimination is allowed, the total

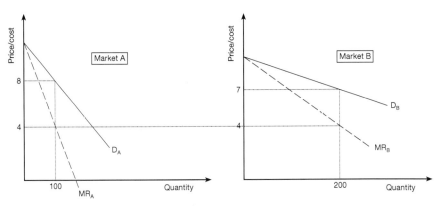

Figure 3.1 Equilibrium of monopoly under price discrimination

---

[117] R Schmalensee, 'Output and Welfare Implications of Monopolistic Third-Degree Price Discrimination' (1981) 71 American Economic Rev 242, 243; Carlton and Perloff, *Modern Industrial Organization*, 306–307.

[118] Chiang and Spatt, 'Imperfect Price Discrimination and Welfare', 155–160, where the authors discuss a second-degree price discrimination model in which the monopolist bundles the product with time in order to discriminate among customers.

[119] Schmalensee, 'Output and Welfare Implications of Monopolistic Third-Degree Price Discrimination' (in a model with constant marginal cost); HR Varian, 'Price Discrimination and Social Welfare' (1985) 75 American Economic Rev 870 (with increasing marginal cost); M Schwartz, 'Third-Degree Price Discrimination and Output: Generalising a Welfare Result' (1990) 80 American Economic Rev 1259 (generalising the result to decreasing marginal cost). This intuition dates back to AC Pigou, *The Economics of Welfare* 284–285 and 288–289 and J Robinson, *The Economics of Imperfect Competition* (London, MacMillan 1933) 203–208.

[120] Tirole, *The Theory of Industrial Organization*, 137.

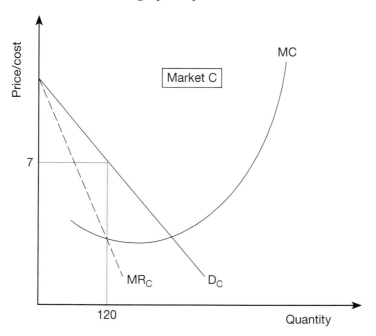

Figure 3.2 Effect of a ban on price discrimination with inelastic aggregate demand

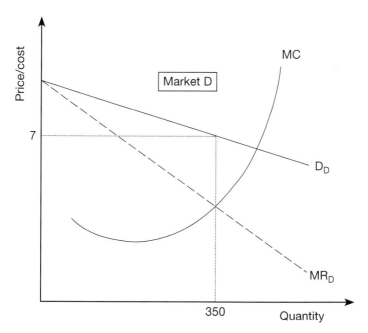

Figure 3.3 Effect of a ban on price discrimination with elastic aggregate demand

output is the sum of the output on market A and the output on market B, so that in this case the firm produces 300 units to sell.

In a market where price discrimination is prohibited there are two possibilities, as shown in Figures 3.2 and 3.3 above: either the resulting aggregated demand is inelastic (market C), in which case the total output decreases, or the aggregate demand is elastic (market D) and then the total output should increase. In the absence of accurate data on the elasticity of demand in markets A and B, it is impossible to predict in the abstract which market outcome will prevail.

The problem is that with price discrimination, some consumers pay a higher price and others a lower price. Under a uniform price regime, some consumers may pay a lower price but other consumers may have to pay a higher price[121] or may have to forgo buying the product altogether. The net effect on consumer surplus depends on the size of these opposing effects. In order to calculate the overall effect on social welfare, the net effect on consumer welfare should be added to the increase in producer welfare minus the deadweight loss. This measure of welfare should then be compared with social welfare under the uniform price regime.

A separate but equally important point is that price discrimination may be an efficient way of recovering fixed costs.[122] In industries where substantial investments that result in fixed costs are required to achieve optimal levels of productive efficiency or product development, a ban on price discrimination could have a negative effect on incentives to invest both *ex ante*, because the ability to price discriminate may be an important factor in the decision to invest, and *ex post*, because the increased profits resulting from price discrimination are a reward for past investment. This, however, cannot be an argument for excluding or severely limiting the application of competition law to price discrimination. It is an argument in favour of including dynamic efficiency considerations in the test for discriminatory abuses.

The above analysis shows that it cannot be asserted with certainty that price discrimination by a dominant firm is never, or only very rarely, socially harmful.[123] Clearly, price discrimination increases the dominant undertaking's profits

---

[121] Unless first-degree price discrimination occurs, under second or third-degree price discrimination consumers are only imperfectly sorted so that it is possible that some consumers pay a price lower than their reservation value.

[122] This is uncontroversial as a general proposition: see D Ridyard, 'Exclusionary Pricing and Price Discrimination Abuses under Article 82—An Economic Analysis' (2002) 23 ECLR 286, 286–287 and D Geradin and N Petit, 'Price Discrimination under EC Competition Law: Another Antitrust Doctrine in Search of Limiting Principles?' (2006) 2 J Comp L & Econ 479, 484–485. This intuition has its origins in the seminal article by FP Ramsey, 'A Contribution to the Theory of Taxation' (1927) 37 Economic Journal 47.

[123] Even in one of the most balanced discussions of this issue, the bias is clearly towards defending the pro-competitive effects of price discrimination: see O'Donoghue and Padilla, *The Law and Economics of Article 82 EC*, 558–600, who argue that price discrimination is 'generally positive or ambiguous', thus implying that price discrimination is unlikely to be detrimental. There is no serious discussion of the negative effects of price discrimination that have been identified in the literature.

but this circumstance alone is far from conclusive. Certain well recognized exclusionary practices, which do not entail profit sacrifice, also increase the dominant undertaking's profits. This is, for instance, the case with margin squeeze, where the conduct is profitable as long as the value of forgone sales on the input market is more than offset by increased market power rents on the downstream market. Not to mention exploitative abuses that fall foul of the law notwithstanding the fact that their only purpose is to increase the dominant undertaking's profits. Nor can it be assumed that any conduct that results in increased profits is beneficial because 'it has a knock-on effect on investment'.[124] The profits made by a dominant undertaking, which, it bears repeating, has substantial and durable market power and is shielded from effective competition by significant barriers to entry, may well be reinvested in the business but may also be dissipated in rent-seeking activities, appropriated by managers, or eroded by X-inefficiencies.

As complex as it may be, the examination of the welfare effects of price discrimination is only the first step in framing the test for discriminatory abuses. Under competition law, a reduction in social welfare *per se* is not a criterion under which conduct by a dominant firm is held to be abusive. The increased deadweight loss resulting from price discrimination compared to uniform prices can only be *indirectly* addressed if the prices charged by the dominant undertaking to the high-valuation customers are exploitative. Excessively high prices may well be applied only in a segment of the market. Therefore, they could be part of a price discrimination strategy. This, however, is a form of exploitative abuse and not a form of discriminatory abuse. Therefore, it falls to be assessed under the exploitative abuse test.[125] And, of course, as explained above, price discrimination may be exclusionary, in which case it is assessed under the relevant test for anti-competitive exclusion. This further demonstrates that purely discriminatory abuses must take place on intermediate markets. Price discrimination vis-à-vis final consumers can be either exploitative or result in the exclusion of rivals. There is no other conceivable anti-competitive effect. On intermediate markets, however, beyond the exclusion of rivals and the direct exploitation of customers, price discrimination may generate distortions in the competitive relationship between the suppliers or the customers of the dominant undertaking in a way that harms long-term social welfare.[126] The economic analysis of this type of price discrimination differs significantly from the welfare analysis of price discrimination vis-à-vis final customers. To this kind of market-distorting price discrimination the discussion must now turn.

---

[124] O'Donoghue and Padilla, *The Law and Economics of Article 82 EC*, 559.

[125] See 282–284 below.

[126] Geradin and Petit, 'Price Discrimination under EC Competition Law: Another Antitrust Doctrine in Search of Limiting Principles?', 517–521, would limit discriminatory abuses to practices that distort competition on downstream markets and practices that distort competition between the downstream division of a dominant undertaking and its downstream rivals. The latter form of abuse is, however, better analysed as exclusionary because the harm to long-term social welfare results from the exclusion of the competitors of the dominant firm, not from price discrimination as such. On the potential benefits of this type of price discrimination see B Klein and JS Wiley Jr, 'Competitive Price Discrimination as an Antitrust Justification for Intellectual Property Refusals to Deal' (2002) 70 Antitrust LJ 599.

(c) Competitive implications of discrimination on intermediate markets

There may be several models of intermediate market price discrimination and, needless to say, the welfare and competitive implications differ depending on the sets of assumptions relied on and the focus of the analysis.

O'Brien and Shaffer study a model in which downstream competition is based on price and the upstream monopolist applies a two-part tariff in bilateral negotiations with buyers, which remain private. When bilateral negotiations are unconstrained, all MC are the same. The monopolist extracts customer surplus through the fixed fees, which are a function of relative bargaining powers. Average prices therefore differ.[127] If price discrimination is forbidden so that no two-part tariff may be used, the monopolist extracts surplus by setting prices above MC. The retailers add their own mark-up. Downstream prices are higher than in the unconstrained discrimination scenario.[128] If, however, the monopolist could only set a two-part tariff in which the fixed fee and the marginal prices are the same for all customers, it would set the fixed fee in order to extract the entire surplus from the least profitable customer. But marginal prices will be above MC because the constraint on the level of the fixed fees forces the monopolist to internalize downstream competition through marginal prices. Retail prices will be higher than under unconstrained discrimination.[129] Finally, even when the monopolist can privately set discriminatory fixed fees but must set common wholesale costs, retail prices will be higher. Intuitively, this is because the law forbids private negotiations on wholesale prices, which drives prices down to MC.[130] Under all scenarios when discrimination is forbidden, short-term social welfare and consumer welfare are lower than under unconstrained discrimination, although, in certain circumstances, intermediate customers' profits are higher when discrimination is forbidden.[131] This model focuses exclusively on short-term welfare implications and does not examine long-term implications for productivity and, particularly, for downstream customers' incentives to innovate and invest. Furthermore, because of the bargaining model chosen, price discrimination equilibria in which prices are higher than MC do not arise. However, as the authors themselves recognize, there are a number of scenarios in which it is quite plausible that unilaterally negotiated unobservable two-part tariffs will yield prices above MC. When this is the case, comparing social welfare under unconstrained discrimination and when discrimination is prohibited becomes much more difficult.[132] Whatever the strengths and weaknesses of this model, the possibility that price discrimination increases social welfare or the difficulty in determining the welfare effects of price discrimination has very little to say about the optimal competition rules regarding abusive discrimination. The fundamental point is that competition law does not, and should not, forbid price discrimination but attempts to identify the conditions under which price

---

[127] DP O'Brien and G Shaffer, 'The Welfare Effects of Forbidding Discriminatory Discounts: A Secondary Line Analysis of Robinson-Patman' (1994) 10 JL Econ & Org 296, 303–304.
[128] ibid 305–307.   [129] ibid 307–308.   [130] ibid 308–310.
[131] ibid 310–313.   [132] ibid 315.

discrimination on intermediate markets has a market-distorting effect, which is incompatible with the objective of maximizing long-term social welfare.

The analysis of price discrimination on intermediate markets must take into account not only its effect on price and output but also its impact on the firms' strategic choices. Katz considers a model in which a monopolist of an input supplies two downstream firms: a large chain active on multiple markets and a small store active only on one market. The downstream firms compete on quantities, and the large chain can integrate backwards by producing the input itself. In certain circumstances, price discrimination may raise the price to all downstream firms so that social welfare is reduced. The key intuition is that the monopolist's pricing decisions are not simply based on static profit-maximization but take into account the threat of backward integration by the large chain. Results differ depending on the monopolist's incentives to allow backward integration by setting its price so that, *ceteris paribus*, backward integration is profitable. First, suppose that it is not profitable for the monopolist to allow the large chain to integrate backwards. When this is the case, the monopolist must charge the large chain a price which makes it indifferent to the latter whether to opt for integration or outsourcing. If the monopolist cannot price discriminate, it will charge to both customers the price at which the large chain's profitability in the absence of integration is the same as its profitability if it integrates backwards. If the monopolist can price discriminate, however, it will only have to charge the price that makes the chain indifferent between backward integration and outsourcing to the chain. The price to the small store can be higher. As a result of the contraction of the output of the small store, the profitability of the large chain would rise, which in turn would allow the monopolist to raise its price to the large chain.[133] As opposed to what happens in final product markets, where price discrimination generally means that some consumers pay a higher price and some a lower price, in this model all prices rise. Consider now how the decision of the monopolist to let the large chain integrate may change under either the price discrimination regime or the uniform pricing regime. The monopolist decides whether to allow backward integration by comparing its profits at prices that prevent integration with profits when integration takes place. The monopolist's profits at prices that prevent integration are higher under price discrimination. On the other hand, its profits post-integration do not depend on its ability to price discriminate because there will be only one customer left on the market. Therefore, price discrimination is more likely to prevent backward integration than uniform pricing. The welfare effects of price discrimination depend, *inter alia*, on whether backward integration is efficient. Backward integration results in a duplication of upstream fixed costs but creates an upstream duopoly in place of the former monopoly. Its welfare effects depend on whether the increase in industry output offsets the loss of productive efficiency.[134] As with other economic models, policy implications are not easy to draw. But the analysis

---

[133] ML Katz, 'The Welfare Effects of Third-Degree Price Discrimination in Intermediate Good Markets' (1987) 77 American Economic Rev 154, 161.
[134] ibid 163–164.

shows that there is no basis in economics to maintain that price discrimination on intermediate markets is almost always beneficial because, in its absence, all prices, or the average market price, would rise. In the absence of price discrimination prices may either fall or rise, depending on the market context.

Price discrimination on intermediate markets may have a negative effect on productive efficiency by favouring inefficient firms over efficient ones. Yoshida analyses a model in which a monopolist of an upstream input supplies downstream firms which use both the monopolist's input α and a mixture of other inputs β. Downstream firms compete on quantities. The uniform price regime is compared to a regime where third-degree price discrimination takes place. The monopolist is assumed to face independent linear demands and to have constant MC so that its output is the same under uniform pricing or price discrimination. This allows the analysis to focus on the impact on downstream costs and output.[135] When moving from the uniform pricing equilibrium to the price discrimination equilibrium, more efficient firms are harmed by price discrimination. The market shares of more efficient firms decrease while the market shares of less efficient firms increase. Intuitively, this may be because more efficient firms have a higher willingness to pay for the input. A price discriminating monopoly will charge them a higher price. If all downstream firms can be ordered in α-β-efficiency so that, given any two firms i and j, $\alpha_i > \alpha_j$ implies $\beta_i > \beta_j$, welfare always decreases.[136] If, however, some firms are more α-efficient compared to others but less β-efficient, welfare is reduced only for certain parameterizations.[137] What is striking about this model is that an increase in downstream output is found to be a sufficient condition for a welfare loss. Because price discrimination is profitable to the monopolist and the downstream output increase raises consumer welfare, the entire loss accrues at the level of the intermediate industry due to the subsidizing of less efficient firms.[138] Two key insights may be derived from this analysis. The first is that in intermediate markets, and unlike in final markets, an increase in total output and, therefore, in the welfare of the final consumers cannot predict whether price discrimination is beneficial or detrimental. The second is that price discrimination has the potential to impair equal opportunities on the intermediate market by favouring inefficient undertakings over efficient ones. The distortion of competition which results from altering the cost structures of the downstream firms is not only detrimental to social welfare and productivity in the short term but may impair the long-term ability of efficient undertakings to invest and innovate.

Finally, the welfare losses of price discrimination on intermediate markets may result from distortions that price discrimination induces in the choice of technologies. This type of harm is particularly serious as it negatively affects dynamic efficiency and impairs long-term productivity growth. DeGraba discusses a

---

[135] Yoshida, 'Third-Degree Price Discrimination in Input Markets: Output and Welfare', 240–242.

[136] ibid 244.   [137] ibid 245.   [138] ibid 246.

model in which the upstream monopolist charges low-cost producers a higher price and high-cost producers a lower price. This, at first sight, counter-intuitive scenario arises when the monopolist can observe downstream demand and has an incentive to charge a higher price to the producer who faces the more inelastic downstream demand. When demand is linear, as in the model in question, a lower MC will correspond to a more inelastic demand. In the short term, welfare decreases because the firms with a higher MC will produce more and the firms with the lower MC will produce less than under uniform pricing.[139] What is even more interesting is the long-term impact on the downstream producers' investment incentives. Because the subsidy, which is the result of price discrimination, artificially reduces the difference in the downstream firms' MC, there will be a distorted incentive to adopt technologies with lower fixed costs and higher MC than would be optimal for social welfare. In the long term, even the monopolist is harmed because the higher MC of downstream firms lead to a decrease in the demand for the upstream input.[140] The harm to longterm productivity could not be clearer. This model is highly stylized and can hardly be generalized. The entire edifice rests on the idea that a downstream buyer with a lower MC and higher demand pays more for an input. This will not often be the case, particularly when the upstream seller is not a monopolist protected by insurmountable entry barriers. Large buyers are generally offered quantity discounts. They may have significant bargaining power if they are able to make a credible threat of switching to other suppliers. Furthermore, larger orders may result in lower transaction costs or more efficient planning of production. Even a monopolist may be expected to pass on at least some MC reductions to its customers. On the other hand, a model in which a monopolist charges more to customers with lower MC and inelastic demand is not entirely implausible. An example could be a port operator charging higher fees to ferry operators with low MC that face a higher but less elastic downstream demand because they run at peak times on important commuter routes. If lower fees are charged to ferry operators facing a more elastic demand because they are more expensive or less convenient, this may discourage investment in technologies which reduce MC, such as computer passenger reservation systems.

(d) *The market-distorting discrimination test*

The economic analysis of price discrimination demonstrates that, beyond exclusionary and exploitative conduct, there may be a case for prohibiting price discrimination on intermediate markets that distorts the competitive relationship between suppliers or buyers of the dominant firm. However, there is absolutely no case for banning price discrimination *per se*. Price discrimination may be harmful or

---

[139] P DeGraba 'Input Market Price Discrimination and the Choice of Technology' (1990) 80 American Economic Rev 1246, 1247–1249.
[140] ibid 1249–1252.

beneficial depending on the circumstances. The welfare effects of price discrimination on intermediate markets depend crucially on three factors:

1. The effect of price discrimination on the productive and dynamic efficiency of the intermediate firms;

2. Whether, in the absence of price discrimination, output is higher or lower (this condition is less important on intermediate markets but still relevant because output-expanding price discrimination is prima facie beneficial to long-term social welfare);

3. The impact of a ban of price discrimination on the dynamic efficiency of a dominant firm both *ex ante*, because the ability to price discriminate may be an important factor in the decision to invest, and *ex post*, because the increased profits resulting from price discrimination are a reward for past investment.

Given that the implications of potentially abusive conduct for allocative and dynamic efficiency are relevant to all abuses, the hallmark of the test for abusive discrimination is the impact on the efficiency of intermediate firms. Discrimination is abusive when it places customers or suppliers of the dominant undertaking at a competitive disadvantage notwithstanding the fact that, in the absence of the discrimination, they would be as efficient as their competitors. Firms that are equally efficient are denied equality of opportunities on the market. This is precisely the same rationale as the rationale of the as efficient competitor test applied to exclusionary abuses.

F. The consumer harm test

(1) General formulations of the consumer harm test

The consumer harm test focuses on the effect of the conduct on price and output.[141] The test has a clear advantage for those who argue that the objective of competition law is or should be the maximization of consumer welfare.[142] However, the test is also consistent with the objective of maximizing long-term social welfare and may even perform, on average, better than a social welfare test in achieving a social welfare objective.[143]

---

[141] Salop, 'Exclusionary Conduct, Effect on Consumers, and the Flawed Profit-Sacrifice Standard', 329–330. In *Brooke Group*, the Supreme Court held that a dangerous probability of recoupment is a prerequisite for a finding of liability under s 2 of the Sherman Act thus adopting a consumer harm test for predation. Without recoupment, predatory pricing produces lower aggregate prices in the market and consumer welfare is enhanced. Under a social welfare standard, however, below cost pricing is inefficient regardless of recoupment: SC Salop, 'Question: What is the Real and Proper Antitrust Welfare Standard? Answer: The True Consumer Welfare Standard', presented to the Antitrust Modernization Commission (4 November 2005) 6.

[142] See Ch 2, n 74 above.   [143] See 45–49 above.

There are various formulations of the test. Salop describes it as follows:[144]

Under this standard, one would conclude that exclusionary conduct violates the antitrust laws if it reduces competition without creating a sufficient improvement in performance to fully offset these potential adverse effects on prices and thereby prevent consumer harm.

Areeda and Hovenkamp define exclusionary conduct as acts that:[145]

(1) are reasonably capable of creating, enlarging, or prolonging monopoly power by impairing the opportunities of rivals; and
(2) either (2a) do not benefit consumers at all, or (2b) are unnecessary for the particular consumer benefits that the acts produce, or (2c) produce harms disproportionate to the resulting benefits.

Hovenkamp has further argued that the allegedly anti-competitive conduct 'must be reasonably susceptible of judicial control, which means that the court must be able to identify the conduct as anti-competitive and either fashion a penalty producing the correct amount of deterrence or an equitable remedy likely to improve competition'.[146]

(2) Advantages of the consumer harm test

The strength of the consumer harm test is that it focuses on the effect of conduct on price and output. The question the test asks is not simple to answer but, at least, it is clear. Conduct is anti-competitive only if it harms customers.

The consumer harm test is also consistent with the objectives of competition law. Lower prices, larger output, and better or new products are key drivers of long-term social welfare and productivity. Obviously, they are not the only drivers of social welfare and productivity because productive efficiency and innovation in production processes are equally important. However, in a well-functioning market it can be expected that firms will pass on lower costs, at least in part, to consumers by way of lower prices, better services, or investment in R&D. There could, of course, be cases where productive efficiencies outweighing any negative effects on price and output are not passed on to consumers and yet they increase long-term social welfare. However, there are reasons for believing that such cases should be rare. Theoretical research has shown that the consumer harm test may force firms to choose more socially desirable options than a social welfare test.[147] Furthermore, the test requires consumer harm in the first place. A dominant firm

---

[144] Salop, 'Exclusionary Conduct, Effect on Consumers, and the Flawed Profit-Sacrifice Standard', 330.

[145] Areeda and Hovenkamp, *Antitrust Law: An Analysis of Antitrust Principles and Their Application*, 651a, 72.

[146] Hovenkamp, 'Exclusion and the Sherman Act', 148–150.

[147] B Lyons, 'Could Politicians Be More Right than Economists? A Theory of Merger Standards' Revised Centre for Competition and Regulation (CCR) Working Paper CCR 02-1 (European University Institute, 2003); DJ Neven and L-H Röller, 'Consumer Surplus vs Welfare Standard in a Political Economy Model of Merger Control' (2005) 23 Intl J Ind Org 829; J Farrell and ML Katz, 'The Economics of Welfare Standards in Antitrust', Competition Policy Center, Institute of Business and Economic Research (UC Berkeley, 20 July 2006).

simply has to ensure that its conduct, which harms competitors and generates efficiencies, does not harm consumers. Also, it is not a condition that the conduct in question must benefit consumers. Only if consumers are harmed as a result of the conduct does it have to be shown that the efficiencies the conduct generates are passed on to consumers and outweigh any negative effects on them.

A further strength of the test is that it allows for a wider consideration of the effects of the conduct under review, both positive and negative.[148] There is a growing recognition that the 'balancing' of the negative effect on output, prices, and innovation and the benefits of the efficiencies is not, and cannot be, a rigorous quantification and weighing-up of opposing welfare effects. Nor is this 'balancing' exercise an open-ended weighing-up of the social benefits and costs of the conduct under review. The process has been described as a sliding-scale standard in which the higher the evidence of consumer harm is, the more compelling is the evidence of efficiencies which the fact-finder will require.[149] Areeda and Hovenkamp describe the standard as a 'proportionality enquiry'.[150] This allows an assessment of unilateral conduct in the round without requiring quantification and balancing of opposing effects on price, output, costs, and innovation in the short and long term, which would, in most if not all circumstances, be either impossible or speculative.

(3) Problems of over- and under-enforcement associated with the consumer harm test

One of the main disadvantages of the consumer harm test is that it is both over-inclusive and under-inclusive.

The test may be over-inclusive and deter conduct that generates efficiencies because, if conduct clearly increases market power but also generates substantial efficiencies, a dominant undertaking risks infringing the competition rules unless it can be shown that the pass-through of the efficiencies to consumers outweighs any price increase. This is a difficult task, and the risk of enforcement action and a finding of infringement may lead dominant firms to abandon conduct that would generate efficiencies and be beneficial to social welfare in the long term. Therefore, the test may discourage competition on the merits.[151] The phrase 'competition on the merits' refers to competition which harms rivals because of superior efficiency. Therefore, if the dominant undertaking's conduct generates efficiencies and would make business sense in the absence of the exclusion of rivals, it must be considered as 'competition on the merits' and, thus, lawful. The consumer welfare test

---

[148] For the adoption of a broad consumer welfare balancing test, see *United States v Microsoft Corp* 253 F 3d 34, 58–59 (DC Cir 2001). In that case, the DC Circuit held that, to be condemned as exclusionary, a monopolist's act must cause harm to the competitive process and, thereby, harm to consumers. If the plaintiff successfully establishes a prima facie case under s 2 of the Sherman Act, the defendant may proffer a 'procompetitive justification' for its conduct, for instance greater efficiency or enhanced consumer appeal. If the justification is not rebutted, the plaintiff must show that the anti-competitive effect outweighs the pro-competitive justification.

[149] Salop, 'Exclusionary Conduct, Effect on Consumers, and the Flawed Profit-Sacrifice Standard', 332–333.

[150] Areeda and Hovenkamp, *Antitrust Law*, 651a, 72.

[151] On the concept of competition on the merits, see 170–171 below.

may deter competition on the merits because the dominant firm may be unsure as to whether the effect of the efficiencies on consumers outweighs the negative effect of the restriction of competition. The risk of false positive errors and over-deterrence cannot simply be addressed by adjusting the standard of proof (a quantitative adjustment) rather than by changing the liability standard (a qualitative adjustment).[152] The standard of proof does have an important role to play in striking the right balance between different enforcement risks. However, the standard of proof is in itself an uncertain threshold. It is not possible to say with certainty what would be considered proof beyond reasonable doubt or on the balance of probabilities. Nor is it even possible to predict what evidence will be available when enforcement action is taken. More fundamentally, to adopt a standard that gives rise to a systematic risk of false convictions and over-deterrence only to raise the standard of proof to reduce such a risk seems illogical unless no other test could perform better as a matter of substance. And, at least in certain circumstances, the naked exclusion test and the as efficient competitor test are clearly superior to the consumer harm test.

On the other hand, it must be emphasized that the consumer harm test, especially if reinforced by a heightened standard of proof, may also give rise to systematic false acquittals and under-deterrence. In the same way as it is difficult for a dominant firm to assess *ex ante* whether its conduct does, on balance, harm consumers, it may be very difficult for a competition authority or claimant to prove that the conduct was likely to have such an effect. The difficulty that a competition authority or claimant faces in proving consumer harm in turn means that the test can operate to encourage dominant firms to engage in, rather than deterring them from, anti-competitive conduct *ex ante*.

(4) Administrability of the consumer harm test

In addition to its over- and under-inclusive nature, the other main criticism of the consumer welfare test is that it is not administrable.[153] The foundation of this argument is that in order to determine the effect of the dominant undertaking's conduct on consumer welfare, a long-term market-wide balancing exercise would be required. Clearly, a static market-wide balancing test, which focused on short-term effects, would be under-inclusive. Such a test would not be suitable for the assessment of conduct that does not harm consumers in the short-term. For instance, predation, which increases consumer welfare in the short-term, would always be lawful under a static consumer harm test. Furthermore, the test requires the balancing of all the positive and negative effects of the conduct under review on consumer welfare. To give only one example, if the exclusion of a rival increases the

---

[152] As suggested by Salop, 'Exclusionary Conduct, Effect on Consumers, and the Flawed Profit-Sacrifice Standard', 353–354 and Salop 'The Controversy over the Proper Antitrust Standard for Anticompetitive Exclusionary Conduct', 493–494.

[153] Werden, 'Identifying Exclusionary Conduct under Section 2: The "No Economic Sense" Test', 428–432; Melamed, 'Exclusive Dealing Agreements and Other Exclusionary Conduct—Are There Unifying Principles?', 379–388.

dominant undertaking's market power and its productive efficiency, two effects of price and output have to be assessed: the tendency of market power to increase prices and the extent to which lower production costs are reflected in lower prices. The conduct under review is abusive only if it results in increased prices. Therefore, dominant undertakings, when deciding on their market strategies *ex ante*, and competition authorities and courts, when determining whether the dominant undertaking's conduct was lawful *ex post*, would have to balance any harm to consumers caused by the market power resulting from the exclusion of rivals against any benefit resulting from the allegedly unlawful conduct in the long term. This presupposes information or assumptions not only about the effect of the conduct in question on prices but also about the value for consumers of product improvements and innovation and the degree of pass-through of productive efficiencies. Information about the long-term effects of competition law intervention on incentives for innovation and risk-taking would also be needed.[154] Some US commentators argue that this task is not only beyond the ability of a jury,[155] but also beyond the competence of competition authorities and courts.[156] Furthermore, it would not give dominant undertakings sufficient guidance to enable them to comply with the law without forgoing pro-competitive behaviour.[157] The proponents of the consumer harm tests respond by pointing out that consumer harm analysis is routinely carried out in merger cases and does not appear to give rise to insurmountable problems.[158] However, merger analysis is, in most legal systems, carried out by notifying the relevant competition authority of the proposed transaction. Therefore, firms may certainty obtain *ex ante* while, as regards abuse of dominance, they have to assess their own conduct by themselves. To say that the dominant undertaking would be required to carry out an *ex ante* assessment of the impact of its conduct on consumer welfare,[159] addresses the problem only in part. Clearly, an *ex ante* assessment rules out the risk that conduct that was perfectly lawful when first devised and implemented could become retroactively unlawful because of unpredictable market developments. It does not follow, however, that an *ex ante* assessment of the net long-term effect of conduct on price, output, and innovation is any less complex. It seems, therefore, that this criticism of the consumer welfare test is justified. The complexity of a test does not mean, of course, that it cannot be applied. But it is an incentive to search for an alternative test whenever possible, which is what this chapter has done.

---

[154] Werden, 'Identifying Exclusionary Conduct under Section 2: The "No Economic Sense" Test', 431.

[155] ibid 432; Elhauge, 'Defining Better Monopolization Standards', 317.

[156] Melamed, 'Exclusive Dealing Agreements and Other Exclusionary Conduct—Are There Unifying Principles?', 381.

[157] ibid 381–382.

[158] Salop, 'The Controversy over the Proper Antitrust Standard for Anticompetitive Exclusionary Conduct', 493.

[159] Salop, 'Exclusionary Conduct, Effect on Consumers, and the Flawed Profit-Sacrifice Standard', 343.

(5) Exploitative abuses and consumer harm

Exploitative abuses consist in the imposition of prices that are significantly and persistently higher[160] or trading conditions that are significantly and persistently more onerous than those that would have prevailed under effective competition.[161] There is no doubt, therefore, that exploitative abuses are assessed under a consumer harm test.

The key problem of exploitative abuses in competition policy relates to whether intervention is appropriate at all. Some argue that the cost of enforcement errors in this area is very high because a prohibition of prices that may appear excessive under the consumer harm test may deter investment both by the firm in question and by other firms. This would be highly detrimental to social welfare.[162] On the other hand, the cost of non-intervention may not be high when entry forces dominant firms to lower their prices.[163] The fundamental flaw of this argument is that when high profits are necessary to reward investment or to finance future investment, they are not exploitative. An investment, which includes remuneration for a firm's risk, must be compensated in a competitive market. Therefore, unless the measurement of the competitive return on the investment of the dominant firm is impossible or excessively difficult, there is no reason why a prohibition of excessive prices should in any way discourage investment. Nor are excessive prices necessarily 'self-correcting'. Generally, excessive prices imposed by a dominant firm are not 'self-correcting' because a firm is not dominant unless it has substantial and durable market power, that is, substantial market power protected by significant barriers to entry.[164] Furthermore, what matters in terms of attracting entry is not the

---

[160] The requirements of 'significance' and 'persistency' are necessarily implied in the prohibition of exploitative abuses by dominant undertakings. There are many circumstances in which an undertaking may apply supra-competitive prices or trading conditions but, if it is not dominant, any economic profits would be competed away by the entry or expansion of rivals. Similarly, there are many circumstances in which an undertaking may charge prices or apply trading conditions that are not the same as those that would have prevailed under conditions of effective competition. For instance, any undertaking selling a differentiated product may in the short-term earn some economic profits. To prohibit any discrepancy between price and marginal cost would be absurd and give rise to a form of price regulation enforcing MC pricing across all industries.

[161] A crucial problem is, in practice, to devise a workable methodology to determine when prices are excessive and when trading conditions are exploitative. This problem falls outside the scope of the normative analysis in this chapter, which aims at identifying the key elements of an optimal legal test rather than the types of evidence (whether of fact or opinion given by experts) that, in the circumstances of each individual case, are capable of proving that prices or trading conditions are exploitative. For further references on this topic, see Ch 8, n 77 below.

[162] DS Evans and AJ Padilla, 'Excessive Prices: Using Economics to Define Administrable Legal Rules' (2005) 1 J Comp L & Econ 97, 114–116.

[163] ibid 115–116.

[164] M Motta and A de Streel, 'Excessive Pricing and Price Squeeze under EU Law' in CD Ehlermann and I Atanasiu (eds), *European Competition Law Annual 2003: What Is an Abuse of a Dominant Position?* (Oxford, Hart Publishing 2006) 91, 108, make this error when they distinguish regulation, which applies to markets 'where there are legal barriers to entry and/or significant market failures' and competition law, which 'generally applies to markets where competitive forces are in principle free to operate'. The authors were perhaps focusing on legal barriers to entry but the effect of legal or other entry barriers on the ability of the dominant firm to harm long-term social welfare may not be significantly different although the source of the impediment to entry is different.

pre-entry price but the expected post-entry price, which is unrelated to whether the pre-entry price was excessive or not.[165]

A better argument against a prohibition of exploitative abuses is that any conceivable legal test other than an outright ban on prices x per cent higher than a given measure of cost, would be so complex to administer that there would be many enforcement errors and no *ex ante* certainty for dominant firms.[166] Is non-intervention then the solution? If it is true that excessive prices imposed by a dominant firm are not self-correcting, the right answer would have to be no. Prices above the competitive level imposed by a dominant firm clearly reduce social welfare in the short term. The presence of significant barriers to entry means that the harm is likely to continue in the long term. Furthermore, the unconstrained power to charge supra-competitive prices in the long term is likely to reduce the incentives of the dominant firm to increase its own productive efficiency and to invest in product improvements. When the exploitative abuse occurs on intermediate markets, further harm may arise because the customers of the dominant firm must pay a monopoly price for an input. This may have two consequences, which will be exacerbated if the input makes a significant contribution to downstream costs. First, there may be inefficient substitution towards a different input. Secondly, lower profits may result in lower investment incentives on the intermediate market. Therefore, excessive prices are capable of harming social welfare and productivity in the long term. When they are the result of the ability of a dominant firm to exercise substantial and durable market power, the case for intervention is made in theory, provided that an administrable test can be designed.

The problem of the test can be divided into two issues. First, should intervention be limited to certain special circumstances so that structural conditions over and above dominance may act as a further safeguard against the risk of false convictions and over-deterrence? Secondly, should there be any further requirements relating to the competitive harm in addition to the reduction of social welfare that is inherent in the charging of prices above the competitive level?

As regards potential structural screens, the dominant position is a prime candidate to act as an element of an enhanced intervention threshold. A mere dominant position, which grants substantial and durable market power but is consistent with the existence of a competitive fringe, is not sufficient to justify a prohibition of excessive prices. Customers clearly have alternatives to turn to, although they may not be able to switch their entire requirements to competitors. Therefore, there is a degree of price discipline on the market albeit lower than the competitive pressure that would be consistent with effective competition on that market. When this is the case, imposing a price cap on the dominant undertaking would give rise to a significant risk of distorting the functioning of the market and the normal dynamics of competition with a competitive fringe. On the other hand,

---

[165] A Ezrachi and D Gilo, 'Are Excessive Prices Really Self-Correcting?' (2009) 5 J Comp L & Econ 249, 255–257.

[166] Motta and de Streel, 'Excessive Pricing and Price Squeeze under EU Law', 109.

an appropriately defined enhanced dominance threshold may limit interventions to markets where the magnitude of the distorting effect of price regulation is lowest and the competitive harm of exploitative abuses is highest. Moreover, an enhanced dominance threshold may reduce, at least to a certain extent, the risk of error inherent in the assessment of excessive prices. Fewer markets, where harm is more likely to occur and be of a larger scale, would be subject to the prohibition and any errors would have a more limited over-deterrent effect across the economy. However, it would be too narrow an approach to limit intervention to cases in which there are 'insurmountable legal barriers to entry'.[167] Natural monopolies and *de facto* monopolies are in precisely the same position as legal monopolies,[168] provided that entry on a sufficient scale to exercise effective competitive pressure on the dominant firm is either impossible or unlikely in the long term. But nor should, the requirement that the market be characterized by 'high and non-transitory barriers to entry'[169] be sufficient. These conditions would be moot, as they are inherent in a finding of dominance.[170] It is also questionable whether it would be appropriate to require that the dominant position is the result of current or past exclusive or special rights[171] or that it 'is not the result of past investment or innovations'.[172] Such requirements would be difficult to apply in practice. On liberalized markets for example, a dominant position is often in part the result of past exclusive or special rights and in part of investment. Furthermore, it is difficult to conceive of circumstances in which a dominant position is not the result of any investment or innovation. Any business requires some investment. But, more importantly, the exploitative abuse test must take into account the need to reward investment when determining whether a price is excessive. Therefore, there is no need to introduce this further screen at the dominance stage over and above the presence of a monopolist or quasi-monopolist protected by such barriers to entry that entry is impossible or unlikely in the long term.

With regard to potential competitive harm screens, the question arises of whether an additional requirement relating to competitive harm could perform the role of a further screening device to avoid false convictions and over-deterrence. In order to perform this function of minimizing error costs, consumer harm must be distinct from, and additional to, the mere charging of supra-competitive prices or the imposition of excessively onerous trading conditions. The reason for this is that otherwise a consumer harm requirement would

---

[167] Evans and Padilla, 'Excessive Prices: Using Economics to Define Administrable Legal Rules', 119–120.

[168] Exclusive rights or special rights granted to particular undertakings by the State and conferring on them a monopoly or quasi-monopoly are, in substance if not in form, the same as a legal monopoly. The term legal monopoly should, therefore, include monopolistic or quasi-monopolist positions resulting from the granting of special or exclusive rights, although, in theory, other undertakings are allowed to operate in the market.

[169] Motta and de Streel, 'Excessive Pricing and Price Squeeze under EU Law', 109–110.

[170] See Ch 10 below.

[171] Motta and de Streel, 'Excessive Pricing and Price Squeeze under EU Law', 110.

[172] Evans and Padilla, 'Excessive Prices: Using Economics to Define Administrable Legal Rules', 119.

be redundant because prices significantly and persistently above the competitive level or excessively onerous trading conditions invariably cause some consumer harm. Therefore, the law should go further and require proof of demonstrable consumer harm distinct from, and additional to, the harm that derives from the mere payment of an excessively high price or the imposition of excessively onerous conditions.[173] Examples of such additional harm are:

1. The prevention of the development of a differentiated product, or the emergence of a new product, or the reduction of innovation[174]—thus, excessive prices that significantly deter investment by downstream firms would cause consumer harm;

2. The impact of short-term high prices on long-term prices if short-term prices significantly increase long-term prices, for instance through forward products (such as options and futures);[175]

3. The manifest inability of the dominant undertaking to meet demand in circumstances in which it is not possible for other undertakings to enter the market or to expand output.[176]

G. Conclusion

The above analysis shows that no single test for abuse of dominance is conceivable in theory and as a matter of enforcement policy. Not even for exclusionary abuses is it possible to design one test that optimally balances enforcement risks for all conceivable abusive practices. This does not mean, however, that the law is left without clear guiding principles so that competition law is in reality a set of ad hoc solutions perhaps suited to the facts of individual cases but devoid of any underpinning rationale. On the contrary, economic theory and enforcement policy principles can be examined in the light of the normative objective of competition law to yield a number of tests that, by themselves or in combination with each other, are capable of determining with a sufficient degree of accuracy whether conduct by a dominant firm is abusive.

---

[173] ibid 119–120, where the authors argue that it may be appropriate to prohibit excessive prices when, *inter alia*, there is 'a risk that those prices may prevent the emergence of new goods and services in adjacent markets'. The substantial consumer harm screen proposed here is wider but rests on the same idea that proof of specific and distinct consumer harm is a key safeguard against the risk of enforcement errors and over-deterrence.

[174] See eg the EU case law on refusal to license an IP right: Joined Cases C-241/91 P and C-242/91 P *Radio Telefis Eireann (RTE) and Independent Television Publications Ltd (ITP) v Commission* [1995] ECR I-743 (*Magill*); Case C-418/01 *IMS Health GmbH & Co OHG v NDC Health GmbH & Co KG* [2004] ECR I-5039; Case T-201/04 *Microsoft Corp v Commission* [2007] ECR II-3601 *(Microsoft I)*.

[175] *German Electricity Wholesale Market* [2009] C36/8 *(E.ON)* recitals 35–38.

[176] Case C-41/90 *Klaus Höfner and Fritz Elser v Macrotron GmbH* [1991] ECR I-1979.

Exclusionary abuses may be assessed under tests of intent, the as efficient competitor test, and the consumer harm test. Behaviour that has the sole or overwhelmingly predominant purpose of harming competition, has no conceivable redeeming virtue either by way of economic efficiencies or otherwise, and is reasonably capable of causing competitive harm can be prohibited under a naked exclusion test. Because of the low risk of false convictions and over-deterrence, when conduct is nakedly exclusionary an inquiry into its capability of excluding equally efficient competitors or harming consumers would be wasteful. It is, of course, always open to the dominant undertaking to rebut the evidence of naked exclusion or to adduce evidence that the conduct realizes efficiencies. However, if the test is properly applied so that it is limited only to the most egregiously anti-competitive conduct, the instances in which efficiency justifications are successful should be rare. The controversy is likely to focus on factual issues relating to whether the conduct is nakedly exclusionary in the first place. Beyond the naked abuse test, intent by itself is not suitable as a general test for abuse of dominance. It may, however, play three important roles. First, it may be an element of the test when a certain type of conduct is capable of producing significant competitive harm but a finding of infringement based solely on objective factors would be subject to a systematic high risk of false acquittals. Secondly, proof of intent may be required to condemn certain practices in addition to proof of anti-competitive effects when a finding of infringement based on objective factors only would be subject to a systematic risk of false convictions. Thirdly, evidence of intent may be relevant to prove the objective elements of the test. In this case, however, intent is not a test but the object of circumstantial evidence.

The as efficient competitor test, while unsuitable as the only test for exclusionary abuses, has significant advantages in terms of protection of the competitive process, consistency with the goals and the normative foundations of competition law, and legal certainty. The under-inclusive nature of the test is not a problem as long as it is accepted that the as efficient competitor test is not the only abuse test. The over-inclusive nature of the test can be addressed by allowing the dominant undertaking to adduce evidence to the effect that conduct that excludes equally efficient competitors is, on balance, beneficial. In other words, as under the naked exclusion test, the dominant undertaking must always be allowed to adduce appropriately substantiated arguments that the conduct generates efficiencies. The consumer harm test has two strengths: it is consistent with the objective of competition law to maximize social welfare in the long term and it allows for a wider consideration of the negative and positive effects of the conduct in a principled way, namely by focusing exclusively on their impact on consumers. Nevertheless, because it is complex to apply, it is inferior to the naked exclusion test and the as efficient competitor test whenever these tests can be applied without significant shortcomings. Furthermore, while the consumer harm test has been criticized as being over-inclusive and over-deterrent, in reality proof of consumer harm is exacting.

Requiring proof of consumer harm thus biases the test towards false acquittals and under-deterrence. Therefore, the consumer harm test should apply when the risk of false convictions and over-deterrence is high.[177]

Exploitative abuses are clearly assessed under the consumer harm test. The controversy relates to whether intervention is warranted at all. This chapter concludes that there is no theoretical reason to exclude the application of competition law to such abuses. It is important, however, that, in addition to proof of prices or trading terms significantly and persistently above those that would have prevailed under conditions of effective competition, two further requirements should be fulfilled to guard against the risk of false convictions and over-deterrence. First, an enhanced dominance threshold should be required so that exploitative abuses may only be committed by a monopolist or quasi-monopolist protected by such barriers to entry that entry is impossible or unlikely in the long term. Secondly, the test for exploitative abuses should require proof of consumer harm different from, and additional to, the mere charging of an excessive price or the mere imposition of an excessively onerous trading condition.

Beyond exclusionary and exploitative conduct, there may be a case for prohibiting discrimination on intermediate markets that distorts the competitive relationship between downstream buyers of the dominant firm. However, there is absolutely no case for banning price discrimination per se. A price discrimination test would have to balance three factors: (a) the effect of price discrimination on the productive and dynamic efficiency of the intermediate firms; (b) whether, in the absence of price discrimination, output is higher or lower; and (c) the impact of a ban of price discrimination on the dynamic efficiency of the dominant firm both *ex ante*, because the ability to price discriminate may be an important factor in the decision to invest, and *ex post*, because the increased profits resulting from price discrimination are a reward for past investment. Because the second and third factors are relevant to all types of abuse, the hallmark of abusive discrimination is the impairment of the ability to compete of firms that, in the absence of the discrimination, would be as efficient as their competitors and are thus denied equal competitive opportunities by the behaviour of the dominant undertaking.

All abuse tests discussed in this chapter describe the elements that a competition authority or claimant must prove in order to establish a prima facie case of abuse. As is clear from the discussion of each test, it is always possible that conduct that fails the test is in fact not harmful or that it may even be beneficial to long-term social welfare because it produces efficiencies or has certain other cognizable benefits. From a normative point of view, all that it is possible to say with any certainty is that such a defence must be available and that, in theory, efficiencies

---

[177] This is the approach adopted by the EU courts to refusal to supply by a vertically integrated dominant undertaking: see Cases C-241/91 P and 242/91 P *Magill*, para 54; Case T-504/93 *Tiercé Ladbroke SA v Commission* [1997] ECR II-923, para 131; C-418/01 *IMS*, para 37; Case T-201/04 *Microsoft I*, paras 643–647.

or other cognizable benefits would have to be assessed as to their nature, magnitude, and likelihood and compared with the competitive harm resulting from the conduct under review. The precise scope of the objective justification defence and the details of the assessment of the proportionality of the benefits of the conduct compared to the competitive harm it causes are quintessentially legal questions. They will be discussed in Chapter 3 in the context of the analysis of the abuse tests under EU law.

PART II
LEGAL FOUNDATIONS

4

The Objective of Article 102

A. Introduction

The normative analysis carried out in the previous chapters provides the theoretical framework within which Article 102 can be interpreted, but does not shed any light on the objective of Article 102 itself. The objective of Article 102 is not determined by the theory of competition law deemed preferable or soundest from time to time. The question is not a matter of economics or political economy, it is a legal question. Economics, political economy, and historical developments are the context in which the hermeneutics of Article 102 takes place. They are factors that may contribute to the clarification of the legal meaning of the provision but they are incapable, in themselves, of providing a definitive answer to the problem of its objective.

As a preliminary point of method, it is important to distinguish objectives, rules, and tests. The objective is the ultimate goal pursued by competition law; its raison d'être. In this context, only immediate objectives are relevant, namely those objectives which, in law, play a role in the interpretation of the rules. Side effects of competition, beneficial from a social or political point of view but irrelevant in a teleological interpretation of the EU competition rules, are not objectives for the purposes of this study. Rules are the prohibitions, prescriptions, and authorizations to be found in the texts of the Treaties and secondary EU legislation, such as the EU Merger Regulations[1] or Commission block exemption Regulations.[2]

---

[1] Council Regulation (EEC) 4064/89 of 21 December 1989 on the control of concentrations between undertakings [1990] OJ L257/13 ('1989 Merger Regulation') and Council Regulation (EC) 139/2004 of 20 January 2004 on the control of concentrations between undertakings [2004] OJ L24/1 ('2004 Merger Regulation').

[2] eg Council Regulation (EEC) 19/65 of 2 March 1965 on the application of Article 81(3) of the Treaty to certain categories of agreements and concerted practices [1965] OJ L36/533; Council Regulation (EEC) 2821/71 of 20 December 1971 on application of Article 85(3) of the Treaty to categories of agreements, decisions and concerted practices [1971] OJ L285/46; Council Regulation (EC) 1215/1999 of 10 June 1999 amending Regulation (EEC) 19/65 on the application of Article 81(3) of the Treaty to certain categories of agreements and concerted practices [1999] OJ L148/1; Commission Regulation (EC) 772/2004 of 27 April 2004 on the application of Article 81(3) of the Treaty to categories of technology transfer agreements [2004] OJ L123/11; Commission Regulation (EU) 267/2010 of 24 March 2010 on the application of Article 103(3) of the Treaty on the Functioning of the European Union to certain categories of agreements, decisions and concerted practices in the insurance sector [2010] OJ L83/1; Commission Regulation (EU) 330/2010 of 20

Tests are further specifications or articulations of the rules that courts and competition authorities,[3] and particularly the Union courts, have developed and continue to develop to spell out in greater detail the circumstances in which the EU competition rules apply. A simple example illustrates this tripartite distinction. Social welfare is a potential objective of competition law. The prohibition of concerted practices having as their object the prevention, restriction, or distortion of competition within the internal market is a rule set out in Article 101 TFEU. The application of such a prohibition to the exchange of confidential information that appreciably reduces the market independence of the participant undertakings by substituting practical cooperation for the normal risks of competition[4] is a further specification or articulation of the rule that spells out the circumstances in which a certain arrangement must be characterized as a concerted practice, having as its object the prevention, restriction, or distortion of competition. It is, therefore, a test.[5]

This chapter indentifies the objective of Article 102 through a process of literal and teleological interpretation. The conclusions reached through this hermeneutical process are tested by looking at the *travaux préparatoires* of the Treaty of Rome. Then, the case law on Articles 101 and 102 and the EU Merger regime are examined. Finally, conclusions are drawn.

B. Interpretation of Article 102

(1) The general prohibition of an abuse of a dominant position

The text of Article 102 has remained unchanged since the signing of the Treaty of Rome establishing the European Economic Community,[6] save for the substitution of the words 'internal market' for 'common market' by the Lisbon Treaty.[7]

April 2010 on the application of Article 101(3) of the Treaty on the Functioning of the European Union to categories of vertical agreements and concerted practices [2010] OJ L102/1; Commission Regulation (EU) 461/2010 of 27 May 2010 on the application of Article 101(3) of the Treaty on the Functioning of the European Union to categories of agreements and concerted practices in the motor vehicle sector [2010] OJ L129/52.

[3] For a similar understanding and use of the word 'test', see A-L Sibony, *Le Juge et le raisonnement économique en droit de la concurrence* (Paris, LGDJ 2008) 462–469.

[4] Case 48/69 *Imperial Chemical Industries Ltd v Commission* [1972] ECR 619, para 64; Joined Cases 40/73 to 48/73, 50/73, 54/73 to 56/73, 111/73, 113/73, and 114/73 *Coöperatieve Vereniging 'Suiker Unie' UA v Commission* [1975] ECR 1663 (*Suiker Unie*), paras 173–174; Case T-7/89 *SA Hercules Chemicals NV v Commission* [1991] ECR II-1711, paras 259–260, upheld in Case C-51/92 P *SA Hercules Chemicals NV v Commission* [1999] ECR I-4235.

[5] This terminology is adopted for the sake of clarity and is purely descriptive. Its value lies in setting out a coherent taxonomy and achieving linguistic precision.

[6] Treaty establishing the European Economic Community 25 March 1957 ('Treaty of Rome') 25 March 1957, 298 UNTS 11 1973 Gr Brit TS No I (Cmd 5179-II).

[7] Treaty of Lisbon [2007] OJ C306/1.

The current text of Article 102 reads as follows:

Any abuse by one or more undertakings of a dominant position within the internal market or in a substantial part of it shall be prohibited as incompatible with the internal market in so far as it may affect trade between Member States.

Such abuse may, in particular, consist in:

(a) directly or indirectly imposing unfair purchase or selling prices or other unfair trading conditions;

(b) limiting production, markets or technical development to the prejudice of consumers;

(c) applying dissimilar conditions to equivalent transactions with other trading parties, thereby placing them at a competitive disadvantage;

(d) making the conclusion of contracts subject to acceptance by the other parties of supplementary obligations which, by their nature or according to commercial usage, have no connection with the subject of such contracts.

The first sentence of Article 102 appears to give little guidance on the objectives of the prohibition. The two requirements that, first, the dominant position must be held within the internal market, or in a substantial part of it,[8] and that, secondly, the abuse is prohibited only insofar as it may affect trade between Member States,[9] are purely jurisdictional thresholds. They do not define the elements of a dominant position or an abuse. Rather, they establish the circumstances in which an abuse of a dominant position becomes relevant under EU law and, therefore, capable of being assessed under Article 102. The concept of the internal market is, in this context, geographical, indicating the location of the abuse.

The two substantive requirements in the first sentence of Article 102, namely abuse and dominant position, are not defined. The only element that provides an indication as to why an abuse of a dominant position is prohibited is the provision that such conduct is 'incompatible with the internal market'. This phrase refers to the principle that the rules on competition are an integral part of the legal regime of the internal market. But it also indicates that the functioning of the internal market requires that an abuse of a dominant position be prohibited. The crucial question then becomes why an abuse of a dominant position is incompatible with the internal market. Plainly, Article 102 does not apply only to conduct that has a market-partitioning effect in the sense that it re-erects the barriers to free trade that the Treaties abolish. None of the four examples of abuse in Article 102 is necessarily market-partitioning, although all of them may, in certain circumstances, result in the compartmentalization of national markets. A clear parallel can be drawn

---

[8] Joined Cases 40/73 to 48/73, 50/73, 54/73 to 56/73, 111/73, 113/73, and 114/73 *Suiker Unie*; Case 26/75 *General Motors Continental NV v Commission* [1975] ECR 1367; Case 7/82 *Gesellschaft zur Verwertung von Leistungsschutzrechten mbH (GVL) v Commission* [1983] ECR 483; Case C-247/86 *Société alsacienne et lorraine de télécommunications et d'électronique (Alsatel) v SA Novasam* [1988] ECR 5987; Case C-393/92 *Municipality of Almelo v NV Energiebedrijf Ijsselmij* [1994] ECR I-1477; Case T-229/94 *Deutsche Bahn AG v Commission* [1997] ECR II-1689.

[9] Commission Notice—Guidelines on the effect on trade concept contained in Articles 81 and 82 of the Treaty [2004] OJ C101/07 ('Guidelines on the effect on trade concept'); Joined Cases 6/73 and 7/73 *Istituto Chemioterapico Italiano SpA and Commercial Solvents Corp v Commission* [1974] ECR 223 (*Commercial Solvents*); Case 27/76 *United Brands Co v Commission* [1978] ECR 207.

with Article 101. Article 101(1) prohibits 'as incompatible with the internal market' all agreements between undertakings, decisions by associations of undertakings, and concerted practices which may affect trade between Member States and have as their object or effect the prevention, restriction, or distortion of competition within the internal market. However, Article 101(1) does not prohibit only market-partitioning agreements. Article 101(1)(a), for example, prohibits agreements that directly or indirectly fix the purchase or selling prices or any other trading conditions. Such agreements may not have any market-partitioning object or effect. This would be the case for a cartel covering the whole territory of the European Union and open to be joined by new undertakings wishing to enter the EU market. Such an agreement would not have any market-partitioning effect but is, nonetheless, prohibited. Nor does the incompatibility with the internal market derive from the fact that the abuse may affect trade between Member States. The effect on trade between Member States is a separate requirement from the incompatibility with the internal market.[10] An abuse is prohibited as incompatible with the internal market even if it increases trade.[11]

Since the first sentence of Article 102 does not textually define the meaning of abuse of a dominant position, it is necessary to verify whether any indications can be found in the illustrative list of abuses in Article 102(a) to (d).

(2) The illustrative list

The list of abuses set out in Article 102(a) to (d) does not provide an exhaustive definition of conduct that may be an abuse.[12] This is clear from the text of the provision, which reads: 'Such abuse may, in particular, consist in . . .'. As a consequence of this, the Court of Justice has consistently held that the practices listed in Article 102(a) to (d) must be assessed in the context of Article 102 as a whole.[13] Thus, the objective of Article 102 may be derived from the description of the individual practices, from Article 102 as a whole, and from Article 102 construed in the context of the Treaties.

Article 102(a) provides that an abuse of a dominant position may consist in directly or indirectly imposing unfair purchase or selling prices or other unfair trading conditions. This provision is generally interpreted as prohibiting exploitative abuses, such as charging excessively high prices,[14] or imposing unfair contractual

---

[10] And it is not a substantive element of the abuse but a jurisdictional threshold: Guidelines on the effect on trade concept, para 12.

[11] ibid para 34.

[12] Case 6/72 *Europemballage Corp and Continental Can Co Inc v Commission* [1973] ECR 215 (*Continental Can*); Case C-333/94 P *Tetra Pak International SA v Commission* [1996] ECJ I-5951 (*Tetra Pak II*); Case C-95/04 P *British Airways plc v Commission* [2007] ECR I-2331.

[13] Case C-333/94 P *Tetra Pak II*; Case C-95/04 P *British Airways*.

[14] Case 78/70 *Deutsche Grammophon Gesellschaft mbH v Metro-SB-Großmärkte GmbH & Co KG* [1971] ECR 487; Case 27/76 *United Brands*; Case 26/75 *General Motors Continental*; Case 226/84 *British Leyland v Commission* [1986] ECR 3263; Joined Cases C-147/97 P and C-148/97 P *Deutsche Post AG v Gesellschaft für Zahlungssysteme mbH (GZS) and Citicorp Kartenservice GmbH* [2000] ECR I-825.

terms on customers.[15] However, Article 102(a) is equally capable of being applied to exclusionary abuses. Without doing any violence to the ordinary meaning of the language, a price against which an equally efficient competitor is unable to compete may be described as unfair. Article 102, however, does not define what 'unfair' means. Logically, therefore, unfair must be defined in the light of the objective of Article 102.

Article 102(b) provides that an abuse of a dominant position may consist in limiting production, markets, or technical development to the prejudice of consumers. The term 'production' denotes the amount of output. Limiting production involves reducing market output. The term 'market' means an arrangement in which buyers and sellers transact with one another. Therefore limiting a market involves limiting the possibilities for sellers and buyers to transact with one another. The French text uses 'débouchés', which may be translated as 'outlets'. This concept of limitation of markets, therefore, denotes limitations of output by denying customers access to certain products. 'Technical development' means dynamic efficiency, or, in other words, innovation in production technologies or product development. Limitation of technical development, therefore, is the same as a negative effect on dynamic efficiency. This may consist in a reduction of the rivals' incentives or ability to innovate. It may also consist in the dominant undertaking's own lack of innovation incentives.[16] Furthermore, the limitation of production, markets, or technical development must be 'to the detriment of the consumers'. However, consumer detriment would appear to be already captured by the test of limitation of production, markets, or technical development. Output restrictions (limitation of production or markets) and lower levels of innovation (limitation of technical development) harm consumers. It is necessary, therefore, to search for a meaning of the consumer harm test in relation to practices that already, in themselves, would appear to harm consumers. The answer is that the consumer harm required under Article 102(b) is an enhanced form of consumer detriment over and above a

---

[15] Case 27/76 *United Brands*; Case C-333/94 P *Tetra Pak II*; *Der Grüne Punkt—Duales System Deutschland* [2001] OJ L166/1, upheld in Case T-151/01 *Der Grüne Punkt—Duales System Deutschland GmbH v Commission* [2007] ECR II-1607, appeal dismissed in Case C-385/07 P *Der Grüne Punkt—Duales System Deutschland GmbH v Commission* [2009] 5 CMLR 19.

[16] R O'Donoghue and AJ Padilla, *The Law and Economics of Article 82 EC* (Oxford, Hart Publishing 2006) 199–200, construe Art 102(b) as setting out the general test of foreclosure. It is difficult to say whether Art 102(b) refers to foreclosure. On the one hand, it can be argued that, if it had done, it would have explicitly said so. On the other hand, limitation of markets may well be construed as denying customers access to the dominant undertaking's competitors. As argued in the text, Art 102(b) probably refers to certain types of foreclosure that are prohibited under an enhanced consumer harm test. It would appear that O'Donoghue and Padilla take the view that it would be desirable if all exclusionary conduct could be assessed under Art 102(b). The authors are guided in their analysis by their belief that consumer welfare should be both the objective of Art 102 and the test for abuse. The case law has assessed exclusionary conduct both under Art 102(a) (eg Case T-271/03 *Deutsche Telekom AG v Commission* [2008] ECR II-477, para 167, upheld in Case C-280/08 P *Deutsche Telekom AG v Commission* [2010] OJ C346/4) and 102 (b) (eg Joined Cases C-241/91 P and C-242/91 P *Radio Telefís Eireann (RTE) and Independent Television Publications Ltd (ITP) v Commission* [1995] ECR I-743 (*Magill*), para 54) and, in any event, makes it absolutely clear that there is a general concept of abuse derived from the interpretation of Art 102 as a whole: Case C-333/94 P *Tetra Pak II*, para 37.

mere restriction of output, markets, or innovation. Thus, the consumer harm test under Article 102(b) may consist in a specific form thereof, such as the prevention of the emergence of a new or differentiated product.[17]

It goes without saying that no argument can be based on Article 102(b) to say that consumer welfare is the objective of Article 102. It is significant that consumer harm is only relevant under one of the four abuses in the illustrative list. If consumer harm had been the test under Article 102, the first sentence of the provision would have prohibited 'any abuse of a dominant position to the detriment of consumers'. This is, plainly, not the case.

Article 102(c) provides that an abuse of a dominant position may consist in applying dissimilar conditions to equivalent transactions with other trading partners, thereby placing them at a competitive disadvantage. This provision is generally understood as prohibiting anti-competitive discrimination and, in particular, price discrimination.[18] It requires that some form of discrimination be established between two or more customers or suppliers of the dominant undertaking. Furthermore, the discriminatory conditions must place a trading partner of the dominant undertaking at a 'competitive disadvantage'. This phrase is not defined but, on a literal interpretation, it would appear to require that the discriminated firm's ability to compete must be materially diminished vis-à-vis its competitors. This form of anti-competitive discrimination enshrines the principle of equality of opportunities. The importance of this principle cannot be underestimated. It is significant that Article 102(c) sets out this principle as an example of abuse. It means that non-discrimination and equality of opportunities may be free-standing constitutive elements of the abuse whether or not the conduct is also limiting output, markets, or technical development to the detriment of consumers under Article 102(b) or consists in unfair prices or other trading conditions under Article 102(a). However, the principle of non-discrimination and equality of opportunities obviously requires further refinement. It cannot be the case that, if the dominant undertaking grants a customer a discount, the same discount must be granted to all other customers. The key lies in the concept of 'competitive disadvantage', which, not being defined in the text of Article 102, must be construed in accordance with the objective of that Article.

Article 102(d) provides that an abuse of a dominant position may consist in making the conclusion of contracts subject to acceptance by the other parties of supplementary obligations that, by their nature or according to commercial usage, have no connection with the subject of such contracts. This provision is probably

---

[17] The issue arises in particular in refusal to supply cases: see Joined Cases C-241/91 P and C-242/91 P *Magill*; Case C-7/97 *Oscar Bronner GmbH & Co KG v Mediaprint Zeitungs- und Zeitschriftenverlag GmbH & Co KG* [1998] ECR I-7791; Case C-418/01 *IMS Health GmbH & Co OHG v NDC Health GmbH & Co KG* 5039 [2004] ECR I-5039; Case T-201/04 *Microsoft Corp v Commission* [2007] ECR II-3601 (Microsoft I).

[18] Case T-203/01 *Manufacture française des pneumatiques Michelin v Commisson* [2003] ECR II-4071 (*Michelin II*); Case C-95/04 P *British Airways*; Case C-333/94 P *Tetra Pak II*; Case C-310/93 *BPB Industries plc and British Gypsum Ltd v Commission* [1995] ECR I-865 (*British Gypsum*); *Deutsche Post AG—Interception of cross-border mail* [2001] OJ L331/40.

the narrowest in Article 102. It is also different from the other practices listed in Article 102 because it does not contain any clear indication of the constitutive elements of the abuse beyond the mere description of a commercial practice. In particular, the fact that the tying practice is in accordance with commercial usage in the industry does not mean that the dominant undertaking's conduct is not an abuse.[19] As a result, very little can be derived from Article 102(d) which can provide meaningful guidance on the definition of abuse.

(3) The internal market

(a) The link between the competition rules and the internal market

In the light of the few clues which are to be found in the text of Article 102 itself, the key element which appears capable of casting light on the objective of the prohibition is the definition of the abuse as 'incompatible with the internal market'. Whether or not the position was unclear before the Lisbon Treaty, there is now no doubt that the EU competition rules have the objective of ensuring the correct functioning of the internal market.[20]

This results, in the first place, from a literal interpretation of the EU competition rules. An abuse of a dominant position under Article 102, or an agreement between undertakings under Article 101, is prohibited 'as incompatible with the internal market'. This wording has been in place since the Treaty of Rome of 1957, apart from the change from 'common market' to 'internal market'.

The interpretation of the EU competition rules in the overall framework of the Treaties confirms this conclusion. Article 3 TFEU provides that the Union shall have exclusive competence on the 'establishing of the competition rules necessary for the functioning of the internal market'. The European Union, therefore, has no competence to regulate competition as such, whatever its beneficial objectives are believed to be, but only to regulate competition to the extent that is necessary for the functioning of the internal market. Article 3 TEU does not include competition as one of the objectives of the Union, but does include among them the establishment of the internal market.[21] This is technically not a change to the previous legal framework. Competition law was never an objective of the European Community[22] or the European Union.[23] However, it was at least arguable that a system ensuring that competition in the internal market, as an activity of the Community, was not distorted was an intermediate

---

[19] Case C-333/94 P *Tetra Pak II*, para 37.
[20] Case C-52/09 *Konkurrensverket v TeliaSonera Sverige AB* (17 February 2011) (*TeliaSonera*), paras 20–21.
[21] Art 3(3) TEU provides: 'The Union shall establish an internal market. It shall work for the sustainable development of Europe based on balanced economic growth and price stability, a highly competitive social market economy, aiming at full employment and social progress, and a high level of protection and improvement of the quality of the environment. It shall promote scientific and technological advance.'
[22] See Art 3 EC, which listed competition as an activity of the European Community and not as an objective.
[23] Art 2 TEU.

goal directly relevant to the general objectives of the Community as set out in Article 2 EC.[24] Currently, competition law has the immediate objective of ensuring the functioning of the internal market. Its ultimate objective, which is to achieve the ultimate goals of the Union as set out in Articles 2 and 3(1) TEU,[25] is not its direct aim but is attained insofar as the competition rules contribute to the proper functioning of the internal market. Protocol (27) on the Internal Market and Competition makes it clear that 'the internal market as set out in Article 3 of the Treaty on European Union includes a system ensuring that competition is not distorted'. The immediate, practical significance of this Protocol is to clarify that Article 352 TFEU can be used as a legal basis on which to implement measures in the field of competition. Its more general effect is, however, to restate that competition is part of the objectives of the Union only insofar as it falls within the broader internal market objective. The text of the Treaty establishing a Constitution for Europe did provide that free and undistorted competition was an objective of the Union,[26] but the constitutional Treaty never came into force and that provision was deliberately not reproduced in the Treaty of Lisbon. The contingent reasons why this happened may be historically and politically interesting,[27] but cannot change the legal effect of the choice of the Member States and the clear meaning of the current texts of the Treaties. There is no doubt, therefore, that the immediate objective of the EU competition rules is the proper functioning of the internal market. The problem of identifying the purpose of the EU competition rules becomes, therefore, the problem of identifying the objective of the internal market, and the role of competition in achieving that objective.

---

[24] Art 2 EC read as follows: 'The Community shall have as its task, by establishing a common market and an economic and monetary union and by implementing common policies or activities referred to in Articles 3 and 4, to promote throughout the Community a harmonious, balanced and sustainable development of economic activities, a high level of employment and of social protection, equality between men and women, sustainable and non-inflationary growth, a high degree of competitiveness and convergence of economic performance, a high level of protection and improvement of the quality of the environment, the raising of the standard of living and quality of life, and economic and social cohesion and solidarity among Member States.'

[25] On these objectives, see 116–121 below.

[26] Treaty establishing a Constitution for Europe [2004] OJ C303/1 ('European Constitution'), Art I-3: 'The Union shall offer its citizens an area of freedom, security and justice without internal frontiers, and an internal market where competition is free and undistorted.' It is worth noting that the link between the internal market and competition was still present but had a different significance. Competition was not necessary for the functioning of the internal market but the internal market was a space in which competition was to be free and undistorted. Art I-3 of the constitutional Treaty not only made competition a free-standing objective alongside the internal market but, arguably, defined the internal market as being characterized by free and undistorted competition.

[27] It is well known that France, probably for reasons of domestic politics, asked and obtained an amendment to the text of the Treaty of Lisbon, which reproduced Art I-3 of the constitutional Treaty, excising any reference to competition in what is now Art 3 TEU. Other Member States obtained, in return, the concession that a protocol be signed making it clear that the internal market included competition as a necessary element and that the residual legal basis for harmonization measures, which is now Art 352 TFEU, could be used to implement measures in the field of competition.

(b) *The internal market and economic freedom*

Article 26 TFEU provides that 'the internal market shall comprise an area without internal frontiers in which the free movement of goods, persons, services and capital is ensured in accordance with the provisions of the Treaties'.

The structure of the internal market rests on four pillars: free movement of goods,[28] persons,[29] services,[30] and capital.[31] The free movement of goods and services provisions are more directly related to the EU competition rules, which apply to undertakings engaged in the supply of goods or services, although clearly the competitive structure of national industries affects, and is affected by, the free movement of labour and capital.

Even by focusing only on the free movement of goods and services provision, it is still not possible to clarify whether the law of the internal market is based on an economic freedom or on an anti-protectionist rationale.[32] The very fact that the competition rules are a building block of the internal market makes it difficult to argue that the latter are only concerned with the removal of protectionist measures. If only protectionist measures were banned it would be difficult to understand why anti-competitive practices that are not straightforwardly market-partitioning are prohibited. Under an economic freedom rationale the competition rules protect the right of firms to trade within the internal market without unjustified impediments. The free movement rules guard against impediments put in place by the State. But impediments to economic freedom may also be put in place by some undertakings against other undertakings. These non-State impediments must be prohibited because they offend against the same fundamental economic freedom.

The prohibition of exploitative abuses and cartels can also be explained under an economic freedom rationale. The internal market guarantees undertakings the freedom to trade within the European Union. This freedom gives them access to all national markets and allows them to reap the benefits of increased volumes of trade, economies of scale, and wider access to sources of supply. This freedom, however, can be abused not only by excluding other undertakings from the benefits of the internal market but also by exploiting market power to the detriment of society. It would be illogical to allow undertakings to expand and grow only to allow them to reap private benefits to the detriment of the economy as a whole.

It appears, therefore, that the competition rules are consistent with the concept of the internal market as safeguarding the economic freedom of economic agents to conduct economic activity within the European Union. However, the concept of freedom is not self-sufficient because the content of the freedom must be determined by a further objective.[33] In order to define the economic freedom that the internal market and, as a result, the competition rules protect, it is therefore necessary to define the objectives of the internal market.

---

[28] Art 34 TFEU.   [29] Art 45 TFEU.   [30] Art 56 TFEU.   [31] Art 63 TFEU.

[32] See J Snell, 'The Notion of Market Access: A Notion or a Slogan?' (2010) 47 CML Rev 437, 470–472.

[33] For the proof of this proposition, see 18–21 above.

(c) *The social welfare objective of the internal market*

In the search for the objectives of the internal market, the focus is on those objectives that can be translated into legal concepts and rules, which may be defined as immediate objectives. For the purpose of the present inquiry, objectives that are of a purely political nature or are the intended consequence of market integration, but do not relate to the legal framework of the internal market, are disregarded unless they are relevant to the immediate objectives.

Unfortunately, the Treaties do not provide a specific statement of the objectives of the internal market. Article 3(3) TEU, after providing that 'the Union shall establish an internal market', adds that the Union:

…shall work for the sustainable development of Europe based on balanced economic growth and price stability, a highly competitive social market economy, aiming at full employment and social progress, and a high level of protection and improvement of the quality of the environment. It shall promote scientific and technological advance.

It is unclear whether this statement is a clarification of the aims of the internal market or whether it sets out further objectives of the Union. In all likelihood, Article 3(3) clarifies what the goals of the internal market are, while setting out some further objectives. If this is correct, then this provision would support the idea that the objective of the internal market is the economic welfare of the peoples of Europe. Because the purpose of this inquiry is to identify the objective of the internal market as the objective of the EU competition rules, the relevant factors to be taken into account are those of an economic nature. From this perspective, it is clear that the objective of the internal market is not the maximization of short-term social or consumer welfare but economic growth, competitiveness, and scientific and technological advance. Economic growth, in particular, relates to the growth of the value of production of society.[34] Article 3(3) explains further that what the Union aims for is a 'highly competitive social market economy'. Because the immediate focus of the analysis is on economic factors, the key words appear to be 'competitive' and 'market'. A competitive economy is an economy where the largest and highest quality output is produced at the lowest possible cost. A competitive economy is, therefore, an economy where productivity is high.[35] The particular emphasis placed on scientific and technological advance, which relates to dynamic efficiency, illustrates this point. A highly productive economy is characterized by high quality products, which command high prices on the market, and efficient production processes, which lower the cost of production and increase output. 'Market' relates to an environment where goods and services are freely exchanged between suppliers

---

[34] Under Art 3(3), economic growth must have certain features in that it must not be inflationary and must be balanced across the various sectors of the economy. These features relate to monetary and industrial policy and not, or at least not directly, to the competitive structure of the industry within the internal market.

[35] ME Porter, *The Competitive Advantage of Nations* (New York, The Free Press 1990) 6.

and consumers. The market is the virtual place where competition occurs and is functioning effectively where the largest and highest quality output is produced at the lowest possible cost. The concept of market economy is consistent with the concepts of economic growth and competitiveness.

The focus of all these elements, or their common denominator, is productivity. The concept of productivity can be adopted as the synthesis of economic growth, competitiveness, market economy, and scientific and technological advance. These elements are also the key determinants of the economic welfare of the society. Productivity grows when the value of production grows and the cost of production relative to the value of production diminishes. A higher value of production at lower costs maximizes social welfare. As regards the timeframe of the objective, Article 3(3) sets out the principle of the sustainable development of Europe, which means that productivity and social welfare must grow over the long term. Therefore, Article 3(3) indicates that the objective of the internal market is to promote long-term social welfare in the European Union.

This interpretation of Article 3(3) focuses on the economic objective of the internal market because it is its economic objective that determines the content and function of the competition rules as a key element of economic policy. However, this interpretation is consistent with the non-economic goals of the internal market and, in particular, with the economy's 'social' attribute in Article 3(3). 'Social' market economy means that the free market principle finds its limit in the principles of solidarity and respect for human dignity and human rights, and that long-term productivity growth must go hand in hand with the aim of achieving full employment and social cohesion.[36] This social dimension of the market economy is compatible with the promotion of long-term productivity growth. Economic growth is compatible with full employment, while increased productivity of labour results in higher salaries. A society where more skilled and highly paid jobs are created fares better in terms of social cohesion than an economy where economic growth is based on unskilled, low paid labour. But even an internal market that fosters long-term productivity growth may not produce, automatically, equal opportunities to participate in the society's wealth or a socially just allocation of resources. Policies other than free trade and competition should then intervene. It would be wrong to distort the objectives of the competition rules in order to achieve pure social justice objectives. This would be the case if a consumer welfare objective were to be assigned to EU competition law on the assumption that to do so would achieve a more socially just distribution of resources. Redistribution in a social market economy is not necessarily redistribution from producers to consumers. It could be redistribution from one market to another or from one region to

---

[36] For more on social market economy, see P Koslowski, *The Social Market Economy: Theory and Ethics of the Economic Order* (Berlin, Springer 1998); N Barry, 'The Social Market Economy' (1993) 10 Social Philosophy and Policy 1; W Möschel, 'Competition as a Basic Element of the Social Market Economy' (2001) 2 EBOR 713; W Möschel, 'Competition Policy From An Ordo Point of View' in A Peacock and H Willgerodt (eds), *German Neo-Liberals and The Social Market Economy* (London, MacMillan 1989) 142.

another. There is no indication in the Treaties that a feature of the social market economy is a redistribution of wealth from producers to consumers.[37]

The interpretation of the economic objective of the internal market as the maximization of long-term productivity and social welfare is also consistent with the protection of the environment, which represents a guiding principle in sustainable economic growth under Article 3(3) TEU. Economic growth must be oriented towards production processes and products that are the most efficient in terms of their impact on the environment and contribute to its improvement. A society is prepared to place a higher value on these processes and products and this is reflected in higher prices and, therefore, in a higher value of production. Scientific and technical development must also contribute to the preservation and improvement of the environment. A social market economy aims to achieve this environmental objective through a free market which includes undistorted competition.[38] High productivity also allows industry to improve standards required by social objectives, such as the protection of health and safety and the improvement of the quality of the environment.[39]

The objective of the internal market to promote long-term social welfare though productivity growth can be translated into a workable objective of the competition rules. Moreover, a long-term social welfare objective is, from a theoretical and normative point of view, the appropriate objective of competition law.[40] The focus on long-term productivity is, however, important because it emphasizes that this should be achieved not only through an alignment of prices with marginal costs but through maximizing productive and dynamic efficiency. The Court of Justice in *TeliaSonera* endorsed a long-term social welfare objective of the TFEU competition rules while at the same time emphasizing the link between the competition rules and the internal market. The Court affirmed the link between Article 3(3) TEU and Article 3(1)(b) TFEU and stated the objective of the TFEU competition rules as 'the well-being of the European Union', which the Court said included the welfare of producers, consumers, and the public interest.[41] The reference to the 'public interest' must be understood in the context of the framework of the Treaties and not in relation to unspecified public policies that should be pursued

---

[37] Any redistributive objective would in any event be extraneous to competition policy: see 41–43 above.

[38] Direct conflicts between the environmental objective and the maximization of long-term social welfare and productivity cannot be ruled out. On the conflicts between competition law and non-competition objectives, see G Monti, 'Article 81 EC and Public Policy' [2002] CML Rev 1057; C Townley, *Article 81 EC and Public Policy* (Oxford, Hart Publishing 2009); A Komninos, 'Resolution of Conflicts in the Integrated Article 81 EC' in C-D Ehlermann and I Atanasiu (eds), *European Competition Law Annual 2004: The Relationship between Competition Law and (Liberal) Professions* (Oxford, Hart Publishing 2006) 451. This book does not deal with the general topic of the conflict between competition law and other policy objectives. However, it addresses the issue of how other policy objectives are taken into account in the test for abuse: see 317–321 below.

[39] Porter, *The Competitive Advantage of Nations*, 6.　　　　[40] See Ch 2 above.

[41] Case C-52/09 *TeliaSonera*, paras 20–22. The social welfare objective of the competition rules had already been affirmed by the Court of Justice on several occasions under the previous Treaties: see Case C-94/00 *Roquette Frères SA v Directeur général de la concurrence, de la consommation et de la répression des fraudes* [2002] ECR I-9011, para 42 and Joined Cases 46/87 and 227/88 *Hoechst AG v Commission* [1989] ECR 2859, para 25.

by the competition rules. The 'public interest' in question is, therefore, the economic objective of the internal market under Article 3(3), which is the long-term social welfare of the European Union, comprising the values and preferences of the model of society envisaged in the Treaties over and above a merely monetary measure of surplus.

(d) The competition rules and the objectives of the Union

The long-term social welfare objective of the TFEU competition rules affirmed in *TeliaSonera* can be further elucidated by examining the objective of the competition rules in the light of the objectives of the Union as set out in Articles 2 and 3 TEU. Technically, this interpretative process would have to take place in two stages. First, the objective of the internal market would have to be interpreted in the light of the objectives of the Union. Secondly, the objective of the competition rules would have to be interpreted in the light of the objective of the internal market. However, as a matter of logic, the transitive property means that it is possible to discuss directly the objective of the competition rules in the light of the objectives of the Union.

The Union's aim is 'to promote peace, its values and the well-being of its peoples'.[42] The Union's values are the 'respect for human dignity, freedom, democracy, equality, the rule of law and respect for human rights, including the rights of persons belonging to minorities. These values are common to the Member States in a society in which pluralism, non-discrimination, tolerance, justice, solidarity and equality between women and men prevail.'[43] It is necessary to examine each of these aims and values and their relevance to the objective of the competition rules. Not all the objectives and values of the European Union may be achieved by each of the EU policies or activities at the same time. Peace, for instance, is one of the most important objectives of the Treaties and, historically, the main one. Economic integration results in interpenetration of markets, social cohesion, and cultural exchanges that establish peace on a long-lasting foundation. It is clear, though, that the aim of promoting peace cannot be translated into the legal purpose of the competition rules. The same can be said of democracy and tolerance. Other objectives are also clearly extraneous to competition policy such as respect for human dignity, democracy, respect for human rights and the rights of the minorities, solidarity, and equality between women and men. The competition rules must be applied in a way that respects these values, but these values are not in themselves the objective of the competition rules.[44] Justice evokes a substantive rather than

---

[42] Art 3(1) TEU.   [43] Art 2 TEU.

[44] A different view was put forward by the first generation of ordoliberal thinkers who believed that a pluralistic market structure was necessary to preserve democracy and that market power could be dangerously turned into political power: F Böhm, 'Demokratie und ökonomische Macht' in Institut für ausländisches und internationals Wirtschaftsrecht, *Kartelle und Monopole im modernen Recht: Band l* (Karlsruhe, CF Müller 1961) 120, stating very clearly that: 'Das Problem der ökonomischen Macht ist gleichbedeutend mit dem Problem der privaten Macht'; W Eucken, *Die Grundlagen der Nationalökonomie* (9th edn Berlin, Springer 1989) 169.

procedural concept.[45] This is particularly true in the context of Article 2 TFEU, where procedural fairness is described by equality (which includes formal equality), pluralism, and non-discrimination. Because competition law is concerned with the process of rivalry rather than directly with an outcome,[46] justice is not in itself capable of being an objective of competition law. While it is possible to describe as just the allocation of resources which results from a fair and free process such as undistorted competition, in this case the definition of justice presupposes the definition of a fair and free process and not vice versa.[47] Other objectives, such as the rule of law, relate to the process of applying the competition rules but have nothing to do with their substantive objective.

On the other hand, freedom, equality, pluralism, and non-discrimination are prima facie relevant to the competition discourse. Economic freedom, equality of opportunities, and non-discrimination are principles capable of being the normative foundations of the competition rules. None of these objectives, however, is specific enough to solve the problem of the definition of competition.[48] The well-being of the European peoples, on the other hand, is capable of being interpreted as the welfare of the society. In fact, this would appear to be the ordinary meaning of the words. In the light of a social welfare objective, the principles of freedom, equality, pluralism, and non-discrimination acquire a specific content within the competition law field. Freedom is the right to contribute to the long-term welfare of society through the exercise of an economic activity unhindered by the conduct of firms, which reduces long-term social welfare by restricting the process of market rivalry. From the consumer's point of view, freedom is the right to obtain goods and services on a market where firms compete effectively and are unhindered by the welfare-reducing conduct of their competitors. Non-discrimination, equality of opportunities, and pluralism describe an effective competitive process in which all firms and consumers have the opportunity to participate unhindered by restrictions of rivalry that harm social welfare. The principles of freedom, equality of opportunities, and non-discrimination are the expression of the social welfare objective. It is the social welfare objective that draws the line between the conflicting freedoms of different firms and consumers. And it is the social welfare objective that explains why certain inequalities are justified and others are not. Given the link between the competition rules, the internal market, and long-term social welfare, highlighted in the previous section, the objective of the competition rules is fully consistent with the objectives of the Union.

It could be argued that the well-being of the European peoples is also capable of being interpreted as a consumer welfare objective, perhaps on the basis that all persons are consumers while not all may be producers. This argument is, however, not tenable. The well-being of European peoples relates to the whole

[45] eg a substantive interpretation of social justice was put forward by J Rawls, *A Theory of Justice* (Rev edn Harvard, Harvard University Press 1999).

[46] See 22–23 above.

[47] R Nozick, *Anarchy, State, and Utopia* (New York, Basic Books 1974).

[48] As explained at 18–24 above.

of the society. There is no textual reference in Article 3 which would suggest that the Union's aim is not the welfare of the society as a whole but the welfare of consumers. The distributional objective inherent in the principle of solidarity is not capable of being pursued through competition policy and is better achieved by other means.[49] In any event, the objective of long-term social welfare is consistent with the long-term welfare of consumers. The protection of an effective competitive process, which results in lower costs, larger and higher quality output, and innovation, also delivers lower quality-adjusted prices to consumers. The rejection of a consumer welfare objective is simply a recognition that EU competition law is not concerned with lower short-term prices for consumers at the expense of productive and dynamic efficiency. Long-term productivity growth delivers higher producer and consumer welfare, higher salaries, higher returns on capital, and sustainable development. An exclusive focus on short-term consumer welfare would be contrary to the objectives of the Union. On the other hand, the competition rules protect consumers by ensuring effective competition and a well-functioning internal market characterized by sustainable economic growth, competitive industries, and technical progress.[50]

(4) Historical background and *travaux préparatoires*

(a) A methodological gloss

The interpretation of Article 102 in the framework of the Treaties leads to the conclusion that its objective is to maximize long-term social welfare. To corroborate this conclusion, this section examines the *travaux préparatoires* of the Treaty of Rome to understand whether the drafters of the Treaty had any specific concept of competition in mind. It is important to emphasize, however, that the weight of the *travaux préparatoires* as an aid to the interpretation of Article 102 is limited. The objective of Article 102 must be determined, first and foremost, based on its textual and teleological interpretation in the overall framework of the Treaties as currently in force. The very fact that the *travaux préparatoires* have been released only decades after the Treaty came into force demonstrates that they were not intended to be used in its interpretation. Nevertheless, given that more than fifty years after the drafting of Article 102 it is still not clear what the purpose of the provision is, a discussion of the *travaux préparatoires* may provide some corroboration in favour of one or another interpretation.

---

[49] For the proof of this proposition, see 41–43 above.

[50] Joined Cases C-468/06 P to C-478/06 P *Sot Lélos kai Sia EE v GlaxoSmithKline AEVE Farmakeftikon Proionton* [2008] ECR I-7139, para 68, where the Court said that 'in the light of the Treaty objectives to protect consumers by means of undistorted competition and the integration of national markets, the Community rules on competition are also incapable of being interpreted in such a way that, in order to defend its own commercial interests, the only choice left for a pharmaceuticals company in a dominant position is not to place its medicines on the market at all in a Member State where the prices of those products are set at a relatively low level'.

(b) *The Treaty establishing the European Coal and Steel Community*

The competition provisions of the Treaty of Rome have their closest precedent in Articles 65 and 66 of the Treaty establishing the European Coal and Steel Community (the 'ECSC Treaty'). These provisions, however, are different from the competition provisions of the Treaty of Rome in two ways. First, they were adopted in the context of the establishment of a common market in one specific sector which was considered to be of significant strategic importance.[51] Secondly, unlike the Treaty of Rome, the ECSC Treaty made provisions for the control of concentrations.[52] The structure of the industry and the risk of excessive consolidation were seen as major problems at the time, while the focus of the Treaty of Rome was initially on anti-competitive collusive and unilateral practices and not on concentrations. On the other hand, the general objectives of the ECSC Treaty bore a strong resemblance to the objectives of the Treaty of Rome.[53] The prohibition of cartels in the ECSC Treaty was linked to the objective of establishing a common market in coal and steel characterized by economic growth and high productivity. The Schuman declaration of 9 May 1950 made clear that the ECSC was intended to ensure market integration and the expansion of production 'in contrast to international cartels, which tend to impose restrictive practices on distribution and the exploitation of national markets'.[54] Consumer welfare is totally absent.

(c) *From the ECSC Treaty to the Spaak Report*

Following the signing of the ECSC Treaty, European integration experienced four difficult years, with the French proposal for a European Defence Community eventually being rejected by the French national assembly.[55] In 1955, the initiative was taken to convene an inter-governmental conference in Messina to discuss the further steps for European integration. The Benelux countries had issued a joint memorandum calling for further integration in the specific sectors of transport, energy, and the pacific use of atomic energy, but also more generally the establishment of a common market with no quantitative restrictions and customs duties.[56] The Messina conference embraced this programme, although the final resolution did not fully reflect the Benelux memorandum. In particular, the Resolution agreed the objective of the establishment of a common market and took the view that its implementation required the study of a number of questions, including 'l'élaboration de règles assurant le jeu de la concurrence au sein du marché commun

---

[51] This is clear from Art 3 ECSC, which set out the tasks of the Community including the achievement of a number of industrial policy objectives, such as stability of supply within the common market and the maintenance of conditions under which undertakings had the incentive to develop and improve their production potential avoiding the irresponsible depletion of resources.

[52] See Art 66 ECSC.   [53] Compare Art 2 ECSC and Art 2 of the Treaty of Rome.

[54] Declaration by Robert Schuman, French Foreign Minister, 9 May 1950 (the 'Schuman Declaration').

[55] J Pinder, *The Building of the European Union* (3rd edn Oxford, OUP 1998) 8–9.

[56] Négociations des traités instituant la CEE et la CEEA (1955–1957), CM3. Réunion des ministres des affaires étrangères, Messine, 01–03.06.1955, CM3/NEGO/006, Mémorandum des pays Benelux aux six pays de la CECA (18 mai 1955).

de manière à exclure notamment toute discrimination nationale'.[57] Competition was seen, from the very beginning, as being an indispensable element of the common market. However, there is little in the Resolution on the definition and the objectives of competition and, in any event, not too much should be read into a high-level political statement of this kind.[58] Nevertheless, three points are worth noting. First, economic integration was described as indispensable 'pour maintenir à l'Europe la place qu'elle occupe dans le monde, pour lui rendre son influence et son rayonnement, et pour augmenter d'une manière continue le niveau de vie de sa population'.[59] The only objective of an economic nature which would then be adopted in the final text of the Treaty of Rome was the well-being of the European peoples, which, as explained above, relates to long-term social welfare. Secondly, competition is described as the 'jeu de la concurrence', which denotes a dynamic process. Thirdly, there is an emphasis on 'national discrimination', an ambiguous phrase where the adjective may mean the adoption of practices which are discriminatory between two or among several states, or discrimination on the basis of nationality.[60]

The Resolution of the Messina conference established an inter-governmental committee under the presidency of the Belgian Minister of Foreign Affairs, Paul-Henri Spaak. The report of the Heads of Delegation to the Ministers of Foreign Affairs (the 'Spaak Report') constituted the basis for the subsequent negotiation of the Treaty of Rome by the inter-governmental conference for the common market and the Euratom.

The Spaak Report set out the purpose of the inclusion of competition law in the Treaty in a very general way. This should not come as a surprise, as the Report was a high-level political document. Nevertheless, the objective of the common market was described with sufficient clarity as the creation of an area of common economic policy 'constituant une puissante unité de production, et permettant une expansion continue, une stabilité accrue, un relèvement accéléré du niveau de vie, et le développement de relations harmonieuses entre les États qu'il réunit'.[61]

---

[57] Négociations des traités instituant la CEE et la CEEA (1955–1957), CM3. Réunion des ministres des affaires étrangères, Messine, 01–03.06.1955, CM3/NEGO/006, Résolution adoptée par les ministres des Affaires étrangères des Etats membres de la CECA, réunis à Messine (1er au 3 juin 1955).

[58] The Minutes of the inter-governmental conference shed little further light on the objectives of the common market and the competition rules. In fact, competition was not discussed by the Ministers of foreign affairs. The main concerns of the conference were of a political nature, particularly the position of Europe in the relations between the USSR and the Western Bloc, the pace of economic integration, and broader political issues: see Négociations des traités instituant la CEE et la CEEA (1955–1957), CM3. Réunion des ministres des affaires étrangères, Messine, 01–03.06.1955, CM3/NEGO/006, Procès-verbal de la conférence de Messine (1er au 3 juin 1955).

[59] Négociations des traités instituant la CEE et la CEEA (1955–1957), CM3. Réunion des ministres des affaires étrangères, Messine, 01–03.06.1955, CM3/NEGO/006, Résolution adoptée par les ministres des Affaires étrangères des Etats membres de la CECA, réunis à Messine (1er au 3 juin 1955).

[60] This idea that discrimination based on nationality should be prohibited as part of the competition regime was rejected in the Treaty of Rome: see 130 below.

[61] Comité intergouvernemental créé par la conférence de Messine. Rapport des chefs de délégation aux ministres des Affaires étrangères. Bruxelles: Secrétariat, 21 avril 1956—Rapport des

The main concern, which underlies the need for a common market, was, therefore, productivity and economic growth.[62] Compartmentalized national markets were considered to be an obstacle to the achievement of the economies of scale necessary to exploit modern technologies efficiently. National monopolies were held to be inefficient because they were not subject to competitive pressure. A common market would make undertakings subject to constant pressure to invest to improve their productive efficiency and the quality of their products. At the same time, better division of labour and increased security of supply would eliminate waste of resources and non-economical activities.[63] Normal conditions of competition free from State intervention and anti-competitive practices were deemed key to the effective functioning of the common market.[64] Competition rules applicable to undertakings were necessary to avoid a situation where 'dual pricing' took the place of customs duties, dumping endangered efficient production, and market-partitioning by undertakings replaced the division of the national markets.[65] It is important to notice that consumer welfare is completely absent from this analysis. An efficient allocation of resources was a relevant objective, but alongside productivity and economic growth.[66] The objective of increasing the standard of living is not seen as the consequence of marginal cost pricing, but as the outcome of a process of market integration that fostered high productivity and economic growth. As explained above, the Treaty of Rome and the subsequent Treaties adopted the approach of the Spaak Report by envisaging a common market, now an internal market, with the primary objective of fostering long-term productivity growth and social welfare.[67]

Chapter 1 of Title II of the Spaak Report set out in greater detail the principles on which the competition rules should be based. The Title opened with the statement that it was necessary to examine the conditions that would ensure that the common market leads to an efficient allocation of resources, the raising of the standard of living, and a faster rate of economic growth.[68] Probably because of the steer from the Messina Conference resolution, the first issue to be discussed

---

chefs de délégation aux ministres des Affaires étrangères (Bruxelles, 21 avril 1956) ('Spaak Report'), Première Partie, Le Marché Commun, Introduction, I.

[62] ibid Avant-Propos.   [63] ibid Première Partie, Le Marché Commun, Introduction, I.
[64] ibid Première Partie, Le Marché Commun, Introduction, II.B.   [65] ibid.
[66] ibid where the objective of the widening of the markets and competition is described as 'assurer la répartition la plus rationelle des activités et le rythme le plus favorable d'expansion'.
[67] Art 2 of the Treaty of Rome read as follows: 'The Community shall have as its task, by establishing a common market and progressively approximating the economic policies of Member States, to promote throughout the Community a harmonious development of economic activities, a continuous and balanced expansion, an increase in stability, an accelerated raising of the standard of living and closer relations between the states belonging to it.' Art 3(f) provided: 'For the purposes set out in Article 2, the activities of the Community shall include, as provided in this Treaty and in accordance with the timetable set out therein:...(f) the institution of a system ensuring that competition in the common market is not distorted'. The concept that better summarizes these objectives from an economic perspective is long-term social welfare, which combines economic growth with increased living standards. Subsequent amendments to the Treaty of Rome have remained faithful to the basic idea that the objective of the internal market is to foster the long-term welfare of society: see 113–121 above.
[68] Spaak Report, 53.

was the problem of discrimination based on nationality or residence. However, there was a clear recognition that the achievement of the common market itself would render discrimination unfeasible, since the opportunity for a customer to buy from another undertaking in the same Member State would make dual pricing unsustainable.[69] The same line of reasoning was applied to anti-dumping.[70] This statement is important. It shows that the concern of the Spaak Report was to sideline the issue of discrimination on grounds of nationality in favour of an approach that considered the competitive implications of discrimination. This approach would, eventually, prevail during the negotiations of the Treaty.

Addressing the problem of monopolies, by which the Spaak Report meant both anti-competitive agreements ('ententes') and anti-competitive unilateral conduct ('position de monopole'), the first question related to the issue of discrimination. Given that the achievement of the common market would render discrimination unsustainable, the Spaak Report stated that intervention in the case of discrimination would be justified only if two conditions are satisfied: (a) the customer is practically obliged to accept the discriminatory conditions; (b) the discriminatory conditions have an effect on competition between customers.[71] This approach is clearly reflected in Article 102(c), which has not changed since the Treaty of Rome, in that the provision requires not only discrimination but also competitive disadvantage. Turning to the treatment of agreements and unilateral conduct, the Spaak Report highlighted that the Treaty must prevent those agreements or that conduct which could jeopardize the fundamental objectives of the common market. The link between the competition rules applicable to the undertakings and the objectives of the common market, now the internal market, is reflected in the text of Articles 101 and 102 which prohibit anti-competitive agreements and abuses of a dominant position as 'incompatible with the internal market'. This does not mean, however, that the concern of the drafters and, now, the purpose of Articles 101 and 102 are to prohibit practices that have a market-partitioning effect. The Spaak Report made it absolutely clear that while market-partitioning practices were to be banned because they re-establish the division of the markets,[72] the intended benefits of the common market were productivity, economic growth, and innovation. This is evident in the recommended prohibition of agreements limiting production or technical progress because, the Spaak Report stated, such agreements would harm productivity growth.[73] Finally, the Spaak Report recommended prohibiting the 'absorption' or 'domination' of the market by one undertaking. The reason for

---

[69] ibid 53–54.

[70] ibid 54. It is interesting to note that in earlier drafts of the Treaty anti-dumping provisions were included in Title II La Politique du Marché Commun, Chapter 1, Les Règles de Concurrence, Section 1 Les normes applicables aux entreprises. Art 41 of the Projet d'Articles en vue de la rédaction du Traité instituant la Communauté du marché européen allowed Member States to maintain or introduce anti-dumping legislation for the transitional period and gave the Commission the power to invite Member States to modify legislation which was unduly restrictive: Conférence intergouvernementale pour le marché commun et l'euratom, Secrétariat, Projet d'articles en vue de la rédaction du Traité instituant la Communauté du marché européen, Bruxelles, le 17 juillet 1956 Mar Com 17 (MAE 175 f/56 gd) 39.

[71] Spaak Report, 55.   [72] ibid 55.   [73] ibid 56.

the recommendation was that such a situation would eliminate one of the essential advantages of a vast market, namely reconciling the deployment of the means of mass production with the maintenance of competition.[74] Essentially, the prohibition would have resulted in a form of merger control. This recommendation was not adopted in the Treaty.

As for the drafting technique, the Report recommended that the competition principles in the Treaty should be sufficiently precise to allow the Commission, as the executive of the future European Economic Community, to adopt the appropriate implementing regulations.[75] On the other hand, the Report also guarded against drafting rigid rules, as competition was not a field where the solutions could be fixed from day one and provide answers to all questions that might arise.[76]

In conclusion, there are three points arising from the Spaak Report that are worth highlighting. The first is that the objective of the common market and the competition rules was not consumer welfare, but the well-being of the peoples of Europe to be achieved by economic growth, productivity, and innovation. The second is a rejection of the idea that discrimination on grounds of nationality was a competition concern. The third is the alignment of the objectives of the common, now the internal, market and the competition rules as economic growth, productivity, and innovation.

(d) The drafting of the text of Article 102

The drafting guidelines set out in the Spaak Report are reflected in the Projet d'articles of 17 July 1956.[77] Title II, La Politique du Marché Commun, Chapter 1, Les Règles de Concurrence, Section 1, Normes applicables aux entreprises, opened with Article 40, proclaiming that the establishment of the common market implies that customers benefit from conditions analogous to those existing in an internal market.[78] Article 41 dealt with anti-dumping legislation.[79] Article 42 dealt with monopolies ('les monopoles') and applied to agreements and what is now the abuse of a dominant position.[80] That Article declared incompatible with the common market: (a) the fact of exercising, when setting the price or conditions for comparable transactions, vis-à-vis sellers or buyers in competition with each other, by virtue of agreements or because of the exploitation of a dominant position on the market, a discrimination which prejudices them compared to their competitors; (b) monopolistic situations or practices having the following

---

[74] ibid: '...il conviendra d'empêcher...l'absorption ou la domination du marché d'un produit par une seule entreprise parce qu'elle éliminerait l'un des avantages essentiels d'un vaste marché, qui est de concilier l'emploi des techniques de production de masse et le maintien de la concurrence'.

[75] ibid: 'Les principes inscrits dans le traité doivent être assez précis pour permettre à la Commission européenne de prendre des règlements généraux d'exécution....'. Such regulations 'auront pour objet d'élaborer les règles détaillées concernant la discrimination, d'organiser un contrôle des opérations de concentration, et de mettre en pratique une interdiction des ententes qui auraient pour effet une répartition ou une exploitation des marchés, une limitation de la production ou du progrès technique'.

[76] ibid.

[77] Conférence intergouvernementale pour le Marché commun et l'Euratom, Secrétariat, Project d'articles en vue de la rédaction du Traité instituant la Communauté du marché européen.

[78] ibid 38.   [79] ibid 39.   [80] ibid 40.

forms: (b.1) partitioning of markets through agreements between undertakings; (b.2) agreements having as their object the limitation of production or technical progress; and (b.3) absorption or domination of the market of a product by one undertaking.[81] Unilateral effects were addressed in two contexts. The first was the prohibition of discriminatory practices placing customers or suppliers of the dominant undertaking at a competitive disadvantage. The second was the prohibition of absorption or domination of the market by one undertaking. The intention was probably to prohibit a dominant position or the acquisition of a dominant position and not—or not only—its abuse. This interpretation is borne out by footnote 1, referring to the prohibition in question, which asked whether it should be the subject of a special examination, given that it did not relate to a practice but to a situation as such ('une situation en tant que telle').[82]

On 4 September 1956, the French delegation presented a proposal with some significant changes to the 17 July project. The French proposal contained a general prohibition on discrimination with no requirement of competitive disadvantage. Article 42 of the Project was substantially redrafted, the key changes being the following: (a) a general prohibition of practices, whether agreements or monopolistic, having as their object or possible effect the impediment of competition—this draft introduced the distinction between object and effect now in Article 101 TFEU; (b) the prohibition of the absorption or domination of the market by an undertaking but with the important addition 'ou un groupe d'enterprises', which is the first trace of the concept of collective dominance in the draft Treaty; (c) the possibility of exempting anti-competitive practices and situations if certain conditions are satisfied; and (d) the prohibition of the same practices whether achieved by agreement between undertakings or by a monopolistic undertaking.[83]

The first reading of Articles 40 to 43 of the Projet d'articles Doc Mar Com 17 ('the Project of 17 July 1956') took place on 3 to 5 September 1956.[84] The German delegation proposed to delete the general prohibition on discrimination and to set out in the Treaty establishing the European Economic Community a general principle that all discrimination based on nationality and causing harm or disadvantage to an economic entity be prohibited. It further proposed to provide for a system aimed at preventing undertakings in a monopoly situation abusing that situation. The same control should apply to undertakings in a situation of oligopoly and acting in concert.[85]

The approaches of the French and the German delegations to undertakings in a monopoly situation were very different. The French delegation proposed that the same regime should apply to agreements and monopolies.[86] Furthermore, the French proposal maintained the prohibition of dominance as such and even

---

[81] ibid.   [82] ibid (fn 1).

[83] Conférence intergouvernementale pour le Marché commun et l'Euratom, Secrétariat, Groupe du Marché commun, Dispositions Remplaçant l'Article 42 du document Mar. Com. 17, Proposition présentée par la délégation française 2–3.

[84] Extrait du procès-verbal des réunions des 3–5 septembre 1956 du Groupe du Marché commun de la conférence intergouvernementale pour le Marché commun et l'Euratom (MAE 252/56).

[85] ibid 2.   [86] ibid 3.

extended it to what is now known as collective dominance. The German delegation, on the other hand, argued that monopolies should only be subject to abuse
control.[87] The rationale for the proposal was that monopolies and oligopolies are
not necessarily incompatible with a competition regime. What was necessary,
according to the German delegation, was not to prohibit monopolies themselves
but the abuses to which certain monopolist situations might lead.[88]

On 10 September 1956, the German delegation presented a draft alternative
to both the 17 July draft and the French proposal.[89] The general prohibition on
discrimination was much more restrictive. Only discriminatory practices of an
undertaking that disadvantaged customers or suppliers in competition with each
other because of their nationality were prohibited.[90] The prohibition of agreements
and the prohibition of abusive exploitation of a dominant position were contained
in two different Articles. Article 42b of the German proposal would have prohibited the abusive exploitation of the position of public or private undertakings not
subject to any significant competition ('concurrence sérieuse'). The term 'exploiter'
appears for the first time in the draft of what would then become Article 102. It
is, therefore, worth explaining that the use of this term, which still appears in the
French text of the TFEU, does not refer to the category of so-called exploitative
abuses. The exploitation in question was not the exploitation of customers or, for
a buyer in a dominant position, of sellers. It was the exploitation of the dominant
position, that is, the misuse of the undertaking's advantageous position of strength
on the market.[91]

It is clear that there is a striking similarity between the draft Article proposed
by the German delegation and what would become the final text of Article 86 of
the Treaty of Rome (now Article 102 TFEU). It is, therefore, necessary to examine the differences between the German proposal and both the French proposal
and the text of 17 July in more depth. First, the German proposal contained a
definition of dominance as the situation in which an undertaking does not have
to face any significant competition. It was not the size of the undertaking which

---

[87]　ibid 3. The Italian and the Dutch delegations agreed: ibid 4.
[88]　Secrétariat, Memento interne, Groupe du Marché Commun, 3 et 4 septembre 1056 Fascicule 5,
Brussels, le 7 septembre 1956, 5 et 6, statement by Mr M Müller-Armack.
[89]　Projet (remis par M Tiesing) Bruxelles, le 10 septembre 1956 MAE 252 f756 mv.
[90]　ibid.
[91]　P Akman, 'Searching for the Long-Lost Soul of Article 82 EC' (2009) 29 OJLS 267, 296 and fn
148, states that 'the texts of Article 82 EC in French and German' support the view that Art 82 was
intended to prohibit exploitation of the dominant undertaking's suppliers or customers. The French
text reads: 'Est incompatible avec le marché commun et interdit... d'exploiter de façon abusive une
position dominante...'. The German text reads: 'Mit dem Gemeinsamen Markt unvereinbar und
verboten ist die missbräuchliche Ausnutzung einer beherrschenden Stellung...'. Presumably, the
author takes the view that the French verb 'exploiter' and the German noun 'Ausnutzung' mean
'exploitation' of a person or entity. However, these terms also mean abuse in a sense close to the ety-
mology of the word both in English (from a Latin stem *ab*-use) and in German (*aus*-nutzen): to gain,
get an advantage from something, often with a pejorative connotation. The meaning of the term is
given by the context. In Art 102 it is given by the object (in French) and genitive (in German): what
is exploited is not a customer or supplier but the dominant position itself. 'Exploiter de façon abusive
une position dominante' and 'die missbräuchliche Ausnutzung einer beherrschenden Stellung' mean
the abusive use of a dominant position for the dominant undertaking's own benefit. Quite *how* the
dominant position may be abused is left unclear.

mattered as such but the lack of effective competitive pressure. Secondly, the German draft unequivocally prohibited only the abuse of a dominant position rather than merely its acquisition or possession. Thirdly, it set out a number of circumstances in which the conduct of a dominant undertaking could be considered abusive. This list would become, with some significant changes, the current illustrative list in Article 102. It was deliberately drafted in flexible and ambiguous language.[92] The list was probably not intended to describe types of conduct that may be abusive, let alone *per se* abusive, but circumstances or scenarios in which the dominant undertaking could commit an abuse. This is suggested by the use of the gerund in the following grammatical construction: '. . . doit être interdit, le fait . . . d'exploiter abusivement leur position, notamment—en demandant ou proposant des prix. . . .—en exerçant une discrimination. . . .—en limitant la production. . . .—en prétendant subordonner . . .'. While the language was both inelegant and ambiguous, the fact that the first indent simply referred to the dominant undertaking requiring or even merely proposing prices and conditions, without any further qualification, strongly suggests that the list did not describe abusive practices but possible scenarios in which an abuse could occur. Otherwise, the first indent would have prohibited a dominant undertaking from proposing prices or conditions, which would be absurd. The language of the illustrative list changed significantly through the subsequent drafts.

The Dutch delegation and, for some Articles, the Dutch and the Belgian delegations jointly, presented alternative proposals.[93] Following meetings on 5 to 7 November 1956, it was decided to confer on a smaller group the task of drafting a new 'projet d'articles', taking into account the discussion and leading to a significant reduction of the alternative texts.[94] Following further discussions and proposals, a new text was drafted and presented by the Dutch delegation on 15 November 1956.[95] Article 40 still set out a general prohibition of discrimination but the German and Italian delegations proposed its deletion. The treatment of

---

[92] An abuse could be found when the dominant undertaking required or proposed prices or conditions, when it exercised an unjustified discrimination against buyers or sellers in the conclusion of contracts, when it limited production or markets or technical or economic progress, and, finally, when it purported to make the conclusion of contracts conditional upon the acceptance, by the trading partner, of goods or services which, because of their nature or according to commercial usage, could not be linked: Projet (remis par M Tiesing) Bruxelles, le 10 septembre 1956 (MAE 252 f756 mv).

[93] The four proposals can be read in a synoptic table in Conférence intergouvernementale pour le Marché commun et l'Euratom, Secrétariat, Tableau synoptique des projets d'articles soumis par les délégations concernant les règles de concurrence applicables aux entreprises, Bruxelles, le 16 septembre 1956.

[94] Extrait du procès-verbal des réunions des 6–7 novembre 1956 du Groupe du Marché commun de la conférence intergouvernementale pour le Marché commun et l'Euratom (MAE 525/56).

[95] Conférence intergouvernementale pour le Marché commun et l'Euratom, Secrétariat, Projet de Rédaction sur les règles de concurrence (proposé par la délégation néerlandaise) Bruxelles, le 15 novembre 1956 (MAE 547 f/56 dvl). For the text following the second reading, see : Conférence intergouvernementale pour le Marché commun et l'Euratom, Secrétariat, Groupe du Marché commun, Projet de Rédaction sur les règles de concurrence établi le 20 novembre 1956 par un groupe d'experts compte tenu des échanges de vues intervenues le 19 novembre 1956 en groupe restreint (MAE 602 f/56 js).

agreements (now termed 'accords') and monopolies was kept separate according to the original German proposal. Article 41 applied to anti-competitive agreements. Article 42(a) resembled very closely the current text of Article 102. Compared to the original German proposal, there was no longer a definition of dominance. Following the original French proposal, the abuse could be committed by one or *more* undertakings. The language introducing what is now the illustrative list appeared to set out forms of conduct that may be abusive rather than setting out circumstances in which an abuse might occur. The first indent referred to prices or conditions 'non équitables', an adjective that was introduced in the Dutch proposal of 15 November 1956.[96] In the second indent, the limitation of production, markets, or technical progress, which the Spaak Report had considered detrimental to productivity and the German proposal purported to prohibit without qualification, was considered abusive if it occured 'au prejudice des consommateurs'. The third indent did not simply describe a situation in which the dominant undertaking exercised unjustified discrimination against buyers and sellers. It set out in more detail that an abuse may consist in 'appliquer à l'égard de partenaires commerciaux des conditions inégales à des prestations équivalentes et leur infliger de ce fait un désavantage dans la concurrence'. In particular, there was a requirement that the discrimination must place an undertaking at a competitive disadvantage vis-à-vis other undertakings, following the initial approach in the Spaak Report.[97] The final indent closely resembled the German proposal by describing situations in which the dominant undertaking made the conclusion of contracts conditional upon 'l'acceptation, par les partenaires, de prestations supplémentaires qui, en raison de leur nature ou des usages commerciaux, n'ont pas de lien avec l'objet de ces contrats'.

The Dutch text was examined on second reading on 13 to 15 November 1956. At that meeting, the German delegation opposed the concept of discrimination on grounds of nationality set out in Article 40 of the draft on the basis that it was useless and too rigid in competition law.[98] The Italian delegation supported the German proposal. No substantial discussion took place on the abuse of a dominant position.[99] The draft articles were finally approved by the Group on the common market of the inter-governmental conference on 27 to 29 November 1956 and transmitted to the Heads of the delegations. Following the German and Italian opposition, the general prohibition on discrimination on grounds of nationality was deleted because it was held to fall outside the scope of the competition rules.[100] The Committee of the heads of the Delegations approved the draft on 6 December

---

[96] ibid.   [97] Spaak Report, 55.

[98] Secrétariat, Memento interne, Groupe du Marché Commun 13, 14 et 15 novembre 1956, Fascicule 10, Brussels, le 20 novembre 1956, Examen en seconde lecture des règles de concurrence.

[99] There was only a statement by M Hyzen advocating a consistent treatment of agreements and abuse of dominance. However, France supported the text as drafted and this isolated call for consistency was not followed-up: ibid 3.

[100] Extrait du procès-verbal des réunions des 27–29 novembre 1956 du Groupe du Marché commun de la conférence intergouvernementale pour le Marché commun et l'Euratom (MAE 705/56).

1956.[101] The main change was the application of Section 1 to private undertakings only.[102] There were no comments on the abuse of dominance provisions.[103]

The final text of Article 86, now Article 102 EC, resembles very closely the text approved on 6 December 1956. The only differences are the following: (a) the language introducing the illustrative list was changed to the current version—the amendment is arguably purely stylistic compared to the text approved on 6 December 1956 but possibly more restrictive than the text in the German proposal of 10 September 1956; (b) Article 86(c) was subject to purely stylistic changes—the provision continues to require both discrimination against other undertakings that are customers or suppliers of the dominant undertaking and a competitive disadvantage as the effect of the discrimination; (c) Article 86(d) was also subject to purely stylistic changes.

(e) Long-term social welfare in the travaux préparatoires

It is not easy to maintain that the drafters of the Treaty had in mind a particular concept of competition or a particular test to be applied to determine whether a dominant undertaking abuses its position. However, the fundamental statement in the Spaak Report, which saw the competition rules as having the purpose of achieving the objective of raising the standard of living through an efficient allocation of resources, a faster rate of economic growth, high productivity, and innovation, was never contradicted and was reflected in the link between Articles 85 and 86, Article 3(f), and Article 2 of the Treaty of Rome.[104] The link between the competition rules, the internal market, and the objectives of the Union is still firmly embedded in the architecture of the current Treaties.

Furthermore, it is impossible to maintain that somehow the German delegation introduced ordoliberal concepts in EU competition law and in Article 102 in particular.[105] On the contrary, the German proposal rejected the ordoliberal idea that monopolies should be prohibited as such,[106] or forced to behave as if

---

[101] Conférence intergouvernementale pour le Marché commun et l'Euratom, Secrétariat, Comité des chefs de délégation, Rédaction approuvée par le Comité des chefs de délégation au cours de sa séance du 6 décembre 1956 concernant Titre II—Chapitre 1: Les Règles de Concurrence, Section 1: Normes applicables aux entreprises (MAE 788 f/56 mts).

[102] ibid 2 (fn 1).

[103] See also the Extrait du procès-verbal de la réunion du 6 décembre 1956 du Comité des Chefs de délégation de la conférence intergouvernementale pour le Marché commun et l'Euratom (MAE 781/56).

[104] See n 67 above.

[105] This is, however, what is generally assumed: see D Hildebrand, *The Role of Economic Analysis in the EC Competition Rules* (3rd edn Alphen aan den Rijn, Kluwer Law International 2009) 11–12.

[106] Ordoliberalism advocated the model of 'complete competition' according to which market power should be diffused as far as possible, see W Eucken, 'Die Wettbewerbsordnung und ihre Verwrklichung' (1949) 2 ORDO 1, 64: 'Wirtschaftliche Macht sollte in einer Wettbewerbsordnung nur soweit bestehen wie sie notwendig ist, um die Wettbewerbsordnung aufrecht zu erhalten.' Some ordoliberal thinkers believed that market power may be diffused even if the market structures tend to be oligopolistic or even monopolistic, depending on the configuration of the other factors conditioning competition, see Hildebrand, *The Role of Economic Analysis in the EC Competition Rules*, 161. Monopolies should be prohibited where possible. A firm or group of firms with economic power over customers and competitors was structurally inconsistent with the concept of complete competition. Thus, the competition authority's primary mandate was to detect and punish cartels and

they had been subject to competition.[107] The aim of the German proposal of 10 September 1956 was precisely to put beyond doubt that monopolies were not prohibited as such, but only if they engaged in abusive conduct. While the concept of abusive conduct was undefined, there is no indication whatsoever that the ordoliberal 'as if' standard was being proposed. What the German delegation said was that certain monopolistic situations might lead to abuse. This is hardly an endorsement of the 'as if' standard. Nor was the ordoliberal concept of 'Leistungswettbewerb' ever mentioned or hinted at.[108] That the German delegation had in mind an economic concept of competition rather than the political theories of the ordoliberals is also apparent in the definition of dominant position in the German proposal, which referred to the absence of any significant competitive pressure as the hallmark of dominance.[109]

As regards the consumer welfare objective, while references to consumers were added during the drafting process in what are now Article 101(3)[110] and

---

other agreements between competitors. Where a monopoly position was not based on an agreement between competitors, the task of the competition authority was more difficult. Ordoliberalists distinguished between 'avoidable' and 'unavoidable' monopolies. Avoidable monopolies occurred where one firm had won the competitive battle against its rivals and was consequently in a position to distort competition. Unavoidable monopolies occurred in cases of natural monopoly or where the monopoly position stemmed from a legally protected right. In order to be able to protect the competitive process, in cases of avoidable monopolies a competition authority had to have the power to require that firms divest themselves of components of their operations or otherwise eliminate their monopoly positions, see Eucken, 'Die Wettbewerbsordnung und ihre Verwirklichung', 68: 'Das Monopolamt hat die Aufgabe, vermeidbare Monopole aufzulösen.'

[107] Some ordoliberals recognized that some monopolies, eg natural monopolies, were unavoidable. They believed that unavoidable monopolies should be regulated according to a principle of 'behaviour analogous to competition'. The task of the competition authority was to ensure that monopolists behaved as if they were subject to complete competition. Eucken, 'Die Wettbewerbsordnung und ihre Verwrklichung', 68, expresses this idea in the clearest terms: 'Ziel der Monopolgesetzgebung und der Monopolaufsicht ist es, Träger wirtschaftlicher Macht zu einem Verhalten zu veranlassen, als ob vollständige Konkurrenz bestünde. Das Verhalten des Monopolisten hat "wettbewerbsanalog" zu sein.' This approach was called the 'as if' standard. Leonhard Miksch, who was a leading student of Walter Eucken's, was the main proponent of the 'as if' standard: see L Miksch, *Wettbewerb als Aufgabe: Grundsätze einer Wettbewerbsordnung* (2nd edn Godesberg, Helmut Küpper 1947).

[108] It is generally argued that ordoliberalism influenced the early application of Arts 101 and 102, and, to a certain extent, still does. Hildebrand claims that ordoliberal thinking had a direct influence on EU competition policy (see Hildebrand, *The Role of Economic Analysis in the EC Competition Rules*, 163–165). According to Ahlborn and Grave, 'due to the huge impact ordoliberalism had on EC competition policy, many of the ordoliberal concepts have been hard-wired into the system, even when at times the link to ordoliberalism has been obscured or forgotten', see C Ahlborn and C Grave, 'Walter Eucken and Ordoliberalism: An Introduction from a Consumer Welfare Perspective' (2006) 2 Competition Policy International 197, 206. Whish, on the other hand, warns that the role of ordoliberalism may have been exaggerated: R Whish, *Competition Law* (6th edn Oxford, OUP 2009) 21–22.

[109] Projet (remis par M Tiesing) Bruxelles, le 10 septembre 1956 (MAE 252 f756 mv).

[110] There was no mention of consumers in the original text of Art 42 of the draft of 17 July 1956: see Conférence intergouvernementale pour le Marché commun et l'Euratom, Secrétariat, Project d'articles en vue de la rédaction du Traité instituant la Communauté du marché européen. The condition that the benefits under what is now Art 101(3) must be passed on to consumers appeared in the French proposal: Conférence intergouvernementale pour le Marché commun et l'Euratom, Secrétariat, Groupe du Marché commun, Dispositions Remplaçant l'Article 42 du document Mar Com 17, Proposition présentée par la délégation française, 2–3.

Article 102(b), there was no discussion of consumer welfare as the objective of the competition rules or of consumers as the main or only beneficiaries of the competition regime. The drafting process strongly suggests that references to consumers were included in relation to specific tests as limits to the application of certain provisions, but not as the expression of a general principle that the EU competition rules had the exclusive objective of benefiting consumers.

As regards price discrimination, which is the only form of abuse of dominance which was expressly considered, the drafters made a conscious choice to include a requirement of competitive disadvantage in what is now Article 102(c), while discrimination based on nationality, without more, was not considered to be a competition issue and was deleted from the competition provisions of the Treaty.

Overall, the analysis of the *travaux préparatoires* of the Treaty of Rome corroborates the validity of the interpretation of the objective of the EU competition rules as the maximization of long-term social welfare.

C. The problem of the objective of the EU competition rules in the case law and secondary legislation

(1) Integrated analysis of Article 102, Article 101, and merger control

This section examines the case law and secondary legislation on the objective of the EU competition rules. Of course, the case law and secondary legislation cannot change the objective the Treaties assign to the competition rules. However, a general analysis of the case law and secondary legislation on the objective of the EU competition rules serves the purpose of verifying the conclusions reached by a textual and teleological interpretation of the Treaties.

The analysis of the objective of Article 102 in the case law and in secondary legislation must be carried out in an integrated fashion. It is indisputable that Article 102 aims at achieving the objective of the internal market as set out in the Treaties. So does Article 101. As a consequence, the objective of both provisions must be the same as a matter of law. It is also indisputable that the two EU merger control regulations, the 1989 Merger Regulation[111] and the 2004 Merger Regulation,[112] have as their legal basis Article 103 as well as Article 352 TFEU. This means that the Merger Regulations are, in part, implementations of Articles 101 and 102 and, in part, implementations of the general objectives of competition policy and the internal market, as set out in the Treaties. Merger control must, therefore, have the same objective as Articles 101 and 102.

---

[111] 1989 Merger Regulation. [112] 2004 Merger Regulation.

(2) The EU competition rules and the objectives of the Treaties

(a) Article 102

The case law on Article 102 has repeatedly emphasized the link between the prohibition of abuse of a dominant position, as an essential component of the legal regime of the internal market, and the general objectives of the European Union. Already in *Continental Can*, the Court of Justice held that undistorted competition was necessary 'to promote throughout the Community a harmonious development of economic activities' as provided by Article 2 EEC.[113] The aim of Articles 101 and 102 was to safeguard the principles and attain the objectives set out in Articles 2 and 3 EEC as in force at the time.[114] This approach was confirmed in *Hoffmann-La Roche*.[115] However, there has also been a trend in the case law that assumes that competition is an end in itself. This trend had emerged already in the early cases, which appear to elevate the establishment of a system of undistorted competition, which was, until the Lisbon Treaty came into force, an activity of the Community set out in Article 3 EC, to an objective in its own right.[116] On a closer reading, however, the case law only establishes that Article 102 aims at ensuring that competition is not distorted and protects a competitive market structure.[117] The Court has often refrained from defining what a competitive market structure or undistorted competition is, though it is clear that the definition of these concepts must be based on the objectives of the Treaties.[118] A notable exception is the judgment of the Court of Justice in *TeliaSonera*, which endorses a long-term social welfare objective reflecting societal values and preferences in addition to a purely monetary measure of supplier and consumer surplus.[119]

(b) Article 101

The case law on Article 101 confirms that the concept of competition in EU law must be construed in the light of the objectives of the Treaties.

Already in *Société Technique Minière*, the Court of Justice, reasoning that anti-competitive conduct is only prohibited when it has an effect on trade between Member States and that the Treaty prohibits anti-competitive conduct as 'incompatible with the common market [now the internal market]', held that an interference with competition is relevant under Article 101(1) only when 'it may be

---

[113] Case 6/72 *Continental Can*, para 24.   [114] ibid para 25.

[115] Case 85/76 *Hoffmann-La Roche & Co AG v Commission* [1979] ECR 461, para 125.

[116] Case 27/76 *United Brands*, para 63; Case 322/81 *NV Nederlandsche Banden Industrie Michelin v Commission* [1983] ECR 3461 (*Michelin I*), para 29.

[117] In the case law on Art 102, the formula adopted since Case 6–72 *Continental Can*, para 26, is to the effect that Art 102 is aimed not only at practices which may cause prejudice to consumers directly, but also at those which are detrimental to them through their impact on an effective competition structure. The formula has been repeatedly reaffirmed. See, for instance, Case C-95/04 P *British Airways*, para 106.

[118] While never clearly stated, this proposition is implicit in the case law. Case 6–72 *Continental Can*, para 26, for instance, refers to the competitive structure envisaged in Art 3 of the Treaty of Rome, which listed activities aimed at achieving the objectives set out in Art 2.

[119] Case C-52/09 *TeliaSonera*, paras 20–22, relying on Case C-94/00 *Roquette Frères*, para 42 and Joined Cases 46/87 and 227/88 *Hoechst*, para 25.

assumed that there is a possibility that the realization of a single market between Member States may be impeded'.[120] Similarly, in *Consten and Grundig*, the Court reiterated that, when examining whether an agreement has an effect on trade between Member States, 'what is particularly important is whether the agreement is capable of constituting a threat, either direct or indirect, actual or potential, to freedom of trade between Member States in a manner which might harm the attainment of the objectives of a single market between states'.[121] Dealing with the applicability of Article 101 to vertical agreements, the Court went on to say:[122]

An agreement between producer and distributor which might tend to restore the national divisions in trade between Member States might be such as to frustrate the most fundamental objectives of the Community. The Treaty, whose Preamble and content aim at abolishing the barriers between States, and which in several provisions gives evidence of a stern attitude with regard to their reappearance, could not allow undertakings to reconstruct such barriers. Article 85(1) [now Article 101(1)] is designed to pursue this aim, even in the case of agreements between undertakings placed at different levels in the economic process.

Thus, it was the market-partitioning object that justified the strict treatment of intra-brand agreements conferring absolute territorial protection on a distributor. In laying down this principle, the Court confined itself to setting out a legal test. It did not discuss the objective of Article 101 or the internal market. However, the judgment is consistent with the objective of the internal market to foster long-term productivity growth. This is apparent from the Court's statement of the negative effects of the agreement: (a) higher prices in the French market; (b) excessive inter-brand differentiation dampening inter-brand competition; and (c) diminished incentives for distributors to behave efficiently, taking into account that distribution costs were a significant proportion of total costs.[123]

The reluctance to discuss the objective of Article 101 is a recurrent feature of the case law. In *Metro I*,[124] the Court of Justice ruled on the compatibility of a selective distribution system for electrical equipment with Article 101 TFEU.[125] The Court held that the requirement that competition shall not be distorted implied 'the existence on the market of workable competition, that is to say the degree of

---

[120] Case 56/65 *Société Technique Minière (LTM) v Maschinenbau Ulm GmbH (MBU)* [1966] ECR 235. See also Case 23/67 *Brasserie de Haecht v Wilkin* [1967] ECR 407, 415.

[121] Joined Cases 56/64 and 58/64 *Etablissements Consten SàRL and Grundig-Verkaufs-GmbH v Commission* [1966] ECR 299 (*Consten and Grundig*). On this case, see A Jones and B Sufrin, *EU Competition Law: Text, Cases, and Materials* (4th edn Oxford, OUP 2011) 204–209; G Amato, *Antitrust and the Bounds of Power* (Oxford, Hart Publishing 1997) 49; Whish, *Competition Law* 604–605; DG Goyder, *Goyder's EC Competition Law* (5th edn Oxford, OUP 2009) 43; V Korah, *An Introductory Guide to EC Competition Law and Practice* (9th edn Oxford, Hart Publishing 2007) 6–7, 59–61, and 68–69; O Odudu, 'Interpreting Article 81(1): Demonstrating Restrictive Effect' (2001) 26 EL Rev 261, 271–272.

[122] Joined Cases 56/64 and 58/64 *Consten and Grundig*, 340.   [123] ibid 343.

[124] Case 26/76 *Metro SB-Großmärkte GmbH & Co KG v Commission* [1977] ECR 1875 (Metro I).

[125] Selective distribution systems are now assessed in the light of Commission Regulation (EU) 330/2010 of 20 April 2010 and Commission notice—Guidelines on Vertical Restraints [2010] OJ C130/1. However, the case under review is still important in order to understand the development of the jurisprudence of the EU courts on Art 101 TFEU.

competition necessary to ensure the observance of the basic requirements and the attainment of the objectives of the Treaty, in particular the creation of a single market achieving conditions similar to those of a domestic market'.[126] Thus, the Court recognized the need to define competition in the light of the objectives of the Treaties. The Court, however, refrained from specifying what the objective of the EU competition rules is, perhaps for fear of the unintended consequences that a clear statement of the purpose of those rules might have.

The subsequent case law on Article 101 has been even less generous in discussing the objective of the provision.[127] The Opinion of Advocate General Trstenjak in *The Competition Authority v Beef Industry Development Society* is a notable exception. In a case concerned with whether an agreement between competitors to reduce over-capacity in the industry was a restriction of competition by object, the Advocate General adopted as a starting point the objectives of Article 101:[128]

Article 81 EC [now Article 101 TFEU] protects competition in particular in regard to its function of forming a single market with conditions akin to an internal market and its function of supplying consumers as well as possible. In examining whether an agreement encroaches upon that protected interest, the Community judicature considers whether the agreement limits the freedom of one or more undertakings to determine their policy on the market independently (requirement of independence) and whether that limitation of freedom has an appreciable effect on market conditions.

This definition is a significant step forward compared to the previous case law, in that it not only links competition with the internal market but identifies a further objective, inherent in the internal market, which is capable of constituting a meaningful criterion for the definition of 'restriction of competition', namely consumer welfare ('supplying consumers as well as possible'). The Advocate General also makes a clear distinction between the objective of the law, which is the establishment of the internal market and 'supplying consumers as well as possible', and the test the case law applies, which would ask whether the agreement restricts economic freedom and, if so, whether it has an appreciable effect on the market. The error the Advocate General commits is to identify too readily the objective of the internal market with 'supplying consumers as well as possible'. There is no reasoning to support this proposition. A contextual and teleological interpretation

---

[126] Case 26/76 *Metro I*, para 20.

[127] This includes a number of seminal cases such as Case 262/81 *Coditel SA Compagnie générale pour la diffusion de la télévision v Ciné-Vog Films SA* [1982] ECR 3381 (*Coditel II*); Case 258/78 *LC Nungesser KG v Commission* [1982] ECR 2015; Case 42/84 *Remia BV v Commission* [1985] ECR 2545; Case 161/84 *Pronuptia de Paris GmbH v Pronuptia de Paris Irmgard Schillgallis* [1986] ECR 353; Case C-234/89 *Stergios Delimitis v Henninger Bräu AG* [1991] ECR I–935; Case C-250/92 *Gøttrup-Klim ea Grovvareforeninger v Dansk Landbrugs Grovvareselskab AmbA* [1994] ECR I-5641; Case T-112/99 *Métropole télévision (M6) v Commission* [2001] ECR II-2459; Joined Cases T-374/94, T-375/94, T-384/94, and T-388/94 *European Night Services Ltd (ENS) v Commission* [1998] ECR II-1533; Case C-309/99 *JCJ Wouters, JW Savelbergh and Price Waterhouse Belastingadviseurs BV v Algemene Raad van de Nederlandse Orde van Advocaten* [2002] ECR I-1577; Case T-328/03 *O2 (Germany) GmbH & Co OHG v Commission* [2006] II-1231.

[128] Opinion of AG Trstenjak in Case C-209/07 *The Competition Authority v Beef Industry Development Society Ltd* [2008] ECR I-8637 (*Irish Beef*) para 42. The Court did not follow the AG in this analysis.

of Articles 1, 2, and 3 TEU and 3, 101, and 102 TFEU demonstrates that it is long-term social welfare rather than consumer welfare that is the objective of the internal market and the EU competition rules.

(c) Merger control

The 1989 Merger Regulation provided that a concentration 'which creates or strengthens a dominant position as a result of which effective competition would be significantly impeded in the common market or in a substantial part of it shall be declared incompatible with the common market'.[129] The 2004 Merger Regulation provides that a concentration 'which would significantly impede effective competition, in the common market or in a substantial part of it, in particular as a result of the creation or strengthening of a dominant position, shall be declared incompatible with the common market'.[130] While the test has changed, the reason for the prohibition remains the same: certain concentrations are incompatible with the internal market.[131] As in Articles 101 and 102, this points to the objective of merger control as being the same as the objective of the internal market, namely long-term social welfare.

The case law under the 1989 Merger Regulation contains little in terms of analysis of its objective.[132] *Kali and Salz* was the first case in which the Court of Justice expanded upon the objective of the Regulation, but merely to point out the purpose of ensuring undistorted competition as a necessary element of the internal market.[133] This clarifies the point that the objective of merger control, as those of Articles 101 and 102, is to be derived from the objective of the internal market. On the other hand, *Kali and Salz* also confirms the trend in the case law to refrain from a clear statement of purpose of the EU competition rules. Similarly, in *Gencor v Commission*, the Court of First Instance, dealing with the relevance of market shares in the assessment of collective dominance, stated that the 1989 Merger Regulation reflected 'the general objective assigned by Article 3(g) of the Treaty, namely the establishment of a system ensuring that competition in the common

---

[129] 1989 Merger Regulation, Art 2(3).   [130] 2004 Merger Regulation, Art 2(3).

[131] This conclusion is confirmed by the recitals of the Regulations: 1989 Merger Regulation, recitals 1 and 2 and 2004 Merger Regulation, recital 2.

[132] There are some tautological statements. See for instance Case C-12/03 P *Commission v Tetra Laval BV* [2005] ECR I-987, para 73: 'the purpose of the Regulation...is to prevent the creation or strengthening of dominant positions capable of significantly impeding effective competition in the common market or a substantial part thereof', upholding Case T-5/02 *Tetra Laval BV v Commission* [2002] II-4381. Most cases are, however, narrowly concerned with the application of the legal test rather than with a broader analysis of the objective of merger control: Case T-310/01 *Schneider Electric SA v Commission* [2002] ECR II-4071; Case T-342/99 *Airtours plc v Commission* [2002] ECR II-2585; Case T-464/04 *Independent Music Publishers and Labels Association (Impala) v Commission* [2006] ECR II-2289 (*Impala*), set aside on appeal (but not on this issue) in Case C-413/06 P *Bertelsmann AG and Sony Corporation of America v Independent Music Publishers and Labels Association (Impala)* [2008] ECR I-4951 (*Impala*).

[133] Joined Cases C-68/94 P and C-30/95 P *French Republic v Commission* [1998] ECR I-1375 (*Kali and Salz*), paras 168–171; applied in Case T-102/96 *Gencor Ltd v Commission* [1999] II-753, paras 148–151.

market is not distorted', and then went on to apply the case law on Article 102 by analogy.[134]

The analysis of the Merger Regulations and the merger case law is consistent with the conclusion that the objectives of EU competition law are those of the internal market. However, probably because the Regulations are secondary legislation, there has been even less meaningful discussion of the objective of the law in merger control than under Articles 102 and 101.

(3) Rejection of consumer welfare as an objective of EU competition law

On the back of a growing literature arguing that consumer welfare is, or should be, the objective of the EU competition rules,[135] arguments have been raised before the EU courts to the effect that certain agreements or conduct did not infringe Article 101 or 102 respectively because they did not harm consumer welfare. The Court of Justice has, however, firmly rejected the proposition that harm to consumers is the only test under Article 101 or 102, thus casting significant doubts on whether consumer welfare is the objective of the EU competition rules.

As regards Article 102, the issue was raised squarely in *British Airways*.[136] In that case, the dominant undertaking argued that its rebate system was not an infringement of Article 102 because it did not harm consumers as required by Article 102(b). Advocate General Kokott stated that Article 102 forms part of a system designed to protect undistorted competition within the internal market. As a consequence, Article 102, like the other EU competition rules, is not designed only or primarily to protect the immediate interests of individual competitors or consumers, but to protect the structure of the market and thus competition 'as an institution'. When competition 'as an institution' is impeded, consumers may also be harmed. Therefore, consumers are indirectly protected by safeguarding the process of competition.[137] The Court of Justice, while not explicitly adopting the Advocate General's analysis, rejected British Airways' argument that the conduct in question could only be abusive if it caused prejudice to consumers. The Court pointed out, relying on *Continental Can*,[138] that Article 102 is aimed not only at practices that may cause prejudice to consumers directly, but also at those that are

---

[134] Case T-102/96 *Gencor*, paras 199–205. More generally, it is settled case law that the concept of dominant position under the Merger Regulations is the same as under Art 102: Joined Cases C-68/94 P and C-30/95 P *Kali and Salz*; Case T-102/96 *Gencor*; Case T-342/99 *Airtours*; Case T-464/04 *Impala*, set aside on appeal (but not on this issue) in Case C-413/06 P *Impala*.

[135] J Stuyck, 'EC Competition Law After Modernisation: More than Ever in the Interest of Consumers' (2005) 28 Journal of Consumer Policy 1; P Marsden and P Whelan, ' "Consumer Detriment" in the EC and UK Competition Law' (2006) 27 ECLR 569; Akman, 'Searching for the Long-Lost Soul of Art 82 EC', 267–303; M Kellerbauer, 'The Commission's New Enforcement Priorities in Applying Article 82 EC to Dominant Companies' Exclusionary Conduct: a Shift towards a More Economic Approach?' (2010) 31 ECLR 175.

[136] Case C-95/04 P *British Airways*, upholding Case T-219/99 *British Airways plc v Commission* [2003] ECR II-5917.

[137] Opinion of AG Kokott in Case C-95/04 P *British Airways*, para 68.

[138] Case 6/72 *Continental Can*, para 26.

detrimental to them through their impact on an effective competition structure.[139]
Consumers are thus protected not by prohibiting only those practices that are
detrimental to consumer welfare, but also by preserving an effective competitive
structure. It follows that a competitive structure cannot be defined as a structure
that maximizes consumer welfare, or a negative effect on consumer welfare would
be a necessary element of the test. The competitive structure of the market, which
Article 102 protects, must be defined in the light of the objective of the EU competition rules within the framework of the Treaties, which, as explained above, can be
synthetically described as the promotion of long-term social welfare. Consumers
clearly benefit from the maximization of long-term social welfare but producers
benefit too. It is the welfare of the society as a whole, not the welfare of consumers,
that EU competition law aims to protect. The issue was placed beyond doubt by
the Court of Justice in *TeliaSonera*, where the objective of the TFEU competition
rules, and of Article 102 in particular, was said to be 'to prevent competition from
being distorted to the detriment of the public interest, individual undertakings
and consumers, thereby ensuring the well-being of the European Union'.[140]

   This approach is consistent with the case law on Article 101. In *GlaxoSmithKline*,
a case concerned with dual pricing of pharmaceutical products aimed at preventing parallel trade from Spain to other Member States, the Fourth Chamber
(extended composition) of the Court of First Instance stated that the objective of
Article 101(1) is the protection of the welfare of the final consumer.[141] On appeal,
the Court of Justice set aside the reasoning of the Court of First Instance on this
point.[142] The Court's reasoning rests on three pillars. First, the Court relied on its
own precedents on agreements preventing parallel trade.[143] This is in itself significant because it demonstrates that the Court was unwilling to reverse or revisit
established doctrines in the light of a novel consumer welfare theory, however
vocally and enthusiastically supported by certain business, academic, and prac-
titioner quarters. Secondly, the Court said that agreements aimed at partitioning
national markets or making the interpenetration of national markets more difficult have as their object the restriction of competition within the meaning of
Article 101.[144] The Court interpreted Article 101 in the light of the objectives
of the Treaties, which include market integration. It is clear, therefore, that consumer welfare was not held to be the objective of Article 101. Thirdly, the Court
noted that the protective purpose of Article 101 is wider than the protection of

---

[139] Case C-95/04 P *British Airways*, paras 103–108.
[140] Case C-52/09 *TeliaSonera*, para 22.
[141] Case T-168/01 *GlaxoSmithKline Services Unlimited v Commission* [2006] ECR II-2969,
para 118, where the Court stated 'the objective assigned to Article 81(1) EC . . . is to prevent undertakings, by restricting competition between themselves or with third parties, from reducing the welfare
of the final consumer of the products in question'.
[142] Joined Cases C-501/06 P, C-513/06 P, C-515/06 P, and C-519/06 P *GlaxoSmithKline Services
Unlimited v Commission* [2009] ECR I-9291, paras 58–67.
[143] ibid para 59, relying on Case 19/77 *Miller International Schallplaten v Commission* [1978] ECR
131 and Joined Cases 32/78 and 36/78 to 82/78 *BMW Belgium v Commission* [1979] ECR 2435.
[144] Joined Cases C-501/06 P, C-513/06 P, C-515/06 P, and Case C-501/06 P *GlaxoSmithKline*,
para 61.

consumers. The Court made three points: (a) nothing in Article 101 indicates that 'only those agreements which deprive consumers of certain advantages may have an anti-competitive object'; (b) Article 101, like other EU competition rules, 'aims to protect not only the interests of competitors or of consumers, but also the structure of the market and, in so doing, competition as such'; and (c) as a consequence, 'for a finding that an agreement has an anti-competitive object, it is not necessary that final consumers be deprived of the advantages of effective competition in terms of supply or price'.[145] The most significant part of the judgment is the statement that Article 101 *and* the other EU competition rules, including, therefore, Article 102, protect competitors, consumers, and the structure of the market. This can be read as an endorsement of a social welfare objective over a consumer welfare objective and of a long-term objective over a short-term one.

The link between the EU competition rules and long-term social welfare rather than consumer welfare is even clearer in cases where there is no direct impact from the anti-competitive practice on consumer prices. A notable example is *T-Mobile Netherlands v Raad van bestuur van de Nederlandse Mededingingsautoriteit*. In that case, the Dutch mobile phone operators had exchanged confidential informa-tion relating to the remuneration payable to dealers for certain subscriptions.[146] Having restated that the purpose of Article 101 is not only to protect competitors or consumers but also the structure of competition, the Court of Justice held that 'in order to find that a concerted practice has an anti-competitive object, there does not need to be a direct link between that practice and consumer prices'.[147] Therefore, the fixing of an element of the dealers' remuneration was not anti-competitive because it resulted in higher consumer prices, which was established on the facts[148] and open to the Court as a way of condemning the practice under review. It was anti-competitive because it allowed the firms in question to distort competition, namely to put in place conditions of competition on the market that differed from the conditions of normal competition.[149] The rationale for the pro-hibition must be found in the objectives of the Treaties and, in particular, in the objective of promoting long-term productivity growth. Collusion on the dealers' remuneration diminishes the mobile phone operators' and the distributors' incen-tives to maximize distributional efficiencies. Inefficient suppliers would not be penalized through higher fees charged by distributors and efficient distributors would not benefit from increased fees charged to the suppliers. This is capable of harming productivity whether or not final prices are affected. Ultimately, dimin-ished suppliers' and distributors' incentives to maximize efficiencies in distribution are likely to harm consumers. But harm to final consumers is neither a necessary nor a sufficient condition for the application of Article 101.

The *GlaxoSmithKline* and *T-Mobile Netherlands* cases implicitly overrule earlier statements of the Court of First Instance purporting to say that consumer welfare is the ultimate objective of the EU competition rules. One such case is *Österreichische*

---

[145] ibid para 63.
[146] Case C-8/08 *T-Mobile Netherlands BV v Raad van bestuur van de Nederlandse Mededingingsautoriteit* [2009] ECR I-4529.
[147] ibid para 39.   [148] ibid para 37.   [149] ibid paras 31–35.

Postsparkasse v Commission, where the Court of First Instance had to rule on whether a customer of the infringing undertaking had a legitimate interest which entitled him to complain to the Commission about an infringement of the EU competition rules.[150] The Court held that a customer who is harmed in his economic interests by an alleged infringement of EU competition law has a legitimate interest to make a complaint to the Commission.[151] The Court went on to say:[152]

It should be pointed out in this respect that the ultimate purpose of the rules that seek to ensure that competition is not distorted in the internal market is to increase the well-being of consumers. That purpose can be seen in particular from the wording of Article 81 EC [Article 101 TFEU]. Whilst the prohibition laid down in Article 81(1) EC [Article 101(1) TFEU] may be declared inapplicable in the case of cartels which contribute to improving the production or distribution of the goods in question or to promoting technical or economic progress that possibility, for which provision is made in Article 81(3) EC [Article 101(3) TFEU], is inter alia subject to the condition that a fair share of the resulting benefit is allowed for users of those products. Competition law and competition policy therefore have an undeniable impact on the specific economic interests of final customers who purchase goods or services. Recognition that such customers—who show that they have suffered economic damage as a result of an agreement or conduct liable to restrict or distort competition—have a legitimate interest in seeking from the Commission a declaration that Articles 81 EC and 82 EC [Articles 101 TFEU and 102 TFEU] have been infringed contributes to the attainment of the objectives of competition law.

The Court is undeniably correct in saying that consumers who have suffered loss have a legitimate interest in seeking an infringement decision from the Commission. This contributes to the attainment of the objectives of EU competition law because it empowers those who have been harmed by an alleged infringement to make a complaint to the Commission. It is far from clear, however, that this has anything to do with the ultimate objective of EU competition law. The statement as to the objective of competition law was not necessary to the Court's ruling. Legitimate interest is capable of being construed independently of the objective of competition law. The objective of competition law determines what a restriction of competition is. The definition of legitimate interest is a different question and may be resolved by focusing on the nature of the interest affected and the causal link between the effect on a relevant interest and the alleged infringement. Following the Court's reasoning in *Österreichische Postsparkasse*, however, competitors would have no standing to complain to the Commission because the objective of competition law is the protection of consumer welfare. This is not only contrary to the established practice on standing in Commission proceedings[153]

---

[150] Joined Cases T-213/01 and T-214/01 *Österreichische Postsparkasse AG v Commission* [2006] ECR II-1601.

[151] ibid, para 114.   [152] ibid, para 115.

[153] Commission Notice on the handling of complaints by the Commission under Articles 81 and 82 of the EC Treaty [2004] OJ C101/65, para 36.

and the case law of the EU courts on standing under Article 263 TFEU[154] but also the case law on the right to damages for breaches of the EU competition rules. As regards the standing of claimants in proceedings for the recovery of damages, EU law does not adopt the protective purpose doctrine of German law[155] or the antitrust injury doctrine of US law[156] to determine the complainant or claimant's standing in competition proceedings.[157] The EU law rule is that if a person suffered loss as a result of an infringement of the competition rules, he is entitled to recover damages, provided there is a causal link between the infringement and the loss.[158] If issues of standing were to be determined in the light of a purported consumer welfare objective of EU law, the case law would have given standing only to consumers. Nor can any argument be derived from the mention of consumers in Article 101(3) or, indeed, in Article 102(b). Again, the argument would prove too much. Focusing on Article 101(3), if the condition that a fair share of the benefits of an agreement, which falls under Article 101(1), must accrue to consumers demonstrates that the purpose of Article 101 is to protect consumers, then why is detriment to consumers not mentioned in Article 101(1)? This would be even more striking because the burden of proof as regards the conditions under Article 101(3) is on the undertakings concerned. It would then be for the undertakings to prove the gravamen or essential element of the offence, while the authority or claimant would have to prove only a restriction of competition. More importantly, consumer benefits are not sufficient to absolve an undertaking from an infringement of Article 101. An agreement that restricts competition but benefits consumers may still be an infringement of Article 101 if it eliminates all competition. But if

[154] Competitors are routinely given standing either to challenge a decision to reject a complaint or accept commitments in Art 101 or 102 or merger proceedings (eg Case T-170/06 *Alrosa Company Ltd v Commission* [2007] ECR II-2601) or to intervene in proceedings brought by the addressees of the decision (eg Case C-385/07 P *Der Grüne Punkt—Duales System Deutschland*).

[155] The protective purpose doctrine is well established under German tort law, where the claimant is only entitled to compensation if he suffers harm as a consequence of the violation of a norm the purpose of which was to protect a person in the position of the claimant from the harm in question. See M Ruffert, 'Rights and Remedies in European Community law: A Comparative View' [1997] CML Rev 307, 311–312. This concept is not alien to English tort law. In English law, a cause of action in tort arises from the breach of a duty imposed by statute if it can be shown that the 'statutory duty was imposed for the protection of a limited class of the public and that Parliament intended to confer on members of that class a private right of action for breach of the duty': *X (minors) v Bedfordshire County Council* [1995] 2 AC 633, 731, (Lord Browne-Wilkinson). On the tort of breach of statutory duty, see R Buckley, 'Breach of Statutory Duty' in A Dugdale and M Jones (eds), *Clerk & Lindsell on Torts* (20th edn London, Sweet & Maxwell 2010) 565.

[156] In *Brunswick Corp v Pueblo Bowl-O-Mat, Inc* 429 US 477 (1977), the US Supreme Court required that, in order to recover damages, a plaintiff must show antitrust injury, defined as 'injury of the type the antitrust laws were intended to prevent and that flows from that which makes defendants' acts unlawful' (ibid 429 US 489).

[157] The Court of Justice implicitly rejected the protective purpose doctrine in a case concerned with the right to damages for a breach of Art 101: see Joined Cases C-295/04 P to C-298/04 P *Vincenzo Manfredi v Lloyd Adriatico Assicurazioni SpA* [2006] ECR I-6619. See also R Nazzini, 'Potency and Act of the Principle of Effectiveness: The Development of Competition Law Remedies in Community Law' in C Barnard and O Odudu (eds), *The Outer Limits of European Union Law* (Oxford, Hart Publishing 2009) 401, 421–422.

[158] Case C-453/99 *Courage Ltd v Bernard Crehan* [2001] ECR I-6297, para 26; Joined Cases C-295/04 P to C-298/04 P *Vincenzo Manfredi v Lloyd Adriatico Assicurazioni SpA*, para 90 (on the right to damages) and paras 61–62 (on the requirement of causation).

consumer welfare is the ultimate purpose of the law, it would be absurd for the law to prohibit an agreement that benefits consumers. Therefore, consumer welfare cannot be the ultimate objective of Article 101. Of course, it can be objected that preserving competition in the long term is also beneficial to consumers. But then the argument in favour of consumer welfare as the objective of Article 101 loses all weight because the preservation of competition in the long term, while beneficial to consumer welfare, is also beneficial to social welfare, productivity, economic growth, and the competitiveness of the industry. It is wholly arbitrary to pick out one of the long-term benefits of an effective competitive process and elevate it to the only objective of EU competition law, perhaps because of its political or populist attraction.

The rejection of consumer welfare as the objective of EU competition law does not mean that the protection of consumers is irrelevant under the competition rules. Article 12 TFEU provides that 'consumer protection requirements shall be taken into account in defining and implementing other Union policies and activities'. It is noteworthy that consumer protection is not one of the objectives of the Union but a principle to be taken into account when defining and implementing EU policies and activities. The objective of fostering long-term social welfare through the protection of competition is consistent with consumer protection requirements because consumers, as members of the wider society, which includes producers and workers, benefit from the pursuit of such an objective. An illustration of how the EU courts apply competition law, taking into account consumer protection, is *Sot Lélos kai Sia*, a case in which the Court of Justice was asked to rule on whether a dominant undertaking's refusal to meet orders in full for the purpose of limiting parallel trade in its pharmaceutical products was an infringement of Article 102.[159] The Court's starting point was the need to protect effective competition, understood in terms of constraint on price exerted by alternative sources of supply.[160] A dominant undertaking that refuses to supply its customers in the Member State of export with the effect of eliminating all effective competition from them in the Member State of import thus infringes Article 102.[161] The Court then emphasized the importance of market integration, which brings about benefits in terms of supply and prices for final consumers in the Member State of import.[162] However, the 'objectives to protect consumers by means of undistorted competition and the integration of national market' prevented an interpretation of the EU competition rules which would result in a dominant undertaking finding it more rational not to supply a low price market at all in order to avoid parallel imports.[163] As a consequence, a dominant undertaking must be allowed to protect its own commercial interests by refusing to accept orders that are 'out of the ordinary'.[164] Adopting a wider approach than in the *GlaxoSmithKline* and *T-Mobile Netherlands* cases, the Court considered and rejected the dominant undertaking's argument that parallel

---

[159] Joined Cases C-468/06 P to C-478/06 P *Sot Lélos kai Sia EE v GlaxoSmithKline AEVE Farmakeftikon Proionton*, paras 9–27.

[160] ibid para 64, in the light of paras 53, 55, and 56.

[161] ibid para 35.   [162] ibid paras 65–66.   [163] ibid para 68.

[164] ibid paras 69–71.

trade did not benefit the final consumer by pointing out that parallel trade exercises a downward pressure on prices in the Member State of import.[165]

Sot Lélos kai Sia does not do much to shed light on the objective of the EU competition rules. The approach of the Court, however, appears to be an attempt to integrate consumer protection requirements in a wider framework rather than to adopt consumer welfare as the objective of EU competition law. Such an approach differs significantly from the Opinion of Advocate General Jacobs in *Synetairismos Farmakopoion Aitolias & Akarnanias (Syfait) v GlaxoSmithKline*,[166] a reference in the same national case, which was, however, declared inadmissible.[167] The Advocate General considered that parallel trade could result in products not being marketed, or being marketed later, in low-price Member States, and in diminished incentives for pharmaceutical firms to invest in R&D of new products. Such a negative effect on 'output and consumer welfare' meant that the conduct under review was not abusive.[168] Advocate General Ruiz-Jarabo Colomer, in the *Sot Lélos kai Sia* case, took a more orthodox view and focused on the objective of protecting freedom of trade between Member States, relying on the case law on free movement of goods to support his view that price regulation in the Member States did not justify a practice by a dominant undertaking aimed at preventing parallel imports.[169]

(4) Fairness

(a) Fairness and equally efficient competitors

The case law of the EU courts contains clear statements to the effect that the competition rules protect freedom and fairness. Notwithstanding the harsh criticism that some commentators have levelled at this approach,[170] it is impossible to deny

---

[165] Ibid paras 52–57.
[166] Opinion of AG Jacobs in Case C-53/03 *Synetairismos Farmakopoion Aitolias & Akarnanias (Syfait) v GlaxoSmithKline plc* [2005] ECR I-4609.
[167] ibid.
[168] ibid paras 89–95. Formally, the AG dealt with the issue as an objective justification but he took the view that the distinction between abuse and objective justification was 'somewhat artificial': ibid para 72.
[169] Opinion of AG Ruiz-Jarabo Colomer in Joined Cases C-468/06 P to C-478/06 P *Sot Lélos kai Sia EE v GlaxoSmithKline AEVE Farmakeftikon Proionton*, paras 53: 'it is evident that the intention of GSK is contrary to the objectives of the Treaty, since it affects freedom of trade between Member States to an extent which might harm the attainment of a single market', and 88: 'Although the prohibition contained in Article 28 EC [Article 34 TFEU] cannot be invoked against undertakings, the obligation not to impede the objectives of the Treaty, and in particular freedom of trade between Member States, applies to them in the form of Articles 81 EC and 82 EC [Articles 101 and 102 TFEU], which state that conduct which causes the artificial partitioning of national markets and impairs competition is incompatible with the Treaty. It is therefore appropriate to mention the case-law of the Court of Justice on the free movement of goods, at least inasmuch as it concerns the partitioning of national markets.' At para 87, the AG relied on Joined Cases C-267/95 P and C-268/95 P *Merck & Co Inc v Primecrown Ltd* [1996] ECR I-6285 for the proposition that price regulation does not justify a derogation from the principle of the free movement of goods, which he applied by analogy under Art 102 TFEU.
[170] IS Forrester, 'Article 82: Remedies in Search of Theories?' (2005) 28 Fordham Intl LJ 919, 919–920; Korah, *An Introductory Guide to EC Competition Law and Practice* 14.

that EU competition law is concerned with fairness.[171] In fact, fairness is part of the tests set out in Articles 101(3), which requires, as a condition for its application, that a 'fair share' of the benefits of an agreement caught by Article 101(1) be passed on to consumers, and Article 102(a), which lists as a possible abuse the imposition of 'unfair' prices or other trading conditions. Therefore, the problem is not whether EU competition law is, or should be, concerned with fairness but what fairness means in EU competition law. The answer lies in the definition of the objective of the EU competition rules, namely the promotion of long-term social welfare. Fairness must be interpreted in the light of that objective and not as a free-standing concept. It is simply impossible, as a matter of principled theory and logic, to define fairness independently of the objective being pursued.[172]

Deutsche Telekom illustrates the meaning of fairness in EU competition law.[173] In that case, the Commission decided that Deutsche Telekom had abused its dominant position by imposing 'unfair prices in the form of a margin squeeze to the detriment of competitors'.[174] The Commission held that there is 'an abusive margin squeeze if the difference between the retail prices charged by a dominant undertaking and the wholesale prices it charges its competitors for comparable services is negative, or insufficient to cover the product-specific costs to the dominant operator of providing its own retail services on the downstream market'.[175] The Court of First Instance upheld this approach, stating that there is a margin squeeze if, given the wholesale and retail prices of the dominant undertaking, an equally efficient competitor would not be able to offer its services otherwise than at a loss.[176] The Court of Justice agreed.[177] Unfairness has, therefore, a very specific meaning in this case. It does not denote any harm to a competitor or any disadvantage that a smaller firm may suffer by reason of its lesser size or financial resources. Nor does it require a level playing field as such, in which all firms have the 'right' to be viable on the market. Unfairness denotes a practice of a dominant firm that excludes an equally efficient competitor from the market. From the point of view

---

[171] There is no evidence that the origin of this terminology had anything to do with ordoliberal thinking, not least because it appeared first in the Dutch proposal (see 129–130 above). For the ordo-liberals, competition was necessary not only for market performance but also to protect fairness and equality of opportunities on the market: F Böhm, 'Freiheit und Ordnung in der Marktwirtschaft' (1971) 22 ORDO 11, 20: 'Denn vom Wettbewerb hängt nicht nur der Leistungspegel ab, der den Wachstumspolitikern verständlicherweise zunächst am Herzen liegt, sondern auch der *Freiheits-, Gleichheits- und Gerechtigkeitsgehalt des markwirtschaftlichen Systems.*' All members of the society had to perceive the market as fair with equal opportunities to all market participants. Since market power implied that the market was unfair, market power was an obstacle to social integration: W Eucken, *Grundsätze der Wirtschaftpolitik* (6th edn Tübingen, JCB Mohr 1990) 185. Eucken, 'Die Wettbewerbsordnung und ihre Verwrklichung', 27, argued that: 'Wie der Rechtsstaat so soll auch die Wettbewerbsordnung einen Rahmen schaffen, in dem die freie Betätigung des einzelnen durch die Freiheitssphäre des anderen begrenzt wird und so die menschlichen Freiheitsbereiche ins Gleichgewicht gelangen.' On the political dimension of competition law see also Eucken, *Grundsätze der Wirtschaftpolitik* 150–168 and W Röpke, *Civitas Humana* (Erlenbach-Zürich, Eugen Rentsch 1946) 372.

[172] See 21–24 above.   [173] Case T-271/03 *Deutsche Telekom*.

[174] *Deutsche Telekom AG* [2003] OJ L263/9, recital 201.   [175] ibid recital 107.

[176] Case T-271/03 *Deutsche Telekom*, paras 186–194.

[177] Case C-280/08 P *Deutsche Telekom*, para 167. See also Case C-52/09 *TeliaSonera*, para 34.

of the competitor, a practice is unfair when it forces it to incur losses in order to stay on the market even if it is as efficient as the dominant undertaking. This idea of fairness is consistent with the objective of promoting long-term social welfare. Firms that are less efficient than the dominant one must not be protected because to do so would entail productive inefficiency even if consumer welfare increased in the short term. The loss of productive efficiency is not justified by lower prices because EU competition law is not concerned with short-term consumer welfare but with firms' incentives to lower their costs and improve their products in the long term.

In EU law, a system of undistorted competition also requires equality of opportunities among firms in terms of access to the market and actual competition. In *Connect Austria Gesellschaft für Telekommunikation GmbH v Telekom-Control-Kommission*,[178] Austrian legislation provided that frequencies in the DCS 1800 band could be allocated to a public undertaking holding a dominant position on a relevant market in the mobile telecommunications sector[179] without the payment of an additional fee. Other undertakings were charged a fee for the allocation of frequencies in the same band.[180] The Court of Justice held that the Austrian legislation was in breach of Articles 102 and 106(1) TFEU, as it distorted competition because it did not ensure equal opportunities for firms.[181] It could be argued that the judgment is limited to the telecoms sector or regulated sectors. It is undoubtedly true that the regulatory framework features prominently in the case[182] and that equality of opportunities may have been considered particularly important in a recently liberalized market.[183] However, the Court affirmed the principle of equality of opportunities in the discussion of Articles 102 and 106(1) without any reference to the regulatory framework or the need to interpret the competition rules differently in a recently liberalized or regulated sector. Nor is it possible

---

[178] Case C-462/99 *Connect Austria Gesellschaft für Telekommunikation GmbH v Telekom-Control-Kommission and Mobilkom Austria AG* [2003] ECR I-5197.

[179] The Court identified three possible relevant market definitions: ibid para 76.

[180] ibid paras 18–20 and 28.

[181] ibid paras 80–88 and 95. Given that the dominant undertaking had been charged a fee for the GSM 900 licence, the Court recognized that if the overall fees paid by the dominant undertaking for the GSM 900 and the DCS 1800 bands were equivalent in economic terms to the fees paid by its competitors for the DCS 1800 band, equality of opportunities would be observed: ibid paras 89–95.

[182] ibid paras 3–17 and 96–118. A stronger argument for limiting the principle to regulated sectors could be made on the facts of Joined Cases C-327/03 P and C-328/03 P *Bundesrepublik Deutschland v ISIS Multimedia Net GmbH und Co KG* [2005] ECR I-8877, where the Court applied the principle of equality of opportunities to determine the legality of charges for the allocation of telephone numbers under Art 11(2) of Directive (EC) 97/13 of 10 April 1997 on a common framework for general authorisations and individual licences in the field of telecommunications services [1997] OJ L117/15. The third condition of Art 11(2) of the Directive required Member States to take into account the need to foster the development of innovative services and competition. While the Court reasoned in terms of Art 102 and undistorted competition (ibid paras 39–44), it was applying a provision in a regulated sector and not the competition rules of the TFEU (see, in particular, para 45, where the Court referred to the policy objective of 'making a significant contribution to the entry of new operators into the market').

[183] The Court pointed out that the claimant was 'a new entrant on the market' (Case C-462/99 *Connect Austria*, para 85) and that the dominant undertaking was 'a former monopoly which already enjoys a number of advantages' (ibid para 96).

to maintain that the principle only applies to State measures when Article 102 is applied in conjunction with Article 106(1). Following its settled case law, in *Connect Austria* the Court said that Articles 106(1) and 102 prevent Member States from adopting measures that inevitably lead a public undertaking or an undertaking having special or exclusive rights to abuse its dominant position.[184] It then relied on the definition of abuse under Article 102[185] and went on to state that 'a system of undistorted competition, as laid down in the Treaty, can be guaranteed only if equality of opportunities is secured as between the various economic operators'.[186] The principle of equality of opportunities has since been reaffirmed by the Court of Justice in *MOTOE*, a case relating to the power of an organizer of motorcycling events to veto the granting of administrative authorizations for the carrying out of such events by its competitors.[187] Equality of opportunities is, therefore, a general principle of EU competition law, which is not limited to the assessment of State measures under Article 106(1).

The Court of First Instance applied the principle of equality of opportunities to determine the issue of which products must be included in the margin squeeze test in *Deutsche Telekom*. In that case, the Court held that, under Article 102, undertakings must have equal opportunities to compete within the single market.[188] This means that competitors must be able to compete on an equal footing with the dominant undertaking. In *Deutsche Telekom*, the dominant undertaking provided access to its unbundled local loop, which could be used by competitors to offer a number of downstream services. Those services included analogue, ISDN, and

---

[184] Case C-462/99 *Connect Austria*, para 80; Case C-18/88 *Régie des télégraphes et des téléphones v GB-Inno-BM SA* [1991] ECR I-5941, para 20; Case C-242/95 *GT-Link A/S v De Danske Statsbaner (DSB)* [1997] ECR I-4449, paras 33–34; Case C-203/96 *Chemische Afvalstoffen Dusseldorp BV v Minister van Volkshuisvesting, Ruimtelijke Ordening en Milieubeheer* [1998] ECR I-4075, para 61.

[185] Case C-462/99 *Connect Austria*, para 81; Case 85/76 *Hoffmann-La Roche*, para 90; Case 322/81 *Michelin I*, para 73.

[186] Case C-462/99 *Connect Austria*, para 83. See also Case C-202/88 *French Republic v Commission* [1991] ECR I-1223, a case concerned, *inter alia*, with the review of the legality of a Commission Directive adopted under Art 106(3) TFEU providing that Member States were to entrust the function of drawing up the specifications for telecommunications terminal equipment, monitoring their application, and granting type-approval to a body independent of the firms active on the market. In that case, the Court said at para 51: 'It should be observed that a system of undistorted competition, as laid down in the Treaty, can be guaranteed only if equality of opportunity is secured as between the various economic operators. To entrust an undertaking which markets terminal equipment with the task of drawing up the specifications for such equipment, monitoring their application and granting type-approval in respect thereof is tantamount to conferring upon it the power to determine at will which terminal equipment may be connected to the public network, and thereby placing that undertaking at an obvious advantage over its competitors.' The case relates, again, to a State measure but the principle of equality of opportunities is laid down in general fashion as an element of the system of undistorted competition envisaged in the Treaties. In Case C-18/88 *Régie des télégraphes et des téléphones v GB-Inno-BM* the Court relied on para 51 of Case C-202/88 *French Republic v Commission* in the more specific context of Arts 102 and 106(1) TFEU.

[187] Case C-49/07 *Motosykletistiki Omospondia Ellados NPID (MOTOE) v Elliniko Dimosio* [2008] ECR I-4863, para 51.

[188] Case T-271/03 *Deutsche Telekom*, para 198, upheld in Case C-280/08 P *Deutsche Telekom*, paras 219–222 and 230–243. The Court of First Instance relied on Case C-462/99 *Connect Austria*, para 83, and Joined Cases C-327/03 P and C-328/03 P *Bundesrepublik Deutschland v ISIS Multimedia Net*, para 39. The Court of Justice cited in addition Case C-49/07 *MOTOE*, para 51.

ADSL retail access services and call services. The Commission had excluded call services from the margin squeeze calculation. It had determined the price charged for wholesale access and compared it to a weighted average of the prices charged for analogue, ISDN, and ADSL retail access services.[189] The Court of First Instance upheld the decision on the ground that equality of opportunities among economic players required that the dominant undertaking's equally efficient competitors could reflect their wholesale costs in their retail prices. If they could not, they could be forced to offset the losses incurred on providing access services through higher call charges. This would 'distort competition in telecommunications markets'.[190] The Court of Justice upheld the Court of First Instance's judgment in full, with specific reference to equality of opportunities as a free-standing legal principle under Article 102.[191]

The above analysis demonstrates that fairness is not an objective of the EU competition rules. It is a test which must be interpreted consistently with the objective of fostering long-term social welfare. Such an objective requires, in particular, that all equally efficient firms must be able to compete on an equal footing without being prejudiced as a result of the ability of dominant firms to exclude them for reasons other than superior efficiency.[192]

(b) Fairness and less efficient competitors

The strict rule against the protection of less efficient competitors in EU law is qualified with regard to undertakings that may become as efficient as the dominant firm within a reasonable timeframe but are prevented from doing so precisely because of the allegedly abusive conduct. For this to occur, the market must be characterized by early mover's advantages of the dominant firm or demand-related efficiencies such as learning curves, network effects, or economies of scale. Alternatively, the alleged abuse may involve multi-market conduct whereby the dominant undertaking is able to rely on economics of scope that cannot be replicated by entrants because simultaneous entry to all markets concerned is unrealistic.[193]

To understand how socially harmful exclusion of less efficient competitors may occur, it is sufficient to focus on the analysis of abuses that take place within the framework of only one relevant market. If the market is characterized by strong learning effects,[194] at the time of entry, an entrant's costs, all other things being equal, are by definition higher than those of the incumbent. The entrant may

---

[189] Case T-271/03 *Deutsche Telekom*, paras 106–111.

[190] ibid para 199. See also paras 196–198, where the Court referred to the relevant EU regulatory framework for telecommunications and pointed out that separate consideration of access charges and call charges was required by the EU regulatory principle of tariff rebalancing. This case could, therefore, be read as limiting the application of equality of opportunities to a regulated sector where such a principle reflects a specific regulatory objective.

[191] Case C-280/08 P *Deutsche Telekom*, paras 233.

[192] On the as efficient competitor test see Ch 7 below.

[193] See eg DW Carlton and M Waldman, 'The Strategic Use of Tying to Preserve and Create Market Power in Evolving Industries' (2002) 33 RAND Journal of Economics 194.

[194] Learning effects occur when cost reductions are achieved because of experience gained over time. Average costs decline while cumulative output increases. For an example of the standard

become as or more efficient than the incumbent only by being on the market long enough and by moving along its learning curve. Thus, to use a numerical example, if, at the time of entry, the incumbent's average cost is £20 and the entrant's average cost is £25, the incumbent may inflict losses on the entrant by charging a price of £21. The argument that the entrant is less efficient than the incumbent and, there-fore, that its exclusion from the market would not harm long-term social welfare and productivity would be fallacious. Because of learning effects, the entrant may achieve an average cost (AC) of £18 after he has produced a certain output. The incumbent's above-cost price cut, however, may have the effect of preventing the entrant from producing the output required to achieve the maximum cost reduc-tion achievable. Exactly the same principle applies to other early movers' advan-tages or demand-related efficiencies, such as network effects or economies of scale. As a consequence, an exclusionary price need not be below the dominant under-taking's costs.[195]

The Commission Guidance on Article 102 recognizes this problem. While the Commission appears to set a safe harbour for prices that are not capable of excluding an equally efficient competitor,[196] this safe harbour is qualified by the statement that anti-competitive foreclosure, which the Commission defines as foreclosure leading to consumer harm, may also occur when the prices of the dominant undertaking exclude a less efficient competitor. The constraint exerted by a less efficient competitor must be assessed dynamically because 'in the absence of an abusive practice such a competitor may benefit from demand-related advantages, such as network and learning effects, which will tend to enhance its efficiency'.[197]

This principle is consistent with the objectives of Article 102. If there are signifi-cant demand-related efficiencies and the abuse prevents the entrant from becom-ing as efficient as the dominant undertaking by denying him the benefit of such efficiencies, exclusion would appear to be likely to harm long-term social welfare and productivity. If each time economies of scale, learning by doing, or network effects are significant, the incumbent is allowed to exclude the rival, the efficiency

treatment of learning effects in industrial organization literature, see D Besanko et al, *Economics of Strategy* (5th edn Hoboken NJ, Wiley 2010) 95–101.

[195] OE Williamson, 'Predatory Pricing: A Strategic and Welfare Analysis' (1977) 87 Yale LJ 284, 303–304. E Elhauge, 'Why Above-Cost Price Cuts to Drive out Entrants Are Not Predatory: and the Implications for Defining Costs and Market Power' (2003) 112 Yale LJ 681, 779–782, accepts that if an entrant will become as efficient as the incumbent and this is not at the expense of the incumbent's efficiency, then entry of potentially as efficient competitors is beneficial. However, he goes on to argue that, if this is the case, capital markets will fund any necessary start-up losses: ibid 782–786. The assumption of efficient capital markets, however, cannot be generalized: D Gale and M Hellwig, 'Incentive Compatible Debt Contracts: The One-Period Problem' (1985) 52 Rev Econ Stud 647; RM Townsend, 'Optimal Contracts and Competitive Markets with Costly State Verification' (1979) 21 Journal of Economic Theory 265; DW Diamond, 'Financial Intermediation and Delegated Monitoring' (1984) 51 Rev Econ Stud 393.

[196] Communication from the Commission—Guidance on the Commission's enforcement pri-orities in applying Article 82 of the EC Treaty to abusive exclusionary conduct by dominant under-takings [2009] OJ C45/7 ('Guidance on Art 102'), para 23.

[197] ibid para 24.

and innovation incentives of the dominant undertaking and its rivals would be materially weakened. The dominant undertaking would be given carte blanche to protect its market power in circumstances in which social welfare would be improved without any long-term sacrifice in productive efficiency. Firms which can achieve the same efficiency as the incumbent would be deterred from entering. Entry would only take place if the entrant were more efficient than the dominant undertaking so that it could offset any disadvantage resulting from switching costs or demand-related efficiencies, or could offer a new product, which improved significantly on the product of the dominant undertaking. Considering that the market in question is, by definition, already characterized by substantial market power protected by significant barriers to entry and unconstrained by customers, this would be too high a hurdle to set for entry to occur.

Finally, prohibiting the exclusion of potentially equally efficient competitors is not contrary to the principle of equality of opportunities between the dominant undertaking and its competitors,[198] provided that two conditions are met: (a) the competitor is likely to become as efficient as the dominant undertaking within a reasonable period of time; and (b) conduct by the dominant undertaking that fulfils the other conditions for abuse is preventing the competitor from becoming at least as efficient as itself.

(5) Economic freedom

A number of cases describe a restriction of competition as a restriction of the economic freedom of competitors or customers. This is true of the case law under both Articles 102 and 101.

The case law on rebates is illustrative of the role of the economic freedom concept under Article 102. In *Michelin I*, the Court of Justice ruled that to determine whether a rebate system applied by a dominant firm was abusive it was necessary to consider 'all the circumstances' and 'to investigate whether, in providing an advantage not based on any economic service justifying it, the rebate tends to remove or restrict the buyer's freedom to choose his sources of supply, to bar competitors from access to the market, to apply dissimilar conditions to equivalent transactions . . . or to strengthen the dominant position by distorting competition'.[199] The Court placed considerable weight on the 'pressure' on dealers to reach the annual target,[200] on the limitation of the customer's 'freedom of choice and independence',[201] and on the position of 'dependence' in which dealers found themselves.[202] However, the restriction of freedom was not the only element of the analysis. The Court also relied on the exclusion of competitors.[203] The question to be asked is whether the restriction of freedom test would have been capable of sustaining a finding of abuse regardless of the exclusionary rationale. The answer is clearly no. If competitors had been able to offer comparable discounts, the dealers' economic freedom would not

---

[198] See 74–76 above.   [199] Case 322/81 *Michelin I*, para 73.   [200] ibid paras 81 and 84.
[201] ibid para 85.   [202] ibid.   [203] ibid paras 82, 84, and 85.

have been restricted for the very simple reason that they could have switched to the dominant firm's competitors without incurring any significant additional costs. The same conclusion would hold if the dominant firm had no actual or potential competitors. No restriction of freedom could be envisaged in such a market. The economic freedom protected in *Michelin I* is, therefore, the freedom to be able to select one's suppliers based on competitive market forces. The primary concept is that of competition, to be defined in the light of the objective of fostering long-term social welfare. The concept of economic freedom derives from the concept of competition. It constitutes its individualization. The Court of Justice clearly hinted at this doctrine when it said in *Michelin I* that the effect of the rebates under review was 'calculated to prevent dealers from being able to select freely at any time in the light of the market situation the most favourable of the offers made by the various competitors and to change supplier without suffering any appreciable economic disadvantage'.[204] At the same time, a restriction of economic freedom is the vehicle through which the exclusionary effect is achieved. In the absence of the restriction, customers would choose other suppliers, who are perhaps as efficient or even more efficient than the dominant firm. Again, the Court explained this by saying that the rebates limited the dealers' choice of supplier and made access to the market more difficult for competitors.[205] The restriction of freedom can be seen as the cause of the exclusionary effect. This interpretation of *Michelin I* is borne out by the analysis of the subsequent case law, which has recast the test for anti-competitive rebates as requiring an exclusionary effect whereby the restriction of the customer's freedom is an element of the exclusionary strategy of the dominant firm.[206]

The case law under Article 101 appears to make a distinction between the restriction of the freedom to trade and the restriction of commercial freedom. In *Bayerische Motorenwerke AG v ALD Auto-Leasing D GmbH*, the Court of Justice was asked to rule on the compatibility of a prohibition imposed by BMW on its dealers to supply cars to independent leasing companies unless the lessee's residence or seat was within the dealer's territory.[207] The Court said that the agreement amounted to absolute territorial protection for BMW dealers in relation to the lessees within their territories. The Court added:[208]

Furthermore, the agreement reduces each dealer's freedom of commercial action in so far as each individual dealer's choice of customer is confined exclusively to those leasing companies which have concluded contracts with lessees established within that dealer's contract territory.

---

[204] ibid para 85.   [205] ibid.   [206] Case C-95/04 P *British Airways*, para 69.
[207] Case C-70/93 *Bayerische Motorenwerke AG v ALD Auto-Leasing D GmbH* [1995] ECR I-3439, paras 1–14.
[208] ibid para 91. See also Case C-306/96 *Javico International and Javico AG v Yves Saint Laurent Parfums SA (YSLP)* [1998] ECR I-1983, para 13: 'As far as agreements intended to apply within the Community are concerned, the Court has already held that an agreement intended to deprive a reseller of his commercial freedom to choose his customers by requiring him to sell only to customers established in the contractual territory is restrictive of competition within the meaning of Article 85(1) of the Treaty [now Article 101(1) of TFEU].'

The use of the term 'furthermore' might suggest that the restriction of commercial freedom is a totally independent basis for the finding of a restriction of competition. However, this is quite difficult to justify as a matter of logic. Any contract which the law considers binding under certain conditions results in a limitation of freedom. But not all contracts are restrictions of competition. The answer lies in the observation, which ought to be uncontroversial, that if the agreement under review had not conferred absolute territorial protection, the restriction of the dealers' commercial freedom under the contract would have been irrelevant. The restriction of freedom is an infringement of Article 101 because it limits the dealers' opportunities to trade within the internal market. The primary reason for the prohibition is the market-partitioning object and effect of the agreement, not the restriction of freedom *per se*.

As far as a more general concept of commercial or economic freedom is concerned, it is now well established that not all restrictions of commercial freedom are restrictions of competition. The Court of First Instance in the *Métropole* case recognized that 'it is not necessary to hold, wholly abstractly and without drawing any distinction, that any agreement restricting the freedom of action of one or more of the parties is necessarily caught by the prohibition laid down in Article 85(1) of the Treaty [now Article 101(1) TFEU]'.[209] This proposition, which has since been endorsed by the Court of Justice,[210] is uncontroversial since agreements that are not restrictive by object can only be found to have an anti-competitive effect following a thorough market inquiry.[211] A restriction of freedom cannot, therefore, by definition be a sufficient condition for a finding of infringement under Article 101. The very concept of economic freedom can only be defined in the light of the objective of the protection of competition. The economic freedom which EU competition protects is, therefore, the freedom of economic agents not to be limited in their economic activity by any behaviour of firms that reduces market rivalry so as to harm social welfare in the long term. On this analysis, freedom is the individualization of the objective concept of competition, which the Treaties protect.

D. Conclusion

This chapter searched for the objective of Article 102. The literal interpretation of Article 102 sheds little light on its objective. The only element that points to the purpose of the prohibition is the requirement that abuses of a dominant position are prohibited as 'incompatible with the internal market'. Therefore, the purpose

---

[209] Case T-112/99 *Métropole télévision (M6)*, para 76.
[210] Case C-309/99 *JCJ Wouters v Algemene Raad van de Nederlandse Orde van Advocaten*, para 97.
[211] Settled case law: see Case 56/65 *Société Technique Minière (LTM) v Maschinenbau Ulm (MBU)*; Case 23/67 *Brasserie de Haecht v Wilkin*; Case C-234/89 *Stergios Delimitis v Henninger Bräu*; Joined Cases T-374/94, T-375/94, T-384/94, and T-388/94 *European Night Services Ltd (ENS)*; Case T-328/03 *O2 (Germany) GmbH & Co OHG*.

of Article 102 must be determined in the light of the objectives of the internal market. This is absolutely clear given the wording of Article 3 TFEU and Protocol (27) on the Internal Market and Competition.

The objectives of the internal market are manifold and can be divided into economic and social objectives. However, not all objectives can be pursued at the same time by all EU policies. Given the economic nature of the EU competition rules, what is needed to identify their objective is to discover the economic objective of the internal market. A literal interpretation of Article 3(3) reveals that the economic objective of the internal market is to maximize long-term social welfare through productivity growth. Therefore, this is also the objective of the EU competition rules and Article 102 in particular. The maximization of long-term social welfare is consistent with the pursuit of the aims and values of the Union set out in Articles 2 and 3 TEU. Detailed analysis of the *travaux préparatoires* of the Treaty of Rome corroborates the validity of the interpretation of the objective of the EU competition rules as the maximization of long-term social welfare through productivity growth. There is no trace in the *travaux préparatoires* of any significant ordoliberal influence on the drafting of the competition provisions of the Treaty.

The case law on Articles 102 and 101 and on mergers and the EU Merger Regulations contain little discussion on the objective of the competition rules. However, they are clearly inconsistent with a consumer welfare objective. On the other hand, they are compatible with a long-term social welfare objective whereby consumers also benefit from effective competition resulting in higher productivity and social welfare. The case law on Article 102 provides one of the clearest instances of the Court of Justice endorsing a long-term social welfare objective reflecting the values and preferences of the society.[212]

Fairness is not an objective of Article 102. It is a test which must be interpreted consistently with the objective of maximizing long-term social welfare. Such an objective requires, in particular, that all equally efficient firms must be able to compete on an equal footing without being prejudiced as a result of the ability of dominant firms to exclude them for reasons other than superior efficiency. This principle means that, under Article 102, a less efficient competitor must not be protected unless: (a) the competitor is likely to become as efficient as the dominant undertaking within a reasonable period of time; and (b) conduct by the dominant undertaking that fulfils the other conditions for abuse is preventing the competitor from becoming at least as efficient as itself.

Economic freedom is the individualization of the objective purpose of competition law. It is competition law seen through the lense of the relevant interests of individual firms and consumers. The economic freedom which EU competition protects is, therefore, the freedom of economic agents not to be limited in their economic activity by any behaviour of firms that reduces market rivalry so as to harm social welfare in the long term.

---

[212] Case C-52/09 *TeliaSonera*, paras 20–22.

The conclusions reached in this chapter are consistent with the normative theory of competition law developed in Chapter 2. Chapter 3 examined the abuse tests on the basis of the normative theory of competition law set out in Chapter 2. Therefore, the conclusions of Chapters 2 and 3 can be applied to the development of the abuse tests in the following chapters.

5

The General Framework of the Abuse Tests in EU Law

A. Introduction

Considerable uncertainty and a significant degree of controversy surround the tests that determine whether conduct is abusive under Article 102. The publication by the Commission of the Guidance on Article 102 in 2009 has hardly contributed to solving the problem.[1] In striking contrast with other sets of guidelines,[2] the Guidance on Article 102 is limited to explaining how the Commission will set its enforcement priorities.[3] It is not guidance on the substantive tests for abuse. It applies only as a matter of administrative discretion. Its force before national competition authorities and courts is, at most, weakly persuasive.[4] More fundamentally, the Guidance is not always consistent with the case law of the EU courts. Therefore, even if it could be valid as an exercise of administrative discretion on the part of the Commission, it carries limited weight in the substantive assessment of unilateral conduct under Article 102 before the EU courts and the national courts.

---

[1] Communication from the Commission—Guidance on the Commission's enforcement priorities in applying Article 82 of the EC Treaty to abusive exclusionary conduct by dominant undertakings ('Guidance on Art 102') [2009] OJ C45/7.

[2] eg Communication from the Commission—Notice—Guidelines on the application of Article 81(3) of the Treaty [2004] OJ C101/97 (The 'Guidelines on Art 101(3)'); Guidelines on the application of Article 81 of the EC Treaty to technology transfer agreements [2004] OJ C101/2; Guidelines on Vertical Restraints [2000] OJ C291/1; Guidelines on the assessment of horizontal mergers under the Council Regulation on the control of concentrations between undertakings [2004] OJ C31/5 ('Guidelines on Horizontal Mergers'). Guidelines on the assessment of non-horizontal mergers under the Council Regulation on the control of concentrations between undertakings [2008] OJ C265/6 ('Guidelines on Non-horizontal Mergers').

[3] Guidance on Art 102, paras 2 and 3.

[4] AC Witt, 'The Commission's Guidance Paper on Abusive Exclusionary Conduct—More Radical Than it Appears?' (2010) 35 EL Rev 214, 230–234; M Kellerbauer, 'The Commission's New Enforcement Priorities in Applying Article 82 EC to Dominant Companies' Exclusionary Conduct: A Shift towards a More Economic Approach?' (2010) 31 ECLR 175, 184–186; G Monti, 'Article 82 EC: What Future for the Effects-Based Approach?' (2010) 1 Journal of European Competition Law & Practice 2, 8; LL Gormsen, 'Why the European Commission's Enforcement Priorities on Article 82 EC Should be Withdrawn' (2010) 31 ECLR 45, 46–50; LL Gormsen, *A Principled Approach to Abuse of Dominance in European Competition Law* (Cambridge, CUP 2010) 150–164; MA Gravengaard and N Kjaersgaard, 'The EU Commission Guidance on Exclusionary Abuse of Dominance—and Its Consequences in Practice' (2010) 31 ECLR 285, 286–288.

The focus of this inquiry must be on the teleological interpretation of Article 102 and on how the case law has construed and applied the prohibition. The problem is that the case law on Article 102 has developed in a haphazard fashion, with cases often decided in a way which reflected the preoccupation of reaching the right outcome on a particular set of facts rather than the need to set out clear rules and principles applicable in future cases. As a result, it would be impossible to explain each and every case in the light of overarching principles and structured rules. Some cases are decided on their own facts and, as such, have very little precedential value. Other cases are simply wrongly decided, at least insofar as they set out principles and rules applicable to future cases. But throughout the web of the leading cases on Article 102 some common threads are always to be seen. These threads combine to form a clearly recognizable and coherent analytical structure that borrows its logical framework from the principle of proportionality.[5] The test always asks whether the conduct of the dominant undertaking prima facie restricts competition or exploits the restriction of competition inherent in the dominant position in a way that runs counter to the purpose of Article 102. The test could be rephrased as asking whether the conduct under review causes competitive harm. Bearing in mind that the purpose of Article 102 is to maximize long-term social welfare through effective competition, competitive harm can thus be defined as a restriction of competition or an exploitation of the dominant position that harms social welfare in the long term.[6] This does not mean, however, that in each and

---

[5] G de Búrca, 'The Principle of Proportionality and its Application in EC Law' (1993) 13 YEL 105; N Emiliou, *The Principle of Proportionality in European Law: A Comparative Study* (London, Kluwer Law International 1996); T Tridimas, *The General Principles of EC Law* (2nd edn Oxford, OUP 2006) 136–241; FG Jacobs, 'Recent Developments in the Principle of Proportionality in European Community Law' in E Ellis (ed), *The Principle of Proportionality in the Laws of Europe* (Oxford, Hart Publishing 1999) 1; T Tridimas, 'Proportionality in Community Law: Searching for the Appropriate Standard of Scrutiny' in E Ellis (ed), *The Principle of Proportionality in the Laws of Europe* (Oxford, Hart Publishing 1999) 65; K Lenaerts and P van Nuffel, *Constitutional Law of the European Union* (2nd edn London, Sweet & Maxwell 2005) 109–114; J Steiner, L Woods, and C Twigg-Flesner, *EU Law* (9th edn Oxford, OUP 2006) 128–130; A Arnull et al, *Wyatt & Dashwood's European Union Law* (5th edn London, Sweet & Maxwell 2006) 240–244; P Craig, *EU Administrative Law* (Oxford, OUP 2006) 631–637; C Barnard, *The Substantive Law of the EU* (3rd edn Oxford, OUP 2010) 81–82 and 497–498; TC Hartley, *The Foundations of European Community Law* (6th edn Oxford, OUP 2007) 151; S Douglas-Scott, *Constitutional Law of the European Union* (2nd edn London, Sweet & Maxwell 2004) 183–185; P Craig and G de Búrca, *EU Law: Text, Cases and Materials* (4th edn Oxford, OUP 2007) 544–551; JH Jans, 'Proportionality Revisited' (2000) 27 LIEI 239; J Christoffersen, *Fair Balance: Proportionality, Subsidiarity and Primarity in the European Convention on Human Rights* (The Hague, Martinus Nijhoff Publishers 2009) 31–226; A Stone Sweet and J Mathews, 'Proportionality, Judicial Review and Global Constitutionalism' in G Bongiovanni, G Sartor, and C Valentini (eds), *Reasonableness and Law* (Dordrecht and London, Springer 2009) 173; A Arnull, 'Gambling with Competition in Europe's Internal Market' (2009) 30 ECLR 440; C Barnard, 'Restricting Restrictions: Lessons for the EU from the US?' (2009) 68 CLJ 575; A Mowbray, 'A Study of the Principle of Fair Balance in the Jurisprudence of the European Court of Human Rights' (2010) 10 Human Rights L Rev 289; T-I Harbo, 'The Function of the Proportionality Principle in EU Law' (2010) 16 ELJ 158.

[6] This reasoning may appear to be circular but is, in fact, deductive because competitive harm is defined in the light of the objective of Art 102, which was established independently in Ch 4 above. More fundamentally, however, we would agree with the idea that 'formal objections such as the argument about "circular reasoning", which can easily be cited at any time in the study of

every case a reduction of long-term social welfare must be proved. The case law infers competitive harm from the types of anti-competitive effects that need to be established under the test applicable to the facts the case. These are the effects that, typically, mean that a certain type of harm occurs. Anti-competitive effects are only relevant because they are presumed to cause competitive harm, and thus run counter to the purpose of Article 102, according to the normal course of events.[7] If the conduct has anti-competitive effects and, therefore, is presumed to cause competitive harm, the next question is to determine whether the conduct under review generates efficiencies or has other cognizable benefits and does so in a proportionate way.[8]

This chapter identifies the key principles of the abuse test under Article 102. It starts by laying down the conceptual and contextual premises of the test under Article 102. These are the development of proportionality as an analytical structure and the application of the principle of proportionality in Union law in general and under Article 101 in particular. The chapter goes on to analyse the proportionality test under Article 102 and the key principles that shape the concept of abuse, namely the definition of abuse in the case law, effective competition, and the 'doctrine' of the special responsibility of the dominant undertaking. Then, the chapter examines the causal link between dominance, conduct, and effect. Finally, conclusions are drawn.

B. The proportionality test in context

(1) Proportionality as an analytical structure

Proportionality is, first and foremost, an analytical structure.[9] It is, strictly speaking, not a test because 'it does not, in itself, produce substantive outcomes'.[10] Proportionality is a procedure for the assessment of complex socio-economic phenomena when such an assessment requires consideration of different, often opposing, factors. In legal reasoning, proportionality is perhaps what in the past two

---

first principles, are always sterile when one is considering concrete ways of investigating. When it comes to understand the matter at hand, they carry no weight and keep us from penetrating into the field of study': M Heidegger, *Being and Time* (J Macquarrie and E Robinson trs, Malden MA USA, Blackwell Publishing 2010) 27.

[7] Under the previous Treaties, the case law established that conduct was abusive when it impaired an effective competitive structure within the meaning of Art 3(1)(g) EC: see eg 85/76 *Hoffmann-La Roche & Co AG v Commission* [1979] ECR 461, para 38; Case C-95/04 P *British Airways plc v Commission* [2007] ECR I-2331, para 106. Because Art 3(1)(g) contained what could be termed 'intermediate objectives', effective competition in itself was simply a means to achieve the general objectives set out in Art 2 EC. This teleological link between Art 102, the protection of the competitive process, and the objectives of the Union is still fundamentally the same under the current Treaties: see the discussion in Ch 4 above.

[8] eg Case C-95/04 P *British Airways plc v Commission* [2007] ECR I-2331, para 86.

[9] A Stone Sweet and J Mathews, 'Proportionality Balancing and Global Constitutionalism' (2008) 47 Columbia Journal of Transnational Law 73, 75–77.

[10] ibid 77.

centuries was the syllogism: a way of thinking about legal norms and applying them in a predictable fashion. The demise of syllogistic legal reasoning and the advent of proportionality can be explained by the increasing complexity of the social and economic matrix to which the law currently applies. The syllogistic structure can account for the subsuming of facts under a generally applicable rule. It is, however, less apt to explaining the weighing-up and balancing of different interests and factors. This was the very strength of the syllogism in the era of the liberal State when formal equality was the key guiding principle in the application of the law. The law must apply equally to equal situations. The exercise of judgment was limited to the correct interpretation of the rules and the ascertainment of the facts. The application of the rules was a logical comparison between the facts as judicially proven and the rule as judicially interpreted. With the evolution of the liberal state into the modern pluralistic democracy based on the model of social market economy, both the State and the individual have expanded their respective spheres. The conflict between objectives, interests, and values can no longer be resolved by the application of general and abstract norms based on a hierarchical approach. The resolution of the conflict requires a balancing exercise. The application of the rule becomes more complex. A mere comparison between the rule as judicially interpreted and the facts as judicially proven is no longer sufficient. To arrive at the right outcome, the court must weigh different factors against each other. Proportionality is a procedure for a meaningful and yet predictable application of rules that require consideration of different interests or factors in order to reach a decision on the case at hand.

Proportionality as an analytical structure is used in very different contexts and with different functions, including the control of discretion, the setting of a standard for judicial review, the definition of the scope of legal norms, the rationalization of the power of judges, and the balancing of different interests or rights.[11] Under Article 102, proportionality is a structured way of assessing the negative and positive effects of the conduct of dominant undertakings. Its content as a test depends on the definition of anti-competitive effects and objective justification. Its main benefit is to allow the consideration of the different effects of the conduct under review while retaining rationality in decision-making and the predictability of outcomes.

(2) Proportionality as a general principle of EU law

Competition law does not exist or develop in isolation. It forms part of the fabric of Union law. Proportionality under Article 102 is an extension and application of the analytical structure of proportionality as a general principle of Union law.

Under Article 5(1) TEU, the primary function of the principle of proportionality is to govern the exercise of the competences of the Union. Article 5(4) TEU

---

[11] A Andenas and S Zleptnig, 'Proportionality in WTO: A Comparative Perspective' (2007) 42 Texas Intl LJ 371, 384–387.

provides that 'under the principle of proportionality, the content and form of Union action shall not exceed what is necessary to achieve the objectives of the Treaties'.[12] But the principle of proportionality has a much wider scope in that action by Member States in the sphere of EU law is also subject to a proportionality scrutiny, in particular when it seeks to restrict rights conferred by EU law. It must already be clear from the brief discussion of proportionality as an analytical structure that the tests applied to review the legality of Union acts or Member States' action within the sphere of EU law cannot be the same as the proportionality test under Article 102 because the content of the tests is different. The analytical structure, however, is similar. Therefore, drawing a parallel with the proportionality test as a general principle of EU law may help to clarify some of the reasoning in the case law on Article 102.

A useful analogy to help explain the nature of the Article 102 test is the case law on restrictions on trade in goods between Member States under Articles 34 to 36 TFEU. Articles 34 and 35 prohibit quantitative restrictions on imports and exports and all measures having equivalent effect between Member States. They mirror the prohibition of restrictions of competition in Article 101(1). Article 36 provides for the power of Member States to impose restrictions on trade 'justified on grounds of public morality, public policy or public security; the protection of health and life of humans, animals or plants; the protection of national treasures possessing artistic, historic, or archaeological value; or the protection of industrial and commercial property'. However, these 'restrictions shall not…constitute a means of arbitrary discrimination or a disguised restriction on trade between Member States'.

The case law interprets these provisions in the light of the principle of proportionality. This principle, however, applies not only to the exceptions under Article 36 but also to the definition of the scope of prohibition of measures having equivalent effect to a quantitative restriction on trade. The wide definition of such measures in *Dassonville* is qualified by the application of the *Cassis de Dijon* 'rule of reason' and the *Keck* exception. The test can be stated as follows: (a) Article 34 applies to 'all trading rules enacted by Member States which are capable of hindering, directly or indirectly, actually or potentially' intra-EU trade;[13] (b) if a measure discriminates between national products and products imported from another Member State, the prohibition in Article 34 applies and the measure under review can only be allowed if the State proves that the measure is justified under Article 36; (c) indistinctly applicable measures having a negative impact on imports fall outside the prohibition under Article 34 if they relate to 'selling arrangements' that apply 'to all affected traders operating within the national territory and provided they affect in the same manner, in law and in fact, the marketing of domestic products and of those from other Member States';[14]

---

[12] See also Protocol (2) on the Application of the Principles of Subsidiary and Proportionality [2010] OJ C83/206.

[13] Case 8/74 *Procureur du Roi v Benoît and Dassonville* [1974] ECR 837, para 5.

[14] Joined Cases C-267/91 P and C-268/91 P *Criminal Proceedings Against Bernard Keck and Daniel Mithouard* [1993] ECR I-6097, para 16; T Connor, 'Accentuating the Positive: The "Selling Arrangement", the first Decade, and Beyond' (2005) 54 ICLQ 127.

(d) pending EU-wide harmonization, an indistinctly applicable measure which hinders intra-EU trade within the meaning of *Dassonville* and *Keck* can also escape the prohibition under the *Cassis de Dijon* 'rule of reason' if it is 'necessary in order to satisfy mandatory requirements relating in particular to the effectiveness of fiscal supervision, the protection of public health, the fairness of commercial transactions and the defence of the consumer' and it is proportionate to the objective to be achieved.[15] *Keck* and *Cassis de Dijon* apply a proportionality inquiry to the definition of the restriction in the first place. Thus, certain measures are not a restriction on trade because they are selling arrangements affecting market access of foreign and domestic products in the same way or because they pursue a mandatory requirement and are proportionate to it. On the other hand, measures that are restrictive of trade can be justified under Article 36 if they pursue one of the objectives set out in that Article and are proportionate to the objective pursued.

A clear statement of the proportionality test under Article 36 can be found in the Opinion of Advocate General Poiares Maduro in *Leppik*. The case concerned Finnish legislation requiring an import licence for the importation of substances containing more than 80 per cent of undenatured ethyl alcohol. The Advocate General described the proportionality test as a structured way of balancing different interests. Once a revelant interest has been indentified—in that case one of the objectives set out in Article 36—the proportionality test asks three further questions: (a) whether the measure is suitable to achieving the objective;[16] (b) whether an alternative measure is available that would achieve the objective as effectively while being less restrictive;[17] and (c) whether the level of protection afforded to the objective being pursued is commensurate to the interference with intra-EU trade that it causes.[18] The Court in *Leppik* did not refer to this last limb of the proportionality test.[19] This may have been because of the wide margin of appreciation left to Member States when the objective pursued is the protection of human life and public health.[20] More generally, because of the risk of encroachment on the discretion of the Member States in pursuing legitimate public policy objectives, the Court of Justice may refrain from ascertaining whether the benefits of the measures are proportionate to the harm caused. But this is not always the case. In *Danish Bottles*, the Court of Justice reviewed a Danish regulation restricting the import into Denmark of drinks that were not in approved containers and, as a consequence, could not be returned through a comprehensive system for the collection of used containers. They could only be returned to the retailer who sold them. The Court said that the system of approved-only containers ensured a very high

---

[15] Case 120/78 *Rewe-Zentrale AG v Bundesmonopolverwaltung für Branntwein* [1979] ECR 649 (*Cassis de Dijon*), para 8.
[16] Opinion of AG Poiares Maduro in Case C-434/04 *Criminal Proceedings Against Jan-Erik Anders Ahokainen and Mati Leppik* [2006] ECR I-9171 (*Leppik*), para 24.
[17] ibid para 25.   [18] ibid para 26.
[19] Case C-434/04 *Leppik*, paras 31 and 40.   [20] ibid para 33.

re-use rate and, therefore, a very high degree of protection of the environment.[21] However, the Court added:[22]

The system for returning non-approved containers is capable of protecting the environment and, as far as imports are concerned, affects only limited quantities of beverages compared with the quantity of beverages consumed in Denmark owing to the restrictive effect which the requirement that containers should be returnable has on imports. In those circumstances, a restriction of the quantity of products which may be marketed by importers is disproportionate to the objective pursued.

The Court was reviewing whether the degree of protection of the environment achieved by the system under review justified the restriction of trade and found that it did not. A lower degree of protection was therefore required.[23] This clearly demonstrates that the proportionality test in EU law allows a comparative assessment of the harms and benefits of the measure or conduct under review.

(3) The proportionality framework under Article 101

An even closer analogy to Article 102 is Article 101. Article 101(1) prohibits agreements, concerted practices, and decisions by associations of undertakings having as their object or effect the restriction, prevention, or distortion of competition. Article 101(3) provides that the prohibition in Article 101(1) does not apply if four conditions are met: (a) the agreement improves the production or distribution of goods or promotes technical or economic progress; (b) it gives consumers a fair share of the benefits in question; (c) it is indispensable to achieving the benefits; and (d) it does not result in the elimination of all competition on the market concerned. The bifurcated structure of Article 101 can be seen as a proportionality framework for the balancing of different effects: the restriction of competition under Article 101(1) and productive and dynamic efficiency under Article 101(3).[24] But the proportionality principle is not limited to the structured balancing of the negative and positive effects of an agreement. It also affects the assessment of the restriction of competition under Article 101(1). This is done in innumerable ways that are sensitive to the facts of each individual case. Three examples will suffice to clarify the point.

---

[21] Case 302/86 *Commission v Kingdom of Denmark* [1988] ECR 4607 (*Danish Bottles*) para 20.

[22] ibid para 21.

[23] See also Case C-169/91 *Council of the City of Stoke-on-Trent and Norwich City Council v B & Q plc* [1992] ECR I-6635, para 15: 'Appraising the proportionality of national rules which pursue a legitimate aim under Community law involves weighing the national interest in attaining that aim against the Community interest in ensuring the free movement of goods'. The Court went on to conflate the no less restrictive means test with the balancing test: 'In that regard, in order to verify that the restrictive effects on intra-Community trade of the rules at issue do not exceed what is necessary to achieve the aim in view, it must be considered whether those effects are direct, indirect or purely speculative and whether those effects do not impede the marketing of imported products more than the marketing of national products' (ibid).

[24] O Odudu, *The Boundaries of EC Competition Law: The Scope of Article 81* (Oxford, OUP 2006) 131–146.

Under Article 101(1), the principle of proportionality applies first of all to determine whether a contractual restriction that is necessary for the achievement of a
legitimate business purpose amounts to a restriction of competition. In *Remia*, the
Court of Justice held that non-compete clauses between the seller and the buyer
of an undertaking were not prohibited by Article 101(1) if they were necessary to
give effect to the transfer of the business in question.[25] In *Pronuptia*, the Court
of Justice considered the positive effects on competition of distribution franchise
agreements. The franchisor is able to reap a reward for his investment in branding
and know-how without investing his own capital, while the franchisees, which
would not have been in the position of investing to the same extent, benefit from
the branding and know-how of the franchisor. As a consequence, restrictive clauses
that are strictly necessary to protect the know-how and assistance provided by the
franchisor are not 'restrictions of competition' within the meaning of Article 101(1).
Franchise agreements promote inter-brand competition in circumstances in which
the franchisor would not have made the additional investment to expand its business or enter new markets.[26] *Nungesser* was also concerned with increased inter-
brand competition offsetting negative effects on intra-brand competition. The
Court ruled on the validity of a decision by the Commission prohibiting an exclusive licence of plant breeder's rights reinforced by absolute territorial protection. The
judgment clarifies the scope of the earlier *Consten and Grundig* case[27] and limits it
to market-partitioning agreements having the object of conferring absolute territorial protection on the licensee, thereby insulating national markets through collusive behaviour.[28] On the other hand, the Court held that an open exclusive licence,
whereby the licensor undertook not to grant any more licences within the contractual territory and not to compete with the licensee within its exclusive territory,
falls outside the scope of Article 101(1) on the grounds that in the absence of such
exclusivity an undertaking in a Member State other than the State where the owner
of the rights is established 'might be deterred from accepting the risk of cultivating
and marketing that product; such a result would be damaging to the dissemin-
ation of a new technology and would prejudice competition in the Community
between the new product and similar existing products'.[29] In *Gøttrup-Klim*,[30] the

---

[25] Case 42/84 *Remia BV v Commission* [1985] ECR 2545.

[26] Case 161/84 *Pronuptia de Paris GmbH v Pronuptia de Paris Irmgard Schillgallis* [1986]
ECR 353.

[27] Joined Cases 56/64 and 58/64 *Etablissements Consten SàRL and Grundig-Verkaufs-GmbH v
Commission* [1966] ECR 299, holding that a trade mark licence conferring absolute territorial protection on the licensee was an infringement of Art 101(1).

[28] Case 258/78 *LC Nungesser KG v Commission* [1982] ECR 2015.

[29] ibid para 57. In the subsequent Case 27/87 *Louis Erauw-Jacquery v La Hesbignonne SC* [1988]
ECR 1919, the Court ruled on the prohibition on the licensee of plant breeder's rights to sell, export,
or assign basic seeds used for propagation as opposed to seeds that are developed from basic seeds
and can be used for agricultural purposes, with which Case 258/78 *Nungesser* was concerned. It held
that a developer of basic seeds must be able to restrict propagation to growers he selects as licensees.
However, it is not clear whether the Court so held in consideration of the investment needed to
develop basic seeds or because the right to restrict propagation of basic seeds was the subject-matter
of the right in question rather than a mode of its exercise.

[30] Case C-250/92 *Gøttrup-Klim ea Grovvareforeninger v Dansk Landbrugs Grovvareselskab AmbA*
[1994] ECR I-5641.

Court of Justice considered a provision in the statute of a cooperative purchasing association prohibiting the members from joining any other association in direct competition with it. The Court held the provision under review not to infringe Article 101(1) insofar as it was 'restricted to what is necessary to ensure that the cooperative functions properly and maintains its contractual power in relation to producers'.[31] In its judgment, the Court expressly considered 'beneficial effects on competition'[32] and 'adverse effects on competition'.[33] This case law is generally considered to establish an ancillary restraint doctrine whereby conduct that is 'necessary to enable the parties to an agreement to achieve a legitimate commercial purpose' falls outside Article 101(1) even if it restricts competition.[34]

The principle of proportionality also requires that an agreement must be assessed in the overall context in which the agreement is made and produces its effects having particular regard to its non-competition objectives. If the agreement has certain effects that are restrictive of competition but these restrictive effects are inherent in the pursuit of a legitimate non-competition objective and proportionate to it, the agreement does not infringe Article 101(1). In *Wouters*, the Court of Justice held that regulations made by the Bar Council of the Netherlands prohibiting lawyers from entering into partnership with accountants, had the effect of restricting competition but did not infringe Article 101(1) because they did not go beyond what was necessary in order to ensure the proper practice of the legal profession.[35] In *Meca-Medina*, the Court of Justice held that anti-doping rules inherent in the pursuit of integrity, objectivity, and ethical values of competitive sport and proportionate to the pursuit of these objectives did not fall within the scope of Article 101(1). The Court referred explicitly to the proportionality test and examined whether the anti-doping rules in question were 'limited to what is necessary to ensure the proper conduct of competitive sport'.[36]

Finally, Article 101(1) only applies to agreements having an appreciable effect on competition. The Court of Justice in *Völk v Vervaecke* held that an agreement falls outside the prohibition in Article 101(1) 'where it has only an insignificant

---

[31] ibid para 45.   [32] ibid para 34.   [33] ibid para 35.

[34] R Whish, *Competition Law* (6th edn Oxford, OUP 2008) 124–126. See, generally, 'Guidelines on Art 101(3)', paras 28–31, adopting the doctrine of ancillary restraints as explained in Case T-112/99 *Métropole Télévision (M6), Suez-Lyonnaise des eaux, France Télécom and Télévision Française 1 SA (TF1) v Commission* [2001] ECR II-2459. For a critical review of the approach in the *Métropole* case and the Guidelines, see R Nazzini, 'Article 81 EC Between Time Present and Time Past: A Normative Critique of "Restriction of Competition" in EU law' (2006) 43 CML Rev 497.

[35] C-309/99 *JCJ Wouters, JW Savelbergh and Price Waterhouse Belastingadviseurs BV v Algemene Raad van de Nederlandse Orde van Advocaten* [2002] ECR I-1577, para 97–109.

[36] Case C-519/04 P *David Meca-Medina and Igor Majcen v Commission* [2006] ECR I-6991 (*Meca-Medina*), paras 42–55. This case casts considerable doubt on the view taken by G Monti, 'Article 81 EC and Public Policy' (2002) 39 CML Rev 1057, 1087, who believed that Case 309/99 *Wouters* incorporates the *Cassis de Dijon* 'rule of reason' into Art 101(1), so that a restriction of competition would not be prohibited under Art 101(1) if it pursues a mandatory requirement of public policy of a Member State and the restriction is inherent in the pursuit of this objective. The integrity of sport is not a mandatory requirement of the public policy of a Member State. It could, perhaps, still be considered a regulatory requirement given that the case concerned the International Olympic Committee, a body established under public international law exercising regulatory functions in relation to certain sporting events: R Whish, *Competition Law*, 129.

effect on the market, taking into account the weak position which the persons concerned have on the market of the product in question'.[37] The Commission Notice on Agreements of Minor Importance now sets out the thresholds below which agreements are deemed by the Commission not to have an appreciable effect on competition.[38] The doctrine of appreciability is not explicitly linked to the principle of proportionality but is an expression of the same idea: under the doctrine of ancillary restraints or the *Wouters* test a restriction is proportionate to a legitimate aim, while under the doctrine of appreciability a restriction is of insufficient magnitude to justify the application of Article 101(1). Proportionality delineates the boundaries of what amounts to a restriction of competition as well as determining when an interference with the competitive process is not a restriction of competition because it pursues a legitimate objective in a proportional way.

C. Proportionality under Article 102

(1) The proportionality framework in the case law

Under Article 102, the case law applies a proportionality test which asks, first, whether the conduct under review prima facie causes competitive harm and, secondly, whether it is objectively justified.

The definition of tests of competitive harm relies on the identification of anti-competitive effects that are presumed to harm long-term social welfare based on the balancing of the risk and cost of enforcement errors. The case law has developed a number of tests to determine whether conduct by a dominant undertaking is prima facie abusive. These correspond to the intent test,[39] the as efficient competitor test,[40] and the consumer harm test.[41] Which test or tests apply in a given case depends on the balancing of the risks and costs of false acquittals and under-deterrence and the risks and costs of false convictions and over-deterrence associated with the type of conduct under review. The lower the risks and costs of false convictions and over-deterrence, the stricter the test. As the risks and costs of false convictions and over-deterrence increase, the test becomes more lenient for the dominant undertaking and a competition authority or claimant is required to meet a higher threshold to make out a prima facie case.

It must be borne in mind that the abuse tests developed in the case law are judicial statements of the necessary elements that a competition authority or claimant must prove to justify a finding of abuse, provided that no other evidence is adduced that is inconsistent with the conduct under review running counter to the purpose of Article 102. The abuse tests in the case law may be described as crystallized presumptions establishing a prima facie case of abuse. They are neither absolute

---

[37] Case 5/69 *Franz Völk v SPRL Ets J Vervaecke* [1969] ECR 295.
[38] Commission Notice on agreements of minor importance which do not appreciably restrict competition under Article 81(1) of the Treaty establishing the European Community (*de minimis*) [2001] OJ C368/13 (the 'Commission Notice on Agreements of Minor Importance').
[39] See Ch 6 below.   [40] See Ch 7 below.   [41] See Ch 8 below.

prohibitions of certain forms of conduct nor do they exhaust the infinite variety of abusive business practices and valid business justifications that may be relevant under Article 102. In particular, if a prima facie case of abuse is established, it is always open to the dominant undertaking to adduce sufficient evidence tending to show that its conduct is objectively justified.[42]

While the principle of proportionality manifests itself mainly in the balance between prima facie anti-competitive effects and objective justification, it is important to note that the same principle also affects what is a prima facie abuse. This is particularly clear when the case law applies a test of reasonableness or proportionality *stricto sensu* to determine whether the conduct causes competitive harm. In *Compagnie Maritime Belge*, one of the abuses consisted in the request by the members of a dominant shipping conference that the Zairean authorities enforced an agreement which gave the conference's members the exclusive right to carry all cargo within the operation of the conference to and from Zaire. The agreement allowed for 'derogations' with the consent of both parties but the conference was not minded to give its consent.[43] The Court of First Instance held that a dominant undertaking 'which enjoys an exclusive right with an entitlement to agree to waive that right is under a duty to make reasonable use of the right of veto conferred on it by the agreement in respect of third parties' access to the market'.[44] The Court went on to say that the members of the conference did not do so when they insisted that the agreement be strictly complied with, thus excluding from the market their only competitor with an initial market share of only 2 per cent. It was also relevant that the conduct was part of an exclusionary plan,[45] which on the facts excluded the validity of any pro-competitive justification. More generally, the case law establishes that a dominant undertaking is entitled to take reasonable and proportionate steps to protect its commercial interests when they are under threat but not if the purpose of the conduct is to strengthen the dominant position and abuse it.[46] This doctrine recognizes that either the conduct under review is a reasonable and proportionate reaction to a commercial threat and, therefore, lawful or it is an abuse of a dominance position and, therefore, prohibited. The reasonable and proportionate protection of legitimate commercial interests is not an objective justification because it is inherently incompatible with a prima facie

---

[42] On objective justification, see Ch 9 below.

[43] *Cewal, Cowac and Ukwal* [1993] OJ L34/20, recitals 20–27 and 63–72.

[44] Joined Cases T-24/93 to T-26/93 and T-28/93 *Compagnie Maritime Belge Transports SA v Commission* [1996] ECR II-1201, para 108, upheld on appeal in Joined Cases C-395/96 P and C-396/96 P *Compagnie Maritime Belge Transports SA v Commission* [2000] ECR I-1365, paras 72–88.

[45] Joined Cases T-24/93 to T-26/93 and T-28/93 *Compagnie Maritime Belge*, paras 102–109.

[46] Case C-27/76 *United Brands Co and United Brands Continentaal BV v Commission* [1978] ECR 207, para 189; Case T-203/01 *Manufacture Française des Pneumatiques Michelin v Commisson* [2003] ECR II-4071 (*Michelin II*), para 55; Case T-65/89 *BPB Industries plc and British Gypsum Ltd v Commission* [1993] ECR II-389 (*British Gypsum*), para 69, appeal dismissed in Case C-310/93 P *BPB Industries plc and British Gypsum Ltd v Commission* [1995] ECR I-865 (*British Gypsum*); Case T-301/04 *Clearstream Banking AG and Clearstream International SA v Commission* [2009] ECR II-3155, para 132; Case T-321/05 *AstraZeneca AB v Commission* [2010] OJ C221/33, on appeal in Case C-457/10 P *AstraZeneca AB v Commission* [2010] OJ C301/18.

abuse. The strengthening of the dominant position is not the pursuit of a legitimate commercial interest. Therefore, if the purpose of the conduct is to strengthen the dominant position, it is by definition not the reasonable and proportionate pursuit of a legitimate commercial interest. In *Compagnie Maritime Belge*, selective price cuts by a quasi-monopolist against the only competitor were found not to be a reasonable and proportionate response to entry.[47] In *United Brands* the refusal to supply an established customer by a dominant undertaking with a strong consumer brand was not the reasonable and proportionate protection of legitimate commercial interests if the customer was abiding by normal commercial practice and the reason for the refusal was that the customer was promoting the products of a competitor.[48]

The principle of proportionality applies even more clearly in the assessment of objective justification. A prima facie abuse is not necessarily an infringement of Article 102 if the conduct is objectively justified. The proportionality framework for objective justification has been spelt out most clearly by the Court of Justice in *British Airways*:[49]

Assessment of the economic justification for a system of discounts or bonuses established by an undertaking in a dominant position is to be made on the basis of the whole of the circumstances of the case... It has to be determined whether the exclusionary effect arising from such a system, which is disadvantageous for competition, may be counterbalanced, or outweighed, by advantages in terms of efficiency which also benefit the consumer. If the exclusionary effect of that system bears no relation to advantages for the market and consumers, or if it goes beyond what is necessary in order to attain those advantages, that system must be regarded as an abuse.

The Court set out a proportionality test that resembles the test adopted by the case law on the fundamental freedoms. First, a legitimate objective must be identified, in this case the pursuit of efficiency. Secondly, the conduct under review must be suitable to achieving the objective. The Court expressed the suitability test by requiring that the conduct have 'some relation to the advantages for the market and consumers'. The Advocate General explained this test in *Leppik* as requiring that 'the measure at issue must indeed contribute to achieving the aim pursued'.[50] Thirdly, the conduct must not go beyond what is necessary to achieve the objective being pursued. This means that there must be no less restrictive means to achieve the same level of advantages with comparable efforts on the part of the dominant undertaking.[51] Fourthly, the Court of Justice in *British Airways* explicitly

---

[47] Joined Cases T-24/93 to T-26/93 and T-28/93 *Compagnie Maritime Belge*, para 148.

[48] Case 27/76 *United Brands*, para 182.

[49] Case C-95/04 P *British Airways*, para 86.

[50] Opinion of AG Poiares Maduro in Case C-434/04 *Leppik*, para 24.

[51] Again, a parallel with the Opinion of AG Poiares Maduro in ibid para 25 reveals that the same analytical structure is being applied: 'The second test concerns the necessity of the measure. To put it more precisely: it concerns the question whether an alternative measure is realistically available that would protect the Member State's legitimate interests just as effectively, but would be less restrictive of the free movement of goods. In other words: could the Member State, by directing a similar

required a balancing exercise: the advantages must counterbalance or outweigh the disadvantages. And, finally, consumers must benefit.[52]

In conclusion, the test under Article 102 can be stated as follows: (a) Does the conduct under review prima facie cause competitive harm? The reasonable and proportional pursuit of a legitimate commercial objective is incapable of being even a prima facie abuse; (b) if the conduct prima facie causes competitive harm, it is relevant to determine whether: (b.1) it produces efficiencies (or pursues some other legitimate objective);[53] (b.2) it is suitable to achieving the efficiencies; (b.3) it is the least restrictive means of achieving them; (b.4) the benefits of the conduct, for both producers and consumers, outweigh the potential competitive harm; and (b.5) the conduct benefits consumers.

(2) The proportionality framework in the Guidance on Article 102

In 2009, the European Commission published the Guidance on the Commission's enforcement priorities in applying Article 102 to abusive exclusionary conduct by dominant undertakings. The Guidance adopts a proportionality test that asks, first, whether the conduct under review restricts competition and, then, allows the dominant undertaking to raise a defence of objective justification.

The Guidance puts forward a single abuse test that determines whether conduct is prima facie abusive. The test relies on the concept of anti-competitive foreclosure and applies, albeit as a prioritization tool, to all exclusionary abuses.[54] Anti-competitive foreclosure is defined as foreclosure 'having an adverse impact on consumer welfare, whether in the form of higher price levels than would have otherwise prevailed or in some other form such as limiting quality or reducing consumer choice'.[55] The Commission explains this test as requiring the likelihood that, as a result of the exclusion or marginalization of competitors, the dominant undertaking will be in a position profitably to increase or maintain prices above the competitive level or negatively to affect the non-price parameters of competition such as choice, innovation, and quality.[56] Such an exercise can rely on qualitative as well as on quantitative evidence.[57] Finally, the negative impact on consumers is not necessarily the impact on final consumers but may be the impact on the immediate customers of the dominant undertaking.[58]

By setting out this consumer harm test the Commission is not requiring distinct proof of substantial customer harm resulting from the infringement but the likelihood, which may be exclusively inferred from qualitative factors, that the foreclosure of competitors strengthens or maintains the dominant position. This is inherent in all exclusionary abuses, as the *Hoffmann-La Roche* definition makes

---

amount of its resources into an alternative measure, achieve the same result at a lower cost to intra-Community trade?'

[52] The objective justification test is discussed in detail in Ch 9 below.

[53] On the objectives that may be pleaded as part of an objective justification defence, see Ch 9 below.

[54] Guidance on Art 102, paras 19–22.   [55] ibid para 19.

[56] ibid para 19, read in conjunction with para 11.   [57] ibid para 19.   [58] ibid.

clear.[59] This interpretation of the Guidance is corroborated by the factors that the Commission considers relevant to establishing anti-competitive foreclosure. These factors, which the Commission clarifies are not necessarily cumulative, are the following:[60]

1. The position of the dominant undertaking;

2. The conditions on the relevant market, in particular barriers to entry and expansion;

3. The position of the dominant undertaking's competitors, the competitive significance of foreclosed competitors, and the counter-strategies available to rivals;

4. The position of customers or input suppliers, the selectivity of the conduct, the strategic significance of customers or suppliers for rivals, the strategies available to customers;

5. The extent of the conduct;

6. Evidence of actual foreclosure;

7. Direct evidence of any exclusionary strategy, including evidence of intent.

As well as setting out a general framework for the assessment of anti-competitive foreclosure, the Guidance puts forward specific tests applicable to individual abuses.[61] The approach in the Guidance is problematic because, while the Commission is not completely ignoring the case law, it is nevertheless constantly putting forward different tests or expressing the legal tests in a way that does not reflect judicial precedent.[62] However, what is clear is that the Commission adopts the same analytical framework as the case law does in setting out flexible tests under which a prima facie abuse may be established subject to objective justification.

As regards objective justification, the Guidance on Article 102 explains that a dominant undertaking may be able to justify its conduct on the ground that it produces efficiencies that guarantee that no harm to consumers is likely to arise.[63] In the Commission's view, four cumulative conditions must be fulfilled:[64]

1. The efficiencies have been, or are likely to be, realized as a result of the conduct;

2. The conduct is indispensable to the realization of those efficiencies. There must be no less anti-competitive conduct that is capable of producing the same efficiencies;

---

[59] Case 85/76 *Hoffmann-La Roche*, para 91. On this case, see 169–171 below.

[60] Guidance on Art 102, para 20.

[61] ibid paras 32–46 (on exclusive dealing), 37–45 (conditional rebates), 47–62 (on tying and bundling), 63–74 (on predation), and 75–90 (on refusal to supply and margin squeeze).

[62] See Ch 6 below, on the intent tests and Ch 7 below, on the as efficient competitor test. These chapters explain why proof of consumer harm is not required under these tests. See also Ch 8 below, on the consumer harm test, which demonstrates that the consumer harm test adopted by the Commission has a lower threshold than the test adopted in the case law, at least as far as refusal to license IP rights is concerned.

[63] Guidance on Art 102, paras 28–31.   [64] ibid para 30.

3. The likely efficiencies brought about by the conduct outweigh any likely negative effects on competition and consumer welfare in the affected markets; and

4. The conduct does not eliminate effective competition.

This test is different from and stricter than that set out in *British Airways*.[65] However, although the content of the test is not consistent with the case law and with Article 102 itself, the Guidance on Article 102 adopts the same proportionality framework.[66] The overall test in the Guidance on Article 102, therefore, reflects the principle of proportionality.

D. The limited usefulness of the definition of abuse in *Hoffmann-La Roche*

Article 102 protects effective competition as a driver of long-term social welfare and productivity growth. The first question of the proportionality test is whether the conduct under review causes competitive harm. But what degree of interference with the process of effective competition justifies a prima facie finding of abuse? A partial answer in relation to exclusionary abuses, and at quite a general level, can be found in *Hoffmann-La Roche*.

In *Hoffmann-La Roche*, the dominant undertaking had entered into supply contracts with its largest customers which either provided for a formal exclusivity or quasi-exclusivity obligation or granted the buyer a 'fidelity rebate' designed as an incentive for the buyer to purchase all or most of its requirements from the dominant undertaking.[67] Upholding the infringement decision adopted by the Commission, the Court set out a definition of abuse, which would be highly influential in future cases:[68]

The concept of abuse is an objective concept relating to the behaviour of an undertaking in a dominant position which is such as to influence the structure of a market where, as a result of the very presence of the undertaking in question, the degree of competition is weakened and which, through recourse to methods different from those which condition normal competition in products and services on the basis of the transactions of commercial operators, has the effect of hindering the maintenance of the degree of competition still existing on the market or the growth of that competition.

---

[65] Case C-95/04 P *British Airways*, para 86. The case law does not require that the net effect of the conduct on consumers is positive or neutral. It simply requires that the efficiencies benefit consumers. Furthermore, there is no requirement in the case law that the conduct under review does not eliminate effective competition. For a detailed analysis, see 306–311 below.

[66] It goes without saying that in a system based on the rule of law an administrative authority is not entitled to change the legal rules that it has the duty to enforce. Therefore, the relevant parts of the Guidance will be discussed in detail in the following chapters in the light of Art 102 and the case law. A different problem is whether the Commission, given its limited resources, is entitled to select from among cases that could all be infringements of the competition rules as a matter of prioritization. On this topic, see WPJ Wils, 'Discretion and Prioritisation in Public Antitrust Enforcement, in Particular EU Antitrust Enforcement' (2011) 34 World Competition (forthcoming).

[67] Case 85/76 *Hoffmann-La Roche*.   [68] ibid para 91.

Formally, there are three key elements of the test. First, the conduct must be capable of influencing the structure of the market ('Verhaltenweisen... die die Struktur eines Marktes beeinflussen können'). Secondly, there must be recourse to methods different from those that condition normal competition in products and services on the basis of the transactions of commercial operators ('Verwendung von Mitteln..., welche von den Mitteln eines normalen Produkt- oder Dienstleistungswettberbs auf der Grundlage der Leistungen der Markbürger abweichen'). Thirdly, the behaviour must be capable of hindering the maintenance of the degree of competition still existing on the market or the growth of that competition ('Verhaltenweisen... die die Aufrechterhaltung des auf dem Markt noch bestehenden Wettbewerbs oder dessen Entwicklung... behindern...'). The third element is expressed in the German text with the same construction as the first (*können* governs *behindern*). The first and the third elements express the same idea that the conduct must have a negative effect on competition. Therefore, the test can be reformulated as follows: the test for abuse asks whether the conduct under review is capable of restricting competition by means other than competition on the merits.[69] This test is quintessentially vague. The requirement that there must be an effect on market structure in the form of an impediment to competition is obvious: an exclusionary abuse must, by logical necessity, have some exclusionary effect. But *Hoffmann-La Roche* neither defines nor explains what type of exclusionary effect is required. As regards the likelihood of the exclusionary effect, the use of *können* provides little guidance. *Können* expresses the possibility or potential of the effect occurring. It does not suggest any given degree of probability, whether high or low, although the effect cannot be impossible or highly unlikely. Finally, the requirement that the means by which the exclusion of competitors is achieved must be different from normal competition is, again, self-evident. If a competitor loses market share because the dominant undertaking introduces an improved version of its product that consumers value more than the competitor's, this is clearly not an abuse. But the concept of competition on the merits is not, in itself, a sufficiently defined legal concept to enable clear boundaries to be drawn that allow behaviour to be placed within or outside them. Richards LJ, in the English Court of Appeal, recognized this when he said that normal competition is not 'a concept with a legal definition, or at least a sufficiently hard-edged concept that it can be determined as a matter of law whether a particular factual situation does or does not amount to normal competition'. Rather, 'whether there has been recourse to methods different from those which condition normal competition is a question of expert appreciation'.[70] This statement perhaps goes too far. While competition on the merits is not a clear-cut legal rule, it is a guiding

---

[69] 'Competition on the merits' is an alternative phrase used in the case law to denote the concept of 'normal competition' in Case 85/76 *Hoffmann-La Roche*: see eg Case T-65/98 *Van den Bergh Foods Ltd v Commission* [2003] ECR II-4653, para 157, appeal dismissed in Case C-552/03 P *Unilever Bestfoods (Ireland) Ltd v Commission* [2006] ECR I-9091; Opinion of AG Kokott in Case C-95/04 P *British Airways plc v Commission* [2007] ECR I-2331, para 24.

[70] *National Grid plc v Gas and Electricity Markets Authority* [2010] EWCA Civ 114, [2010] UKCLR 386, para 41.

principle. Normal competition is behaviour which is consistent with the objective of Article 102 in that it contributes to increasing social welfare and productivity in the long term. Competition is 'normal' when it is rational commercial conduct consistent with the profit-maximizing strategy of a non-dominant undertaking. What distinguishes the conduct of a dominant undertaking as abnormal is the ability to harm competition which is the hallmark of dominance. Competition is 'on the merits' when it is based on superior efficiency rather than on means that reflect the ability to harm competition that is constitutive of the dominant position. These principles are specific enough to provide guidance in individual cases. They are, however, not immediately operational tests. Ultimately, what is and is not competition on the merits must be determined in relation to the form, purpose, and effect of the conduct under review in each individual case.

The above analysis makes it clear that it is not possible to say that the use of the term *Produkt- oder Dienstleistungswettberb* in *Hoffmann-La Roche* in any way reflects Eucken's concept of *Leistungswettberb* as opposed to *Behinderungswettbewerb*.[71] While this terminology and the overall tone of the judgment might suggest that ordoliberal thinking influenced the Court in the case, the language of the case is too vague to justify the conclusion that the Court adopted or endorsed an ordoliberal concept of abuse. The use of the term *Produkt- oder Dienstleistungswettberb* is perfectly consistent with the meaning of *Leistung* as 'result' or 'outcome' of effort or work[72] or the legal meaning of 'performance of an obligation' (in this case contractual).[73]

In conclusion, *Hoffmann-La Roche* establishes the general principle that conduct is abusive when it restricts competition by means other than behaviour based on efficiency or consistent with the normal profit-maximizing strategy of a non-dominant undertaking. Such a principle must be applied in the light of the tests discussed in Chapters 6 to 9. It is not an immediately operational test itself.

---

[71] In his 'complete competition' model, Eucken distinguishes two types of competition: 'performance competition' (*Leistungswettbewerb*) and 'impediment competition' (*Behinderungswettbewerb*). The former occurs in completely competitive markets, whereas the latter indicates a lack of complete competition: W Eucken, 'Die Wettbewerbsordnung und ihre Verwrklichung' (1949) 2 ORDO 1. Loyalty rebates, exclusive agreements, and predation are examples of impediment competition and must thus be prohibited (ibid): 'Jede Art des "Behinderungswettbewerbes", also Sperren jeglicher Form, Treurabatte, Exklusivverträge und Kampfpreise gegen Aussenseiter mit dem Ziel der Vernichtung oder Abschreckung sind zu verbieten.'

[72] At para 90 (Case 85/76 *Hoffmann-La Roche*, para 90), the Court talks about 'einen nicht auf Leistungen begründeten und folglich verfälschten Wettbewerb'. The natural meaning of 'nicht auf Leistungen begründeten' is 'not based on the result of [its own] work'. The phrase is similar to the idea of 'growth or development as a consequence of a superior product' or 'business acumen' in the US case law; see *United States v Grinnell Corp* 384 US 563 (1966) 570–571; *Verizon Communications Inc v Law Offices of Curtis V Trinko LLP* 540 US 398, 407 (2004) 410, 124 S Ct 872, 157 L Ed 2d 823.

[73] At para 90 the Court talks about 'wirtschaftlichen Leistung', meaning 'commercial transaction' or 'performance of a commercial obligation' (Case 85/76 *Hoffmann-La Roche*, para 90). At para 91, the Court explains the concept of *Leistungswettberb* by referring to the 'Leistungen der Markbürger', the transactions or contractual performances of the merchants (ibid para 91). The usage of *Leistung* in this context appears to denote commercial transactions as a nexus of obligations to be performed which justify each other in a contractual setting.

E. *Continental Can* and the concept of effective competition

The concept of abuse clearly requires, at the very minimum, that the conduct of the dominant undertaking restricts competition or exploits a restriction of competition. But what is the level of competitive pressure that Article 102 aims at protecting? The answer was given early on by the Court of Justice in *Continental Can*.[74]

In *Continental Can*, the Commission had prohibited the acquisition by Continental Can through its subsidiary Europemballage of approximately 80 per cent of the shares and convertible debentures in a competitor. The merger eliminated competition in the relevant markets.[75] The Court had to define the concept of abuse from first principles. The aim of Articles 101 and 102 was 'the maintenance of effective competition within the [internal market]'.[76] The elimination of competition would be contrary to the objective of promoting 'throughout the [Union] a harmonious development of economic activities'.[77] An infringement of Article 102 is committed 'if an undertaking in a dominant position strengthens such position in such a way that the degree of dominance substantially fetters competition, ie that only undertakings remain in the market whose behaviour depends on the dominant one'.[78] If this happens, 'the objectives of the Treaty are circumvented by an alteration of the supply structure which seriously endangers the consumer's freedom of action in the market'.[79] This reasoning can be entirely explained in terms of the allocative inefficiency of market power. An increase in market power which results from the acquisition of a competitor is an abuse if 'the degree of dominance reached substantially fetters competition'.[80] Allocative inefficiency harms consumers and this explains the references to the consumer's freedom of action. The restriction of freedom is seen as an effect of the 'alteration to the supply structure'[81] and is a way of describing the consequences of a substantial increase in market power. In this context, the Court famously adopted a distinction between two types of abuse: practices which may harm consumers directly[82] and practices which may harm consumers indirectly through their impact on an effective competitive structure.[83] Notwithstanding the somewhat misleading language used by the Court, which might suggest that Article 102 was concerned mainly with exploitative abuses rather than with exclusion, the judgment focused strongly on the protection of effective competition as the objective of Article 102. This concept was derived directly from the objectives of the Treaty as in force at the time. The objective that the current Treaties assign to Article 102 is the promotion of long-term social welfare. As a consequence, effective competition within the meaning of *Continental Can* is the degree of competition that ensures that, on a given market, long-term social welfare is maximized. This interpretation of the concept of effective competition

---

[74] Case 6/72 *Europemballage Corp and Continental Can Co Inc v Commission* [1973] ECR 215 (*Continental Can*), para 18.

[75] ibid para 28.   [76] ibid para 25.   [77] ibid para 24.   [78] ibid para 26.
[79] ibid para 29.   [80] ibid para 26.   [81] ibid para 29.   [82] ibid para 26.
[83] ibid.

was confirmed by the Court of Justice in the Article 102 case *Metro I*, where the Court held that Article 101 protected 'workable competition' defined as 'the degree of competition necessary to ensure the basic requirements and the attainment of the objectives of the EEC Treaty'.[84] 'Workable competition' must be read as 'effective competition' in this context in order to avoid confusion with the concept of workable competition discussed below.[85] This has been conclusively clarified by the Court of First Instance in *GlaxoSmithKline*, where 'effective competition' was defined as 'the degree of competition necessary to ensure the attainment of the objectives of the Treaty'.[86]

It is important to underline that the concept of effective competition does not correspond to concepts such as perfect competition, workable competition, or complete competition. It is a legal concept whose meaning is entirely determined by the Treaties. Economics plays a key role in clarifying this concept but has no normative function in this regard.

Effective competition is clearly different from perfect competition. Perfect competition is a model in which each firm is a price taker. Supply and demand must be sufficiently fragmented. There must be no barriers to entry. Prices must be perfectly transparent. Products must be homogenous. When these conditions are satisfied, prices equal MC and allocative efficiency is maximized. Clearly, this model has nothing to say about the competition that Article 102 aims at protecting.

Effective competition is not the same as the ordoliberal concept of 'complete competition' under which market power should be as diffused as possible to avoid any firm or group of firms exercising power over competitors or customers that would limit their market freedom.[87] Effective competition is consistent with market power insofar as market power is a driver of productivity and innovation and does not result in anti-competitive conduct causing a reduction of social welfare in the long term.

Perhaps the concept that is closer to effective competition is that of workable competition. Workable competition may be defined as 'the most desirable forms of competition selected from those that are practically possible, within the limits set by conditions we cannot escape'.[88] The crux of this theory is that once any one of the conditions of perfect competition is not met, the optimal outcome is not necessarily achieved by striving to meet the other conditions. For instance, if instead of an atomistic supply structure there are few large sellers, the homogenous character of the product and perfect price transparency are not necessarily

---

[84] 26/76 *Metro SB-Großmärkte GmbH & Co KG v Commission* [1977] ECR 1875 (*Metro I*), para 20.

[85] See eg A Jones and B Sufrin, *EU Competition Law: Text, Cases, and Materials* (4th edn Oxford, OUP 2011) 33–34.

[86] T-168/01 *GlaxoSmithKline Services Unlimited v Commission* [2006] ECR II-2969, para 109.

[87] See eg W Eucken, 'Die Wettbewerbsordnung und ihre Verwrklichung'. For a summary of these concepts in English, see D Hildebrand, *The Role of Economic Analysis in the EC Competition Rules* (3rd edn Alphen aan den Rijn, Kluwer Law International 2009) 161.

[88] JM Clarke, 'Toward a Concept of Workable Competition' (1940) 30 American Economic Rev 241, 242.

desirable.[89] The main policy implication of this theory was to discourage intervention against any perceived departure from the model of perfect competition. Imperfect competition could be 'fairly healthy and workable'.[90] Workable competition is still, therefore, an abstract economic model: it seeks to identify the best outcome when the first best is not available. Furthermore, because its benchmark remains perfect competition, the model is still exclusively concerned with allocative efficiency. Its usefulness, however, is the intuition that there can be a healthy competitive process even when the market is characterized by constraints that make perfect competition impossible and that the optimal outcome does not depend on how closely the structure of the industry or the competitive process resembles perfect competition. The concept of effective competition shares this conceptual premise but develops it in the light of the framework of the Treaties. Effective competition is a legal concept. Its aim is not to identify the most desirable solution for a given industry but to provide a benchmark against which conduct that is potentially harmful to long-term social welfare can be assessed. As a consequence, effective competition is the degree of competitive pressure that, given all constraints inherent in the structure of the market and the nature of the product and independent of abusive conduct of the dominant undertaking, would maximize social welfare in the long term.

F. The special responsibility of the dominant undertaking

The case law repeatedly affirms that a dominant undertaking has a special responsibility not to impair undistorted competition in the internal market. This formula originates in *Michelin I*, where the Court of Justice, in the context of market definition, considered that the strong preference of the Dutch dealers for Michelin tyres, due to their superior technology and the wider range of Michelin's products compared to its competitors' ranges, meant that 'a dealer established in the Netherlands normally cannot afford not to sell Michelin tyres'.[91] In response to the argument that, in this way, the dominant undertaking would be penalized because of its superior efficiency, the Court said:[92]

A finding that an undertaking has a dominant position is not in itself a recrimination but simply means that, irrespective of the reasons for which it has such a position, the undertaking concerned has a special responsibility not to allow its conduct to impair genuine undistorted competition on the [internal market].

The Court of Justice was not laying down a test for abuse. It was saying that an undertaking may be dominant because of its superior efficiency. This is not in itself an infringement of Article 102. Superior efficiency is not penalized. However, if an undertaking is dominant, whether because of superior efficiency or for any other

---

[89] Clarke, 'Toward a Concept of Workable Competition', 249.   [90] ibid 256.
[91] Case 322/81 *NV Nederlandsche Banden Industrie Michelin v Commission* [1983] ECR 3461 (*Michelin I*), paras 55–56.
[92] ibid para 57.

reason, it has a 'special responsibility' not to impair undistorted competition in the internal market. Since *Continental Can* and *Hoffmann-La Roche* had already defined the abuse as conduct that restricts effective competition in the internal market, the concept of 'special responsibility' in *Michelin I* simply expressed the idea that Article 102 singles out dominant firms—this is the meaning of the adjective 'special'—by prohibiting them from engaging in conduct which is abusive under that provision. Nothing more can or should be read into this concept of 'special responsibility'. 'Special responsibility' is not a legal doctrine because it does not define legal rules. It is a short-hand to describe and explain their operation. Importantly, the doctrine of special responsibility must not be used as a formula according to which duties and liabilities can be imposed on the dominant undertaking. Duties and liabilities can be imposed on the dominant undertaking only under tests that concretize the general precepts of Article 102 in the light of its objective. Only to this extent can 'special responsibility' become a legal doctrine. But then it would add nothing to the definition of the abuse because it would only say that a dominant undertaking has a special responsibility not to abuse its dominant position within the meaning of Article 102.

The majority of cases refer to the concept of special responsibility in its descriptive function. In *Irish Sugar*, for example, the Court of First Instance recited the *Michelin I* formula but only to set out, in general terms, the legal framework that applies to dominant undertakings under Article 102.[93] In *Compagnie Maritime Belge*, the Court of Justice adopted the same approach when it referred to the special responsibility of a liner conference that held a collective dominant position.[94] The Court then referred to the special responsibility two more times in relation to specific abuses. The liner conference had an agreement with the relevant authorities of Zaire. The agreement granted the conference the exclusive right to carry cargo by sea between Zaire and certain European ports. Derogations were allowed but only with the mutual agreement of both parties. When the Zairean authorities permitted the only competitor of the conference to operate on the routes in question, the conference requested strict compliance with the agreement. The Court recalled the concept of special responsibility and went on to say that the conference 'sought to rely on the contractual exclusivity . . . in order to remove its only competitor from the market'.[95] It was not the special responsibility that characterized the conduct as abusive. It was its exclusionary purpose. The same can be said about the Court's reliance on the concept of special responsibility in the assessment of the abuse consisting in the application of selective above-cost price cuts aimed at excluding the conference's only competitor. The reference to the special responsibility was useful in explaining that the scope of the Article 102 prohibition depends on the facts of each individual case. The abusive nature of the conduct under review, however, did not depend on and was not derived from a purported doctrine of special responsibility but from the features of the market, the degree of dominance, and the aim

---

[93] Case T-228/97 *Irish Sugar plc v Commission* [1999] ECR II-2969, para 112.
[94] Joined Cases C-395/96 P and C-396/96 P *Compagnie Maritime Belge*, para 37.
[95] ibid paras 72–88.

of the pricing strategy.[96] In some complex Article 102 cases, the EU courts feel perfectly able to rule on the abuse without any reference to the special responsibility of the dominant undertaking, which would be an error of law if this were a legal doctrine in some way constitutive of the concept of abuse.[97]

In conclusion, the concept of special responsibility serves the useful purpose of describing the scope of the prohibition that applies to dominant undertakings. The Union courts have thus clarified, by reference to the special responsibility, that the scope of the prohibition is not defined by bright-line rules but depends on the facts of each individual case.[98] Yet again, nothing should be read in this statement other than a recognition that the scope of the prohibition is not set once and for all but depends on the facts of each case and, in particular, on the degree of dominance,[99] the magnitude of the competitive harm,[100] the objective being pursued,[101] and the means employed to achieve it.[102]

G. Causal link between dominance, conduct, and effect

(1) Causal link between dominance and competitive harm

The conventional wisdom is that Article 102 does not require a causal link between dominance and abuse.[103] Two leading cases lend support to this proposition. In *Continental Can*, the Court was asked to rule on whether a dominant undertaking's

---

[96] ibid paras 114–121.

[97] eg Joined Cases C-468/06 P to C-478/06 P *Sot Lélos kai Sia EE v GlaxoSmithKline AEVE Farmakeftikon Proionton* [2008] ECR I-7139; Case C-418/01 *IMS Health GmbH & Co OHG v NDC Health GmbH & Co KG* [2004] ECR I-5039.

[98] eg Joined Cases C-395/96 P and C-396/96 P *Compagnie Maritime Belge*, para 114: 'the actual scope of the special responsibility imposed on a dominant undertaking must be considered in the light of the specific circumstances of each case which show that competition has been weakened'; Case C-333/94 P *Tetra Pak International SA v Commission* [1996] ECR I-5951 (*Tetra Pak II*), para 25: 'the actual scope of the special responsibility imposed on a dominant undertaking must be considered in the light of the specific circumstances of each case which show a weakened competitive situation', upholding Case T-83/91 *Tetra Pak International SA v Commission* [1994] ECR II-755 (*Tetra Pak II*), para 115.

[99] The classic example is Joined Cases C-395/96 P and C-396/96 P *Compagnie Maritime Belge*, para 119: 'It is sufficient to recall that the conduct at issue here is that of a conference having a share of over 90% of the market in question and only one competitor. The appellants have, moreover, never seriously disputed, and indeed admitted at the hearing, that the purpose of the conduct complained of was to eliminate G & C from the market.'

[100] eg Case T-65/89 *British Gypsum*, para 68: 'the conclusion of exclusive supply contracts in respect of a substantial proportion of purchases constitutes an unacceptable obstacle to entry to that market'.

[101] The objectives pursued by the dominant undertaking must relate 'to the defence of the legitimate interests of an undertaking engaged in competition on the merits': Case T-321/05 *AstraZeneca*, para 672.

[102] The means employed are subject to a test of reasonableness and proportionality: see Joined Cases T-24/93 to T-26/93 and T-28/93 *Compagnie Maritime Belge*, para 148.

[103] R Whish, *Competition Law*, 201–202. See, however, convincingly T Eilmansberger, 'How to Distinguish Good from Bad Competition under Article 82: In Search of Clearer and More Coherent Standards for Anti-Competitive Abuses' (2005) 42 CML Rev 129, 140–142, arguing that the causal link is not between dominance and conduct but between dominance and competitive harm.

acquisition of a competitor was an abuse. The applicant argued that an abuse could only be committed if the dominant position was the 'means through which the abuse is effected'. The Court's answer was that Article 102 had the objective of protecting undistorted competition in the internal market. Therefore, the strengthening of the dominant position of an undertaking may be an abuse, 'regardless of the means and procedure by which it is achieved', if it has a negative impact on an effective competitive structure. The question of 'the link of causality' was 'of no consequence'.[104] In *Hoffmann-La Roche*, a case concerning exclusivity arrangements and rebates conditional on the customer purchasing all or most of its requirements from the dominant undertaking, the Court of Justice disagreed with the applicant's argument that 'the use of economic power bestowed by a dominant position is the means whereby the abuse has been brought about'.[105] *Continental Can* and *Hoffmann-La Roche* relate to a narrow concept of 'but for' causation between dominance and conduct. They mean that, for an abuse to be established, it is not required that dominance be the 'but for' or *sine qua non* cause of the abusive conduct.[106] Non-dominant undertakings may be able to carry out the same conduct. Any other interpretation would exclude from the scope of application of Article 102 a wide range of practices that may restrict competition and harm long-term social welfare but can also be carried out by non-dominant undertakings.

While dominance need not necessarily be the means through which the abuse is effected, it is far from clear that the law does not require a link between dominance and abuse. The case law defines dominance as 'a position of economic strength enjoyed by an undertaking that enables it to prevent effective competition being maintained on the relevant market by giving it the power to behave to an appreciable extent independently of its competitors, customers, and ultimately consumers'.[107] If dominance is the ability to impair effective competition and, as *Continental Can* and *Hoffmann-La Roche* establish, the abuse must have a negative impact on an effective competitive structure, it seems odd, to say the least, to conclude that dominance and abuse are not linked. The Court of Justice in *Tetra Pak II* explicitly required that there must be a link between dominance and abuse.[108] It is true that the Court was dealing with the issue of whether the abuse could take place on a market where the undertaking concerned was not dominant. But the Court considered that the requirement of a link between dominance and abuse was generally established when the abuse took place on the dominated market, while such a link was 'normally not present where conduct

---

[104] Case 6/72 *Continental Can*, para 27.   [105] Case 85/76 *Hoffmann-La Roche*, para 91.
[106] Eilmansberger, 'How to Distinguish Good from Bad Competition under Article 82', 141–142.
[107] Case 27/76 *United Brands*, para 65; Case 322/81 *Michelin I*, para 29; C-311/84 *Centre Belge d'Études de Marché—Télémarketing (CBEM) v SA Compagnie Luxembourgeoise de Télédiffusion (CLT) and Information Publicité Benelux (IPB)* [1985] ECR 3261 *Télémarketing*, para 16; Case 30/87 *Corinne Bodson v Pompes Funèbres des Régions Libérées SA* [1988] ECR 2479, para 26; Case C-396/96 *Compagnie Maritime Belge*, para 34; Case T-65/98 *Van den Bergh Foods*, para 154; Case T-128/98 *Aéroports de Paris v Commission* [2000] ECR II-3929, para 147; Case T-321/05 *AstraZeneca*, para 239.
[108] Case C-333/94 P *Tetra Pak II*, para 27.

on a market distinct from the dominated market produces effects on that distinct market'.[109] The position, therefore, is that a link is always required not that a link is only required in multi-market abuses. This is consistent with the text of Article 102, which prohibits an 'abuse by one or more undertakings of a dominant position' not an abuse by one or more dominant undertakings.[110] Article 102, therefore, is not a prohibition of socially harmful conduct that applies only to dominant undertakings but is a prohibition of conduct that is socially undesirable because it is carried out by dominant undertakings. In particular, conduct by a dominant undertaking is prohibited when, by impairing an effective competitive structure, it harms social welfare in the long term. Only undertakings having the ability to restrict effective competition can bring about the type of competitive harm that Article 102 aims at preventing. This demonstrates that a causal link must exist between dominance and the competitive harm that is relevant under Article 102. However, causation cannot be the basis for distinguishing between conduct that is abusive *per se* and conduct that is abusive because of its effects. This distinction would be based on whether market power is the means by which the abuse is committed or the condition for anti-competitive effects to occur in the form of a manipulation of market structure. Tying and refusal to supply would be in the former category, while exclusivity, rebates, or acquisitions of competitors or competing technologies would fall into the latter category.[111] These implications drawn from the causation requirement are not well founded. Whether the dominant undertaking engages in refusal to supply or anti-competitive rebates, the anti-competitive effect is the same: the reduction of competitive pressure causing harm to long-term social welfare.[112] Article 102 considers dominance as a necessary condition for harm to occur but not for the conduct to take place. Any firm can refuse to supply a rival or grant retroactive discounts that result in incremental sales below cost. Dominance is a necessary condition for neither form of conduct. But it is a necessary condition for either form of conduct to reduce competition and harm long-term social welfare within the meaning of Article 102.

The above considerations demonstrate that Article 102 envisages a causal link between dominance and competitive harm. Since the abuse tests under Article 102 rely on anti-competitive effects to presume competitive harm, this also means that dominance must be an integral element of the assessment of anti-competitive effects.

---

[109] ibid.

[110] Eilmansberger, 'How to Distinguish Good from Bad Competition under Article 82', 141.

[111] ibid 143–146.

[112] On the importance of the effect rather than the form of the conduct in the assessment of the abuse, see I Lianos, 'The Price/Non Price Exclusionary Dichotomy: A Critical Appraisal' (2009) 2 Concurrences 34, 39 and I Lianos, 'Categorical Thinking in Competition Law and the "Effects-based" Approach in Article 82 EC' in A Ezrachi (ed), *Article 82 EC: Reflections on Its Recent Evolution* (Oxford: Hart Publishing 2009) 19, 45–48.

(2) Multi-market abuses

(a) Input/output and complementary products

The need for a causal link between dominance and abuse comes into sharp focus in the analysis of multi-market abuses. Competitive harm may occur when dominance, conduct, and effect exist or take place in different markets. Multi-market abuses are, therefore, prohibited under Article 102. However, the risk is of false positives and over-deterrence is high. Once a dominant position is established on one market, normal competitive conduct on other markets may be prohibited or deterred even if it is incapable of harming or unlikely to harm competition. The need to prove a link between dominance and abuse is, therefore, particularly acute whenever the abuse concerns more than one market.

To understand the different permutations of multi-market abuses, it is useful to distinguish vertical and horizontal foreclosure. Vertical foreclosure occurs when the conduct and the foreclosure effect are at different levels of the supply chain. Typically, the abusive conduct takes place on an input market (the 'upstream market') but the foreclosure effect takes place on the market for the output for which the input is used (the 'downstream market'). The incentive to engage in anti-competitive conduct is the maintenance, strengthening, or acquisition of downstream market power. The ability to exclude is based on the control of a bottleneck input, which is necessary for downstream firms to compete. Horizontal foreclosure occurs when the conduct and the foreclosure effects take place at the same level of the supply chain, namely on the same market or on markets that are equally close to the final consumer.[113]

As regards vertical foreclosure, the link between dominance, conduct, and effect is constituted by the ability and the incentive of an undertaking dominant on the market for an input to harm competition by foreclosing downstream rivals who are also upstream competitors.[114] The plausibility of competitive harm in this context is a given in the post-Chicago economic literature.[115]

---

[113] On the distinction between vertical and horizontal foreclosure, see European Commission, DG Comp, 'DG Competition discussion paper on the application of Article 82 of the Treaty to exclusionary abuses' (Brussels, December 2005) (the 'DG Comp Discussion Paper on Art 102') paras 69–73.

[114] C-7/97 *Oscar Bronner GmbH & Co KG v Mediaprint Zeitungs- und Zeitschriftenverlag GmbH & Co KG* [1998] ECR I-7791; Case C-241/91 P and C-242/91 P *Radio Telefis Eireann (RTE) and Independent Television Publications Ltd (ITP) v Commission* [1995] ECR I-743 (*Magill*); *Wanadoo España v Telefónica* [2008] OJ C83/6; Case 311/84 *Télémarketing*; Case C-418/01 *IMS*; Case T-201/04 *Microsoft Corp v Commission* [2007] ECR II-3601 (*Microsoft I*); Case T-271/03 *Deutsche Telekom AG v Commission* [2008] ECR II-477, appeal dismissed in Case C-280/08 P *Deutsche Telekom AG v Commission* [2010] OJ C346/4; Case T-301/04 *Clearstream Banking*.

[115] There is now a vast literature on vertical foreclosure, which bears witness to the complexity of this topic. See also, for further references, JM Vernon and DA Graham, 'Profitability of Monopolization by Vertical Integration' (1971) 79 Journal of Political Economy 924; R Schmalensee, 'A Note on the Theory of Vertical Integration' (1973) 81 Journal of Political Economy 442; FR Warren-Boulton, 'Vertical Control with Variable Proportions' (1974) 82 Journal of Political Economy 783; M Katz and C Shapiro, 'On the Licensing of Innovations' (1985) 16 RAND Journal of Economics 504; P Aghion and P Bolton, 'Contracts as a Barrier to Entry' (1987) 77 American Economic Rev 388; J Farrell and NT Gallini, 'Second-Sourcing as a Commitment: Monopoly Incentives to Attract

More complicated is the application of Article 102 to multi-market horizontal foreclosure. The easiest case is that of complementary products. It is well established in economic theory[116] that an undertaking dominant on the market for a primary product may have the ability and incentive to harm competition by foreclosing the market for a complementary product by forcing or inducing customers not to buy the complementary products sold by competitors. The ability to do so results from the dominant position on the primary market, which means that there are no or poor substitutes for the dominant undertaking's primary product. The incentive to do so may be the acquisition, maintenance, or strengthening of dominance in the secondary market, the primary market, or a third, emerging market. The classic examples of this type of abuse are tying, pure bundling, or bundled discounts whereby customers are forced or induced to purchase the dominant undertaking's complementary products rather than its competitors' products.[117]

(b) Neighbouring markets

The risk of false convictions and over-deterrence increases significantly in cases where the dominant undertaking is dominant in the market for product A and the potentially abusive conduct takes place on the market for product B but A

Competition' (1988) 103 Quarterly Journal of Economics 673; MA Salinger, 'Vertical Mergers and Market Foreclosure' (1988) 103 Quarterly Journal of Economics 345; MK Perry, 'Vertical Integration: Determinants and Effects' in R Schmalensee and RD Willig (eds), *Handbook of Industrial Organization: Vol I* (Amsterdam, North Holland 1989); O Hart and J Tirole, 'Vertical Integration and Market Foreclosure' (1990) Brookings Papers on Economic Activity (Microeconomics) 205; P Bolton and MD Whinston, 'Incomplete Contracts, Vertical Integration, and Supply Assurance' (1993) 60 Rev Econ Stud 121; Z Chen and TW Ross, 'Refusals to Deal, Price Discrimination and Independent Service Organizations' (1993) 2 Journal of Economics and Management Strategy 593; B Caillaud, B Jullien, and P Picard, 'Competing Vertical Structures: Precommitment and Renegotiation' (1995) 63 Econometrica 621; J Vickers, 'Competition and Regulation in Vertically Related Markets' (1995) 62 Rev Econ Stud 1; G Gaudet and N Long, 'Vertical Integration, Foreclosure and Profits in the Presence of Double Marginalisation' (1996) 5 Journal of Economics and Management Strategy 409; C-TA Ma, 'Option Contracts and Vertical Foreclosure' (1997) 6 Journal of Economics and Management Strategy 725; C Stefanadis, 'Downstream Vertical Foreclosure and Upstream Innovation' (1997) 45 Journal of Industrial Economics 445; MH Riordan, 'Anticompetitive Vertical Integration by a Dominant Firm' (1998) 88 American Economic Rev 1232; Z Chen and TW Ross, 'Refusal to Deal and Orders to Supply in Competitive Markets' (1999) 17 Intl J Ind Org 399; JP Choi and Y Sang-Seung, 'Vertical Foreclosure with the Choice of Input Specifications' (2000) 30 RAND Journal of Economics 717; WS Comanor and P Rey, 'Vertical Restraints and the Market Power of Large Distributors' (2000) 17(2) Rev Ind Org 135; T Chipty, 'Vertical Integration, Market Foreclosure, and Consumer Welfare in the Cable Television Industry' (2001) American Economic Rev 428; S Martin, H-T Normann, and CM Snyder, 'Vertical Foreclosure in Experimental Markets' (2001) 32 RAND Journal of Economics 466; G Chemla, 'Downstream Competition, Foreclosure and Vertical Integration' (2003) 12 Journal of Economics and Management Strategy 261; S Caprice, 'Incentive to Encourage Downstream Competition under Bilateral Oligopoly' (2005) 12(9) Economics Bull 1; CC de Fontenay and JS Gans, 'Vertical Integration in the Presence of Upstream Competition' (2005) 36 RAND Journal of Economics 544.

[116] eg MD Whinston, 'Tying, Foreclosure, and Exclusion' (1990) 80 American Economic Rev 837; DW Carlton and M Waldman, 'The Strategic Use of Tying to Preserve and Create Market Power in Evolving Industries' (2002) 33 RAND Journal of Economics 194; JP Choi and C Stefanidis, 'Tying, Investment, and the Dynamic Leverage Theory' (2001) 32 RAND Journal of Economics 52.

[117] Case T-30/89 *Hilti AG v Commission* [1990] ECR II-163; Case T-83/91 *Tetra Pak II* upheld on appeal in Case C-333/94 P *Tetra Pak II*; Case T-201/04 *Microsoft I*; *Coca-Cola* [2005] OJ L253/21; *Napier Brown—British Sugar* [1988] L284/41.

and B are neither input-output products nor complementary products. There is, therefore, no link between the products as such. These markets may be defined as neighbouring markets, as there is some proximity or link between them besides the relationship of input/output or complements between the products in question.

The first type of case involves the dominant undertaking deploying a multi-market punishment system against customers who deal with competitors. If this kind of behaviour constitutes the enforcement of exclusionary arrangements on the market where the undertaking is dominant, it is abusive. In *British Gypsum*, an undertaking dominant on the plasterboard market had entered into a number of abusive exclusive arrangements with its customers on that market. In addition, it had adopted a policy on the neighbouring plaster market that prioritized orders at times of shortages, giving preference to loyal customers over customers who also dealt with competitors on the plasterboard market. The Court of First Instance held that this conduct could be abusive, provided two conditions were fulfilled. The first was that 'distributors which are victims of the alleged practices, must be present in both markets'.[118] The second was that 'the functioning of the plaster market must display certain particular characteristics'[119] in that the conduct of the dominant undertaking on the non-dominated market had to be capable of 'affecting the functioning of that market'.[120] Reformulating the second condition, the dominant undertaking must have the ability to harm customers on the non-dominated market.

In *British Gypsum*, the dominant undertaking had implemented abusive exclusionary practices on the dominated market. The abuse on the non-dominated market reinforced the abuse on the dominated market. It is not clear whether conduct exclusively taking place on the non-dominated market where the customers are essentially the same as those on the dominated market can be abusive if it forecloses the dominated market. By analogy with the *Tetra Pak II* doctrine,[121] which does not require an abuse to be established on the dominated market, the answer must be in the affirmative.

An even more complicated situation arises when the conduct and the anti-competitive effects both take place on the non-dominated market. In *Tetra Pak II*, the European Commission found that Tetra Pak was dominant on the EU-wide markets for aseptic packaging machines and cartons and had a leading market position on the EU-wide markets for non-aseptic packaging machines and cartons.[122] In the aseptic systems sector, Tetra Pak had a market share of 90 to 95 per cent.[123] In the non-aseptic systems sector, Tetra Pak had market shares fluctuating between 48 and 55 per cent, with the second largest rival, Elopak, at about 27 per cent.[124] Elopak had for some considerable time been trying to enter

---

[118] Case T-65/89 *British Gypsum*, para 93, upheld on appeal in Case C-310/93 *British Gypsum*, para 11.

[119] Case T-65/89 *British Gypsum*, para 93.   [120] ibid.

[121] Case C-333/94 P *Tetra Pak II*.

[122] *Tetra Pak II* [1992] OJ L72/1, recitals 99–101. On market definition see ibid recitals 92–98.

[123] ibid recital 12 and Case T-83/91 *Tetra Pak II*, para 13.

[124] *Tetra Pak II*, recital 13 and Case T-83/91 *Tetra Pak II*, para 14.

the aseptic sector.[125] Its complaint related to a number of exclusionary practices in the non-aseptic sector, including predatory pricing[126] and the tying of Tetra Pak machines and cartons.[127] The Commission found that Tetra Pak had abused its dominant position in the aseptic markets by engaging in abusive conduct on the non-aseptic markets.[128] The theory of harm in the decision did not rely on the incentive of the dominant undertaking to prevent Elopak from entering the aseptic sector, which would appear consistent with the facts of the case, but on the ability to harm competition on the non-dominated market resulting from the dominant position on a neighbouring market.

The EU courts upheld this approach.[129] The Court of Justice, however, emphasized that special circumstances must be present for conduct on non-dominated markets producing effects only on those markets to be deemed abusive.[130] Special circumstances were present in that case because 'the quasi-monopoly enjoyed by Tetra Pak on the aseptic markets and its leading position on the distinct, though closely associated, non-aseptic markets placed it in a situation comparable to that of holding a dominant position on the markets in question as a whole'.[131] The special circumstances consisted in the following factors:[132]

1. Tetra Pak's virtual monopoly in the aseptic sector;[133]

2. Tetra Pak's high market shares in the non-aseptic sector;[134]

3. The customers of Tetra Pak in one sector were potentially also customers in the other sector and 35 per cent of Tetra Pak customers bought both aseptic and non-aseptic machines and cartons;[135]

4. Tetra Pak's ability to offset losses in one line of business or geographical location against profits in another line of business or geographical location;[136]

5. Tetra Pak's ability to focus its efforts in the non-aseptic sector given that it faced no competitive threat in the aseptic sector;[137]

6. The presence of the key suppliers on both sectors;[138]

7. The overall position of strength on both sectors considered together.[139]

This test is confusing. The EU courts did not spell out clearly the legal question in relation to which the relevance of the links between the two markets had to be

---

[125] Case T-83/91 *Tetra Pak II*, para 120.   [126] *Tetra Pak II*, recital 5.
[127] ibid recitals 116–117.   [128] ibid recital 104.
[129] Case T-83/91 *Tetra Pak II*, paras 117–122 and, on appeal, Case C-333/94 P *Tetra Pak II*, paras 21–33.
[130] Case C-333/94 P *Tetra Pak II*, para 27.   [131] ibid para 31.
[132] These factors are described and discussed, with varying degrees of emphasis, in the Commission decision and the judgments of the courts: see *Tetra Pak II*, recitals 101–102 and 104; Case T-83/91 *Tetra Pak II*, paras 118–122; Case C-333/94 P *Tetra Pak II*, paras 27–31.
[133] Case C-333/94 P *Tetra Pak II*, para 28.   [134] ibid para 28.
[135] Case T-83/91 *Tetra Pak II*, para 119 and Case C-333/94 P *Tetra Pak II*, para 29.
[136] *Tetra Pak II*, recital 101.
[137] Case T-83/91 *Tetra Pak II*, para 121 and Case C-333/94 P *Tetra Pak II*, para 29.
[138] Case T-83/91 *Tetra Pak II*, para 120 and Case C-333/94 P *Tetra Pak II*, para 29.
[139] Case T-83/91 *Tetra Pak II*, paras 118 and 122 and Case C-333/94 P *Tetra Pak II*, para 28.

assessed. The only clue can be found in the judgment of the Court of Justice, which requires a 'link' between dominance and abuse.[140] This must be the starting point of the analysis. The Court of Justice must have considered the links between the dominated and the non-dominated market as being relevant to establishing the required link between dominance and abuse. But a link between dominance and abuse can only mean that dominance gives the undertaking in question either the ability or the incentive to harm competition. There is no other conceivable link. On the facts, the most likely theory of harm was that Elopak was trying to enter the dominated market. Predation on the neighbouring market was a way of protecting market power on the dominated market. However, because the Commission and the courts focused exclusively on the effect on the non-dominated markets, the maintenance or strengthening of the dominant position could not have provided the incentive to harm competition. The link between dominance and abuse was, therefore, primarily in the ability to exclude.[141] The ability to exclude cannot be assessed in the abstract but needs to be examined in relation to each type of abuse. As regards predation, the ability to harm competition could have consisted in the asymmetric access to equity and finance of Tetra Pak and Elopak.[142] This could, for instance, explain the reference to Tetra Pak's ability to 'concentrate its efforts' on the non-dominated markets.[143] This reasoning is, however, absent in the Commission decision and the judgments of the EU courts. All that was established in this case was that there was a list of factors that linked two markets. The relevance of these factors was not explained. Nor was the test in relation to which relevance had to be assessed.

It is even more difficult to explain why, because of the close links with the dominated markets, Tetra Pak was able to harm competition by tying two products in respect of neither of which it was dominant. This conclusion in *Tetra Pak II* is not only unsupported by convincing legal reasoning but also, probably, wrong on the facts. The only possible theory of harm applicable in the case was that the undertaking dominant in the aseptic system markets, by reducing rivals' profitability in the non-aseptic system markets, was making it unprofitable for them to enter the aseptic system markets. This theory of harm resembles Carlton and

---

[140] Case C-333/94 P *Tetra Pak II*, para 27.

[141] *Tetra Pak II*, recital 105: 'Tetra Pak has used the association which exists between the four markets in question to commit abuses on the non-aseptic markets, abuses which it could not have committed in the absence of its dominant position on the aseptic markets, whether they involve practices aimed at eliminating competitors or their products, predatory or discriminatory prices, or indeed the imposition on Tetra Pak product users of unfair contractual terms'.

[142] The theory of harm could have been financial predation, assuming that capital markets are not perfect. See J Tirole, *The Theory of Industrial Organization* (Cambridge Mass, MIT Press 1988) 379; LG Telser, 'Cutthroat Competition and the Long Purse' (1966) 9 Journal of Law and Economics 259; D Gale and M Hellwig, 'Incentive Compatible Debt Contracts: The One-Period Problem' (1985) 52 Rev Econ Stud 647; RM Townsend, 'Optimal Contracts and Competitive Markets with Costly State Verification' (1979) 21 Journal of Economic Theory 265; DW Diamond, 'Financial Intermediation and Delegated Monitoring' (1984) 51 Rev Econ Stud 393. For the Chicago School position, which is sceptical of financial predation, see GJ Stigler, 'Imperfections in the Capital Market' in GJ Stigler, *The Organization of Industry* (reprinted Chicago, The University of Chicago Press 1983) 113, and H Bork, *The Antitrust Paradox: A Policy at War with Itself* (New York, The Free Press 1993) 147–148.

[143] Case C-333/94 P *Tetra Pak II*, para 29; Case T-83/91 *Tetra Pak II*, para 121.

Waldman's two-period entry game. However, in Carlton and Waldman the tied product was complementary to the tying product and the incumbent had a monopoly on the tying product.[144] In *Tetra Pak II*, the non-aseptic system markets were not complementary to the aseptic system markets, and Tetra Pak was not dominant on the tying market in the non-aseptic sector. Therefore, dominance on the aseptic system markets did not give rise to the ability to exclude rivals from the non-aseptic markets, although it may have explained the incentive to exclude. This issue was not addressed by the Court of Justice on appeal even if one of the pleas related specifically to the multi-market nature of the abuse. One possible explanation for this error was that Tetra Pak was also accused of having engaged in predatory pricing in the non-aseptic sector.[145] As explained above, in relation to predatory pricing on non-dominated markets, the judgment of the Court of Justice is probably correct on the facts even if the legal reasoning is wanting. It would appear that Tetra Pak raised the issue of multi-market abuse before the Court of Justice in general and not in relation to each specific abuse.[146] As a result, the issue of tying may have not been raised specifically or may have been overlooked. Be that as it may, neither economic theory nor EU case law supports the proposition that the mere fact that an undertaking is dominant on a neighbouring market confers on it the ability to exclude rivals by engaging in tying on other markets where it is not dominant. There is no relevant 'link' between dominance and the abuse in these circumstances.[147] The inescapable conclusion is that, to the extent that the Court found that tying was abusive in the absence of dominance on the tying market, *Tetra Pak II* was wrongly decided and should not be followed.

Another possible theory of multi-market abuse is based on reputation. An undertaking dominant on market A may engage in predation in market B, on which it is not dominant, to signal to rivals that it will engage in the same behaviour should they decide to enter the dominated market. In *Ministre de l'économie, des finances et de l'emploi v GlaxoSmithKline France*, the French Cour de cassation upheld the judgment of the Cour d'appel setting aside the decision of the Conseil de la concurrence which had found predation in non-dominated market with the purpose of protecting a dominated market by building a reputation for predation. The Cour de cassation held that there was no proof of sufficient links between the two markets (other than the fact that they both related to non-regulated sales to hospitals) and no proof that potential entrants to the dominated market could be

---

[144] Carlton and Waldman, 'The Strategic Use of Tying to Preserve and Create Monopoly Power in Evolving Industries', 195–197.

[145] Case T-83/91 *Tetra Pak II*, paras 16–20.

[146] Case C-333/94 P *Tetra Pak II*, paras 21–23.

[147] The Court, therefore, misapplied the test for multi-market abuses it had correctly stated (ibid para 27): 'It is true that application of Article [102] presupposes a link between the dominant position and the alleged abusive conduct, which is normally not present where conduct on a market distinct from the dominated market produces effects on that distinct market. In the case of distinct, but associated, markets, as in the present case, application of Article [102] to conduct found on the associated, non-dominated, market and having effects on that associated market can only be justified by special circumstances.'

deterred by predation on the non-dominated market. The Court, however, did not rule out, as a matter of law, the possibility of this type of multi-market abuse.[148]

(c) The test for multi-market abuses

Dominance, abuse, and effect may exist or take place on different markets. The key is that there must be a link between dominance and abuse. This means that dominance must give the undertaking in question either the ability or the incentive to harm competition. This test is sensitive to the nature of the abuse. The required links between the dominated and the non-dominated market must be assessed under this test and not in the abstract. For instance, the presence of the same competitors on both the dominated and the non-dominated market is not a relevant link under the *British Gypsum* doctrine of abuse on a non-dominated market as imposing a switching cost on customers on the dominated market. What matters in this scenario is the presence of the same customers on both markets and the ability of the dominant undertaking to affect the functioning of the non-dominated market by harming customers on that market. On the contrary, in a multi-market predatory strategy based on reputational effects, what counts is that the competitors on the non-dominated market where predation occurs are potential entrants to the dominated market, and predation can effectively work as a signalling strategy that deters entry. The permutations are as many as there are potential multi-market exclusionary strategies and depend on the facts of each case. It is clear, however, that the factors listed in the Court of Justice's judgment in *Tetra Pak II* do not automatically mean that an abuse may be found when conduct and anti-competitive effects occur on markets where the dominant undertaking is not dominant. The question in each case is whether dominance gives the undertaking concerned either the ability or the incentive to harm competition.

H. Conclusion

This chapter examined the analytical framework of the test for abuse under Article 102 and the key doctrines that shape the general concept of abuse. Given the lack of clarity which plagues this area of the law, it is necessary first of all to define the concepts of competitive harm and anti-competitive effects. Competitive harm is a restriction on competition or an exploitation of the dominant position that harms social welfare in the long term. Anti-competitive effects are the effects of the conduct on a relevant market from which it is possible in law to presume competitive harm. Thus, competitive harm and anti-competitive effects can sometimes be used interchangeably because competitive harm includes anti-competitive effects and anti-competitive effects are presumed to cause competitive harm.

---

[148] Case 08-14503 *Cour de cassation, chambre commerciale, Ministre de l'économie, des finances et de l'emploi v GlaxoSmithKline France* 17 March 2009 (French Supreme Court).

The test under Article 102 can be described as a proportionality test stated as follows: (a) does the conduct under review prima facie cause competitive harm? The reasonable and proportional pursuit of a legitimate commercial objective is incapable of being even a prima facie abuse; (b) if the conduct prima facie causes competitive harm, it is relevant to determine whether: (b1) it produces efficiencies; (b.2) it is suitable to achieving the efficiencies; (b.3) it is the least restrictive means of achieving them; (b.4) the benefits of the conduct, for both producers and consumers, outweigh the potential competitive harm; and (b.5) the conduct benefits consumers. This is consistent with proportionality as a general principle of Union law and with the analytical structure of the test under Article 102.

Hoffmann-La Roche establishes that conduct is abusive when it restricts competition by means other than behaviour based on efficiency or consistent with the normal profit-maximizing strategy of a non-dominant undertaking. This definition is, in itself, of limited use in defining operational abuse tests. It is, however, important in that it clarifies that both the conduct of the dominant undertaking and its effect are constitutive elements of the abuse.

Article 102 protects effective competition within the meaning of *Continental Can* and *Metro I*, namely the degree of competition that ensures that, on a given market, long-term social welfare is maximized. Market power and prices above marginal cost are consistent with effective competition when they increase social welfare in the long term, for instance because they are necessary for the ability and incentive of firms to invest in new productive technologies or in the development of new products. This concept of competition is a legal concept that reflects a teleological interpretation of the competition rules of the TFEU and is not the same as the economic construct of perfect competition, the ordoliberal idea of 'complete competition', or Clark's theory of 'workable competition'.

The often cited 'doctrine' of the special responsibility of the dominant undertaking is not a legal doctrine capable of influencing the application of Article 102. It is a descriptive way of expressing the idea that a form of conduct that is unobjectionable if carried out by a non-dominant firm may infringe Article 102 if carried out by a dominant undertaking.

Contrary to what is almost universally believed, Article 102 envisages a causal link between dominance and abuse. This causal link, however, is not a 'but for' causation requirement between dominance and a form of conduct that may be abusive. The causal link must be established between dominance and competitive harm. Therefore, dominance must be an integral part of the assessment of competitive harm. Since the abuse tests under Article 102 rely on anti-competitive effects to presume competitive harm, this requirement means that dominance must be an integral element of the assessment of anti-competitive effects. Proof of the causal link between dominance and anti-competitive effects is particularly important in multi-market abuses where it is necessary to prove that dominance gives the undertaking in question either the ability or the incentive to harm competition by engaging in abusive conduct or causing anti-competitive effects on market on which it is not dominant.

PART III

TESTS OF ABUSE

6

The Tests of Intent

A. Introduction

The previous chapter has demonstrated that the minimum requirements of the abuse are a restriction of effective competition or the exploitation of a restriction of effective competition and conduct that is not based on efficiency and is not consistent with the profit-maximizing behaviour of a non-dominant undertaking. Given these broad parameters, the scope of the special responsibility depends on the facts of each individual case.

This chapter examines the test of intent under Article 102. Chapter 3 concluded that intent by itself is not suitable as a general test for abuse of dominance. However, a naked exclusion test as a test of intent may apply to the conduct of a dominant undertaking which has the sole or overwhelmingly predominant purpose of harming competition, has no conceivable redeeming virtue either by way of economic efficiencies or otherwise, and is reasonably capable of causing competitive harm. Beyond nakedly abusive conduct, Chapter 3 argued that intent may play three important roles. First, it may be an element of the test when a certain type of conduct is capable of causing significant competitive harm but a finding of infringement based on objective factors alone would be subject to a systematic high risk of false acquittals. Secondly, proof of intent may be required to condemn certain practices in addition to proof of anti-competitive effects when a finding on infringement based on objective factors alone would be subject to a systematic risk of false convictions. Thirdly, evidence of intent may always be relevant to prove the objective elements of the test. In this case intent is not a test but the object of circumstantial evidence. Union law relies on all three roles of intent in the application of the competition rules.

As a preliminary observation it is necessary to clarify whether the definition of abuse as an objective concept[1] in the case law bars reliance on intent as a test[2]

---

[1] Case 85/76 *Hoffmann-La Roche & Co AG v Commission* [1979] ECR 461, para 91.

[2] This could appear to be the view of the General Court in Case T-321/05 *AstraZeneca AB v Commission* [2010] OJ C221/33, para 359, under appeal in Case C-457/10 P *AstraZeneca AB v Commission* [2010] OJ C301/18, where the Court held that proof of the intention of the dominant undertaking to mislead patent offices was not necessary but the intent was still a relevant factor to be taken into account even if the finding of infringement 'should primarily be based on an objective finding that the abusive conduct actually took place'. In fact, intent as a test does not mean that it is not necessary for the conduct to take place. Intent clarifies whether the conduct is anti-competitive rather than competition on the merits.

or as evidence[3] in EU competition law. The answer is that the definition of abuse sets out a general principle that applies as a default position: Article 102 does not make the intent to harm competition a necessary condition for a finding of abuse. This does not mean, however, that intent cannot be an element of the test in relation to specific forms of conduct where, in the absence of proof of intent, it would be impossible to establish whether the conduct under review is anti-competitive or not. The case law on predation adopts precisely this approach.[4] And, of course, when intent is an element of the test it is never the only test: pure subjective intention cannot run counter to the purpose of Article 102. Anti-competitive intent must have been implemented in conduct, ie as a minimum, capable of achieving the intended result in its market context. In this sense, even when intent is part of the abuse test, abuse is and remains an objective concept. *A fortiori*, evidence of intent may be relevant to establishing objective factors that are constitutive elements of the abuse test.[5]

This chapter discusses the naked abuse test in EU law and then examines the role that intent plays as an element of the test in predation, abuse of rights, and tying. The relevance of evidence of intent is discussed next. The conclusions set out the main findings of the inquiry into the role of intent under Article 102.

B. The naked abuse test

(1) Naked abuse as a general test

From a normative perspective, the naked exclusion test can be stated to be a prima facie prohibition of behaviour that has the sole or overwhelmingly predominant purpose of harming competition, has no conceivable redeeming virtue either by way of economic efficiencies or otherwise, and is reasonably capable of causing competitive harm. EU law appears to be in line with this approach. A dominant undertaking may engage in a practice which is so clearly anti-competitive that the law dispenses with proof of other indicators of anti-competitive effect, such as the exclusion of an equally efficient competitor or consumer harm. The Guidance on Article 102 explains:[6]

There may be circumstances where it is not necessary for the Commission to carry out a detailed assessment before concluding that the conduct in question is likely to result in consumer harm. If it appears that the conduct can only raise obstacles to competition and

---

[3] Although the relevance of evidence of intent in EU competition law is not seriously disputable: see Case C-202/07 P *France Télécom SA v Commission* [2009] ECR I-2369, para 98 and the Communication from the Commission—Guidance on the Commission's enforcement priorities in applying Article 82 of the EC Treaty to abusive exclusionary conduct by dominant undertakings [2009] OJ C45/7 ('Guidance on Art 102') para 20.

[4] Case 62/86 *AKZO Chemie BV v Commission* [1991] ECR I-3359, para 72; Case T-83/91 *Tetra Pak International SA v Commission* [1994] ECR II-755 (*Tetra Pak II*), para 151, upheld in Case C-333/94 P *Tetra Pak International SA v Commission* [1996] ECR I-5951 (*Tetra Pak II*); Case C-202/07 *France Télécom*, para 98; Guidance on Art 102, paras 20 and 66.

[5] Guidance on Art 102, para 20.   [6] ibid para 22.

that it creates no efficiencies, its anti-competitive effect may be inferred. This could be the case, for instance, if the dominant undertaking prevents its customers from testing the products of competitors or provides financial incentives to its customers on condition that they do not test such products, or pays a distributor or a customer to delay the introduction of a competitor's product.

The case law and the Commission practice support this proposition. In particular, the naked abuse test has been applied to distributional practices, the provision of misleading information to patent offices, and the abuse of court proceedings.

In *Tetra Pak II*, the Commission found that it was abusive for Tetra Pak to buy competitors' machines and obtain undertakings from customers that they would cease using them in order to prevent the testing of such machines and deprive competitors of trade references for their products.[7] The Commission's approach in *Tetra Pak II* received judicial endorsement by the Court of First Instance in *Irish Sugar*, where the dominant undertaking agreed with two customers to swap its own products for those of a competitor and threatened the customers in question that if they did not agree to the swap they would lose certain preferential discounts on the dominant undertaking's products.[8] The same approach was applied in *Intel*, a case concerning rebates granted by the dominant undertaking to its customers that allegedly foreclosed from the market Intel's only competitor AMD. The Commission distinguished two types of rebate. Rebates conditional upon the customer purchasing part of its requirements from Intel were assessed as 'conditional rebates'.[9] Rebates conditional upon the customer delaying, cancelling, or otherwise restricting the commercialization of products based on the microprocessor of AMD were assessed as 'naked restrictions'.[10] The difference lay in the fact that a payment conditional upon a customer obtaining all or most of its requirements from the dominant undertaking does not have as its sole or overwhelmingly predominant purpose the restriction of competition. Furthermore, it may have efficiency justifications because, for instance, it allows the supplier to pass to the customers lower costs resulting from the achievement of economies of scale in production or distribution. A more thorough assessment of the exclusionary effects of the practice is, therefore, necessary. On the other hand, payments by Intel to its customers on condition that the launch of specific AMD-based products was delayed or cancelled or their commercialization restricted had no conceivable explanation other than the exclusion of AMD.[11] Therefore, for such 'naked restrictions', it was not appropriate to conduct the as efficient competitor test, which the Commission applied to the other rebates.[12] In terms of the analysis of the effect of the conduct, it was held sufficient to prove that the payments were a material factor in the customer delaying, cancelling, or otherwise restricting the planned

---

[7]   *Tetra Pak II* [1992] OJ L72/1, recitals 71–83 and 165.

[8]   Case T-228/97 *Irish Sugar plc v Commission* [1999] ECR II-2969, paras 226–235, upheld in Case C-497/99 P *Irish Sugar plc v Commission* [2001] ECR I-5333. The grounds for appeal to the Court of Justice concerned the finding of a dominant position and not the abuses.

[9]   *Intel* [2009] OJ C227/13, recitals 920–1642. The decision is under appeal in Case T-286/09 *Intel Corp v Commission* [2009] OJ C220/41.

[10]   *Intel*, recitals 1643–1683.   [11]   ibid recital 1680.   [12]   ibid recital 1667.

commercialization of specific competitor's products for which there was consumer demand. As a result, consumers were deprived of a choice, which they would have otherwise had.[13] The delayed or failed commercialization of AMD-based products for which there was consumer demand was held to be an anti-competitive effect within the meaning of the case law,[14] although the Commission was adamant that the case law did not require proof of the 'effects of the conduct and its impact on the market'.[15]

The naked abuse test was also applied in *AstraZeneca*, a case concerning the making of misleading representations to patent offices aimed at obtaining exclusive rights to which AstraZeneca was not entitled. The General Court said that the conduct in question 'constituted a practice based exclusively on methods falling outside the scope of competition on the merits' and 'solely serves' to exclude competitors.[16] Another abuse consisted in AstraZeneca applying for the deregistration of the marketing authorizations for the capsule formulation of its drug in certain Member States as a consequence of the decision to withdraw the capsule formulation from the market and to launch a new tablet formulation instead. The intended effect of this conduct was to prevent parallel importers and suppliers of generic alternatives to the drug in question from relying on the capsule market authorization in order to market their own products instead of having to comply with more onerous regulatory requirements. This conduct delayed generic entry and impaired parallel imports.[17] The General Court upheld this analysis on the grounds that the conduct under review 'was only such as to ... obstruct or delay the market entry of generic products'.[18] The Court framed the test as follows:[19]

... in the absence of grounds connected with the legitimate interests of an undertaking engaged in competition on the merits and in the absence of objective justification, an undertaking in a dominant position cannot use regulatory procedures solely in such a way as to prevent or make more difficult the entry of competitors on the market.

The problem with the naked abuse test in *AstraZeneca* is that the Court understood the test as being purely objective.[20] However, a purely objective test of naked abuse coupled with a low threshold of anti-competitive effects based on the capability to foreclose[21] gives rise to too high a risk of false convictions and over-deterrence. Intent must be a necessary requirement of the naked abuse test so as to ensure that only conduct that is genuinely anti-competitive and lacks any valid business justification is prohibited without a full inquiry into the effects on the market under either the as efficient competitor test or the consumer harm test. This conclusion is reinforced by the analysis of the case law on abusive litigation. In *ITT Promedia*, it was alleged that a dominant undertaking had committed an abuse by bringing court proceedings against a competitor. The Court of First Instance adopted the following cumulative tests framed by the Commission: (a) the proceedings cannot

---

[13] ibid recitals 1652, 1655, 1664, and 1666.   [14] ibid recitals 1672 and 1675.
[15] ibid recital 1674.   [16] Case T-321/05 *AstraZeneca*, para 608.
[17] *Generics/AstraZeneca* [2006] OJ L332/24, recitals 777–862.
[18] Case T-321/05 *AstraZeneca*, para 676.   [19] ibid para 817.   [20] ibid para 356.
[21] ibid para 824.

reasonably be considered as an attempt to establish the rights of the undertaking concerned and can therefore only serve to harass the opposite party; and (b) they are conceived within the framework of a plan whose goal is to eliminate competition.[22] The Court added that access to a court is a general principle common to the legal traditions of the Member States and protected by the ECHR. As a consequence, initiating legal proceedings can only constitute an abuse in exceptional circumstances and the criteria set out by the Commission must be construed narrowly.[23] The high risk of false convictions and over-deterrence leads to the application of the naked exclusion test: the abuse of court proceedings can only constitute an infringement of Article 102 if the litigation has the sole or overwhelmingly predominant purpose of harming competition, which the Court understood as a test of intent. While this test is partly based on the constitutional status of the right to access to a court, the more fundamental rationale of guarding against the risk of false convictions and over-deterrence applies with equal force to regulatory procedures.

(2) Naked abuse and free trade

(a) Free trade as a key driver of long-term social welfare

In the light of the EU objective of establishing an internal market based on the free movement of good and services, the case law and the Commission practice consider prima facie abusive conduct that has the sole or overwhelmingly predominant purpose of restricting free trade and is reasonably capable of doing so. The naked exclusion test applies even if the conduct in question is not necessarily prima facie incapable of realizing any conceivable efficiencies. Efficiencies are not irrelevant and can always be pleaded as an objective justification but even their plausibility is not such as to displace the very strong inference of competitive harm that the law draws from the fact that the practice in question is inimical to one of the most fundamental principles of the European Union. The reason is that EU law regards free trade as key to the maximization of social welfare in the long term. As a consequence, conduct by a dominant undertaking runs counter to the objective of Article 102 if it has the sole or overwhelming purpose of restricting free trade and is reasonably capable of doing so.

(b) Above-cost rebates

Above-cost discounts may exceptionally be an infringement of Article 102 if they have the sole purpose of restricting intra-EU trade. Because a key indicator of anti-competitive intent is often the targeting of undertakings that are more likely to switch to foreign competitors, these rebates may also result in the application of different prices to different customers that do not reflect a difference in costs. This discriminatory element is, however, better understood in the context of the exclusionary objective of the rebate rather than as the element of a free-standing

---

[22] Case T-111/96 *ITT Promedia NV v Commission* [1998] ECR II-2937, para 55.
[23] ibid paras 60–61.

discriminatory abuse under Article 102(c). An instructive example of this approach is *BPB Industries*,[24] where the Commission found that BPB Industries and its subsidiary British Gypsum (together 'British Gypsum') had committed an abuse of dominant position on the British and Irish plasterboard markets by granting rebates conditional upon the customers agreeing to purchase plasterboard exclusively from British Gypsum.[25] British Gypsum was a quasi-monopolist in both Great Britain and Northern Ireland, with market shares between 90 and 100 per cent on both markets.[26] In Northern Ireland, in particular, the rebates in question were intended to prevent Spanish imports into the market, and achieved this end.[27] The Court of First Instance upheld the findings of abuse.[28] As regards the Irish market, the Court held that British Gypsum's rebates infringed Article 102 on two grounds. First, they discriminated against importers and aimed at dissuading them from purchasing plasterboard from Spain.[29] Secondly, 'any form of loyalty rebate through which the supplier endeavours, by means of financial advantages, to prevent its customers from obtaining supplies from competitors constitutes an abuse within the meaning of Article [102] of the Treaty'.[30] For the latter proposition, the Court relied on *Michelin I*, but it is clear that this was a misapplication of that case. *Michelin I* requires an assessment of 'all the circumstances' before a rebate system may be found to be unlawful.[31] In fact, *British Gypsum* is better understood as a case in which selective fidelity rebates by a quasi-monopolist had the sole prima facie purpose of restricting free trade. This doctrine was further refined in *Irish Sugar*,[32] a case where the Commission found that Irish Sugar had abused its single and, prior to a certain date, collective[33] dominant position on the retail and industrial markets for granulated sugar in the Republic of Ireland. In the context of a general policy of protecting its home markets from imports from other Member States and competing sugar packers in the Republic of Ireland, Irish Sugar adopted a policy of 'border rebates' granted to selected customers established in the border

---

[24] *BPB Industries plc* [1989] OJ L10/50.

[25] ibid recitals 123–130 (in relation to the abuse on the British market) and 148–152 (in relation to the abuse on the Irish market).

[26] ibid recitals 24, 41, and 114–121.   [27] ibid recitals 148.

[28] Save for a minor aspect relating to the duration of the abuse consisting in prioritizing orders placed by loyal customers in the case of shortages of plaster: see Case T-65/89 *BPB Industries plc and British Gypsum Ltd v Commission* [1993] ECR II-389 (*British Gypsum*), upheld on appeal in Case C-310/93 *BPB Industries plc and British Gypsum Ltd v Commission* [1995] ECR I-865 (*British Gypsum*). The grounds of appeal to the Court of Justice did not involve a finding of abuse in relation to the rebates in Great Britain and Northern Ireland except for the issue of the applicability of Article 101(3) TFEU: see ibid paras 6–9.

[29] Case T-65/89 *British Gypsum*, para 119.   [30] ibid para 120.

[31] Case 322/81 *NV Nederlandsche Banden Industrie Michelin v Commission* [1983] ECR 3461 (*Michelin I*), para 73.

[32] *Irish Sugar plc* [1997] OJ L258/1, partly upheld in Case T-228/97 *Irish Sugar* (which set aside the finding of selective low prices to customers of a French competition on the industrial sugar market and reduced the fine).

[33] The collective dominant position was held by Irish Sugar as producer and Sugar Distributors Limited, a subsidiary of Irish Sugar carrying out the distribution function for the group. However, prior to 1990, Irish Sugar had contested that it controlled SDL. The Commission found that, prior to 1990, Irish Sugar and SDL were collectively dominant: see *Irish Sugar*, recitals 111–113. In the text, references to Irish Sugar or the dominant undertaking will include both Irish Sugar and SDL unless the context clearly requires otherwise.

area with Northern Ireland. The border rebate was unrelated to objective economic factors. Rather, 'it was used and modulated whenever it was considered that the price difference between Northern Ireland and Ireland might have induced cross-border sales'.[34] This practice was part of a much wider exclusionary strategy.[35] The Court of First Instance upheld the finding of infringement on the ground that the border rebates constituted a barrier to the achievement of the internal market and were 'prejudicial to the outcome of effective and undistorted competition, especially with regard to the interests of consumers'.[36] However, the Court recognized, implicitly, the risk of false convictions and over-deterrence that a prohibition of above-cost price cuts carries with it. Therefore, it limited the application of the prohibition of above-cost price cuts designed to prevent parallel imports to 'an undertaking holding a dominant position as extensive as that enjoyed by the applicant',[37] which held 88 per cent of the relevant market.[38] The border rebates were also found to be discriminatory and, therefore, abusive within the meaning of Article 102(c).[39] However, the way in which the Court rejected the argument that the border rebates were a legitimate reaction to competition from imports shows that the market-partitioning purpose of the rebate was a constitutive element of the abuse.[40] In the absence of the market-partitioning purpose, it would have been inconceivable to hold that reacting to competitive pressure by lowering prices above cost was a discriminatory abuse under Article 102(c). Therefore, it would have been preferable to sustain the finding of abuse exclusively on the ground of the market-partitioning effects of the conduct. The discriminatory nature of the practice was, of course, relevant. It is clear that if Irish Sugar had lowered its prices to all Irish customers, such conduct would not have been abusive unless it had been predatory. But discrimination was an element of a market-partitioning strategy, not the primary cause of the anti-competitive effect. This explains why there is no real analysis of 'competitive disadvantage' in this case: the primary harm of the border rebates was harm to intra-EU trade.

(c) Refusal to supply

It is a prima facie abusive for a dominant undertaking to discontinue or limit supplies to existing customers with the sole or overwhelmingly predominant purpose of restricting free trade. This principle appears to be the true *ratio* of the *Sot Lélos kai Sia* case.[41] In that case, a dominant pharmaceutical company had discontinued

---

[34] *Irish Sugar*, recitals 57–69 and 128–135.
[35] Additional practices aimed at limiting imports were to put pressure on a State-owned carrier not to transport imported sugar, to agree with retailers to exchange a competitor's sugar with the dominant undertaking's sugar, and to apply a fidelity rebate. Furthermore, Irish Sugar engaged in abusive price discrimination against customers who did not export the processed products by granting exporters an export rebate and discriminated against sugar packers who bought sugar to compete with Irish Sugar's downstream retail business. Finally, it offered the major food wholesalers a rebate conditional on the achievement of a growth target: *Irish Sugar*, recitals 43–44, 46–53, 70–84, 120–122, 124–127, and 136–154.
[36] Case T-228/97 *Irish Sugar*, para 185.   [37] ibid para 185.
[38] ibid para 186. The market in question is the retail sugar market.
[39] ibid para 183.   [40] ibid para 185.
[41] Joined Cases C-468/06 P to C-478/06 P *Sot Lélos kai Sia EE v GlaxoSmithKline AEVE Farmakeftikon Proionton* [2008] ECR I-7139.

or reduced supplies to Greek wholesalers with the purpose of preventing them from engaging in parallel trade.[42] The Court of Justice considered that parallel trade in medicinal products benefits the final consumer but added that it was not necessary to rule on whether the dominant undertaking had to take into account such benefits when assessing whether its conduct complied with Article 102.[43] This strongly suggests that the Court was here explaining why parallel trade enjoys a strong degree of protection in EU law but was not setting out a legal test. The test was rather that a dominant undertaking cannot refuse to meet the orders of an existing customer 'for the sole reason that that customer…exports part of the quantities ordered to other Member States with higher prices' unless the orders in question are 'out of the ordinary'.[44] The behaviour under review was analysed as a form of refusal to supply liable to eliminate all competition from the parallel importers in question in the Member States of import.[45] This characterization of the behaviour in *Sot Lélos kai Sia* is mistaken. One of the precedents on which the Court of Justice relied was *Commercial Solvents*, a case concerned with vertical foreclosure, namely with the refusal of a vertically integrated dominant undertaking to supply an input to an upstream customer who is also a downstream competitor.[46] In *Sot Lélos kai Sia*, the refusal to supply concerned not an input but the final product that customers would simply buy in one Member States and resell in another Member State. The other precedent on which the court relied was *United Brands*, a case in which the dominant undertaking stopped supplying a customer because the latter had become heavily engaged in the promotion and sale of the products of a competitor. The effect of the practice was to deter other customers from stocking and promoting competitors' products. The refusal to supply was, therefore, a way of enforcing a single branding strategy. It had nothing to do with either vertical foreclosure or the prevention of parallel imports.[47] The question in *Sot Lélos kai Sia* was different: in what circumstances does a dominant undertaking's interference with free trade run counter to the purpose of Article 102? The Court answered that question when it recalled that the case law had already established that 'a practice by which an undertaking in a dominant position aims to restrict parallel trade in the products that it puts on the market constitutes abuse of that dominant position'. This was, in particular, when the effect of the practice was to neutralize the benefits of lower prices that 'may' apply elsewhere in the European Union or 'to create barriers to re-importations which come into competition with the distribution network' of the dominant undertaking.[48] This principle would explain why the ruling in *Sot Lélos kai Sia* is limited to ordinary orders of established customers. A dominant undertaking is under no duty to expand production in order to allow

---

[42] ibid paras 9–13.   [43] ibid paras 52–57.

[44] ibid paras 70–71.   [45] ibid paras 33–39.

[46] Cases 6/73 and 7/73 *Istituto Chemioterapico Italiano SpA and Commercial Solvents Corp v Commission* [1974] ECR 223 (*Commercial Solvents*).

[47] Case 27/76 *United Brands Co and United Brands Continentaal BV v Commission* [1978] ECR 207, paras 163–203.

[48] Joined Cases C-468/06 P to C-478/06 P *Sot Lélos kai Sia*, para 37, relying on Case 26/75 *General Motors Continental NV v Commission* [1975] ECR 1367 and 226/84 *British Leyland plc v Commission* [1986] ECR 3263.

parallel trade to develop. But if it is already selling its products it cannot engage in practices that have the sole or overwhelmingly predominant purpose of impeding intra-EU trade in its products.

(d) Raising rivals' costs

Excessive prices or excessively onerous contractual terms may be an abuse of dominance when their sole or overwhelmingly predominant purpose is to restrict free trade. The case law and the Commission practice, however, are rather confused and may be read as suggesting that these practices are abusive because they are exploitative of customers. In reality, excessive prices or excessively onerous trading conditions that can only serve the purpose of preventing intra-EU trade are prohibited not because they are exploitative of customers but because they raise the costs of undertakings engaging in intra-EU trade which is liable to be restricted as a result.

In *General Motors*, the Court held that General Motors had a monopoly on the market for the inspection of imported motor vehicles of its own make in order to verify their conformity with specifications approved by the Belgian authorities.[49] The Court said that an abuse may consist in the charging of a price 'which is to the detriment of any person acquiring a motor vehicle imported from another Member State'.[50] A price 'which is excessive in relation to the economic value of the service provided' was, therefore, not abusive *per se* but only to the extent that it limited parallel imports.[51] The Court added that an excessive price could also be abusive when it led to 'unfair trade' under Article 102(a) but there is no reason to believe that the Court was setting out a second, alternative test, given that it did not explain what 'unfair trade' under Article 102 meant.

In *British Leyland*, the Court of Justice applied *General Motors* to a very similar set of facts, this time relating to the issuing of certificates of conformity for left-hand-drive cars re-imported into the United Kingdom.[52] The Court relied on *General Motors* but understood that judgment as prohibiting a legal monopoly from charging a price that is disproportionate to the economic value of the service provided.[53] However, *General Motors* establishes that an excessive price is abusive when it prevents parallel imports. *British Leyland* suggests that Article 102 imposes on a legal monopoly a duty not to charge a price that is disproportionate to the economic value of the product or service. Insofar as the Court was relying on *General Motors* as a precedent, this conclusion is based on a misunderstanding of the *ratio* of that case. Nor was it necessary on the facts of the case at hand, as British Leyland—in very much the same way as, allegedly, General Motors more than a decade earlier[54]—was charging excessively high fees for certificates

---

[49] Case 26/75 *General Motors*, paras 4–10. The monopoly arose because Belgian law granted General Motors the exclusive right to carry out such inspections.
[50] ibid para 11.   [51] ibid para 12.   [52] Case 226/84 *British Leyland*.
[53] ibid para 27.
[54] The decision of the Commission was set aside by the Court of Justice on the facts: Case 26/75 *General Motors*, paras 13–24.

of conformity in order to prevent parallel imports of cars of its own make to the United Kingdom.[55]

General Motors was applied by the Commission in *DPAG—Interception of Cross-Border Mail*, a case in which the Commission held that the German public postal operator Deutsche Post AG (DPAG) had abused its dominant position on the German market for the forwarding and delivery of incoming cross-border letter mail.[56] A number of companies based in Germany or in third countries used the British Post Office (BPO) for bulk mail deliveries to Germany, which allowed them to realize appreciable cost savings compared to collection and delivery in Germany.[57] The Commission made it clear that it investigated DPAG's overall pattern of behaviour rather than focusing on individual elements of its anti-competitive strategy in isolation.[58] The abuse consisted in the intercepting, surcharging, and delaying of in-coming cross-border mail.[59] In particular, based on legal arguments that the Commission found to be incompatible with EU law, DPAG required BPO to pay the difference between the full domestic tariff and the terminal dues payable under the *Reims II* agreement.[60] This surcharge was found to be an excessive price as it was 25 per cent above the average cost of the service.[61] The Commission recalled that the case law prohibits excessive pricing if it has the effect of 'curbing parallel trade or of unfairly exploiting customers'.[62] However, it relied for this proposition on *General Motors*, which was only concerned with parallel trade and, therefore, with the exclusionary effect of excessive pricing. On the facts, *DPAG—Interception of Cross-Border Mail* was also only about trade restrictions. DPAG's conduct was aimed at weakening a foreign competitor. Higher charges and delays incurred by BPO might have resulted in UK customers shifting their business to DPAG on the UK market for outgoing cross-border letter mail.[63] More broadly, DPAG was trying to force the customers of BPO to send mail to Germany from Germany. In this way, by preventing senders from using the most efficient delivery service for their bulk mail within the European Union, DPAG was preventing trade within the internal market and thus harming productivity growth which crucially requires producing a unit of output at the lowest possible cost, including through localizing production, distribution, and services in the country where they are most efficient. Therefore, the conclusion that a price that exceeds the average cost by 25 per cent is abusive in itself regardless of its effect of impeding free trade must be regarded as wrong in law and contrary to the objective of Article 102. *DPAG—Interception of Cross-Border Mail* is not an excessive pricing case but an application of the naked exclusion test to conduct having the sole or overwhelmingly predominant purpose of impeding trade.

---

[55] This is clear from the overall facts of the case: see Case 226/84 *British Leyland*, paras 11–34.
[56] *Deutsche Post AG—Interception of Cross-Border Mail* [2001] OJ L331/40 (*DPAG—Interception of cross-border mail*).
[57] ibid recitals 8–78.   [58] ibid recital 104.   [59] ibid recitals 104 and 120.
[60] See *Reims II* [1999] OJ L275/17.
[61] *DPAG—Interception of cross-border mail*, recital 156.   [62] ibid recital 155.
[63] ibid recital 132.

(e) Discrimination

Consistently with the key role that free trade plays in the internal market as a driver of productivity and social welfare in the long term, discriminatory behaviour having the sole or overwhelmingly predominant purpose of restricting trade is abusive under Article 102. The anti-competitive harm of such practices is not the competitive distortion caused by upstream non-cost reflective prices but the restriction of trade. It is preferable, therefore, not to refer to Article 102(c) in relation to this form of abuse.

Applying dissimilar conditions to equivalent transactions to customers depending on the extent to which they engage in intra-EU trade is prima facie abusive. In *United Brands*, the dominant undertaking United Brands Company (UBC) applied different prices for identical quantities of green bananas sold on the same terms at the two European ports of Bremerhaven and Rotterdam. The prices differed depending on the Member State of the destination of the goods.[64] The Commission held that this practice was an impediment to intra-EU trade.[65] The Court of Justice upheld the Commission's decision, placing even more emphasis on the detriment to the single market as an anti-competitive effect of the discriminatory practice.[66] The Court said that the discriminatory prices were 'obstacles to the free movement of goods'.[67] This effect was exacerbated by the prohibition against distributors reselling bananas when still green[68] and by a quota system whereby UBC determined the quantities allocated to each customer.[69]

Discrimination aimed solely at restricting competition from foreign competitors is also prima facie abusive. In *Irish Sugar*, a notable example of market-partitioning price discrimination was the export rebate which the dominant undertaking granted to industrial customers who exported their final product.[70] The Commission held that the system was abusive under Article 102(c) because the rebates were not consistently applied to all exporters and because they discriminated between non-exporting and exporting customers even if the transaction was identical and even if these two categories of customer did not compete with each other.[71] The Court upheld the Commission decision on the basis that the rebates in question were designed to prevent customers who were engaged in export trade, and therefore more exposed to foreign suppliers of sugar, from switching to foreign suppliers for their requirements.[72] Article 102(c) was relied on in very general, almost abstract, terms.[73] The Court identified two anti-competitive effects. The first was a distortion of the competitive process due to the prices being determined not by supply and demand on the Irish market but by the location of the buyer

---

[64] *Chiquita* [1976] OJ L95/1.   [65] ibid.

[66] Case 27/76 *United Brands*, paras 223–234.   [67] ibid para 232.

[68] ibid paras 232 and 130–162 (on the abusive nature of the resale prohibition clause). The Commission had not relied on UBC's resale prohibition clause as a reinforcing factor of the market-partitioning discrimination.

[69] ibid para 232. This quota allocation system was not the object of a finding of infringement and is not further described or discussed in the judgment.

[70] *Irish Sugar*, recitals 70–72, 136–144, and 157.   [71] ibid recitals 136–138.

[72] Case T-228/97 *Irish Sugar*, para 139.   [73] ibid para 140.

of the end product.[74] This is, however, not an anti-competitive effect. Even when a dominant undertaking price discriminates, it is always the interaction of supply and demand that determines market output. The test set out by the Court is meaningless and incapable of sustaining the finding of abuse. However, the Court identified a second anti-competitive effect in the exclusion of foreign producers of sugar. The rebates 'placed the applicant's competitors on the industrial sugar market who were based outside Ireland at a competitive disadvantage'.[75] This form of 'competitive disadvantage' is not the competitive disadvantage required under Article 102(c). It is a restriction of intra-EU trade. The Court put this beyond doubt when it said that the rebates under review served 'to maintain, and even reinforce, the isolation of the industrial sugar market in Ireland'.[76] The export rebate under review should have been characterized as a naked restriction of intra-EU trade rather than a discriminatory abuse under Article 102(c).

Applying dissimilar conditions to equivalent transactions depending on the nationality or residence of the customers is prima facie abusive. In *Corsica Ferries Italia Srl v Corpo dei Piloti del Porto di Genova*,[77] an association of undertakings enjoying a legal monopoly on the market for pilotage services in the port of Genoa applied a tariff that discriminated in favour of vessels authorized to carry on cabotage. Cabotage is the provision of shipping services between the ports of one State. Only vessels flying the Italian flag could be authorized to engage in cabotage in Italy and, as a matter of fact, undertakings owning these vessels were predominantly Italian. As a result of the discriminatory tariff, vessels sailing between ports of different Member States were charged higher fees than cabotage vessels for the same pilotage services. The Court of Justice held that this practice amounted to discrimination on the ground of nationality and was in breach of the freedom to provide maritime services as regulated at the time.[78] In response to a further question by the referring court, the Court of Justice also ruled that Italy was in breach of Articles 106 and 102 because, by approving the discriminatory tariff, it induced the dominant undertaking to which it had granted the exclusive right to provide pilotage services in the port of Genoa to abuse its dominant position by applying dissimilar conditions to equivalent transactions within the meaning of Article 102(c).[79] Importantly, the Court did not mention the further requirement of Article 102(c), namely 'competitive disadvantage'. This is even more striking if one considers that the Court had examined the 'disadvantage' resulting from the restriction of the freedom to provide services. The disadvantage was, mainly, the increased cost that the discriminatory tariff imposed on an undertaking providing shipping services in Italy from other Member States compared to an Italian undertaking.[80] The absence of analysis of competitive disadvantage under Article 102(c) can be explained by the fact that the prohibition of discrimination on grounds of nationality or residence applies regardless of a specific disadvantage to the person

---

[74] ibid para 141.   [75] ibid para 145.   [76] ibid para 147.
[77] Case C-18/93 *Corsica Ferries Italia Srl v Corpo dei Piloti del Porto di Genova* [1994] ECR I-1783.
[78] ibid paras 17–37.   [79] ibid para 43.   [80] ibid para 21.

exercising the freedom, which is distinct from the discrimination itself.[81] This principle was applied in *1998 Football World Cup*, where the French Committee for the organization of the 1998 Football World Cup (CFO) had applied conditions for the sales of certain tickets to the general public which discriminated in favour of customers residing in France. Although the Commission examined the case as an exploitative abuse, the better view is that the abuse was a form of discrimination that restricted free trade within the European Union.[82]

The principle that discrimination against undertakings engaged in intra-EU trade or in favour of domestic undertakings is abusive under Article 102 was also applied in *Portuguese Republic*. In that case, the Portuguese airport authority applied a system of landing charges under which domestic flights benefited from a 50 per cent discount. In theory, all EU undertakings could operate domestic flights.[83] However, the Court of Justice held that a measure favouring domestic flights affected 'free competition' in that it granted an advantage to customers depending on the degree to which they were engaged in purely domestic trade.[84] The Court also held that a rebate system under which landing charges were progressively reduced based on the number of landings[85] was discriminatory because the higher thresholds could be met only by the largest customers of the dominant undertaking.[86] These rebates infringed Article 102(c) because they favoured 'certain airlines, in this case de facto the national airlines, and where the airports concerned are likely to enjoy a natural monopoly for a very large portion of their activities'.[87] While the Court used language suggesting that a rebate system that benefits only the largest customers of the dominant undertaking and is not objectively justified is abusive under Article 102(c),[88] the better view is that this part of the judgment rests on the same rationale and pursues the same policy objective as the ruling on the discriminatory discounts in favour of domestic flights. The Court should have made it clearer that the fact that only the national carriers could achieve the highest thresholds was not only relevant but necessary to the finding of abuse. The discounts resulted in a *de facto* discrimination between national and foreign carriers. This is why it was possible to conclude that they were abusive only on the basis of the very significant differences in the average rates applied to

---

[81] See Arts 59 and 65 of the EC Treaty establishing the European Economic Community 25 March 1957, which the Court of Justice applied in the *Corsica Ferries* case. See now Arts 56 and 61 TFEU.

[82] *1998 Football World Cup* [2000] OJ L5/55.

[83] Case C-163/99 *Portuguese Republic v Commission* [2001] ECR I-2613, paras 3 and 61.

[84] Case C-163/99 *Portuguese Republic*, para 66, relying on Case C-381/93 *Commission v French Republic* [1994] ECR I-5145.

[85] For a detailed analysis of the rebates, see Case C-163/99 *Portuguese Republic*, para 4 and *Portuguese Airports* [1999] OJ L69/31, recital 2.

[86] Case C-163/99 *Portuguese Republic*, para 52.

[87] ibid para 56 and *Portuguese Airports*, recital 26: 'the *de facto* effect of this system, therefore, is to favour the national carriers, ie TAP and Portugalia'.

[88] Case C-163/99 *Portuguese Republic*, para 53.

different carriers[89] without any analysis of competitive disadvantage on the down-stream market. The abuse was, therefore, a form of naked exclusion restricting intra-EU trade rather than a discriminatory abuse under Article 102(c).

(f) Naked exploitation

Article 102 prohibits exploitative abuses when they limit production, markets, and technical development to the detriment of consumers. Exploitative abuses are assessed under the consumer harm test.[90] However, there may be exceptional circumstances in which a naked exploitation test is applicable. A naked exploita-tion test would condemn conduct that has the sole or overwhelmingly predom-inant purpose of limiting production, markets, or technical development to the prejudice of consumers,[91] has no conceivable redeeming virtue either by way of efficiencies or otherwise, and is reasonably capable of causing competitive harm. This test may be met when the following conditions are present: (a) an undertak-ing obtains a monopoly or quasi-monopoly on the basis of a commitment to adopt a course of conduct which is sufficiently specified at the time when the commit-ment is made; (b) other undertakings rely on the commitment to their detriment; and (c) the now monopolist or quasi-monopolist breaches its commitment for no other conceivable reason than to exploit its market power to the detriment of its customers. A case in which this may occur is when, in the context of a standard setting process, the holder of an IP right relevant to the proposed standard obtains a dominant position on the basis of a commitment to charge a certain price,[92] its

---

[89] *Portuguese Airports*, recital 25. The Court seemed more concerned with the excessive level of the discount for the highest threshold: Case C-163/99 *Portuguese Republic*, para 54.

[90] See 275–282 below.

[91] A dominant position is not prohibited as such. Therefore, exploitative abuses must consist in more than simply charging the profit-maximizing price that is rational for the dominant undertak-ing to apply. See 275–277 below.

[92] Currently, the commitment is generally a FRAND or RAND commitment. It is questionable whether the concept of FRAND or RAND meets the proposed test that the commitment must be to adopt a course of conduct which is sufficiently specified. On the concept of FRAND or RAND see DG Swanson and WJ Baumol, 'Reasonable and Non-Discriminatory (RAND) Royalties, Standards Selection, and Control of Market Power' (2005) 73 Antitrust LJ 1 and A Layne-Farrar, AJ Padilla, and R Schmalensee, 'Pricing Patents for Licensing in Standard-Setting Organizations: Making Sense of Frand Commitments' (2007) 74 Antitrust LJ 707. The FRAND standard to assess royalties and other licensing terms is adopted in the Commission Notice—Guidelines on the application of Article 81 of the EC Treaty to technology transfer agreements [2004] OJ C101/2. As regards exclusive cross-licences that create an industry standard, the Commission explains that 'it will normally be required that the technologies which support such a standard be licensed to third parties on fair, reasonable and non-discriminatory terms' (ibid para 164). As regards technology pools, the Commission states: 'Where the pool has a dominant position on the market, royalties and other licensing terms should be fair and non-discriminatory and licences should be non-exclusive. These requirements are neces-sary to ensure that the pool is open and does not lead to foreclosure and other anti-competitive effects on down stream markets. These requirements, however, do not preclude different royalties for dif-ferent uses. It is in general not considered restrictive of competition to apply different royalty rates to different product markets, whereas there should be no discrimination within product markets. In particular, the treatment of licensees should not depend on whether they are licensors or not. The Commission will therefore take into account whether licensors are also subject to royalty obligations' (ibid para 226). See also the Communication from the Commission—Guidelines on the applicabil-ity of Article 101 of the Treaty on the Functioning of the European Union to horizontal co-operation

future customers rely on such a commitment by making significant sunk investments, and, after the adoption of the standard, the now dominant undertaking, without any conceivable reason other than to exploit its market power, breaches its commitment.[93] The application of the naked abuse test would mean that in such a case the dominant undertaking may be found to have abused its dominant position purely on the basis of the breach of a sufficiently specified commitment without any analysis of consumer harm, which is otherwise invariably required for exploitative abuses.

This approach should not be extended beyond the deliberate breach of a commitment which resulted in the undertaking in question becoming a monopolist or quasi-monopolist and on which its customers relied to their detriment. In particular, the charging of a price in excess of a regulatory benchmark applicable in the industry may be used in the assessment of excessive prices but does not constitute naked exploitation.[94] Only to the extent that the regulatory benchmark reflects the competitive price, for instance the price that allows the undertaking in question to cover the long-term economic cost of the business, can it be used to determine whether a price is excessive. Therefore, a regulatory benchmark is not a substitute for the Article 102 tests but may be relevant to their application to the facts of an individual case.

C. Intent and the risk of systematic false convictions

(1) Predation

(a) *The problem*

The test of intent can be used to guard against the risk of false convictions when conduct has the potential of harming competition but may also be consistent with competition on the merits, and the cost of enforcement errors is very high. This

---

agreements [2011] OJ C11/1, corrigenda [2011] OJ C33/20 (the 'Horizontal Guidelines'), paras 285 and 287–291.

[93] See, in the EU, *Rambus* [2010] OJ L30/14. In the United States, there has been more extensive litigation: see eg *Broadcom Corp v Qualcomm Inc* 501 F 3d 297 (3d Cir 2007); *Rambus Inc v Federal Trade Commission* 522 F3d 456 (DC Circuit 2008), cert denied *Federal Trade Commission v Rambus Inc* 129 S Ct 1318, 173 L ed 2d 586 (2009).

[94] This is the approach the Court of Justice adopted in Case 66/86 *Ahmed Saeed Flugreisen and Silver Line Reisebüro GmbH v Zentrale zur Bekämpfung unlauteren Wettbewerbs eV* [1989] ECR 803, para 43, for the assessment of the exploitative nature of air tariffs. The Court said that 'certain interpretative criteria for assessing whether the rate employed is excessive may be inferred from Directive 87/601/EEC, which lays down the criteria to be followed by the aeronautical authorities for approving tariffs. It appears in particular from Article 3 of the directive that tariffs must be reasonably related to the long-term fully allocated costs of the air carrier, while taking into account the needs of consumers, the need for a satisfactory return on capital, the competitive market situation, including the fares of the other air carriers operating on the route, and the need to prevent dumping'. The Court did not say that a tariff in excess of the regulated tariff was abusive but that the regulated tariff provided 'interpretative criteria' for the application of the test under Art 102.

is particularly the case in relation to predation. The Commission Guidance on Article 102 defines predation as follows:[95]

A dominant undertaking engages in predatory conduct by deliberately incurring losses or forgoing profits in the short-term . . . so as to foreclose or be likely to foreclose one or more of its actual or potential competitors with a view to strengthening or maintaining its market power, thereby causing consumer harm.

Predation is a costly and risky strategy for a dominant undertaking,[96] and often there will be more rational means to achieve the intended anti-competitive ends.[97] On the other hand, in settings where capital markets are imperfect or an entrant does not have perfect information about the cost of the incumbent, predation may be a plausible exclusionary strategy.[98] The question is how to distinguish predatory from pro-competitive low prices. In the first place, the case law relies on a cost test: if the dominant undertaking is not covering its costs, the conduct in question is capable of excluding an equally efficient competitor.[99] However, the mere fact that a dominant undertaking's revenue is not high enough to cover its costs is not always sufficient to infer that the conduct under review is likely to harm social welfare in the long term. There may be reasons why total costs (TC) have not been recovered other than the intention to exclude competitors. In particular, when the dominant undertaking is recovering its variable cost but not its full fixed costs, in the short term it may still be rational for the dominant undertaking not to discontinue production. Stopping production may entail an even greater loss if at least some fixed costs are being recovered. Exit may be costly if there was a sunk cost of entry. Market demand may be falling, thus leading to a situation of

---

[95] 'Guidance on Art 102', para 63.

[96] H Bork, *The Antitrust Paradox: A Policy at War with Itself* (New York, The Free Press 1993) 149–152. For a lucid rebuttal of the simplistic Chicago School argument espoused by Bork, see OE Williamson, 'Williamson on Predatory Pricing II' (1979) 88 Yale LJ 1183, 1184–1186.

[97] LG Telser, 'Cutthroat Competition and the Long Purse' (1966) 9 Journal of Law and Economics 259; JS McGee, 'Predatory Price Cutting: The Standard Oil (NJ) Case' (1958) 1 Journal of Law and Economics 137, 137–141.

[98] J Tirole, *The Theory of Industrial Organization* (Cambridge Mass, MIT Press 1988) 365 and 379; PL Joskow and AK Klevorick, 'A Framework for Analyzing Predatory Pricing Policy' (1979) 89 Yale LJ 213, 230–231; J Roberts, 'A Signaling Model of Predatory Pricing' (1986) 38 Oxford Economic Papers (supplement) 75; D Sharfstein, 'A Policy to Prevent Rational Test-Market Predation' (1984) 2 RAND Journal of Economics 229; P Milgrom and J Roberts, 'Predation, Reputation and Entry Deterrence' (1982) 27 Journal of Economic Theory 280; D Kreps and R Wilson, 'Reputation and Imperfect Information' (1982) 27 Journal of Economic Theory 253; D Fudenberg and J Tirole, 'A "Signal-Jamming" Theory of Predation' (1986) 17 RAND Journal of Economics 366; G Saloner, 'Predation, Mergers and Incomplete Information' (1987) 18 RAND Journal of Economics 165.

[99] Case 62/86 *AKZO*, paras 71–74; Case C-333/94 P *Tetra Pak II*, para 41; Case C-202/07 P *France Télécom*, para 109. A crude cost test based on AVC was first proposed by PH Areeda and DF Turner, 'Predatory Pricing and Related Practices under Section 2 of the Sherman Act' (1975) 88 Harv L Rev 697. This test has since been subject to rigorous and well-founded criticism: FM Scherer, 'Predatory Pricing and the Sherman Act: A Comment' (1976) 89 Harv L Rev 869; WJ Baumol, 'Quasi-Permanence of Price Reductions: A Policy for Prevention of Predatory Pricing' (1980) 89 Yale LJ 1; Joskow and Klevorick, 'A Framework for Analyzing Predatory Pricing Policy', 242–245. See also JA Ordover and RD Willig, who endorse Joskow and Klevorick's structural analysis in their article 'An Economic Definition of Predation: Pricing and Product Innovation' (1981) 91 Yale LJ 8, 10–13.

overcapacity. The market may be expanding and the dominant undertaking may not have reached the new minimum efficient scale. Therefore, prices below average total cost (ATC) but above average variable costs (AVC) in themselves do not allow an inference of predation in themselves. But, the fact remains that firms must recover their TC in the long term in order to stay on the market. Prices below long-run average total costs (LRATC) set by a dominant undertaking can exclude an equally efficient competitor. However, more than a mere price/cost test is required to establish a prima facie case of predation when the dominant undertaking is recovering its AVC.

(b) Inadequacy of the recoupment test

One way of distinguishing predation from pro-competitive conduct is to determine whether the dominant undertaking is likely to recoup the losses incurred by engaging in the conduct under review after the exclusion of rivals.[100] Many commentators argue that recoupment should be a necessary element of the predation test.[101] Recoupment would constitute an additional filter, which contributes to minimizing the risk of false convictions and over-deterrence. Furthermore, if recoupment is not probable, predation would benefit consumers and should not be prohibited.[102] And, finally, recoupment would guard against regulatory capture because it helps to distinguish between harm to competitors who wish to be shielded from aggressive competition and harm to the market. The latter

---

[100] This is the expression of a more general scepticism about predatory pricing and abuse of dominance in general in some jurisdictions. See eg *Stearns Airport Equipment Co Inc v FMC Corp* 170 F3d 518 (5th Cir 1999) 527–528, where the United States 5th Appeals Circuit read the three leading Supreme Court cases on predation *Matsushita Electric Industrial Co Ltd v Zenith Radio Co* 475 US 574 (1986); *Cargill Inc v Monfort of Colorado, Inc* 479 US 104 (1986); and *Brooke Group Ltd v Brown & Williamson Tobacco Corp* 509 US 209 (1993) as expressing 'extreme skepticism' of predatory pricing claims both because of the difficulty in distinguishing predation from pro-competitive pricing and because of 'the consensus among economists that such schemes are difficult if not impossible to successfully complete and thus unlikely to be attempted by rational businessmen'.

[101] V Korah, *An Introductory Guide to EC Competition Law and Practice* (9th edn Oxford, Hart Publishing 2007) 195–197; EP Mastromanolis, 'Predatory Pricing Strategies in the European Union: A Case for Legal Reform' (1998) 19 ECLR 211, 219–223; P Bolton, JF Brodley, and MH Riordan, 'Predatory Pricing: Strategic Theory and Legal Policy' (2000) 88 Georgetown LJ 2239, 2267–2270; M Lorenz, M Lübbig, and A Russel, 'Price Discrimination, a Tender Story' (2005) 26 ECLR 355, 359; RJ Van den Bergh and PD Camesasca, *European Competition Law and Economics: A Comparative Perspective* (2nd edn London, Sweet & Maxwell 2006) 294–295; MS Gal, 'Below-Cost Price Alignment: Meeting or Beating Competition? The France Télécom Case' (2007) 28 ECLR 382, 383.

[102] This was one of the reasons why the Supreme Court of the United States in *Brooke Group* required that 'the plaintiff must demonstrate that there is a likelihood that the predatory scheme alleged would cause a rise in prices above a competitive level that would be sufficient to compensate for the amounts expended on the predation, including the time value of the money invested in it'. See also the Opinion of AG Mazák in Case C-202/07 *France Télécom*, para 74, where he said: 'where there is no possibility of recoupment, consumers and their interests should, in principle, not be harmed. I may note here that I share the view of AG Jacobs who in his Opinion in *Oscar Bronner* stated that "the primary purpose of Article [101 TFEU] is to prevent distortion of competition and in particular to safeguard the interests of consumers—rather than to protect the position of particular competitors".' The Court did not follow the AG's Opinion on this point (see Case C-202/07 *France Télécom*, paras 103–113).

only occurs when the dominant firm is able to raise prices and restrict output in the post-predation phase. However, proof of recoupment defined as a quantitative comparison between the predatory losses or forgone revenues and the gain from predation would be an unreliable indicator of the competitive harm that Article 102 aims to avoid. To understand why recoupment is not necessary for harm to long-term social welfare to occur, it may be instructive to consider the example of an entrant who is more efficient than the dominant firm. When this is the case, the latter may be forced to apply very deep price cuts in order to exclude the rival. Post-exclusion profits may not be sufficient to offset the losses incurred but the net effect of predation on social welfare and productivity is still negative because of the loss in productive efficiency—the less efficient firm remains in the market—and allocative efficiency—prices are higher after exit than they would have been in the absence of exclusion and there is a deadweight loss.[103] In this scenario, the dominant firm is not recouping its investment in predation but is simply protecting its market power.[104] It may be argued that if the dominant firm faces a more efficient rival and is unable to recoup the losses incurred by predating through discounted post-predation profits at least equal to the predatory losses, then it would be rational for such a firm to exit the market. This argument does not take into account the cost of exit, which the firm in question avoids by predating. So as long as the sum of the cost of exit plus the post-predation profits equals the predatory losses, predation is rational. Given that predation in EU law is only prohibited if engaged in by dominant firms, a significant cost of exit will almost inevitably be present.[105] Furthermore, when dominant undertakings engage in predation, they do so based on an *ex ante* assessment. They do not quantify precisely how much predation would cost and how much they would gain if predation is successful. They consider a number of objective factors that are relevant to the assessment of the costs and benefits of predation. These key elements of the decision-making process are the cost of the predation, the expected gain, and its likelihood of success. Based on these factors, the decision to engage in predation is not, or at least not necessarily, led by complex economic modelling or quantitative analysis but is a matter of judgment. This decision-making process is then reflected in conduct that is the implementation of the predatory strategy.

---

[103] C Ritter, 'Does the Law of Predatory Pricing and Cross-Subsidisation Need a Radical Rethink?' (2004) 27 World Competition 613, 644–645.

[104] ibid 645–646, Ritter argues that unprofitable predation may be preferable to an even less desirable outcome. This would be the case when the whole sequence—the predation and the post-predation phases—is '*less disastrous* than under the continued presence of the new entrant (or aggressive competitor) over the same period'. While this intuition is correct and accords with business reality, it is highly questionable whether, if the new entrant is more efficient than the incumbent, 'hardly any predatory strategy will seem unreasonable, provided that they carry even a remote possibility of excluding the maverick competitor'. There are a number of possible alternatives, the most obvious of which, discussed in the text, is exit.

[105] Other strategies would be open to the dominant firm. One may be repositioning, for instance by scaling down production and retreating to a niche segment of the market. The same analytical framework that applies to exit can be adapted to non-exit strategies. Repositioning will have a cost, which, as the cost of exit, must be taken into account in the assessment of the rationality of predation.

Furthermore, a predatory strategy does not necessarily involve recoupment. A dominant undertaking may be deterring entry through a signalling strategy or by building a reputation for predation in a multi-market context.[106] Finally, a requirement to prove recoupment would 'make it difficult to bring a successful case' because of the measurement problems that a competition authority or claimant would have to overcome, particularly when the rival is not excluded but forced to raise its prices in an oligopolistic market.[107] As a matter of enforcement policy, it is desirable for intervention to be possible before the harmful effects of the predatory conduct have occurred.[108] Proof of recoupment, therefore, could only be proof of the ability to recoup in the future. This exercise would either rely on structural factors already inherent in the assessment of dominance or would be in the form of the modelling of a future market setting post-exclusion. In the former case, recoupment would not perform the role of guarding against the risk of false convictions and over-deterrence because it would not add anything to the analysis of dominance and below-cost pricing. In the latter case, proof of recoupment would have to rely on assumptions about future market developments that would be speculative, to say the least, and unlikely to meet the standard of proof required in legal proceedings. As a consequence, the risk of false acquittals and over-deterrence would increase disproportionately.

(c) The test of intent in predation

Unlike recoupment, intent may be a suitable test to determine whether below-cost prices are predatory. If a dominant undertaking applies below-cost prices with the intent of eliminating a competitor by resorting to means that fall outside the scope of competition on the merits, the conduct is likely to run counter to the purpose of Article 102 as long as it is reasonably capable of causing competitive harm. The case law adopts this approach when it requires that—if prices are above AVC but below ATC, the conduct of the dominant undertaking is abusive only if there is proof of a plan to eliminate a competitor.[109] Proof of intent is not required if prices are below AVC because the case law considers that, prima facie, such prices can have no other purpose than the elimination of a competitor.[110] When prices are below AVC intent is, therefore, not irrelevant but presumed.

The question arises of whether a 'plan' or 'intent' to eliminate a competitor is a test of intent or rather an objective assessment of the conduct in its market context.

---

[106] Ritter, 'Does the Law of Predatory Pricing and Cross-Subsidisation Need a Radical Rethink?', 639–641; R O'Donoghue and AJ Padilla, *The Law and Economics of Article 82 EC* (Oxford, Hart Publishing 2006) 255; J Temple Lang and R O'Donoghue, 'Defining Legitimate Competition: How to Clarify Pricing Abuses under Article 82 EC' (2002) 26 Fordham Intl LJ 83, 144–145.

[107] O'Donoghue and Padilla, *The Law and Economics of Article 82 EC*, 255; Temple Lang and O'Donoghue, 'Defining Legitimate Competition: How to Clarify Pricing Abuses under Article 82 EC', 144–145.

[108] Ritter, 'Does the Law of Predatory Pricing and Cross-Subsidisation Need a Radical Rethink?', 642; O'Donoghue and Padilla, *The Law and Economics of Article 82 EC*, 256.

[109] Case 62/86 *AKZO*, paras 71–74; Case C-333/94 P *Tetra Pak II*, para 41; Case C-202/07 P *France Télécom*, para 109.

[110] Case 62/86 *AKZO*, para 71; Case C-202/07 P *France Télécom*, para 109.

In *AKZO*, the Court held that certain price quotations could only be explained by AKZO's 'intention to damage' its competitor ECS.[111] In the same case, the Court of Justice considered that AKZO's pricing policies had the 'aim of damaging ECS's viability'.[112] In *Tetra Pak II*, the Court of First Instance relied on evidence of 'eliminatory intent', a 'plan for eliminating' Tetra Pak's competitor Elopak, and an 'eliminatory strategy'.[113] The Court also held that, when prices were above AVC but below ATC, the *AKZO* rule required the ascertainment of 'the strategy of the undertaking in a dominant position'.[114] The Court of Justice used the phrase 'economic purpose' in relation to prices below AVC and 'intention' in relation to prices above AVC but below ATC.[115] In *France Télécom*, the Court of First Instance referred to 'a plan for eliminating a competitor'[116] and 'intention to eliminate competition'.[117] The Court of Justice used the phrases 'plan having the purpose of eliminating a competitor'[118] and, in relation to prices below AVC, 'economic objective'[119] and 'eliminatory intent'.[120] Disposing concisely of the argument of the applicant that the Court of First Instance had relied only on subjective elements to establish a predatory plan, the Court of Justice said that 'although the Court of First Instance referred to a "strategy to preempt" the market by WIN, it none the less deduced this from objective factors such as that undertaking's internal documents'.[121] Thus, reliance on internal documents was sufficient to establish intention. It is clear, therefore, that the test is a test of subjective intent but intent may be inferred exclusively from circumstantial evidence and must have been implemented in conduct capable of achieving the intended result not only in the abstract but in its market context.

(d) Recoupment as predatory incentive

Intent is superior to recoupment as a predation test. However, recoupment may be relevant evidence of motive or incentive to predate under the intent test. In *France Télécom*, the Court of Justice held that predation is prohibited because it is a practice with 'the sole economic objective' of eliminating competitors 'with a view, subsequently, to profiting from the reduction of the degree of competition still existing on the market'.[122] This definition of predation already demonstrates that the existence of an incentive to predate is relevant to prove intent. The Court, however, dispensed with proof of recoupment when the 'eliminatory intent of the undertaking at issue could be presumed in view of that undertaking's application

---

[111] Case 62/86 *AKZO*, para 102.   [112] ibid para 103. See also paras 108 and 109.
[113] Case T-83/91 *Tetra Pak II*, para 151. See also para 190, where the Court talks about 'eliminatory intent'.
[114] ibid para 187.   [115] Case C-333/94 P *Tetra Pak II*, paras 40–42.
[116] Case T-340/03 *France Télécom SA v Commission* [2007] ECR II-107, para 130. See also para 209, which talks about 'a plan of predation'.
[117] ibid para 197.
[118] Case C-202/07 *France Télécom*, para 109. See also para 111, where the Court uses similar terminology.
[119] ibid para 109.   [120] ibid para 110.   [121] ibid para 98.   [122] ibid para 107.

of prices lower than average variable costs'.[123] But the Court also clarified that recoupment was an element of a predatory strategy that may be relevant in rebutting a defence of objective justification for prices below AVC and in proving a predatory strategy if prices are above AVC but below ATC.[124] *Tetra Pak II*, a case where the Court of Justice said that proof of recoupment was not necessary to establish predation,[125] was understood as dispensing with proof of recoupment when prices are below AVC.[126] The problem with this attempt at distinguishing *Tetra Pak II* is that in that case there were also instances of prices above AVC but below ATC.[127] This error is, however, not fatal to the reasoning in *France Télécom*. *France Télécom* is consistent with *Tetra Pak II* because it simply clarifies that recoupment is not necessarily irrelevant in the analysis of predation. *Tetra Pak II* still stands as authority for the proposition that recoupment is not a necessary element of the predation test.

A separate question arises as to whether proof of the impossibility of recoupment is inconsistent with a finding of abuse. In *France Télécom*, the Court held that this is not the law.[128] It could be argued that this ruling is counter-intuitive because if there is no way in which a dominant undertaking can benefit from predation, this is strong evidence that the conduct is not abusive as it cannot harm social welfare in the long term. However, it is important to focus on the reason why the Court considered that the impossibility of recoupment was not incompatible with a finding of abuse. Even if the dominant undertaking cannot recoup its losses, predation allows it to 'reinforce its dominant position . . . so that the degree of competition existing on the market, already weakened precisely because of the presence of the undertaking concerned, is further reduced and customers suffer loss as a result of the limitation of the choices available to them'.[129] The strengthening or even only the maintenance of a dominant position may, however, be considered a form of recoupment.[130] The Court was thus rejecting the definition of recoupment as a comparison of future gains with current losses. The Court was not saying that proof of lack of incentive to predate is compatible with a finding of predation. EU law, however, considers that the strengthening or maintenance of a dominant position is a sufficient predatory incentive. It is permissible to infer this condition from the elements relevant to the assessment of dominance[131] as long as the market structure is not likely to change significantly post-exclusion.

---

[123] ibid para 110. [124] ibid para 111. [125] Case C-333/94 P *Tetra Pak II*, para 44.
[126] Case C-202/07 *France Télécom*, para 110. [127] ibid para 42.
[128] ibid para 112. [129] ibid.
[130] Commission Guidance on Art 102, para 71, where the Commission states that consumer harm occurs when 'the conduct would be likely to prevent or delay a decline in prices that would otherwise have occurred'. While the consumer harm test is not relevant in predation analysis, this is a correct definition of a form of recoupment as incentive to predate.
[131] G Niels and H Jenkins, 'Reform of Article 82: Where the Link between Dominance and Effects Breaks Down' (2005) 26 ECLR 605, 606; M Moura e Silva, 'Predatory Pricing under Article 82 and the Recoupment Test: Do Not Go Gentle Into That Good Night' (2009) 30 ECLR 61, 66; M Motta, 'The European Commission's Guidance Communication on Article 82' (2009) 30 ECLR 593, 596. See also Van den Bergh and Camesasca, *European Competition Law and Economics*, 294, who argue that 'when analysing a complaint of predatory pricing, the extent of monopoly power, the conditions for market entry, and the effects that a dynamic competi-

This understanding of recoupment is not dissimilar to the approach adopted in the Guidance on Article 102.[132] However, and contrary to what the Guidance on Article 102 may appear to suggest, consumer harm is not a separate element of the predation test. The constitutive elements of the test are the application of prices below a relevant measure of costs, predatory intent, and the absence of objective justification. The focus of the intent test is on the strategy of the dominant undertaking not on the prediction of its future outcome.

(e) The no economic sense test as a test of intent

The no economic sense test asks whether conduct tends to restrict competition and would make no economic sense but for its effect of restricting competition and thus creating or maintaining monopoly power.[133] In the European Union, the test may appear to find some support in the case law.[134] In *AKZO*,[135] the Court of Justice held that prices below average variable costs 'by means of which a dominant undertaking seeks to eliminate a competitor must be regarded as abusive'. The Court explained the rationale for the test in the following way:[136]

A dominant undertaking has no interest in applying such prices except that of eliminating competitors so as to enable it subsequently to raise its prices by taking advantage of its monopolistic position, since each sale generates a loss, namely the total amount of the fixed costs (that is to say, those which remain constant regardless of the quantities produced) and, at least, part of the variable costs relating to the unit produced.

Subsequent cases have relied upon this predation test, often emphasizing the no economic sense rationale for the 'rule'.[137] However, in *AKZO* itself the Court of Justice set out a second test which strongly indicates the adoption of the as efficient competitor test in conjunction with a test of intent. The Court said that prices

---

tive process has on costs should be carefully examined in order to determine whether a sufficient degree of monopoly power could be acquired in the long run'. This test is not dissimilar to the strengthening of dominance test adopted by the Court of Justice in Case C-202/07 *France Télécom*, para 112.

[132] Guidance on Art 102, para 70: 'Generally speaking, consumers are likely to be harmed if the dominant undertaking can reasonably expect its market power after the predatory conduct comes to an end to be greater than it would have been had the undertaking not engaged in that conduct in the first place, that is to say, if the undertaking is likely to be in a position to benefit from the sacrifice.'

[133] See 66–72 above.

[134] See also the Guidance on Art 102, paras 59 and 60–63, which defines predation as involving an element of 'sacrifice' of short-term revenues. The analysis of sacrifice in the Guidance on Art 102, however, is not an endorsement of the no economic sense test. Rather, it is a definitional element to be understood in the context of a test of exclusion of as efficient competitors leading to consumer harm: see ibid paras 64–69.

[135] Case 62/86 *AKZO*.   [136] ibid para 71.

[137] Case T-83/91 *Tetra Pak II*, para 148 (relying on Case 62/86 *AKZO*, para 71) and paras 150: 'by their scale and their very nature, the purpose of such losses, which cannot reflect any economic rationale other than ousting Elopak, was unquestionably to strengthen Tetra Pak's position on the markets in non-aseptic cartons . . .' and 189 (relating to the UK market and repeating almost literally the same statement), upheld on appeal in Case C-333/94 P *Tetra Pak II*, para 41: '. . . prices below average variable costs must always be considered abusive. In such a case, there is no conceivable economic purpose other than the elimination of a competitor, since each item produced and sold entails a loss for the undertaking.'

above AVC but below ATC 'must be regarded as abusive if they are determined as part of a plan for eliminating a competitor'.[138] The Court went on to explain:[139]

Such prices can drive from the market undertakings which are perhaps as efficient as the dominant undertaking but which, because of their smaller financial resources, are incapable of withstanding the competition waged against them.

The Court of Justice clarified why proof of intent is not required when prices are below AVC in *France Télécom*, when it explained that 'prices below average variable costs must be considered prima facie abusive inasmuch as, in applying such prices, an undertaking in a dominant position is presumed to pursue no other economic objective save that of eliminating its competitors'.[140] The no economic sense test for prices below AVC is, therefore, a test of intent. Furthermore, because the Court used the phrase 'prima facie' and the verb 'presumed', it follows that it is open to the dominant undertaking to rebut the inference of predation not only by adducing evidence of an objective justification but also by displacing the presumption of intent, though in practice the two defences will almost always be indistinguishable.

(f) *The predation test in the Guidance on Article 102*

The Guidance on Article 102 defines predation as conduct by a dominant undertaking which deliberately incurs losses or forgoes profits in the short term so as to foreclose its rivals with a view to strengthening or maintaining its market power, thereby causing consumer harm.[141] The 'sacrifice' element of the predation test[142] is met if short-term revenues are lower than could have been expected from a reasonable alternative conduct.[143] Prices below average avoidable costs (AAC) are seen as a clear indication of sacrifice.[144] The Commission would then ask three further questions in its prioritization exercise. The first is whether the conduct is capable of excluding an equally efficient competitor.[145] The second is whether the conduct is likely to cause consumer harm.[146] The third is whether the conduct produces efficiencies that outweigh the harm to consumers.[147] Clearly, the Commission is attempting to apply the as efficient competitor test in conjunction with the consumer welfare test. Without any explanation, the Commission declines to follow the case law and sets out an alternative test of consumer harm. Quite apart from being contrary to the fundamental tenets of a system based on the rule of law, such an approach is not based on a sound enforcement policy. The case law has developed a perfectly workable test which is in line with the purpose of Article 102. In particular, as this chapter demonstrates, the case law is right to reject a consumer harm

---

[138] Case 62/86 *AKZO*, para 72. This test has also been relied upon in a number of subsequent cases but with no reference to the as efficient competitor rationale: Case T-83/91 *Tetra Pak II*, para 149.

[139] Case 62/86 *AKZO*, para 72.   [140] Case C-202/07 P *France Télécom*, para 109.

[141] Guidance on Art 102, para 59.   [142] ibid paras 59 and 60–63.

[143] ibid para 61.   [144] ibid para 64.   [145] ibid paras 64–65.

[146] ibid paras 66–68.   [147] ibid para 69.

test for predation, adopting a test of intent instead.[148] The Commission Guidance, therefore, carries no weight as a statement of the law and, given its deliberate disregard of a case law which gives effect to the purpose of Article 102, there must be serious doubts even as to whether it can be saved as a prioritization tool.

(2) Abuse of contractual rights

A particularly acute enforcement problem arises when a dominant firm exercises a right which is in itself unassailable under EU competition law but whose exercise may run counter to the purpose of Article 102. Clearly, because *ex hypothesi* the existence of the right is unobjectionable, the risk of false convictions and over-deterrence is very high. EU competition law distinguishes abuse of court proceedings and regulatory procedures from abuse of contractual rights. As explained above, abuse of court proceedings and regulatory procedures is examined under the naked abuse test.[149] As regards abuse of contractual rights, EU law adopts a broader test of intent.

In *Compagnie Maritime Belge*, one of the abuses consisted in the request by the members of a dominant shipping conference that the Zaire authorities should enforce an agreement which gave the conference's members the exclusive right to carry all cargo within the operation of the conference to and from Zaire. The agreement allowed for 'derogations' with the consent of both parties but the conference was not minded to give its consent.[150] The Court of First Instance said:[151]

…an undertaking in a dominant position which enjoys an exclusive right with an entitlement to agree to waive that right is under a duty to make reasonable use of the right of veto conferred on it by the agreement in respect of third parties' access to the market.

The Court went on to say that the members of the conference did not do so when they insisted that the agreement be strictly complied with, thus excluding from the market their only competitor with an initial market share of only 2 per cent. It was also relevant that the conduct was part of an exclusionary plan.[152] Therefore, when dealing with abuse of contractual rights, the case law adopts a cautious approach. *Compagnie Maritime Belge* considered that a relevant element of the case was the anti-competitive intent of the dominant undertaking. This was in addition to the objective factors relating to the exclusionary effect of the conduct. Intent plays the role of guarding against the risk of false convictions and over-deterrence where it

---

[148] See 203–209 above.

[149] See 190–191 above. Yet a different problem arises in relation to the abuse of IP rights: see 269–272 below.

[150] *Cewal, Cowac and Ukwal* [1993] OJ L34/20, recitals 20–27 and 63–72.

[151] Joined Cases T-24/93 to T-26/93 and T-28/93 *Compagnie Maritime Belge Transports SA v Commission* [1996] ECR II-1201, para 108, upheld on appeal in Joined Cases C-395/96 P and C-396/96 P *Compagnie Maritime Belge Transports SA v Commission* [2000] ECR I-1365, paras 72–88.

[152] Joined Cases T-24/93 to T-26/93 and T-28/93 *Compagnie Maritime Belge*, paras 102–109.

is particularly difficult to distinguish abusive conduct from the normal exercise of rights.

D. Intent and the risk of systematic false acquittals

(1) Tying

(a) The problem

Tying occurs when two products, A and B, are marketed so that customers buying A, the tying product, must also buy B, the tied product. B, however, can also be purchased as a stand-alone product.[153] Article 102(d) lists tying as one of the possible abuses, providing that an abuse may consist in 'making the conclusion of contracts subject to acceptance by the other parties of supplementary obligations which, by their nature or according to commercial usage, have no connection with the subject of such contracts'. It goes without saying, however, that this definition is purely illustrative. Tying may be abusive beyond the circumstances described in Article 102(d). For instance, it is well established that tying may be abusive when there is a natural link between the two products,[154] or when the tying is in accordance with commercial usage.[155] What counts is whether the tying is abusive under the general principles of Article 102.[156]

The assessment of tying under Article 102 has given rise to a degree of uncertainty and controversy.[157] There is a perception that the EU courts apply a rule

---

[153] Guidance on Art 102, para 48.   [154] Case C-333/94 P *Tetra Pak II*, para 37.

[155] Case T-83/91 *Tetra Pak II*, para 137, upheld on appeal in Case C-333/94 P *Tetra Pak II*, paras 35–37; T-201/04 *Microsoft Corp v Commission* [2007] ECR II-3601 (*Microsoft I*), para 940.

[156] Case T-201/04 *Microsoft I*, para 942.

[157] See, also for further references, J-Y Art and GS McCurdy, 'The European Commission's Media Player Remedy in its Microsoft Decision: Compulsory Code Removal Despite the Absence of Tying or Foreclosure' (2004) 25 ECLR 694; M Dolmans and T Graf, 'Analysis of Tying Under Article 82 EC: The European Commission's Microsoft Decision in Perspective' (2004) 27 World Competition 225; D Ridyard, 'Tying and Bundling—Cause for Complaint?' (2005) 26 ECLR 316; K-U Kühn, R Stillman, and C Caffarra, 'Economic Theories of Bundling and Their Policy Implications in Abuse Cases: An Assessment in Light of the Microsoft Case' (2005) 1 European Competition Journal 85; Van den Bergh and Camesasca, *European Competition Law and Economics*, 264–276; O'Donoghue and Padilla, *The Law and Economics of Article 82 EC*, 477–518; FEG Diaz and AL Garcia, 'Tying and Bundling under EU Competition Law: Future Prospects' (2007) 3 Competition Law International 13; J Langer, *Tying and Bundling as a Leveraging Concern under EC Competition Law* (Alphen aan den Rijn, Kluwer Law International 2007); CE Mosso et al, 'Article 82' in J Faull and A Nikpay (eds), *The EC Law of Competition* (2nd edn Oxford, OUP 2007) 313, 368–373; R Thompson and J O'Flaherty, 'Article 82' in P Roth and V Rose (eds), *Bellamy & Child European Community Law of Competition* (6th edn Oxford, OUP 2008) 909, 998–1004; R Whish, *Competition Law* (6th edn Oxford, OUP 2008) 679–687; E Rousseva, *Rethinking Exclusionary Abuses in EU Competition Law* (Oxford, Hart Publishing 2010) 219–257 and 396–403.

of *per se* illegality to tying[158] that is wholly inappropriate.[159] On the other hand, some argue that the case law, far from establishing a form of *per se* illegality, is a balanced approach that leads to reasonable results.[160] The Guidance on Article 102 considers that, in addition to dominance on the tying market,[161] three more factors are relevant to the analysis of tying: (a) the tying and the tied product must be distinct; (b) tying forecloses competitors on the tied market; and (c) it leads to consumer harm.[162] These elements are only partly consistent with those identified in the case law. First, the case law also requires that customers be coerced to obtain the tied product if they wish to purchase the tying product.[163] However, in the Guidance on Article 102 this requirement is inherent in the very definition of tying. Therefore, in this respect, there is no material difference between the case law and the Guidance on Article 102. Secondly, it is not entirely clear that the case law requires proof of foreclosure as there are precedents suggesting that, generally, foreclosure in inherent in a tying practice.[164] Finally, the case law does not appear to require consumer harm as a free-standing element of the test.

(b) *The enforcement risks associated with tying*

The assessment of the anti-competitive effects of tying is complex. The simplest theory of harm would be based on leveraging: a monopolist in market A has the ability and the incentive to obtain a monopoly in a competitive market B if it makes the purchase of product A conditional on also purchasing product B. In this way, the monopolist will earn a monopoly profit in market A and a monopoly profit in market B, instead of a monopoly profit in market A and no economic profit in market B. The Chicago critique easily demolished this simplistic theory of harm, at least for settings where the tying and the tied product are bought in fixed proportions and the tied market is perfectly competitive. A monopoly in market A can never extract more than the value $v_a + v_b$ that consumers place on A + B. Any bundled price exceeding $v_a + v_b$ would result in no sales. Any increase in the price of B would result in lower sales of A unless the monopolist also lowered the price of A. It follows that a producer of A and B that has a monopoly on market A can

---

[158] eg DS Evans, AJ Padilla, and MA Salinger, 'A Pragmatic Approach to Identifying and Analysing Legitimate Tying Cases' in CD Ehlermann and I Atanasiu (eds), *European Competition Law Annual 2003: What Is an Abuse of a Dominant Position?* (Oxford, Hart Publishing 2006) 556, 558.

[159] C Ahlborn, DS Evans, and JA Padilla, 'The Antitrust Economics of Tying: A Farewell to Per Se Illegality' (2004) 49 Antitrust Bull 297, 289–290.

[160] Dolmans and Graf, 'Analysis of Tying Under Article 82 EC: The European Commission's Microsoft Decision in Perspective', 226–238 and 242–244.

[161] This is not controversial: *Eurofix-Bauco v Hilti* [1988] L65/19, recital 70; Case T-30/89 *Hilti AG v Commission* [1990] ECR II-1439, para 85; *Microsoft* [2007] OJ L32/23 (*Microsoft I*) recitals 310–314 and Art 2(b); *Microsoft (tying)* [2010] OJ C36/7 (*Microsoft II*) recitals 17 and 24–30. For an exception see *Tetra Pak II*, upheld in Case T-83/91 *Tetra Pak II*, paras 117–122 and, on appeal, Case C-333/94 P *Tetra Pak II*, paras 21–33.

[162] Guidance on Art 102, para 50.

[163] *Microsoft I*, recitals 843–876 and Case T-201/04 *Microsoft I*, paras 1031–1058.

[164] *Microsoft I*, recital 841 and Case T-201/04 *Microsoft I*, paras 868, 1035, and 1036

only extract one monopoly profit on markets A and B.[165] The policy implication of the single monopoly profit theorem was that, because the monopolist of the tying product has no incentive to tie in order to obtain monopoly power on the tied market, which he cannot achieve, if tying takes place it must have an efficiency rationale. Efficiency justifications for tying are numerous and depend on the nature of the products concerned and the features of the markets, but the Chicago School identified, in particular, efficient price discrimination through the use of tying as a metering device,[166] the protection of the monopolist's goodwill by excluding inferior products from the tied markets,[167] technological interdependence,[168] economies of scale or scope,[169] and evasion of price regulation.[170]

In response to the Chicago critique, the post-Chicago literature shows convincingly that a dominant undertaking may have an incentive to tie in order to protect or strengthen its market power on the tying market, to acquire or protect market power on the tied market, or to acquire market power on a related emerging market.[171] The circumstances in which this may happen, however, often require knowledge of market data that is not normally available. Whinston's model, for instance, yields different results depending on the customers' valuations of the products in question, whether the incumbent commits to tying, and whether the products are independent or complementary. In the case of independent products, assuming economies of scale on the tied market, if the dominant undertaking did not commit to tying, the tying makes no difference to the decisions of rival firms as

---

[165] Bork, *The Antitrust Paradox*, 372–373; RA Posner, *Antitrust Law: An Economic Perspective* (2nd edn University of Chicago Press, Chicago 2001) 198–199; GJ Stigler, 'United States v Loew's Inc: A Note on Block Booking' (1963) Sup Ct Rev 152, 152–152.

[166] Posner, *Antitrust Law*, 199–200; Bork, *The Antitrust Paradox*, 376–378. Bork (ibid para 378) also identifies cases in which tying as a metering device is not a means to price discriminate, for instance when a durable product, however requiring maintenance services, is sold, and the tying of this product with components sold in variable quantities helps the seller distinguish between heavy users who will need more costly maintenance services and light users who will have lower maintenance requirements. In this example, tying allows charging heavy and light users different prices for the maintenance services, but the different prices are cost-justified and, therefore, not discriminatory.

[167] Posner, *Antitrust Law*, 201–202; Bork, *The Antitrust Paradox*, 379–380.

[168] Bork, *The Antitrust Paradox*, paras 379–380.

[169] ibid paras 378–379. While Bork speaks about economies of scale, the lower costs result from the production or distribution of distinct components as a bundle, which suggests that the correct terminology should be economies of scope.

[170] ibid para 376, where the author argues that if the price of the tying product is regulated or subject to a cartel, the tying may have the effect of remedying the distortion. The benefits of tying when the tying product is subject to a cartel are obvious. As for the case of evasion of government regulation, Bork argues that the remedy does not lie in the antitrust laws (ibid para 381). Interestingly, the Commission now sees evasion of price regulation in the tying market as an anti-competitive effect of tying: Guidance on Art 102, para 57 ('if the prices the dominant undertaking can charge in the tying market are regulated, tying may allow the dominant undertaking to raise prices in the tied market in order to compensate for the loss of revenue caused by the regulation in the tying market').

[171] MD Whinston, 'Tying, Foreclosure, and Exclusion' (1990) 80 American Economic Rev 837; DW Carlton and M Waldman, 'The Strategic Use of Tying to Preserve and Create Market Power in Evolving Industries' (2002) 33 RAND Journal of Economics 194; JP Choi and C Stefanidis, 'Tying, Investment, and the Dynamic Leverage Theory' (2001) 32 RAND Journal of Economics 52.

to whether to be active in the tied market. Exclusion is not possible.[172] The reason is that, in the absence of commitment, the dominant undertaking has an incentive to charge the short-term profit-maximizing price for the bundle. With or without tying, the incumbent will charge the same price and make the same profit. The Chicago critique applies. If, however, commitment is possible, tying may exclude an equally efficient competitor.[173] If the dominant undertaking has irreversibly committed to tying, it will have an incentive to lower the price of the bundle below the independent pricing level. This may force the entrant to exit or reduce its output.[174] Whinston extended the model to the case of heterogeneous valuations for the tying product and found that exclusion was more plausible in the absence of commitment than with commitment. The reason for this is that a commitment to tying could backfire in this scenario if a sufficient number of consumers had a valuation for the tying product below the cost of production. Furthermore, with tying, the tied market becomes differentiated, with a bundle supplied by the incumbent and a stand-alone product supplied by the entrant. Product differentiation increases the profits of the entrant.[175] In this setting, however, exclusion becomes plausible in the absence of commitment because it allows the incumbent to price discriminate between high and low valuation consumers of the tying product.[176] Yet different results obtain in the case of complementary products, where the Chicago critique applies with more force because a higher price for the tied product has the effect of eroding monopoly profits on the tying market. Here, the incentive to tie results from the existence of competitively supplied alternatives to the tying product or further uses of the tied product.[177]

Quite apart from the complexity of post-Chicago models, the welfare implications of tying remain unclear, even when tying can exclude an equally efficient competitor. Carlton and Waldman caution that the social welfare implications of their model of leveraging market power to a newly emerging market are ambiguous because the entrant's incentive to enter the tied market is the prospect of monopoly profits in the emerging market. Therefore, entry may in fact decrease social welfare.[178] This static welfare analysis, however, has only limited weight under Article 102, which has the objective of maximizing social welfare in the long term by protecting effective competition. Allowing an incumbent to exclude equally efficient competitors through means other than superior efficiency is likely to lead to X-inefficiencies and lower investment incentives in the long term. Therefore, a *per se* legality approach to tying, which would render this practice immune under EU competition law, would not only be against the text of Article 102(d) but also inconsistent with the purpose of Article 102 as a whole. Given that a *per se* prohibition of tying is unjustified[179] and non-intervention would run counter to

---

[172] Whinston, 'Tying, Foreclosure, and Exclusion', 842–843.   [173] ibid 843–846.
[174] ibid 844.   [175] ibid 846–847.   [176] ibid 848–850.   [177] ibid 850–856.
[178] Carlton and Waldman, 'The Strategic Use of Tying to Preserve and Create Market Power in Evolving Industries', 213.
[179] KN Hylton and M Salinger, 'Tying Law and Policy: A Decision-Theoretic Approach' (2001) 69 Antitrust LJ 469.

the purpose of Article 102, it is necessary to identify a test capable of determining when tying is anti-competitive without deterring pro-competitive behaviour.

(c) *Intent and incentive for anti-competitive tying*

To overcome the impasse that the complexity of the analysis of tying entails, the Commission has put forward a test of consumer harm. The Guidance on Article 102 requires proof of foreclosure leading to consumer harm,[180] stating that consumer harm may occur on 'the tied market, the tying market, or both at the same time'.[181] The Court of First Instance in *Microsoft I*, however, held that the finding that Microsoft's conduct protected market power on the tying market and aimed at monopolizing emerging markets was not necessary to establish the abuse. Proof of foreclosure on the tied market was sufficient.[182] The Court's scepticism about a consumer harm test is probably due to the realization that it is very difficult, perhaps impossible in practice, to prove that tying raises prices, restricts output, or depresses investment incentives. A tying practice under scrutiny by a competition authority or court is generally ongoing and may be sustainable in the long term. When this is the case, there will be no evidence of the counterfactual. To model prices, output, and innovation in a market setting without the tying practice can certainly be done but is unlikely ever to meet the standard of proof required in legal proceedings. As a consequence, the risk of false acquittals and under-deterrence would increase significantly. On the other hand, to say that tying deprives consumers of a wider choice of products is tantamount to recognizing that proof of foreclosure is sufficient: if competitors are excluded and offer a product that is not homogenous, this form of consumer harm is inherent in the foreclosure itself. This would raise the risk of false convictions and over-deterrence.

Consumer harm performs poorly as a tying test. Instead, intent could play a key role in determining whether a tying practice is anti-competitive.[183] A test of intent would place more emphasis on the strategic motivations of the dominant undertaking and would then verify that the conduct is capable, in the market context, of protecting or strengthening the dominant undertaking's market power on the tying market, acquiring or protecting market power on the tied market, or acquiring market power on a related emerging market.

The intent test in tying is perfectly administrable and reflects the practice of the Commission since *Tetra Pak II*. In that case, the Commission found that by tying cartons to machines, Tetra Pak foreclosed competition for cartons because the carton markets were the markets in which Tetra Pak was more vulnerable to competition. In this way, Tetra Pak 'artificially' limited 'competition to the area in which its position is strongest because equipment, in particular aseptic equipment, is the area in which its technological lead is greatest and entry barriers are at their highest'.[184] In *Hilti*, Hilti had been able to preserve and strengthen its

---

[180] Guidance on Art 102, paras 52–58 and 19–20.   [181] ibid para 52.
[182] Case T-201/04 *Microsoft I*, paras 1031–1090 and, in particular, para 1058.
[183] M Lao, 'Reclaiming a Role for Intent Evidence in Monopolization Analysis' (2004) 54 American University L Rev 151, 192–199.
[184] *Tetra Pak II*, recital 146.

dominant positions on the markets for nail guns, Hilti-compatible cartridges, and Hilti-compatible nails. Hilti's strategy was to use its dominant position on the markets where barriers to entry were highest, namely the markets for nail guns and Hilti-compatible cartridges, in order to reinforce its dominance on the market where it was most vulnerable, namely the market for Hilti-compatible nails.[185] In *Microsoft I*, the Court of First Instance considered that the foreclosure of competitors on the tied market was sufficient to establish the anti-competitive effect of tying.[186] The Commission, however, had gone further, particularly in the analysis of indirect network effects and actual foreclosure. Microsoft had an incentive to exclude because the market would have tipped at some point, giving it substantial market power on the media player market protected by high entry barriers created by the anti-competitive conduct itself. But why did Microsoft have an incentive to do so given that the Chicago critique demonstrates that, generally, a monopolist can only extract one monopoly profit on the tying and the tied market? The Commission identified two reasons.[187] The first was the protection of Microsoft's market power on the client PC operating system market. Media players could be used as platforms for 'limited purpose' programmes such as media applications calling upon the application programming interfaces exposed by media players. A development of this model to 'general purpose' applications would pose a threat to Windows as the dominant PC operating system, as applications could run on media players regardless of the underlying operating system. Media players in conjunction with Java technologies could significantly reduce the importance of the operating system. By foreclosing the media player market, Microsoft protected its dominant position on the operating system market.[188] Furthermore, Microsoft's monopolization of the media player market would increase the barriers to entry to the operating system market because it would force a potential entrant to offer a Microsoft-compatible media player.[189] The issue did not arise on appeal.[190] The second reason why Microsoft had an incentive to tie was the acquisition of market power on emerging markets. The monopolization of the media player market allowed Microsoft to gain a 'significant advantage in other business areas such as those for content encoding software, format licensing, wireless information device software, DRM solutions and online music delivery'.[191] Adopting the same approach, in *Microsoft II* the Commission took the preliminary view that the tying of Microsoft's web browser, Internet Explorer, to Windows was a strategy to preserve Microsoft's dominant position on client PC operating systems.[192]

A test of intent for tying would always require proof of capability to foreclose on the tied market. Without foreclosure on the tied market, the dominant undertaking would not be able to protect or strengthen its market power on the tying market, to acquire or protect market power on the tied market, and to acquire market power on a related emerging market. The case law and the Commission's practice

---

[185] *Eurofix-Bauco v Hilti*, recital 74.
[186] Case T-201/04 *Microsoft*, paras 1031–1059.   [187] *Microsoft I*, recitals 971–977.
[188] ibid recital 972. See recital 43 for an explanation of the functionality of 'Java technologies'.
[189] ibid recital 974.   [190] Case T-201/04 *Microsoft I*, paras 1031–1090.
[191] ibid recital 975 (footnotes omitted).   [192] *Microsoft II*, recitals 57–58.

are consistent with this approach and in no way support the idea that certain 'classic tying cases' infringe Article 102 regardless of foreclosure effects.[193] In *Eurofix-Bauco v Hilti*, the Commission established that Hilti's competitors would not be able to achieve the economies of scale necessary to compete effectively if they did not supply Hilti-compatible products[194] and that Hilti had been able to limit severely effective competition from independent producers of Hilti-compatible nails.[195] The issue did not arise before the EU courts. Therefore, the EU courts could not have ruled on the foreclosure requirement. In *Tetra Pak II*, Tetra Pak argued that the Commission found the tying of cartons to machines to be an infringement of Article 102 without considering whether these practices 'had any real effect on competition'.[196] The Court of First Instance rejected this argument on the ground that the tying clauses had to be appraised in the context of the other twenty-four contractual clauses under review, the 'effect' of which was 'an overall strategy aiming to make the customer totally dependent on Tetra Pak for the entire life of the machine once purchased or leased, thereby excluding in particular any possibility of competition at the level both of cartons and of associated products'.[197] The Court went on to comment on the 'object' of certain other clauses which 'could' be considered abusive in themselves. Importantly, these clauses did not include the terms obliging customers to purchase only Tetra Pak cartons from Tetra Pak for use with Tetra Pak machines.[198] In *Microsoft I*, the Commission examined in depth the foreclosure on the tied market.[199] The Court of First Instance endorsed this approach.[200] The Guidance on Article 102 is in line with this approach when it states that, for tying to be investigated by the Commission as a matter of priority, the exclusion of competitors from the tied market is invariably required.[201]

E. Evidence of intent as circumstantial evidence

Even when intent is not a constitutive element of the abuse, evidence of intent may be relevant to prove objective elements of the test.[202] This general approach is adopted in the Guidance on Article 102. The Commission considers that it

---

[193] This interpretation of the case law is widespread and led both the Commission and the Court of First Instance into error, albeit in obiter dicta, in *Microsoft I*, recital 841 and Case T-201/04 *Microsoft I*, paras 868, 1035, and 1036. N Economides and I Lianos, 'The Elusive Antitrust Standard on Bundling in Europe and in the United States in the Aftermath of the Microsoft case' (2009) 76 Antitrust LJ 483, 536, follow the traditional view and believe that the pre-*Microsoft* case law adopted a 'quasi-per se test' to the foreclosure element of tying.

[194] *Eurofix-Bauco v Hilti*, recital 70.　　　[195] ibid recital 72.

[196] Case T-83/91 *Tetra Pak II*, para 128.　　[197] ibid para 135.　　[198] ibid.

[199] *Microsoft I*, recitals 843–951.　　[200] Case T-201/04 *Microsoft I*, paras 1031–1058.

[201] Guidance on Art 102, para 52.

[202] Evidence of intent may, of course, be relevant for purposes that do not strictly fall within the constitutive elements of the abuse. For instance, evidence of intent may be relevant for the purposes of characterizing the abuse as a single overall infringement, which has significant implications, not least for the application of the limitation period: see eg Case T-321/05 *AstraZeneca*, paras 892–895 and *Prokent-Tomra* [2008] OJ C219/11, recital 392, upheld in Case T-155/06 *Tomra Systems ASA v Commission* [2010] OJ C288/31, under appeal in Case C-549/10 P *Tomra Systems ASA v Commission* [2011] OJ C63/18.

may rely on direct evidence of an exclusionary strategy such as internal documents or threats to competitors as evidence of anti-competitive foreclosure because such evidence 'may be helpful in interpreting the dominant undertaking's conduct'.[203]

It is important, however, to distinguish evidence of intent under the intent test, which is direct evidence—ie evidence of a primary fact[204]—and evidence of intent under a purely objective test, which is circumstantial evidence—ie evidence from which the existence of a primary fact may be inferred. An illustration of the confusion that may arise is *AstraZeneca*, a case in which the dominant supplier of Losec, a drug for the treatment of gastro-intestinal conditions, was accused of making misleading representations to the patent offices of certain Member States in order to obtain an extension of the duration of the exclusive right guaranteed by its patent over the active molecule of Losec. The General Court held that the 'misleading nature of representations made to public authorities must be assessed on the basis of objective factors'. Proof of the 'deliberate nature' or 'bad faith' of the dominant undertaking was not required.[205] However, the Court added that 'intention...also constitutes a relevant factor which may, should the case arise, be taken into consideration by the Commission'. Whether the dominant undertaking intended 'to resort to practices falling outside the scope of competition on the merits' may 'support the conclusion that the undertaking concerned abused a dominant position, even if that conclusion should primarily be based on an objective finding that abusive conduct actually took place'.[206] *AstraZeneca* is an application of the naked exclusion test. The naked exclusion test is better described as a test of intent. The Court, therefore, was wrong in holding that the intent of the dominant undertaking to harm competition was not required. As regards nakedly exclusionary conduct, the test of intent plays an important limiting role because it ensures that only conduct that is part of an anti-competitive strategy is prohibited by Article 102; otherwise there is a risk that the test may be over-expansive and catch conduct that is harmless under Article 102 (although it may be prohibited under other legal rules). The Court in *AstraZeneca* considered circumstantial evidence what was instead direct evidence.

In order to be relevant, evidence of subjective intention must relate to the intention to engage in conduct that does not fall within the scope of competition on the merits. In a predation case, for instance, intention must relate to a deliberate loss-making strategy that is only profitable because it excludes equally efficient competitors and allows the dominant undertaking to maintain or strengthen its market power. Evidence of the subjective intention of increasing or maintaining market share or overcoming a competitor would not be evidence of intention to engage in conduct that does not fall within the scope of competition on the merits. In some

---

[203] Guidance on Art 102, para 20.

[204] A primary fact is a fact that the law requires to be established, by proof or otherwise, in order for given legal effects to arise. A secondary fact is a fact from which the existence of a primary fact may be inferred. For instance, intent is a primary fact in the offence of murder. Motive is a secondary fact from which intent may be inferred.

[205] Case T-321/05 *AstraZeneca*, para 356.   [206] ibid para 359.

cases, this distinction between a generic intention to compete aggressively and a specific intention to behave in an anti-competitive way is not clearly drawn. As a result, internal documents that only reveal a generic intention to compete aggressively are mistakenly relied on as evidence of abuse. In *Tomra*, for instance, the Commission held that the dominant undertaking had abused its dominant position on five national markets for high-end reverse vending machines by entering into exclusive dealing arrangements,[207] individualized quantity commitments,[208] and individualized rebate schemes.[209] The Commission took the view that internal documents seized on Tomra's premises evidenced a policy of limiting entry, denying competitors growth opportunities, eliminating competitors through acquisitions, and tying customers by means of exclusive or preferred supplier agreements.[210] Reliance on this evidence for the purpose of establishing an exclusionary strategy is troublesome. The language relied on in *Tomra* as evidence of anti-competitive intent did not reveal any anti-competitive strategy because it did not relate to the anti-competitive means by which the exclusion of competitors would be achieved. References to exclusivity in internal documents are, therefore, neutral. Whether such references are evidence of anti-competitive intent depends on whether exclusivity is anti-competitive. Exclusivity, however, is not abusive by its very nature.[211] Therefore, the evidence in question was irrelevant and its use to establish the abuse could not fail to be prejudicial because it was based on a circular reasoning, which assumed that exclusivity was anti-competitive, which was instead the matter to be proved. The General Court, however, upheld the decision on this point. The Court applied the right legal principle, namely that internal documents may be evidence of an exclusionary strategy, but did not examine the content of the documents.[212] As a consequence, the Court failed to state the reasons for its ruling and distorted the evidence by assuming that references to practices that the Commission considered to be anti-competitive was evidence of anti-competitive intent.

F. Conclusion

This chapter concludes that, contrary to the received wisdom, intent plays an important role in determining whether conduct runs counter to the purpose of Article 102. Abuse, however, remains an objective concept because evidence of subjective intent is never sufficient, by itself, to establish a prima facie case of abuse. The conduct must be capable in its market context of causing competitive harm. Furthermore, intent can be inferred from purely objective factors so that direct

---

[207] *Prokent—Tomra*, recitals 286–296.   [208] ibid recitals 297–313.
[209] ibid recitals 314–329.   [210] ibid recitals 97–108.
[211] This is what the Commission had in mind: see ibid recitals 100–101, where the Commission identified an internal policy of using exclusive or *de facto* exclusive agreements as a means to grow or respond to competition, and recital 290, where the Commission stated that 'exclusivity obligations, because they require customers to purchase all or significant parts of their demand from a dominant supplier, have by their nature a foreclosing capability'. However, exclusivity must be examined under the as efficient competitor test: see 245–248 below.
[212] Case T-155/06 *Tomra*, paras 33–41.

proof of subjective intent is not necessary. With these important qualifications, intent plays three roles in shaping the abuse tests under Article 102.

First, intent constitutes the centre of gravity of the naked abuse test, which prohibits conduct that has the sole or overwhelmingly predominant purpose of harming competition, has no conceivable redeeming virtue either by way of efficiencies or otherwise, and is reasonably capable of causing competitive harm.

Secondly, intent complements the test of foreclosure of as efficient competitors in predation to guard against a systematic risk of false convictions and over-deterrence, particularly when the prices of the dominant undertaking are above AVC but below ATC. Recoupment is relevant to this test as predatory incentive. Intent also guards against the risk of systematic false convictions and over-deterrence in relation to the abuse of contractual rights, where it complements a test based on the reasonable exercise of the right and the foreclosure of competitors.

Thirdly, intent guards against the risk of systematic false acquittals and under-deterrence in tying, where it complements the test of foreclosure on the tied market by requiring proof of the anti-competitive incentive to tie defined as the protection, strengthening, or acquisition of market power by the dominant undertaking on the tied market, the tying market, or a related emerging market.

As well as being an element of the test in the circumstances highlighted above, intent may cast light on the objective elements of the abuse tests. However, care must be exercised in distinguishing whether evidence of intent is direct evidence or circumstantial evidence. Direct evidence of intent must relate to the anti-competitive purpose of the conduct under review under the relevant test. Circumstantial evidence of intent must relate to the anti-competitive elements of the conduct other than intent itself. Finally, it is of fundamental importance that evidence of anti-competitive intent be distinguished from evidence of the generic intent to carry out the practice under review. Generic intent to carry out the practice under review cannot be evidence of the anti-competitive elements of the conduct in question. Specific reference to methods of competition falling outside the scope of competition on the merits is required for such evidence to be admissible as evidence of abuse.

7

The As Efficient Competitor Test

A. Introduction

Under the as efficient competitor test, conduct is prima facie abusive if it is capable of excluding a competitor that is at least as efficient as the dominant undertaking.[1]

The as efficient competitor test has received strong judicial endorsement in predatory pricing[2] and margin squeeze[3] but not in other pricing abuses, in particular rebates.[4] When the as efficient competitor test applies, the case law is clear that consumer harm is not a necessary element of the test. This is in stark contrast with the Guidance on Article 102, which would appear always to require proof of consumer harm, albeit only for the purpose of prioritization of cases. Furthermore, the Guidance on Article 102 applies the as efficient competitor approach to evaluate not only predation[5] and margin squeeze[6] but also conditional rebates.[7] More generally, the as efficient competitor test also plays the role of a 'safe harbour'. This means that, when the allegedly abusive conduct consists in exclusionary prices, the Commission will normally only intervene if the prices of the dominant undertaking are below its costs.[8] However, the Commission points out that 'in certain circumstances a less efficient competitor may also exert a constraint which should be taken into account when considering whether particular price-

---

[1] For a normative discussion of the test, see 72–92 above.

[2] Case 62/86 *AKZO Chemie BV v Commission* [1991] ECR I-3359; Case T-83/91 *Tetra Pak International SA v Commission* [1994] ECR II-755 (*Tetra Pak II*), upheld in Case C-333/94 P *Tetra Pak International SA v Commission* [1996] ECR I-5951 (*Tetra Pak II*); Case T-340/03 *France Télécom SA v Commission* [2007] ECR II-107, upheld in Case C-202/07 P *France Télécom SA v Commission* [2009] ECR I-2369.

[3] Case T-271/03 *Deutsche Telekom AG v Commission* [2008] ECR II-477, upheld in Case C-280/08 P *Deutsche Telekom AG v Commission* [2010] OJ C346/4; Case C-52/09 *Konkurrensverket v TeliaSonera Sverige AB* (17 February 2011) (*TeliaSonera*).

[4] eg Case 322/81 *NV Nederlandsche Banden Industrie Michelin v Commission* [1983] ECR 3461 (*Michelin I*); T-203/01 *Manufacture Française des Pneumatiques Michelin v Commisson* [2003] ECR II-4071 (*Michelin II*); Case T-219/99 *British Airways plc v Commission* [2003] ECR II-5917, upheld in Case C-95/04 P *British Airways plc v Commission* [2007] ECR I-2331; Case T-155/06 *Tomra Systems ASA v Commission* [2010] OJ C288/31, under appeal in Case C-549/10 P *Tomra Systems ASA v Commission* [2011] OJ C63/18.

[5] Communication from the Commission—Guidance on the Commission's enforcement priorities in applying Article 82 of the EC Treaty to abusive exclusionary conduct by dominant undertakings [2009] OJ C45/7 ('Guidance on Art 102'), paras 63–74.

[6] ibid para 80.   [7] ibid paras 37–45.   [8] ibid paras 23–27.

based conduct leads to anticompetitive foreclosure'. As explained in Chapter 3, this dynamic application of the as efficient competitor test recognizes the under-inclusive nature of the test. Many abuses are rational precisely because they deny competitors the benefit of demand-related efficiencies and force them to operate on an inefficient scale. The exclusion of competitors who are not yet as efficient as the dominant undertaking but could become as or even more efficient than the dominant undertaking in the absence of the abusive conduct is likely to harm social welfare in the long term. Therefore, unlike the exclusion of less efficient competitors, the exclusion of potentially equally efficient competitors is a legiti-mate concern under Article 102.[9]

This chapter is structured as follows. First, it examines the development of the as efficient competitor test in predation and, in particular, the cost benchmarks that are relevant to the application of the test. Next, it examines the extension of the test to margin squeeze, above-cost rebates, mixed bundling, and exclusivity. Then, it discusses discriminatory abuses as a further extension of the as efficient competitor test. In discrimination, the efficiency benchmark is not the dominant undertak-ing because the latter does not compete on the market where the anti-competitive effects occur. Rather, the efficiency benchmark are the undertakings benefiting from the discrimination. Discrimination is capable of affecting the ability to com-pete of firms that are as efficient as firms benefiting from the discrimination and are placed at a competitive disadvantage because of the dominant undertaking's conduct. Finally, conclusions are drawn.

B. Predatory conduct

(1) Predation and exclusion of as efficient competitors

The test for predation in the case law is unequivocally based on the as efficient competitor principle.[10] In *AKZO*, the Court of Justice held that prices below AVC are presumed to be predatory, while prices above AVC but below ATC are abusive if they are part of a plan to eliminate a competitor.[11] The Court explic-itly relied on the as efficient competitor rationale in relation to prices above AVC and below ATC[12] but the same rationale applies *a fortiori* when prices are below average variable costs.[13] Unlike the subsequent US *Brooke Group* case,[14] and similarly to a number of US appellate courts' decisions,[15] the price-cost

---

[9] See 74–76 above.
[10] For the literature on predation, see 201–210 above. This chapter builds upon the conclusions that Ch 6 reached on predation as an anti-competitive strategy.
[11] Case C-62/86 *AKZO*, paras 71–72.   [12] ibid para 72.
[13] The price/cost test in *AKZO* has been consistently applied by the EU courts in predation cases: see, Case C-333/94 P *Tetra Pak II*, para 41 and Case C-202/07 P *France Télécom*, para 109.
[14] *Brooke Group Ltd v Brown & Williamson Tobacco Corp* 509 US 209 (1993).
[15] *Northeastern Telephone Co v AT & T* 651 F2d 76 (2nd Cir 1981), cert denied, 455 US 943 (1982); *MCI Communications Corp v American Telephone and Telegraph Co* 708 F2d 1081, 1132–1133 (7th Cir 1983), cert denied, 464 US 891, 104 SCt 234 (1983); *Borden Inc v Federal Trade Commission* 674 F2d 498 (6th Cir 1982) vacated on other grounds, 461 US 940 (1983).

test is explicitly linked to the equally efficient competitor test. Moreover, EU law has clearly rejected the consumer harm test for the assessment of predation. Thus, proof of (the likelihood of) recoupment is not a requirement for establishing an abuse of predatory pricing.[16] Since recoupment is the effect of the conduct on consumer welfare, recoupment is the consumer harm element of the abuse of predatory pricing. It is to protect the interests of consumers that the US Supreme Court in *Brooke Group* required proof of a dangerous probability of recoupment for a finding of predation under section 2 of the Sherman Act.[17] In EU law, on the other hand, the capability of the conduct to eliminate an equally efficient competitor with anti-competitive intent[18] is sufficient to sustain a finding of abuse subject to any objective justification that the dominant undertaking may have.[19] Chapter 6 has already demonstrated that the intent test adopted by the EU courts is superior to the consumer harm test. This chapter focuses on the as efficient competitor element of the test, which is not only relevant to predatory conduct but also to margin squeeze, rebates, mixed bundling, and exclusivity.

(2) The problem of the permissible cost benchmarks

The as efficient competitor test often relies on cost benchmarks to determine whether conduct by the dominant undertaking is capable of excluding as efficient competitors. It is, therefore, of fundamental importance to understand what principles govern the choice of the appropriate cost benchmarks. This is particularly the case when a cost benchmark which has not been adopted in the case law is nevertheless applied in an individual case. A clear example is the choice of cost benchmarks in the Guidance on Article 102, which does not follow the cost measures endorsed by the Court of Justice. The Court of Justice in *AKZO* used AVC and ATC as cost benchmarks.[20] The Commission Guidance on Article 102 adopts two cost measures that differ, in certain respects, from AVC and ATC. They are AAC and long-run average incremental

---

[16] Case T-83/91 *Tetra Pak II*, para 150, upheld in Case C-333/94 P *Tetra Pak II*, paras 39–44; Case T-340/03 *France Télécom*, paras 224–230, upheld in Case C-202/07 P *France Télécom*, paras 110–113.

[17] *Brooke Group*, 224: 'Recoupment is the ultimate object of an unlawful predatory pricing scheme; it is the means by which a predator profits from predation. Without it, predatory pricing produces lower aggregate prices in the market, and consumer welfare is enhanced. Although unsuccessful predatory pricing may encourage some inefficient substitution toward the product being sold at less than its cost, unsuccessful predation is in general a boon to consumers.'

[18] Case C-333/94 P *Tetra Pak II*, para 44: 'It must be possible to penalize predatory pricing whenever there is a risk that competitors will be eliminated. The Court of First Instance found…that there was such a risk in this case. The aim pursued, which is to maintain undistorted competition, rules out waiting until such a strategy leads to the actual elimination of competitors'. The principle was confirmed in Case T-340/03 *France Télécom*, para 227, upheld in Case C-202/07 P *France Télécom*, paras 110–112.

[19] On objective justification, see Ch 9 below.

[20] Case C-62/86 *AKZO*, paras 71–72; Case C-333/94 P *Tetra Pak II*, para 41; Case C-202/07 P *France Télécom*, para 109

cost (LRAIC).[21] The problem of the cost benchmarks is not an issue of fact to be determined on a case-by-case basis but a legal question to be answered in the light of the as efficient competitor principle.

The Court of Justice in *AKZO* defined variable cost as the cost that varies 'depending on the quantities produced'.[22] AVC is the variable cost per unit of output.[23] TC is the sum of 'fixed costs plus variable costs'.[24] While there is no definition of fixed costs in the case, such a definition follows from the definition of variable cost. Therefore, fixed costs are costs that do not vary depending on the quantities produced. ATC equals the TC per unit of output. These cost concepts in *AKZO* are borrowed from microeconomic theory. Thus, AVC, which can only be plotted in the short run, is the variable cost per unit of output. The AVC curve plots the short-run AVC against the level of output. The ATC curve captures the relationship between cost per unit of output and the level of output. A perfectly competitive and productively efficient firm would organize its costs of production to attain the lowest point on the ATC curve. MC represents the change in total cost for each unit of change in the output. Generally, MC decreases at low outputs because of the benefits from greater specialization, but increases after a point because each additional worker can only produce a successively smaller rise in the output (known as the law of diminishing returns). The MC curve intersects the AVC and ATC curves at their minimum points. The average fixed cost (AFC) curve continuously falls since the same amount of fixed costs is being spread over more units as the output is increased. These cost curves are represented in Figure 7.1 below.

ATC can be plotted in the short run or in the long run. The short-run average total cost (SRATC) curves and the LRATC curve coincide at certain points, for instance Q1 in Figure 7.2 below, and it is at these points that fixed plant and equipment is

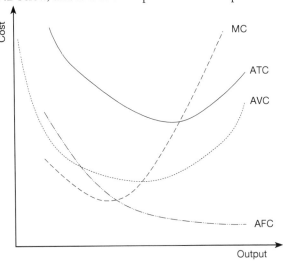

Figure 7.1 The short-term costs of a firm

[21] Guidance on Art 102, para 26.   [22] Case C-62/86 *AKZO*, para 71.
[23] ibid.   [24] ibid para 72.

optimal for the given level of output. For all other outputs there is either too much or too little of the inputs and the SRATC curve lies above the LRATC curve. The LRATC curve represents the boundary between attainable and unattainable costs and is formed from the envelope of SRATC curves as shown. The lowest point on the firm's LRATC curve, Q_0, represents the output at which long-run costs are minimized. As the firm moves along the LRATC curve from the left end point to Q_0, economies of scale increase. Beyond Q_0 there are increasing diseconomies of scale. If average revenue falls below the LRATC then the firm is making a loss in the long run. In the absence of other incentives, it is rational for such a firm to exit the market.

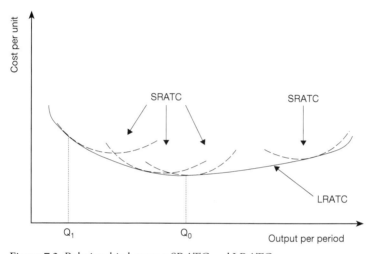

Figure 7.2 Relationship between SRATC and LRATC

The MC and MR determine the firm's output decision. A firm will produce up to the point where MC equals MR. This explains why the Court in *AKZO* chose AVC and ATC as the cost benchmarks in predation analysis. MC determines the profit-maximizing (or loss-minimizing) output that a firm produces. The predation test, however, is not concerned with whether a firm is producing more or less than the optimal output. Clearly, if a firm's price is below its MC, this would be an indication of irrational market behaviour. Such behaviour could be explained by the aim of excluding a competitor. However, because the objective of the test is to infer whether the pricing policy of the dominant undertaking is capable of excluding an as efficient competitor, more robust inferences can be drawn from the implications of the pricing policy under review for temporary shutdown decisions and exit decisions of an equally efficient competitor. If the dominant undertaking is making such a loss that it would be rational to cease production in the short term, an exclusionary strategy may be inferred. This is the case when prices are below AVC.[25] If prices are below AVC, the

---

[25] Case C-202/07 P *France Télécom*, para 110, where the Court held that proof of recoupment is not necessary 'in circumstances where the eliminatory intent of the undertaking at issue could be presumed in view of that undertaking's application of prices lower than average variable costs'.

dominant undertaking could simply cease production and be better off. There may be benign reasons why it does not do so but the prices in question call for an explanation. If the dominant undertaking is not recovering its ATC, an equally efficient competitor having to match the dominant undertaking's prices would exit the market in the long term. In the short term, however, it is still rational for the dominant undertaking to produce because it is recovering its variable costs and, possibly, part of its fixed costs. Therefore, a competition authority or claimant must prove a predatory strategy to establish a prima facie case of predation. These concepts are illustrated by Figures 7.3 to 7.6 below, which represent four possible profit or loss outcomes for a firm in the short run. To simplify the graphs, it is assumed that price = average revenue (AR) = MR but, for present purposes, nothing turns on this assumption. As shown in Figure 7.3 below, the firm might make an economic profit, represented by area ABCD, if the sale price is higher than the ATC of producing the optimal output. If the price the firm sells its products at coincides with the minimum ATC, then the firm breaks even because it recovers its TC, including the opportunity cost of capital. The firm makes a normal profit but not an economic profit. This corresponds to Figure 7.4 below. In Figures 7.5 and 7.6 below, the price is set below the minimum ATC, thus meaning that the firm will make an economic loss, equal to the areas EFGH and IJKL in each case. One can see from the graphs that the economic loss is significantly greater if the firm chooses to price the product below AVC instead of pricing between AVC and ATC. In the short run the firm may choose to continue to produce if the price lies between AVC and ATC, but would choose to exit the market if this continued in the long run. In the short run we would expect a firm to stop producing if price fell below average AVC.

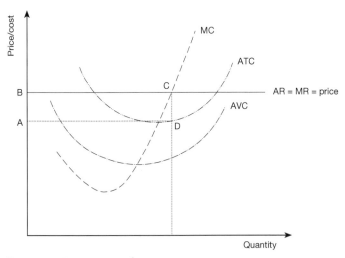

Figure 7.3 Economic profit

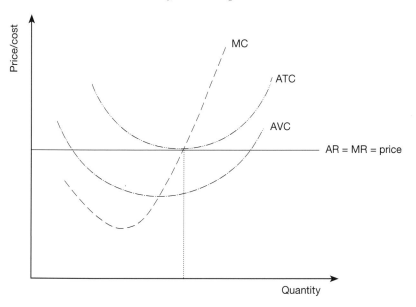

Figure 7.4 Break-even point

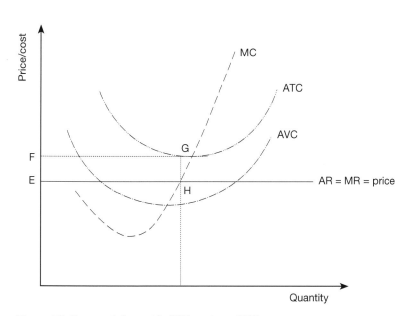

Figure 7.5 Economic loss with AVC < price < ATC

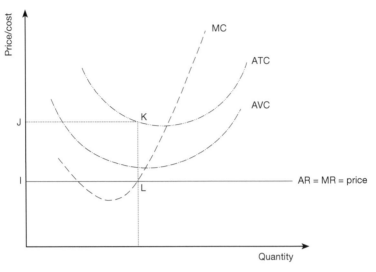

Figure 7.6 Economic loss with price < AVC

The analysis of the rationale for the *AKZO* price/cost tests clarifies whether cost benchmarks other than AVC and ATC may be used under Article 102. The answer is in the affirmative provided that the cost benchmark allows the drawing of an inference of predation under the *AKZO* test. Therefore, prices must be regarded as predatory whenever, at those prices, it would be more rational for the firm to cease production or not to increase output in the first place. The appropriate cost benchmark is whatever measure of cost determines the firm's short-term shutdown decision in the industry. Furthermore, if there is proof of an anti-competitive strategy, prices would be predatory whenever they have an impact on the profitability of the firm such that, if persistent for a sufficiently long period of time, the firm would exit the market. The appropriate cost benchmark is whatever measure of cost determines the firm's exit decision in the long term.

Are the cost benchmarks put forward by the Commission in the Guidance on Article 102 consistent with this analysis? The Commission defines AAC as 'the average of the costs that could have been avoided if the company had not produced a discrete amount of (extra) output, in this case the amount allegedly the subject of abusive conduct'.[26] AVC and AAC are the same if the dominant undertaking does not incur any fixed cost in producing the incremental output that is alleged to be the subject of abusive conduct. However, AAC will be higher than AVC if the dominant undertaking incurs a fixed cost in producing that extra output. For instance, predation may entail not only a price cut but also adding extra capacity or launching an advertising

---

[26] Commission Guidance on Art 102, para 26 fn 18.

campaign.[27] This is consistent with the *AKZO* test for prices below AVC. *Ex ante*, the dominant undertaking should not have increased output in the first place. By analogy with the short-term shutdown decision, the mere fact that prices are below AAC, therefore, warrants a presumption of predation. However, when using AAC, it is of fundamental importance to adopt an *ex ante* perspective. If a firm expected to recover AAC *ex ante* but the business decision turns out to be wrong, it cannot be said any longer that it is more rational for the firm to discontinue production, because a sunk cost has been incurred. This means, in practice, that if prices are between AVC and AAC, the presumption of predation must be supported by proof of a predatory strategy. This is not entirely inconsistent with the general approach in the Commission Guidance on Article 102, which regards prices below AAC as evidence of sacrifice but not as sufficient evidence to raise a presumption of predation.[28]

The Commission defines LRAIC as 'the average of all the (variable and fixed) costs that a company incurs to produce a particular product'.[29] The LRAIC does not include only the fixed costs incurred during the period of the alleged abuse but all the fixed (and variable) costs attributable to a given product in the long term. For single product undertakings, ATC and LRAIC are the same.[30] For multi-product undertakings, the measure of LRAIC solves the problem of the allocation of common costs, which was not addressed in the *AKZO* case.[31] It can thus be concluded that LRAIC serves the same function as ATC. It determines whether it would be rational for an equally efficient competitor to exit the market should prices fall persistently below this cost measure over the long term.

C. Margin squeeze

The case law has now clearly extended the principle established in the *AKZO* case in relation to predatory pricing to all pricing practices of a dominant undertaking. Thus, in *Deutsche Telekom*, the Court of Justice relied on *AKZO* to hold that the margin squeeze test is based on the prices and strategy of the dominant undertaking.[32] This general principle in the assessment of pricing practices rests on two pillars: legal certainty[33] and equality of opportunities.[34]

---

[27] ibid para 64, fn 40, which explains that the sunk cost of adding extra capacity would be an element of AAC but not of AVC.

[28] ibid paras 67–73.   [29] ibid para 26, fn 18.   [30] ibid.

[31] On some technical aspects of cost allocation, see OXERA, 'Assessing Profitability in Competition Policy Analysis', Economic Discussion Paper 6, OFT657 (July 2003) 92–96, which gives a good overview of the problems. See also the Commission Recommendation of 19 September 2005 on accounting separation and cost accounting systems under the regulatory framework for electronic communications [2005] OJ L266/64, which adopts the principle of causality in cost allocation.

[32] Case C-280/08 *Deutsche Telekom*, paras 198–199. See also Case C-52/09 *TeliaSonera*, para 41, relying on Case C-62/86 *AKZO*, para 74 and Case C-202/07 P *France Télécom*, para 108. See also *Wanadoo España v Telefónica* [2008] OJ C83/6, recital 546, under appeal in Case T-336/07 *Telefónica SA v Commission* [2007] OJ C269/55.

[33] Case T-271/03 *Deutsche Telekom*, para 192, upheld in Case C-280/08 *Deutsche Telekom*, para 203.

[34] Case T-271/03 *Deutsche Telekom*, para 199, upheld in Case C-280/08 *Deutsche Telekom*, paras 230–234.

A margin squeeze results from the spread between the upstream and downstream prices of a vertically integrated undertaking dominant on the upstream market.[35] When downstream competitors of the dominant undertaking purchase an upstream input from such an undertaking and compete with it on the downstream market, the dominant undertaking may have the ability and incentive to increase the price of the upstream input or decrease the price of the downstream product in order to raise the costs or erode the revenues of its downstream rivals. The spread between the upstream and the downstream prices of the dominant undertaking is unfair within the meaning of Article 102(a) when it is capable of excluding a downstream competitor which is at least as efficient as the dominant undertaking.[36] This exclusionary effect may arise when the difference between the upstream price (charged to the downstream competitors of the dominant undertaking) and the downstream price (charged to the retail customers of the dominant undertaking) is either negative or insufficient to cover the dominant undertaking's downstream costs.[37] The problem of the relevant measure of cost is, essentially, the same as in predation.[38] The solutions should, in principle, be the same. However, the question has only recently received attention in margin squeeze cases. In the early case of *Napier Brown— British Sugar*, the test was whether the dominant undertaking would cover its own 'cost of transformation'. The concept of 'cost of transformation' was not defined, although, on the facts, it is clear that the costs in question were the costs of repackaging and selling the sugar, which were the downstream variable costs excluding the cost of the input.[39] In *Deutsche Telekom*, the Commission held that, in the circumstances of that case, there was a margin squeeze if the

---

[35] Margin squeeze is a free-standing abuse in EU law although many elements of the test are still controversial: J Kavanagh, 'Assessing Margin Squeeze under Competition Law' (2004) 3 Comp Law 187; P Crocioni, 'Price Squeeze and Imputation Test: Recent Developments' (2005) 26 ECLR 558; D Geradin and R O'Donoghue, 'The Concurrent Application of Competition Law and Regulation: The Case of Margin Squeeze Abuses in the Telecommunications Sector' (2005) 1 J Comp L & Econ 355; R O'Donoghue and AJ Padilla, *The Law and Economics of Article 82 EC* (Oxford, Hart Publishing 2006) 303–350; L Colley and S Burnside, 'Margin Squeeze Abuse' (2006) 2 European Competition Journal 185; MF Alvarez-Labrador, 'Margin Squeeze in the Telecommunications Sector: An Economic Overview' (2006) 29 World Competition 247; M Polo, 'Price Squeeze: Lessons from the Telecom Italia Case' (2007) 2 J Comp L & Econ 453; DW Carlton, 'Should "Price Squeeze" be a Recognized Form of Anticompetitive Conduct?' (2008) 4 J Comp L & Econ 271; R Thompson and J O'Flaherty, 'Article 82' in P Roth and V Rose (eds), *Bellamy & Child European Community Law of Competition* (6th edn Oxford, OUP 2008) 909, 993–998; E Rousseva, *Rethinking Exclusionary Abuses in EU Competition Law* (Oxford, Hart Publishing 2010) 417–422; G Faella and R Pardolesi, 'Squeezing Price Squeeze under EC Antitrust Law' (2010) 6 European Competition Journal 255; TT Nguyen, 'Price Squeezing: Linkline in the United States—No Link to the European Union' (2010) 41 Intl Rev IP & Comp L 316; FF Duncan, 'No Margin for Error: The Challenges of Assessing Margin Squeeze in Practice' (2010) 9 Comp Law 124.

[36] Case C-280/08 *Deutsche Telekom*, paras 163, 167, 169, and 183; Case C-52/09 *TeliaSonera*, paras 31, 32, and 39. The as efficient competitor test includes the potentially as efficient competitor test (ibid para 45), recognizing that the costs of the competitors may have to be taken into account if the dominant undertaking controls an infrastructure whose costs have already been amortized or has cost advantages attributable to the dominant position (presumably, for instance, economies of scale).

[37] Case T-271/03 *Deutsche Telekom*, paras 34–46.   [38] See 223–229 above.

[39] *Napier Brown—British Sugar* [1988] OJ L284/41, recital 66.

difference between wholesale and retail prices resulted in a margin which was 'insufficient to cover the product-specific costs to the dominant operator of providing its own retail services on the downstream market'.[40] Product-specific costs are the costs incurred to provide the retail products excluding the costs of the network, but including the costs of any special equipment required to provide network access to end-users and maintenance, customer care, and billing costs.[41] The costs of the different services provided were averaged, based on the same weighting used for the calculation of the price of the services, namely the number of lines actually sold by the dominant undertaking and their price.[42] Fixed costs were spread over the average life of a subscription.[43] Thus, it would appear that the product-specific costs included all avoidable downstream costs arising from the sale of the retail product to the end-user. This is consistent with the predation test, which presumes the exclusion of as efficient competitors when the dominant undertaking charges prices below AAC. AAC in this case were the same as AVC over the life of a subscription. The dominant undertaking challenged specific aspects of this methodology before the Court of First Instance, which upheld the Commission decision in full. There was, however, no challenge to the measure of cost used by the Commission. This is understandable given that AAC or AVC is the lowest cost measure that could be employed. In *Telefónica*, the Commission adopted LRAIC as the downstream cost measure.[44] This was justified on the grounds that competitors' decisions to invest were based on the total incremental costs of providing a given output and that in margin squeeze cases it was necessary to assess the competitors' ability to compete in the long term.[45] A further justification was that in network industries fixed costs are high and variable costs are low. In order to be viable, an undertaking must price above variable costs.[46] Therefore, a price above variable cost may be exclusionary. This reasoning should not be limited to network industries.[47] Whether fixed costs are significantly higher than variable costs will have an implication for how much LRAIC and AVC diverge but does not mean that, conceptually, a decision to invest in a low-fixed cost industry depends on variable cost. The investment decision will still depend on the incremental cost of the project. However, if fixed costs are low or even non-existent, the incremental cost of the project will be close to, or the same as, its variable costs. LRAIC remains the appropriate measure of cost whenever the exclusionary strategy is sustainable in the long term and there is evidence of an exclusionary strategy.[48]

---

[40] *Deutsche Telekom AG* [2003] OJ L263/9, recital 107.   [41] ibid recitals 139 and 155–158.
[42] ibid recitals 116 and 159.
[43] ibid recital 159. This is not entirely clear in the decision but follows necessarily from the fact that upstream and downstream one-off charges were divided by the average life of a subscription: see ibid recitals 148 and 151.
[44] *Wanadoo España v Telefónica* [2008] OJ C83/6 (*Telefónica*) recitals 316–324, under appeal in Case T-336/07 *Telefónica and Telefónica de España v Commission* [2007] OJ C269/55.
[45] *Telefónica*, recitals 317–318.   [46] ibid recital 317.
[47] See the discussion of the case law and the cost tests in predation at 223–229 above.
[48] Consistent with the predation test: see 223-229 above.

The AAC test in *Deutsche Telekom AG* and the LRAIC test in *Telefónica* are consistent with the cost tests in predation analysis. The higher measure of cost used in *Telefónica*, however, begs the question of whether the application of a mere cost test is sufficient to establish a prima facie case of abuse. In predation, when prices are below ATC or LRAIC but above AVC or AAC, proof of anti-competitive intent is required. The test of intent performs the role of guarding against the risk of false convictions and over-deterrence because, when prices lie between AVC and ATC, there may be pro-competitive explanations for below-cost prices in the short term. The probability that such prices may be predatory is further diminished because predation is a risky strategy. The dominant undertaking is deliberately incurring losses to protect or strengthen its dominant position. Exclusionary practices entailing a profit sacrifice are inherently less attractive for a dominant undertaking than practices that can exclude equally efficient competitors without forcing the dominant undertaking to incur any losses. Margin squeeze is one such practice. Because the exclusionary effect results from the modulation of upstream and downstream prices, the vertically integrated dominant undertaking may well be profitable on an end-to-end basis while still excluding equally efficient downstream competitors.[49] Compared to predation, margin squeeze is thus a more plausible exclusionary strategy, which means that the risk of false convictions and over-deterrence is also lower. Therefore, it is justified not to require proof of anti-competitive intent when, given its actual downstream prices, the downstream division of the dominant undertaking would recover a notional AVC or AAC but not a notional ATC or LRAIC calculated on the basis of the input price charged to competitors upstream.

D. Conditional above-cost rebates

(1) Protection of less efficient undertakings incompatible with Article 102

Considerable debate surrounds the assessment of conditional rebates[50] that do not result in average market prices or average prices charged to a particular customer being below cost.[51] The case law adopts different approaches to different forms of

---

[49] *Telefónica*, recitals 329–349.
[50] The Commission defines conditional rebates as 'rebates granted to customers to reward them for a particular form of purchasing behaviour': Guidance on Art 102, para 37. This definition is broadly consistent with the case law and will be adopted in this book.
[51] D Ridyard, 'Exclusionary Pricing and Price Discrimination Abuses under Article 82—An Economic Analysis' (2002) 23 ECLR 286; J Temple Lang and R O'Donoghue, 'Defining Legitimate Competition: How to Clarify Pricing Abuses under Article 82 EC' (2002) 26 Fordham Intl LJ 83, 91–115; A Heimler, 'Below-Cost Pricing and Loyalty-Inducing Discounts: Are They Restrictive and, If So, When?' (2005) 1 Competition Policy International 149; HG Kamann and E Bergmann, 'The Granting of Rebates by Market Dominant Undertakings under Article 82 of the EC Treaty' (2005) 26 ECLR 83; G Federico, 'When Are Rebates Exclusionary?' (2005) 26 ECLR 477; D Spector, 'Loyalty Rebates: An Assessment of Competition Concerns and a Proposed Structured Rule of Reason' (2005) 1 Competition Policy International 89; C Ahlborn and D Bailey, 'Discounts, Rebates and Selective Pricing by Dominant Firms: A Trans-Atlantic Comparison' (2006) 2 European Competition Journal 101; O'Donoghue and Padilla, *The Law and Economics of Article 82 EC*, 374–406; RJ Van den Bergh and PD Camesasca, *European Competition Law and Economics: A Comparative Perspective*

rebates. In *Hoffmann-La Roche*, the Court of Justice held that a dominant undertaking may not apply, either by agreement with the customer or unilaterally, a system of rebates conditional on the customer obtaining all or most of its requirements from the undertaking in a dominant position.[52] If the rebate is not conditional upon exclusivity or quasi-exclusivity, the case law adopts a full market inquiry test. In *Michelin I*, the Court of Justice held that it was necessary to examine all the circumstances, including in particular 'the criteria and rules for the grant of the discount' and whether the discount provided 'an advantage not based on any economic service justifying it'. The rebates would have an anti-competitive effect if they tended 'to remove or restrict the buyer's freedom to choose his sources of supply, to bar competitors from access to the market, to apply dissimilar conditions to equivalent transactions with other trading parties or to strengthen the dominant position by distorting competition'.[53] This test is in principle compatible with the as efficient competitor test. A rebate restricts the customer's freedom to choose its sources of supply and forecloses competitors only if as efficient competitors are unable to match it. If they are, then the rebate is competition on the merits. The problem is that, the case law and the Commission practice have applied this test in a very formalistic way.[54] Thus, if a rebate is a quantity rebate, it is deemed to reflect productive efficiencies.[55] A quantity rebate is a discount 'granted on invoice according to

---

(2nd edn London, Sweet & Maxwell 2006) 260–264; CE Mosso et al, 'Article 82' in J Faull and A Nikpay (eds), *The EC Law of Competition* (2nd edn Oxford, OUP 2007) 313, 381–388; Thompson and O'Flaherty, 'Article 82', 972–978; R Whish, *Competition Law* (6th edn Oxford, OUP 2008) 719–726; D Geradin, 'A Proposed Test for Separating Pro-Competitive Conditional Rebates from Anti-Competitive Ones' (2009) 32 World Competition 41; L Kjølbye, 'Rebates under Article 82 EC: Navigating Uncertain Waters' (2010) 31 ECLR 66; Rousseva, *Rethinking Exclusionary Abuses in EU Competition Law*, 173–218; I Van Bael and J-F Bellis, *Competition Law of the European Community* (5th edn Alphen aan den Rijn, Kluwer Law International 2010) 817–830.

[52] Case 85/76 *Hoffmann-La Roche & Co AG v Commission* [1979] ECR 461, para 89.

[53] Case 322/81 *Michelin I*, para 73. This test has been applied in the subsequent cases: see eg Case T-203/01 *Michelin II*, para 60 and Case T-155/06 *Tomra*, para 214.

[54] Joined Cases 40/73 to 48/73, 50/73, 54/73 to 56/73, 111/73, 113/73, and 114/73 *Coöperatieve Vereniging 'Suiker Unie' UA v Commission* [1975] ECR 1663 (*Suiker Unie*); Case 322/81 *Michelin I*; Case 27/88 *Solvay & Cie v Commission* [1989] ECR 3355; Case C-53/92 P *Hilti AG v Commission* [1994] ECR I-667; *BPB Industries plc* [1989] OJ L10/50, upheld in Case T-65/89 *BPB Industries plc and British Gypsum Ltd v Commission* [1993] ECR II-389 (*British Gypsum*), appeal dismissed in Case C-310/93 P *BPB Industries plc and British Gypsum Ltd v Commission* [1995] ECR I-865 (*British Gypsum*); Case T-30/91 *Solvay SA v Commission* [1995] ECR II-1775, uphead in Cases C-286/95 P *Commission v Imperial Chemical Industries plc (ICI)* [2000] ECR I-2341; Case C-333/94 P *Tetra Pak II*; Case T-228/97 *Irish Sugar plc v Commission* [1999] ECR II-2969, upheld in Case C-497/99 P *Irish Sugar plc v Commission* [2001] ECR I-5333; Joined Cases T-24/93 to 26/93 and 28/93 *Compagnie Maritime Belge Transports SA v Commission* [1996] ECR II-1201 (*Compagnie Maritime Belge*) upheld in Joined Cases C-395/96 P and 396/96 P *Compagnie Maritime Belge Transports SA v Commission* [2000] ECR I-1365; Case C-163/99 *Portugal v Commission* [2001] ECR I-2613; Case T-203/01 *Michelin II*; Case T-219/99 *British Airways* upheld in Case C-359/01 P *British Sugar plc v Commission* [2004] ECR I-4933; Case C-95/04 P *British Airways*; Case T-151/01 *Der Grüne Punkt—Duales System Deutschland GmbH v Commission* [2007] ECR II-1607, upheld in C-385/07 P *Der Grüne Punkt—Duales System Deutschland GmbH* [2009] ECR I-6155; Joined Cases T-57/01 and T-58/01 *Solvay v Commission* [2009] ECR II-4621; Case T-155/06 *Tomra*.

[55] Case T-203/01 *Michelin II*, para 85; Case 322/81 *Michelin I*, para 71; Case 85/76 *Hoffmann-La Roche*, para 90; Case C-163/99 *Portuguese Republic v Commission* [2001] ECR I-2613, para 50; Opinion of AG Mischo in Case C-163/99 *Portuguese Republic*, para 106; Case T-155/06 *Tomra*, para 212.

the size of the order'.[56] This statement of the law must be understood as saying that the rebate in question is presumptively lawful unless it is predatory. This 'safe harbour' is consistent with the as efficient competitor test. A quantity discount cannot exclude an as efficient competitor unless it is below cost. However, the case law has taken a very restrictive approach to retroactive rebates, namely rebates that reward a certain purchasing behaviour of the customer. Typically, the rebate would apply on total turnover once a certain threshold or progressively higher thresholds triggering progressively higher discounts are met. These rebates have been held to infringe Article 102 on the basis on the following elements: (a) their retroactive rather than incremental application;[57] (b) the length of the reference period and the size of the rebate, from which it can be inferred that there is a strong incentive for the customer to reach the rebate thresholds given the magnitude of the potential discounts;[58] (c) the asymmetry between the market share of the dominant undertaking and the market shares of its competitors, which suggests that the latter would not be able to offer rebates to be spread on a turnover comparable with that of the dominant undertaking;[59] (d) whether the rebates are individually negotiated,[60] although standard form rebates can also be abusive;[61] and (e) the non-transparent operation of the rebate system for the customers.[62] This test can clearly result in the protection of inefficient competitors.[63] However, Chapters 2 and 3 demonstrate that, because the objective of Article 102 is not to protect consumer welfare but to enhance social welfare in the long term, the protection of less efficient competitors is contrary to the purpose of Article 102 unless: (a) the competitor is likely to become as efficient as the dominant undertaking within a reasonable period of time; (b) conduct by the dominant undertaking that fulfils the other conditions for abuse is preventing

---

[56] Case T-203/01 *Michelin II*, para 85.

[57] Case C-95/04 P *British Airways*, paras 73–74, where the incentive effect of the rebate is linked to its retroactive nature; Case T-203/01 *Michelin II*, paras 88 and 95; Case T-155/06 *Tomra*, paras 183 and 260.

[58] Case 322/81 *Michelin I*, paras 80–81; Case T-219/99 *British Airways*, paras 273, 274, and 295; Case T-203/01 *Michelin II*, paras 85 and 95.

[59] Case 322/81 *Michelin I*, para 82; Case T-219/99 *British Airways*, paras 276–278, upheld in Case C-95/04 P *British Airways*, paras 71 and 75–76. In the analysis of the foreclosure effect, the Court of Justice followed closely the Opinion of AG Kokott in Case C-95/04 P *British Airways*, paras 48–53.

[60] Case C-95/04 P *British Airways*, paras 71–72; Case T-155/06 *Tomra*, paras 76–87.

[61] Case T-203/01 *Michelin II*, para 67–74.

[62] Case 322/81 *Michelin I*, para 83; *Intel* [2009] OJ C227/13, recitals 942–948, under appeal in Case T-286/09 *Intel Corp v Commission* [2009] OJ C220/41.

[63] The case law has been criticized by commentators: B Sher, 'Price Discounts and *Michelin II*: What Goes Around, Comes Around' (2002) 23 ECLR 482; J Kallaugher and B Sher, 'Rebates Revisited: Anti-Competitive Effects and Exclusionary Abuse under Article 82' (2004) 25 ECLR 263, 263–272; Kamann and Bergmann, 'The Granting of Rebates by Market Dominant Undertakings under Article 82 of the EC Treaty'; D Waelbroeck, '*Michelin II*: A Per Se Rule Against Rebates By Dominant Companies?' (2005) 1 J Comp L & Econ 149; O'Donoghue and Padilla, *The Law and Economics of Article 82 EC*, 375–377; G Monti, *EC Competition Law* (Cambridge, CUP 2007) 162–173; V Korah, *An Introductory Guide to EC Competition Law and Practice* (9th edn Oxford, Hart Publishing 2007) 154–158; J Goyder, *Goyder's EC Competition Law* (5th edn Oxford, OUP 2009) 329–333; R Whish, *Competition Law*, 724–725; Rousseva, *Rethinking Exclusionary Abuses in EU Competition Law*, 180–184. See, however, L Gyselen, 'Rebates: Competition on the Merits or Exclusionary Practice?' in C-D Ehlermann and I Atanasiu (eds), *European Competition Law Annual 2003: What Is an Abuse of a Dominant Position?* (Oxford, Hart Publishing 2006) 287.

the competitor from becoming at least as efficient as itself.[64] It is clear, therefore, that there are only two bases for prohibiting above-cost conditional rebates: either they exclude an equally efficient competitor or they exclude a competitor that would be likely to become as efficient as the dominant undertaking in the absence of the allegedly exclusionary conduct.

(2) Static application of the as efficient competitor test

The Commission's approach to conditional rebates changed significantly with the publication of the Commission Guidance on Article 102.[65]

The Commission defines conditional rebates as rebates that reward customers for a particular purchasing behaviour.[66] This definition includes rebates granted on condition that the customer purchases its requirements exclusively from the dominant undertaking or does not deal with a particular competitor, as well as discounts granted on the attainment of given purchasing thresholds. As regards the latter discounts, a distinction is drawn between incremental rebates and retroactive rebates. Incremental rebates apply a discount to all units purchased in excess of the threshold. Retroactive rebates apply the discount to all units purchased in the relevant period, below and above the threshold, once the threshold has been attained.[67] An incremental rebate of 10 per cent off a list price of £10 with a threshold of 100 units means that the customer will pay £9 for all units he purchases in excess of 100. In the same example, a retroactive rebate means that the customer will not only pay £9 for all units he purchases in excess of 100 but he is also entitled to a retroactive discount of 10 per cent on the 100 units he has already purchased. On attaining the threshold, the customer is entitled to £100 retroactive discount in addition to the 10 per cent discount on all the extra units he buys. Therefore, retroactive rebates may have a more severe foreclosure effect.[68] This is not because there is anything inherently sinister or anti-competitive in retroactive rebates. In fact, any retroactive rebate may be designed as an incremental one. In the previous example, the retroactive rebate could be turned into an incremental one by providing that, on the attainment of 100 units, the customer is entitled to 10 free units and then a discount of 10 per cent on all extra units purchased. Simply, on the same percentage discounts and thresholds, a retroactive rebate results in a larger discount because it is applied to a larger quantity.

The Commission considers that rebates resulting in a average price which is above the relevant cost benchmark may foreclose competitors because they allow the dominant undertaking to leverage the market power it has on the non-contestable share of demand in order to prevent customers from switching

---

[64] See 75–76 above.
[65] LL Gormsen, 'The European Commission's Priority Guidelines on Article 82 EC' (2009) 14 Communications Law 83, 86; Rousseva, *Rethinking Exclusionary Abuses in EU Competition Law*, 389–395; M Kellerbauer, 'The Commission's New Enforcement Priorities in Applying Article 82 EC to Dominant Companies' Exclusionary Conduct: a Shift Towards a More Economic Approach?' (2010) 31 ECLR 175, 183–186; MA Gravengaard and N Kjaersgaard, 'The EU Commission Guidance on Exclusionary Abuse of Dominance and its Consequences in Practice' (2010) 31 ECLR 285; L Kjølbye, 'Rebates under Article 82 EC: Navigating Uncertain Waters'.
[66] Guidance on Art 102, para 37.   [67] ibid.   [68] ibid para 40.

to competitors for the contestable share of demand. The non-contestable share of demand is defined as 'the amount that would be purchased by the dominant undertaking in any event'. The contestable share of demand is defined as 'the amount for which the customer may prefer to be able to find substitutes'.[69] A conditional rebate may foreclose an equally efficient competitor if the effective price[70] that the competitor must offer to compensate a customer for the loss of the rebate is below the relevant cost benchmark. The effective price is calculated on the 'relevant range'. In incremental rebates, the relevant range is the incremental units that the customer considers switching. For retroactive rebates, the relevant range is the units that 'can realistically be switched to a competitor'.[71] For retroactive rebates, the relevant range is, therefore, the same as the contestable share.

To illustrate this analysis, consider a retroactive rebate of 8 per cent off a £5 list price on all units purchased once the threshold of 600 units is reached. If the total demand of the customer is 1,000, the contestable share is 400, and the MC or AVC (or AAC) of the dominant undertaking is constant at £4.50, the rebate results in foreclosure of an equally efficient competitor. If the customer switches 400 units to a competitor, it loses the entire discount. The whole amount of the discount forgone must, therefore, be applied to the whole of the contestable share. The price that a competitor would need to offer to compensate the customer for the loss of the discount (the effective price) is £4. At that price, as shown in Figure 7.7 below, an equally efficient competitor would have made a loss represented by the area below the MC, or AVC, line (area DEFG).

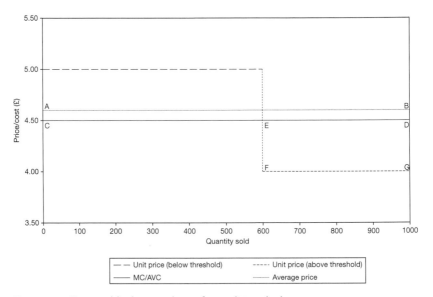

Figure 7.7 Contestable share analysis of a conditional rebate

---

[69] ibid para 39; *Intel*, recitals 1009–1036.
[70] For the definition of effective price, see Guidance on Art 102, para 41.
[71] ibid para 42.

The dominant undertaking can afford to sell at this price since the average price it is charging the customer (£4.60) is still above its MC (£4.50), which yields a supra-competitive profit represented by area ABCD.

Another way of expressing the same concept is that the rebate creates a switching cost for the customer if it wishes to purchase from a competitor of the dominant undertaking. Figure 7.8 below compares the customer expenditure if the threshold for the retroactive discount is not achieved with the customer expenditure if it is achieved. It is clear that as the quantity purchased increases the more incentive there is for the customer to purchase from the largest supplier, that is, the one offering the discount above a certain threshold, since the expenditure difference increases strictly with the quantity purchased.

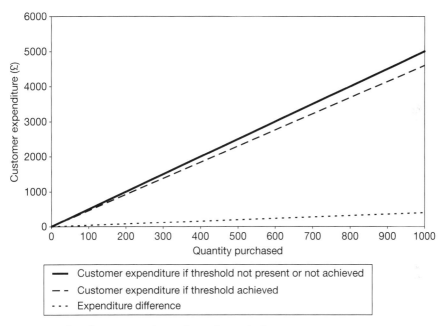

Figure 7.8 Switching cost analysis of a conditional rebate

It may be instructive to compare this analysis with the so-called 'suction effect' theory, which, regrettably, has been endorsed in the case law, albeit only as a factor that may legitimately be taken into account rather than as a test.[72] For simplicity, in Figure 7.9 below, we imagine that the customer only wants to buy one unit more than the threshold (in this case 601). Then, for each quantity purchased from the dominant firm, we calculate the price that the competitor must offer on a per unit

[72] Case T-155/06 *Tomra*, para 267.

basis to tempt the customer to buy the remaining units from them. We see that as the customer's order approaches the threshold, the price the competitor must offer decreases rapidly and, eventually, becomes negative.

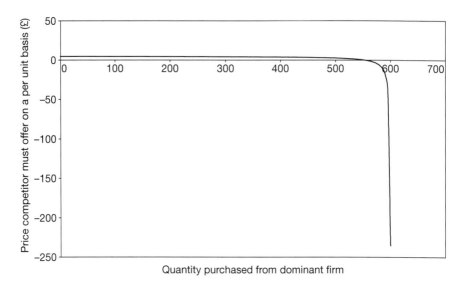

Figure 7.9 Suction effect analysis of a conditional rebate

This way of analysing the rebate does not take into account the fact that competition does not take place on a per unit basis but in relation to a certain share of the customer's demand that the competitor is able to satisfy, in this example up to 400 units. Therefore, the 'suction effect theory' is patently inadequate to explain why the rebate would foreclose an equally efficient competitor. Rightly, the Commission does not adopt this approach in the Guidance on Article 102. Rather, the calculation of the effective price over the relevant range provides the basis for a price/cost test similar to the predation test. The Commission envisages that, if the effective price is below the AAC of the dominant undertaking, the rebates will be capable of excluding equally efficient competitors.[73] If the effective price is above the AAC of the dominant undertaking but below its LRAIC, the Commission will investigate whether competitors have 'realistic and effective counter-strategies' to compete against the price schedule of the dominant undertaking. If they do not, the rebate will be considered capable of foreclosing an equally efficient competitor.[74] In addition to the price/cost analysis, the Commission also considers that an individualized volume threshold is more likely to be anti-competitive because it can be designed based on the non-contestable share of each customer. A standardized volume threshold may be too low for some customers and too high for others.

<hr />

[73] Guidance on Art 102, para 44; *Intel*, recital 1038.   [74] Guidance on Art 102, para 44.

However, a standardized threshold may approximate the requirements of most customers and thus have a foreclosure effect.[75] Finally, if the rebates are capable of foreclosing an equally efficient competitor, the Commission will examine whether the foreclosure will lead to consumer harm, applying the general framework in paragraph 20 of the Guidance.[76]

The Commission's approach comes close to the correct assessment of the foreclosure effect of a rebate system with three important qualifications. First, the analysis of whether competitors have 'realistic and effective counter-strategies' to overcome the effect of the dominant undertaking's pricing schedule is an element of the as efficient competitor test which is always necessary in the assessment of conditional rebates. If competitors are able to deploy 'realistic and effective counter-strategies', the rebate is incapable of excluding equally efficient competitors whether the effective price is below or above AAC. Secondly, if the rebate is capable of excluding an equally efficient competitor, no separate proof of consumer harm is required. The principle of fairness and equality of opportunities requires that equally efficient competitors be allowed to compete on an equal footing with the dominant undertaking.[77] In reality, the Guidance on Article 102 only envisages a very weak inference of consumer harm based on the recycling of elements already relevant to the assessment of dominance and foreclosure.[78] This flaw is, therefore, not fatal. There is in principle no harm in the Commission explaining in its decisions how a level playing field between the dominant undertaking and its equally efficient competitors would benefit consumers, as long as it is clear that this is not part of the legal test. Thirdly, there is no ground on which it is possible to distinguish rebates that result in an effective price below AAC and those that result in an effective price above AAC and below LRAIC. In this respect, the right analogy for conditional rebates is not predation but margin squeeze. Predation is a risky strategy that cannot be carried out indefinitely. Like margin squeeze, rebates are a strategy that can be carried out profitably for an indefinite period of time.[79] Rebates should, therefore, be prohibited regardless of proof of an anti-competitive strategy whenever prices are below the measure of cost that determines the firms' exit decisions on the market under review.

(3) Dynamic application of the as efficient competitor test

Exclusionary rebates may be used by a dominant undertaking to prevent competitors from benefiting from demand-related efficiencies such as economies of scale or network effects. Competitors may not exit the market but will have higher costs and, thus, be less able to exert effective competitive pressure on the dominant undertaking. This theory of harm may be at the heart of the EU case

---

[75] ibid para 45.   [76] ibid paras 38 and 20.

[77] The Court of Justice Case has unequivocally rejected the argument that consumer harm is a necessary element of the test for anti-competitive rebates: Case C-95/04 P *British Airways*, paras 105–108.

[78] See eg the analysis of consumer harm in *Intel*, recitals 1605–1614.

[79] Case T-155/06 *Tomra*, para 267

law that condemns rebates having a foreclosure effect without any inquiry into whether the rebates foreclose as efficient or potentially as efficient competitors. If this is the unexpressed rationale of the case law, then it is a legitimate concern under Article 102. However, in the assessment of the exclusion of potentially equally efficient competitors the risk of false convictions and over-deterrence is high. Rebates may be exclusionary even if the effective price is above the dominant firm's LRAIC. It may be difficult to estimate whether competitors would be likely to become as efficient as the dominant undertaking within a reasonable timeframe in the absence of exclusion. An error would result in the protection of less efficient firms, which runs counter to the objective of Article 102. Therefore, while a price/cost test may be inappropriate, so would a test of mere foreclosure. What is required is an enhanced intervention threshold that minimizes the risk of false convictions and over-deterrence while condemning rebates that are truly anti-competitive. Candidate tests are intent or consumer harm. However, a test of intent would perform poorly because rebates always have pro-competitive justifications as well as possible anti-competitive effects. It would be impossible to distinguish in practice whether the strategy of the dominant firm was to foreclose rivals or enhance its own efficiency. A consumer harm test would also be inadequate to address the enforcement risk concerns relating to rebates. If consumer harm is understood as a reduction of choice on the market, then the exclusion of any competitor offering a differentiated product, no matter how inefficient, would be sufficient to prohibit above-cost rebates. If consumer harm is rigorously understood as a reduction in output and increase in price, it would be very difficult to prove to the required legal standard. This would be contrary to the effectiveness of Article 102. But more fundamentally, the constraint exerted by an inefficient competitor is likely to increase output on a highly concentrated market. A consumer harm test could thus lead to the protection of inefficient competitors contrary to the purpose of Article 102.

By a process of exclusion, there is only one option that makes it possible to prohibit rebates that foreclose potentially equally efficient competitors consistently with the effectiveness and purpose of Article 102: to require proof of actual effects. This was the approach adopted in *Deutsche Post*.[80] The Commission held that Deutsche Post AG and its predecessor undertakings (together 'DPAG') abused their dominant position on the German market for mail-order parcel services by implementing a system of fidelity rebates from 1974 to 2000 and by predation from 1990 to 1995. Legally, the analysis relied heavily on *Hoffmann-La Roche*. However, in reality, the Commission carried out a thorough analysis of the actual effects of the rebates. The cornerstone of the effects analysis was the consideration that the market was characterized by significant economies of scale. The creation of an infrastructure for mail-order services would be a significant sunk cost. To operate efficiently, an undertaking had to reach a scale of at least 100 million parcels

---

[80] *Deutsche Post AG* [2001] OJ L125/27.

or catalogues, which corresponded to two major customers.[81] By granting fidelity rebates, DPAG prevented competitors from reaching a minimum efficient scale.[82] The foreclosure effect resulted from the fact that competitors were 'compelled to offer discounts to offset the loss which customers suffer if they have a smaller percentage of their parcels distributed by DPAG'.[83] By the same token, customers were deterred from setting up their own delivery divisions which, once the minimum efficient scale had been reached, could have competed with DPAG.[84] By necessary implication, the Commission recognized that competitors could only rationally enter the market on a relatively small scale. Once they had built up a significant and stable foothold, they could make the sunk investment necessary to compete with DPAG head-on. Until they did that, given their smaller scale, competitors could only handle a part, probably a reasonably small part, of each customer's requirements. No customer could, therefore, switch his business to a competitor of DPAG entirely. The Commission was able to point to empirical evidence from which it could be inferred that the market was foreclosed, including DPAG's stable market share at more than 85 per cent for ten years with no other undertaking competing at national level[85] and the total absence of entry of undertakings from other Member States.[86]

The decision in *Deutsche Post* seems well founded in law and in policy. There is no absolute requirement for a quantitative analysis of foreclosure of potential as efficient competitors as long as uncontradicted evidence of foreclosure demonstrates the following cumulative elements:

1. The loss of the rebate constitutes a significant switching cost[87] for the customer;

2. The market is characterized by very significant sunk cost and demand-related efficiencies;

3. It is not rational for an undertaking to enter on the same scale as that of the dominant undertaking;

4. Competitors have the ability to achieve a minimum efficient scale or to become as efficient as the dominant undertaking because of the market demand for their services and their own cost structure and access to finance;

5. The rebates have *in fact* prevented competitors from achieving a minimum efficient scale or from becoming as efficient as the dominant undertaking. Proof of actual foreclosure effect is necessary.

---

[81] ibid recitals 32 and 37.
[82] ibid recital 37.   [83] ibid recital 39.   [84] ibid recital 38.   [85] ibid recital 32.
[86] ibid recital 42.
[87] Switching costs can be defined as the real or perceived costs that are incurred when changing supplier, but which are not incurred by remaining with the current supplier: see C McSorley, AJ Padilla, and M Williams, 'Switching Costs' DTI Economic Discussion Paper 5 (15 April 2003) 1; J Farrell and C Shapiro 'Dynamic Competition with Switching Costs' (1988) 19 RAND Journal of Economics 123; DW Carlton and M Waldman, 'Competition, Monopoly and Aftermarkets' (2010) 26 JL Econ & Org 54, 55–71.

The above requirements are demanding. However, they are the only way to ensure that the prohibition of above-cost rebates that exclude potentially equally efficient competitors is consistent with the purpose of Article 102.

E. Unconditional above-cost rebates

Exceptionally, unconditional above-cost rebates may be found abusive in the application of the dynamic as efficient competitor test. The leading case in point is *Compagnie Maritime Belge*.[88] The Commission found that the members of a liner conference had abused their collective dominant position by implementing targeted above-cost price cuts designed to drive their only competitor (G & C) out of the market—a practice then known in the maritime trade as 'fighting ships'.[89] The Commission explained that, regardless of whether or not Cewal's conduct resulted in actual losses, it is an abuse for a collectively dominant liner conference to subsidize lower but above-cost rates by the conference's normal freights charged on its other sailings. The effect of such a practice might be to exclude from the market an equally efficient competitor with 'lesser financial capacity'.[90] The Court of First Instance upheld the finding of abuse on the rather shaky foundation that a dominant undertaking cannot react to entry, expansion, or any competitive initiative by a rival by conduct whose real purpose is to strengthen its dominant position.[91] This was what the liner conference members were doing when they applied above-cost price cuts with the intention of driving their only competitor out of the market.[92]

The Advocate General attempted to clarify the position.[93] He started from the general principle that 'non-discriminatory price cuts by a dominant undertaking which do not entail below-cost sales should not be regarded as being anticompetitive'.[94] This was for two reasons. The first reason was that above-cost price cuts benefit consumers.[95] However, this is also true of predatory prices. The problem is that low prices that increase consumer welfare in the short-term may harm social welfare and productivity in the long-term if they exclude equally efficient competitors or even competitors who could become as efficient as the dominant undertaking but for the alleged abuse. The second reason, which is well founded, is that above-cost price cuts are generally not capable of excluding equally efficient competitors, and EU competition law should 'not offer less efficient undertakings a safe haven against vigorous competition even from dominant undertakings'.[96] This statement is immediately qualified because, according to the

---

[88] *Cewal, Cowac and Ukwal* [1993] OJ L34/20, upheld on this point in Joined Cases T-24/93 to T-26/93 and T-28/93 *Compagnie Maritime Belge* and, on appeal, in Joined Cases C-395/96 P and C-396/96 P *Compagnie Maritime Belge*.

[89] *Cewal, Cowac and Ukwal*, recital 32.   [90] ibid recital 82.

[91] Joined Cases T-24/93 to T-26/93 and T-28/93 *Compagnie Maritime Belge*, para 146.

[92] ibid paras 147–148.

[93] Opinion of AG Fennelly in Joined Cases C-395/96 P and C-396/96 P *Compagnie Maritime Belge*.

[94] ibid para 132.   [95] ibid.   [96] ibid.

Advocate General, different considerations should apply if the dominant undertaking has a quasi-monopoly, price cuts are selective, or their aim is to eliminate all competition.[97] None of these factors, however, in isolation or in combination with each other, justifies a departure from the general principle stated by the Advocate General that less efficient competitors should not be protected. Nor does the selectivity of the price cuts, which the Advocate General suggested should be a necessary element of the test.[98] Finally, the Advocate General commented that the process of sharing revenue losses is a form of recoupment.[99] This explains the strategy of the collectively dominant undertaking: excluding a competitor by forgoing profits and allocating revenue losses to members. But, again, no explanation is given as to why this would justify a departure from the principle that less efficient competitors should not be protected. Perhaps the Advocate General's insistence on the degree of the conference's market power approaching a monopoly[100] and the complete absence of any analysis of whether G & C might have been or become as efficient as Cewal's members suggest that what the Advocate General might have had in mind was that, when the market is dominated by a quasi-monopolist, even not equally efficient entrants should be allowed to compete. The Court of Justice, however, did not endorse this approach. In upholding the finding of abuse, the Court said that liner conferences provide adequate and efficient scheduled maritime transport services. As a consequence, when a single conference has a dominant position on a particular market, its customers 'would have little interest in resorting to an independent competitor, unless the competitor were able to offer prices lower than those of the liner conference.'[101] This means that the competitor had to overcome a switching cost as a result of which it was not sufficient for him simply to match the prices of the dominant undertaking. The features of the market meant that a competitor could not be as efficient as the dominant undertaking as soon as it entered the market. This was the reason why a departure from the principle that less efficient firms should not be protected under Article 102 was justified: the Court was applying the dynamic as efficient competitor test. However, conscious of the risks of false convictions and over-deterrence that the application of Article 102 to unconditional above cost-price cuts entails, the Court set out three additional safeguards: (a) the dominant undertaking must be a monopolist or quasi-monopolist; (b) the price cuts must be selective and applied as part of an anti-competitive strategy; (c) the price cuts must be capable of eliminating all residual competition on the market so as to result in the maintenance or strengthening of the dominant undertaking's market power, including the protection of supra-competitive profits on other markets or market segments.[102] These conditions may be relaxed only

---

[97] ibid. The AG also mentioned that price cuts could be implemented 'with relative autonomy from costs'. Perhaps he meant that in the maritime transport sector short-term fixed costs are very high and the MC of transporting an additional container may be very low once capacity has been fixed (ibid para 133). The point was not addressed by the Court of Justice and is, in principle, irrelevant.

[98] ibid paras 132, 135, and 137.   [99] ibid para 136.

[100] It is in this Opinion that the term 'superdominance' was first used: see ibid para 137.

[101] Joined Cases C-395/96 P and C-396/96 P *Compagnie Maritime Belge*, para 116.

[102] ibid paras 117–119.

when unconditional above-cost price cuts are ancillary to a wider exclusionary strategy so that, while not abusive in themselves, they run counter to the purpose of Article 102 because they reinforce the effect of other abusive practices.[103]

F. Mixed bundling

Mixed bundling occurs when two or more products are available either together or separately 'but the sum of the prices when sold separately is higher than the bundled price'.[104]

There is no case law explicitly discussing the legal tests applicable to multi-product rebates.[105] The Commission Guidance on Article 102 adopts the as efficient competitor test. Therefore, if competitors are either already selling identical bundles or are realistically able to do so, the pricing practice of the dominant undertaking can only be abusive if the price of the bundle as a whole is predatory.[106] If, however, competitors are not realistically able to supply identical bundles, the test considers whether the incremental price of a product in the bundle is below the LRAIC of supplying that product. If this is the case, the bundling is likely to exclude an equally efficient competitor.[107]

The approach adopted by the Commission is similar to the analysis of multi-product rebates in the UK case of *BSkyB*.[108] BSkyB granted certain wholesale

---

[103]   See eg *Eurofix-Bauco v Hilti* [1988] OJ L65/19, recitals 46 and 80, upheld on this point in Case T-30/89 *Hilti AG v Commission* [1990] ECR II-163, para 100. The issue did not arise on the appeal to the Court of Justice in Case C-53/92 P *Hilti AG v Commission* [1994] I-667.

[104]   Guidance on Art 102, para 48.

[105]   For the previous practice of the Commission, see *Coca-Cola* [2005] OJ L253/21; *Coca Cola*, European Commission, XIXth Report on Competition Policy (Brussels, Office for Official Publications of the European Communities 1989) para 50; European Commission, 'The European Commission Accepts an Undertaking from Digital Concerning its Supply and Pricing Practices in the Field of Computer Maintenance Services', Press Release of 10 October 1997 IP/97/868. For the practice in mergers, see *GE/Amersham* (Case COMP/M.3304) [2004] OJ C74/5 and Guidelines on the assessment of non-horizontal mergers under the Council Regulation on the control of concentrations between undertakings [2008] OJ C265/6 ('Guidelines on Non-horizontal Mergers'), paras 93–118.

[106]   Guidance on Art 102, para 61.

[107]   ibid paras 59–61. The Commission would also look further at whether the practice is likely to cause consumer harm: ibid paras 19, 21. For an interesting analysis close to the Commission's current approach, see DA Crane, 'Mixed Bundling, Profit Sacrifice, and Consumer Welfare' (2006) 55 Emory LJ 55. See also B Nalebuff, 'Bundling, Tying, and Portfolio Effects: Part 1—Conceptual Issues', DTI Economics Paper No 1 (February 2003) and B Nalebuff, 'Bundling as an Entry Barrier' (2004) 119 Quarterly Journal of Economics 159. In the US, much debate has been generated by *LePage's Inc v 3M (Minnesota Mining and Manufacturing Co)* 324 F3d 141 (3rd Cir 2003) (en banc) cert denied, 124 S Ct 2932 (2004), a case which appears to adopt an unstructured rule of reason approach to bundled discounts: see eg RA Epstein, 'Monopoly Dominance or Level Playing Field? The New Antitrust Paradox' (2005) 72 U Chi L Rev 49, 71–72; RA Posner, 'Vertical Restraints and Antitrust Policy' (2005) 72 U Chi L Rev 229, 238–240; TA Lambert, 'Evaluating Bundled Discounts' (2005) 89 Minn L Rev 1688, 1722–1723.

[108]   Decision of the Director General of Fair Trading No CA98/20/2002, *BSkyB Investigation: Alleged Infringement of the Chapter II Prohibition* (Case CP 01916-00, 17 December 2002) (*BSkyB*). Two applications to vary the decision under the Competition Act 1998, s 47, as in force from 1 April 2003 to 19 June 2003, were rejected in Decision of the Office of Fair Trading under Section 47

bundled discounts which, allegedly, foreclosed entry to the wholesale premium channel market.[109] The DGFT applied a two-limb test: (a) whether the discount resulted in average prices of incremental units below their incremental costs;[110] (b) whether an actual or realistic potential foreclosure effect existed (likelihood of foreclosure).[111] Because certain distributors had not received the discounts in question and all of them had moved away from the relevant range during the relevant period, the discounts were found not to be likely to have a foreclosure effect.[112] As for the distortion of downstream competition, the DGFT found evidence that this had not happened.[113]

The application of the as efficient competitor test is consistent with the insight that while multi-product rebates are a form of bundling, the bundling is achieved through a pricing strategy. The key factor is, therefore, whether equally efficient competitors can compete effectively against the price schedule of the dominant undertaking. An open question is whether Article 102 allows for alternative tests to cater for circumstances in which single-product competitors of the dominant undertaking cannot enter all the relevant markets at the same time and their costs are higher than the LRAIC of the dominant undertaking precisely because the bundling prevents them from achieving demand-related efficiencies that would reduce their costs. The answer must be in the affirmative. There is nothing in Article 102 that requires the application of a price/cost test to mixed bundling. Therefore, when single-product competitors are prevented from being as efficient as the dominant undertaking by the conduct under review, mixed bundling may be assessed under the test of intent by analogy with tying[114] or under the dynamic as efficient competitor test by analogy with single-product rebates.[115] On the other hand, there is no basis for assessing mixed bundling under a consumer harm test. Mixed bundling is a strategy that can be sustainable in the long term. Speculating on whether prices would be lower without the mixed bundling would either amount to little more than saying that the foreclosure of any competitor is likely to increase prices (or reduce choice) or be a wholly theoretical exercise prone to significant errors and unsuitable to being verified in legal proceedings.

G. Exclusivity

Exclusivity may be defined as the obligation of a customer to purchase goods or services on a given market exclusively or to a large extent from the dominant undertaking.[116] The Guidance on Article 102 appears to adopt a consumer harm test by stating that the Commission will intervene when consumers as a whole

---

Relating to Decision CA98/20/2002: Alleged Infringement of the Chapter II Prohibition by BSkyB (29 July 2003) (*BSkyB s 47 decision*).

[109] *BSkyB*, para 601.   [110] ibid paras 613–614.   [111] ibid para 639.
[112] ibid para 639.   [113] ibid para 644.   [114] See 211–217 above.
[115] See 239–242 above.
[116] Guidance on Art 102, para 33. This definition is consistent with the definition in Case 85/76 *Hoffmann-La Roche*, para 89. The dominant undertaking may enter into exclusive contracts for the

do not benefit. However, the assessment of the factors that the Commission may take into account points in the direction of the as efficient competitor test. First, the Commission states that consumers are more likely to be harmed when the demand side of the market is fragmented.[117] Fragmentation of demand is a factor that allows a dominant undertaking to exploit the lack of coordination of buyers. If the demand of each individual buyer is not sufficient to attract entry because of significant sunk costs or economies of scale on the market, when a buyer decides to buy from the dominant undertaking he exerts a negative externality on the other buyers. Therefore, a competitor can be excluded from the market even if he is as efficient as the dominant firm. Secondly, exclusive purchasing obligations are more likely to be harmful when the rivals of the dominant undertaking are not yet present on the market.[118] When this is the case, exclusivity may act as a barrier to entry. For instance, a bundle of long-term exclusive contracts may prevent an entrant from obtaining a share of demand sufficient to compensate the entry investment within the time frame required by the investors. This, again, may be the case even if the entrant is as efficient as the dominant undertaking. Thirdly, a non-contestable share of demand may give a supplier the ability and incentive to foreclose the share of demand open to competition by entering into exclusive purchasing arrangements with customers.[119] If the supplier makes an all or nothing offer, the customer will accept it as long as the cost of doing so is lower than the cost of not purchasing the product in question. As efficient competitors may be unable to compensate the customer for the losses made by not purchasing from the dominant undertaking. Fourthly, if competitors can compete on equal terms with the dominant undertaking, exclusive purchasing obligations are unlikely to be anti-competitive unless their durations make switching very difficult or impossible.[120] Arguably, the anti-competitive effect of long duration of the contracts is only plausible if, at the time when the long-term exclusive contracts were entered into, the foreclosed competitors either were not present on the market or could not compete with the dominant undertaking on equal terms. Finally, the Guidance requires proof of consumer harm but consumer harm is simply inferred from the exclusion of equally efficient competitors: because equally efficient competitors cannot compete effectively or competitors cannot become as efficient as the dominant undertaking, prices are likely to be higher, output lower, and innovation incentives negatively affected. This form of reasoning is simply a way of explaining the rationale for the as efficient competitor test and does not make proof of consumer harm a necessary element of the test.

There is some support for the Commission's approach in the case law. In *Suiker Unie*, the Court of Justice held that exclusivity may be an abuse if competitors are left with no available distribution channels through which they can market their

---

supply of an important input: *Greek Lignite* [2008] OJ C93/3 (summary decision), on appeal in Case T-169/08 *DEI v Commission* [2008] OJ C183/24.

[117] Guidance on Art 102, para 34.   [118] ibid para 36.   [119] ibid.
[120] ibid.

products on a sufficiently large scale.[121] This approach was somewhat undermined by *Hoffmann-La Roche*, where the Court of Justice said that exclusivity between a dominant undertaking and its customers was an abuse because such arrangements are not competition on the merits but are designed to restrict or eliminate altogether the customer's freedom to choose his sources of supply and to deny other undertakings access to the market.[122] Since *Hoffmann-La Roche*, however, and despite an apparent deference to this case as a precedent,[123] the case law has been moving away from a strict *per se* prohibition. In *British Gypsum*, the Court of First Instance held that exclusive dealing was only abusive when it applied to 'a substantial proportion of purchases'. In these circumstances, exclusivity would be 'an unacceptable obstacle' to market entry.[124] In *Van den Bergh*, the Court of First Instance said that an ice cream supplier had abused its dominant position by offering an exclusive freezer cabinet free of charge to retailers who did not have their own freezer cabinet or a freezer cabinet supplied by a competitor. The tying of 40 per cent of outlets on the relevant market was an abuse because it 'has the effect of foreclosing competitors even if there is demand for their products'.[125] Thus, the Court relied on three factors in order to presume a foreclosure effect: dominance, exclusivity, and the size of the foreclosed share of demand.

The case law suggests that, prima facie, it is an abuse for a dominant undertaking to enter into exclusive purchasing obligations affecting a substantial share of market demand. Given that the protection of inefficient competitors would be contrary to the purpose of Article 102, this approach must be understood as establishing a presumption that the application of exclusivity to a substantial share of demand gives rise to a presumption that competitors are excluded from the market even if they are as efficient as the dominant undertaking or that they are prevented from becoming as efficient as the dominant undertaking within a reasonable timeframe. It is then for the dominant undertaking to adduce sufficient evidence tending to show that the exclusive purchasing obligations either are not capable of foreclosing (potential) equally efficient competitors or produce efficiencies that rebut the prima facie case of abuse under the objective justification test. The Commission's approach, albeit as a matter of prioritization, would appear to require a more thorough market analysis. In fact, the two approaches may not differ significantly as the factors to be taken into account under the Commission's approach are likely to be at least implied in a finding of dominance. If individual buyers are able to counteract a supplier's ability to exclude competitors or have the ability and incentive to coordinate to neutralize the supplier's attempts to exclude from the market equally efficient firms, the supplier is not dominant. Similarly, the ability of rivals to compete on an equal footing for the entire market demand is incompatible with

---

[121] Joined Cases 40/73 to 48/73, 50/73, 54/73 to 56/73, 111/73, 113/73, and 114/73 *Suiker Unie*, para 486.

[122] Case 85/76 *Hoffmann-La Roche*, para 90.

[123] See eg Case T-155/06 *Tomra*, para 208 and *Intel*, recital 920, where only lip service is paid to the ruling in *Hoffmann-La Roche*.

[124] Case T-65/89 *British Gypsum*, paras 66–68.

[125] Case T-65/98 *Van den Bergh Foods Ltd v Commission* [2003] ECR II-4653, paras 159–160, upheld in Case C-552/03 P *Unilever Bestfoods (Ireland) Ltd, formerly Van den Bergh Foods Ltd v Commission* [2006] ECR I-9091.

a finding of dominance. The same must be said if long-term exclusive contracts are incapable of deterring new entrants.[126] The case law, therefore, appears to adopt a pragmatic approach to exclusivity that avoids duplicating the analysis already carried out when dominance is examined as a threshold issue. The Commission's approach, on the other hand, is not wrong in law and simply makes explicit when examining the conduct of the dominant undertaking the analysis that the presumption adopted by the case law infers from the finding of dominance.

H. Discrimination

(1) Article 102(c) as the exclusive legal basis

Discrimination occurs when a supplier sells the same product to two consumers at different prices and the price difference does not reflect the different costs of supplying the product. The same definition applies, *mutatis mutandis*, to the application of different trading terms to transactions entailing the same cost for the supplier. From a normative point of view, there may be a case for prohibiting price discrimination on intermediate markets that distorts the competitive relationship between suppliers or buyers of the dominant firm. Three factors are relevant to the test: (1) the effect of price discrimination on the productive and dynamic efficiency of the intermediate firms; (2) whether, in the absence of price discrimination, output is higher or lower—output-expanding price discrimination is prima facie beneficial to long-term social welfare and productivity and the strongest evidence would be needed to rebut this presumption; (3) the impact of a price discrimination ban on the dynamic efficiency of the dominant firm both *ex ante*—because the ability to price discriminate may be an important factor in the decision to invest and *ex post*—because the increased profits resulting from price discrimination are a reward for past investment.[127] Article 102(c) provides that an abuse may consist in applying dissimilar conditions to equivalent transactions with other trading parties, thereby placing them at a competitive disadvantage. Unlike under Article 102(b), there is no requirement that the discrimination be to the detriment of consumers. The test for a prima facie abuse under Article 102 focuses, therefore, on 'competitive disadvantage', that is, on the effect of price discrimination on the productive and dynamic efficiency of the suppliers or customers of the dominant undertaking. This is also the *only* test for abusive discrimination as a free-standing abuse under Article 102. The reason is simple. Price discrimination as a free-standing abuse must result in upstream or downstream competitive distortions. There is no other theoretically conceivable harm to long-term social welfare that is distinct from the harm caused either by the exclusion of rivals or by the exploitation of customers. It also follows that discrimination as a free-standing abuse simply cannot occur if the discriminatory prices or trading terms are applied to final consumers. Discrimination vis-à-vis final consumers is not prohibited under Article 102(c).

---

[126] On the concept of dominance, see Ch 10 below.   [127] See 88–92 above.

'Trading parties' are manifestly undertakings involved in the supply of goods or services on a market. Nor can final consumers be placed at a 'competitive disadvantage', as they do not compete with each other on a market. Any form of price discrimination vis-à-vis final consumers can be abusive only if it is either exploitative or exclusionary.[128]

(2) Criticism of the application of Article 102(c) to exclusionary conduct

Notwithstanding that Article 102(c) is clear in requiring proof of competitive disadvantage, and not just of disadvantage, there has been a tendency in the case law to condemn exclusionary abuses also as discrimination, with little or no analysis of downstream market distortions.[129] This case law is not only wrong in law but generates a substantial risk of over-deterring price discrimination that is harmless or pro-competitive.[130] Whether or not an exclusionary abuse also results in discriminatory prices or trading terms for the customers of the dominant undertaking is irrelevant as a matter of law.[131] An example of this mistaken approach to Article 102(c) is *Clearstream*. Clearstream was the only provider of primary clearing and settlement services[132] for securities issued under German law to central security depositories and international central securities depositories.[133] It was also

---

[128] This was the case in *1998 Football World Cup* [2000] OJ L5/55, recitals 74, 77, 84, and 88–114, where discriminatory arrangements for the sale of World Cup tickets that discriminated in favour of French residents were held to be exploitative under Art 102(b).

[129] Case 85/76 *Hoffmann-La Roche*; Case 322/81 *Michelin I*; *Napier Brown—British Sugar*; *Irish Sugar plc* [1997] OJ L258/1, upheld in Case T-228/97 *Irish Sugar*, appeal dismissed in Case C-497/99 P *Irish Sugar*; *BPB Industries*, upheld in Case T-65/89 *British Gypsum*, para 94, appeal dismissed in Case C-310/93 *British Gypsum*; Case T-229/94 *Deutsche Bahn AG v Commission* [1997] ECR II-1689, upheld on appeal in Case C-436/97 P *Deutsche Bahn AG v Commission* [1999] ECR I-2387. From now on, the text will focus on discrimination vis-à-vis the customers of the dominant undertaking. The same considerations apply to discrimination vis-à-vis its suppliers.

[130] D Geradin and N Petit, 'Price Discrimination under EC Competition Law: Another Antitrust Doctrine in Search of Limiting Principles?' (2006) 2 J Comp L & Econ 479, 488–489.

[131] There are few cases that recognize this explicitly. For instance, *Cewal, Cowac and Ukwal*, recital 83 held that the abuse was both exclusionary and discriminatory but the Court of First Instance in Joined Cases T-24/93 to T-26/93 and T-28/93 *Compagnie Maritime Belge*, para 150, held that the characterization of the abuse as discrimination was irrelevant. The issue was not taken up before the Court of Justice: Joined Cases C-395/96 P and C-396/96 P *Compagnie Maritime Belge*, paras 99–121. This is similar to the earlier case *Vitamins* [1976] OJ L223/27, recitals 24 and 26, where the Commission characterized loyalty rebates as also discriminatory under Art 102(c) but the Court of Justice dealt with the abuse only as an exclusionary one: see Case 85/76 *Hoffmann-La Roche*, para 90 in particular. However, other cases appear to include discrimination in the test for the assessment of exclusionary abuses: Case C-280/08 P *Deutsche Telekom*, para 175; Case C-95/04 P *British Airways*, para 67; Case 322/81 *Michelin I*, para 73; Case C-52/09 *TeliaSonera*, para 28. This case law, however, can be explained as setting out a list of relevant matters of fact that include discrimination as evidence of targeting in exclusionary abuses, which may be a material fact depending on the circumstances.

[132] Primary clearing and settlement services were defined as clearing and settlement carried out by the final depository of the securities. Secondary clearing and settlement services were defined as clearing and settlement carried out by intermediaries, ie persons who do not have the final custody of the securities: see Case T-301/04 *Clearstream Banking AG and Clearstream International SA v Commission* [2009] ECR II-3155, paras 13–14.

[133] *Clearstream* [2009] C165/7, recitals 201 and 215; ibid paras 47–74.

active in the provision of secondary clearing and settlement of cross-border securities transactions together with Euroclear Bank ('Euroclear').[134] Clearstream discriminated against Euroclear with respect to direct access to Clearstream's primary
clearing and settlement services.[135] The abuse in question was clearly exclusionary
but was also characterized as discrimination under Article 102(c). The analysis
by the Court of First Instance of the requirement of 'competitive disadvantage' is
almost non-existent.[136] The Court was content to note that the application of discriminatory fees for a period of five years by a monopolist to a customer 'could not
fail to cause' that customer 'a competitive disadvantage'.[137] Thus it clearly failed to
provide reasons as to the key element of market-distorting price discrimination,
namely the effect of the discrimination on the downstream competitive process.
As in the other cases that apply a very low threshold under Article 102(c) when the
abuse is also exclusionary,[138] the judgment can be explained on the ground that
the discrimination in question was, in reality, part of a wider exclusionary strategy.
The Court must have felt that the risk of a false conviction or over-deterrence in the
case at hand was low once an exclusionary abuse had been established. However,
this approach fails to consider the precedential value of individual cases. Thus, the
astonishing superficiality with which the case law addresses the requirement of
competitive disadvantage when the abuse is also exclusionary, risks creating a precedent that may be applied to purely market-distorting discrimination. This trend
in the case law is plainly wrong and must be urgently revised. There is nothing to
be gained in applying Article 102(c) to exclusionary abuses with a lower threshold
of 'competitive disadvantage'. There is, however, much to be feared because that
lower threshold may be applied to purely market-distorting price discrimination.
This would be not only manifestly contrary to the language of Article 102(c) but
would also give rise to systematic false convictions and grossly disproportionate
over-deterrence of legitimate pro-competitive discounting. The Commission has
perhaps become aware of this acute problem that plagues the law on Article 102.
Thus, in *Intel*, the Commission analysed a number of rebates conditional upon
customers obtaining all or most of their requirements from the dominant undertaking exclusively as a foreclosing practice and not under Article 102(c), although,
arguably, the rebates resulted in different unit prices depending on whether or not
the customers agreed to grant Intel exclusivity or quasi-exclusivity.[139]

(3) Market-distorting discrimination and competitive disadvantage

Article 102(c) applies to discriminatory conduct by a dominant undertaking vis-à-vis
upstream or downstream undertakings. The competitive harm relevant under Article
102(c) is not the exclusion of rivals of the dominant undertaking but the negative impact
on the upstream or downstream competitive process that results from distortions in the

---

[134] Case T-301/04 *Clearstream*, para 143 and *Clearstream*, recital 236.
[135] Case T-301/04 *Clearstream*, paras 5–24.
[136] Opinion of AG Kokott in Case C-95/04 P *British Airways*, para 130.
[137] Case T-301/04 *Clearstream*, para 194.   [138] See n 129 above.
[139] See *Intel*, where there is no discussion of a potential discriminatory abuse.

productive or dynamic efficiency of the suppliers or customers of the dominant undertaking. Therefore, the key element of the test under Article 102(c) is that discrimination must cause a competitive disadvantage to certain upstream or downstream undertakings vis-à-vis others. The law presumes that such a disadvantage is detrimental to long-term social welfare.[140] The problem is that the case law and decisional practice of the Commission have not so far clearly established a test for competitive disadvantage.[141]

An attempt to frame a meaningful test of discrimination is *Soda-Ash—Solvay 2003*.[142] The rebates applied by the dominant undertaking were exclusionary but they were also prohibited as discriminatory under Article 102(c).[143] Even customers who bought all their requirements from the dominant undertaking could pay 'substantially' different unit prices.[144] As a result, the price discrimination 'had a considerable effect upon the costs of the undertakings affected'. The input in question was 70 per cent of the raw material batch cost and 13 per cent by weight of the finished product. From this the Commission inferred that the discrimination affected the 'profitability and competitive positions' of the customers.[145] However, the inference that a considerable impact on costs affects competition is problematic. As a general proposition, cost variations, even when significant, do not necessarily distort downstream competition. Significant cost variations may simply reduce the profits of certain customers. But in industries where there are no significant investment requirements and as long as the rate of return of downstream firms remains above or at the cost of capital, anti-competitive effects are unlikely. The price discrimination simply transfers surplus from customers of the dominant undertaking to the dominant undertaking itself. This could amount to an exploitative abuse but is not sufficient to establish a discriminatory abuse. Therefore, a presumption that whenever the price discrimination significantly affects the costs of downstream competitors there is a 'competitive disadvantage' under Article 102(c) is not warranted. It is worth emphasizing that this provision requires not only a 'disadvantage' but a 'competitive disadvantage'. Any reduced profits would certainly be a

---

[140] The requirement that there must be discrimination, namely that dissimilar conditions must be applied to similar transactions, is necessary but not sufficient and does not relate to the competitive harm that Article 102 aims at deterring or remedying.

[141] The literature bears witness to the lack of clarity and the problems to which the case law of the EU courts has given rise: B Klein and JS Wiley Jr, 'Competitive Price Discrimination as an Antitrust Justification for Intellectual Property Refusals to Deal' (2002) 70 Antitrust LJ 599; D Ridyard, 'Exclusionary Pricing and Price Discrimination Abuses under Article 82—An Economic Analysis' (2002) 23 ECLR 286; P Muysert, 'Price Discrimination—An Unreliable Indicator of Market Power' (2004) 25 ECLR 350; D Glynn, 'Article 82 and Price Discrimination in Patented Pharmaceuticals: The Economics' (2005) 26 ECLR 135; M Lorenz, M Lubbig, and A Russell, 'Price Discrimination, a Tender Story' (2005) 26 ECLR 355; O'Donoghue and Padilla, *The Law and Economics of Article 82 EC*, 552–561; MA Gravengaard, 'The Meeting Competition Defence Principle—A Defence for Price Discrimination and Predatory Pricing?' (2006) 27 ECLR 658; Geradin and Petit, 'Price Discrimination under EC Competition Law: Another Antitrust Doctrine in Search of Limiting Principles?'; CE Mosso et al, 'Article 82', 388–390.

[142] *Soda-Ash—Solvay* [1991] OJ L152/21 (*Soda-Ash—Solvay 1991*), annulled in Case T-32/91 *Solvay SA v Commission* [1995] ECR II-1825, upheld on appeal in Joined Cases C-287/95 P and C-288/95 P *Commission v Solvay SA* [2000] ECR I-2391. The decision was readopted in *Soda-Ash—Solvay* [2003] OJ L10/10 (*Soda-Ash—Solvay 2003*). The readopted decision will be cited.

[143] *Soda-Ash—Solvay 2003*, 181–185.

[144] ibid recitals 183–184.   [145] ibid recital 185.

disadvantage but do not necessarily affect an undertaking's ability to compete. This is also consistent with the objective of Article 102 which is not to protect individual interests in a given level of surplus, even if a negative effect on the surplus of an individual customer is the result of the exercise of market power, but to prevent effective competition being distorted to the detriment of long-term social welfare.

A modest step forward in the assessment of competitive disadvantage was made in *British Airways*. The case concerned, yet again, exclusionary rebates that were also found to be discriminatory within the meaning of Article 102(c).[146] The scheme resulted in different rates of commission being paid for the same revenue generated by the sale of British Airways' tickets and was not justified by any efficiencies accruing to the dominant undertaking or by the service provided by the travel agents.[147] Proof of competitive disadvantage involved the analysis of downstream competition. Thus, it was relevant that travel agents competed among themselves by promoting their services or by passing on part of the commission to their customers.[148] Commission income financed promotional expenditure and lower fares.[149] When an agent dealt with a large airline, 'the agent's income would be significantly affected by the type of commission offered by the powerful airline'.[150] Therefore, discriminatory levels of commission distorted the ability of travel agents to compete with each other.[151] This test can be recast as an as efficient competitor test. Significant differences in the rates of commission would have affected the ability of equally efficient travel agents to compete in a way that did not reflect their comparative efficiency but reflected the turnover they achieved with the dominant undertaking.

The Court of First Instance upheld the Commission's finding of abuse on the grounds that prices were discriminatory and competition among travel agents was intense.[152] The Court must have implied, therefore, that a lower commission revenue significantly affected downstream margins and thus the ability of downstream undertakings to promote their services and lower their prices. The Advocate General placed emphasis on the finding of the Court below that competition among travel agents was intense.[153] She considered that one further element was necessary in the analysis of competitive disadvantage, namely that the commission schemes under review 'could lead to sharp and significant variations in the income of the individual travel agents'.[154] So while the Advocate General rightly considered the reasoning of the Court of First Instance to be 'extraordinarily scanty' on the issue of price discrimination, she expressed the view that the Court did not commit an error of law.[155] Without referring to the opinion of the Advocate General, the Court of Justice nevertheless clarified that, since Article 102(c) aims at avoiding distortions of competition in the internal market, competitive disadvantage must be understood as a distortion of the competitive relationship between customers or suppliers of the dominant undertaking.[156] This ruling

---

[146] *Virgin/British Airways* [2000] OJ L30/1, upheld in Case T-219/99 *British Airways*, appeal dismissed in Case C-95/04 P *British Airways*.

[147] *Virgin/British Airways*, recitals 109–110.   [148] ibid recital 111.   [149] ibid.

[150] ibid recital 32.   [151] ibid recital 111.

[152] Case T-219/99 *British Airways*, paras 233–240.

[153] Opinion of AG Kokott in Case C-95/04 P *British Airways*, para 127.

[154] ibid para 128.

[155] ibid para 130.   [156] Case C-95/04 P *British Airways*, paras 143–144.

conclusively establishes that a mere financial disadvantage is not sufficient to establish competitive disadvantage under Article 102(c). *A fortiori*, it is also beyond doubt that mere price discrimination is not an abuse.[157]

British Airways clarifies that competitive advantage is a necessary element of the test for abusive discrimination but is unclear on the type and intensity of anti-competitive effects that may justify a finding of abuse.[158] A better approach was adopted in *Alpha Flight Services/Aéroports de Paris*, a decision that, unlike *British Airways*, concerned discrimination that was not also exclusionary.[159] In *Alpha Flight Services/Aéroports de Paris*, ADP was dominant on the market for airport management services at the Paris airports. ADP charged a lower fee for self-handling than for the provision of ground handling services to third parties. Furthermore, it charged different levels of fee to different customers. The Commission held that these fees were discriminatory and abusive because they had a 'significant effect'[160] on competition on the ground handling services market and on the air transport market.[161] Because the market-distorting effect took place on a downstream market on which the dominant undertaking was not present,[162] there was no need for the dominant undertaking to have any intention to harm competition.[163] The finding that the discriminatory fees were an 'important part of a supplier's cost structure'[164] was only the starting point of the analysis. More importantly, the fees affected MC and, therefore, were reflected in the downstream prices.[165] As a result, competitors paying the highest fee were forced either to lose customers or to reduce their margins.[166] This distorted the airlines' choice between self-handling and outsourcing ground handling to third parties. The choice between the two business models was not based on their relative efficiency but on the artificial cost differences created by the upstream price discrimination.[167] The distortion was significant because ground handling accounted for a large proportion of the airlines' operating costs. The airlines' choice of suppliers was based on the price of

---

[157] ibid para 144, where the Court said very clearly that mere discrimination is not sufficient and that competitive disadvantage must be proved separately.

[158] The threshold appears to be quite low. See ibid para 145: '...there is nothing to prevent discrimination between business partners who are in a relationship of competition from being regarded as being abusive as soon as the behaviour of the undertaking in a dominant position tends, having regard to the whole of the circumstances of the case, to lead to a distortion of competition between those business partners. In such a situation, it cannot be required in addition that proof be adduced of an actual quantifiable deterioration in the competitive position of the business partners taken individually.' The question of the standard of anti-competitive effect is discussed at 294–300 below.

[159] *Alpha Flight Services/Aéroports de Paris* [1998] OJ L230/10, upheld in Case T-128/98 *Aéroports de Paris v Commission* [2000] ECR II-3929, appeal dismissed in Case C-82/01 P *Aéroports de Paris v Commission* [2002] ECR I-9297.

[160] *Alpha Flight Services/Aéroports de Paris*, recital 109.

[161] ibid recitals 32–34, 67, and 109–133.

[162] Case T-128/98 *Aéroports de Paris*, para 164. This downstream market-distorting effect is different from the commission of the abuse on a market other than the dominated market, which is limited to exceptional circumstances: see Case C-333/94 P *Tetra Pak II*, para 25.

[163] Case T-128/98 *Aéroports de Paris*, para 173.

[164] *Alpha Flight Services/Aéroports de Paris*, recital 109.

[165] ibid recitals 109, 32–34, and 38.   [166] ibid recital 110.

[167] ibid recitals 67, 131, and 132; Case T-128/98 *Aéroports de Paris*, para 215; Case C-82/01 P *Aéroports de Paris*, para 116.

the service but the price of the service did not reflect the efficiency of the supplier. Therefore, 'the quality and efficiency of the services concerned are liable to be considerably affected owing to the distortions of competition between suppliers'.[168] Further anti-competitive effects occurred on the air transport markets. The quality of ground handling services was an important element of airlines' competitive strategies in differentiating themselves and meeting the demands and expectations of the passengers.[169] The price discrimination effectively subsidized self-handling compared to ground handling services provided by third parties. Because only the airlines with a large volume of traffic at the Paris airports were able to operate a self-handling service efficiently, these airlines enjoyed an advantage over airlines that had no choice but to use the more expensive third party ground handling services.[170] However, negative effects on markets other than the immediate upstream or downstream market were rightly held not to be necessary for a finding of abuse at least when a distortion of competition between the customers of the dominant undertaking is established.[171]

Alpha Flight Services/Aéroports de Paris sets out the right test for market-distorting price discrimination. The case was upheld by the EU courts and, unlike *British Airways*, was concerned with discrimination that did not have exclusionary effects. The test requires proof of the following elements to establish a prima facie case of competitive disadvantage: (a) the discrimination must affect significantly the costs of the downstream undertakings; and either (b) these significant differences in cost affect the parameters of competition, including price, output, or innovation; or (c) there is a negative effect on the productive or dynamic efficiency of certain undertakings compared to others. The test requires, therefore, a significant distortion of downstream competition. It is worth noting that the threshold is higher than the effect generally required for an abuse under Article 102. This is, however, justified, because of the need to guard against the risk of false convictions and over-deterrence due to the pervasive nature of discrimination and its ambiguous welfare effects. Unlike in other multi-market abuses, the dominant undertaking has no incentive to harm competition.[172] A test of intention to guard against the risk of false convictions and over-deterrence would make no sense. Consumer harm as an alternative way of minimizing enforcement risks and costs would also be inappropriate. Determining the level of output either on the market where the dominant undertaking is active or on the market where the undertakings subject to discrimination compete with each other would be a highly speculative exercise and set the intervention threshold too high. Proof of consumer harm caused by the discrimination would certainly be evidence of a distortion of downstream competition. But imposing the burden of proving consumer harm on a competition authority or a claimant would run counter to the effectiveness of Article 102(c). The requirement to prove a significant distortion of competition appears to strike

---

[168] *Alpha Flight Services/Aéroports de Paris*, recital 131.   [169] ibid recital 132.
[170] ibid recitals 120, 123, and 130 and Case T-128/98 *Aéroports de Paris*, para 218.
[171] Case T-128/98 *Aéroports de Paris*, para 218.   [172] See 211–217 above.

the right balance between preserving the *effet utile* of the provision, while guarding against the risk of false convictions and over-deterrence.

I. Conclusion

This chapter discussed the as efficient competitor test and came to the conclusion that the test applies to a much wider range of conduct than either the Guidance on Article 102 or the case law appears to suggest. Importantly, when the as efficient competitor test applies, there is no requirement also to prove consumer harm.

The archetype of the as efficient competitor test is the predation test. Chapter 6 has already demonstrated that predation is examined under the intent test. This chapter shows that the required intensity of foreclosure is determined by the as efficient competitor test. Predatory conduct must be capable of foreclosing an equally efficient competitor. To decide whether this test is met, the law compares the price and the costs of the dominant undertaking. Although the actual cost benchmarks used in any given case are not, strictly speaking, part of the legal test, the relevant cost benchmarks must be consistent with the as efficient competitor principle. This means that they must be the cost benchmarks that either determine temporary shutdown decisions or definitive exit decisions in a given industry.

When the as efficient competitor principle is applied to other abuses, it is necessary to draw a distinction between predation, which is a risky strategy and one which cannot be carried out indefinitely, and pricing practices such as margin squeeze, rebates, mixed bundling, and exclusivity, which do not require any profit sacrifice and are sustainable in the long term. The latter practices are examined under the as efficient competitor test without any requirement to prove intent or consumer harm. However, mixed bundling can also be examined under the intent test by analogy with tying as an alternative to the as efficient competitor test. When this is the case, mere foreclosure is sufficient provided that there is proof of anti-competitive intent.

The as efficient competitor test can be applied dynamically. This means that a practice can be exclusionary when it forecloses competitors that could become as efficient as the dominant undertaking within a reasonable period of time but are prevented from doing so by the allegedly abusive conduct. When this test applies, however, the only approach which is consistent with the purpose of Article 102 is to require proof of actual effects. Alternatively, unconditional above-cost price cuts may be prohibited under very stringent conditions, namely if they reinforce another anti-competitive practice or if they are applied by a monopolist or quasi-monopolist as part of an exclusionary strategy with the effect of eliminating all residual competition on the part of potentially as efficient competitors, which in turn results in the maintenance or strengthening of the dominant position.

The as efficient competitor test also applies to determine whether discrimination that is neither exclusionary nor exploitative is abusive under Article 102(c). Discrimination under Article 102(c) is abusive if, and only if, it produces significant distortions of upstream or downstream competition. Therefore, abusive market-distorting discrimination must place upstream or downstream undertakings at a competitive disadvantage vis-à-vis equally efficient undertakings. This means that the following elements must be established: (a) the discrimination must affect significantly the revenues or costs of the upstream or downstream undertakings; and either (b) these significant differences in revenues or cost affect the parameters of competition, including price, output, or innovation; or (c) there is a negative effect on the productive or dynamic efficiency of certain undertakings compared to others.

The tests applied by the Commission and by the EU courts are not always consistent with the principles set out in this chapter on the basis of a purposive interpretation of Article 102. Particularly in the areas of rebates and discrimination, the EU courts should urgently review the current case law to bring it into line with the legal framework established by the Treaties.

8

The Consumer Harm Test

A. Introduction

The consumer harm test asks whether the conduct of the dominant undertaking results in higher prices, lower output, or reduced product innovation. The test is not necessarily the manifestation of a consumer welfare objective of the competition rules but is consistent with the achievement of long-term social welfare.[1] Therefore, the test may be applied under Article 102 even if this provision does not aim at maximizing some measure of consumer welfare but long-term social welfare. However, as the previous chapters have amply demonstrated, consumer harm is not the only test under Article 102. While the Commission envisages applying a diluted consumer harm test in its prioritization of investigations into alleged exclusionary abuses,[2] the case law adopts the consumer harm test in a much narrower set of cases.

This chapter examines the consumer harm test in vertical foreclosure, focusing on refusal to supply and margin squeeze. Next, it discusses the exploitative abuse test, which requires actual consumer harm. Then, it analyses the possibility that consumer harm may be the default test under Article 102 for practices that do not follow under other tests either directly or by analogy. Finally, conclusions are drawn.

B. The consumer harm test in vertical foreclosure

(1) The concept of vertical foreclosure

Foreclosure may have different forms that call for different types of analysis. There are, essentially, three types of foreclosure identified in the case law. First, single-market foreclosure occurs when an undertaking dominant in market A forecloses a competitor from market A. Predation, anti-competitive rebates, and exclusive contracts may all result in single-market foreclosure. Secondly, vertical foreclosure takes place when a dominant undertaking active on an upstream or downstream

---

[1] See 45–49 above.

[2] Communication from the Commission—Guidance on the Commission's enforcement priorities in applying Article 82 of the EC Treaty to abusive exclusionary conduct by dominant undertakings [2009] OJ C45/7 ('Guidance on Art 102'), paras 19–21.

market forecloses access to the market where it may not be dominant. Vertical foreclosure presupposes the existence of two markets or production stages: a market or production stage for a component and a market for a product that incorporates the component. A vertically integrated dominant undertaking's refusal to supply an indispensable input to a downstream competitor and margin squeeze are the clearest example of vertical foreclosure. The third type of foreclosure is horizontal foreclosure, which refers to an undertaking dominant in market A foreclosing access to market B where markets A and B are at the same level of the distribution chain. Tying and bundling are the archetypes of horizontal foreclosure.

Refusal to supply and margin squeeze are the two main types of vertical foreclosure practice relevant under EU law. In EU law, the consumer harm test has been developed mainly in relation to refusal to supply.

(2) Refusal to supply

(a) *The problem of balancing investment incentives and competitive harm*

Generally, refusal to supply occurs when an undertaking abuses its dominant position by refusing to supply products or services to a customer. The consumer harm test, however, has been applied to behaviour that may be described as vertical refusal to supply. Vertical refusal to supply is a refusal to supply that is applied as part of a vertical foreclosure strategy. Vertical foreclosure refers to the behaviour of a vertically integrated undertaking that is not only dominant on a market for an important input but is also active on the market where its upstream customers intend to use the input. The control of the input gives the undertaking the ability to exclude downstream firms. The presence of the dominant undertaking on the downstream market gives such an undertaking the incentive to exclude.[3]

---

[3] The problems relating to refusal to supply have been widely discussed in the literature, with an emphasis on the need for a cautious approach or even restraint in intervention: see TE Kauper, 'Article 86, Excessive Prices, and Refusals to Deal' (1990) 59 Antitrust LJ 441, 449–455; P Areeda, 'Essential Facilities: An Epithet in Need of Limiting Principles' (1990) 58 Antitrust LJ 841; J Temple Lang, 'Defining Legitimate Competition: Companies' Duties to Supply Competitors and Access to Essential Facilities' (1994) 18 Fordham Intl LJ 437; D Ridyard, 'Essential Facilities and the Obligation to Supply Competitors under UK and EC Competition Law' (1996) 17 ECLR 438; B Doherty, 'Just What Are Essential Facilities?' (2001) 38 CML Rev 397; C Stothers, 'Refusal to Supply as Abuse of a Dominant Position: Essential Facilities in the European Union' (2001) 22 ECLR 256; DW Carlton, 'A General Analysis of Exclusionary Conduct and Refusal to Deal— Why *Aspen* and *Kodak* are Misguided' (2001) 68 Antitrust LJ 659; R Pitofsky, D Patterson, and J Hooks 'The Essential Facilities Doctrine under US Antitrust Law' (2002) 70 Antitrust LJ 443; P Crocioni and C Veljanovski, 'Price Squeezes, Foreclosure and Competition Law: Principles and Guidelines' (2003) 4 Journal of Network Industries 28; AJ Meese, 'Property, *Aspen*, and Refusals to Deal' (2005) 73 Antitrust LJ 81; RJ Van den Bergh and PD Camesasca, *European Competition Law and Economics: A Comparative Perspective* (2nd edn London, Sweet & Maxwell 2006) 276–280; R Incardona, 'Modernisation of Article 82 EC and Refusal to Supply: Any Real Change in Sight?' (2006) 2 European Competition Journal 337; A Stratakis, 'Comparative Analysis of the US and EU Approach and Enforcement of the Essential Facilities Doctrine' (2006) 27 ECLR 434; CI Nagy, 'Refusal to Deal and the Doctrine of Essential Facilities in US and EC Competition Law: A Comparative Perspective and a Proposal for a Workable Analytical Framework' (2007) 32 EL Rev 664; CE Mosso et al, 'Article 82' in J Faull and A Nikpay (eds), *The EC Law of Competition* (2nd edn Oxford, OUP 2007) 313, 353–365; U Muller and A Rodenhausen, 'The Rise and Fall of the

Vertical refusal to supply should be treated with caution. As stated in a general theoretical proposition known as the Chicago School single monopoly profit theorem, a vertically integrated monopolist can maximize its profits by setting the upstream price of the output equal to its marginal cost. There is no incentive, therefore, to foreclose downstream firms.[4] However, this general proposition does not hold true in all market settings. In particular, it is not true when the upstream firm is not a monopolist and downstream customers are able to switch to competitors for their requirements. If customers resort to a second-sourcing strategy, upstream rivals of the dominant undertaking can, over time, become more efficient and erode the dominant firm's upstream market power. Furthermore, when the vertically integrated dominant undertaking faces competition downstream, it may be able to divert sales from its downstream competitors to its downstream division by raising its downstream customers' costs. If post-exclusionary downstream profits are higher than post-exclusionary upstream forgone revenues, this strategy is rational for the dominant undertaking.[5] However, it is not socially desirable because firms which, on the downstream market, are as efficient as the dominant undertaking are foreclosed. This may cause a loss of productive efficiency and also, potentially, of dynamic efficiency if downstream firms could have invested in new production processes or product development. In short, downstream competition does matter to long-term social welfare. In particular, whenever increased downstream competition increases downstream output, a refusal to supply an upstream input to downstream firms may harm long-term social welfare.[6]

Essential Facility Doctrine' (2008) 29 ECLR 310; A Andreangeli, 'Interoperability as an "Essential Facility" in the Microsoft Case—Encouraging Competition or Stifling innovation?' (2009) 34 EL Rev 584; E Rousseva, *Rethinking Exclusionary Abuses in EU Competition Law* (Oxford, Hart Publishing 2010) 81–132 and 412–416.

[4] RA Posner, *Antitrust Law: An Economic Perspective* (2nd edn Chicago, University of Chicago Press 2001) 224–225; H Bork, *The Antitrust Paradox: A Policy at War with Itself* (New York, The Free Press 1993) 140–141. This is recognized in the Guidelines on the assessment of non-horizontal mergers under the Council Regulation on the control of concentrations between undertakings [2008] OJ C265/6 ('Guidelines on Non-horizontal Mergers'), para 44.

[5] Guidelines on Non-horizontal Mergers, paras 40–43.

[6] There is ample support for this conclusion in the economic literature, although it must be cautioned that economic models often rely on strong assumptions. Furthermore, equilibrium outcomes are hardly ever unequivocal in terms of their welfare effects. However, it cannot be seriously disputed that in market settings that are consistent with the features of the dominant position under Art 102, a firm controlling a bottleneck input may have the ability and the incentive to exclude rivals so as to harm long-term social welfare. For proof of the principles distilled in the text and further references see P Rey and J Tirole, 'A Primer on Foreclosure' in M Armstrong and R Porter (eds), *Handbook of Industrial Organisation: Vol III* (Amsterdam, North Holland 2007) 418; JM Vernon and DA Graham, 'Profitability of Monopolization by Vertical Integration' (1971) 79 Journal of Political Economy 924; R Schmalensee, 'A Note on the Theory of Vertical Integration' (1973) 81 Journal of Political Economy 442; FR Warren-Boulton, 'Vertical Control with Variable Proportions' (1974) 82 Journal of Political Economy 783; M Katz and C Shapiro, 'On the Licensing of Innovations' (1985) 16 RAND Journal of Economics 504; P Aghion and P Bolton, 'Contracts as a Barrier to Entry' (1987) 77 American Economic Rev 388; J Farrell and NT Gallini, 'Second-Sourcing as a Commitment: Monopoly Incentives to Attract Competition' (1988) 103 Quarterly Journal of Economics 673; MA Salinger, 'Vertical Mergers and Market Foreclosure' (1988) 103 Quarterly Journal of Economics 345; MK Perry, 'Vertical Integration: Determinants and Effects' in R Schmalensee and RD Willig (eds), *Handbook of Industrial Organization: Vol I* (Amsterdam, North

From a long-term social welfare perspective, refusal to supply should be treated with caution because too wide a duty to supply would have a negative impact on the long-term investment incentives of both the dominant undertaking and its competitors.[7] Forcing a firm to share the product of its investment with its competitors calls for a trade-off between maximizing *ex post* social welfare and productivity and preserving optimal *ex ante* incentives to invest. Property rights, in particular IP rights, have the function of providing undertakings with incentives to invest in new products, infrastructures, and technologies. Freedom of contract is the cornerstone of a market economy in which a firm is at liberty to decide when, to whom, and on which terms to sell its products in order to recoup its investments. If the advantages obtained as a result of investments are required to be shared with other undertakings or the conditions and terms of supply are subject to regulation, a firm is no longer free to devise the business strategy it thinks fit to recoup its investment. As a result, the expected return on the investment and, therefore, the incentive to invest may be reduced.[8] A further difficulty affecting market-wide investment incentives is the free-rider problem. Investment is costly and risky. If the results of investment, be it a superior product, an invention protected by a patent, or an indispensable infrastructure, had to be shared with competitors, each undertaking would wait for competitors to make the investment and then reap the benefits of it by claiming access to the product, patent, or infrastructure in question. Therefore, no undertaking would have any incentive to invest *ex ante*.[9]

Holland 1989); O Hart and J Tirole, 'Vertical Integration and Market Foreclosure' (1990) Brookings Papers on Economic Activity (Microeconomics) 205; P Bolton and MD Whinston, 'Incomplete Contracts, Vertical Integration, and Supply Assurance' (1993) 60 Rev Econ Stud 121; Z Chen and TW Ross, 'Refusals to Deal, Price Discrimination and Independent Service Organizations' (1993) 2 Journal of Economics and Management Strategy 593; B Caillaud, B Jullien, and P Picard, 'Competing Vertical Structures: Precommitment and Renegotiation' (1995) 63 Econometrica 621; J Vickers, 'Competition and Regulation in Vertically Related Markets' (1995) 62 Rev Econ Stud 1; G Gaudet and N Long, 'Vertical Integration, Foreclosure and Profits in the Presence of Double Marginalisation' (1996) 5 Journal of Economics and Management Strategy 409; C-TA Ma, 'Option Contracts and Vertical Foreclosure' (1997) 6 Journal of Economics and Management Strategy 725; C Stefanadis, 'Downstream Vertical Foreclosure and Upstream Innovation' (1997) 45 Journal of Industrial Economics 445; MH Riordan, 'Anticompetitive Vertical Integration by a Dominant Firm' (1998) 88 American Economic Rev 1232; Z Chen and TW Ross, 'Refusal to Deal and Orders to Supply in Competitive Markets' (1999) 17 Intl J Ind Org 399; JP Choi and Y Sang-Seung, 'Vertical Foreclosure with the Choice of Input Specifications' (2000) 30 RAND Journal of Economics 717; WS Comanor and P Rey, 'Vertical Restraints and the Market Power of Large Distributors' (2000) 17(2) Rev Ind Org 135; T Chipty, 'Vertical Integration, Market Foreclosure, and Consumer Welfare in the Cable Television Industry' (2001) American Economic Rev 428; S Martin, H-T Normann and CM Snyder, 'Vertical Foreclosure in Experimental Markets' (2001) 32 RAND Journal of Economics 466; G Chemla, 'Downstream Competition, Foreclosure and Vertical Integration', (2003) 12 Journal of Economics and Management Strategy 261; S Caprice, 'Incentive to Encourage Downstream Competition under Bilateral Oligopoly' (2005) 12(9) Economics Bull 1; CC de Fontenay and JS Gans, 'Vertical Integration in the Presence of Upstream Competition' (2005) 36 RAND Journal of Economics 544.

  [7] Opinion of A-G Jacobs in Case C-7/97 *Oscar Bronner GmbH & Co KG v Mediaprint Zeitungs- und Zeitschriftenverlag GmbH & Co KG* [1998] ECR I-7791, para 57; Case C-418/01 *IMS Health GmbH & Co OHG v NDC Health GmbH & Co KG* [2004] ECR I-5039, para 48.

  [8] Guidance on Art 102, para 75.

  [9] ibid. See also Opinion of AG Jacobs in Case C-7/97 *Oscar Bronner*, para 57: 'the justification in terms of competition policy for interfering with a dominant undertaking's freedom to contract

Long-term social welfare and productivity would be harmed if the very application of Article 102 resulted in sub-optimal investments. Under Article 102, long-term productive and dynamic efficiency considerations prevail over short-term allocative efficiency. Any policy that favoured the latter to the detriment of long-term investment incentives would, therefore, be contrary to Article 102. On the other hand, the control of an indispensable input, even when it is the outcome of investment and innovation, may give an undertaking the ability and incentive to exclude rivals, with negative consequences not only for short-term social welfare but also for long-term incentives to invest. A dominant undertaking, shielded from competitive pressure, may not be spurred on to behave efficiently and make further socially optimal investments. Rivals who are denied access to the market will have no incentives to finance investments in further innovation. Failure to license a technology may negatively affect follow-on innovation. Therefore, there is no reason to believe that allowing a dominant undertaking to exclude rivals by refusing to supply them with an indispensable input will never be harmful to social welfare in the long term. An optimal legal test would prohibit anti-competitive exclusion while preserving market-wide investment incentives. If it is possible to design such a rule, it would be consistent with the objectives of Article 102 to prohibit refusals to supply that are likely to harm social welfare in the long term, while respecting the firms' proprietary rights and freedom of contract whenever the exercise of such rights and freedom causes no competitive harm or whenever to encroach upon them would have a detrimental effect on long-term market-wide investment incentives.

Given the high risk of discouraging investment inherent in the imposition on dominant upstream firms of a duty actively to assist their downstream competitors, EU law requires a higher intervention threshold for refusal to supply. The precise scope of the test or tests for vertical refusal to supply is, however, not entirely clear. An element common to all types of refusals to supply is that the input must be 'indispensable' to the customer. The case law also requires a particularly severe exclusionary effect, with formulations ranging from the elimination of the competitor requesting access to the elimination of all competition on the downstream market. Finally, the case law appears to treat refusals to supply any input in general differently from refusals to license an IP right. A refusal to license IP rights is abusive only in 'exceptional circumstances'.[10] The exceptional circumstances identified in the case law overlap in part with the elements of the general refusal to

---

often requires a careful balancing of conflicting considerations. In the long term it is generally pro-competitive and in the interest of consumers to allow a company to retain for its own use facilities which it has developed for the purpose of its business. For example, if access to a production, purchasing or distribution facility were allowed too easily there would be no incentive for a competitor to develop competing facilities. Thus while competition was increased in the short term it would be reduced in the long term. Moreover, the incentive for a dominant undertaking to invest in efficient facilities would be reduced if its competitors were, upon request, able to share the benefits. Thus the mere fact that by retaining a facility for its own use a dominant undertaking retains an advantage over a competitor cannot justify requiring access to it.'

[10] Joined Cases C-241/91 P and C-242/91 P *Radio Telefis Eireann (RTE) and Independent Television Publications Ltd (ITP) v Commission* [1995] ECR I-743 (*Magill*), para 50; Case C-418/01

supply test but add the condition that the refusal to supply must cause consumer harm in the form of the prevention of the emergence of a new product for which there is consumer demand or deterrence of innovation.[11] A further qualification that applies to refusals to license IP rights is that a dominant undertaking cannot be required to adopt a course of conduct that deprives it of the substance of the IP right in question.[12]

In contrast to what appears to be the current case law, the Guidance on Article 102 adopts a unified approach to refusal to supply. The Guidance explains that the Commission will consider refusal to supply as an enforcement priority if three conditions are met: (a) the refusal relates to an input 'that is objectively necessary to be able to compete effectively on a downstream market'; (b) 'the refusal is likely to lead to the elimination of effective competition on the downstream market'; and (c) 'the refusal is likely to lead to consumer harm'.[13] The objective necessity or indispensability of the input and the foreclosure effect are elements of the consumer harm test because consumer harm must be caused by the foreclosure of competitors resulting from the refusal to supply an indispensable or objectively necessary input.

(b) Indispensability

The requirement of indispensability or objective necessity relates to the dominant undertaking's ability to exclude. It is an element of the assessment of dominance and an indication of the capability of the conduct to cause harm. It functions as a filter to identify cases that are clearly not problematic. If the input is not indispensable, no competition concern arises under Article 102. As an element of the abuse test, its significance is that of a first indicator of the capability of the conduct to cause consumer harm through a severe restriction of competition. As a matter of law, there is no reason to define a special category of indispensability as 'essential facilities'.[14] The term may be used in a descriptive way to denote a certain type of

---

IMS, para 35; Case T-201/04 *Microsoft Corp v Commission* [2007] ECR II-3601 (*Microsoft I*), para 331.

[11] Contrast Case 6/73 *Istituto Chemioterapico Italiano SpA and Commercial Solvents Corp v Commission* [1974] ECR 223 (*Commercial Solvents*) and Case 311/84 *Centre Belge d'Etudes de Marché—Télémarketing (CBEM) v SA Compagnie Luxembourgeoise de Télédiffusion (CLT) and Information Publicité Benelux (IPB)* [1985] ECR 3261 (*Télémarketing*) with Case C-241/91 and C-242/91 P *Magill*; Case C-418/01 *IMS*; and Case T-201/04 *Microsoft I*.

[12] For the clearest statement of this principle, see Case 238/87 *AB Volvo v Eric Veng (UK) Ltd* [1988] ECR 6211.

[13] Guidance on Art 102, para 81.

[14] The terminology is occasionally used by the Commission: *Sea Containers v Stena Sealink* [1994] OJ L15/8, recital 66 and *ENI* [2010] OJ C352/8 (summary decision), recitals 39 and 56. The use of the term in competition law originates in the US: *MCI Communications Corp v American Telephone and Telegraph Co* 708 F2d 1081, 1132–1133 (7th Cir) cert denied, 464 US 891, 104 SCt 234 (1983). See also H Hovenkamp, *Federal Antitrust Policy: The Law of Competition and Its Practice* (St Paul, Thompson/West Publishing 2005) 309–314. On the essential facilities 'doctrine' in EU law, see, in addition to the literature cited at n 3 above, V Korah, 'Access to Essential Facilities under the Commerce Act in Light of Experience in Australia, the European Union and the United States (2000) 31 Victoria University of Wellington L Rev 231 and A Capobianco, 'The Essential Facility

indispensable input but no legal consequences flow from such a description over and above the application of the general refusal to supply test.

The Commission Guidance on Article 102 considers that an input is indispensable when it is objectively necessary for firms to be able to exercise an effective competitive constraint on the market. An input is not indispensable when competitors can obtain access to an efficient alternative source of supply in the foreseeable future.[15] In the case law, the term 'indispensable' was first used by the Court of Justice in the *Télémarketing* case but with little guidance on its precise meaning.[16] Some more clarity was provided in the later case of *Magill*, where three broadcasters held a factual and, to the extent that the information was protected by copyright, legal monopoly over their own television listings.[17] Each dominant undertaking published its own weekly television guide and prevented others from publishing weekly listings. Without the right to reproduce the programme schedule of each broadcaster, it was impossible for third parties or each dominant undertaking to publish a comprehensive weekly television guide. The concept of indispensability implicitly adopted by the Court was the legal impossibility of replicating the input.[18] However, in *IMS*, the Court held that indispensability was not limited to the legal or technical impossibility to replicate the input but included cases in which to replicate the input is 'not economically viable for production on a scale comparable to that of the undertaking which controls the existing product or service'.[19] The case concerned a copyrighted grid which divided the territory of Germany into 1,860 areas or bricks (the '1860 brick structure'). Pharmaceutical companies received data disaggregated at the level of each brick and organized their supplies based on that structure. As a result, the 1860 brick structure was a *de facto* industry standard. In *Oscar Bronner*, the Court of Justice defined indispensability as the absence of a potential realistic alternative to the upstream input as a result of technical, legal, or economic obstacles capable of making it impossible or unreasonably difficult for an undertaking with a market share comparable to that of the dominant undertaking to replicate the input either on its own or together with other undertakings. It is not sufficient that such alternative inputs as there may be are less 'advantageous' than the input owned by the dominant undertaking or that the undertaking requesting access cannot replicate the input because of its smaller size.[20] In *Microsoft I*, the concept of indispensability was significantly broadened. The question was how to assess whether a certain degree of interoperability between Microsoft client PC operating system Windows and third party

---

Doctrine: Similarities and Differences between the American and European Approaches' (2001) 26 EL Rev 548.

[15] Guidance on Art 102, para 83.

[16] Case 311/84 *Télémarketing*, para 26. The term 'indispensable' was not used in Case 6/73 *Commercial Solvents* although the input in that case was probably indispensable on the facts.

[17] *Magill TV Guide/ITP, BBC and RTE* [1989] OJ L78/43 (*Magill*), recital 22, upheld in Case T-69/89 *Radio Telefis Eireann v Commission* [1991] II-485 (*Magill*), appeal dismissed in Joined Cases C-241/91 P and C-242/91 P *Magill*.

[18] *Magill*, recital 23; Case T-69/89 *Magill*, para 63; Joined Cases C-241/91 P and C-242/91 P *Magill*, paras 47 and 53.

[19] Case C-418/01 *IMS*, para 28.   [20] Case C-7/97 *Oscar Bronner*, paras 43–46.

work group server operating systems was 'indispensable' for undertakings operating on the work group server operating system market. The Court of First Instance held that any degree of interoperability which did not allow Microsoft's rivals on the work group server operating system market to compete 'viably' on the market would fall short of the standard required under Article 102 because it would not allow effective competition to take place on the market.[21] *Microsoft I* is consistent with *Tiercé Ladbroke*, where the Court of First Instance examined indispensability in relation to the ability of downstream firms to compete effectively. The applicant submitted that the sound and pictures of French races were indispensable for the provision of the off-course taking of bets. The Court disagreed. The betting shop operator seeking to obtain a licence to televise the French races had a 'significant position' on the Belgian market as regards bets on French races. Moreover, bets were placed before the beginning of the race so that whether or not the race was televised could not have a decisive influence on the placing of the bet. This analysis implies that the input was not indispensable because it did not prevent the applicant from competing effectively.[22]

The indispensability requirement must be understood as being relevant to the dominant undertaking's ability to harm competition. In *IMS*, the Court held that it is not necessary that there is a market for the upstream product. The determinative issue is whether there are two different production stages with an upstream input being indispensable for the supply of the downstream product. The Court explained this requirement in terms of the existence of a potential or even hypothetical upstream market.[23] The Guidance on Article 102 adopts the approach in *IMS* and explains that it is not necessary 'for the refused product to have been already traded: it is sufficient that there is demand from potential purchasers and that a potential market for the input at stake can be identified'.[24] When this is the case, the input is not a product because it is not supplied on a market. The analysis of indispensability, therefore, does not relate to the objective features of a product but to the dominant undertaking's ability to harm competition. It is questionable whether this requirement should be relaxed further and extended to inputs that are not in existence but would be profitable to develop if the market power rents of the downstream division of the dominant undertaking are not taken into account. In *ENI*, a commitments decision, the Commission took the preliminary view that ENI did not invest in additional capacity on its gas pipelines because third party access to increased capacity on the gas transport market would have boosted competition on the downstream gas supply markets to the detriment of ENI's own downstream business. ENI decided to forgo the higher upstream profits that would have been generated by the sale of the additional capacity on ENI's pipelines in order to protect its downstream market power.[25] This decision can be explained in the light of the policy objective to use Article 102 to foster competition on recently liberalized markets. However, second-guessing the investment

---

[21] Case T-201/04 *Microsoft I*, para 229.
[22] Case T-504/93 *Tiercé Ladbroke SA v Commission* [1997] ECR II-923, paras 131–132.
[23] Case C-418/01 *IMS*, paras 44–45.   [24] Guidance on Art 102, para 79.
[25] *ENI*, recitals 55–60.

decisions of dominant undertakings, even if they control indispensable inputs or 'essential facilities', risks imposing an *ex ante* regulatory obligation of uncertain content that may distort optimal investment incentives. While the Commission practice suggests that certain undertakings singled out as holders of 'essential facilities' may have such an obligation under Article 102 TFEU,[26] the EU courts have not yet ruled on this issue. Given that the risk of competitive distortions is particularly acute in this area, it appears that, at the very least, it should be necessary to prove that the under-investment strategy has been carried out with anti-competitive intent as a way of guarding against the risk of false conviction and over-deterrence.[27]

The case law discussed above considers an input indispensable when it would be impossible or unprofitable (and, therefore, not viable) for a competitor as efficient as the dominant undertaking and operating on the same scale to replicate the input so that, without the input supplied by the dominant undertaking, downstream firms cannot compete effectively. With the important qualification relating to the requirements applicable to the hypothetical competitor requesting access, the Guidance on Article 102 is, therefore, consistent with the case law. Because indispensability is a necessary but not sufficient indicator of consumer harm, the test can be stated as a 'safe harbour': if the input is not indispensable, the refusal to supply is not capable of causing consumer harm.

(c) Intensity of the exclusionary effect

Refusal to supply is only abusive if the consumer harm results from a restriction of competition. However, the case law is not clear as to the type of foreclosure effect required.

Formally, the case law applies three tests. The first test would apply to the refusal to supply an input in general. The elimination of all competition on the part of the undertaking requesting access would appear to be sufficient. In *Commercial Solvents*, the Court of Justice held that the required exclusionary effect of a refusal to supply by a dominant undertaking that decided to integrate downwards was the elimination of all competition on the part of the downstream competitor requesting access. On the facts, however, the foreclosed competitor was one of the principal suppliers of the downstream product in the single market.[28] In *Oscar Bronner*, the Court of Justice applied the case law on IP rights to the refusal to allow access to a distribution system plainly not protected by IP rights. It did so, however, in a hypothetical form[29] and applying the foreclosure test of elimination of competition on the part of the undertaking requesting access instead of the more stringent

---

[26] In addition to *Sea Containers v Stena Sealink* and *ENI* see also *Flughafen Frankfurt/Main AG* [1998] OJ L72/30.

[27] In *ENI*, the deliberate nature of ENI's conduct was considered relevant to the analysis: *ENI*, recital 60.

[28] Case 6/73 *Commercial Solvents*, para 25. In *Télémarketing*, the test was framed as the 'possibility of eliminating all competition from another undertaking': Case 311/84 *Télémarketing*, paras 26–27.

[29] Case C-7/97 *Oscar Bronner*, para 41: 'even if that case-law on the exercise of an intellectual property right were applicable to the exercise of any property right'.

test of elimination of all competition required by the case law on IP rights.[30] In that case, however, the input was not indispensable so that it was not possible to draw any inferences as to the capability of the conduct to exclude all competitors or only some. The second test would apply to refusals to license IP rights, which would appear to be abusive only if it leads to the elimination of all competition on the market. In *Magill*, the Court of Justice considered that the 'exceptional circumstances' in which a refusal to grant a copyright licence was abusive included the fact that, by the refusal, the dominant undertaking reserved to itself the down-stream market excluding all competition on that market.[31] The third test was adopted in *Microsoft I*, where the Court of First Instance sought to strike a balance between the two alternatives of elimination of a competitor and elimination of all competition, and construed 'elimination of all competition' as 'elimination of effective competition'.[32] Elimination of competition thus means that competitors are marginalized or substantially weakened to the extent that they do not exert any effective competitive pressure on the dominant undertaking.[33]

Are different tests in relation to different types of refusal to supply justified? The answer must be in the negative. There is no principled basis on which it is possible to distinguish refusal to supply any product or service, grant access to a physical infrastructure, and refusal to license IP rights. This is not because of a formalistic analogy that relies on the theory that IP rights are a form of property.[34] The key point is that the risk of false convictions and over-deterrence in limiting the free-dom of an undertaking to choose its business partners and dispose of its assets is the same whenever a dominant undertaking is required to supply its rivals in order to enable them to compete more effectively. The equivalence in the balance of error costs is clear if one considers that, if IP rights protect investment, so does the right to property more generally, at least insofar as property is used as a produc-tive asset. Freedom of contract is also essential to preserve investment incentives in a market economy. By selling its products to whomever it chooses at whatever price and on whatever terms it thinks fit, a firm maximizes its profits so as to be able to cover its economic costs, including the cost of capital expressed as the rate of return required by investors. Nor should it be assumed that IP rights are more valuable to the society than other property rights. Modest innovations may be patented, while major investments may result in physical infrastructures or high-quality products that are not covered by IP rights. The same harm to society that would result from too wide a duty to license IP rights would result from too wide a duty to grant access to physical infrastructures or supply competitors with superior inputs not protected by IP rights. Therefore, the intervention threshold should be the same. And because of the high risk of false convictions and over-deterrence in refusal to supply cases, the higher foreclosure threshold indentified in the case law should apply. The case law sets the higher bar for refusal to license IP rights,

---

[30] ibid.

[31] Case C-241/91 and C-242/91 P *Magill*, para 56, applied in Case C-418/01 *IMS*, para 47.

[32] Case T-201/04 *Microsoft I*, para 563. 　　[33] ibid paras 570, 575–579, and 580–612.

[34] An analogy rightly criticized by I Lianos, 'Competition Law and Intellectual Property Rights: Is the Property Rights' Approach Right?' in J Bell and Claire Kilpatrick (eds), *Cambridge Yearbook of European Legal Studies* (Oxford, Hart Publishing 2006) 153.

which is abusive if it leads to the elimination of all competition on the market. This threshold should apply to all refusal to supply cases. The test of elimination of an individual competitor should not be sufficient to establish an infringement. This conclusion is already inherent in the case law on the refusal to supply an input that is not protected by IP rights. Even if this case law applies a test of elimination of all competition on the part of the competitor requesting access, in reality the test is one of elimination of all competition. This is because indispensability is an objective concept and does not relate to the position of the competitor requesting access. Therefore, if the refusal to supply is capable of excluding a competitor, it must be capable of excluding all competitors.

The foreclosure test for refusal to supply should be elimination of all competition for all types of input. However, elimination of all competition does not mean that no undertaking must be left on the market. The Court of First Instance in *Microsoft I* was right to say that elimination of all competition means elimination of all effective competition. The presence of a few marginalized competitors with significantly higher costs than the dominant undertaking, who are either on the market at the behest of the dominant undertaking or obtain a substantially inferior input, does not prevent a refusal to supply being abusive, provided that the remaining competitors do not exercise *any* effective competitive pressure on the dominant undertaking.

The above analysis shows that the Commission Guidance on Article 102 adopts the right approach in considering the elimination of effective competition as a necessary element in all refusal to supply cases, without drawing any further distinctions.[35] The Commission, however, is not correct when it suggests that the elimination of all effective competition may simply be inferred from the indispensability of the input.[36] The indispensability of the input is a necessary but not sufficient condition for the exclusionary effect of the refusal to supply. Proof of the effect of the refusal on downstream competition is a necessary and free-standing element of the test. The Commission itself identifies a number of factors that are relevant to the impact of the refusal on downstream competition, such as the market share of the dominant undertaking and its ability to expand output, the number of competitors who are affected, and the degree of substitutability between the products of the dominant undertaking and the products of the foreclosed competitors.[37]

(d) Raising rivals' costs

In the light of the above analysis, it is highly questionable whether the foreclosure test should be weakened to include instances in which the refusal to supply simply raises rivals' costs.

In *British Midland v Aer Lingus*, the abuse was Aer Lingus's refusal to provide interline facilities to British Midland when the latter entered the London Heathrow–Dublin route.[38] British Midland could compete effectively and operate profitably over time. The refusal to supply, however, raised its costs and shrank

---

[35] Guidance on Art 102, para 85.   [36] ibid.   [37] ibid.
[38] *British Midland v Aer Lingus* [1992] OJ L96/34, recitals 14–30.

its revenues. This is a much lower threshold than the elimination of all effective competition. The case can be explained on the ground that the Commission was pursuing a policy of encouraging competition in civil aviation markets, which, at the relevant time, were subject to regulatory restrictions, extensive industry cooperation, and capacity constraints. Furthermore, Aer Lingus had provided interlining facilities to British Midland before on other routes. The refusal to interline was clearly a reaction to entry aimed at protecting the dominant position on the relevant market.[39] It was also contrary to widespread industry practice, whereby interlining was only refused because of difficulties in currency conversion or doubts about the creditworthiness of the airline requesting the facility.[40]

Clearstream Banking is also in conflict with the principle that the refusal to supply must eliminate all effective competition. In that case, the dominant undertaking delayed granting a downstream competitor access to its indispensable upstream clearing and settlement services.[41] The delay related only to access to primary clearing and settlement of registered shares transactions while access was already provided in relation to bearer shares.[42] The Court of First Instance set out all the foreclosure tests applied in the case law: the *Microsoft I* test of elimination of all effective competition,[43] the *Oscar Bronner* test of elimination of competition on the part of the undertaking requesting access,[44] and the *Michelin II* test[45] requiring that the allegedly abusive conduct tended to restrict competition or was capable of doing so.[46] On the facts, the Court held that the refusal to supply hindered the competitor's 'capacity to provide comprehensive, pan-European and innovative services'. This 'harmed competition in the provision of cross-border secondary clearing and settlement services'.[47] This test is hardly a test of elimination of all competition, whether at all or on the part of a particular undertaking. The Court applied a test of 'tendency' to restrict competition, which flies in the face of clear precedents and significantly lowers the enhanced intervention threshold that the case law adopts in refusal to supply cases.

The requirement that the refusal to supply must be likely to eliminate all effective competition should not be relaxed further. This requirement is imposed by the case law in order to enhance the intervention threshold and achieve an optimal balance between preserving *ex ante* investment incentives and avoiding *ex post* competitive harm. If any refusal to supply which raises rivals' costs may be abusive, dominant undertakings supplying a more efficient input would be under a duty to supply it to rivals. This is precisely what the case law on refusal to supply seeks to avoid. *British Midland v Aer Lingus* can be explained as a case limited to its facts in a particular conjuncture of the development of the airline industry. The same can perhaps be said of *Clearstream Banking*, a case concerned with the emergence of a

---

[39] ibid recital 26.   [40] ibid recitals 25 and 30.

[41] Case T-301/04 *Clearstream Banking AG and Clearstream International SA v Commission* [2009] ECR II-3155, paras 93–138.

[42] ibid para 102.   [43] ibid para 148.   [44] ibid para 147.

[45] T-203/01 *Manufacture Française des Pneumatiques Michelin v Commisson* [2003] ECR II-4071 (*Michelin II*), para 239.

[46] Case T-301/04 *Clearstream*, para 144.   [47] ibid para 149.

pan-European market in settlement and clearing. The precedential value of these cases is, therefore, very limited.

(e) Clarifying the consumer harm test in refusal to supply

Consumer harm as a separate element of the test for vertical refusal to supply is clearly required when the refusal relates to an IP right. In *Magill*, the Court of Justice held that an 'exceptional circumstance' in that case was that the refusal to license prevented the emergence of a new product for which there was potential consumer demand.[48] In *Tiercé Ladbroke*, the Court of First Instance held that the refusal to supply sound and pictures of French horse races to a Belgian betting shop operator was not abusive because it did not prevent the emergence of a new product.[49] The Court of Justice in *IMS* clarified that the indispensability test and the consumer harm test are cumulative and not alternative.[50] In *Microsoft I*, the refusal to license did not prevent the emergence of a completely new product, ie a product which would be in a different product market. Rather, it prevented the development of differentiated products with improved features that customers would value. The Court of First Instance held that the new product test must be read in the context of Article 102(b). The test is, therefore, harm to consumers. Consumers may be harmed not only as a result of limitation of production or markets but also because of reduced innovation.[51] Less availability of differentiated products[52] and lower incentives to innovate for the dominant undertaking's competitors[53] amounted to consumer harm. This test is consistent with the previous case law. In *IMS* the new product was defined, albeit implicitly, as a product which may be within the existing product market but which must have additional features for which there is potential demand.[54] Assuming that the evidence supported the Commission's findings, *Microsoft I* was, therefore, rightly decided. However, specific harm must be shown by evidence independent of the mere exclusion of competitors. A mere inference of harm from exclusion does not satisfy the test. It follows that the Court of First Instance erred in law when it applied to Microsoft's refusal to license the principle that Article 102 prohibits not only conduct which may prejudice consumers directly but also practices which harm them by impairing an effective competitive structure.[55] As the Court of Justice made absolutely clear in *IMS*, this general principle does not apply to refusal to license IP rights, which is only abusive if a consumer harm test is met.

It is important to highlight that the consumer harm test in relation to IP rights responds to the need to protect the subject-matter of such rights. The case law establishes that the consumer harm caused by a vertical refusal to license must consist in reduced availability of differentiated products or lower innovation and not simply in higher prices and lower output. This is because the very subject-matter of an IP right is the right to prevent anybody else from reproducing the protected invention,

---

[48] Case C-241/91 and C-242/91 P *Magill*, para 54.
[49] Case T-504/93 *Tiercé Ladbroke*, para 131.   [50] Case C-418/01 *IMS*, para 37.
[51] Case T-201/04 *Microsoft I*, paras 643–647.   [52] ibid paras 650–652.
[53] ibid paras 653–654.   [54] Case C-418/01 *IMS*, para 49.
[55] Case T-201/04 *Microsoft I*, para 664.

mark, creative work, or information. The same considerations, however, do not necessarily apply to the right to physical property, which consists in the exclusive enjoyment of an asset but not in the right to prevent anybody else from producing or acquiring similar assets. The case law recognizes this difference in that it dispenses with proof of consumer harm when the refusal to supply does not relate to an IP right. In *Commercial Solvents*, a case concerning refusal to supply an indispensable raw material, the Court did not require a finding of consumer harm for an abusive refusal to supply to be established. Instead, the Court took the view that the impairment of an effective competitive structure in the European Union was sufficient. The Court, however, added that the impairment of an effective competitive structure harmed consumers indirectly.[56] This could only mean that a negative impact on an effective competitive structure is also likely to result in higher prices, lower quality, and less innovation on the market. In *Clearstream*, a case concerning refusal to supply services, the Court of First Instance held that the conduct under review harmed innovation and, ultimately, customers of cross-border secondary clearing and settlement services.[57] The Commission had also found a negative impact both on innovation and on output.[58] Neither the Commission nor the Court, however, set out consumer harm as a free-standing and necessary element of the abuse test. It appears, however, that this distinction between physical property and IP rights is wholly unjustified. As explained above, there is a strong analogy between physical assets used for business purposes, freedom of contract, and IP rights in the need to preserve *ex ante* investment incentives and reward past investments. Therefore, the requirement for separate proof of consumer harm as a way of guarding against the risk of false convictions and over-deterrence applies with equal force to all refusal to supply cases. This would only be an incremental development of the case law, which already requires proof of elimination of all effective competition. In a vertical foreclosure setting, the elimination of all effective competition would generally lead to consumer harm unless downstream competition would add no value in terms of increase in output or product quality. Proof of consumer harm would thus amount to proof that downstream firms are likely to increase market output or product quality or, which is the same, that they do not have the incentive simply to replicate the products and the prices of the dominant undertaking in a market that is not likely to expand.

The form of consumer harm to be proved in vertical refusal to supply in general differs from the consumer harm test in refusal to license IP rights. When the refusal to supply does not relate to IP rights, the more stringent test of negative effect on product differentiation, development of new products, or innovation does not apply. That test is mandated by the subject-matter of IP rights, which is the exclusive right to the use of an invention, mark, creative work, or information. To allow that invention, mark, creative work, or information simply to be reproduced or used to duplicate the products already supplied by the dominant undertaking,

---

[56] Case 6/73 *Commercial Solvents*, para 32; Case 6/72 *Europemballage Corp and Continental Can Co Inc v Commission* [1973] ECR 215 (*Continental Can*), para 26.

[57] Case T-301/04 *Clearstream*, para 149.

[58] *Clearstream* [2009] OJ C165/7, recitals 228, 231, and 232.

even if to do so would expand output, would negate the very subject-matter of the IP right and have a disproportionately negative effect on investment incentives.[59] As regards the right to physical property and freedom of contract, there is no reason for requiring this enhanced consumer harm test. The test can simply be consumer harm, including higher prices and lower output.

It follows from the above analysis that, as a general proposition, the Commission Guidance on Article 102 is right when it applies a consumer harm test to all cases of refusal to supply.[60] There are, however, two points on which the Guidance is at odds with the case law and should be revised. The first is that the Guidance defines consumer harm as a situation in which 'the negative consequences of the refusal to supply in the relevant market outweigh over time the negative consequences of imposing an obligation to supply'.[61] This balancing exercise may be required in the context of objection justification but not as part of the consumer harm test. The second is that the Commission does not differentiate between refusal to supply in general and refusal to license IP rights. However, the consumer harm test for refusals to supply in general simply asks whether prices are likely to be higher, output lower, or follow-on innovation reduced as a consequence of the refusal to supply. For IP rights, the test is stricter,

---

[59] Only to this extent and for this reason should a different abuse test apply to IP rights. The literature focuses generally on either a proprietary rationale or on an innovation rationale to support the proposition that IP rights should be treated differently: see T R Lewis and D A Yao, 'Some Reflections on the Antitrust Treatment of Intellectual Property' (1995) 63 Antitrust LJ 603; V Korah, 'The Interface Between Intellectual Property and Antitrust: The European Experience' (2001) 69 Antitrust LJ 801; L Pepperkorn, 'IP Licences and Competition Rules: Striking the Right Balance' (2003) 26 World Competition 527; DT Keeling, *Intellectual Property Rights in EU Law: Vol 1* (Oxford, OUP 2003) 297–401; T Hays, *Parallel Importation under European Union Law* (London, Sweet & Maxwell 2004) 168–214; SD Anderman, 'Does the Microsoft Case offer a New Paradigm for the "Exceptional Circumstances" Test and Compulsory Copyright Licenses under EC Competition Law?' (2004) 1(2) Competition L Rev 7; J Killick, '*IMS* and *Microsoft* Judged in the Cold Light of IMS' (2004) 1(2) Competition L Rev 23; C Ritter, 'Refusal to Deal and "Essential Facilities": Does Intellectual Property Require Special Deference Compared to Tangible Property?' (2005) 28 World Competition 281; H Hovenkamp, MD Janis, and MA Lemley, 'Unilateral Refusals to License' (2006) 2 J Comp L & Econ 1; D Kanter, 'IP and Compulsory Licensing on Both Sides of the Atlantic—An Appropriate Antitrust Remedy or a Cutback on Innovation?' (2006) 27 ECLR 351; ML Montagnani, 'Predatory and Exclusionary Innovation: Which Legal Standard for Software Integration in the Context of the Competition Versus Intellectual Property Rights Clash?' (2006) 37 Intl Rev IP & Comp Law 304; V Korah, *An Introductory Guide to EC Competition Law and Practice* (9th edn Oxford, Hart Publishing 2007) 335–359; A Roughton, 'Intellectual Property Rights' in P Roth and V Rose (eds), *Bellamy & Child European Community Law of Competition* (6th edn Oxford, OUP 2008) 813; YS Katsoulacos, 'Optimal Legal Standards for Refusals to License Intellectual Property: A Welfare-Based Analysis' (2008) 5 J Comp L & Econ 269; A Devlin, 'The Stochastic Relationship Between Patents and Antitrust' (2008) 5 J Comp L & Econ 75; FOW Vogelaar, 'The Compulsory Licence of Intellectual Property Rights under the EC Competition Rules: An Analysis of the Exception to the General Rule of Ownership Immunity from Competition Rules' (2009) 6 Competition L Rev 117; L Kjølbye, 'Article 82 EC as Remedy to Patent System Imperfections: Fighting Fire with Fire?' (2009) 32 World Competition 163; L Zhang, 'Refusal to License Intellectual Property Rights under Article 82 EC in Light of Standardisation Context' (2010) 32 EIPR 402; S Anderman and H Schmidt, *EU Competition Law and Intellectual Property Rights: The Regulation of Innovation* (2nd edn Oxford, OUP 2011).

[60] Guidance on Art 102, paras 86–88.   [61] ibid para 86.

requiring proof of a negative effect on product differentiation, the development of new products, or innovation.

(f) Refusal to supply an existing customer

The case law applies a different test to the discontinuance of supplies to an existing customer. In *United Brands*, the Court of Justice said that a dominant undertaking with a strong brand valued by consumers could not 'stop supplying a long-standing customer who abides by regular commercial practice, if the orders placed by that customer are in no way out of the ordinary'.[62] In *Sot Lelos kai Sia*, the Court of Justice confirmed this principle in the case of a dominant undertaking which refused to supply customers engaging in parallel trade.[63]

The Commission Guidance on Article 102 supports the idea that disruption of previous supplies should be treated more strictly than refusal to supply a new customer. The Commission justifies this view by noting that a customer may have made relationship-specific investments. Furthermore, if a dominant undertaking has in the past found it rational to supply a customer, it will be presumed that 'supplying the input does not imply any risk that the owner receives inadequate compensation for the original investment'. The burden would shift on to the dominant undertaking 'to demonstrate why circumstances have actually changed in such a way that the continuation of its existing supply relationship would put in danger its adequate compensation'.[64]

The case law and the Commission practice are totally unjustified. There is no reason to distinguish the refusal to supply a new customer from the decision to stop supplying an existing customer. In both cases, the dominant undertaking is disposing freely of its property, products, or IP rights and interfering with this freedom carries a risk of reducing *ex ante* investment incentives. Paradoxically, this approach gives dominant undertakings the incentive to restrict supplies in the first place, for fear of being locked into contractual relationships that, if terminated, would give rise to a prima facie case of abuse.

On closer analysis, the case law on the EU courts setting out this approach has nothing to do with vertical foreclosure. In *United Brands*, the dominant undertaking stopped supplying a customer because the latter had become heavily engaged in the promotion and sale of the products of a competitor. The effect of the practice was to deter other customers from stocking and promoting competitors' products. The refusal to supply was, therefore, a way of enforcing a single branding strategy. It had nothing to do with the ability and incentive of the supplier of an indispensable input to exclude downstream competitors.[65] When refusal to supply is used to enforce another anti-competitive practice, it must be examined under the test applicable to the main abuse. The test applicable to refusals to supply that enforce an exclusivity strategy is, therefore, the as efficient

---

[62] Case 27/76 *United Brands Co and United Brands Continentaal BV v Commission* [1978] ECR 207, para 182. See also *Napier Brown—British Sugar* [1988] OJ L284/41, recitals 63 and 64.
[63] Joined Cases C-468/06 P to C-478/06 P *Sot Lélos kai Sia EE v GlaxoSmithKline AEVE Farmakeftikon Proionton* [2008] ECR I-7139, paras 49 and 70–71.
[64] Guidance on Art 102, para 84.   [65] Case 27/76 *United Brands*, paras 163–203.

competitor test.[66] In *Sot Lelos kai Sia*, the refusal to supply had the sole prima facie purpose of restricting intra-EU trade.[67] That reason alone was sufficient to hold that it constituted a prima facie infringement of Article 102 in application of the naked exclusion test.[68] There was no need for the Court to rely on the misguided principle that a dominant undertaking cannot discontinue supplies to an existing customer abiding by normal commercial practice if its orders are in no way out of the ordinary.

The above analysis does not mean that discontinuing supplies to an existing customer can never be an abuse of a dominant position. It means that the test must be the same as for refusal to supply a new customer. Whether the circumstance that the dominant undertaking was supplying the customer in question will help to establish a prima facie case of abuse depends on the facts and evidence of each individual case and in no way relieves a competition authority or claimant from proving that all the elements of the legal test have been met.

(3) Margin squeeze as a vertical foreclosure strategy

The Commission Guidance on Article 102 characterizes margin squeeze as a form of refusal to deal. As a consequence, a duty to deal appears to be a necessary element of the test.[69] However, the Court of Justice in *TeliaSonera* categorically excluded the notion that margin squeeze presupposes a duty of the dominant undertaking to supply the input to competitors under the refusal to supply test.[70] In *TeliaSonera*, the Advocate General took the opposite view. His reasoning rested on three pillars. First, there is a substantive analogy: margin squeeze is a vertical foreclosure strategy analogous to refusal to supply. There is 'no independent competitive harm caused by the margin squeeze over and beyond the harm which would result from a duty-to-deal violation at the wholesale level'. And there is no material difference between imposing a duty to deal at wholesale level and imposing a duty to

---

[66] See 245–248 above. The Guidance on Art 102 recognizes this principle at para 77.

[67] Joined Cases C-468/06 P to C-478/06 P *Sot Lélos kai Sia*, paras 65–66.

[68] See 193–195 above. The Guidance on Art 102, para 77, accepts that refusals to supply that prevent parallel imports are subject to a different test, although it does not set out a framework for the assessment of this type of behaviour.

[69] Guidance on Art 102, paras 80–81.

[70] Case C-52/09 *Konkurrensverket v TeliaSonera Sverige AB* (17 February 2011) (*TeliaSonera*), paras 56–59. Curiously, the Commission argued that margin squeeze does not presuppose a duty to deal, thus contradicting its own admittedly quite ambiguous Guidance on Art 102. The Guidance, para 82, relaxes the requirement for the imposition of a duty to supply in circumstances where it is clear that such a duty would not have a negative effect on investment incentives, for instance because the dominant undertaking has a duty to supply imposed by regulation compatible with EU law or because the dominant position was acquired under the protection of special or exclusive rights or financed by state resources. This approach reflects the analysis in *Wanadoo España v Telefónica* [2008] OJ C83/6, recitals 299–308, under appeal in Case T-336/07 *Telefónica SA v Commission* [2007] OJ C269/55. In the US, in the absence of an upstream antitrust duty to deal, wholesale prices charged to rivals cannot be challenged and, therefore, no margin squeeze abuse is conceivable. The conduct of a vertically integrated dominant firm is only exclusionary if downstream prices are predatory: *Pacific Bell Telephone Co v Linkline Communications Inc* 129 S Ct 1109, 172 L Ed 2d 836 (2009).

deal at given wholesale and retail prices.[71] Secondly, there is a decision-theoretic analogy: the risk and costs of false convictions and over-deterrence, in particular as regards investment incentives, are the same in both cases. If the dominant under-taking does not have a duty to deal, to impose on it a duty to charge upstream and downstream prices that allow as efficient downstream firms to compete effectively would reduce the dominant undertaking's investment incentives.[72] Thirdly, there is an argument *a fortiori*: if the dominant undertaking can 'harm' its competitors by refusing to supply them, why can it not harm them by charging upstream and downstream prices that make it difficult for them to compete?[73] The Advocate General's reasoning is convincing. His conclusion is confirmed by the observation that a margin squeeze remedy must compel the dominant undertaking to supply the input. The ability to foreclose in a margin squeeze case derives from the dominant undertaking's control of a bottleneck input and its incentive rests on the protection of the supra-competitive profits of the vertically integrated structure by restricting downstream competition. In order to restrict downstream competi-tion, a dominant undertaking may refuse to supply the upstream input altogether. However, in certain circumstances, the dominant undertaking may have a legal duty to supply arising independently of competition law[74] or may find it profitable to supply the input but at a price that does not allow competitors to exercise effec-tive competitive pressure downstream. A margin squeeze remedy would require the dominant undertaking to set upstream and downstream prices so that equally efficient competitors can cover their downstream costs. However, in the absence of a duty to deal, the dominant undertaking could at this point simply stop supplying the input. A margin squeeze remedy must, therefore, include the duty to supply the input. Otherwise, any margin squeeze remedy would have the perverse effect of acting as an incentive for the dominant undertaking to behave in a more anti-competitive way. The Court of Justice in *TeliaSonera*, however, misunderstood the margin squeeze test. The Court might have been induced in error because mar-gin squeeze consists in the modulation of upstream and downstream prices. The refusal to supply test must, therefore, necessarily be complemented by the as effi-cient competitor test. This does not mean, however, that margin squeeze is a form of customer foreclosure analogous to predation, rebates, or exclusivity. But, regret-tably, an analogy with non-vertical foreclosure is what the Court probably had in mind when it said that it would be absurd to hold that all abuses relating to the

---

[71] Opinion of AG Mazák in Case C-52/09 *TeliaSonera*, para 16.

[72] ibid para 21. Less convincing is the observation that the dominant undertaking could be forced to raise downstream prices (ibid), as this may occur whether or not there is an upstream duty to deal in order to avoid a margin squeeze.

[73] ibid.

[74] For instance, the dominant undertaking may be subject to a regulatory obligation to supply compatible with EU law: see Guidance on Art 102, para 82 and Opinion of AG Mazák in Case C-52/09 *TeliaSonera*, paras 18 and 21. However, the effectiveness of a margin squeeze remedy cannot depend on an obligation to supply that does not arise under Article 102. And, in any event, there is no reason why a regulatory obligation to supply, whether or not it is compatible with EU law, should be automatically taken as implying the same assessment of the risk and cost of false convictions and over-deterrence that underpins the refusal to supply test under Art 102.

dominant undertaking's prices or trading terms presuppose a duty to deal.[75] Thus, the Court failed to distinguish horizontal foreclosure practices in which the dominant undertaking only deals with customers and vertical foreclosure practices in which the issue is whether and, if so, on what terms, the dominant undertaking must deal with its competitors so as to allow them to compete effectively. It is only in relation to vertical foreclosure that Article 102 requires the conditions for a duty to deal to be established as a safeguard against over-deterrence of market-wide investments. To have failed to recognize this principle on the basis of an obvious misunderstanding of different types of abuse weakens significantly the persuasiveness of *TeliaSonera* as a precedent, and the Court of Justice is urged to overrule it at the first available opportunity.

C. Exploitative abuses

(1) The need for limiting principles

Article 102 prohibits excessive prices and exploitative trading conditions applied by a dominant undertaking.[76] There is no difficulty in interpreting this prohibition as the prohibition of prices significantly and persistently higher or trading conditions significantly and persistently more onerous than those that would have prevailed under effective competition.[77] Furthermore, precisely because excessive

---

[75] Case C-52/09 *TeliaSonera*, para 58.

[76] Case 27/76 *United Brands*, para 248; Case 66/86 *Ahmed Saeed Flugreisen and Silver Line Reisebüro GmbH v Zentrale zur Bekämpfung unlauteren Wettbewerbs eV* [1989] ECR 803, para 43; Case 395/87 *Ministère Public v Jean-Louis Tournier* [1989] ECR 2521 (*Tournier*) para 34. See also Cases 110/88, 241/88, and 242/88 *François Lucazeau v Société des Auteurs, Compositeurs et Editeurs de Musique (SACEM)* [1989] ECR 2811 (*Lucazeau*), which concerns the same dispute between French discothèque operators and the French copyright management society SACEM. The judgment of the Court of Justice is in substantially the same terms as Case 395/87 *Tournier*, which was a reference in related criminal proceedings.

[77] The analysis of the evidence that may be used to prove that prices or trading terms are significantly and persistently higher or more onerous than those that would have prevailed under effective competition, falls outside the scope of this monograph. Suffice it to say that the case law and Commission practice appear to adopt several types of test: (a) price/cost tests: Case 27/76 *United Brands* and *Scandlines Sverige AB v Port of Helsingborg* (Case COMP/A.36.568/D3, 23 July 2004) (*Port of Helsingborg*); (b) tests relying on cross-market comparisons: Case 30/87 *Corinne Bodson v Pompes Funèbres des Régions Libérées SA* [1988] ECR 2479 (*Bodson*) and Case 395/87 *Tournier*; (c) proportionality tests seeking a balance of interests between the supplier and its customers: Case 127/73 *Belgische Radio en Televisie v SV SABAM and NV Fonior* [1974] ECR 313 (*BRT v SABAM*); Case 395/87 *Tournier*, para 45; *Tetra Pak II* [1992] OJ L72/1, recitals 106–145, upheld in Case T-83/91 *Tetra Pak International SA v Commission* [1994] ECR II-755 (*Tetra Pak II*), appeal dismissed in Case C-333/94 P *Tetra Pak International SA v Commission* [1996] ECR I-5951 (*Tetra Pak II*); *Der Grüne Punkt—Duales System Deutschland* [2001] OJ L166/1, upheld in Case T-151/01 *Der Grüne Punkt—Duales System Deutschland GmbH v Commission* [2007] ECR II-1607, appeal dismissed in Case C-385/07 P *Der Grüne Punkt—Duales System Deutschland GmbH* [2009] ECR I-6155; Case C-52/07 *Kanal 5 Ltd v STIM* [2008] ECR I-9275, paras 28–29 and 31. Another, controversial, way of assessing whether prices are exploitative is to examine the profitability of the dominant undertaking: see Decision of the Director General of Fair Trading No CA98/2/2001 *Napp Pharmaceutical Holdings Ltd and Subsidiaries*, OFT (30 March 2001) (*Napp*), paras 223–229, partly upheld on appeal (but fully upheld on the point in question) in *Napp Pharmaceutical*

prices are supra-competitive prices and exploitative trading conditions are conditions that are more onerous than those that would prevail under effective competition, there is no doubt that Article 102 adopts a test of actual consumer harm for exploitative abuses. The appropriate legal basis for the prohibition of exploitative abuses, therefore, is Article 102(b), which proscribes the limitation of production, markets, and technical development to the detriment of consumers. This seems preferable to relying on Article 102(a), which prohibits unfair prices and trading conditions.[78] Article 102(a) applies to exclusionary practices.[79] If it also applied to exploitative abuses, the term 'unfair' used in that provision would have two very different meanings. More fundamentally, Article 102(a), on its terms, does not require proof of consumer harm, while exploitative abuses undoubtedly require proof of actual consumer harm.

While there is no textual difficulty in reading Article 102(b) as prohibiting exploitative abuses, the question is whether such a prohibition is consistent with the purpose of Article 102. The answer was provided in Chapter 3, which established that the prohibition of exploitative conduct is compatible with a competition regime which has the objective of maximizing long-term social welfare.[80] However, when such a prohibition is in place, it is of fundamental importance to provide for appropriate safeguards against the risk of over-deterrence and competitive distortions inherent in a rule proscribing exploitative behaviour. From a normative point of view, two safeguards may apply: an enhanced dominance threshold or proof of consumer harm that is different from, and additional to, the mere charging of an excessive price or the mere imposition of an excessively onerous trading condition.[81] The case law and the decisional practice of the Commission do not explicitly require either of these conditions. However, they are consistent with them: in practice, purely exploitative abuses have been found only if an enhanced dominance threshold or proof of consumer harm over and above the mere application of supra-competitive prices or trading terms have been established. Furthermore,

---

Holdings Ltd (No 4) v Director General of Fair Trading [2002] CAT 1, [2002] Comp AR 13, [2002] ECC 13 (*Napp v DGFT*), permission to appeal was refused by the Competition Commission Appeal Tribunal in *Napp Pharmaceutical Holdings Ltd v Director General of Fair Trading (No 5)* [2002] CAT 5, [2002] Comp AR 259, and further application for leave rejected by the Court of Appeal in *Napp Pharmaceutical Holdings Ltd v Director General of Fair Trading (No 5)* [2002] EWCA Civ 796, [2002] 4 All ER 376. See also UK Competition Commission, *Market Investigation into Supply of Bulk Liquefied Petroleum Gas for Domestic Use* (Competition Commission, 29 June 2006) paras 5.2–5.16 and Appendices J and K and UK Competition Commission, *Store Cards Market Investigation* (Competition Commission, 7 March 2006) (*Store Cards Market Investigation*) paras 866–880. For an overview on profitability measures in competition analysis, see OXERA, 'Assessing Profitability in Competition Policy Analysis' Economic Discussion Paper 6 (OFT657, July 2003).

[78] The case law does refer to Art 102(a) as prohibiting excessive prices and exploitative trading conditions: Case 27/76 *United Brands*, para 248; Case 26/75 *General Motors Continental NV v Commission* [1975] ECR 1367, para 12; Case 30/87 *Bodson*; Case 395/87 *Tournier*, para 34. But see Case C-52/07 *Kanal 5*, where the Court of Justice did not refer to 'unfair' prices under Art 102(a).

[79] Case C-52/09 *TeliaSonera*; Case C-280/08 P *Deutsche Telekom AG v Commission* [2010] OJ C346/4, para 172.

[80] See 97–100 above.   [81] See 98–100 above.

in EU law exploitative abuses can also be prohibited when they are the result of anti-competitive exclusion.

(2) Enhanced dominance test

Article 102 and EU case law are absolutely clear that the mere fact that an undertaking holds a dominant position is not in itself an infringement of Article 102.[82] A constituent element of the dominant position is substantial and durable market power.[83] Therefore, an undertaking with substantial and durable market power does not, because of this fact alone, infringe Article 102. But substantial and durable market power is precisely the ability to charge a price persistently and significantly above the competitive level. It follows that the prohibition of excessive prices must require more than dominance and the charging of prices persistently and significantly above the competitive level.

The case law and the enforcement practice of the Commission supports the proposition that purely exploitative abuses may be found if the dominant undertaking is a legal or *de facto* monopolist or quasi-monopolist. Collecting society cases are predicated on the premise that the collecting society holds a *de facto* monopoly vis-à-vis rights-holders and users. The EU courts assumed that rights-holders and users had no choice but to deal with the national collecting society.[84]

A natural monopoly is, obviously, a *de facto* monopoly. In *Port of Helsingborg*, one of the alleged abuses was that the Port of Helsingborg charged an excessive port fee to ferry operators. The Commission defined the market as the provision of port services and facilities to ferry operators transporting passengers and vehicles on the Helsingborg–Elsinore route.[85] The Port of Helsingborg was the only undertaking on the relevant market and there was 'no possibility for any other

---

[82] Art 102 prohibits the abuse of a dominant position not a dominant position as such. The case law is absolutely settled and uncontroversial: Case 322/81 *NV Nederlandsche Banden Industrie Michelin v Commission* [1983] ECR 3461(*Michelin I*), para 57; Joined Cases C-395/96 P and C-396/96 P *Compagnie Maritime Belge Transports v Commission* [2000] ECR I-1365, para 37; Case C-52/09 *TeliaSonera*, para 24.

[83] Guidance on Art 102, paras 8–11. This is the best interpretation of the case law that defines dominance as the ability to behave independently of its competitors, customers, and final consumers: see eg Case 85/76 *Hoffmann-La Roche & Co AG v Commission* [1979] ECR 461, para 38; Case 27/76 *United Brands*, para 65; Case C-280/08 P *Deutsche Telekom*, para 170; Case C-52/09 *TeliaSonera*, para 23.

[84] Case 395/87 *Tournier*, para 6; Joined Cases 110/88, 241/88, and 242/88 *Lucazeau*, para 7; Case 127/73 *BRT v SABAM*, paras 3 and 5; Case C-52/07 *Kanal 5*, paras 7, 16, 17, and 21.

[85] *Port of Helsingborg*, recitals 72–77. This market definition may appear excessively narrow but was probably based on the idea that the hypothetical monopolist would find it profitable to increase the competitive price of the services in question by 5% to 10%. Ferry operators transporting passengers and/or vehicles on the Helsingborg-Elsinore route had no alternative to using the port of Helsingborg. However, the problem is that ferry operators may transport fewer passengers or operate less frequently, thus reducing the profitability of the port. Passengers had alternatives to the ferry and, in particular, the Øresund Bridge. The Commission rejected this argument, stating that the customers using the port and the bridge were different: see ibid recital 73. But the question was whether downstream demand could discipline the price charged by the port to the ferry operators—a question that the decision does not address adequately.

undertaking to enter the upstream market as regards the provision of port facilities and services at Helsingborg'.[86]

Legal monopolies and exclusive or special rights granted to certain undertakings by the State and conferring on them a dominant position could also give rise to the special responsibility not to make use of the situation of weakened competition on the market in order to charge excessive prices or impose excessively onerous contractual terms. In *Corinne Bodson v SA Pompes Funèbres des Régions Libérées*, undertakings belonging to the same group held exclusive concessions to provide certain funeral services in a number of French communes.[87] The Court of Justice held that the relevant factors for the assessment of whether the group of undertakings in question held a dominant position included 'the size of the market share held by the group which is shielded from any competition at all as a result of the exclusive concession' and 'the influence of that monopolistic situation on the position of the group with regard to supplies of goods and services not covered by the exclusive concession'.[88] The presence of legal barriers was material to the conclusion of the Court that an excessive pricing abuse was possible on the facts of the case. Furthermore, the case law and the decisional practice of the Commission has established that Article 106,[89] in conjunction with Article 102(b), is infringed when an undertaking holding exclusive or special rights is unable to meet customer demand.[90] Article 106(1) is not a free-standing provision but operates a *renvoi* to other provisions of the TFEU, including Article 102. The inability to meet demand is a limitation of output that prejudices consumers. This is the definition of exploitative abuse. Therefore, it must be an abuse, for an undertaking holding exclusive or special rights, to limit production, markets, and technical development to the prejudice of consumers even when the dominant undertaking is not compelled to do so by a State measure.

When the dominant position amounts to a legal, natural, or *de facto* monopoly or is the consequence of exclusive or special rights granted by the State, the impossibility or difficulty of entry will generally be an inherent feature of the market. However, in relation to purely exploitative abuses, it is important to make this condition explicit. The features of the market, which have just been described, are not necessarily incompatible with entry. A legal monopoly may be displaced if the relevant legislation is going to be repealed to open the market to competition,

---

[86] ibid recital 79.   [87] Case 30/87 *Bodson*.   [88] ibid.

[89] Art 106(1) TFEU reads as follows: 'In the case of public undertakings and undertakings to which Member States grant special or exclusive rights, Member States shall neither enact nor maintain in force any measure contrary to the rules contained in the Treaties, in particular to those rules provided for in Article 18 and Articles 101 to 109'. On Art 106, see JL Buendia Sierra, 'Article 86: Exclusive Rights and Other Anti-Competitive State Measures' in Faull and Nikpay (eds), *The EC Law of Competition*, 593–655 and JL Buendia Sierra, *Exclusive Rights and State Monopolies under EC Law: Article 86 (former Article 90) of the EC Treaty* (Oxford, OUP 1999).

[90] eg Case C-41/90 *Klaus Höfner and Fritz Elser v Macrotron GmbH* [1991] ECR I-1979 (*Höfner and Elser*); Joined Cases C-180/98 P to C-184/98 P *Pavel Pavlov v Stichting Pensioenfonds Medische Specialisten* [2000] ECR I-6451; Case C-67/96 *Albany International BV v Stichting Bedrijfspensioenfonds Textielindustrie* [1999] ECR I-5751; *Dutch Courier Services* [1990] OJ L10/47; *Spanish Courier Services* [1990] OJ L233/19.

a natural monopoly consisting in an 'essential facility' may become obsolete because of technological advances, and a *de facto* monopoly may be displaced by an innovative entrant even if entry has not taken place in the past. A prohibition of exploitative abuses in these circumstances would be superfluous. The condition relating to entry barriers ensures that the prohibition of excessive prices is necessary because entry is unlikely to correct the market failure.[91]

(3) Enhanced consumer harm test

Article 102 does not prohibit dominance. This means that something more than dominance must be required before exploitative prices or trading conditions can be prohibited. One option is to require a higher dominance threshold. Alternatively, an enhanced consumer harm test could be applied. Purely exploitative abuses are prohibited under Article 102(b). Therefore, they must be 'to the prejudice of consumers'. Consumer harm, however, is inherent in the charging of supra-competitive prices. As a result, a requirement to prove consumer harm would not be capable of limiting the application of the prohibition of exploitative abuses so as to guard against the risk of market distorting and over-deterrence. Therefore, the question is whether the law should go further and require proof of demonstrable consumer harm distinct from, and additional to, the harm that derives from the mere payment of an excessively high price or the imposition of excessively onerous conditions.[92] The case law and the enforcement practice of the Commission have so far identified three cases in which this may occur. The first example is based on the case law on refusal to license IP rights: the prevention of the development of a differentiated product or the emergence of a new product, or the reduction of innovation.[93] Thus, excessive prices that deter investment in production technologies or product development by downstream firms would cause consumer harm. The second example is the impact of short-term prices on long-term prices. *E.ON* was a commitments decision concerning the exploitation of a collective dominant position. The limiting principle of exploitative abuses consisting in the requirement of an enhanced dominance threshold is clearly not applicable to collective dominance. However, the Commission took the preliminary view that E.ON had withheld generation capacity on the German wholesale market for electricity, a limitation of production amounting to an exploitative abuse. Intervention was justified because the conduct in question not only had the short-term impact of raising prices significantly at times of peak demand but also increased the prices of forward products

---

[91] For a similar conclusion based on error cost analysis, see DS Evans and AJ Padilla, 'Excessive Prices: Using Economics to Define Administrable Legal Rules' (2005) 1 J Comp L & Econ 97, 119–120.

[92] Evans and Padilla, ibid 119–120 argue that it may be appropriate to prohibit excessive prices when, *inter alia*, there is 'a risk that those prices may prevent the emergence of new goods and services in adjacent markets'. The substantial consumer harm test proposed here is wider but rests on the same idea that proof of specific and distinct consumer harm is a key safeguard against the risk of enforcement errors and over-deterrence.

[93] Joined Cases C-241/91 P and C-242/91 P *Magill*; Case C-418/01 *IMS*; Case T-201/04 *Microsoft I*.

(such as options and futures), which were based on short-term prices.[94] This long-term effect of the abuse must go beyond the persistent charging of excessive prices made possible by the presence of barriers to entry. Current prices must determine future prices regardless of whether the dominant undertaking continues to be dominant over the period under consideration. The third example is established in the case law on Article 106(1) read in conjunction with Article 102(b): the manifest inability of the dominant undertaking to meet demand in circumstances in which it is not possible for other undertakings to enter the market or to expand output. In *Höfner and Elser*, the Court of Justice held that a public employment agency having the exclusive right to provide recruitment services could not avoid breaching Article 102(b) if it was manifestly unable to meet market demand and other undertakings could not legally provide those services.[95] It may be argued that in any case of prices above MC there will be unmet demand from customers whose willingness to pay equals MC. However, this condition is more stringent because it requires not only proof of excessive prices but also proof of actual or potential market demand for the product over and above the mere existence of consumers whose willingness to pay for the product is lower than its current price and higher than, or equal to, its MC.

(4) Post-exclusionary exploitation test

A third case in which exploitative abuses would not amount to a prohibition of dominance as such is when the exploitation is made possible by exclusionary conduct. The leading case on post-exclusionary exploitation is *United Brands*. The Court of Justice considered United Brands' distribution strategy to be exclusionary and market-partitioning.[96] On the facts of the particular case at hand,[97] the Court held that a dominant undertaking infringes Article 102 if it makes use of its dominant position in order to obtain commercial benefits which it would not have obtained in conditions of effective competition.[98] This test requires a causal link between dominance and abuse. Dominance was defined as the ability to prevent effective competition.[99] The cause of the exploitative abuse could only be the actual exercise of the dominant undertaking's ability to exclude rivals. Therefore, exploitation in *United Brands* was made possible by exclusion.

An illustration of this approach is the UK case of *Napp*. Napp, the dominant supplier of a slow release morphine product called MST, had engaged in predation

---

[94] *German Electricity Wholesale Market* [2009] C36/8 (*E.ON*) recitals 35–38. In the case of collective dominance an enhanced dominance threshold would be very difficult to define and apply.

[95] Case C-41/90 *Höfner and Elser*.

[96] Case 27/76 *United Brands*, paras 159, 182–203, and 233.

[97] ibid para 250: '*In this case* charging a price which is excessive because it has no reasonable relation to the economic value of the product supplied would be such an abuse' (emphasis added).

[98] ibid para 249.

[99] The Court defined dominance as a position of 'economic strength', which gives an undertaking the ability 'to prevent effective competition being maintained on the relevant market by giving it the power to behave to an appreciable extent independently of its competitors, customers and ultimately of its consumers': ibid para 65.

in the hospital segment of the market, which was open to competition. This had allowed Napp to charge excessive prices in the community segment of the market, where there were high barriers to entry and switching costs.[100] The Competition Commission Appeal Tribunal (CCAT) endorsed the OFT's view and categorized Napp's ability to charge excessive prices in the community sector as a form of 'recoupment'.[101] At the CCAT, the OFT argued that the excessive pricing abuse was not free-standing, but depended upon Napp's exclusionary conduct in the hospital segment, which enabled Napp to charge excessive prices in the community segment.[102] However, the CCAT did not construe this argument as meaning that excessive pricing could only be abusive if it was made possible by the dominant undertaking's exclusionary behaviour. The CCAT considered that such a contention would have been wrong in law.[103] In the light of the analysis in this chapter, it may be doubted whether the CCAT was correct. While Napp was super-dominant, with market shares in excess of 90 per cent,[104] the reason why successful entry was more difficult was that Napp engaged in predatory behaviour.[105] In the absence of predation, entry would not have been impossible or very unlikely even in the long term. Therefore the OFT was right to characterize the excessive pricing abuse as dependent on the exclusionary abuse.

It is questionable whether this doctrine should be extended further to exploitative prices made possible by anti-competitive behaviour that is not an infringement of Article 102. In *Rambus*, the Commission accepted commitments in a case in which Rambus was accused of charging excessive royalties for the use of patented technology relating to dynamic random access memory (DRAM).[106] Rambus was alleged to be dominant on the worldwide market for DRAM interface technology, comprising the technology needed for the interoperability between a DRAM chip and the other components of a PC.[107] These royalties could not have been claimed if Rambus had not intentionally deceived a standard-setting organization and its members by not disclosing the existence of patents and patent applications relating to technology relevant to the adopted standard.[108] This 'patent ambush' was

---

[100] *Napp*, paras 142–143. In fact, at the time of the decision, a commentator rightly noted that 'it may seem somewhat unusual for a decision that appears in essence to be about discriminatory pricing to refer so centrally to excessive and predatory pricing': M Furse, 'Caught Napping: DGFT and Napp Pharmaceutical Holdings Ltd' (2001) 22 ECLR 477, 479. As the same commentator acknowledged, this approach was consistent with the OFT, *Guideline on Assessment of Individual Agreements and Conduct* (OFT414, 1999) then in force (Furse, 'Caught Napping', 479, also for the quotation from the guideline in question). This approach would also be consistent with the OFT, *Assessment of Conduct: Draft Competition Law Guideline for Consultation* (OFT414a, 2004) paras 3.4–3.5. In other words, by a conscious policy choice, the OFT regards price discrimination as abusive on a case-by-case basis, focusing on whether it is exclusionary or exploitative or, it should be added, it has both effects, as in *Napp*. This approach is not easy to reconcile with certain precedents of the EU courts: M Furse, 'Monopoly Price Discrimination, Article 82 and the Competition Act' (2001) 22 ECLR, 149, 154–155.
[101] *Napp v DGFT*, paras 261 and 299.   [102] ibid paras 364–365.   [103] ibid para 434.
[104] *Napp*, paras 96–100.   [105] ibid paras 168–180.   [106] *Rambus* [2010] OJ L30/14.
[107] ibid recitals 16, 17, and 26.
[108] ibid recital 27. There is now a significant literature on the intersection between competition law and standard setting. Also for further references, see I Rahnasto, *Intellectual Property Rights, External Effects and Antitrust Law* (Oxford, OUP 2005); J H Park, *Patents and Industry Standards* (Cheltenham,

arguably the cause of Rambus's dominant position. Had another standard been adopted, which would have probably been the case if Rambus had disclosed the existence of the patents and patent applications in question, Rambus's technologies would have been irrelevant to the standard.[109] The exploitative abuse in *Rambus* depended upon exclusionary conduct by a non-dominant undertaking: Rambus became dominant and, thus, capable of charging excessive royalties because of the exclusion. The exclusionary element of the abuse, however, would not be prohibited under Article 102.[110] In theory, it would be possible to devise a test that defined non-abusive exclusionary conduct that, in conjunction with a limitation of production, markets, or technical development to the prejudice of consumers under Article 102(b), could amount to an exploitative abuse that would not simply punish dominance as such. However, this approach would effectively sanction the acquisition of dominance by a non-dominant undertaking by means that are not prohibited by the EU competition rules. The unilateral acquisition of a dominant position is not an infringement of the competition rules, no matter how objectionable the conduct in question might be under other legal rules or non-legal norms. And a dominant position is not prohibited as such. The combination of these two principles rules out the proposition that the mere charging of excessive prices by an undertaking that became dominant by means other than competition on the merits can be an infringement of Article 102. In *Rambus*, there was in fact an alternative basis for a finding of abuse: Rambus held a super-dominant position and entry was impossible or highly unlikely even in the long-term, given that the industry was locked into the standard.[111] This would have justified a prohibition of excessive prices on the basis of the enhanced dominance threshold condition.

D. Consumer harm as the default test for exclusionary abuses

The intent test, the as efficient competitor test, and the consumer harm test in vertical foreclosure apply to a wide range of business practices. Novel forms of potential abuses must be assessed under one of these tests depending on the closest

---

Edward Elgar Publishing 2010); M Valimaki, 'A flexible Approach to RAND Licensing' (2008) 29 ECLR 686; DG Swanson and WJ Baumol, 'Reasonable and Non-Discriminatory (RAND) Royalties, Standards Selection, and Control of Market Power' (2005) 73 Antitrust LJ 1; JG Sidak, 'Patent Hold-up and Oligopsonistic Collusion in Standard-Setting Organizations' (2009) 5 J Comp L & Econ 123; G Ohana, M Hanse, and O Shah, 'Disclosure and Negotiation of Licensing Terms Prior to Adoption of Industry Standards: Preventing Another Patent Ambush?' (2003) 24 ECLR 644; MC Naughton and R Wolfram, 'The Antitrust Risks of Unilateral Conduct in Standard Setting, in the Light of the FTC's case against Rambus Inc' (2004) 49 Antitrust Bull 69; M Lemley, 'Intellectual Property Rights and Standard-setting Organizations' (2002) 90 California L Rev 1889; A Layne-Farrar, AJ Padilla, and R Schmalensee, 'Pricing Patents for Licensing in Standard-Setting Organizations: Making Sense of Frand Commitments' (2007) 74 Antitrust LJ 707; J Farrell et al, 'Standard Setting, Patents, and Hold-Up' (2007) 74 Antitrust LJ 603.

[109] *Rambus*, recitals 43–46.

[110] The Commission placed significant emphasis on Rambus's intentionally deceitful behaviour by which it acquired a super-dominant position on the market: ibid recitals 27–29 and 40–43.

[111] ibid recitals 19–25 and 47.

analogy. Thus, conduct that has the sole or overwhelmingly predominant purpose of harming competition, has no conceivable benefits whether in the form of efficiencies or otherwise, and is capable of causing competitive harm, clearly fails the naked abuse test whether or not the particular type of conduct under review has been found abusive in the past. Pricing abuses are examined either under the as efficient competitor test if they are sustainable in the long term and do not entail forgoing revenues or under the as efficient competitor test in conjunction with the intent test if they are not sustainable in the long term and entail a profit sacrifice. Vertical foreclosure is examined under the consumer harm test if there is no pricing element or under the consumer harm test in conjunction with the as efficient competitor test if there is a pricing element. Multi-market abuses are assessed under the intent test or, if there is a pricing element, under the as efficient competitor test. However, the question arises as to whether there is a default test applying to exclusionary practices[112] that are incapable of being subsumed under one of the tests in question either directly or by analogy. The Article 102 tests are ways of identifying conduct that is likely to run counter to the purpose of Article 102, which is to maximize long-term social welfare. Therefore, the logical answer would be that the default test is a reduction of social welfare in the long term. However, such a test would be very difficult to administer, in particular because the prediction of long-term developments are ill-suited to be proved to the standard that the legal process requires. An alternative would be to rely on the consumer harm test. As explained in Chapter 2, consumer harm as a test is consistent with the protection of social welfare and could even perform better that a social welfare standard in achieving a social welfare objective.[113] Furthermore, a consumer harm element is implied in all the Article 102 tests. This is obvious for the consumer harm test but also applies to the intent tests and the as efficient competitor test.

The naked abuse test implies an element of consumer harm in the form of the maintenance or strengthening of the dominant position. This element is inherent in the capability of the conduct to exclude rivals without any other conceivable explanation. If a dominant undertaking implements conduct of this kind, the inevitable consequence is that the dominant position will be maintained or strengthened, whereas if rivals had not been excluded they would have exercised some constraint on the dominant undertaking's market power. The other intent tests require proof of specific intent in relation either to the exclusion of competitors by conduct that does not fall within the scope of competition on the merits[114] or in relation to the maintenance, strengthening, or acquisition of market power.[115] The as efficient competitor test implies consumer harm in the form of the

---

[112] The problem relates to exclusionary practices. Exploitation can only conceivably be assessed under the consumer harm test. Discrimination can only be assessed either under the naked abuse test if it is based on nationality, residence, or the extent to which firms engage in intra-EU trade, or under Art 102(c) if it is market-distorting discrimination. There is no conceivable type of purely discriminatory conduct running counter to the purpose of Article 102 other than market-partitioning or market-distorting discrimination.

[113] See 45–49 above.   [114] This is the case of the intent test in predation: see 201–210 above.

[115] See the discussion on tying at 215–217 above.

strengthening or maintenance of the dominant position. The presence on a domi-nated market of a competitor who is at least as efficient as the dominant under-taking or capable of becoming as efficient as the dominant undertaking within a reasonable time frame is likely to result in larger output and lower prices. Consumer harm can be seen as the common denominator of all the Article 102 tests, although the intent tests and the as efficient competitor test dispense with proof of consumer harm. This does not mean that consumer harm is irrelevant. It only means that the law considers separate proof of consumer harm unnecessary.[116]

An example where the case law resorted to consumer harm as a default test is the assessment of conduct that alters the market structure by the acquisition of undertakings or assets. Such a conduct is prima facie abusive if it strengthens the dominant position. The Court of Justice applied this test to the acquisition by the dominant undertaking of one of its competitors.[117] The strengthening of a dominant position by the acquisition of exclusive rights may also constitute an abuse.[118] This type of conduct and, in particular, the acquisition of sole or joint control over previously independent undertakings now constitutes a merger under the EU Merger Regulation, provided the acquisition has an EU-dimension.[119] The consumer harm test under Article 102 is consistent with the test under the EU Merger Regulation.[120]

E. Conclusion

Consumer harm is not the only abuse test under Article 102. The intent tests and the as efficient competitor test apply without the requirement also to demon-strate consumer harm. However, allocative inefficiency in the form of the main-tenance, strengthening, or acquisition of market power in an affected market is implied in all abuse tests even if the law dispenses with proof of a negative effect on allocative efficiency. The Guidance on Article 102 does not state the law when it appears to require proof of consumer harm for the investigation of all exclu-sionary abuses.

Proof of consumer harm is required in all vertical foreclosure cases and not only, as the case law appears to suggest, when the refusal to supply relates to IP rights. This is the case even if a particularly severe foreclosure effect must also be proved.

---

[116] On allocative efficiency as objective justification, see 309–310 below.

[117] Case 6/72 *Continental Can.*

[118] Case T-51/89 *Tetra Pak Rausing SA v Commission* [1990] ECR II-309 (*Tetra Pak I*), upholding *Tetra Pak I (BTG-licence)* [1988] OJ L272/27.

[119] Council Regulation (EC) 139/2004 of 20 January 2004 on the control of concentrations between undertakings [2004] OJ L24/1 ('2004 Merger Regulation'), replacing Council Regulation (EEC) 4064/89 of 21 December 1989 on the control of concentrations between undertakings [1989] OJ L395/1 ('1989 Merger Regulation').

[120] Art 2(2) and (3) of the 2004 Merger Regulation, replacing the 1983 Merger Regulation, as interpreted by the Commission in the Guidelines on the assessment of horizontal mergers under the Council Regulation on the control of concentrations between undertakings [2004] OJ C31/5 ('Guidelines on Horizontal Mergers') and in the Guidelines on Non-horizontal Mergers.

The reason is that to impose on a dominant undertaking an active duty to assist its competitors may have a significant negative effect on market-wide investment incentives. Because under the long-term social welfare objective of Article 102 dynamic efficiency is particularly important, an enhanced intervention threshold is needed. Consumer harm plays the role of safeguarding against the risk of false convictions and over-deterrence in this area. When a refusal to supply relates to IP rights, consumer harm must be in the form of the prevention of the emergence of new or differentiated products or reduced innovation. This is because of the need to protect the very subject-matter of the IP right, which is the power to prevent anybody from reproducing the invention, mark, creative work, or information without the consent of the holder of the IP right. Therefore, a mere decrease in output or higher prices are not sufficient proof of consumer harm if the undertakings requesting a licence would limit themselves to reproducing the products of the dominant undertaking. The Guidance on Article 102 states the law correctly when it adopts a unified approach to all refusals to supply. However, in failing to draw a distinction between IP rights and other inputs, the Guidance does not recognize the need to protect the subject-matter of IP rights. Even as a prioritization exercise, this is problematic because it could draw unwarranted attention to refusals to license that pose no risk to competition.

Margin squeeze is a form of vertical foreclosure. A duty to supply the upstream input is a necessary element of the abuse. The Court of Justice's misunderstanding of the test in *TeliaSonera* weakens significantly the persuasiveness of the case and should be reviewed by the Court at the earliest opportunity.

Exploitative abuses are examined under a test of actual consumer harm. However, because dominance is not prohibited in itself, a finding of abuse requires more that a mere finding that a dominant undertaking is charging its profit-maximizing price. Three alternative tests apply as limiting principles in this area: (a) an enhanced dominance test under which exploitative abuses can only be committed by monopolies or quasi-monopolies or the holders of special or exclusive rights within the meaning of Article 106 and if entry on a sufficient scale to counteract the abuse is unlikely in the long term; (b) an enhanced consumer harm test under which an exploitative abuse can also be prohibited when the conduct causes consumer harm distinct from, and additional to, the mere charging of prices or application of trading terms persistently and significantly higher or more onerous than the prices or terms that would prevail under conditions of effective competition; and (c) a post-exclusionary exploitation test under which exploitative conduct can also be prohibited when it is the result of anti-competitive exclusion.

The intent tests, the as efficient competitor test, and the consumer harm test in vertical foreclosure and exploitative practices cover a wide range of conduct. Most anti-competitive practices will be subsumed under one of the tests examined in Chapters 6 to 8 either directly or by analogy. However, for novel business practices that are incapable of being subsumed under one of the established tests by analogy, consumer harm applies as a default test. This is consistent with the long-term social welfare objective of Article 102, which can be achieved by the application of a consumer harm test. Furthermore, the intent tests and the as efficient competitor test imply a consumer harm element at least in the form of the maintenance, strengthening, or acquisition of market power on an affected market, although they dispense with proof of consumer harm. Finally, a consumer harm test is sufficient to guard against the risk of false convictions and over-deterrence. Consumer harm is a demanding test. As the case law on refusal to supply shows, when proof of consumer harm is required it is not sufficient to infer harm from the exclusion of a competitor; otherwise, the test would be meaningless. It is necessary to produce evidence proving to the required legal standard that prices will be higher, output lower, and innovation reduced as a result of the alleged infringement not based on an abstract theory but in the specific circumstances of the market or markets under review. This is not a light burden for a competition authority or claimant to discharge.

9

Defences

A. Introduction

The intent tests, the as efficient competitor test, and the consumer harm test apply to establish a prima facie case of abuse. Prima facie abusive conduct is prohibited unless the dominant undertaking raises a defence that is capable of displacing the presumption of abuse. The nature and scope of the defences available under Article 102 are, however, unclear. To bring some clarity to a confused area of the law, it is necessary first of all to distinguish mere defences or rebuttals of a prima facie case from objective justification. Mere rebuttals are defences that do not plead a new primary fact but simply challenge the inference of infringement drawn under the prima facie test either by adducing new evidence or by disputing the weight or probative force of the evidence relied on by the competition authority or claimant. Objective justification is a defence that pleads a new primary fact from which consequences are drawn that are incompatible with a finding of abuse and compatible with the purpose of Article 102 of maximizing long-term social welfare.

Mere defences are potentially infinite and depend on how the dominant undertaking decides to attack the presumption of abuse that arises on the evidence adduced by the competition authority or the claimant. Their study belongs to the realm of forensic science and advocacy not to the analysis of the substantive law. However, the case law has developed a mere defence that deserves special attention: a dominant undertaking is entitled to take reasonable and proportionate steps to protect its commercial interests when they are under threat but not if the purpose of the conduct is to strengthen the dominant position and abuse it.[1] This defence requires the application of a test of proportionality to determine whether the conduct under review is prima facie abusive in the first place. Therefore, it can

---

[1] Case 27/76 *United Brands Co and United Brands Continentaal BV v Commission* [1978] ECR 207, para 189; Case T-203/01 *Manufacture Française des Pneumatiques Michelin v Commisson* [2003] ECR II-4071 (*Michelin II*), para 55; Case T-65/89 *BPB Industries plc and British Gypsum Ltd v Commission* [1993] ECR II-389 (*British Gypsum*), para 69, upheld in Case C-310/93 P *BPB Industries plc and British Gypsum Ltd v Commission* [1995] ECR I-865 (*British Gypsum*); Case T-301/04 *Clearstream Banking AG and Clearstream International SA v Commission* [2009] ECR II-3155, para 132; Case T-321/05 *AstraZeneca AB v Commission* [2010] OJ C221/33, para 672, under appeal in Case C-457/10 P *AstraZeneca AB v Commission* [2010] OJ C301/18.

be described as a proportionality defence. The meeting competition defence is a proportionality defence.[2]

Objective justification introduces a new primary fact[3] which is capable of displacing the presumption that the prima facie abusive conduct is harmful to long-term social welfare. Two types of benefits may be pleaded under objective justification: benefits that fall under allocative, productive, or dynamic efficiency and benefits such as environmental or social improvements that, while capable of increasing the long-term welfare of society, do not fall within the categories of economic efficiencies. It is thus possible to distinguish a narrower efficiency defence and a broader social welfare defence. This distinction, however, is made purely on the basis of the type of benefit pursued. The legal test of objective justification is in all material respects the same.

In the light of the conclusions of this chapter on the allocation of the burden of proof, whether the defence is a mere rebuttal or pleads a new primary fact, the competition authority or claimant always bears the legal burden of proof. The dominant undertaking only bears the burden of adducing sufficient evidence to substantiate its defence so that the competition authority or claimant acquires the burden of disproving it. However, the proportionality defence test is different from the objective justification test. Mere defences do not require a balancing of the negative and beneficial effects of the conduct under review. The proportionality test only asks whether the conduct pursues a legitimate commercial interest, is suitable to the pursuit of the commercial interest in question, and does not go beyond what is necessary to achieve its objective. The reason is that a mere defence is incompatible with the very possibility of establishing a prima facie case. Since no prima facie case can be established in the first place, there is no negative effect that can be balanced against the benefits of the conduct. On the other hand, the pleading of the pursuit of a social welfare objective, whether in the form of efficiencies or otherwise, is an objective justification. Because a prima facie case has been established and, therefore, anti-competitive effects have been proven, the proportionality test under objective justification requires a balancing of positive and negative effects by asking whether the competitive harm is disproportionate to the benefits achieved.

This chapter starts by examining the burden of proof and the standard of anti-competitive effects. The burden of proof and the standard of anti-competitive effects determine the boundaries between what must be proved by a competition authority or claimant to establish a prima facie case and the point at which defences

---

[2] This chapter will discuss in detail the meeting competition defence as it raises issues of fundamental principle under Art 102. Proportionality defences are, however, not a closed category. For an interesting analysis of when a dominant undertaking may be entitled to incur start-up losses, which may be described as a 'start-up losses' defence, see *Wanadoo España v Telefónica* [2008] OJ C83/6 (*Telefónica*), recitals 323–382 and 526–540, under appeal in Case T-336/07 *Telefónica and Telefónica de España v Commission* [2007] OJ C269/55.

[3] This is the case even for allocative efficiency pleaded as an objective justification when the prima facie case is established under a consumer harm test. A consumer harm test proves consumer harm as a result of the maintenance, strengthening, or acquisition of market power to the detriment of consumers. Allocative efficiency as an objective justification pleads the output expanding effect of the conduct under review that results from facts other than market power.

become relevant. Next, proportionality defences are discussed, with a focus on the meeting competition defence. The chapter goes on to examine the proportionality framework of the objective justification defence, distinguishing between the efficiency defence and the social welfare defence. Finally, conclusions are drawn.

B. Burden of proof and evidential burden

The rules on the burden of proof (or legal burden) determine which party bears the risk of the lack of proof of a material fact at the end the proceedings. The allocation of the legal burden may determine the outcome of the case and often does so in complex cases where it is impossible to ascertain all material facts. A key guiding principle in the allocation of the burden of proof from a policy perspective is the preference for false convictions or false acquittals. An analysis of the substantive scope of Article 102 would, therefore, be incomplete without an examination of the rules on the burden of proof.[4]

All legal systems of the EU Member States contain rules on the burden of proof providing who must prove what in legal proceedings in order to secure a certain outcome.[5] The legal burden of proof may be defined as the burden of persuading the tribunal of fact, to the required standard and on the whole of the evidence, of the truth of the facts in issue.[6] If the party bearing the legal burden fails to persuade the tribunal of fact of the truth of any of the facts in issue, it will fail to secure a favourable outcome in relation to the whole or part of the proceedings.[7] Common law systems distinguish between this legal burden and the evidential burden. The

---

[4] The same reasoning applies, with less force, to the standard of proof. However, the better view is that the rules on the standard of proof are governed by national law provided that the principles of equivalence and effectiveness are observed: see Opinion of AG Kokott in Case C-8/08 *T-Mobile Netherlands BV v Raad van bestuur van de Nederlandse Mededingingsautoriteit* [2009] ECR I-4529, paras 81–93 and Regulation 1/2003, recital 5. The rules on the standard of proof are, therefore, not regarded by Union law as falling within the scope of the substantive prohibition in Art 102. On the other hand, the Court in *T-Mobile*, contrary to the Opinion of the AG, ruled that presumptions are part of the substantive scope of the prohibition of Art 101(1): see paras 50–53. The same conclusion must apply to Art 102.

[5] For a comparative analysis of the rules relating to the burden of proof, see M Kazazi, *Burden of Proof and Related Issues: A Study on Evidence before International Tribunals* (The Hague, Kluwer Law International 1996) and J Kokott, *The Burden of Proof in Comparative and International Human Rights Law: Civil and Common Law Approaches with Special Reference to the American and German Legal Systems* (The Hague, Kluwer Law International 1998).

[6] See D 22.3.2, Paul 69 *ad ed*: *ei incumbit probatio qui dicit, non qui negat*. In modern times, the rule was codified in art 1315 of the Napoleonic Code, which provided for the allocation of the burden of proof of civil obligations. Many continental law systems contain a codified rule in their civil codes: see, in Italy, art 2697 cc (codice civile: civil code); in Spain, art 1214 CC (Code civil: Civil code) and art 217 of the Ley de Enjuiciamiento Civil (LEC); in France, art 9 NCPC (nouveau Code de procédure civil: new Code of civil procedure).

[7] R Genin-Meric, 'Droit de la preuve: l'example français' in JM Lebre de Freitas (ed), *The Law of Evidence in the European Union* (The Hague, Kluwer Law International 2004) 137, 159–160; W Brehm, 'Beweisrecht in Deutschland' in Lebre de Freitas (ed), *The Law of Evidence in the European Union*, 179, 180 183; M Serra Dominguez, 'La preuve dans le procès civil espagnol' in Lebre de Freitas (ed), *The Law of Evidence in the European Union*, 381, 381–382; LP Comoglio, *Le prove civili* (Torino: UTET, 2004) 169–205.

evidential burden of the claimant is also known as the establishment of a prima facie case, that is, in the words of a distinguished English judge, 'such evidence as, if believed and left uncontradicted and unexplained, could be accepted' by the tribunal of fact as proof.[8] At common law, in the course of the proceedings, the evidential burden may be acquired by the defendant and shift back to the claimant.[9] The legal burden never shifts but can be allocated between the parties.[10]

In competition cases, the EU courts consistently adopt a framework for the evaluation of evidence that relies on the establishment of a prima facie case and on the distinction between the legal burden and the evidential.[11] However, they do not generally set out the distinction between the legal burden and the evidential burden in a conceptually clear fashion.[12] One notable exception is the Opinion of Advocate General Kokott in the *FEG* case. In that case, the Commission found

---

[8] *Doon Jayasena (Rajapakse Pathurange) v R* [1970] AC 618, 624, *per* Lord Devlin.

[9] The classic analysis is in JB Thayer, *A Preliminary Treatise on Evidence at the Common Law* (London, Sweet & Maxwell 1898) 376–379.

[10] It may be worth making it clear that the shifting of the evidential burden is not an infringement of Art 48(1) of the Charter of Fundamental Rights of the European Union [2010] OJ C83/389 and Art 6(2) ECHR. These safeguards apply in competition proceedings, given their criminal nature for the purpose of the fair trial rights: Case C-235/92 P *Montecatini SpA v Commission* [1999] ECR I-4539, paras 175–176. However, this does not rule out the application of presumptions: ibid para 181 and Joined Cases C-204/00 P, C-205/00 P, C-211/00 P, C-213/00 P, C-217/00 P, and C-219/00 P *Aalborg Portland A/S v Commission* [2004] ECR I-123, paras 79–82 and 132. This is consistent with the jurisprudence of the European Court of Human Rights: *Salabiaku v France* (1991) 13 EHRR 379, para 28; *Hoang v France* (1993) 16 EHRR 53, para 33; *Murray v United Kingdom* (1996) 22 EHRR 29, para 47. Furthermore, the shifting on an evidential burden only, as opposed to placing the legal burden on the defendant, is generally incapable of infringing Art 6(2) ECHR in the first place: *R v DPP, ex p Kebilene* [2000] 2 AC 326; *R v Lambert (Steven)* [2002] 2 AC 545; *R v Johnstone (Robert Alexander)* [2003] UKHL 28, [2003] 1 WLR 1736; *A-G's Reference (No 1 of 2004)* [2004] EWCA Crim 1025, [2004] 1 WLR 2111; *Sheldrake v DPP* [2004] UKHL 43, [2005] 1 AC 264. On this issue, see R Nazzini, 'The Wood Began to Move: An Essay on Consumer Welfare, Evidence and Burden of Proof in Article 82 Cases' (2006) 31 EL Rev 518, 536–538.

[11] This is well established in the case law under Art 101(1): Case 395/87 *Ministère Public v Jean-Louis Tournier* [1989] 2521 (*Tournier*) paras 35–46; Case 48/69 *Imperial Chemical Industries Ltd v Commission* [1972] 619, para 66; Joined Cases C-89/85 P, C-104/85 P, C-114/85 P, C-116/85 P, C-117/85 P, and C-125/85 P to C-129/85 P *A Ahlström Osakeyhtiö v Commission* [1993] I-1307, paras 70–127; Case T-7/89 *SA Hercules Chemicals NV v Commission* [1991] ECR II-1711, para 260; Joined Cases C-189/02 P, C-202/02 P, C-205/02 P to C-208/02 P, and C-213/02 P *Dansk Rørindustri A/S v Commission* [2005] ECR I-5425, paras 132–152; Joined Cases C-204/00 P, C-205/00 P, C-211/00 P, C-213/00 P, C-217/00 P and C-219/00 P *Aalborg Portland*, paras 81 and 82; Case C-199/92 P *Hüls AG v Commission* [1999] ECR I-4287, para 155; and Case C-49/92 P *Commission v Anic Partecipazioni SpA* [1999] ECR I-4125, para 96. Under Art 102, the reliance on tests that are in fact typified presumptions is particularly clear in the case law on predation: Case 62/86 *AKZO Chemie BV v Commission* [1991] ECR I-3359; Case T-83/91 *Tetra Pak International SA v Commission* [1994] ECR II-755 (*Tetra Pak II*) para 148, upheld in C-333/94 P *Tetra Pak International SA v Commission* [1996] ECR I-5951 (*Tetra Pak II*); Opinion of AG Fennelly in Joined Cases C-395/96 P and C-396/96 P *Compagnie Maritime Belge Transports SA v Commission* [2000] ECR I-1365, para 127; Case C-202/07 P *France Télécom SA v Commission* [2009] ECR I-2369, para 109. However, all abuse tests are presumptions of abuse: see eg Case C-163/99 *Portuguese Republic v Commission* [2001] ECR I-2613, para 52 on rebates and Case 78/70 *Deutsche Grammophon Gesellschaft mbH v Metro-SB-Großmärkte GmbH & Co* [1971] ECR 487; Case 40/70 *Sirena Srl v Eda Srl* [1971] ECR 69, para 17; and Case 395/87 *Tournier*, paras 35–46 on exploitative abuses.

[12] The relevance of this distinction between legal and evidential burden in EU law is, however, recognized in the literature: M Brealey, 'The Burden of Proof before the European Court' (1985) 10 EL Rev 250, 255–262 and Nazzini, 'The Wood Began to Move: An Essay on Consumer Welfare, Evidence and Burden of Proof in Article 82 Cases'. For an early essay on how the common law rules of evidence compare with the (then) EEC law on cartels, see JM Joshua, 'Proof in Contested

that a Dutch association of wholesalers of electro-technical fittings had infringed Article 101 TFEU by engaging in a concerted practice relating to prices and discounts. It also found that the result of the concerted practice had been higher prices in the Netherlands market than in other Member States. The parties challenged the decision. The Court of First Instance upheld the Commission on this point, stating that the Commission had observed, without being directly contradicted by the parties, that the prices in the Netherlands were higher than those charged in the other Member States. The Court went on to say that 'the FEG, whilst challenging the assertion that prices are higher in the Netherlands than in neighbouring countries, offered no sound evidence to overturn the latter assertion'.[13] The FEG appealed the point to the Court of Justice, arguing that the Court of First Instance had reversed the burden of proof. The Advocate General in her Opinion laid down a clear distinction between the legal and the evidential burden. She said that the parties have a burden of adducing evidence in support of their respective assertions 'before there is any need to allocate the burden of proof at all'.[14] If the Commission draws conclusions as to the prevailing market conditions based on 'objectively verifiable evidence from stated sources, the undertakings concerned cannot refute the Commission's findings' simply by disputing them. It falls on the undertakings concerned to adduce arguments and evidence that show 'why the information used by the Commission is inaccurate, why it has no probative value, or why the conclusions drawn by the Commission are unsound'.[15] This is not a reversal of the burden of proof but 'the normal operation of the respective burdens of adducing evidence'.[16] Because the FEG had not discharged its burden of adducing evidence, the Advocate General considered that the Court of First Instance 'was able' to uphold the Commission's finding on this point.[17] The Opinion in the *FEG* case, while not using the phrase 'evidential burden', recognizes that the distinction between the legal and the evidential burden, which can be distilled from the common legal traditions of the Member States,[18] is part of the EU law of evidence.[19]

EEC Competition Cases: A Comparison with the Rules of Evidence in Common Law' (1987) 12 EL Rev 315.

[13] Joined Cases T-5/00 and T-6/00 *Nederlandse Federative Vereniging voor de Groothandel op Elektrotechnisch Gebied v Commission* [2003] ECR II-5761, para 337.

[14] Opinion of AG Kokott in Case C-105/04 P *Nederlandse Federative Vereniging voor de Groothandel op Elektrotechnisch Gebied v Commission* [2006] ECR I-8725, para 73

[15] ibid para 74.   [16] ibid.   [17] ibid para 76.

[18] The phenomenon of the shifting of the burden of adducing evidence known as evidential burden is well established in civil law legal systems: see R Genin-Meric, 'Droit de la preuve: l'example français', 147–148; LP Comoglio, *Le prove civili*, 228–231, on Italy; and W Brehm, 'Beweisrecht in Deutschland', 179 and 185. The distinction between legal burden and evidential burden normally applies in the UK in competition cases: see *The Racecourse Association v Office of Fair Trading* [2005] CAT 29, paras 130–134 (a case concerning the prohibition of anti-competitive agreements in the Competition Act 1998, s 2) and *Attheraces Ltd v British Horseracing Board Ltd* [2005] EWHC 3015, [2006] ECC 24, paras 126–127, *per* Etherton J (a case concerning Art 102 and the equivalent UK law prohibition in the Competition Act 1998, s 18) reversed on other grounds in *Attheraces Ltd v British Horseracing Board Ltd* [2007] EWCA Civ 38, [2007] ECC 7.

[19] AG Kokott refers to the terminology of legal and evidential burden in fn 60 of her Opinion in Case C-8/08 *T-Mobile Netherlands BV v Raad van bestuur van de Nederlandse Mededingingsautoriteit*

Under Article 102, the dominant undertaking only bears an evidential burden
in relation to mere defences and objective justification. Article 2 of Regulation
(EC) 1/2003 provides that the burden of proving an infringement of Article 101(1)
or of Article 102 TFEU shall rest on the party or the authority alleging the infringement. The only exception is that the undertaking or association of undertakings
claiming the benefit of Article 101(3) shall bear the burden of proving that the
conditions of that paragraph are fulfilled. Under Article 102, the burden always
rests on the competition authority or party alleging the infringement. The difference between the allocation of the burden of proof under Articles 101 and 102
follows from the very structure of Article 101, which is framed as a prohibition
and an exception. The burden of proving that a prohibition does not apply because
the conduct under review falls within an exception can be placed on the party
invoking the exception.[20] The exception may be implied, as in the *Cassis de Dijon*
mandatory requirements,[21] but it is nevertheless necessary that the structure of
the norm be construed as a prohibition and an exception. The defences to a prima
facie case of abuse under Article 102 are not exceptions to the general principle that
abuse is prohibited. The pursuit of the legitimate objectives relevant under the proportionality defence or the objective justification defence is fundamentally incompatible with a finding of abuse. It is the manifestation of an effective competitive
process. In *Oscar Bronner*, the Court of Justice held that the absence of objective
justification was a necessary condition in determining whether refusal to supply
was an infringement of Article 102.[22] The Court of Justice used the same language
in the *IMS* case.[23] If the behaviour is objectively justified it is not abusive in the
first place.[24] No implied legal burden on the dominant undertaking is, therefore,
conceivable.

The EU courts, while often lacking technical precision in the use of language,
have never said that the dominant undertaking bears a burden of proof and have
always used terminology consistent with the dominant undertaking bearing an
evidential burden only. A few examples will suffice. In *Deutsche Grammophon*,
the Court of Justice held that the difference between the price charged in one

---

[2009] ECR I-4529, although the distinction between the two types of burden was not determinative in that case.

[20] See, by analogy, Case C-17/93 *Criminal Proceedings Against JJJ Van der Veldt* [1994] ECR
I-3537; Case 227/82 *Criminal Proceedings Against Leendert van Bennekom* [1983] ECR 3883, para 40;
and Case C-358/95 *Tommaso Morellato v Unità Sanitaria Locale (USL) n 11 di Pordenone* [1997] ECR
I-1431, para 14, placing on the Member State the burden of proving the defences under Art 36 TFEU
to measures amounting to prohibited restrictions of trade under Arts 34 and 35 TFEU.

[21] Case C-14/02 *ATRAL SA v Belgian State* [2003] ECR I-4431, para 68, placing the burden of
proof on the Member State in relation to the *Cassis de Dijon* 'overriding requirements' because they
are 'exceptions to the free movement of goods' recognized by the case law.

[22] Case C-7/97 *Oscar Bronner GmbH & Co KG v Mediaprint Zeitungs- und Zeitschriftenverlag
GmbH & Co KG* [1998] ECR I-7791, paras 40–41.

[23] Case C-418/01 *IMS Health GmbH & Co OHG v NDC Health GmbH & Co KG* [2004] ECR
I-5039, paras 51–52.

[24] See also the Opinion of AG Kokott in Case C-95/04 P *British Airways plc v Commission* [2007]
ECR I-2331, para 43, where she takes the view that objective justification is a necessary step 'to distinguish abusive from lawful conduct and thus ensure that legitimate price competition does not fall
foul of Article [102 TFEU]'.

Member State by the holder of exclusive distribution rights in sound recordings and the price for the same product re-imported from another Member State may be a 'determining factor' in the assessment of whether the undertaking abused its dominant position 'if unjustified by any objective criteria and if it is particularly marked'.[25] In *Tournier*, the Court held that a comparison of the prices charged by a dominant undertaking with prices in other markets may be 'indicative of an abuse of a dominant position'. It was then for the dominant undertaking 'to justify the difference by reference to objective dissimilarities between the situation in the Member State concerned and the situation prevailing in all the other Member States'.[26] In *Portuguese Republic*, the Court said that the arguments submitted by the Portuguese Republic to justify a discount system which was prima facie abusive were too general and 'insufficient to provide economic reasons to explain specifically the rates chosen for the various bands'.[27] In *Michelin II*, the Court of First Instance held that it is for the dominant undertaking to establish that a discounts system that 'presents the characteristics of a loyalty-inducing rebate system, was based on objective economic reasons'.[28] On the facts, the Court held that Michelin's line of argument was 'too general and [...] insufficient to provide economic reasons to explain specifically the discount rates chosen for the various steps in the rebate system in question'.[29] Thus, the language used in relation to objective justification requires the dominant undertaking to explain and substantiate its plea rather than to prove primary facts. This is consistent with an evidential, not with a legal, burden. Occasionally, the language is more ambiguous. In *British Airways*, the Court of Justice held that 'an undertaking is at liberty to demonstrate that its bonus system producing an exclusionary effect is economically justified'.[30] The verb 'demonstrate' is unclear. It could mean to prove, which would denote a legal burden, but it could also mean to explain and substantiate with evidence, which would denote an evidential burden. The latter meaning is more in line with the way this verb is used in the case law. In *Microsoft*, for instance, the Court of First Instance placed an evidential burden on the dominant undertaking. This is absolutely clear from paragraph 688 of the judgment:[31]

The Court notes, as a preliminary point, that although the burden of proof of the existence of the circumstances that constitute an infringement of Article [102 TFEU] is borne by the Commission, it is for the dominant undertaking concerned, and not for the Commission, before the end of the administrative procedure, to raise any plea of objective justification and to support it with arguments and evidence. It then falls to the Commission, where it proposes to make a finding of an abuse of a dominant position, to show that the arguments and evidence relied on by the undertaking cannot prevail and, accordingly, that the justification put forward cannot be accepted.

---

[25] Case 78/70 *Deutsche Grammophon*. See also Case 40/70 *Sirena*, para 17.

[26] Case 395/87 *Tournier*, paras 35–46.

[27] Case C-163/99 *Portuguese Republic*, paras 55–57; see also paras 61–79 in relation to discrimination and para 73 in relation to Art 106(2) TFEU.

[28] Case T-203/01 *Michelin II*, para 107.   [29] ibid para 109.

[30] Case C-95/04 *British Airways*, para 69.

[31] Case T-201/04 *Microsoft Corp v Commission* [2007] ECR II-3601 (*Microsoft I*), para 688.

There could not be a clearer description of the evidential burden borne by the dominant undertaking in relation to objective justification. However, having reviewed the arguments and the evidence put forward by Microsoft, the Court concluded that 'Microsoft has not demonstrated the existence of any objective justification'. The verb 'demonstrate' is used to denote the evidential burden. The Guidance on Article 102 does little to help clarify the case law. On its terms, the Guidance requires the dominant undertaking 'to provide all the evidence necessary to demonstrate that the conduct concerned is objectively justified' while placing on the Commission the duty to balance the anti-competitive and pro-competitive effects of the conduct.[32] The use of the verb 'demonstrate' gives rise to the same ambiguity as it does in the case law. However, as explained above, the case law uses this verb to denote an evidential burden. Therefore, in the light of the case law the Guidance must be understood as placing on the dominant undertaking an evidential and not a legal burden.

C. Thresholds of anti-competitive effects

As a general principle, for Article 102 to apply, it is not necessary that the anti-competitive effect has actually occurred.[33] Were it otherwise, Article 102 would be deprived of much of its effectiveness.[34] If the prey successfully withstands a predatory attack, if a patent office realizes that the representations made by a dominant undertaking in a patent application are misleading, if a competition authority or court enjoins the dominant undertaking from continuing in an abusive course of conduct before the competitors are forced to exit the market, the conduct of the dominant undertaking does not become lawful. Any other solution would be absurd because it would provide perverse incentives to dominant undertakings to exclude their competitors. If the conduct is unsuccessful, there is no enforcement risk. If the conduct is successful, enforcement action may be incapable of restoring the *status quo ante* and, while heavy fines may be imposed, these will have to be balanced against the market power rents resulting from successful exclusion. The possibility of intervention before exclusion occurs significantly alters this calculation because the risk of a fine does not arise only when exclusion is successful. The dominant undertaking may thus have to pay a fine without benefiting from exclusion.

If intervention must be possible before the allegedly abusive conduct produces the anti-competitive effect, the question of the *ex ante* degree of probability of such an effect becomes crucial. Yet, the EU courts have been particularly inconsistent and elusive in this regard. *Hoffmann-La Roche* uses the verb *können*,

---

[32] Communication from the Commission—Guidance on the Commission's enforcement priorities in applying Article 82 of the EC Treaty to abusive exclusionary conduct by dominant undertakings [2009] OJ C45/7 ('Guidance on Art 102') para 31.

[33] There are, of course, exceptions: see 275–276 above (on exploitative abuses) and 239–242 (on the dynamic application of the as efficient competitor test to rebates).

[34] Case T-201/04 *Microsoft I*, paras 561–562.

expressing capability, ability, or potential,[35] while *Michelin I* uses language suggesting that a mere 'tendency' to foreclose is sufficient.[36] In *Commercial Solvents*, the Court of Justice used 'risk' and 'likelihood' of elimination of a competitor interchangeably.[37] In *Télémarketing*, further different language is adopted, requiring the 'possibility' of the anti-competitive effect.[38] In *Oscar Bronner*, the Court of Justice referred to the likelihood of anti-competitive effects.[39] In *IMS*, both 'likelihood' and the 'capability' were used interchangeably.[40] In *TeliaSonera*, the Court described the degree of probability of the required anti-competitive effect in terms of 'risk' of exclusion,[41] conduct 'capable' of having anti-competitive effects,[42] 'anti-competitive effect which may potentially exclude competitors',[43] and likelihood of exclusion.[44] In the operative part of the judgment, the Court set out the test as asking whether the 'practice produces, at least potentially, an anti-competitive effect'.[45]

Notwithstanding the clear discrepancies in the tests applied in different cases, the first time the EU courts discussed openly the question of the required degree of probability of the anti-competitive effect was in *Microsoft I*. The Commission decision had applied a test of 'risk' of elimination of competition[46] while Microsoft contended that the test should have been one of 'likelihood' or 'high probability'.[47] The Court of First Instance dismissed this argument as purely semantic and 'wholly irrelevant'. The Court ruled that 'risk' and 'likelihood' of elimination of competition are used 'without distinction to reflect the same idea, namely that Article [102] does not apply only from the time when there is no more, or practically no more, competition on the market'.[48] In *British Airways*, the Court of First Instance held that it is sufficient 'to demonstrate that the abusive conduct of the undertaking in a dominant position tends to restrict competition, or, in other words, that the conduct is capable of having, or likely to have, such an effect'.[49] In rejecting the ground of appeal raised by British Airways, the Court of Justice stated that the Court of

---

[35] Case 85/76 *Hoffmann-La Roche & Co AG v Commission* [1979] ECR 461, para 91.

[36] Case 322/81 *NV Nederlandsche Banden Industrie Michelin v Commission* [1983] ECR 3461(*Michelin I*), para 73.

[37] Case 6/73 *Istituto Chemioterapico Italiano SpA and Commercial Solvents Corp v Commission* [1974] ECR 223 (*Commercial Solvents*), paras 25 and 33.

[38] C-311/84 *Centre Belge d'Etudes de Marché—Télémarketing (CBEM) v SA Compagnie Luxembourgeoise de Télédiffusion (CLT) and Information Publicité Benelux (IPB)* [1985] ECR 3261 (*Télémarketing*), paras 26–27.

[39] Case C-7/97 *Oscar Bronner*, paras 38 and 40.

[40] C-418/01 *IMS*, para 47, referring to the concept of 'capability'. The heading of the section, however, uses the word 'likelihood'.

[41] Case C-52/09 *Konkurrensverket v TeliaSonera Sverige AB* (17 February 2011) (*TeliaSonera*), para 43.

[42] ibid paras 63 and 72.   [43] ibid para 64.   [44] ibid para 67.

[45] ibid para 77 and operative part of the judgment.

[46] *Microsoft* [2007] OJ L32/23 (*Microsoft I*), recitals 585, 589, 610, 622, 626, 631, 636, 653, 691–692, 712, 725, 781, 992, and 1070 and Case T-201/04 *Microsoft I*, para 560. It is worth noting that the language of Case T-201/04 *Microsoft I* was English.

[47] Case T-201/04 *Microsoft I*, paras 560–564.   [48] ibid para 561.

[49] Case T-219/99 *British Airways plc v Commission* [2003] ECR II-5917, para 293, upheld in Case C-95/04 P *British Airways*.

First Instance did examine the 'probable effects' of the reward schemes[50] and that the appellant did not seriously deny that its schemes 'tended to affect the situation of competitor airlines'.[51]

This case law is problematic. It is plainly not true, and not only in English but in a number of the languages of the Union, that the phrases used by the EU courts to describe the required probability of the anti-competitive effect have the same meaning. 'Risk' of foreclosure and 'capability' of foreclosure do not have the same meaning as 'likelihood' of foreclosure. Risk has a wide meaning which may denote different degrees of probability including, at its lowest, the mere possibility of something happening. The sentences 'there is a risk of elimination of competition' and 'there is a likelihood of elimination of competition' or 'there is a probability of elimination of competition' have different implications for the degree of probability required. A 20 to 30 per cent probability may be sufficient to establish a risk of elimination of competition, albeit a low one. However, to establish a likelihood or probability of elimination of competition something more than a 50 per cent risk would be required. Without any adjectival qualification, probability or likelihood express the idea of more probable or likely than not, while risk is a mere possibility albeit not a fanciful or imaginary one. Yet another meaning would be attached to the phrase 'capable of eliminating competition'. 'Capability' is the ability or intrinsic quality of producing an effect, not the risk, likelihood, or probability of the effect. Conduct could be capable of eliminating all competition without even a risk of doing so. There is no doubt, therefore, as a matter of language and as a matter of logic, that the different formulations of the test denote different intervention thresholds. In *Microsoft I*, the Court of First Instance dealt with this difficulty by pointing out that all the formulations of the test express the same policy, namely that the Article 102 prohibition applies before the harmful event has occurred.[52] This is undoubtedly true. However, this argument only explains the prospective character of the test. It casts no light on the probability threshold that triggers the application of the prohibition. This was the question that the Court of First Instance was called upon to clarify and which it spectacularly failed to address.

It may be argued that the difference between 'capability', 'risk', and 'likelihood', while established as a matter of language, is irrelevant in practice because competition authorities and courts cannot accurately quantify the probability of foreclosure. They will simply take a view, on the facts of each case, as to whether the conduct under review may result in foreclosure so that intervention under Article 102 is justified. To argue that the law should draw fine distinctions between degrees of probability may be tenable in theory but irrelevant in practice. It may be that this belief underpins the reasoning of the Court of First Instance in *Microsoft I* and the general reluctance of the EU courts to clarify, once and for all, the degree

---

[50] Case C-95/04 P *British Airways*, paras 96–98. The Court did not comment on the significance of the different forms of words which may describe the test of anti-competitive effects under Art 102 such as 'capability', 'likelihood', or 'tendency' to foreclose. The AG had dismissed the difference between these different formulations of the test as 'purely semantic': see Opinion of AG Kokott in ibid para 76.

[51] ibid para 100.   [52] Case T-201/04 *Microsoft I*, paras 561–562.

of probability of anti-competitive effects required under Article 102. It is also perhaps what inspired the Opinion of Advocate General Kokott in *British Airways*, which dismissed the distinction between 'capability' and 'likelihood' as 'purely semantic'.[53] The Advocate General then used at least three formulations of the test interchangeably: capability to foreclose 'not only *in the abstract* but also *in the particular case*',[54] tendency to restrict competition,[55] and likelihood of foreclosure.[56] However, whether or not the EU courts recognize this, the problem is that different tests may yield different results in borderline cases. 'Capability' is clearly the lowest threshold. If the owner of an upstream input without which it is impossible to operate downstream refuses to supply it to potential competitors, the conduct is capable of eliminating all competition on the downstream market. No further inquiry is necessary. Capability is an intrinsic quality of the conduct not its extrinsic effect. In the same example, let it be assumed that there are a few undertakings active on the downstream market using a significantly less efficient input. They can only stay on the market incurring significant losses. However, an investment project is under way which is highly likely (with an 80 per cent probability) to result in the creation of an alternative upstream input which would be as efficient as the current bottleneck product. Downstream competitors are willing to incur losses in order to stay in the market to wait for the new input to become available. Should the project fail, however, there would no longer be any realistic potential alternative to the bottleneck input controlled by the dominant undertaking.[57] In this case, the conduct is capable of foreclosing merely because the refusal to supply relates to an indispensable input. There is also a risk of foreclosure because there is a 20 per cent chance that the alternative input may never be created. The conduct is, however, not likely to foreclose because it is more probable than not that downstream competitors will stay on the market and will become as efficient as the dominant undertaking when the new input becomes available. It is interesting to note that in *Tomra*, the Commission stated that it was sufficient that the conduct under review was capable of foreclosing competitors for an infringement of Article 102 to be established. However, the Commission added that it would also investigate the likely restrictive effects of Tomra's practices.[58] Capability to

---

[53] Opinion of AG Kokott in Case C-95/04 P *British Airways*, para 76.
[54] ibid para 72, emphasis in the original. See also ibid para 71.   [55] ibid para 76.
[56] ibid paras 71 and 77.
[57] A possible objection to this example is that, if the development of an alternative, as efficient input is under way, the current bottleneck is not indispensable. This objection would not be well taken for two reasons. First, indispensability and prospective elimination of competition in refusal to supply cases are two sides of the same coin. If a product is indispensable, the refusal to supply it may result in foreclosure and, vice versa, if lack of access to a product results in competitors being unable to compete, the product in question may be indispensable. Secondly, in *Commercial Solvents*, the Court of Justice considered the bottleneck product indispensable even if alternative inputs were being developed because the latter were only at the experimental stage or not suitable for large-scale production, which is precisely the situation described in the example in question: see Case 6/73 *Commercial Solvents*.
[58] *Prokent-Tomra* [2008] C219/11, recital 285, upheld in Case T-155/06 *Tomra Systems ASA v Commission* [2010] OJ C288/31, under appeal in Case C-549/10 P *Tomra Systems ASA v Commission* [2011] OJ C63/18.

foreclose and likelihood to foreclose are thus seen as two different tests. This novel approach reflected the analytical structure of the Discussion Paper on Article 82, which considered the capability and likelihood of foreclosure as distinct steps in the application of Article 102.[59] The Guidance on Article 102 also recognizes that capability and likelihood to cause competitive harm are two different standards but in a subtler and more ambiguous way. The Guidance adopts a general test of 'likely' anti-competitive effects.[60] However, it also envisages that in certain cases a detailed assessment of the likely effects of the conduct is not required. In particular, this applies to conduct that 'can only raise obstacles to competition and . . . creates no efficiencies'.[61] The use of the verb 'can' indicates that this type of conduct must still be at least capable of harming competition.

Advocate General Kokott, in her opinion in *British Airways*, provides a possible basis, or perhaps the key, for understanding the distinction between likelihood and capability to harm competition when she said that 'conduct of a dominant undertaking is abusive as soon as it *runs counter to the purpose* of protecting competition in the internal market from distortions'.[62] This may explain why different standards of anti-competitive effects apply in different cases. The standard depends on the potential anti-competitive harm associated with the conduct under review and on the risk and cost of false convictions and over-deterrence. Yet, a varying standard to be determined on a case-by-case basis would not be consistent with the principle of legal certainty. The problem is that the case law sets out too many tests and no clear analytical structure for determining which test applies in a given case. It is, therefore, necessary to bring rigour to the language describing the tests of anti-competitive effects and clarify the circumstances in which different tests apply.

As regards the terminology used in the case law to explain the tests, on a closer analysis it becomes clear that the tests can be reduced to two: likelihood of causing competitive harm and capability of causing competitive harm in the actual market context, which could also be expressed as a test of reasonable capability. Nothing would be gained by adopting a further test of 'risk' of causing competitive harm. Risk is too indeterminate a concept. If a lower threshold is required, the test of reasonable capability is able to capture conduct that poses a risk to competition. The same can be said for the test of tendency to cause competitive harm. Tendency appears to be synonymous with capability. Equally, probability and likelihood express the same concept: that conduct must be more likely than not to result in competitive harm. Finally, a test of capability in the abstract would be contrary to the objectives of Article 102. If conduct is not capable of harming long-term social

---

[59] European Commission, DG Comp, 'DG Competition discussion paper on the application of Article 82 of the Treaty to exclusionary abuses' (Brussels, December 2005) (the 'DG Comp Discussion paper on Art 102'), para 58.

[60] Guidance on Art 102, para 20.

[61] ibid para 22. The Commission explains that this 'could be the case, for instance, if the dominant undertaking prevents its customers from testing the products of competitors or provides financial incentives to its customers on condition that they do not test such products, or pays a distributor or a customer to delay the introduction of a competitor's product' (ibid).

[62] Opinion of AG Kokott in Case C-95/04 P *British Airways*, para 69 (emphasis in the original).

welfare in the actual market context in which it takes place, it is irrelevant under Article 102 and its prohibition would only risk stifling normal commercial behaviour for no conceivable gain.

As regards the criteria that should govern which of the two tests of reasonable capability or likelihood of anti-competitive effects applies in a given case, a distinction could be made between intent tests and objective tests. Following the approach in the Guidance on Article 102, the test of reasonable capability of causing competitive harm should apply to conduct that has the sole or overwhelmingly predominant purpose of harming competition and is therefore assessed under the naked abuse test. The risk of false conviction and over-deterrence in prohibiting this type of conduct is low. This approach is all the more justified because conduct that falls within this category may be low-risk from a commercial point of view or may not require a significant profit sacrifice. A dominant undertaking may, therefore, have the incentive to engage in this conduct even if the likelihood of success is only 50 per cent or less. The General Court appears to have adopted this approach in *AstraZeneca*. In relation to the abuse which consisted of making misleading representations to patent offices with the aim of obtaining exclusive rights to which the dominant undertaking was not entitled, the Court said:[63]

In a situation such as that of the present case, where the practices in question—if they are established—cannot, in any way, be regarded as being covered by normal competition between products on the basis of an undertaking's performance, it is sufficient for it to be established that, in view of the economic or regulatory context of which those practices form part, they are capable of restricting competition.

As regards the abuse consisting of the manipulation of regulatory procedures in order to foreclose suppliers of generic drugs and parallel importers, the Court said:[64]

…as regards conduct such as that at issue in the present case—in which regulatory procedures are used without any basis in competition on the merits—evidence that, in view of its economic or regulatory context, that conduct is capable of restricting competition is sufficient to classify it as an abuse of a dominant position.

The same principle should apply to all conduct examined under a test of intent. Intent is a high intervention threshold. When intent is proven, the inescapable conclusion is that the dominant undertaking considered the anti-competitive conduct worthwhile. This means, at the very least, that the dominant undertaking considered the expected gains from the anti-competitive conduct to exceed the expected losses, given the likelihood of success. Proving likely effects would be redundant. Conduct that is implemented with anti-competitive intent runs counter to the purpose of Article 102 as soon as it is reasonably capable of causing the intended harm. The risk of false convictions and over-deterrence is low because the test of intent rules out the probability that the conduct was engaged in for pro-competitive reasons. On the other hand, under the objective tests of exclusion of as

---

[63] Case T-321/05 *AstraZeneca*, para 376.   [64] ibid para 824.

efficient competitors or consumer harm, the conduct of a dominant undertaking runs counter to the objectives of Article 102 only if the specific competitive harms relevant under these tests are likely to materialize. It would be paradoxical, or even absurd, to say that conduct is only prohibited under Article 102 if it excludes an as efficient competitor or causes consumer harm but that conduct that is unlikely to exclude an as efficient competitor or cause consumer harm should be prohibited as soon as a lower threshold of capability is met.

D. Proportionality defences

(1) Structure of the test

Proportionality defences plead the pursuit of a legitimate commercial interest consistent with effective competition leading to the maximization of long-term social welfare. The case law applies a proportionality test: a dominant undertaking must be entitled to take reasonable and proportionate steps to protect its commercial interests when they are under threat unless the purpose of the conduct is to strengthen the dominant position and abuse it.[65] A 'commercial interest' within the meaning of the case law is an interest consistent with the rational profit-maximizing behaviour of a non-dominant undertaking. The proportionality defence does not plead a new primary fact but puts forward a different interpretation of the facts pleaded under the prima facie abuse test. Thus, if the dominant undertaking argues that its conduct is no more than a reasonable and proportionate reaction to competition, this meeting competition defence is limited to providing an explanation of the facts pleaded under the prima facie abuse test that is incompatible with the characterization of the conduct in question as anti-competitive.

The first step in establishing the proportionality defence is to identify a commercial objective the pursuit of which is incompatible with the characterization of the conduct as prima facie abusive. The case law is clear that the strengthening of the dominant position is not the pursuit of a commercial interest consistent with the rational market behaviour of a non-dominant undertaking. If the purpose of the conduct is to strengthen the dominant position, the conduct is by definition not the reasonable and proportionate pursuit of a legitimate commercial interest. Therefore, even above-cost selective price cuts by a quasi-monopolist against the only competitor were found not to be a reasonable and proportionate response to entry.[66] For the same reasons, it is not the reasonable and proportionate pursuit of a legitimate commercial interest for a dominant undertaking with strong consumer brands to discontinue supplies to an established customer to

---

[65] Case 27/76 *United Brands*, para 189; Case T-203/01 *Michelin II*, para 55; Case T-65/89 *British Gypsum*, para 69; Case T-301/04 *Clearstream*, para 132; Case T-321/05 *AstraZeneca*, para 672; Case T-340/03 *France Télécom SA v Commission* [2007] ECR II-107, para 185, upheld in Case C-202/07 P *France Télécom*, paras 41–49

[66] Joined Cases T-24/93 to T-26/93 and T-28/93 *Compagnie Maritime Belge Transports SA v Commission* [1996] ECR II-01201, para 148, upheld on this point in Joined Cases C-395/96 P and C-396/96 P *Compagnie Maritime Belge*.

penalize that customer for promoting the products of a competitor.[67] The legitimate interest pursued must be an objective interest consistent with the rational profit-maximizing behaviour of a non-dominant undertaking. If a dominant undertaking takes advantage of its ability to harm a competitor in a way that runs counter to the purpose of Article 102, it commits an abuse even if its motive is to pursue an otherwise lawful commercial interest. In *Clearstream Banking*, the Court rejected the argument that a prima facie abusive refusal to supply could be justified either as a retaliatory measure against a refusal by the competitor to grant the dominant undertaking access to equivalent services in another Member State[68] or because of the desire of the dominant undertaking to negotiate other elements of the business relationship with the competitor.[69]

For a defence based on the proportionate pursuit of a legitimate commercial interest to be established, it is not sufficient that the commercial interest in question be consistent with the profit-maximizing behaviour of a non-dominant undertaking. The conduct must be suitable to achieving the objective and there must be no less restrictive means of pursuing it. In *British Gypsum*, the Court of First Instance held that the prioritization of deliveries at times of shortage is a legitimate commercial practice that may be pleaded in rebuttal to a prima facie case of abusive discrimination. However, any prioritization system must not result in the exclusion of rivals, as would be the case if customers buying exclusively from the dominant undertaking were given priority over customers buying also from its competitors.[70] The Commission in *BPB Industries* suggested that an acceptable criterion to prioritize deliveries might have been an objective measure of a customer's marketing effort in promoting the product of the dominant undertaking.[71]

(2) The meeting competition defence

The meeting competition defence relies on the assumption that a dominant undertaking pursues a legitimate commercial interest when it does no more than react to competition. The question is whether the conduct of the dominant undertaking is a reasonable and proportionate response to competition. This depends on the conduct in question and, therefore, on the type of abuse under review.

Predation under Article 102 is the application of prices capable of excluding an equally efficient competitor with the intention of harming competition. The meeting competition defence is not linked to any efficiency justification, for instance to the need to win an order to preserve or achieve economies of scale,[72] but rests on the idea that as long as the dominant undertaking matches or undercuts the prices

---

[67] Case 27/76 *United Brands*, para 182. [68] Case T-301/04 *Clearstream*, paras 131–137.
[69] ibid paras 121–130, 134, and 136. [70] Case T-65/89 *British Gypsum*, para 94.
[71] *BPB Industries plc* [1989] OJ L10/50, recital 144.
[72] In this respect, the Opinion of AG Mazák in Case C-202/07 P *France Télécom*, para 95, last sentence and fn 67, is slightly misleading. The question is not whether the law allows for 'circumstances where a dominant undertaking is exceptionally permitted to show that its pricing below average variable cost is objectively justified'. The question is whether the mere fact that such prices, applied on a sufficiently large scale, are the same as, or below those of the competitor by the smallest amount necessary to win the order, justifies prices that are otherwise predatory.

of the competitor to the extent necessary to win the order, there is no abuse.[73] Therefore, allowing the meeting competition defence would be the same as making predation lawful as long as the dominant undertaking only applies the price cuts selectively to respond to the competitor's prices and as long as the dominant undertaking's price cuts are limited to what is necessary to prevent the competitor from winning the order. Under this doctrine, predation would be lawful as long as it minimizes the losses of the dominant undertaking. This would be plainly absurd. The mere fact that below-cost prices capable of excluding an equally efficient competitor and applied as part of a predatory strategy simply match or undercut the competitor's prices to the extent necessary to win the order is not the reasonable and proportionate pursuit of a legitimate commercial interest. It is predation in action. Therefore, the Court if First Instance was right in *France Télécom* when it held that the dominant undertaking was not permitted to align its prices with the prices of its competitors where such prices did not allow the recovery of its variable or total costs.[74]

In margin squeeze cases, the meeting competition defence faces the difficulty that competitors are, by definition, unable to replicate the vertical structure of the dominant undertaking. Therefore, it cannot be a defence for the dominant undertaking to demonstrate that it simply matched its downstream competitors' prices reactively if the price of the bottleneck input is kept at an excessive level. In *Telefónica*, the Commission rejected the meeting competition defence because the dominant undertaking could have lowered its wholesale price to end the margin squeeze.[75] If, on the other hand, the upstream price is cost-reflective and the dominant undertaking's downstream prices are predatory, the meeting competition defence is bound to fail for the same reasons that make it unavailable in predation cases: below-cost pricing that is socially harmful cannot become beneficial simply because the dominant undertaking is matching or undercutting the competitor's prices to the extent necessary to exclude them. This would legalize predation as long as the dominant undertaking minimizes its losses. Finally, if the upstream price is cost-reflective and the downstream prices are not predatory, there is no margin squeeze because no equally efficient competitors can be foreclosed. Therefore, the meeting competition defence is not available in margin squeeze cases.

---

[73] Commentators are divided. Some are in favour of allowing the meeting competition defence: see, U Springer, '"Meeting Competition": Justification of Price Discrimination under EC and US Antitrust Law' (1997) 18 ECLR 251; M Lorenz, M Lübbig, and A Russel, 'Price Discrimination, a Tender Story' (2005) 26 ECLR 355, 359; MA Gravengaard, 'The Meeting Competition Defence Principle—A Defence for Price Discrimination and Predatory Pricing?' (2006) 27 ECLR 658, 667; RJ Van den Bergh and PD Camesasca, *European Competition Law and Economics: A Comparative Perspective* (2nd edn London, Sweet & Maxwell 2006) 295. Others are against: see eg M Waelbroeck, 'Meeting Competition: Is This a Valid Defence for a Firm in a Dominant Position?' in *Studi in onore di Francesco Capotorti: Divenire sociale e adeguamento del diritto—Vol 2* (Milan, Giuffrè 1999) 481, 489. Finally, some look for a middle ground. For instance M Motta, *Competition Policy, Theory and Practice* (Cambridge, CUP 2004) 451, argues that 'matching a competitor's price should not be an accepted defence if it implies prices below average variable costs for the incumbent'.

[74] Case T-340/03 *France Télécom SA v Commission* [2007] ECR II-107, paras 183–187, upheld in C-202/07 P *France Télécom*.

[75] *Telefónica*, recital 639.

When the prices of the dominant undertaking are above its own costs, the principle of equality of opportunities[76] requires that the dominant undertaking is entitled to take advantage of its own efficiency. Therefore, an above-cost price cut that does not go beyond what is necessary to win an order is, as a general principle, not abusive. However, it is unlikely that a prima facie case of anti-competitive unconditional price cuts can be rebutted on the basis of the meeting competition defence. This apparently paradoxical statement must be understood in the light of the very narrowly defined sets of circumstances in which unconditional above-cost price cuts are prohibited under Article 102.[77] Because the threshold for intervention is very high, it follows that the scope for rebuttal is very limited. In *Compagnie Maritime Belge*, a quasi-monopolist applied selective price cuts aimed at excluding from the market its only competitor. The competitor needed to overcome significant switching costs. The price cuts were part of an anti-competitive strategy, and they were applied with the purpose of maintaining or strengthening the dominant position.[78] The Court of First Instance found this conduct to be abusive precisely as an exception to the general principle that dominant undertakings are entitled to protect their legitimate commercial interests by reacting to competition.[79]

Conditional rebates can be examined either under the naked abuse test or under the as efficient competitor test.[80] If the rebates are assessed under the naked abuse test, the meeting competition defence is unavailable. The naked abuse test only applies when the conduct under review has the sole or overwhelmingly predominant purpose of harming competition, has no redeeming virtues, and is reasonably capable of causing the harm intended. This test rules out the very possibility that the conduct could be a reasonable and proportionate competitive reaction. On the other hand, meeting competition is an absolute defence when conditional rebates are assessed under the as efficient competitor test. If the dominant undertaking is replicating, or undercutting by the smallest amount necessary to win the order, a similar price schedule of a competitor, the rebate system is incapable of having any foreclosure effect. If competitors are offering the same rebates, they are able to compete on an equal footing with the dominant undertaking. However, for this defence to succeed, competitors must be realistically able to offer the same effective and average prices as the dominant undertaking, not simply the same contractual percentage discounts and the same thresholds if the thresholds are in practice unlikely to be met. In *Intel*, the Commission rejected Intel's meeting competition

---

[76] Case C-462/99 *Connect Austria Gesellschaft für Telekommunikation GmbH v Telekom-Control-Kommission and Mobilkom Austria AG* [2003] ECR I-5197 (*Connect Austria*), paras 80–88 and 95; Case T-271/03 *Deutsche Telekom AG v Commission* [2008] ECR II-477, para 198, upheld in Case Case C-280/08 P *Deutsche Telekom AG v Commission* [2010] OJ C346/4; and Joined Cases C-327/03 P and C-328/03 P *Bundesrepublik Deutschland v ISIS Multimedia Net GmbH und Co KG* [2005] ECR I-8877, para 39.

[77] Case T-228/97 *Irish Sugar plc v Commission* [1999] II-2969, upheld on appeal in Case C-497/99 P *Irish Sugar plc v Commission* [2001] ECR I-5333; Case T-30/89 *Hilti AG v Commission* [1990] ECR II-163, upheld on appeal in Case C-53/92 P *Hilti AG v Commission* [1994] I-667; Joined Cases T-24/93 to T-26/93 and T-28/93 *Compagnie Maritime Belge*.

[78] Joined Cases T-24/93 to T-26/93 and T-28/93 *Compagnie Maritime Belge*, paras 146–148.

[79] ibid.   [80] See 189–190 and 232–242 above.

defence because Intel had not adduced evidence showing how the rebates under review were structured in order to respond to offers made by AMD.[81] Furthermore, the conditions of the rebate relating to exclusivity or quasi-exclusivity were unnecessary in order to meet price competition because an unconditional lower price would have been sufficient.[82] This approach is rather unstructured but is consistent with the framework of the proportionality defence. AMD was simply not able to replicate Intel's conditional rebates, so Intel's rebates could not, logically, be a reasonable and proportionate reaction to competition.

Meeting competition is an absolute defence to a prima facie case of market-distorting price discrimination under Article 102(c). Meeting competition is clearly a legitimate objective and a non-exclusionary price cut is a suitable means of achieving the objective. Generally, there will be no less restrictive means of winning the order because, in the absence of an exclusionary strategy, the dominant undertaking has the incentive to offer a price no lower than is necessary to win the order. Because meeting competition is a mere defence, no balancing of the harm consisting in the alleged downstream competitive distortion against the benefits of upstream competition is required. In practice, in any event, it is difficult to imagine realistic scenarios in which a customer obtaining lower prices upstream as a result of competitive interaction would gain an advantage that would harm the productive or dynamic efficiency of the downstream industry. If anything, lower upstream prices resulting from upstream competition should increase the efficiency of the downstream industry.

E. Objective justification defences

(1) Structure of the test

The Court of Justice in *British Airways* set out a four limb proportionality test for the assessment of objective justification defences: (a) the conduct must pursue a legitimate objective;[83] (b) it must be suitable to achieving the objective being pursued; (c) it must not go beyond what is necessary to achieve the objective in question; and (d) the benefits of the conduct must counterbalance or outweigh the disadvantages and must benefit consumers.[84]

The Guidance on Article 102 does not refer to objective justification but envisages that the conduct of the dominant undertaking may be justified on the ground that it produces efficiencies. The Guidance then puts forward a test requiring four cumulative conditions to be fulfilled: (a) efficiencies have been, or are likely to be, realized as a result of the conduct; (b) the conduct is indispensable to the realization

---

[81] *Intel* [2009] OJ C227/13, recitals 1631 and 1633. The decision is under appeal in Case T-286/09 *Intel Corp v Commission* [2009] OJ C220/41.

[82] ibid recital 1632.

[83] The objective in question was described as 'advantages in terms of efficiency': Case C-95/04 P *British Airways*, para 86. However, as will be explained in this chapter, the objective justification test is wider and includes any benefits that increase long-term social welfare.

[84] Case C-95/04 P *British Airways*, para 86. See also 166–167 above.

of those efficiencies. There must be no less anti-competitive conduct that is capable of producing the same efficiencies; (c) the likely efficiencies brought about by the conduct outweigh any likely negative effects on competition and consumer welfare in the affected markets; and (d) the conduct does not eliminate effective competition.[85]

It is unclear why the Commission felt it appropriate to formulate a test which differs from the test established in the case law. A plausible explanation is that this departure from the case law aims at achieving consistency with the approach adopted under Article 101. The fact that the conditions for the efficiency defence in the Guidance on Article 102 are similar to the conditions in Article 101(3), as interpreted in the Guidelines on Article 101(3),[86] suggests that this may well be the case. However, this policy aiming for a convergence between the tests under Articles 101 and 102 is completely off the mark. These two provisions apply different tests in the presence of different conditions. The application of Article 102 presupposes a finding of dominance which means that, on the market in question, competition is already weakened. This is taken into account in setting the threshold for establishing a prima facie case of anti-competitive conduct under Article 102.[87] It follows that the conditions necessary to establish an objective justification defence must also be different. This conclusion is unassailable as a matter of law. If the drafters of the Treaty of Rome had wished to achieve consistency between Article 101 and Article 102 they would have reproduced Article 101(3) in Article 102. They did not. The Commission is not entitled to do so in its enforcement policy.[88] This conclusion is also sound as a matter of policy. Articles 101 and 102 aim at preventing two different types of harm. Article 101 aims at preventing the reduction of competition that flows from bilateral or multilateral conduct not

---

[85] Guidance on Art 102, para 30.

[86] Communication from the Commission—Notice—Guidelines on the application of Article 81(3) of the Treaty [2004] OJ C101/97 ('Guidelines on Art 101(3)'), paras 38–116.

[87] The case law is crystal clear in this respect: Case T-65/89 *British Gypsum*, paras 66–67; *Van den Bergh Foods Ltd* [1998] OJ L246/1, upheld in Case T-65/98 *Van den Bergh Foods Ltd v Commission* [2003] ECR II-4653, paras 159–160, appeal dismissed in Case C-552/03 P *Unilever Bestfoods (Ireland) Ltd v Commission* [2006] ECR I-9091. It would not be accurate to say that the Court of First Instance in *Van den Bergh* summarized its analysis under Art 101 thus suggesting that it applied the same 'rule of reason' approach (R O'Donoghue and AJ Padilla, *The Law and Economics of Article 82 EC* (Oxford, Hart Publishing 2006) 360) or that the Court of First Instance 'did not have much to say regarding Article [102], as everything had already been said in reference to Article [101]' (E Rousseva, *Rethinking Exclusionary Abuses in EU Competition Law* (Oxford, Hart Publishing 2010) 545). The Court did not examine all the characteristics of the market afresh but nor did it refer to the analysis under Art 101 as it could have done. It simply relied on three factors in order to presume a foreclosure effect: dominance, exclusivity, and the size of the foreclosed share of demand: see 247 above.

[88] Even less would the Commission be entitled to draw an arbitrary line between Arts 101 and 102 and apply only Art 101 to vertical agreements as argued, perhaps elegantly but ultimately unconvincingly, by Rousseva, *Rethinking Exclusionary Abuses in EU Competition Law*, 433–456 and 460–473. While the fact that the two provisions overlap means, of course, that they can both apply to the same set of facts, it does not follow that it is necessary or appropriate to design an arbitrary line between collusive behaviour, only to be assessed under Art 101, and unilateral conduct falling under Art 102. Such an approach would be against the text of Art 102, which is plainly intended to apply to contractual arrangements: see Art 101(a), (b), and (d). Furthermore, for the reasons set out in the text, this suggestion would also be wrong in policy.

attributable to the position of a single undertaking.[89] The focus of the analysis is on the object or the effect of the individual agreement or network of agreements. Article 102 aims at preventing the negative effect on competition resulting from the unilateral conduct of an undertaking which has the ability and incentive to harm competition. The focus is on the unilateral conduct of the dominant undertaking. Under Article 101, the market power of the undertakings concerned is relevant but there is no need to establish dominance as a threshold question. It is true that, when agreements having potentially anti-competitive effects have been entered into by a dominant undertaking, Article 101 requires the analysis of the same factors that are relevant to a finding of dominance.[90] To conduct an investigation into the distributional practices of a dominant undertaking without having assessed its market power and its ability and incentive to exclude would be to blind oneself to the reality of market dynamics. But this is an argument to apply Article 102 instead of Article 101 because, once dominance is established, Article 102 provides a more appropriate tool for the assessment of conduct as it is tailored to examining the competitive harm caused by a dominant undertaking. The tests under Article 101, on the other hand, have been framed and developed on the basis that no single undertaking has the ability and the incentive unilaterally to harm competition. Indeed, the argument could even go as far as saying that only Article 102, as *lex specialis*, applies to the conduct of a dominant undertaking.

The above analysis already demonstrates that importing the more stringent Article 101(3) test into Article 102 would upset the delicate balance of the different components of the Article 102 test. An examination of the two aspects of the Guidance on Article 102 that differ from the *British Airways* test furnishes conclusive proof of this conclusion. These aspects are the condition relating to the effect on consumers and the condition relating to the elimination of competition.

As regards the condition relating to the effect on consumers, the Court of Justice in *British Airways* merely required that the efficiencies also benefit the consumers. This condition is justified on the ground that it ensures that competition is not restricted to such an extent that the dominant undertaking's incentives to lower costs and invest in new technology and product development are significantly reduced so that, on balance, social welfare is likely to be harmed in the long-term. If sufficient competitive pressure remains on the market to allow consumers to benefit from the prima facie abusive conduct, then long-term efficiency and investment incentives are on balance likely to be preserved notwithstanding the restriction of competition. The consumer benefit limb of the proportionality test is neither a consumer protection requirement nor a consumer welfare test. Had it been either, the Court would have required that the net effect of the conduct on consumers be positive or neutral, while in fact the Court only required that some benefits must accrue to consumers. Therefore, the balancing exercise is not between the harm to consumers resulting from the

---

[89] The same arguments apply to collective dominance, discussed in Ch 11 below. The discussion in the text refers to single dominance for the sake of conciseness

[90] Rousseva, *Rethinking Exclusionary Abuses in EU Competition Law*, 449–451.

maintenance, strengthening, or acquisition of market power and the benefits
to consumers resulting from efficiencies. The balancing is between the benefits of the conduct and the competitive harm. To give a practical example, this
means that if a dominant undertaking's refusal to supply eliminating all effective competition is necessary in order to preserve the dominant undertaking's
ex ante or future investment incentives, a competition authority or court is not
required to balance the harm to consumers resulting from the elimination of
all effective competition against the benefits to consumers resulting from the
dominant undertaking's past or future investments. Instead, what is required
in these circumstances is that the dominant undertaking's investment should
benefit consumers, for instance through the introduction of improved products
or lower-cost technologies that are likely to result in lower prices, and that the
competitive harm caused by the refusal to supply is not disproportionate to the
aim of ensuring that the dominant undertaking's investment incentives are preserved for the benefit of society as a whole. The Court of Justice in *British Airways*
explained this test as an examination of whether the advantages of the conduct
counterbalanced or outweighed the 'exclusionary effect'.[91] This language should
not mislead. The proportionality test does not require a quantitative balancing
of competitive harm and benefits. In *British Airways* itself, the Court said that
the relevant question was whether 'the exclusionary effect' resulting from the
conduct under review 'may be counterbalanced, or outweighed, by advantages
in terms of efficiency which also benefit the consumer'. An exclusionary effect
cannot be quantified. What could be quantified is the reduction in social welfare
caused by the exclusion. But if the Court had required quantification of such an
effect, it would have said so explicitly. On the contrary, it is absolutely clear from
the case law that no quantification of the negative effect of the prima facie abuse
on social welfare is required. The balancing test must, therefore, be a qualitative assessment of the comparative magnitude of the competitive harm and the
benefits resulting from the conduct under review. On one side of the scales there
are the degree of dominance and the extent and intensity of the anti-competitive
effect; on the other side, there are the nature and magnitude of the benefits, the
likelihood and the time frame in which they could arise, and the advantages to
consumers.[92] Consistently with the way in which the case law applies the proportionality test as a general principle of EU law, the test is whether the restriction
of competition is disproportionate to the objectives being pursued.[93] Requiring,

---

[91] Case C-95/04 P *British Airways*, para 86.
[92] A comparison can be drawn with Art 101(3). Under Art 101(3) the structure of the balancing
test is determined by the requirement that consumers must receive a 'fair share' of the benefits of the
agreement. There is no such requirement under Art 102. However, balancing under Art 101(3) is also
a qualitative exercise: see Guidelines on Art 101(3), paras 83–104.
[93] See Case 302/86 *Commission v Kingdom of Denmark* [1988] ECR 4607 (*Danish Bottles*), para
21 (on free movement of goods); Case T-13/99 *Pfizer Animal Health SA v Council of the European
Union* [2002] ECR II-3305, para 411 (on the review of the legality of acts of the Union): 'The Court
observes *in limine* that the principle of proportionality, which is one of the general principles of
Community law, requires that measures adopted by Community institutions should not exceed the
limits of what is appropriate and necessary in order to attain the legitimate objectives pursued by the

as the Commission does, that the net effect of the conduct on consumer welfare be at least neutral, is too high a threshold for objective justification and is at odds with the case law of the Court of Justice. The Commission is allowed to prioritize cases based on criteria that go beyond what is required by law for a finding of infringement but is not allowed to raise the bar for an undertaking to rebut a prima facie finding of abuse. This amounts to the application of a stricter prohibition test than is adopted under Article 102 as interpreted in the case law. It is unlawful for the Commission to apply such a stricter test.

The Guidance on Article 102 also departs from the *British Airways* test by requiring that the conduct of the dominant undertaking must not eliminate effective competition. It is clear why the case law does not envisage such a condition: an abuse that results in the elimination of all effective competition may nevertheless be objectively justified. The most obvious example is refusal to supply. The case law requires that, to establish a prima facie case of abusive refusal to supply, the conduct must be likely to eliminate all effective competition.[94] And yet the same case law unequivocally recognizes that refusal to supply can be objectively justified.[95] The Commission itself accepts that refusal to supply may be objectively justified and, somewhat ironically, adds that it will ensure that the conditions for objective justification which it sets out in the Guidance are met. These conditions include the requirement that effective competition must not be eliminated, which would mean that objective justification would be inapplicable in refusal to supply cases. It is clear that, in requiring evidence that the conduct under review does not eliminate all effective competition, the Commission is acting in breach of Article 102 as interpreted in the case law of the Court of Justice and, therefore, unlawfully.[96]

---

legislation in question, and where there is a choice between several appropriate measures, recourse must be had to the least onerous, and the disadvantages caused must not be disproportionate to the aims pursued'; Case C-331/88 *The Queen v Minister of Agriculture, Fisheries and Food and Secretary of State for Health, ex p Fedesa* [1990] ECR I-4023, para 13 (on the review of the legality of acts of the Union): 'The Court has consistently held that the principle of proportionality is one of the general principles of Community law . By virtue of that principle, the lawfulness of the prohibition of an economic activity is subject to the condition that the prohibitory measures are appropriate and necessary in order to achieve the objectives legitimately pursued by the legislation in question; when there is a choice between several appropriate measures recourse must be had to the least onerous, and the disadvantages caused must not be disproportionate to the aims pursued'; C-67/98 *Questore di Verona v Diego Zenatti* [1999] ECR I-7289, para 37 (on the freedom to provide services): 'Spetta al giudice a quo verificare se la normativa nazionale, alla luce delle sue concrete modalità d'applicazione, soddisfi effettivamente gli obiettivi che possono giustificarla e se le restrizioni da essa imposte non risultino sproporzionate rispetto a tali obiettivi.'

[94] eg Joined Cases C-241/91 P and C-242/91 P *Radio Telefís Eireann (RTE) and Independent Television Publications Ltd (ITP) v Commission* [1995] ECR I-743 (*Magill*) para 56; Case C-418/01 *IMS*, para 47. The Commission itself, rightly, adopts this test in all refusal to supply cases: Guidance on Art 102, para 81.

[95] Case T-69/89 *Radio Telefís Eireann v Commission* [1991] ECR II-485 (*Magill*), para 73 and Joined Cases C-241/91 P and C-242/91 P *Magill*, para 55; Case C-7/97 *Oscar Bronner*, paras 40–41; Case C-418/01 *IMS*, paras 51–52.

[96] The fact that Art 101(3) can apply to dominant undertakings and that the condition of non-elimination of competition can, therefore, be met even if one of the parties to an agreement is dominant (see Case T-395/94 *Atlantic Container Line AB v Commission* [2002] ECR II-875, para 330) does not in any way contradict this conclusion because the threshold for objective justification is different, and more lenient, than the test under Art 101(3). Furthermore, certain abuses, such as

The above analysis has established that the objective justification test in *British Airways* is good law. The Guidance on Article 102 can only be applied insofar as it is consistent with the *British Airways* test, which does not require that the net effect of the conduct under review on consumers must be neutral or positive and that the conduct under review must not eliminate all effective competition.

(2) Efficiency defences

(a) *Allocative efficiency*

Allocative efficiency is a legitimate objective compatible with the long-term social welfare purpose of Article 102. The crucial question under objective justification is whether the conduct of the dominant undertaking is proportionate to the objective pursued. Generally, allocative efficiency defences have failed the least restrictive means limb of the proportionality test. The Commission in *Wanadoo* rejected claims that the predatory conduct was objectively justified because it sought to expand the market on the ground that there was no evidence that output expansion could not be achieved by less restrictive means.[97] In *Intel*, the dominant undertaking claimed that its rebates resulted in lower prices which, presumably, would have enhanced allocative efficiency. The Commission held that the conditions under which the rebates were granted were not necessary to lower prices.[98] In *Michelin I*, the Court held that output expansion could not justify 'such a restriction of the customer's freedom of choice and independence',[99] thus implying that there were other less restrictive means to achieve the objective of increasing sales. In *Telefónica*, the Commission rejected the dominant undertaking's objective justification defence that low prices were necessary in order to increase output in an immature market on the ground that the relevant market was 'still in expansion' but not 'entirely new or in a phase of experimentation'.[100]

Tying may in certain circumstances be justified on the ground that it increases output. The reduction of transaction costs for consumers is a benefit often associated with tying. Because the transaction cost is borne by the customer, lower transaction costs result in larger output. The problem lies in the application of the proportionality framework to the facts of each individual case. First, tying is not suitable for reducing transaction costs when final consumers benefit from an integrated bundle but the tying occurs on an intermediate market. In *Microsoft I*, the Court of First Instance said that 'consumer demand for an "out-of-the-box" client PC incorporating a streaming media player can be fully satisfied by OEMs, who are in the business of assembling such PCs and combining, inter alia, a client PC operating system with the applications desired by consumers'.[101] Tying

---

refusal to supply, do not relate to agreements or concerted practices, so that any parallelism between Art 101(3) and Art 102 breaks down.

[97] *Wanadoo Interactive* (Commission Decision, 16 July 2003) recital 312, upheld in Case T-340/03 *France Télécom*, appeal dismissed in Case C-202/07 P *France Télécom*. The Commission, however, did not carry out a structured proportionality test.

[98] *Intel*, recital 1636.   [99] Case 322/81 *Michelin I*, para 85.

[100] *Telefónica*, recital 626.   [101] Case T-201/04 *Microsoft I*, para 1155.

on an intermediate market is not suitable for reducing transaction costs on the final market if the intermediate resellers of the tying and the tied products could themselves assemble integrated bundles under competitive conditions. The bundle does not have to be imposed by the dominant undertaking. But even when tying takes place at the level of the supply chain where the alleged reduction in transaction costs also occurs, generally mixed bundling is a less restrictive alternative to tying. Provided that the incremental price of each component is not below its LRAIC, consumers would have the choice of buying the bundle, thus saving transaction costs, or buying two stand-alone components. In this way, equally efficient competitors are not foreclosed. In *Microsoft I*, consumer demand for an integrated operating system with media functionality did not justify the tying of Windows and Microsoft Media Player because the Commission decision did not 'prevent Microsoft from continuing to offer the bundled version of Windows and Windows Media Player to consumers who prefer that solution'.[102] While the Court did not apply the proportionality test in a structured way, this appears to be an application of the less restrictive means test: the same objective of offering an integrated solution to those who prefer it can be achieved by mixed bundling. Tying is not required. It is also sometimes argued that tying may be used to internalize the externality that results from the double marginalization effect resulting from two different suppliers with substantial market power selling two complementary products. Because each supplier does not take into account the effect of its own price on the sales of the complementary product, output is lower than in a situation where a single monopolist supplies both products.[103] However, tying is only suitable to expanding output under the double marginalization theory if the tied product is supplied by an undertaking with substantial market power. This is unlikely to arise on the facts of a tying case, where the foreclosure effect on the tied market generally means that the competitors of the dominant undertaking are rather fragmented with none of them having substantial market power. In any event, it is unclear why an undertaking dominant on the tying market would need to tie its products to neutralize a double marginalization effect on complementary markets. Because the dominant undertaking is selling both products, it can internalize the externality simply by pricing the two products so as to maximize profits on the bundle.[104]

---

[102] ibid para 1155.

[103] See eg O'Donoghue and Padilla, *The Law and Economics of Article 82 EC*, 482–483.

[104] K-U Kühn, R Stillman, and C Caffarra, 'Economic Theories of Bundling and Their Policy Implications in Abuse Cases: An Assessment in Light of the Microsoft Case' (2005) 1 European Competition Journal 85, 107–108. The counter-argument by O'Donoghue and Padilla, *The Law and Economics of Article 82 EC*, 483, relying generally on MD Whinston, 'Tying, Foreclosure, and Exclusion' (1990) 80 American Economic Rev 837, is not convincing. Whinston demonstrates that, in certain circumstances, a monopolist has the ability and incentive to exclude a rival from the tied market only if he pre-commits to tying because, when this is the case, profits can only be earned on the bundle and not on the monopolized product: see ibid 844 and 853. However, when there is a double marginalization effect, the dominant undertaking does not need to pre-commit in order to price aggressively. By definition, even without the pre-commitment, it cannot extract all profits from selling the monopolized product because of the highly priced complement sold by the rival. It has, therefore, an incentive independent of any commitment to internalize the externality.

(b) Productive efficiency

The achievement of lower production costs is a legitimate objective compatible with the purpose of Article 102 because increased productivity is a fundamental element of long-term social welfare maximization. Productive efficiency may be improved in particular by increasing the scale of production or by selling two or more products together each time the market is characterized by economies of scale or scope or learning effects. The problem is that exclusionary conduct having the alleged objective of increasing productive efficiency generally fails either the suitability limb or the least restrictive means limb of the proportionality test. This is particularly clear in rebate cases. If increased output results in a reduction of costs, the dominant undertaking is entitled to pass this cost saving to the customer.[105] In *British Airways*, the Court of First Instance held that the retroactive nature of the incentive scheme under review meant that there was 'no objective relation' between a possible benefit for the dominant undertaking arising from the sales of additional tickets and the increased commission rate.[106] This analysis suggests that the incentive scheme failed the suitability test. The same approach was adopted in *Tomra*, where the Commission rejected the argument that the rebates under review allowed the dominant undertaking to realize cost savings or recover fixed costs more efficiently on the following grounds: (a) there was no evidence of how the attainment of the rebate thresholds reduced costs;[107] (b) the form of the rebates was inconsistent with a justification based on cost efficiencies because long-term and less specified contracts attracted better financial terms than large short-term specified orders;[108] (c) the same or similar discount applied to different quantities while different discounts applied to the same quantities;[109] and (d) the individualized character of the schemes demonstrated that their aim was to achieve exclusivity and not productive efficiency.[110] In *Intel*, the dominant undertaking maintained that its rebate schemes resulted in a more efficient utilization of manufacturing capacity by allowing it to exploit economies of scale.[111] The Commission first rejected the defence on the ground that Intel 'has failed to demonstrate what the precise efficiencies in the concrete context of its business relationship with specific OEMs would be',[112] which was an application of the suitability test. The Commission then applied the least restrictive means test and went on to hold that Intel had not substantiated the claim that economies of scale

---

[105] Case C-163/99 *Portugese Republic*, para 49; Case T-228/97 *Irish Sugar*, para 173; Case T-219/99 *British Airways*, para 284 (accepting that in law 'efficiency gains or cost savings' may justify a rebate scheme); Case C-95/04 P *British Airways*, para 84; Case 85/76 *Hoffmann-La Roche*, para 90; Case 322/81 *Michelin I*, para 73; Case T-203/01 *Michelin II*, para 100.

[106] Case T-219/99 *British Airways*, paras 281–285 and 290, upheld in Case C-95/04 P *British Airways*, paras 84–90.

[107] *Prokent—Tomra*, recitals 349 and 354. The issue of objective justification was not raised before the General Court: see Case T-155/06 *Tomra*.

[108] *Prokent—Tomra*, recitals 351–352.   [109] ibid recital 353.

[110] ibid recital 355. The Guidance on Art 102, para 46, considers standardized schemes to be less restrictive than individualized ones.

[111] *Intel*, recital 1637.   [112] ibid recital 1638.

could not be achieved by a less restrictive discounting structure or by an uncon-ditional lower price.[113] Intel also argued that its manufacturing facilities could be utilized in a more cost effective way if it could predict its sales volume and the product mix. Applying the suitability test, the Commission took the view that Intel had not shown the precise cost savings associated with the incremental sales upon which the rebates were conditional. But the Commission also said that the prediction of sales volumes and product mix did not justify conditions relating to the customer's ability to purchase competitors' products,[114] which was an applica-tion of the least restrictive means test.

Telefónica is a rare case in which the Commission applied the balancing limb of the proportionality test. The Commission accepted that 'in case of significant economies of scale or learning effects, in exceptional cases there could be reasons which could justify temporary prices below LRAIC'.[115] However, productive efficiency cannot justify 'a margin squeeze that enables the vertically integrated company to impose losses upon its competitors that it does not incur itself'.[116] Telefónica's low prices could not be justified by the objective of increasing produc-tive efficiencies because there was no evidence that such efficiencies could not have been realized under competitive conditions.[117] In any event, the alleged short-term efficiency gains resulting from the dominant undertaking's conduct would be unlikely to outweigh the long-term negative effects on competition, including rent seeking, 'misallocation of resources, reduced innovation and higher prices'.[118] And, because of Telefónica's downstream market power, efficiency gains were unlikely to be passed on to consumers. As a matter of fact, Spanish broadband prices were 'among the highest in the EU'.[119]

The cost of producing two products together may be lower than the sum of the costs of producing each of them separately.[120] However, the fact that joint production generates efficiencies does not necessarily imply that the products in question must be distributed together.[121] It would appear, therefore, that while economies of scope in production are certainly a legitimate objective that dom-inant undertakings are allowed to pursue under Article 102, joint distribution by tying is generally not suitable to achieving the objective.[122] Tying, however, would be suitable to achieving economies of scope in distribution. The question is whether these practices are the least restrictive means of achieving the objec-tive. Economies of scope in distributing two different products can be achieved by a multi-product rebate whereby the incremental price of each product is above its LRAIC. Such a rebate is unlikely to be exclusionary. At the same time, it is likely to be as effective as tying in realizing economies of scope because any cost

---

[113] ibid.   [114] ibid recital 1639.   [115] *Telefónica*, recital 650.
[116] ibid recital 652.   [117] ibid recital 646.   [118] ibid recital 657.
[119] ibid recital 658.
[120] O'Donoghue and Padilla, *The Law and Economics of Article 82 EC*, 481–482.
[121] Kühn, Stillman, and Caffarra, 'Economic Theories of Bundling and Their Policy Implications in Abuse Cases: An Assessment in Light of the Microsoft Case', 107.
[122] See, however, the Guidelines on Vertical Restraints [2010] OJ C130/1, para 222, which treat joint production and joint distribution without distinguishing between the two.

savings are passed on to consumers, who will buy the bundle if their valuation of it exceeds or equals its cost.

(c) Dynamic efficiency

The Guidance on Article 102 recognizes a broad dynamic efficiency defence in relation to refusal to supply.[123] This approach is consistent with the case law. In *Microsoft I*, the Court of First Instance held that the negative impact of an obligation to license an IP right on the dominant undertaking's incentives to innovate was a permissible objective justification.[124] On the facts, the question is related to *ex ante* incentives. However, the distinction between *ex ante* incentives and *ex post* rewards is largely theoretical. If, historically, without the expectation of exclusive use, the investment would not have been made, this constitutes strong evidence that future investment incentives are also likely to be discouraged.[125] More importantly, the fundamental role of dynamic efficiency in the achievement of the purpose of Article 102 requires that both *ex ante* and *ex post* investment incentives must be relevant under the objective justification test. However, the incentives in question are the incentives of the dominant undertaking. There is no market-wide balancing of investment incentives of the industry as a whole.[126] In *Microsoft I*, the Court set out a two-stage test. First, it was necessary to determine whether the obligation to supply significantly reduced the dominant undertaking's incentives to invest.[127] Secondly, it was necessary to assess whether the significant negative impact on investment incentives might prevail over the 'exceptional circumstances' which gave rise to the alleged abuse. The reference to the 'exceptional circumstances' must be construed as a reference to the competitive harm caused by the refusal to supply, which consists in the elimination of effective competition to the detriment of consumers. The Court itself singled out the limitation of technical development to the prejudice of consumers as an exceptional circumstance relevant to the balancing test.[128] This test is an application of the objective justification proportionality framework. In particular, it is an application of the fourth limb of the proportionality test which requires that the competitive harm must not be disproportionate to the benefits of the conduct under review. The dynamic efficiency

[123] Guidance on Art 102, para 89: 'The Commission will consider claims by the dominant undertaking that a refusal to supply is necessary to allow the dominant undertaking to realise an adequate return on the investments required to develop its input business, thus generating incentives to continue to invest in the future, taking the risk of failed projects into account. The Commission will also consider claims by the dominant undertaking that its own innovation will be negatively affected by the obligation to supply, or by the structural changes in the market conditions that imposing such an obligation will bring about, including the development of follow-on innovation by competitors.'

[124] Case T-201/04 *Microsoft I*, paras 696–712.

[125] See *Microsoft I*, recital 709, where Microsoft's argument related both to the protection of past investments and to the incentives to invest in the future. The *ex ante* and *ex post* perspectives and the impact on future investment incentives are not discussed in the judgment, which refers generally to incentives to innovate: Case T-201/04 *Microsoft I*, paras 668, 689 (with a reference to Microsoft's argument about 'future incentives to invest'), 697, 698 (again referring to Microsoft's argument about 'future' incentives), 699, 701–703, and 706–710.

[126] ibid paras 704–709.   [127] ibid para 701.

[128] ibid para 709. Ultimately, the dynamic efficiency defence was rejected because the dominant undertaking had failed to adduce sufficient evidence to substantiate the issue: ibid paras 698–712.

defence is admissible beyond refusal to supply. Given the importance of dynamic efficiency as a driver of long-term productivity and social welfare maximization, there is no doubt that dynamic efficiency is a legitimate aim under the objective justification test whatever the abuse under consideration.

An alleged margin squeeze is not an abuse if it is a proportionate way of recouping the dominant undertaking's investment in a product or infrastructure. In *Telefónica*, the Commission recognized that dynamic efficiency can substantiate an objective justification defence to a prima facie case of margin squeeze but rejected the defence on the ground that the infrastructure was developed by a former state monopoly using state funds.[129] Furthermore, the Commission held that the dynamic efficiency defence would be rejected if the dominant undertaking developed its infrastructure at a time when it already knew that it would have a regulatory duty to grant access to the infrastructure.[130] This approach is restated in the Commission Guidance on Article 102, probably written in the light of the *Telefónica* case. In fact, the Commission goes even further and explains that it will not apply the refusal to supply test but the broad consumer harm case set out in paragraph 20 of the Guidance when it is 'clear that imposing an obligation to supply is manifestly not capable of having negative effects on the input owner's and/or other operators' incentives to invest and innovate upstream, whether *ex ante* or *ex post*'.[131] The Commission sets out two examples that correspond to the two arguments used to reject the dynamic efficiency defence in *Telefónica*. The first is 'where regulation compatible with [EU] law already imposes an obligation to supply on the dominant undertaking and it is clear, from the considerations underlying such regulation, that the necessary balancing of incentives has already been made by the public authority when imposing such an obligation to supply'.[132] The second is where 'the upstream market position of the dominant undertaking has been developed under the protection of special or exclusive rights or has been financed by state resources'.[133] This approach is fundamentally flawed. An infrastructure may have been developed partly with state funding and partly with private resources and in a competitive environment. This is likely to be the case more and more often in the European Union where former state monopolies have been privatized and previously protected markets have been open to competition for some time. Does this mean that in refusal to supply and margin squeeze cases it is necessary to assess the relative magnitude of the public and private investments in order to determine which test to apply? This approach lacks legal certainty and would result in arbitrary and unpredictable enforcement of Article 102. Nor is the argument based on the *ex ante* knowledge of a regulatory duty to supply any more convincing. Margin squeeze has two elements: a refusal to supply element and a pricing element. A regulatory duty to supply would make the dynamic efficiency defence inapplicable to the refusal to supply element of the margin squeeze, but not to its pricing element unless *ex ante* regulation also required that the dominant undertaking's pricing allowed equally efficient competitors to be viable on the downstream market, in which case the application of Article 102 would be redundant.

---

[129] *Telefónica*, recitals 632–633.   [130] ibid recital 634.
[131] Commission Guidance on Article 102, para 82.   [132] ibid.   [133] ibid.

The approach of the Commission in *Telefónica* and in the Guidance on Article 102 is wrong in policy and does not have any legal basis. In margin squeeze cases, the dominant undertaking is always entitled to adduce sufficient evidence tending to show that the margin squeeze is necessary to recoup its investment. The burden rests on the Commission to prove that the dynamic efficiency defence must be rejected.

A different problem is whether it is permissible, in the context of the dynamic efficiency defence, to take account of the competitors' incentives to invest. In *Telefónica*, the Commission rejected, on the facts, an argument that lowering the upstream access price would have depressed the other operators' incentives to invest in their own infrastructure.[134] The question is whether such an argument is capable, as a matter of law, of substantiating an objective justification defence. *Microsoft I* suggests that it is not. What is relevant is the impact of the prohibition on the dominant undertaking's own investment incentives.[135] At least as far as refusal to supply and margin squeeze are concerned, this would appear to be correct, as the need to preserve market-wide investment incentives and avoid free-riding is accounted for in the enhanced intervention threshold that requires not only the elimination of all effective competition, but also consumer harm before a prima facie case of abuse is established and the issue of objective justification even becomes relevant.

Dynamic efficiency is also relevant in tying cases. Two products may perform better together than if used with other complements. Over time, two products may become so closely associated in the eyes of the consumer, that they become a unitary product because the generality of consumers would not require the functionality of either component without the other's. Improved technical performance and the development of a new, integrated product are forms of dynamic efficiency that are without any doubt legitimate objectives under Article 102. In *Microsoft I*, Microsoft put forward a number of arguments to the effect that unbundling Windows and Media player would result in lower performance or a degradation of the system. The Court rejected those arguments for lack of evidence but accepted, implicitly, that, if substantiated, they could have constituted a valid objective justification.[136] Technological tying appears to be suitable to achieving superior integrated performance or developing a new integrated product. Technological tying, however, must be the least restrictive means of achieving the objective. In order to satisfy this limb of the proportionality test, technical integration must not be the result of a deliberate choice of the dominant undertaking to design complementary products that can only operate optimally together. This would be no more than a commitment to tying that enhances rather than reduces the anti-competitive effects of the practice in question.[137] Therefore, tying must be the result of a genuine technological constraint so that the same result cannot be achieved by mixed bundling or specifying minimum standards or requirements for the tied product. Finally, if tying is the least anti-competitive means of achieving superior performance or the development of a new product,

---

[134] *Telefónica*, recital 635.   [135] Case T-201/04 *Microsoft I*, para 709.
[136] ibid paras 1160 and 1163–1166.   [137] Guidance on Art 102, para 53.

it is necessary to balance the negative effects of tying against its benefits. In this balancing exercise, it must be borne in mind that dynamic efficiency is the most important driver of long-term social welfare, which is the objective of Article 102. Provided that technological tying produces genuine and not insubstantial benefits in terms of product improvement or the development of a new product, the key role of innovation under Article 102 suggests that more weight should be given to dynamic efficiency than to the anti-competitive harm of tying. It is true that tying can also depress the innovation incentives of the competitors of the dominant undertaking. However, the benefits of tying, if established by sufficient evidence adduced by the dominant undertaking, are present and tangible, while lower innovation by the foreclosed firms is likely to be somewhat more remote and speculative. Ultimately, the outcome of the balancing test depends on the facts of each individual case but, importantly, the lack of proof on where the balance lies benefits the dominant undertaking.

Dynamic efficiency also plays a key role in exploitative abuses although, as a general principle, a price that is necessary to recoup investments in the relevant product is not excessive in the first place. The question under objective justification relates to the need for the dominant undertaking to invest in future production process or product development or to recoup or finance investments in other products. An example of such an objective justification relates to the need to recoup investments on other projects which did not result in the manufacturing or commercialization of a successful product and to fund ongoing and future investment projects in other products which may also not be successful.[138] When this is the case, it would be wrong to assess the profitability of a product only in relation to its own cost. Instead, the profitability of a product should be assessed in relation to the cost of a portfolio of projects. This line of argument is often advanced to justify high profits in the pharmaceutical industry, where a successful drug must compensate for several unsuccessful R&D projects and finance ongoing and future research into improved or new drugs. This objective justification was advanced in the UK case of *Napp*.[139] The CCAT rejected this argument on principle rather than on the facts. The CCAT held that whether or not a dominant undertaking engaged in excessive pricing depended on whether the price of the product in respect of which that undertaking is dominant is above the competitive level. The Tribunal went on to say:[140]

In our view, it is not appropriate, when deciding whether an undertaking has abused a dominant position by charging excessive prices in a particular market, to take into account

---

[138] ibid para 89, recognizes that investment in failed projects must be taken into account when examining whether a refusal to supply is objectively justified.

[139] *Napp Pharmaceutical Holdings Ltd (No 4) v Director General of Fair Trading* [2002] CAT 1, [2002] Comp AR 13, [2002] ECC 13 (*Napp v DGFT*), paras 353–361. Permission to appeal was refused by the Competition Commission Appeal Tribunal in *Napp Pharmaceutical Holdings Ltd v Director General of Fair Trading (No 5)* [2002] CAT 5, [2002] Comp AR 259, and a further application for leave was rejected by the Court of Appeal in *Napp Pharmaceutical Holdings Ltd v Director General of Fair Trading (No 5)* [2002] EWCA Civ 796, [2002] 4 All ER 376.

[140] *Napp v DGFT*, ibid para 413.

the reasonableness or otherwise of its profits on other, unspecified, markets comprised in some wider but undefined 'portfolio' unrelated to the market in which dominance exists.

To the extent that the Tribunal was saying that, as a matter of law, investments on other markets can never be taken into account, this statement goes too far. The Tribunal was clearly unimpressed by the way Napp advanced its argument in relation to 'unspecified' markets and an 'undefined' portfolio of projects. But, if substantiated by evidence on the facts of the individual case, the defence must be considered on its merits. To remunerate investors for failed R&D projects is a legitimate aim when a high risk of the failure of individual projects is a systemic feature of the industry so that, in order to be viable, an undertaking must engage in a number of projects some of which, statistically, will fail. When this is the case, the first limb of the proportionality test is satisfied. It is a legitimate objective to remunerate investors for failed projects through supra-competitive profits on successful ones. At the very least, however, the dominant undertaking must adduce evidence of its past, present, and future research projects and the statistical probabilities of failure or success of each project as analysed in its business plans. Secondly, a supra-competitive price is capable of achieving the objective. In fact, it is difficult to identify a different way of achieving the same objective. In order to substantiate this element of the defence, the dominant undertaking must provide, at the very least, evidence of past investments and future investment plans showing how profits from successful products have been used to raise capital for other projects. Thirdly, the supra-competitive price must be the least restrictive way of achieving the aim. This means, in practice, that the dominant undertaking must provide evidence that that level of price is appropriate to finance its portfolio of projects. Fourthly, the harm caused by the excessive prices must not be disproportionate to the incentives for R&D which portfolio pricing creates. This step does not require quantification of the future expected welfare benefits of R&D and the deadweight loss caused by supra-competitive prices. It requires asking whether the harm caused by the excessive prices is disproportionate to the objective of financing a portfolio of risky investments. Because dynamic efficiency is a key driver of long-term productivity growth and social welfare, it would appear appropriate at this stage to give more weight to long-term dynamic efficiency than to short-term allocative efficiency.

(3) Social welfare defences

Objective justification is not limited to the pursuit of objectives that can be strictly subsumed under the categories of allocative, productive, and dynamic efficiency. The purpose of Article 102 is to maximize social welfare in the long term. Therefore, pursuit of any objective that contributes to the maximization of long-term social welfare is a legitimate objective that can be pleaded as an objective justification. Social welfare under Article 102 is not a mathematical calculation of the profits of the industry plus the aggregate difference between consumers' willingness to pay for the products and the price they actually pay. It is a much broader concept that includes everything that contributes to the 'well-being of the European Union'.[141] Thus, social welfare 'incorporates in a positive way everything that an individual might value' as well as 'in a negative way harms to his or her person or property, costs and inconveniences, and anything else that the individual might find distasteful'.[142] Any effects that are capable of increasing the overall well-being of society can be pleaded as an objective justification.[143] The test of suitability, however, performs the role of a limiting principle by ruling out the relevance of benefits that have no objective link with the prima facie abusive conduct. Therefore, in order to escape the prohibition of Article 102, it would not be sufficient to use monopoly profits to finance charitable projects, to increase exports so as to reduce the export country's trade deficit, or to raise the salaries of employees. The reason is that the effect of the objective justification defence must be to invalidate the prima facie inference that the conduct under review is harmful to long-term social welfare. This means that the benefits pleaded under objective justification must be capable of neutralizing the anti-competitive effects of the conduct. Benefits unconnected with the conduct in question are unlikely to do so.[144]

Social welfare defences have been rare under Article 102. One notable exception is *Hilti*, a case where the dominant undertaking argued that it was entitled to prevent the use of competitors' complementary products in conjunction with its own products because of safety concerns.[145] The Court of First Instance held that, when there are public authorities entrusted with the enforcement of rules on the sale of dangerous products and misleading advertising, the dominant undertaking is not allowed to take unilateral measures to ensure the safety of its own products.

---

[141] Case C-52/09 *TeliaSonera*, para 22.

[142] L Kaplow and S Shavell, *Fairness versus Welfare* (Cambridge, Mass and London, England, Harvard University Press 2002) 18 (also for further references).

[143] Some commentators argue that the EU competition rules, and Art 101 in particular, require a balancing of competitive harm and other 'public policy' objectives: see eg G Monti, 'Article 81 EC and Public Policy' (2002) 39 CML Rev 1057 and C Townley, *Article 81 EC and Public Policy* (Oxford, Hart Publishing 2009). In some cases, the social welfare approach and the 'public policy' approach would lead to the same results (eg in the field of environmental benefits). However, the 'public policy' approach is broader and could lead to the balancing of competitive harm against perceived benefits of governmental policy that would have nothing to do with the long-term social welfare purpose of Art 102: in relation to Art 101, see eg G Monti, *EC Competition Law* (Cambridge, CUP 2007) 89–123.

[144] A different question is whether the benefits must accrue on the same market where the anti-competitive effects take place or can accrue on different markets or even to the society as a whole. On the position under Art 101(3), see the Guidelines on Art 101(3), para 43, where the Commission takes the view that normally the benefits of an agreement must accrue in the same market where the agreement restricts competition but that there may be cases where the restriction of competition and the beneficial effects can take place on associated markets if the consumers affected are the same. This approach may be overly restrictive: see Case T-86/95 *Compagnie générale maritime v Commission* [2002] ECR II-1011, para 130, where the Court of First Instance held that under Art 101(3) the relevant benefits are not only the benefits accruing on the relevant market but also, in appropriate cases, the advantages 'for every other market on which the agreement in question might have beneficial effects, and even, in a more general sense, for any service the quality or efficiency of which might be improved by the existence of that agreement'. The same solution should apply under Art 102 provided that there is an objective link between the conduct and the benefits as required under the test of suitability.

[145] Case T-30/89 *Hilti*, para 98.

Instead, it must request the intervention of the competent public authorities, which would result in an impartial adjudication of any disputes between the dominant undertaking and its competitors.[146] The Court was probably applying the test of proportionality by pointing out that there were less restrictive means of achieving the objective. This judgment, however, recognizes that, in law, safety concerns can be a valid objective that a dominant undertaking is entitled to pursue and may plead as an objective justification defence.

While *Hilti* may appear to be a rather isolated case, it is important to emphasize that social welfare defences are admissible under objective justification.[147] Indeed, it is desirable that undertakings, including, or perhaps particularly those which are dominant, should be encouraged to contribute to the welfare of society beyond mere profit-maximization by acting consistently with the values of corporate social responsibility (CSR).[148] The European Commission defines CSR as 'a concept whereby companies integrate social and environmental concerns in their business operations and in their interaction with their stakeholders on a voluntary basis'.[149] CSR can play a key role in contributing to sustainable development, innovation, and the competitiveness of the European industry.[150] More broadly, CSR can contribute to a number of socially desirable objectives, including higher levels of social inclusion, investment in skills development, better innovation performance, environmental benefits, a more positive image of business and entrepreneurs in society, greater respect for human rights, environmental protection and core labour standards, especially in developing countries, and poverty reduction and international development.[151]

It must be emphasized that, while any objectives that contribute to the maximization of social welfare in the long term are relevant under Article 102, the

---

[146] ibid paras 115–118. This part of the judgment was not appealed to the Court of Justice: Case C-53/92 P *Hilti*.

[147] The position is the same under Art 101, where, given the narrower definition of the benefits that may be taken into account under Art 101(3), social welfare defences are admissible under Art 101(1): see Case C-309/99 *JCJ Wouters, JW Savelbergh and Price Waterhouse Belastingadviseurs BV v Algemene Raad van de Nederlandse Orde van Advocaten* [2002] ECR I-1577 and Case C-519/04 P *David Meca-Medina and Igor Majcen v Commission* [2006] ECR I-6991 (*Meca-Medina*). There may be different ways of understanding and expressing this test. For example, AP Komninos 'Non-Competition Concerns: Resolution of Conflicts in the Integrated Article 81 EC', The University of Oxford Centre for Competition Law and Policy Working Paper (L) 08/05 (30 June 2005) 10–14 takes the view that Art 101 as a whole can be balanced against non-competition objectives in a sort of weighing-up of different constitutional values, while P Manzini, 'The European Rule of Reason-Crossing the Sea of Doubt' (2002) 23 ECLR 392, 396–397 and fn 24, argues that this test is an appreciation of the anti-competitive effects in their market context and not in the abstract.

[148] Townley, *Article 81 EC and Public Policy*, 35–37. There is a vast literature on CSR: see, also for further references, M Kerr, R Janda, and C Pitts, *Corporate Social Responsibility: A Legal Analysis* (Toronto, LexisNexis 2009); DJ McBarnet, A Voiculescu, and T Campbell (eds), *The New Corporate Accountability: CSR and the Law* (Cambridge, CUP 2007); R Mares, *The Dynamics of Corporate Social Responsibilities* (Boston, Martinus Nijhoff Publishers 2008); A Crane et al (eds), *Oxford Handbook on Corporate Social Responsibility* (Oxford, OUP 2008).

[149] Communication from the Commission to the European Parliament, the Council and the European Economic and Social Committee Implementing the Partnership for Growth and Jobs: Making Europe a Pole of Excellence on Corporate Social Responsibility, COM(2006) 136 final (Brussels, 22 March 2006) (2006 Communication on CSR).

[150] ibid 3.   [151] ibid 4.

objective justification test applies. This means that the conduct of the dominant undertaking must be suitable to achieving the objective, it must be the least restrictive way of doing so, and the competitive harm caused by the conduct must not be disproportionate to its benefits. Therefore, this test differs from cases in which one EU policy prevails over the competition rules when the Treaties authorize the Union or the Member States to set aside the application of Articles 101 and 102.[152] It also differs from a broad balancing test that would require competition authorities and courts to give prevalence to one or another 'public policy' objective whenever the EU competition rules are applied.[153] Social welfare defences allow the positive effects of the conduct on long-term social welfare to be balanced against the anti-competitive harm. The test is no

---

[152] See eg Art 346(1)(b) TFEU, which provides as follows: 'The provisions of the Treaties shall not preclude the application of the following rules: ... (b) any Member State may take such measures as it considers necessary for the protection of the essential interests of its security which are connected with the production of or trade in arms, munitions and war material; such measures shall not adversely affect the conditions of competition in the internal market regarding products which are not intended for specifically military purposes'. The Treaties may implicitly exempt certain activities from the application of the competition rules: see Joined Cases C-115/97 P to C-117/97 P *Brentjens' Handelsonderneming BV v Stichting Bedrijfspensioenfonds voor de Handel in Bouwmaterialen* [1999] ECR I-6025, paras 50–62 and Case C-67/96 *Albany International BV v Stichting Bedrijfspensioenfonds Textielindustrie* [1999] ECR I-5751, paras 52–64, both concerning collective agreements between workers and employers. The key reasoning of the Court is in paras 59 and 60 of the *Albany* case, which are in substantially the same terms as paras 56 and 57 of the *Brentjens' Handelsonderneming* case. In *Albany*, the Court said at paras 59 and 60: 'It is beyond question that certain restrictions of competition are inherent in collective agreements between organisations representing employers and workers. However, the social policy objectives pursued by such agreements would be seriously undermined if management and labour were subject to Article [101(1)] of the Treaty when seeking jointly to adopt measures to improve conditions of work and employment. It therefore follows from an interpretation of the provisions of the Treaty as a whole which is both effective and consistent that agreements concluded in the context of collective negotiations between management and labour in pursuit of such objectives must, by virtue of their nature and purpose, be regarded as falling outside the scope of Article [101(1)] of the Treaty.' The Court was not balancing non-competition objectives against a restriction of competition in the individual case but was examining whether the Treaty applied to a certain type of agreement. It came to the conclusion that it did not. *Albany* and *Brentjens' Handelsonderneming* are, therefore, authorities for the principle that the Treaties can exempt certain conduct from the application of the competition rules not only explicitly, as in the case of Art 346(1)(b) TFEU, but also by implication. These cases do not support the conclusion that a case-by-case balancing of different objectives is always permissible or even required whenever Art 101 or 102 is applied.

[153] A case-by-case balancing of the desirability of allowing competitive harm in order to achieve a non-economic objective would be beyond the boundaries of justiciability: O Odudu, 'The Wider Concerns of Competition Law' (2010) OJLS 1, 13–14. See, however, Townley, *Article 81 EC and Public Policy*, 53 and 93–98, arguing that policy-linking clauses of the Treaties, now of the TFEU, require that all the policy objectives of the Union be taken into account when implementing any Union policy or activity. However, policy-linking clauses would not appear to have direct effect and to give them direct effect through the application of directly effective provisions would be contrary to the principle of conferral: see, persuasively, Odudu, 'The Wider Concerns of Competition Law', 8–9 and O Odudu, *The Boundaries of EC Competition Law: The Scope of Article 81* (Oxford, OUP 2006) 164–170. On direct effect, see Case 26/62 *NV Algemene Transporten Expeditie Onderneming van Gend en Loos v Nederlandse Administratie der Belastigen* [1963] ECR 1; Case C-253/00 *Antonio Muñoz y Cia SA and Superior Fruiticola SA v Frumar Ltd and Redbridge Produce Marketing Ltd* [2002] ECR I-7289; P Craig, 'Once Upon a Time in the West: Direct Effect and Federalization of EEC Law' (1992) 12 OJLS 453; P Craig and G de Búrca, *EU Law: Text, Cases and Materials* (4th edn Oxford, OUP 2007) 277.

different from efficiency defences. This can be illustrated by considering the case of a vertically integrated dominant undertaking controlling an indispensable input. The dominant undertaking introduces a new version of its product that greatly enhances the functionality of the downstream output but refuses to supply the new product for use by its downstream competitors. If a prima facie case of abusive refusal to supply is established, it is necessary to balance the impact of a duty to supply on the *ex ante* investment incentives of the dominant undertaking against the anti-competitive harm of the refusal to supply. If the same dominant undertaking introduces a less polluting version of its product which is incompatible with the technologies of its downstream competitors, under objective justification it is necessary to balance the environmental benefit of the new product against the competitive harm of the refusal to supply. The question is in all respects the same in both cases: whether the competitive harm is qualitatively disproportionate to the benefit. The allocation of the burden of proof is also the same: the risk of the lack of proof of where the ultimate balance lies rests on the competition authority or claimant. And, most fundamentally, the ultimate objective of the test is the same: to ascertain whether the conduct under review is detrimental to long-term social welfare.

F. Conclusion

This chapter examined the defences available to a prima facie case of abuse. Two preliminary issues, however, had to be clarified first: the burden of proof and the thresholds of anti-competitive effects.. As regards the burden of proof, it is clear that under Article 102 the dominant undertaking does not bear such a burden. The burden of proof rests on the competition authority or claimant who bears the ultimate risk of lack of proof of any material fact. However, when a prima facie case of abuse has been established, the dominant undertaking acquires the burden of adducing sufficient evidence to substantiate a defence. It is then for the competition authority or claimant to disprove the defence. If, at the end of the case and on the whole of the evidence, the competition authority or court is not persuaded to the required standard that the defence is not established, there is no abuse. What may appear to some as a technicality is, therefore, an issue of fundamental importance: the allocation of the burden of proof reflects a preference for false acquittals and under-deterrence under Article 102 once there is sufficient evidence that the conduct under review may be beneficial to long-term social welfare. This is so even if a prima facie case of abuse has been established.

The second preliminary question is when the dominant undertaking acquires the evidential burden of pleading and substantiating a defence. This question calls for the determination of the degree of probability of the anti-competitive effects that the competition authority or claimant must prove. Section C of this chapter concludes that there are two anti-competitive effect standards under Article 102: a test of reasonable capability of the conduct to produce anti-competitive effects and a test of likelihood of anti-competitive effects. The reasonable capability test applies when the conduct is examined under a test of intent. If the dominant undertaking intends to harm competition and its conduct is reasonably capable of causing the intended harm, a further likelihood test would be redundant. The intent test means that the dominant undertaking considered it worthwhile to engage in the anti-competitive conduct given its calculation of the costs and benefits of the conduct in the light of the probability of the anti-competitive objective being achieved. Such conduct runs counter to the purpose of Article 102 whether or not, under an objective test, anti-competitive effects are also likely. On the contrary, when conduct is examined under objective tests, namely the as efficient competitor test applied on its own, and not in conjunction with a test of intent, and the consumer harm test, anti-competitive effects must be more likely than not. Once it is clear that Article 102 prohibits certain conduct because of its anti-competitive effects objectively determined, it would be absurd to hold that the prohibition applies if the anti-competitive effects are unlikely to occur. Beyond the tests of reasonable capability and likelihood, there are no other standards of anti-competitive effects under Article 102. Therefore, the Commission and the courts are strongly discouraged from using vague and uncontrolled terminology such as 'risk', 'potential effects', or 'tend' and 'tendency' even if this terminology may ultimately be construed as referring to either of the established tests.

Defences under Article 102 can be divided into mere defences and objective justification. Mere defences do not plead a new primary fact but are limited to challenging the weight or significance of the evidence adduced by the competition authority or claimant. Proportionality defences are a sub-category of mere defences that deserves special consideration. A dominant undertaking is entitled to pursue a commercial interest consistent with the profit-maximizing conduct of a non-dominant undertaking provided it does so in a reasonable and proportionate way. The conduct must thus pursue a legitimate objective, must be suitable to achieving that objective, and must be the least restrictive way of doing so. A proportionality defence never requires the balancing of the benefits of the conduct against its alleged competitive harm because mere defences do not introduce a new primary fact and, thus, there are no benefits to be balanced against the harm. If a proportionality defence is established, the conduct under review is competition on the merits and there is no competitive harm. If the defence is not established, the conduct under review is prima facie abusive. The meeting competition defence is a proportionality defence raising fundamental issues of principle under Article 102. This chapter concludes that the defence is unavailable in predation and margin squeeze cases. In cases relating to above-cost unconditional price cuts, the defence is also unavailable but for the reason that the abuse test in such cases is construed as a very narrow exception to the general principle that the dominant undertaking is entitled to respond to competition by unconditional above-cost discounts. As regards conditional above-cost rebates, meeting competition is an absolute defence whenever the rebates are examined under the as efficient competitor test. Meeting competition is also an absolute defence, without qualification, to a prima facie case of abusive market-distorting discrimination.

Objective justification is a defence that pleads a new primary fact consisting of benefits that contribute to long-term social welfare maximization. The objective justification test has four limbs: (a) the conduct must pursue a legitimate objective; (b) it must be suitable to achieving the objective being pursued; (c) it must not go beyond what is necessary to achieve the objective in question; and (d) the benefits of the conduct must counterbalance or outweigh the disadvantages and must benefit consumers. This test is set out in the case law and achieves an optimal balance of the values and objectives relevant under Article 102. Therefore, the Guidance on Article 102 is unlawful insofar as it departs from this test by raising the bar for dominant undertakings to substantiate an objective justification defence. The Guidance does so in two respects: by requiring that the net effect of the conduct must be at least neutral for consumers and by requiring that effective competition must not be eliminated. Instead, the objective justification test only requires that some benefits accrue to consumers and does not include a limb relating to the non-elimination of effective competition. These conditions, and particularly the latter, would make the objective justification defence inapplicable in practice in the vast majority of cases and are contrary to the overall scheme of Article 102, which considers favourably conduct that may benefit long-term social welfare, particularly because of dynamic efficiency. It is also relevant that the fourth limb of the proportionality test is not a quantitative balancing of comparable positive and negative effects but a qualitative judgment asking whether the competitive harm is disproportionate to the benefits.

Objective justification defences are of two types: efficiency defences and social welfare defences. Efficiency defences plead that the conduct under review increases allocative, productive, or dynamic efficiency. Social welfare defences plead that the conduct under review increases long-term social welfare, broadly construed as the well-being of the European Union, including the values and the positive and negative preferences of society. The benefits in question include environmental and social benefits, provided that the benefits have an objective relation to the conduct under review. It would not be sufficient, therefore, that monopoly profits are used to finance socially desirable initiatives. It is necessary that the conduct is suitable to achieving the benefits, that it is the least restrictive way of doing so, and that the competitive harm is not disproportionate to the benefits. This test is in no way different and no more difficult to apply than the objective justification test which applies to efficiency defences. More importantly, the ultimate objective of the efficiency defences and the social welfare defences is the same: to ensure that conduct that may be beneficial to long-term social welfare is not prohibited even if a prima facie abuse test is established.

In conclusion, this chapter has demonstrated that defences play an important role under Article 102: they recalibrate the balance of enforcement risks that is biased in favour of false convictions and over-deterrence once a prima facie case of abuse is established. An overly restrictive approach to defences would, therefore, be misguided and contrary to the purpose of Article 102. The problem lies not so much in the admissibility of the defences as a matter of law but in the high evidential requirements that the Commission and the case law appear to place on dominant undertakings. This chapter identified two solutions to this problem: first, the clarification of the evidential nature of the burden on the dominant undertaking and, secondly, an increased relative weight to be given to efficiencies and other social welfare objectives pleaded under objective justification compared to the competitive harm established under a prima facie abuse test.

PART IV

ANALYTIC OF THE CONCEPT
OF DOMINANCE

10

Single Dominance

A. Introduction

Article 102 prohibits 'any abuse ... of a dominant position' but does not define what a 'dominant position' is. During the *travaux préparatoires* of the Treaty of Rome of 1957, the text of Article 42, on first reading, referred to 'l'exploitation d'une position dominante sur le marché', but without defining it.[1] The German proposal of 10 September 1956 envisaged that agreements and abuse of dominance should be dealt with in two different Articles. Article 42b related to abuse of dominance and defined dominant firms as 'entreprises ... qui ne doivent affronter aucune concurrence, ou du moins, aucune concurrence sérieuse'.[2] However, the compromise text of Article 42 presented on 20 November 1956 did not contain any definition of dominance.[3] There is no clear explanation as to why this was agreed, but the final text of Article 86 of the Treaty of Rome, now Article 102 TFEU, reflected this approach. As a result, the definition of dominance is based on the teleological interpretation of Article 102, which led the case law to define the dominant position referred to in Article 102 as a position of economic strength enjoyed by an undertaking that enables it to prevent effective competition being maintained on the relevant market by giving it the power to behave to an appreciable extent independently of its competitors, customers, and ultimately consumers.[4] This defi-

---

[1] Conférence intergouvernementale pour le Marché commun et l'Euratom, Secrétariat, Project d'articles en vue de la rédaction du Traité instituant la Communauté du marché européen, Bruxelles, le 17 juillet 1956 Mar Com 17.

[2] Projet (remis par M Tiesing) Bruxelles, le 10 septembre 1956 MAE 252 f756 mv, Art 42b.

[3] Conférence intergouvernementale pour le Marché commun et l'Euratom, Secrétariat, Groupe du Marché commun, Projet de Rédaction sur le règles de concurrence établi le 20 novembre 1956 par un groupe d'experts compte tenu des échanges de vues intervenues le 19 novembre 1956 en groupe restreint (MAE 602 f/56 js).

[4] Case 27/76 *United Brands Co and United Brands Continentaal BV v Commission* [1978] ECR 207, para 65; Case 85/76 *Hoffmann-La Roche v Commission* [1979] ECR 461, para 38; Case 322/81 *NV Nederlandsche Banden Industrie Michelin v Commission* [1983] ECR 3461 (*'Michelin I'*), para 29; Case C-311/84 *Centre Belge d'Etudes de Marché—Télémarketing (CBEM) v Compagnie Luxembourgeoise de Télédiffusion (CLT) and Information Publicité Benelux (IPB)* [1985] ECR 3261 (*Télémarketing*), para 16; Case 30/87 *Corinne Bodson v Pompes Funèbres des Régions Libérées SA* [1988] ECR 2479 (*Bodson*), para 26; Joined Cases C-395/96 P and C-396/96 P *Compagnie Maritime Belge Transports SA v Commission* [2000] ECR I-1365, para 34; Case T-340/03 *France Télécom SA v Commission* [2007] ECR II-107, para 99, upheld in Case C-202/07 P *France Télécom SA v Commission* [2009] ECR I-2369, para 103; Case T-282/02 *Cementbouw Handel & Industrie BV v Commission* [2006] ECR II-319, para 195; Case T-321/05 *AstraZeneca AB v Commission* [2010] OJ C221/33, para 239,

nition is not self-explanatory. As a result, it has been interpreted differently in different contexts. Two models of dominance are the main contenders: a structuralist model that regards dominance as coextensive with substantial and durable market power,[5] and a behavioural or dynamic model that regards dominance as the ability to harm competition.[6] The choice between these two models has significant implications for the analysis of market power, barriers to entry, and countervailing buyer power.

This chapter discusses the concept of dominance and demonstrates that, under Article 102, dominance is the ability to harm competition.[7] This dynamic concept of dominance is consistent with the objective of Article 102, which is not to address market failures resulting from market power but to prohibit certain unilateral conduct that harms long-term social welfare. Having defined dominance, this chapter goes on to examine the three necessary elements of the dominance test: substantial and durable market power, the presence of dynamic barriers to entry, and the absence of countervailing buyer power.

B. Dominance as the ability to harm competition

Because Article 102 does not define dominance, the Court of Justice was called upon to frame the concept of dominant position through teleological interpretation. This interpretative problem was addressed for the first time in the *United Brands* case.[8] The Court articulated its deductive reasoning in three paragraphs.[9] First, it stated that Article 102 is an application of the general objective then set

---

under appeal in Case C-457/10 P *AstraZeneca AB v Commission* [2010] OJ C301/18; Case C-280/08 P *Deutsche Telekom AG v Commission* [2010] OJ C346/4, para 170; Case C-52/09 *Konkurrensverket v TeliaSonera Sverige AB* [2011] OJ C103/3 (*TeliaSonera*), para 23.

[5] Communication from the Commission—Guidance on the Commission's enforcement priorities in applying Article 82 of the EC Treaty to abusive exclusionary conduct by dominant undertakings [2009] OJ C45/7 ('Guidance on Art 102'), para 11.

[6] This is very clear in certain cases, eg Case 27/76 *United Brands* and Case T-210/01 *General Electric v Commission* [2005] ECR II-5575, both discussed at 328–331, 335–337 and 338–341 below.

[7] In the assessment of single dominance, there is generally no need to examine separately the incentive of the firm in question to harm competition because Art 102 only applies when actual harmful conduct has been implemented. However, as a matter of logic, and in the absence of irrational motives, an undertaking would not commit an abuse, even if it were able to harm competition, if it had no incentive to do so. Normally, the incentive to harm competition is, therefore, relevant to the test of abuse rather than to the test of dominance: see eg the intent test for anti-competitive tying at 211–217 above. However, in oligopolistic collective dominance, the incentive to harm competition is a necessary element of the dominance test: see 372–373 and 382–383 below. These apparently diverging approaches are not inconsistent because dominance and abuse are inextricably intertwined. In principle, they are not even separate tests: dominance is, in fact, an element of the abuse test. It is only as a matter of expediency and judicial economy that dominance is treated as a threshold question: if a firm is not able to harm competition, there is no need to inquire further into the effects of its conduct.

[8] Case 27/76 *United Brands*, paras 58–129. In the previous *Continental Can* case, the need for a definition of dominance did not arise: Case 6/72 *Europemballage Corp and Continental Can Co Inc v Commission* [1973] ECR 215 (*Continental Can*).

[9] Case 27/76 *United Brands*, paras 63–65. The logical structure and wording of these paragraphs is almost identical to para 38 of Case 85/76 *Hoffmann-La Roche*.

out in Article 3 of the Treaty of Rome: the institution of a system ensuring that competition in the internal market is not distorted.[10] Secondly, it summarized the content of the prohibition in Article 102.[11] Thirdly, it defined dominance as 'a position of economic strength enjoyed by an undertaking which enables it to prevent effective competition being maintained on the relevant market by giving it the power to behave to an appreciable extent independently of its competitors, customers, and ultimately consumers'.[12] It follows from the deductive structure of the Court's reasoning and from its teleological method of interpretation that the key constitutive element in the definition is the ability to prevent effective competition being maintained on the relevant market. Because the 'undistorted competition' protected by Article 102 has the objective of promoting long-term social welfare, the ability to prevent effective competition being maintained on the relevant market is the ability to restrict competition in such as way as to harm long-term social welfare. Since dominant firms may harm competition in three ways, namely by exclusionary conduct,[13] by exploitation of customers,[14] or by discrimination,[15] dominance must be defined more generally as an undertaking's ability to cause the competitive harm prohibited by Article 102 or, which is the same, to harm competition within the meaning of Article 102. The Court of Justice in *TeliaSonera* confirmed that this teleological definition of the concept of dominance is still valid under the new Treaties.[16]

The case law explicitly requires that the dominant undertaking must be able to harm competition. Yet, currently the case law and the decisional practice of the Commission place too much emphasis on the economic strength of the undertaking, as a way of describing its substantial and durable market power, and too little

---

[10] Case 27/76 *United Brands*, para 63. The current structure of the TEU and the TFEU is different from the original structure of the Treaty of Rome. However, it is still possible to say that Arts 101 and 102 have the objective of ensuring that competition in the internal market is not distorted. The establishment of a system of undistorted competition was not defined as an objective of the European Economic Community at the time of the Court's ruling in *United Brands*. Nor is it now. However, it is a necessary building block of the internal market: see TFEU, Protocol (27) on the Internal Market and Competition. Therefore, this part of the reasoning of the Court in the *United Brands* case still holds: see Case C-52/09 *TeliaSonera*, paras 20–23.

[11] Case 27/76 *United Brands*, para 64.   [12] ibid para 65.

[13] Joined Cases 40/73 to 48/78, 50/73, 54/73 to 56/73, 111/73, 113/73, and 114/73 *Coöperatieve Vereniging 'Suiker Unie' v Commission* [1975] ECR 1663 (*Suiker Unie*), para 523; Case 27/76 *United Brands*, paras 65–68; Case 85/76 *Hoffmann-La Roche*, para 38; Case 322/81 *Michelin I*, para 30; *ECS/AKZO* [1985] OJ L374/1, recital 18, upheld in Case C-62/86 *AKZO Chemie BV v Commission* [1991] ECR I-3359; Case T-83/91 *Tetra Pak International SA v Commission* [1994] ECR II-755 (*Tetra Pak II*), para 137, upheld in Case C-333/94 P *Tetra Pak International SA v Commission* [1996] ECR I-5951 (*Tetra Pak II*); Case T-203/01 *Manufacture française des pneumatiques Michelin v Commission* [2003] ECR II-4071 (*Michelin II*), paras 197–199; Case C-95/04 P *British Airways plc v Commission* [2007] ECR I-2331, para 58.

[14] Case 66/86 *Ahmed Saeed Flugreisen and Silver Line Reisebüro GmbH v Zentrale zur Bekämpfung unlauteren Wettbewerbs eV* [1989] ECR 803, para 43; Case 395/87 *Ministère Public v Jean-Louis Tournier* [1989] ECR 2521 (*Tournier*), para 34; Case C-52/07 *Kanal 5 Ltd v STIM* [2008] ECR I-9275.

[15] *Alpha Flight Services/Aéroports de Paris* [1998] OJ L230/10, upheld in Case T-128/98 *Aéroports de Paris v Commission* [2000] ECR II-3929, appeal dismissed in Case C-82/01 P *Aéroports de Paris v Commission* [2002] ECR I-9297.

[16] Case C-52/09 *TeliaSonera*, paras 20–23.

emphasis on its ability to exclude rivals. However, the ability to harm competition is as important an element of the definition of dominance as the substantial and durable market power element. Article 102 is not concerned with public intervention in markets that do not function optimally due to market power problems, but with the harmful conduct of firms with substantial and durable market power. If a firm is not able to harm competition, it follows that it is not the type of firm to which Article 102 applies. Furthermore, while on its face the case law appears to devote little attention to the ability of the allegedly dominant undertaking to cause competitive harm, a closer analysis demonstrates that the ability to exclude plays a fundamental role in the assessment of dominance. In *General Electric*, for instance, General Electric's vertical integration was more relevant to General Electric's ability to foreclose than to its durable and substantial market power.[17] The Court of First Instance found that General Electric's leasing subsidiary foreclosed one of the possible routes by which General Electric's rivals could compete with it[18] and that it enabled General Electric to win contracts it would not have otherwise won.[19] Furthermore, General Electric's financing subsidiary, General Electric Capital, had been instrumental in securing *de facto* exclusivity with a major customer. That was sufficient to establish that General Electric Capital contributed to General Electric pre-merger dominance.[20] That dominance is the ability to harm competition is further demonstrated by the frequent description in the case law of the dominant undertaking as an 'unavoidable' or 'obligatory' 'trading partner'.[21] This may be due to product differentiation and brand loyalty,[22] capacity constraints of rivals,[23] or risks and costs associated with switching to competitors.[24] These factors

---

[17] Case T-210/01 *General Electric*, paras 182–242.   [18] ibid para 200.
[19] ibid paras 205–224.   [20] ibid para 225–228.
[21] Case 85/76 *Hoffmann-La Roche*, paras 39–41; Case 7/82 *Gesellschaft zur Verwertung von Leistungsschutzrechten mbH (GVL) v Commission* [1983] ECR 483, para 42; Case T-229/94 *Deutsche Bahn AG v Commission* [1997] ECR II-1689, para 57 ('economic dependence'); Case T-65/98 *Van den Bergh Foods Ltd v Commission* [2003] ECR II-4653, para 156, upheld in Case C-552/03 P *Unilever Bestfoods (Ireland) Ltd, formerly Van den Bergh Foods Ltd v Commission* [2006] ECR I-9091; *Clearstream* [2009] C165/7 (summary decision), recital 224, upheld in Case T-301/04 *Clearstream Banking AG and Clearstream International SA v Commission* [2009] ECR II-3155, para 73 ('indispensable commercial partner') and para 146 ('indispensable trading partner').
[22] Case 322/81 *Michelin I*, para 56 (the Court said that dealers in the Netherlands could not afford not to sell Michelin tyres and that this rendered Michelin 'largely immune to competition'); Case C-62/86 *AKZO*, para 58 (the fact that AKZO offered a range of products wider than that of its main rivals was one of the factors that contributed to AKZO's dominant position); Case T-65/98 *Van den Bergh Foods*, para 156 (Van den Bergh had the most extensive and most popular range of products on the relevant market); *Generics/AstraZeneca* [2006] OJ L332/24, recitals 542 and 552 (AstraZeneca had a first mover advantage in relation to later entrants which was particularly important in the light of doctors' inertia and brand loyalty in prescribing behaviour); *Microsoft* [2007] OJ L32/23 (*Microsoft I*), recitals 516–522 (discussing network effects), upheld in Case T-201/04 *Microsoft Corp v Commission* [2007] ECR II-3601 (*Microsoft I*).
[23] Joined Cases 6/73 and 7/73 *Istituto Chemioterapico Italiano SpA and Commercial Solvents Corp v Commission* [1974] ECR 223 (*Commercial Solvents*), paras 13–16; Case 85/76 *Hoffmann-La Roche*, paras 33–34; *Intel* [2009] OJ C227/13 (summary decision), recital 853, under appeal in Case T-286/09 *Intel Corp v Commission* [2009] OJ C220/41.
[24] *Tetra Pak I (BTG-licence)* [1988] OJ L272/27, recital 37; *IMS Health/NDC: Interim Measures* [2002] OJ L59/18, recital 83; Case T-219/99 *British Airways plc v Commission* [2003] ECR II-5917, para 216, upheld in Case C-95/04 P *British Airways*; *Microsoft I*, recital 463.

may be relevant as barriers to entry or expansion.[25] The description of the dominant undertaking as an unavoidable trading partner, however, reveals that the case law considers these factors also to be directly relevant to the dominant undertaking's ability to harm competition. In a rebate case, for instance, the theory of harm relies on the proof that a share of the dominant undertaking's demand is not contestable by rivals. Customers, therefore, must buy a certain percentage of their requirements from the dominant undertaking. If this is true, the latter may have the ability to leverage the market power it has over the non-contestable share of the demand on the contestable share of the demand. This would be by setting its rebate schedule so that customers have a strong incentive to purchase additional units of the product above the non-contestable share. If there are economies of scale or network effects, entry may be deterred or existing rivals excluded or marginalized.[26] Perhaps even more clearly, dominance is defined as the ability to foreclose downstream rivals in vertical refusal to supply cases. For a vertical refusal to supply to be abusive, the case law requires that the product the dominant undertaking refuses to supply must be an 'indispensable' input.[27] The EU courts regard the 'indispensability' condition as an element of the abuse. It is, instead, better regarded as evidence of dominance relevant to the assessment of the dominant undertaking's ability to exclude rivals.

While the case law on Article 102 does not set out a coherent framework for the analysis of the allegedly dominant undertaking's ability to foreclose, the Guidelines on Non-horizontal Mergers[28] contain a rather extensive examination of the ability of the merged entity to exclude rivals. There is a clear analogy between non-horizontal mergers and the analysis of abuse of dominance under Article 102. Under the 2004 Merger Regulation, the Commission must assess whether a concentration would significantly impede effective competition, in particular as a result of the creation or strengthening of a dominant position in the internal market or a substantial part of it.[29] Dominance under Article 102 is defined as a position of economic strength that enables the undertaking in question to prevent effective competition being maintained on the relevant market by affording it the power to behave, to an appreciable extent, independently of its competitors,

---

[25] Barriers to entry may be provisionally defined as factors that make entry difficult or impossible, thus placing firms wishing to enter the market at a disadvantage vis-à-vis incumbent firms. Barriers to expansion can be provisionally defined as factors that make expansion difficult or impossible. These concepts will be further discussed at 342–355 below. From now on, barriers to entry will include barriers to expansion unless the context clearly requires otherwise.

[26] Guidance on Art 102, paras 37–45; *Intel*, recitals 1574–1575.

[27] Case C-311/84 *Télémarketing*, para 26; Joined Cases C-241/91 P and C-242/91 P *Radio Telefís Eireann (RTE) and Independent Television Publications Ltd (ITP) v Commission* [1995] ECR I-743 ('*Magill*'), para 53–56; Case C-7/97 *Oscar Bronner GmbH & Co KG v Mediaprint Zeitungs- und Zeitschriftenverlag GmbH & Co KG* [1998] ECR I-7791, paras 43–46; Case T-504/93 *Tierce Ladbroke SA v Commission* [1997] ECR II-923, para 132; Case C-418/01 *IMS Health GmbH & Co KG v NDC Health GmbH & Co KG* [2004] ECR I-5039, paras 28–30.

[28] Commission Notice: Guidelines on the assessment of non-horizontal mergers under the Council Regulation on the control of concentrations between undertakings [2008] OJ C265/6 ('Guidelines on Non-horizontal Mergers').

[29] Council Regulation (EC) 139/2004 of 20 January 2004 on the control of concentrations between undertakings ('2004 Merger Regulation') [2004] OJ L24/1, Art 2(2) and (3).

customers and, ultimately, consumers.[30] The two elements of impediment of effective competition and the existence of a dominant position feature in both tests, albeit in different contexts.[31] Furthermore, concerns about non-horizontal mergers relate mainly to foreclosure, as do concerns about abuse of dominance. As a consequence of the focus on foreclosure, the assessment of non-horizontal mergers, which include vertical and conglomerate mergers, often consists in a prospective analysis of the ability of the merged entity to behave in a way which would amount to an abuse under Article 102, provided that the merged entity holds a dominant position. Obviously, the merger test is an *ex ante* assessment, while the abuse test applies to market conduct observable *ex post*. However, this difference relates more to the standard of review and the standard of proof than it does to the substantive analysis of the ability to harm competition. Therefore, the analysis of the ability to harm competition in non-horizontal mergers is capable of casting light on the concept of dominance as the ability to harm competition under Article 102.

In the Guidelines on Non-Horizontal Mergers, the Commission distinguishes different types of foreclosure: (a) input foreclosure in vertical mergers; (b) customer foreclosure in vertical mergers; and (c) tying and bundling. Input foreclosure in vertical mergers is similar to the abuse of refusal to supply an indispensable input and an upstream margin squeeze.[32] In a merger, input foreclosure may raise competition concerns if it relates to an important input,[33] while under Article 102 the input must be indispensable.[34] The nature of the input is not, however, the only element relevant to the ability of the upstream firm to harm competition. Upstream rivals supplying the same product must be capacity constrained, face decreasing returns to scale, offer significantly less efficient alternatives, or have exclusive supply arrangements with the allegedly dominant undertaking.[35]

The analogy between customer foreclosure in vertical mergers and abuse of dominance is less compelling because abusive conduct that forecloses access to customers (as opposed to access to upstream inputs) does not necessarily presuppose that the dominant undertaking is vertically integrated. Nevertheless, it is possible to draw a parallel between the customer foreclosure strategies of a vertically integrated merged entity and the customer foreclosure strategies of a non-vertically integrated dominant undertaking. Vertical integration can be seen as the ultimate customer foreclosure strategy in that a downstream customer becomes part of the upstream undertaking. Thus, customer foreclosure in vertical mergers is analogous to abusive practices that restrict rivals' access to downstream customers. The ability to foreclose access to downstream customers depends on the characteristics of

---

[30] Case 85/76 *Hoffmann-La Roche*, para 38.

[31] The creation or strengthening of a dominant position is not a necessary element of the merger test under the 2004 Merger Regulation, while the existence of a dominant position is a necessary element of the test for abuse under Art 102.

[32] ie a margin squeeze that is the result of an anti-competitively high upstream price.

[33] Guidelines on Non-horizontal Mergers, para 34.

[34] Case C-311/84 *Télémarketing*, para 26; Joined Cases C-241/91 P and C-242/91 P *Magill*, paras 53–56; Case C-7/97 *Oscar Bronner*, paras 43–46; Case T-504/93 *Tierce Ladbroke*, para 132; Case C-418/01 *IMS*, paras 28–30.

[35] Guidelines on Non-horizontal Mergers, para 36.

the market and on the type of conduct in question. In exclusivity and rebate cases, for instance, the ability to exclude depends on the extent to which the allegedly dominant undertaking is an 'unavoidable trading partner',[36] the downstream customers have coordination problems, the market is characterized by economies of scale or scope or network effects,[37] and rivals are able to deploy effective and timely counter-strategies, sustainable over time.[38] The Guidelines on Non-Horizontal Mergers do not discuss customer foreclosure strategies that do not presuppose vertical integration such as predation and margin squeeze resulting from predatory downstream prices. However, the principle that a firm is only dominant if it is able to harm competition still applies. Key factors will be the presence of significant entry barriers, asymmetric access to finance and imperfect capital markets, economies of scale or scope, and network effects.[39]

In conglomerate mergers, competition concerns arise from the ability and incentive of the merged entity to engage in tying or bundling with an overall negative impact on effective competition.[40] The analogy with abuse cases is strong because in both conglomerate mergers and abuse cases the same undertaking supplies two or more products across two or more markets. The factors relevant to the ability to exclude are the characteristics of the products themselves,[41] market power on at least one of the affected markets, with the undertaking in question offering a differentiated product for which there are only a few limited alternatives or rivals being capacity constrained,[42] the presence of a large pool of customers buying all the products concerned,[43] economies of scale, dynamic implications of current demand for future demand, network effects,[44] the ability to commit to a lasting tying or bundling strategy,[45] and the ability of rivals to deploy effective and timely counter-strategies, sustainable over time.[46]

C. Dominance as market power

The case law under Article 102 and the Guidelines on Non-horizontal Mergers confirm that a meaningful analysis of the ability of a firm to harm competition can be carried out. Under this dynamic dominance test, the requirement of a certain level of pre-abuse market power as a condition for a finding of dominance is not a matter of logical necessity because unilateral conduct may cause harm to competition even without any substantial pre-abuse market power. For instance, substantial market power is not a prerequisite for predation. In the presence of asymmetric access to financing, a predatory strategy may be successful because it allows a non-dominant undertaking to obtain market power which it did not

---

[36] ibid.   [37] ibid para 62.   [38] ibid para 67.

[39] eg PL Joskow and AK Klevorick, 'A Framework for Analyzing Predatory Pricing Policy' (1979) 89 Yale LJ 213 and J Tirole, *The Theory of Industrial Organization* (Cambridge Mass, MIT Press 1988) 379.

[40] Guidelines on Non-horizontal Mergers, para 93.   [41] ibid para 98.

[42] ibid para 99.   [43] ibid para 100.   [44] ibid para 101.   [45] ibid para 102.

[46] ibid para 103.

have before.[47] Similarly, in a patent ambush case, an undertaking with no market power at all can obtain substantial and durable market power, or even a monopoly, by concealing the existence of patents that are necessary for a standard adopted in an industry-wide standard-setting process, in which the existence of the patents in question should have been disclosed.[48] Unilateral conduct in such cases may cause harm to long-term social welfare. A definition of dominant position as the ability to harm competition in the absence of pre-abuse market power would be consistent with the objectives of Article 102.[49] There are, however, good reasons for requiring proof of pre-abuse market power in Article 102 cases. Competitive harm caused by purely unilateral conduct is highly unlikely in the absence of some degree of pre-existing market power.[50] Proof of pre-abuse market power does, therefore, act as a filter to sift out cases in which the likelihood of competitive harm is low and, conversely, the likelihood of a false conviction may be very high.[51] Furthermore, to the extent that a false acquittal may occur, conduct which creates market power may be addressed under Article 101, if it does so through agreements, concerted practices, or decisions of associations of undertakings,[52] under

[47] J Church and R Ware, *Industrial Organization: A Strategic Approach* (Boston, McGraw-Hill 2000) 648; M Motta, *Competition Policy: Theory and Practice* (Cambridge, CUP 2004) 443; R O'Donoghue and JA Padilla, *The Law and Economics of Article 82 EC* (Oxford, Hart Publishing 2006) 290–292 and 296; J Vickers, 'Some Economics of Abuse of Dominance', Department of Economics, University of Oxford, Discussion Paper 376 (2007) 3.

[48] eg *Rambus* [2010] OJ C30/14. See G Ohana, M Hansen, and O Shah, 'Disclosure and Negotiation of Licensing Terms Prior to Adoption of Industry Standards: Preventing Another Patent Ambush?' (2003) 24 ECLR 644; EG Petritsi, 'The Case of Unilateral Patent Ambush under EC Competition Rules' (2005) 28 World Competition 25; G Ghidini, *Intellectual Property and Competition Law* (Cheltenham, Edward Elgar 2006) 103–104; KJ Koelman, 'An Exceptio Standardis: Do We Need an IP Exemption for Standards?' (2006) 37 Intl Rev IP & Comp L 823, 838; S Subramanian, 'Patent Trolls in Thickets: Who is Fishing under the Bridge?' (2008) 30 EIPR 182, 186.

[49] It is theoretically conceivable, for instance, to interpret Art 102 as requiring pre-abuse commercial power and the ability to obtain, maintain, or increase market power post-abuse: G Monti, 'The Concept of Dominance in Article 82' (2006) 2 European Competition Journal 31, 38–42.

[50] J Vickers, 'Market Power in Competition Cases' (2006) 2 European Competition Journal 3, 12; F Dethmers and N Dodoo, 'The Abuse of Hoffmann-La Roche: The Meaning of Dominance under EC Competition Law' (2006) 27 ECLR 537, 544; CE Mosso et al, 'Article 82' in J Faull and A Nikpay (eds), *The EC Law of Competition* (2nd edn Oxford, OUP 2007) 313, 321, and 326; G Monti, *EC Competition Law* (Cambridge, CUP 2007) 125; E Arezzo, 'Is There a Role for Market Definition and Dominance in an Effects-based Approach?' in M Mackenrodt, B Conde Gallego, and S Enchelmaier (eds), *Abuse of Dominant Position: New Interpretation, New Enforcement Mechanisms?* (Berlin, Springer 2008) 21, 47.

[51] J Vickers, 'Market Power in Competition Cases' 12; Monti, 'The Concept of Dominance in Article 82', 46–48; G Werden, 'Competition Policy on Exclusionary Conduct: Towards an Effects-based Analysis' (2006) 2 European Competition Journal 53, 55; Monti, *EC Competition Law*, 126–127; E Rousseva, *Rethinking Exclusionary Abuses in EU Competition Law* (Oxford, Hart Publishing 2010) 476.

[52] Communication from the Commission Notice—Guidelines on the application of Article 81(3) of the Treaty [2004] OJ C101/97 ('Guidelines on Art 101(3)'), para 26; S Stroux, 'Article 82—Dominance and Oligopolies' in G Amato and C-D Ehlermann, *EC Competition Law: A Critical Assessment* (Oxford, Hart Publishing 2007) 209, 235–239; Monti, *EC Competition Law*, 155–157; P Roth and V Rose (eds), *Bellamy & Child European Community Law of Competition* (6th edn Oxford, OUP 2008) 913–915 and 940–941.

the 2004 Merger Regulation,[53] or as an exploitative abuse under Article 102.[54] Therefore, the requirement of pre-abuse market power takes account of the risk of conviction and over-deterrence by raising the substantive threshold for intervention. In order to perform this function, pre-abuse market power under Article 102 must be both substantial and durable. The ability of a firm with no substantial and durable market power to harm competition is too remote a possibility to justify the risk of error and over-deterrence that the application of Article 102 to any firm with some degree of market power would entail. Many firms are capable of profitably increasing prices above the competitive level but would be unlikely to have the ability to harm long-term social welfare.[55]

The economic definition of market power must be adapted to the legal requirement of dominance. In EU law, the ability to set prices above MC is only relevant to the extent that it tends to prove that the firm in question has the ability to harm competition. Instead, the Guidance on Article 102 regards the concept of dominance as coextensive with substantial and durable market power. Citing *Hoffmann La-Roche*[56] and *United Brands*,[57] the Commission explains that the notion of independence in the case law is related to the degree of competitive constraint exerted on the dominant undertaking.[58] The Commission goes on to say that 'an undertaking which is capable of profitably increasing prices above the competitive level for a significant period of time does not face sufficiently effective competitive constraints and can thus generally be regarded as dominant'.[59] This definition fails to add that prices must be set significantly above the competitive level. However, the Guidance on Art 102 envisages that the market power of a dominant firm must be substantial.[60] Substantial market power implies the power to set prices significantly above the competitive level. Overall, therefore, the Commission's approach to the effect that dominance requires substantial and durable market power is correct. Yet, dominance is not—as the Commission purports to say—substantial and durable market power. Dominance is the ability to harm competition. The relationship between the concept of dominance as the ability to harm competition and substantial and durable market power as an element of dominance is not, however, easily discernible in the case law. This is probably at the root of the Commission's misunderstanding. The same lack of clarity in the case law has led some commentators to the different conclusion that dominance is commercial power rather than market power. They argue that the case law focuses on whether the dominant undertaking has certain commercial advantages over its rivals, whether it can deploy tactics that cannot be replicated by competitors, and whether it is an unavoidable trading partner for its customers. The case law would not appear to analyse whether the

---

[53] 2004 Merger Regulation, Art 2(2) and (3).

[54] See eg the Commission's commitments decision in *Rambus*.

[55] eg firms in high-technology ('new economy') markets: Mosso, 'Article 82', 331. More broadly, any firm in a differentiated market or in a market characterized by a high rate of innovation may have some market power for a significant period of time. Its market power, however, may not be substantial and may be consistent with effective competition on the market.

[56] Case 85/76 *Hoffmann-La Roche*, para 38. [57] Case 27/76 *United Brands*, para 65.

[58] Guidance on Art 102, para 8. [59] ibid para 11. [60] ibid para 10.

dominant undertaking has the 'power to reduce output and increase prices'.[61] This argument is correct to the extent that dominance is not market power but the ability to harm competition. But the Commission is also correct in that market power is a necessary element of dominance. The leading cases in which dominance was thoroughly examined support this conclusion.

In *United Brands*, the Court of Justice held that market definition was a necessary step for the assessment of the 'economic power of the undertaking concerned'.[62] The Court did not define 'economic power' as the power to set prices above the competitive level. However, the Court held that, in order to determine whether the firm in question was dominant on the relevant market, it was 'necessary first of all to examine its structure and then the situation on the said market as far as competition [was] concerned'.[63] A number of factors relating to the 'structure' of the undertaking may, at first sight, be understood simply as evidence of commercial superiority. In fact, when analysed more closely and in the context of the case as a whole, it becomes clear that these factors are elements of an analysis of market power as a prerequisite for the dominant firm's ability to harm competition. This was apparent, for instance, when the Court examined the dominant firm's vertical integration, noting that it owned large plantations in Central and South America and could secure any additional requirements from independent producers by virtue of contractual arrangements with some of them.[64] Therefore, the Court concluded, the dominant firm 'knows that it can comply with all the requests which it receives'.[65] This conclusion suggests that the Court was examining whether the dominant firm was capacity constrained. The absence of capacity constraints is a relevant factor in a market power analysis. If a firm is not capacity constrained and its competitors are, the former may have a degree of power over price because competitors cannot meet any additional demand. The finding that the dominant firm had constantly invested in R&D in order to improve the productivity of its plantations[66] must also be read as part of a market power assessment. That finding is complemented by the observation that rivals entering the market would have to incur 'large capital investments required for the creation and running of banana

---

[61] Monti, 'The Concept of Dominance in Article 82', 38–43.

[62] Case 27/76 *United Brands*, para 11. The definition of the relevant market has the objective of identifying the short-term competitive constraints on a firm: Commission Notice on the definition of the relevant market for the purposes of Community competition law [1997] OJ C372/5 ('Commission Notice on Market Definition'); Motta, *Competition Policy*, 101–102; J Lücking and S Simon, 'Definition of the Relevant Market' in G Drauz and CW Jones (eds), *EU Competition Law: Volume II—Mergers and Acquisitions* (Leuven, Claeys & Casteels 2006) 151, 151–156; O'Donoghue and Padilla, *The Law and Economics of Article 82 EC*, 63–64; MB Coate and JH Fischer, 'A Practical Guide to the Hypothetical Monopolist Test for Market Definition' (2008) 4 J Comp L & Econ 1031, 1031–1032; C Veljanovski, 'Markets Without Substitutes: Substitution Versus Constraints as the Key to Market Definition' (2010) 31 ECLR 122, 122. The case law considers market definition as a necessary preliminary step in the assessment of dominance: Case 6/72 *Continental Can*, para 32; Case 27/76 *United Brands*, para 10; Case 85/76 *Hoffmann-La Roche*, para 21. Market definition, though a question of great practical importance, is outside the scope of this monograph as it raises problems of a technical nature that are not immediately relevant to the understanding of the core values of Art 102.

[63] Case 27/76 *United Brands*, para 67.   [64] ibid paras 71–76.

[65] ibid para 77.   [66] ibid para 82.

plantations, the need to increase sources of supply in order to avoid the effects of fruit diseases and bad weather'.[67] Therefore, the Court examined the structure of the firm in question not to point out that it had a commercial advantage over its rivals but in order to assess the barriers to entry to the relevant market. The same can be said of the dominant firm's transport and distribution network[68] and its substantial expenditure in advertising.[69] Finally, the Court noted that the dominant firm benefited from economies of scale,[70] which the Court explicitly characterized as a barrier to entry.[71] The Court's analysis of 'the situation with regard to competition' is also consistent with the idea that market power is a necessary condition for a firm to be able to harm competition.[72] The Court found the circumstance that customers continued to buy from the dominant firm, despite the fact that its prices were the highest, to be 'a particular feature of the dominant position' and 'determinative in this case'.[73] In the absence of market power one would expect customers to switch from the supplier with the highest prices to the rivals' cheaper products. The examination of the relevant factors tending to establish dominance culminates in the statement that United Brand's 'economic strength has thus enabled it to adopt a flexible overall strategy directed against new competitors establishing themselves on the whole of the relevant market'.[74] In conclusion, the Court's analysis of dominance in *United Brands* focused mainly on market power but not as an end in itself. Market power is relevant because it gives the dominant firm the ability to harm competition.

The case that most clearly confirms that EU law requires a finding of market power to establish dominance is *Hoffmann-La Roche*.[75] In that case, the Commission had relied on factors relating to the commercial strength or superiority of the dominant firm as probative of dominance. The Court of Justice rejected that approach. First, it held that the stability of an undertaking's market share over time could not be evidence of dominance. The fact that market shares have been stable over time may be the result either of effective competition or of the undertaking's ability to behave independently of competitors.[76] The stability of market shares in itself is, therefore, inconclusive as evidence of dominance.[77] Once dominance has been established, on the other hand, the stability of market shares may be evidence that the dominant position is being maintained.[78] The Court also rejected the argument that the position of Roche as the world's largest vitamins supplier, its turnover, and its worldwide operations were relevant to the assessment of Roche's dominance. The Court held that the competitive assessment had to be carried out market by market and that the volume of overall production across different markets did not in itself give an undertaking a competitive advantage over its competitors. Thus, mere commercial advantages were not considered to be evidence of dominance. On the contrary, while relying on certain structural

---

[67] ibid para 122.   [68] ibid paras 78–81, 83–86, and 122.
[69] ibid paras 87–93 and 122.   [70] ibid para 95.   [71] ibid para 122.
[72] ibid paras 97–129.   [73] ibid para 128.   [74] ibid para 121.
[75] Case 85/76 *Hoffmann-La Roche*.
[76] Namely, the fact that the undertaking is shielded from effective competitive pressure.
[77] Case 85/76 *Hoffmann-La Roche*, para 44.   [78] ibid.

indicators, particularly market shares in absolute terms and market shares relative to the market shares of rivals,[79] the Court held that price pressure would be
incompatible with the existence of a dominant position.[80] However, on the facts,
it found that Roche was 'not subjected to any competitive pressure but by means
of its position is able to adopt a price policy designed to forestall such pressure'.[81]
The concept that dominance is the ability of a firm with market power to harm
competition could not have been expressed more clearly. The link between market
power and the ability to harm competition is also apparent in the Court's analysis of the relevance of the fact that the dominant firm supplied a wider range of
vitamins than its rivals.[82] The Commission had argued the point by saying that
Roche's range of vitamins enabled it to employ a sales and pricing strategy 'far less
dependent than that of the other manufacturers on the conditions of competition
in each market'.[83] The Court held that different vitamins were in different markets
and had to be considered as different products. Therefore, Roche's position was
the same as that of its competitors which supplied other products in the food and
pharmaceutical sectors and could also avail themselves of multi-product marketing strategies.[84] The Court considered this factor relevant because a wide range
of products may be used to devise strategies that exclude rivals unless rivals can
deploy effective counter-strategies. This demonstrates that dominance is the ability to exclude. Market power is a necessary element of the analysis, but not an end
in itself.

The analysis of dominance as requiring a finding of market power is confirmed
by a number of other cases, including *General Electric*,[85] a merger case decided

---

[79] See, in relation to various groups of vitamins, ibid paras 50–52 (relying on a 47% market share
as proof of 'freedom to decide what attitude to adopt when confronted by competition' but discussing additional factors too); paras 53–56 (relying on a market share of 86% as proof of dominance);
paras 59–60 (relying on a market share of, at least, 75% as proof of dominance); paras 61–63 (relying
on a market share of 64.8% and on the market shares of the second and third largest competitors
of 14.8% and 6.3% respectively); and paras 64–66 (relying on a confidential large market share as
proof of dominance which was probably in the region of under 60% and on the market shares of
three competitors and one or more importers).

[80] ibid para 71.   [81] ibid para 76.   [82] ibid paras 45–46.

[83] ibid para 45 (quoting the wording of the Commission's decision).   [84] ibid para 46.

[85] Case T-210/01 *General Electric*. In *General Electric*, the Court of First Instance addressed a
number of issues relating to dominance, both pre- and post-merger. First, the Court ruled on
whether the Commission's finding that General Electric was dominant pre-merger on the market
for large commercial aircraft engines was vitiated by an error of fact or a manifest error of assessment
(ibid paras 92–280). Secondly, the Court dealt with the strengthening of the pre-merger dominant
position on the market for large commercial aircraft engines resulting from the vertical integration of Honeywell's engine starters with General Electric's engines (ibid paras 281–314). Thirdly,
the Court ruled on the conglomerate effects of the proposed merger, which would have combined
General Electric's financing and leasing companies with Honeywell's avionics and non-avionics
products (ibid paras 315–473). Fourthly, the Court ruled on the pleas relating to the areas of horizontal overlaps between the merging parties, namely on the market for jet engines for large regional
aircraft (ibid paras 475–563), in respect of which the Court dealt with pre-merger dominance (ibid
paras 539–542) and the post-merger strengthening of the dominant position (ibid paras 543–563),
on the market for corporate jet aircraft (ibid paras 564–584), and on the market for small marine gas
turbines (ibid paras 564–584). The analysis in the text focuses on the market for large commercial
aircraft engines.

under the 1989 Merger Regulation.[86] On the market for large commercial aircraft engines, General Electric was vertically integrated with an aircraft leasing company holding between 7 and 10 per cent of the market.[87] It was also an undisputed fact that General Electric's finance company, General Electric Capital, gave the General Electric Group better access to the financial markets than its competitors.[88] The Court of First Instance held that the Commission legitimately took vertical integration into account in establishing dominance because the leasing company furthered the sale of General Electric's engines on the market,[89] which was a significant commercial advantage[90] that competitors could not replicate,[91] and foreclosed one of the possible routes to the market which could have been available to competitors.[92] In other words, the Court held that the fact that a seller is vertically integrated with a buyer of its products can be a factor relevant in the assessment of dominance when the same type and degree of vertical integration is not replicable by competitors and forecloses between 7 and 10 per cent of the market. Customer foreclosure strategies constitute a barrier to entry because they reduce the share of demand contestable by competitors. They are also behavioural evidence of a firm's ability to foreclose. Therefore, the Court's approach is consistent with the concept of dominance as market power as a prerequisite for the ability to harm competition. There is no need to interpret this judgment as adopting a vacuous definition of dominance as 'commercial power'.[93] This conclusion is reinforced by the overall approach of the Court. The market behaviour of General Electric's subsidiaries contributed to neutralizing the competitive pressure potentially exerted by its competitors. General Electric's leasing company played a role in securing an exclusive supply contract with the airframe manufacturer for a version of the Boeing 777 (B777X) despite the fact that General Electric's engine was, technically, an inferior product compared to the competing engines. The Court took the view that that General Electric would have lost the contract if the only relevant criteria had been the quality of the product and the price payable

---

[86] Council Regulation (EEC) 4064/89 of 21 December 1989 on the control of concentrations between undertakings [1989] OJ L395/1, corrected version [1990] OJ L257/13, as amended by Council Regulation (EC) 1310/97 of 30 June 1997 amending Regulation (EEC) 4064/89 on the control of concentrations between undertakings [1997] OJ L180/1, corrigendum [1998] OJ L40/17 ('1989 Merger Regulation'). Art 2(3) of the Regulation provided that a concentration, which creates or strengthens a dominant position as a result of which effective competition would be significantly impeded in the common market or in a substantial part of it, shall be declared incompatible with the common market. The EU courts have interpreted the concept of dominance under the 1989 Merger Regulation in the same way as dominance under Art 102: Case T-210/01 *General Electric*, paras 85–87, particularly para 86 (where the Court relies on Case 7/62 *Continental Can*, para 26, for the proposition that the strengthening of a dominant position to such an extent that it significantly impedes competition may be in itself an abuse under Art 102); Case T-2/93 *Air France v Commission* [1994] ECR II-323, para 78; Joined Cases C-68/94 P and C-30/95 P *France v Commission* [1998] ECR I-1375, para 220; Case T-102/96 *Gencor Ltd v Commission* [1999] ECR II-753, para 199; Case T-5/02 *Tetra Laval BV v Commission* [2002] ECR II-4381, para 120.

[87] Case T-210/01 *General Electric*, para 198.   [88] ibid para 201.   [89] ibid para 193.
[90] ibid para 199.   [91] ibid para 200.   [92] ibid.
[93] For this reading of the judgment, see Monti, 'The Concept of Dominance in Article 82', 40–42.

on delivery.[94] Instead, General Electric was able to reverse the competitive outcome.[95] The Court relied on these circumstances to say that General Electric was able to act 'independently' because it was able to devise a commercial strategy that sheltered it 'to a considerable degree from the effects of the immediate commercial pressure of competition' from its rivals.[96] The mere fact that General Electric made financial concessions did not conflict with this finding. Some financial concessions are a normal element of the negotiation process in a bidding market.[97] The Court, therefore, concluded that the circumstances in which General Electric secured the exclusive engine supply contract for the B777X were 'indicative not of the healthy state of competition but of the applicant's market power'.[98] General Electric's leasing subsidiary also played 'an important part in enabling the applicant to supply the engines for an airline aircraft'.[99] Similarly, General Electric Capital gave General Electric a commercial advantage over its rivals, including by enabling it to secure orders in return for loans.[100] On this analysis, the strategic use of General Electric's subsidiaries cannot simply be described as 'commercial power' but is relevant to the assessment of the degree of effective 'competitive pressure' on General Electric and its ability to exclude rivals, thereby maintaining or strengthening its market power. The use of terminology referring to 'commercial levers',[101] 'commercial strength',[102] or the 'power of the applicant's subsidiaries over airlines'[103] does not negate this conclusion but is simply the Court's method of describing, in a realistic way, the dynamics of the market. Equally, the reliance on evidence that may appear to be relatively weak to support specific findings must be understood in the context of the case as a whole and is not inconsistent with a market power analysis. This is confirmed by the assessment of competitive constraints[104] and countervailing buyer power.[105] As regards competitive constraints, General Electric had only two competitors, one of which 'was no longer an effective independent competitor',[106] while the other could not be considered 'as a credible bidder for all engines across all markets and in particular in winning engine exclusivity'.[107] As regards buyer power, the Court upheld the Commission's finding that the constraint exercised by Boeing or Airbus was not sufficient to undermine the conclusion that General Electric was dominant

---

[94] Case T-210/01 *General Electric*, para 213.   [95] ibid.   [96] ibid para 214.

[97] It was disputed whether these concessions were a discount. The Court held that they were not as, it would appear, they did not affect the price payable on delivery: ibid paras 212–213.

[98] ibid para 216.   [99] ibid para 223.

[100] ibid paras 225–228 (relying, in fact, only on one instance in which General Electric Capital made loans to Continental Airlines when the latter company was in financial difficulties in 1993, following which Continental Airlines had chosen General Electric's engines for large commercial aircraft whenever they were available).

[101] ibid para 229   [102] ibid para 242.   [103] ibid para 220.

[104] ibid paras 251–273. In the heading the Court refers to lack or weakness of 'commercial or competitive constraints' (ibid para 251). This language is probably imprecise in the use of the disjunctive 'or' between 'commercial' and 'competitive' and merely descriptive rather than laying down a specific legal definition. It would be unclear, otherwise, what the difference between 'commercial' and 'competitive' constraints might be. In the analysis, the Court does not appear to draw a distinction between two different types of constraint.

[105] ibid paras 274–279.   [106] ibid para 261.   [107] ibid para 273.

on the relevant market.[108] This was because of General Electric's position as the incumbent fleet supplier[109] and because of General Electric's ability to influence the airlines' choice of engine, which in turn restricted the scope for the airframe manufacturers to switch suppliers.[110]

The *General Electric* case, therefore, adopts a concept of dominance as the ability to harm competition that requires the dominant firm to have market power. This is not contradicted by the Court's reliance on market shares as establishing dominance without any need for further inquiry.[111] The relevance of market shares is a purely evidential issue. The Court does not define dominance as the possession of a given market share but considers market shares as 'indicative' of dominance,[112] 'evidence of the existence of a dominant position',[113] or as giving rise to a 'presumption' of dominance.[114] Nor is the Court's language referring to the position of competitors and their 'freedom of action' such as to contradict the assessment of dominance as requiring the possession of market power. The applicant argued that the Commission had failed to address explicitly whether the creation or strengthening of a dominant position had the effect of significantly impeding effective competition in the internal market. The Court held that the finding that a dominant position had been created or strengthened could, in particular cases, be in itself proof of a significant impediment to effective competition.[115] The Court went on to say:[116]

The factors which may be invoked by the Commission in order to establish that an undertaking's competitors lack freedom of action to the degree necessary for a finding that a dominant position has been created or strengthened with regard to that undertaking are often the same as those which are relevant in an appraisal of whether, as a result of such creation or strengthening, competition will be significantly impeded in the common market. Indeed, a factor which significantly affects the freedom of competitors to determine their commercial policy independently is also liable to result in effective competition being impeded.

This language can be explained by considering that economic freedom is the individualization of the objective concept of effective competition. The economic freedom that Article 102 protects is the freedom to participate in the market unhindered by behaviour that harms long-term social welfare. Therefore, the Court of First Instance was right to say that the creation or strengthening of a dominant position can be an impediment to effective competition. The protection of the economic freedom of competitors is, therefore, not an indication that the Court in the *General Electric* case did not carry out a market power analysis.

---

[108] ibid para 279.

[109] ibid para 275.   [110] ibid para 276.

[111] See ibid paras 539–542 (General Electric's pre-merger dominance on the market for large regional jet aircraft engines), paras 543–544 (post-merger dominance on the market for large regional jet aircraft engines), and paras 570–574 (post-merger dominance on the market for corporate jet aircraft engines).

[112] ibid para 167.   [113] ibid para 540.

[114] ibid para 571, relying on the presumption of dominance established in Case C-62/86 *AKZO*, para 60.

[115] Case T-210/01 *General Electric*, para 88.   [116] ibid.

The above analysis clarifies the meaning of the requirement of 'independence' which *United Brands* considered to be the hallmark of dominance.[117] Even a monopolist cannot act independently of its customers. In setting the price at the level where MC equals MR, the pricing behaviour of the monopolist crucially depends on the demand curve, that is, on the preferences of its customers. In an oligopoly, the pricing behaviour of the collectively dominant firms depends on the expected reactions of the rivals, as well as on the demand function. Clearly, this is not the concept of independence that the EU courts have in mind. The key is in the syntax of the definition of dominance in the *United Brands* case: 'a position of economic strength enjoyed by an undertaking which enables it to prevent effective competition being maintained on the relevant market by giving it the power to behave to an appreciable extent independently of its competitors, customers, and ultimately consumers'.[118] The 'independence' of the dominant firm is a consequence of its 'economic strength' and the cause or mode of its ability to restrict competition. The independence of the dominant firm, therefore, must be understood as the inability of the rational market conduct of rivals, customers, and, ultimately, consumers to prevent the dominant undertaking from harming competition. Independence is, therefore, more than just the absence of effective competitive pressure from existing rivals. Any actual or potential behaviour from market players that prevents a firm, however commercially powerful and however large its market share, from harming competition, is incompatible with the existence of the dominant position. The key factors in this analysis are the ease of entry and the presence of powerful customers.

D. Barriers to entry

(1) Dynamic test of barriers to entry

Dominance is the ability of a firm with substantial and durable market power to harm competition. Beyond the long-term market shares of the allegedly dominant undertaking and its competitors,[119] all factors that are capable of conferring

---

[117] Case 27/76 *United Brands*, para 65.   [118] ibid.

[119] The problem of market shares is essentially a matter of determining the relevance and weight of market shares as evidence of a firm's ability to harm competition within the meaning of Art 102. As a purely evidential issue, it is outside the scope of this monograph. It goes without saying, however, that the question is of great practical importance. The Guidance on Art 102, para 14, applies a 'safe harbour' to undertakings with a market share lower than 40%. A different issue is whether market shares can give rise to a presumption of dominance: see: Monti, 'The Concept of Dominance in Article 82', 48–51; Dethmers and Dodoo, 'The Abuse of Hoffmann-La Roche', 541–543; V Korah, *An Introductory Guide to EC Competition Law and Practice* (9th edn Oxford, Hart Publishing 2007) 121–123; R Whish, *Competition Law* (6th edn Oxford, OUP 2008) 175–179. The case law supports at least a permissible inference based on market shares and the absence of factors prima facie capable of invalidating the inference: Case 85/76 *Hoffmann-La Roche*, para 41; Case 322/81 *Michelin I*, paras 32–61; Case C-62/86 *AKZO*, para 60; Case T-30/89 *Hilti AG v Commission* [1990] ECR II-163, paras 92–93, upheld in C-53/92 P *Hilti AG v Commission* [1994] ECR I-667; Case T-228/97 *Irish Sugar plc v Commission* [1999] ECR II-2969, paras 71–104; Case T-321/05 *AstraZeneca*, paras 243–253. Yet another question is the relevance of the comparison between the market share of

substantial and durable market power on a firm are relevant to the assessment of dominance. Furthermore, all factors that are capable of giving a firm the ability to harm competition are also relevant to the assessment of dominance. Barriers to entry or expansion[120] are relevant both to substantial and durable market power and to the ability to harm competition. According to certain economists,[121] economies of scale are a barrier to entry. They contribute to an incumbent firm's durable and substantial market power. But economies of scale are also a factor that may give an incumbent firm with substantial and durable market power the ability to harm competition by making feasible certain exclusionary practices that prevent rivals from becoming as efficient as the incumbent. Other factors, however, are only relevant to a firm's ability to harm competition. Better access to finance, for example, is not a barrier to entry. The mere fact that the incumbent firm has better access to finance does not in itself make entry more costly than is socially optimal. However, in certain circumstances,[122] asymmetric access to finance can give an incumbent firm the ability to harm competition by excluding a new entrant through a predatory strategy. These factors can be described as dynamic barriers to entry because they give an undertaking the ability to exclude rivals to the detriment of long-term social welfare. Their significance is not that they describe a given market structure but that they give a firm the ability to manipulate the dynamics of the market. However, even when barriers to entry are relevant to establishing the requirement of substantial and durable market power, their significance is still dynamic because substantial and durable market power is itself only relevant to a firm's ability to harm competition. Therefore, in EU law, all barriers to entry are dynamic.

In order better to illustrate this concept of dynamic barriers to entry, it may be instructive to dwell on different definitions of barriers to entry in the economic literature[123] and compare them with the EU approach.

Bain was the first to study, in a systematic way, the condition of entry. He proposed to evaluate the 'condition of entry' to an industry 'by the advantages of established sellers in an industry over potential entrant sellers, these advantages being reflected in the extent to which established sellers can persistently raise their price

---

the allegedly dominant firm and the market shares of its competitors: Case 85/76 *Hoffmann-La Roche*, paras 48, 59, and 66; Case T-219/99 *British Airways*, paras 210–211 and 224; Case T-321/05 *AstraZeneca*, paras 246–247 and 251–252.

[120] On the significance of barriers to entry in the assessment of unilateral conduct, see eg OECD, 'Barriers to Entry', Best Practice Policy Roundtables on Competition Policy (2005); T Calvani and J Fingleton, 'Dominance: A Comparative Economic and Legal Analysis' in WD Collins (ed), *Issues in Competition Law and Policy* (Chicago, ABA Press 2008) 845, 849.

[121] J Bain, *Barriers to New Competition: Their Character and Consequences in Manufacturing Industries* (reprinted Fairfield NJ, Augustus M Kelley Publishers 1993) 12 and 53–113.

[122] eg when lenders have imperfect information about the market or when the incumbent can lower the entrant's equity to the extent that the entrant must exit the market or raise its prices to reflect the high costs of borrowing: J Tirole, *The Theory of Industrial Organization* (Cambridge Mass, MIT Press 1988) 379 and PL Joskow and AK Klevorick, 'A Framework for Analyzing Predatory Pricing Policy' (1979) 89 Yale LJ 213, 230–231.

[123] As is done eg by O'Donoghue and Padilla, *The Law and Economics of Article 82 EC*, 117–119 and Monti, *EC Competition Law*, 144–148.

above a competitive level without attracting new firms to enter the industry'.[124] This definition bears a strong resemblance to the definition of dominance in the Guidance on Article 102 as the ability of an undertaking 'of profitably increasing prices above the competitive level for a significant period of time'.[125] This is not surprising. Bain deliberately adopted a structural definition of barriers to entry.[126] More than fifty years later, the Commission adopted a structural definition of dominance as market power. As a result, the list of barriers to entry in the Guidance on Article 102 also resembles Bain's understanding of the condition of entry. The Guidance lists various types of barriers to entry whose common denominator is to create an asymmetry in terms of ease of access to the market between an entrant and the incumbent.[127] Bain considered that barriers to entry would be present in three sets of circumstances: (1) if incumbent firms have absolute cost advantages over entrants; (2) if they have product differentiation advantages; and (3) if the market is characterized by economies of scale.[128] Many of the factors listed by the Commission match Bain's taxonomy. This applies not only to economies of scale but also to privileged access to essential inputs, natural resources, and important technologies, which Bain considered absolute cost advantages.[129] Product differentiation advantages, which Bain defined as 'net price or selling cost advantage, accruing to established firms by reason of buyer preferences for their products, and … price advantages in securing factors of production', correspond to impediments faced by customers in switching to a new supplier. The Commission, however, goes on to acknowledge the existence and significance of dynamic barriers, although only to the extent that they are created by the undertaking's own conduct. Therefore, even in the overall structuralist approach adopted by the Commission, the definition of barriers to entry is, as a minimum, wider than Bain's.

Bain's understanding of barriers to entry was challenged by the Chicago School. Stigler defined a barrier to entry as a 'differentially higher cost of new firms'.[130] Economies of scale and sunk costs are not barriers to entry because they are not asymmetric as between the incumbent and the entrant. The same applies to product differentiation advantages unless the costs of differentiation are different for the incumbent and for an entrant.[131] Like Bain, Stigler did not apply these concepts to competition policy. But the key message was clear: 'barriers to entry'

---

[124] Bain, *Barriers to New Competition*, 3.
[125] Guidance on Art 102, para 11.   [126] Bain, *Barriers to New Competition*, 3.
[127] Guidance on Art 102, para 17: 'Barriers to expansion or entry can take various forms. They may be legal barriers, such as tariffs or quotas, or they may take the form of advantages specifically enjoyed by the dominant undertaking, such as economies of scale and scope, privileged access to essential inputs or natural resources, important technologies, or an established distribution and sales network. They may also include costs and other impediments, for instance resulting from network effects, faced by customers in switching to a new supplier. The dominant undertaking's own conduct may also create barriers to entry, for example where it has made significant investments which entrants or competitors would have to match, or where it has concluded long-term contracts with its customers that have appreciable foreclosing effects. Persistently high market shares may be indicative of the existence of barriers to entry.'
[128] Bain, *Barriers to New Competition*, 13.   [129] ibid 13–14.
[130] GJ Stigler, 'Barriers to Entry, Economies of Scale, and Firm Size' in *The Organization of Industry* (reprinted Chicago, University of Chicago Press 1983) 67.
[131] ibid 67 and 70.

are often simply features of the market that determine the size of firms as costs and demand. Bork applied these principles to competition law. In his view, only predatory conduct amounts to a 'barrier to entry' because it is an artificial obstacle to doing business. All other 'barriers to entry' are simply a cost or risk that all firms in the market must incur. As a consequence, firms who have overcome these 'barriers' are simply more efficient firms.[132]

A step further in the theory of barriers to entry is to recognize that the key question is not whether incumbent firms are protected from entry, or whether certain market features that make entry difficult are equally applicable to all firms or not. The issue is whether a factor that makes entry difficult and, therefore, tends to protect incumbent firms is socially beneficial or not. Social welfare is not a function of the number of firms on the market. Sometimes, in the absence of barriers, entry may be privately profitable but detrimental to society, for instance because of the duplication of fixed costs. When this is the case, an obstacle to entry is not a barrier to entry, whether or not it is inherent in the structure of the market and whether or not incumbent firms had to overcome that obstacle as well.[133] This approach is consistent with the objective of Article 102. Article 102 does not prohibit barriers to entry as such. Nor is it a regulatory provision that enables the State to address structural features of a market whenever they restrict market access by new firms. It is a prohibition of conduct engaged in by firms which have the ability unilaterally to harm long-term social welfare by excluding rivals, exploiting a restriction of competition, or distorting competition between upstream or downstream firms. Although the examination of barriers to entry takes place as a preliminary step in the assessment of the abuse, ultimately a barrier to entry is only relevant under Article 102 if it gives an undertaking the ability to harm long-term social welfare *and* the undertaking in question is actually exploiting this ability. Therefore, barriers to entry in EU law are factors that make entry difficult and, by giving a dominant undertaking the ability to harm competition, are detrimental to long-term social welfare. It is in this sense that the concept of barriers to entry is always dynamic. Barriers to entry are relevant because they make anti-competitive conduct by a dominant undertaking possible and profitable. Even when a barrier to entry appears to be a purely structural factor, such as economies of scale, or a static capital requirement, such as a sunk cost of entry, they are never relevant as such. There is no provision under Article 102 that addresses the effect of structural factors on long-term social welfare. These factors are only relevant insofar as they give the dominant undertaking the ability to harm competition and the dominant undertaking is in fact harming competition. So economies of scale are irrelevant under Article 102 until a dominant undertaking acquires the ability, thanks to economies of scale, to exclude competitors by a distributional practice that prevents them from achieving a minimum efficient scale thus harming social welfare

---

[132] RH Bork, *The Antitrust Paradox* (New York, Basic Books 1978) 310–329.

[133] CC von Weizsäcker, 'A Welfare Analysis of Barriers to Entry' (1980) 11 Bell Journal of Economics 399, 399–401; FM Fisher, 'Diagnosing Monopoly' (1979) 19 Quarterly Review of Economics and Business 7, 23.

in the long term. A sunk cost of entry is irrelevant under Article 102 until it gives an undertaking the ability to discourage entry by foreclosing a given share of demand, thus making it unprofitable for an entrant to sink the entry cost. However, the case law and the Commission enforcement practice have often adopted a structuralist and mechanistic approach to barriers to entry. This is apparent in the analysis of the factors that are normally considered to be barriers to entry. A dynamic approach is, instead, required by Article 102. The current practice of the Commission and the case law of the EU courts have on occasion adopted such an approach, albeit in an embryonic and unstructured way. A significant, but incremental, step forward is, therefore, necessary to bring the current application of Article 102 into line with its purpose and the behavioural concept of dominance that it enacts.

(2) Sunk costs

A sunk cost is a cost of entry to the market that is not fully recoverable upon exit. Substantial sunk costs may contribute to an incumbent undertaking's substantial and durable market power and its ability to harm competition. This is for two reasons. First, sunk costs make entry less likely. As a result, they contribute to a dominant undertaking's incentive to invest in the exclusion of competitors because, entry being less likely post-exclusion, it is more probable that the dominant firm will be able to recoup its investment and continue to earn supracompetitive profits. Secondly, sunk costs may give the dominant firm the ability to discourage entry by committing to, or establishing a reputation for, practices that lower the likely profits of the entrant. If anticipated post-entry profits are lower than required for the entrant to recoup sunk costs in addition to covering any other fixed or variable cost, entry will not occur. In *United Brands*, the Court of Justice held that 'the exceptionally large capital investments required for the creation and running of banana plantations' constituted a barrier to entry.[134] In *Intel*, the Commission established that there were significant sunk costs in the R&D and production of microprocessors based on the x86 architecture (compatible with Windows and Linux operating systems). Together with the substantial economies of scale in production, these factors gave rise to a barrier to entry.[135] This was because not only would a new entrant have to invest significantly to enter the market but also because, in order to operate on an efficient scale, it would have to capture a sizeable share of the market.[136] The dominant undertak-

---

[134] Case 27/76 *United Brands*, para 122.   [135] *Intel*, recitals 854–866.

[136] Sunk costs are routinely part of merger analysis: see eg *JCI/FIAMM* (Case COMP/M.4381) [2009] OJ C241/12, recital 790 (where the Commission considered the costs to be incurred by new suppliers of automotive starter batteries in having their plant certified by the customers to be 'sunk' costs, thus differentiating the position of new entrants, who had to bear that risk, from that of existing suppliers considering expanding production, whose plant had already been certified). See also *Ryanair/AerLingus* (Case COMP/M.4439) [2006] C274/45, recital 621, where the Commission took the view that entry on a given air route would entail high sunk costs for competitors: 'The significant marketing expenditure which are [sic] necessary for any new entrant to establish its brand in Ireland and have access to new customers (and which represent the largest part of expenditure for opening a new route) can be considered as sunk costs should the entry fail.' This analysis was upheld by the

ing thus acquired the ability to exclude rivals by foreclosing a sufficiently large portion of demand.

(3) Economies of scale

Economies of scale arise when average costs fall as output increases. Economies of scale in themselves are not a barrier to entry.[137] They are a feature of the market in respect of which firms must compete. In order to succeed, firms must strive to achieve the lowest possible costs and to capture a share of the market at least equal to the minimum efficient scale of production. This is a parameter of competition, not a barrier to entry. Even if a large incumbent engaged in predatory pricing or entered into widespread exclusivity agreements, an entrant would be able to compete by incurring the same losses or offering the same prices. However, economies of scale combined with additional factors may give rise to a dynamic barrier to entry. In *Intel*, one such additional factor was the sunk costs of entry.[138] A dominant undertaking could discourage entry by committing to, or establishing a reputation for, a practice that denies an entrant a minimum efficient scale. *Ex ante*, entry becomes too risky. *Ex post*, economies of scale may contribute to a dominant undertaking's ability to foreclose competitors who face much higher costs by implementing exclusionary above-cost price cuts. The case law and the Commission practice, however, have sometimes considered economies of scale as contributing to a dominant position without an integrated analysis of all the other factors relevant to the dominant undertaking's ability to harm competition. The elements that contribute to a dominant position are simply listed almost as if it were possible to pick a number of factors at random as long as they are in the abstract capable of being barriers to entry and happen to be present on the facts of the case. An example of this approach may be *BPB Industries*, in which the Commission found that the dominant undertaking enjoyed economies of scale in production.[139] However, the Commission did not explain how economies of scale contributed to the dominant position. On the facts, the dominant undertaking had market shares well above 90 per cent on the relevant British and Irish markets for plasterboard.[140] It offered different forms of discounts to customers on condition that they did not purchase imported plasterboard.[141] Clearly, economies of scale contributed to the concentration of the market. They also explained why competition took place from imports rather than from firms establishing themselves in the United Kingdom. As a result,

---

Court of First Instance in Case T-342/07 *Ryanair Holdings plc v Commission* [2010] OJ C221/35, paras 278–279.

[137] Notwithstanding the fact that the EU courts have occasionally listed economies of scale as contributing to dominance without further analysis: see eg Case 27/76 *United Brands*, para 95.

[138] ibid recitals 854–866.

[139] *BPB Industries plc* [1989] OJ L10/50, recital 116, upheld in Case T-65/89 *BPB Industries plc and British Gypsum Ltd v Commission* [1993] ECR II-389 (*British Gypsum*), appeal dismissed in Case C-310/93 P *BPB Industries plc and British Gypsum Ltd v Commission* [1995] ECR I-865 (*British Gypsum*).

[140] *BPB Industries*, recital 116.   [141] ibid recitals 122–152.

competition was for small portions of demand, and customers remained dependent on the dominant undertaking. This gave the latter the ability to exclude rivals through a system of selective above-cost rebates. This analysis, while consistent with the facts of the case, is absent in the decision. It is instructive to contrast the approach in *BPB Industries* with the more analytical one in *Intel*, where the Commission goes one step further and carries out an integrated analysis of barriers to entry. In order for barriers to entry to play their role in competition analysis, one further step should be made: to examine barriers to entry as relevant to the ability of the dominant undertaking to harm competition in the context of the assessment of the abuse.

(4) Economies of scope and product range

Economies of scope arise when the average costs of producing or distributing two or more products are lower than the average costs associated with only one product. The mere fact that an undertaking has lower costs because it is a multi-product firm is not a barrier to entry. But a wide product range, in combination with other factors such as the 'must stock' quality of one of the products in the range and sunk costs of entry to the 'must-stock' product market, may give the dominant undertaking the ability to exclude competitors.[142] Tying, bundling, and multi-product discounts are practices that are only possible if the dominant undertaking supplies a wide range of products that are purchased, at least to a significant extent, by the same pool of customers. Clearly, a wide product range is never a sufficient condition, even combined with a large market share in one product market, for an undertaking to have the ability to harm competition. But it may be a necessary condition for certain abuses. Its relevance and significance must be established on the facts of each individual case. In *Hoffmann-La Roche*, the Court of Justice held that a wider vitamin range was not a relevant factor in establishing dominance. Competitors could also offer a wide range of products purchased by the same customers, albeit not vitamins, and could therefore counteract any anti-competitive strategy employed by the dominant undertaking.[143] However, it is also possible that undertakings which do not offer a full product range are less effective competitors. In *Friesland/Campina*,[144] the Commission considered that the wholesalers of dairy products in the Netherlands only had limited options to switch to foreign supply as not all foreign suppliers offered a complete product range as compared to Campina and Friesland.[145] Moreover, foreign suppliers often did not supply branded products that could be considered as effective substitutes for the brands of the merging parties.[146]

---

[142] eg *Aérospatiale-Alenia/de Havilland* (Case IV/M.053) [1991] OJ L334/42, recital 30.
[143] Case 85/76 *Hoffmann-La Roche*, paras 45–46.
[144] *Friesland/Campina* (Case COMP/M.5046) [2009] OJ C75/19.   [145] ibid recital 939.
[146] ibid.

(5) Network effects

Direct network effects arise when a consumer's valuation of a product increases as the number of users of the product rises. For instance, the valuation of internet access increases as the number of users of the internet rises, as users can communicate by email, use social network platforms, or share files. Indirect network effects arise when a consumer's valuation for a product increases as the function of the number or quality of complementary products. The valuation of a credit card increases as the number of merchants accepting the card rises.

Network effects may give an undertaking the ability to harm competition. Generally, if all the products on the market are compatible, network effects cannot give rise to a barrier to entry. All firms benefit from market expansion and each firm has the incentive to sell products that consumers value the most at the lowest price in order to gain as large a share of the market as possible. If products are incompatible and no firm has an advantage other than superior efficiency or commercial strategy, again, firms will compete to gain as large a share of the market as possible. The difference is that, once a firm has won the competitive race, it will be more difficult for an existing competitor or a new entrant to gain market share from the leading firm because consumers value the new product less. At that point, network effects may give the leading firm the ability to harm competition in order to protect its market power. In *Microsoft I*, the market was characterized by indirect network effects. Media players are platform software. Content providers and software developers develop content and applications for a given technology and face increased costs in making their products compatible with more than one technology. There are then strong incentives to develop content and applications for the technology which has the widest presence on the market. This in turn raises a barrier to entry for non-compatible technologies. Even if a non-compatible media player were significantly better than Windows Media Player, as long as not enough content and applications were written for it, it would not be able to compete effectively on the market.[147] By tying Windows Media Player with its dominant Windows operating system, Microsoft foreclosed other media players. The strong network effects on the market contributed to its ability to do so.

(6) Switching costs

A switching cost may be defined as the one-off cost that consumers associate with switching from one supplier to another, other than the costs of purchasing the

---

[147] *Microsoft I*, recitals 883–896. Network effects have also been examined in merger cases: see eg *Google/DoubleClick* (Case COMP/M.4731) [2008] OJ C184/10 and *Oracle/Sun Microsystems* (Case COMP/M.5529) [2010] OJ C91/7.

product itself.[148] A useful taxonomy adopted in the management literature[149] is the following:

1. **Economic risk costs.** These are the costs associated with switching to a new supplier about whom the consumer has insufficient information. The consumer, therefore, has to accept the risk of a negative outcome. Thus in *AstraZeneca*, the inertia of doctors in prescribing new drugs was a factor which contributed to reinforce the dominant undertaking's first mover advantage.[150]

2. **Evaluation costs.** Consumers may have to incur costs in looking for, and obtaining information about, a new product.

3. **Learning costs.** The more complex a product and the more differentiated the market, the higher will be the cost of learning to use a new product. In *Oracle/Sun Microsystems*, the costs of retraining staff to support a different database had a negative impact on customers' incentives to switch supplier.[151]

4. **Set-up and monetary loss costs.** Certain products require an initial installation, or time and effort may be required to start the relationship with a new supplier or switching may require relationship-specific investment such as the purchase of new software. In *Oracle/Sun Microsystems*, the costs of moving the data to a new database, recreating the schema describing the data's content and relationships to the database manager, and recreating the software managing the database infrastructure deterred customers from switching to a new supplier.[152]

5. **Benefit loss costs.** These are the costs contractually imposed on a customer for switching to a new supplier. A classic example is a penalty for the early termination of an exclusive supply agreement or the loss of a loyalty rebate.

6. **Personal relationship and brand relationship loss costs.** Breaking 'the bonds of identification' with the supplier's employees with whom the customer interacts or with a strong brand image may be perceived as a cost of switching

---

[148] On switching costs, see R Schmalensee, 'Product Differentiation Advantages of Pioneering Brands' (1982) 27 American Economic Review 349; P Klemperer, 'Markets with Consumer Switching Costs' (1987) 102 Quarterly Journal of Economics 375; J Farrell and C Shapiro, 'Dynamic Competition with Switching Costs' (1988) 19 RAND Journal of Economics 123; A Beggs and P Klemperer, 'Multi-Period Competition with Switching Costs' (1992) 60 Econometrica 651; T Nilssen, 'Two Kinds of Consumer Switching Costs' (1992) 23 RAND Journal of Economics 579; P Klemperer, 'Competition When Consumers Have Switching Costs: An Overview With Applications to Industrial Organization, Macroeconomics, and International Trade' (1995) 62 Rev Econ Stud 515; C McSorley, AJ Padilla, and M Williams, 'Switching Costs', DTI Economic Discussion Paper 5 (15 April 2003) 1.

[149] TA Burnham, JK Frels, and V Mahajan, 'Consumer Switching Costs: A Typology, Antecedents, and Consequences' (2003) 31 Journal of the Academy of Marketing Science 109.

[150] Case T-321/05 *AstraZeneca*, para 83, where, however, doctors' inertia was not explicitly characterized as a switching cost as the issue only arose at market definition stage.

[151] *Oracle/Sun Microsystems*, recital 137. See also *Napp Pharmaceutical Holdings Ltd v Director General of Fair Trading (No 4)* [2002] CAT 1, [2002] Comp AR 13, [2002] ECC 13 (*Napp v DGFT*), para 278, discussing the switching costs of training doctors and nurses to administer a new drug.

[152] *Oracle/Sun Microsystems*, recital 137.

supplier.[153] In EU law, it is well established that brand loyalty may give rise to a switching cost. To overcome customers' loyalty to the incumbent's brand, new firms may have to invest heavily in advertising. This investment is sunk.[154]

This taxonomy gives an idea of how pervasive switching costs are in the economy. To the extent that they are created by suppliers to establish long-lasting relationships with their customers, switching costs are a parameter of competition. However, switching costs may give rise to a barrier to entry because a new firm would have to compensate a customer for the cost of switching. Therefore, the new firm is forced to sell at a price lower than the incumbent's price. Depending on the magnitude of switching costs, a new firm as efficient as, or more efficient than, the incumbent may find entry unprofitable. When this is the case, switching costs may give the incumbent the ability to exclude a competitor by above-cost price cuts.[155]

(7) Vertical integration and exclusive or preferential access to inputs or customers

Firms compete not only by improving the quality of their products or developing new ones, lowering their costs, and reaching out to customers. They also compete in the way they structure their value chain. Vertical integration is a strategic decision made by firms. It is adopted when it is more efficient than outsourcing. When this is the case, a vertically integrated firm will have advantages over firms that must outsource. This does not mean that they are dominant. However, vertical integration may be a barrier to entry in a number of circumstances in which vertical integration gives the vertically integrated firm the ability to harm competition.

First, vertical integration may give a firm better access to key inputs or downstream markets. If, as a consequence, a rival can only have access to inferior inputs or is foreclosed from significant portions of the downstream market, vertical integration contributes to a firm's substantial and durable market power. The same effect of vertical integration may occur if an undertaking has exclusive or preferential access to key inputs or customers through contractual arrangements. In *SFR/Télé 2 France*,[156] SFR, a French undertaking jointly controlled by Vivendi SA and Vodafone Group plc, acquired sole control of the internet access and fixed telephony business of the undertaking Télé 2 France, an undertaking active on the downstream market for the distribution of pay TV services in France through digital

---

[153] Burnham, Frels, and Mahajan, 'Consumer Switching Costs: A Typology, Antecedents, and Consequences', 111–112.

[154] Case 27/76 *United Brands*, paras 91–94; *Michelin* [2002] OJ L143/1 (*Michelin II*) recital 185; *Nestlé/Perrier* (Case IV/M.190) [1992] OJ L356/1, recitals 81 and 83; *Procter & Gamble/VP Schickendanz* (Case IV/M.430) [1994] OJ L354/32, recital 149; *Kimberly-Clark/Scott Paper* (Case IV/M.623) [1996] OJ L183/1, recital 87; *Coca-Cola/Amalgamated Beverages* (Case IV/M.794) [1997] OJ L218/15, recital 137; *The Coca-Cola Company/Carlsberg A/S* (Case IV/M.833) [1998] OJ L145/41, recital 72; *Guiness/Grand Metropolitan* (Case IV/M.938) [1998] OJ L288/24, recital 52.

[155] Joined Cases C-395/96 P and C-396/96 P *Compagnie Maritime Belge*, paras 116–119. On contracts that create a switching cost and may be abusive, see 232–242 and 245–248 above.

[156] *SFR/Télé 2 France* (Case COMP/M.4504) [2007] OJ L316/57.

subscriber line (DSL) technology.[157] Prior to the transaction, Vivendi distributed pay TV programmes directly and through DSL operators but did not have its own DSL distribution division.[158] The Commission took the view that the transaction would give Vivendi the incentive to favour its own DSL distributor, thus weakening the competitive pressure that other DSL distributors exerted over its satellite and terrestrial channels.[159] The anti-competitive effects would be greater because of the barriers to entry to the upstream market for broadcasting rights. In order to compete with Vivendi, other DLS distributors had to acquire broadcasting rights before they could offer any content.[160] However, the acquisition of broadcasting rights was hampered by Vivendi's exclusive agreements with the main providers of the rights.[161] Therefore, the proposed transaction was likely to weaken the emerging competitive pressure exerted by DSL operators on the downstream market in the distribution of pay TV, which was already fragile due to Vivendi's very strong position on all markets for pay TV in France.[162] Thus, the Commission argued that the weakening of downstream competition reinforced 'the very strong positions held by Vivendi on the upstream and intermediate markets', and the strengthening of Vivendi's position on the downstream markets would in turn reinforce its position on the upstream procurement market. Market power at different levels of the supply chain was self-reinforcing 'because of the high degree of vertical integration of the group'.[163]

Secondly, as in *United Brands*,[164] vertical integration may reduce or eliminate capacity constraints or risks in the supply chains. This means that while competitors may be subject to capacity constraints or supply shortages, the vertically integrated firm is not. As a consequence, customers are unable to shift all their requirements to competitors. This may contribute to the durability of market power but can also give the dominant undertaking the ability to exclude rivals by leveraging the market power over the non-contestable share of demand to the contestable share of demand.

Thirdly, vertical integration may give an undertaking the ability to exclude rivals through practices such as refusal to supply or margin squeeze.[165] However, it goes without saying that vertical integration in itself is not a barrier to entry. Vertical integration can amount to a barrier to entry if, and only if, in combination with other factors, it contributes to the dominant undertaking's ability to harm competition. In *Arsenal/DSP*,[166] Velsicol and DSP both produced benzoic acid. Velsicol also produced plasticizers, a downstream product to benzoic acid. Post-merger, Velsicol/DSP would have a very large market share on the input markets (100 per cent or 90 to 100 per cent depending on whether solid benzoic acid was included).[167] Therefore, there was a concern that the merged entity could foreclose access of mono-benzoate and di-benzoate plasticizer producers to

---

[157] ibid recitals 1 and 7.   [158] ibid recital 49.   [159] ibid recitals 84–101.
[160] ibid recitals 96–97.   [161] ibid recital 97.   [162] ibid recital 101.   [163] ibid.
[164] Case 27/76 *United Brands*, paras 70–81.
[165] On refusal to supply and margin squeeze see 229–232 and 258–273 above, respectively. On margin squeeze or a form of vertical foreclosure, see 273–275 above.
[166] *Arsenal/DSP* (Case COMP/M.5153) [2008] OJ C165/14.   [167] ibid recital 280.

benzoic acid by increasing the price of the input.[168] However, the Commission came to the conclusion that the merged entity would have only a limited ability, and in any case no incentive, to foreclose its downstream competitors.[169] The key element of the Commission's analysis was that the foreclosing strategy would not be profitable because it would not divert to the downstream division of the merged entity a sufficiently large share of downstream demand to compensate for the revenues forgone upstream. Furthermore, certain downstream competitors did not exert a significant competitive pressure on the downstream division of the merged entity.[170]

(8) Financial strength

In *AstraZeneca*, the General Court held that the superior financial resources of the dominant undertaking were 'not sufficient in themselves' to establish dominance. However, together with other elements, they allowed the inference that AstraZeneca had 'superior resources to those of its competitors such as to reinforce its market position in relation to them'.[171] In *Hoffmann-La Roche*, on the other hand, the Court of Justice held that the position of the undertaking as the world's largest vitamin manufacturer and within the world's largest pharmaceutical group and the fact that its turnover exceed those of its competitors were irrelevant to the assessment of dominance. The overall volume of production of products belonging to separate relevant markets did not confer on Roche a competitive advantage over its competitors. Furthermore, Roche's competitors were also active worldwide and thus able to deploy global competitive strategies.[172]

The financial strength of an incumbent firm is not in itself a barrier to entry. Nor is it sufficient by itself, or in combination with a very high market share, to establish dominance. However, asymmetric access to finance as between an incumbent firm and entrants may give the former the ability to exclude the latter. In *Hutchison/ RCPM/ECT*, the parties to a concentration in the container terminal sector argued that the likely entry of a new operator would constrain the merged entity because of the new entrant's incentive to price at MC to grow volume. The Commission rejected this argument on the grounds that, in the long-term, an entrant must be able to recover its full costs and, therefore, it cannot price below ATC indefinitely. Furthermore, MC pricing by an entrant would invite a response from the incumbent, who would be in a better position to endure a protracted price war because it had more time to pay back loans and amortize investments and had the backing of a financially strong group.[173] These factors suggested that the merged entity would have more equity capital compared to the entrant and, if needed, would be able to obtain external financing on better terms. On the plausible assumption that

---

[168] ibid recital 272.   [169] ibid recital 313.   [170] ibid recitals 289–310.
[171] Case T-321/05 *AstraZeneca*, para 286.   [172] Case 85/76 *Hoffmann-La Roche*, para 47.
[173] *Hutchison/RCPM/ECT* (Case COMP/JV.55)[2003] OJ L223/1, recital 95.

financial markets are imperfect, these conditions give a dominant undertaking the ability to exclude a rival through predatory pricing.[174]

The financial strength of rivals may also be relevant if it is sufficient to counterbalance potential anti-competitive strategies of the allegedly dominant undertaking. In *Google/DoubleClick* the Commission considered that a potential foreclosing strategy, whereby the merged entity decided to bundle Google's search advertising services[175] or (search) advertising intermediation services[176] with DoubleClick's advertising serving,[177] would be highly unlikely to cause competitors such as Microsoft, Yahoo!, and AOL to cease offering their own services.[178] These rivals were all vertically integrated and had access to considerable financial resources, which would have enabled them to continue to exert significant competitive pressure on the merged entity post-merger.[179]

Finally, financial strength alone is not capable of conferring a dominant position. In *STX/Aker Yards*[180] the market share of the merged entity in the cruise ship market would have been 30 to 35 per cent, whereas the market share of the market leader Fincantieri would have been 40 to 45 per cent. The Commission stated that it is unlikely that an undertaking which is not in a leading market position could become dominant on the basis of financial strength only.[181]

(9) Spare capacity

Spare capacity is a barrier to entry because it may give the dominant undertaking the ability to exclude competitors. Entry depends on expected post-entry profitability and, therefore, expected post-entry output. If the incumbent is committed to maintaining excess capacity and, therefore, is able to increase output significantly in response to entry, entry could become unprofitable. The same principle applies to the expansion of existing rivals. If expansion is costly, because for instance an additional plant must be built, the fact that the market leader has significant excess capacity may discourage expansion.

A special case is when all market participants have excess capacity. In *Hoffmann-La Roche*, undertakings planned capacity over a long period of time. As a consequence, all competitors had unused capacity. Nevertheless, the Court of Justice still held that the dominant undertaking was in a 'privileged position' because it was by itself capable of meeting the entire worldwide demand for the relevant products and the holding of excess capacity did not place it 'in a difficult eco-

---

[174] See 202, n 98 above.

[175] ie the provision of online advertising space for advertisements that appear together with the results of a search: *Google/Double Click*, recitals 11 and 45–56.

[176] ie services provided by advertising networks, advertising exchanges, and media agencies to publishers and advertisers allowing the latter to place advertisements on the web pages through an intermediary, thus avoiding the costs and disadvantages of direct negotiation: ibid recitals 18–25.

[177] ie software hosted on the appropriate server that ensures that advertisements are served on the publisher's web page at the right time and in the right place: ibid recitals 26–30.

[178] ibid recital 357.　　　[179] ibid.

[180] *STX/Aker Yards* (Case COMP/M.4956) [2009] OJ C147/14.　　　[181] ibid recital 87.

nomic or financial situation'.[182] However, if the alleged dominant entity is capacity constrained, while its competitors have spare capacity, this is generally evidence of lack of ability to exclude.[183] The same principle applies when the allegedly dominant undertaking has spare capacity but its competitors' excess capacity is superior.[184]

E. Countervailing buyer power

The Guidance on Article 102 recognizes that customers may be able to neutralize the ability of a leading supplier to increase prices profitably.[185] The Commission's approach reflects the Commission's understanding of dominance as substantial and durable market power. However, its analysis is consistent with the definition of dominance as the ability to harm competition. A supplier with a large market share will not have the ability to exclude rivals, exploit customers, or harm the efficiency of the downstream industry, if customers are sufficiently powerful, well informed, and coordinated to support efficient entry upstream. In EU law, countervailing buyer power must be capable of preventing a seller from harming social welfare in the long term. The short-term welfare implications of countervailing buyer power are of significantly less concern.[186]

---

[182] Case 85/76 *Hoffmann-La Roche*, para 48.

[183] *Thales/Finmeccanica/AAS/Telespazio* (Case COMP/M.4403) [2009] OJ C34/5, recital 327.

[184] *INEOS Group Ltd/Kerling* (Case COMP/M.4734) [2007] OJ C217/3, recital 179.

[185] Guidance on Art 102, para 18. Note that countervailing buyer power relates to the presence of substantial market power on both sides of the market. A different issue is that an undertaking may be dominant as a buyer: see *Virgin/British Airways* [2000] OJ L30/1 and Case T-219/99 *British Airways*, where British Airways was found dominant on the market for the procurement of travel agency services in the United Kingdom.

[186] Instead, the vast literature on monopsony and countervailing buyer power is mainly, albeit not exclusively, concerned with the short-term welfare implications and the short-term market equilibrium of markets with powerful buyers. On monopsony power and countervailing buyer power, see AL Bowley, 'Bilateral Monopoly' (1928) 38 Economic Journal 651; JN Morgan, 'Bilateral Monopoly and the Competitive Output' (1949) 63 Quarterly Journal of Economics 371; JK Galbraith, *American Capitalism: The Concept of Countervailing Power* (New York, Houghton Mifflin 1952); SH Lustgarten, 'The Impact of Buyer Concentration in Manufacturing Industries' (1975) 47 Rev Econ & Stat 125; R McGucken and H Chen, 'Interactions Between Buyer and Seller Concentration and Industry Price-Cost Margins' (1976) 4 Ind Org Rev 123; LA Guth, RA Schwartz, and DK Whitcombe, 'Buyer Concentration Ratios' (1977) 25 Journal of Industrial Economics 241; K Binmore, A Rubinstein, and A Wolinsky, 'The Nash Bargaining Solution in Economic Modelling' (1986) 14 RAND Journal of Economics 176; MV Pauly, 'Monopsony Power in Health Insurance: Thinking Straight While Standing on Your Head' (1987) 6 Journal of Health Economics 73; H Horn and A Wolinsky, 'Bilateral Monopolies and Incentives for Merger' (1988) 19 RAND Journal of Economics 408; MV Pauly, 'Market Power, Monopsony, and Health Insurance Markets' (1988) 7 Journal of Health Economics 111; SE Atkinson and J Kerkvliet (1989) 71 'Dual Measures of Monopoly and Monopsony Power: An Application to Regulated Electric Utilities' (1989) 71 Rev Econ & Stat 250; RD Blair, DL Kaserman, and RE Romano, 'A Pedagogical Treatment of Bilateral Monopoly' (1989) 55 Southern Economic Journal 831; CM Newmark, 'Administrative Control, Buyer Concentration, and Price-Cost Margins' (1989) 71 Rev Econ & Stat 74; U Schumacher, 'Buyer Structure and Seller Performance in US Manufacturing Industries' (1991) 73 Rev Econ & Stat 277; T Chipty 'Horizontal Integration for Bargaining Power: Evidence from the Cable Television Industry' (1995) 4 Journal of Economics and Management Strategy 375; JB Nordemann, 'Buying Power and Sophisticated

The case law and decisional practice recognizes the relevance of countervailing buyer power. In *Italian Flat Glass*, the Court of First Instance set aside a finding of collective dominance on the grounds that, *inter alia*, the Commission had failed to examine whether the presence of a powerful buyer could neutralize the economic power of the three allegedly collectively dominant oligopolists.[187] In *Irish Sugar*, the Court of First Instance rejected, on the facts, the argument that the presence of two powerful buyers was sufficient to rebut a prima facie case of dominance of a seller with a market share of 90 per cent.[188] The Court held that there were a number of customers on the market who were not in a position to constrain the market power of the dominant seller.[189] The commercial strength of the two largest customers was not capable of influencing the prices charged to the other buyers.[190] In *Universal Music Group/BMG Music Publishing*,[191] according to the Commission, it was very likely that, as a result of the merger, Universal would have the ability to increase prices.[192] Apple with its iTunes platform was not considered to have sufficient buyer power to exercise any pressure on Universal. The Universal/BMG repertoire was by far the largest, so that Apple could not credibly threaten to switch to other suppliers but it was limited to threatening not to offer Universal titles on its platform, which in turn would significantly decrease the attractiveness of iTunes.[193]

In other cases, the Commission reached the conclusion that customers had the ability and incentive to act as a counterbalance to the leading seller's ability to harm competition. In *Enso/Stora*, a merger case, the market power of a merged entity with a market share between 50 and 70 per cent and in the presence of high barriers to entry would be constrained by the countervailing buyer power of a buyer with a market share between 60 and 80 per cent and two buyers with market shares between 10 and 20 per cent. The reason was not only the symmetry of market shares between the supply and the demand side. More importantly, the merged entity would be dependent on the leading buyer because if the latter switched supplier, the merged entity could not easily find other purchasers to absorb the

---

Buyers in Merger Control Law: The Need for a More Sophisticated Approach' (1995) 16 ECLR 270; JM Connor, R Rogers, and V Bhagavan 'Concentration and Countervailing Power in the US Food Manufacturing Industries' (1996) 11 Rev Ind Org 473; GF Mathewson and RA Winter, 'Buyer Groups' (1996) 15 Intl J Ind Org 137; CM Snyder 'A Dynamic Theory of Countervailing Power' (1996) 27 RAND Journal of Economics 747; T von Ungern-Sternberg, 'Countervailing Power Revisited' (1996) 14 Intl J Ind Org 507; YK Che and I Gale, 'Buyer Alliances and Managed Competition' (1997) 6 Journal of Economics and Management Strategy 175; PW Dobson and M Waterson, 'Countervailing Power and Consumer Prices' (1997) 107 Economic Journal 418; P Dobson, M Waterson, and A Chu, 'The Welfare Consequences of the Exercise of Buyer Power', OFT Research Paper 16 (September 1998); A Overd, 'Buyer Power' (2001) 22 ECLR 249; I Kokkoris, 'Buyer Power Assessment in Competition Law: A Boon or a Menace?' (2006) 29 World Competition 139; C Doyle and R Inderst, 'Some Economics on the Treatment of Buyer Power in Antitrust' (2007) 28 ECLR 210; OECD, 'Monopsony and Buyer Power', Best Practice Roundtables on Competition Policy (2008).

[187] Joined cases T-68/89, T-77/89, and T-78/89, T-68/89, T-77/89, and T-78/89 *Società Italiana Vetro SpA v Commission* [1992] ECR II-1403 (*Italian Flat Glass*), para 366.

[188] Case T-228/97 *Irish Sugar*, paras 98–104.   [189] ibid para 98.   [190] ibid para 100.

[191] *Universal Music Group/BMG Music Publishing* (Case COMP/M.4404) [2007] OJ L230/12.

[192] ibid recital 386.   [193] ibid recital 383.

output necessary to operate at an efficient capacity. On the other hand, the leading buyer had the ability to develop new capacity with other existing or new suppliers as it already used more than one supplier. It also had the incentive to do so because the cost of the input in question was significant. Unlike in *Irish Sugar*, the countervailing buyer power of the largest buyer would affect the incentives of the merged entity to exercise market power over the smaller customers. This was because the marginalization of the smaller customers would increase the merged entity's dependence on the largest customer. As a result, the Commission found that there was sufficient countervailing buyer power on the market to neutralize the exercise of market power of the merged entity.[194] In *Behringwerke AG/Armour Pharmaceutical Co*, the Commission held that customers on the German plasma-derivative market were sufficiently large, had several suppliers, and were focused on innovation. This allowed smaller sellers or new entrants to establish themselves on the market.[195] In *Syniverse/BSG*, a merger between two undertakings providing technology services to wireless telecommunications companies, mobile network operators were found to have a strong bargaining position by virtue of their relative financial size and the scale of their operations and were thus able not only to influence the buying process but also to sponsor new entry.[196] In *STX/Aker Yards* the Commission found that cruise ship operators had 'a degree of buyer power allowing them to "play" suppliers one against the other in an efficient way'.[197]

F. Conclusion

Under Article 102, dominance is the ability to harm competition to the detriment of long-term social welfare. It is, therefore, a quintessentially behavioural concept. However, the case law and the Commission enforcement practice have often adopted a structuralist approach to dominance. This confusion may originate in the requirement that one of the constitutive elements of dominance is substantial and durable market power. While in theory undertakings with little or no market power may have the ability to harm competition, Article 102 applies only to undertakings with substantial and durable market power. The enforcement costs of applying a prohibition of unilateral conduct to all firms or to all firms with some market power would outweigh its benefits. This does not mean, however, that substantial and durable market power is relevant *per se*. Even less does it mean that dominance is substantial and durable market power as the Guidance on Article 102 appears to say. Article 102 is not a regulatory tool intended to address the market failure resulting from market power. It is a prohibition of unilateral conduct that restricts competition or takes advantage of a market structure in which competition is weakened to the detriment of long-term social welfare.

---

[194] *Enso/Stora* (Case IV/M.1225) [1999] OJ L254/9, recitals 84–97.
[195] *Behringwerke AG/Armour Pharmaceutical Co* (Case IV/M.495), recitals 34–35.
[196] *Syniverse/BSG* (Case COMP/M.4662) [2008] OJ C101/25, recital 99.
[197] *STX/Aker Yards*, recital 153.

Substantial and durable market power is, therefore, an element of the assessment of a firm's ability to act in an anti-competitive way. The main implication of this finding is that dominance must be part and parcel of the assessment of abuse. It is not a separate step, completely detached from the analysis of the harmful conduct, based on a structuralist review of the market. Elements such as the indispensability of the input in refusal to supply, the presence of a non-contestable share in customer-foreclosure strategies, or the inability of competitors to deploy effective counter-strategies to neutralize the anti-competitive behaviour of the undertaking alleged to be dominant, are key factors in the assessment of dominance defined as the ability to harm competition unilaterally.

A fundamental consequence of the definition of dominance as ability to harm competition is that barriers to entry under Article 102 must be examined under a dynamic test. A feature of the market is a barrier to entry only if it contributes, in itself or in combination with other factors, to a firm's ability to foreclose rivals, exploit customers, or harm the efficiency of the downstream or upstream industry to the detriment of long-term social welfare. This test requires an integrated analysis of barriers to entry in the light of the alleged abusive behaviour under review. The case law and the Commission enforcement practice are often out of line with this approach. However, there are notable examples both in the case law and the Commission practice under Article 102 and in the Commission merger practice that show that a dynamic approach to barriers to entry is both administrable and only incrementally different from the current application of Article 102.

Buyers may be able to neutralize a seller's ability to harm competition. Countervailing buyer power requires that the buyer has credible alternatives to purchasing from the seller in question, including switching to existing suppliers, sponsoring new entry, or integrating vertically. It is, however, not sufficient that a dominant undertaking has one or few large customers who may be able to negotiate lower prices than smaller buyers on the market. The presence of large buyers must be such that it neutralizes the harm to long-term social welfare that a dominant seller may cause. In order for this to happen, the structure of demand must be capable of generating incentives for the seller to behave competitively. This is only possible if buyer power exerts competitive pressure on the seller through a credible threat of increased upstream competition. Notwithstanding their overall structuralist approach to dominance, the EU courts and the Commission adopt a dynamic approach to countervailing buyer power which is consistent with the concept of dominance as the ability of a firm to harm long-term social welfare by anti-competitive conduct.

11

Collective Dominance

A. Introduction

Article 102 prohibits any abuse of a dominant position 'by one or more undertakings'. The concept of collective dominance, first recognized by the Court of First Instance in *Italian Flat Glass*,[1] has given rise to a considerable degree of uncertainty and complexity in the development of the legal tests.[2] The reason is that collective dominance has been interpreted as covering tacit oligopolistic collusion[3] as well as

---

[1] Joined Cases T-68/89, T-77/89, and T-78/89 *Società Italiana Vetro Spa v Commission* [1992] ECR II-1403 (*Italian Flat Glass*) para 358.

[2] The concept of collective dominance has generated a vast literature: BJ Rodgers, 'Oligopolistic Market Failure: Collective Dominance Versus Complex Monopoly' (1995) 16 ECLR 21; T Soames, 'An Analysis of the Principles of Concerted Practice and Collective Dominance: a Distinction without a Difference' (1996) 17 ECLR 24; EJ Morgan, 'The Treatment of Oligopoly under the European Merger Control Regulation' (1996) 41 Antitrust Bull 203; JS Venit, 'Two Steps Forward and No Steps Back: Economic Analysis and Oligopolistic Dominance after *Kali & Salz*' (1998) 35 CML Rev 1101; SB Bishop, 'Power and Responsibility: The ECJ's Kali-Salz Judgment' (1999) 20 ECLR 37; PM Fernandez, 'Increasing Powers and Increasing Uncertainty: Collective Dominance and Pricing Abuses' (2000) 25 EL Rev 645; E Kloosterhuis, 'Joint Dominance and the Interaction Between Firms' (2000) 21 ECLR 79; C Gordon and R Richardson, 'Collective Dominance: The Third Way?' (2001) 22 ECLR 416; M Jephcott and C Withers, 'Where to Go Now for EC Oligopoly Control?' (2001) 22 ECLR 295; G Niels, 'Collective Dominance: More than Just Oligopolistic Interdependence' (2001) 22 ECLR 168; O Black, 'Collusion and Co-ordination in EC Merger Control' (2003) 24 ECLR 408; GJ Werden, 'Economic Evidence on the Existence of Collusion: Reconciling Antitrust Law with Oligopoly Theory' (2004) 71 Antitrust LJ 719; O Black, 'Communication, Concerted Practices and the Oligopoly Problem' (2005) 1 European Competition Journal 341; R O'Donoghue and AJ Padilla, *The Law and Economics of Article 82 EC* (Oxford, Hart Publishing 2006) 137–165; D Parker, 'A Screening Device for Tacit Collusion Concerns' (2006) 27 ECLR 424; G Monti, *EC Competition Law* (Cambridge, CUP 2007) 334–338 and 341–342; CE Mosso et al, 'Article 82' in J Faull and A Nikpay (eds), *The EC Law of Competition* (2nd edn Oxford, OUP 2007) 313, 338–344; V Korah, *An Introductory Guide to EC Competition Law and Practice* (9th edn Oxford, Hart Publishing 2007) 124–127; MB Coate, 'Alive and Kicking: Collusion Theories in Merger Analysis at the Federal Trade Commission' (2008) 4 Competition Policy International 145; P Roth and V Rose (eds), *Bellamy & Child European Community Law of Competition* (6th edn Oxford, OUP 2008) 939–946; R Whish, *Competition Law* (6th edn Oxford, OUP 2008) 556–567; J Goyder, *Goyder's EC Competition Law* (5th edn Oxford, OUP 2009) 376–382; FE Mezzanotte, 'Tacit Collusion as Economic Links in Article 82 EC Revisited' (2009) 30 ECLR 137; M Filippelli, 'Collective Dominance in the Italian Mobile Telecommunications Market' (2010) 31 ECLR 81; FE Mezzanotte, 'Using Abuse of Collective Dominance in Article 102 TFEU to Fight Tacit Collusion: The Problem of Proof and Inferential Error' (2010) 33 World Competition 77.

[3] Economic theory moved from the uniform understanding of oligopoly, to be found in the classic works by EH Chamberlain, *The Theory of Monopolistic Competition* (Oxford, OUP, 1966); JS Bain, *Industrial Organisation* (2nd edn New York, John Wiley and Sons 1968); and W Fellner, *Competition*

other instances in which two or more undertakings are linked in such a way that they adopt the same conduct[4] or present themselves as a collective entity[5] on the market because of commercial or structural links or direct or indirect contacts between them. However, oligopolistic collective dominance and non-oligopolistic collective dominance are fundamentally different concepts. The problem of whether undertakings in a concentrated market have the ability and the incentive to restrict output and raise prices is different from the question of whether members of an association of undertakings or a consortium have the ability to harm competition by adopting a common policy on the market. Failure to draw this distinction has led to unnecessary complications in what is already a complex area of the law.

After examining the emergence of the concept of collective dominance, this chapter demonstrates that there are two separate concepts of collective dominance governed by different legal tests. This chapter then goes on to identify the principles that define the scope of abusive conduct by undertakings that are collectively dominant. Finally, conclusions are drawn.

B. The emergence of the concept of collective dominance

Article 102 explicitly provides for the possibility that more than one undertaking can commit an abuse of a dominant position. However, it was only in *Italian Flat Glass* that the Court of First Instance recognized that a dominant position could be held by two or more undertakings. In that case, the Commission had found that three undertakings had engaged in agreements and concerted practices prohibited under Article 101 and had abused their collective dominant position under Article 102.[6] The undertakings concerned controlled more than 80 per cent of the relevant market.[7] They systematically sold products to each other so as to allow each undertaking to offer a full range of products. There was evidence that the market was transparent[8] and that the product was homogenous.[9] The Commission's case under Article 102 was that the position of collective dominance resulted from the agreements and concerted practices which were caught by Article 101.[10] Before the Court, the applicants and the United Kingdom argued that Article 102 was

---

Among the Few (London, Frank Cass & Co 1965), to recognizing a distinction between coordinating and non-coordinating oligopolies. The modern approach starts with the seminal study by GJ Stigler, 'A Theory of Oligopoly' (1964) 72 Journal of Political Economy 44, and is now mainstream: see Werden, 'Economic Evidence on the Existence of Collusion', 719.

⁴ This formulation is adopted in Case C-393/92 *Municipality of Almelo v NV Energiebedrijf Ijsselmij* [1994] ECR I-1477 (*Almelo*), para 42.

⁵ This formulation is adopted in Joined Cases C-395/96 P and C-396/96 P *Compagnie Maritime Belge Transports SA v Commission* [2000] ECR I-1365, para 36.

⁶ Joined Cases T-68/89, T-77/89 and T-78/89 *Italian Flat Glass*. ⁷ ibid para 350.

⁸ ibid paras 18 and 22.

⁹ ibid para 23, quoting the Commission's finding that the undertakings in question manufactured 'identical products'.

¹⁰ ibid paras 350 and 354.

not applicable to the facts of the case as a matter of law.[11] The Court disagreed. It emphasized that Article 102 envisaged the possibility of an abuse by 'one or more undertakings'.[12] 'Undertaking' in Article 102 must have the same meaning as in Article 101. Therefore, collective dominance could not refer to situations in which the links between different business entities are such that they present themselves as an economic unit on the market, as is the case when separate companies belong to the same corporate group and have no decisional independence.[13] Collective dominance refers to circumstances in which two or more separate undertakings are united by such economic links that, by virtue of that fact, together they hold a dominant position vis-à-vis the other operators on the relevant market while remaining separate undertakings.[14] The Court added that this could be the case when two or more undertakings have, through agreements or licences, a technological lead affording them the power to behave to an appreciable extent independently of their competitors, their customers, and ultimately the consumers within the meaning of the definition of dominance in *Hoffman-La Roche*.[15] Ultimately, the Court annulled the decision of the Commission under Article 102 for failure to prove that the undertakings in question presented themselves on the market as a collective entity[16] but held that a finding of collective dominance could not be ruled out as a matter of law.[17]

The Court of Justice confirmed the possibility of a collective dominant position in *Almelo*. In that case, under the relevant Dutch legislation, regional energy distributors were granted a non-exclusive concession for the distribution of energy to local distributors and end-users within a given territory.[18] The general conditions for the supply of electric power by a regional distributor to local distributors contained an exclusive purchasing obligation.[19] This reproduced a clause contained in the model terms and conditions for the supply of electricity of the Association of Operators of Electricity Undertakings in the Netherlands.[20] The Court of Justice held that the clause in question was an agreement between undertakings having a restrictive effect on competition[21] and that the same clause could be an abuse of a collective dominant position by the regional electricity distributors in the Netherlands.[22] The Court stated that for such a collective dominant position

---

[11] ibid paras 340–346.   [12] ibid para 357.
[13] ibid. For a thorough analysis of the concept of undertaking in Union law, see O Odudu, *The Boundaries of EC Competition Law: The Scope of Article 81* (Oxford, OUP 2006) 23–56.
[14] Joined Cases T-68/89, T-77/89, and T-78/89 *Italian Flat Glass*, para 358; Case T-193/02 *Laurent Piau v Commission* [2005] ECR II-209, para 110; Joined Cases C-395/96 P and C-396/96 P *Compagnie Maritime Belge*, para 36.
[15] Joined Cases T-68/89, T-77/89, and T-78/89 *Italian Flat Glass*, para 358.
[16] ibid paras 365–368.   [17] ibid paras 357–359.
[18] Case C-393/92 *Almelo*, paras 4–5   [19] ibid para 35.   [20] ibid para 38.
[21] ibid paras 35–36.
[22] ibid paras 40–45. The Court cited Case 30/87 *Corinne Bodson v SA Pompes Funèbres des Régions Libérées* [1988] ECR 2479. *Bodson*, however, does not explicitly address the question of a collective dominant position. It is true that the Court of Justice consistently refers to a 'group of undertakings' in the part of the judgment dealing with Art 102 but this seems to be on the assumption that the group in question is a single undertaking for the purpose of Arts 101 and 102. The Court had already ruled that if the undertakings in question constitute an economic unit, any agreements between them cannot fall under Art 101. The part of the judgment discussing the issue of dominance opens with the following statement: 'Any anti-competitive behaviour on the part of a group of undertakings

to exist, the undertakings in the group must be linked in such a way that they adopt the same conduct on the market.[23] It was, however, for the national court to consider whether there existed between the regional electricity distributors in the Netherlands links which were sufficiently strong for there to be a collective dominant position in a substantial part of the internal market.[24] *Almelo* may be seen as a case that establishes, as a matter of law, the possibility of a collective dominant position among undertakings operating at the same level of the distribution chain in different markets.[25] However, the Court of Justice did not adopt any market definition. It is arguable that the market for the supply of energy to local distributors may have been national. Regional distributors had a non-exclusive concession for the supply of energy in a given territory and, in the absence of the exclusive purchasing obligation, it is plausible to assume that local distributors and end-customers could have purchased energy from other Dutch regional distributors. The market definition issue was not raised before the Court. Therefore, given that the case law is clear that dominance can only be assessed once a relevant market has been properly defined, the issue must have been left to the national court by necessary implication.[26]

The Court of First Instance further refined the concept of collective dominance in *Gencor*.[27] The Commission had prohibited the integration of Gencor's

---

holding concessions which constitute an economic unit as defined in the case-law of the Court must be considered in the light of Article [102] of the Treaty.' It seems, therefore, that the Court of Justice in *Almelo* incorrectly cited the *Bodson* case as an authority on collective dominance.

[23] Case C-393/92 *Almelo*, para 42. The definition of collective dominance in *Almelo* clearly implies that there must be no competition between the collectively dominant undertakings. See Case C-96/94 *Centro Servizi Spediporto Srl v Spedizioni Marittima del Golfo Srl* [1995] ECR I-2883, paras 33–34 (finding that national legislation providing that a committee with a minority representation of road haulage contractors had the power to recommend road haulage tariffs to be approved and made mandatory by the relevant Minister did not confer on the undertakings concerned a collective dominant position because it did not eliminate competition between them) and Joined Cases C-140/94 P to C-142/94 P *DIP SpA v Comune di Bassano del Grappa* [1995] I-3257, paras 26–27 (finding that national legislation requiring a licence to be obtained before opening a shop in a municipality by a procedure envisaging the advisory opinion of a committee in which established traders were represented, albeit in the minority, did not confer on the established traders a collective dominant position because it did not eliminate competition between them).

[24] Case C-393/92 *Almelo*, para 43.

[25] O'Donoghue and Padilla, *The Law and Economics of Article 82 EC*, 148.

[26] Case 6/72 *Europemballage Corp and Continental Can Co Inc v Commission* [1973] ECR 215 (*Continental Can*) para 32; Case 27/76 *United Brands Co and United Brands Continentaal BV v Commission* [1978] ECR 207, para 10; Case 85/76 *Hoffmann-La Roche & Co AG v Commission* [1979] ECR 461, para 21.

[27] Case T-102/96 *Gencor Ltd v Commission* [1999] ECR II-753; GP Elliott, 'The Gencor Judgment: Collective Dominance, Remedies and Extraterritoriality under the Merger Regulation' (1999) 24 EL Rev 638; V Korah, '*Gencor v Commission*: Collective Dominance' (1999) 20 ECLR 337. *Gencor* was a case under Council Regulation (EEC) 4064/89 of 21 December 1989 on the control of concentrations between undertakings [1989] OJ L395/1, corrected version [1990] OJ L257/13, as amended by Council Regulation (EC) 1310/97 of 30 June 1997 amending Regulation (EEC) 4064/89 on the control of concentrations between undertakings [1997] OJ L180/1, corrigendum [1998] OJ L40/17 ('1989 Merger Regulation'). It is established, however, that the definition of collective dominance under Art 102 is the same as in merger control: Case T-193/02 *Laurent Piau v Commission* [2005] ECR II-209, para 111, concerning an alleged abuse of a collective dominant position under Art 102, where the Court of First Instance adopted the test set out in Case T-342/99 *Airtours plc v Commission* [2002] ECR II-2585, para 62, concerning a case under the 1989 Merger Regulation.

and Lonrho's platinum and rhodium businesses because the concentration would have created a collective dominant position between the merger entity and another undertaking (Amplats).[28] The merger would have reduced the main suppliers of platinum from four to three and, within two years from the decision, to two (because of the exhaustion of Russian stocks). The merged entity and Amplats would have accounted for 60 to 70 per cent and then 80 per cent of the market, with respective market shares of 30 to 35 per cent and then 40 per cent.[29] The Commission took the view that mere oligopolistic interdependence could amount to a collective dominant position.[30] A number of market characteristics were held to make it likely that the duopoly resulting from the concentration and the exhaustion of Russian stocks would have had no incentive to compete effectively but, on the contrary, would have had the incentive to reduce output and raise prices.[31] The Court of First Instance upheld the Commission's decision holding that the creation or strengthening of a collective dominant position between the merged entity and one or more undertakings could be incompatible with the system of undistorted competition that the 1989 Merger Regulation intended to preserve.[32] The Court defined collective dominance as the ability of two or more undertakings acting together, in particular because of factors giving rise to a connection between them, to adopt a common policy on the market and to act, to a considerable extent, independently of their competitors, their customers and, ultimately, of consumers.[33] In rejecting the applicant's argument that the Commission had not established the existence of structural links as required by the case law, the Court stated that the case law (mainly, the *Italian Flat Glass* case) required the existence of economic links, which need not be structural. The concept of economic links includes the relationship of interdependence between the members of a tight oligopoly which, in a market with the appropriate characteristics in particular in terms of market concentration, transparency, and product homogeneity, are able to anticipate one another's behaviour and have therefore a strong incentive to align their conduct on the market, in particular in such a way as to maximize joint profits by restricting production with a view to increasing prices.[34] In *Compagnie Maritime Belge*, the Court of Justice confirmed that agreements or other legal links are not necessary to establish a collective dominant position. Collective dominance may result from 'other connecting factors and would depend on an economic assessment and, in particular, on an assessment of the structure of the market in question'.[35] Thus, the case law in the 1990s gives full effect to the text of Article 102, which prohibits

---

The judgment of the Court of First Instance in the *Piau* case was upheld in Case C-171/05 P *Laurent Piau v Commission* [2006] ECR I-37 but the issue of collective dominance did not arise on appeal: see para 33. The different nature of the analysis, prospective in merger control and retrospective under Art 102, does not impinge on the definition of collective dominance but only on the type of evidence that may be relevant and on the standard of proof.

[28] *Gencor/Lonrho* (Case IV/M.619) [1997] OJ L11/30.　　　[29] ibid recital 181.
[30] ibid recital 140. See Niels 'Collective Dominance: More Than Just Oligopolistic Interdependence', 168–169.
[31] *Gencor/Lonrho*, recital 205.　　　[32] Case T-102/96 *Gencor*, paras 148 and 151.
[33] ibid para 163.　　　[34] ibid para 276.
[35] Joined Cases C-395/96 P and C-396/96 P *Compagnie Maritime Belge*, para 45.

any abuse of a dominant position by one or more undertakings. However, the early case law on collective dominance conflated two fundamentally different concepts of dominance: the ability to harm competition by two or more undertakings acting as a collective entity by virtue of structural or commercial links or direct or indirect contacts and the ability to harm competition of oligopolistic undertakings tacitly coordinating their behaviour. Instead, these two concepts of collective dominance must be separately examined and are subject to completely different legal tests.

C. Non-oligopolistic collective dominance

(1) Horizontal non-oligopolistic collective dominance

(a) *The two-pronged structure of the test*

Horizontal non-oligopolistic collective dominance arises when two or more undertakings act as a collective entity on the same market and have the ability to harm competition because of structural or commercial links or direct or indirect contacts between them. Structural or commercial links or direct or indirect contacts must be sufficient to arrive at the conclusion that two or more undertakings act as a collective entity. Their role must not be limited to facilitating tacit oligopolistic coordination.

The Court of Justice in *Compagnie Maritime Belge* held that the test for non-oligopolistic collective dominance is two-pronged. The first question is whether two or more undertakings act as a collective entity. The second question is whether they are dominant.[36]

(b) *Collective entity test*

The collective entity test requires a thorough analysis of the links between the undertakings in question. Structural links may include interlocking directorships, cross-shareholdings, participation in joint ventures, or participation in trade associations. Commercial links may include cross-licences of relevant technologies or exclusive reciprocal distributorship agreements. Direct contacts include regular exchanges of confidential information relevant to the parameters of competition, such as information on costs, prices, and output. Indirect contacts include the exchange of the same type of information through a third party, for instance in the case of retailers who share information through their common suppliers. Structural or commercial links or direct or indirect contacts need not be unlawful under Article 101. In *Compagnie Maritime Belge*, the Court of Justice upheld a finding of abuse of collective dominance notwithstanding the fact that the arrangements among the members of a dominant liner conference were block-exempted from the application of Article 101(1).[37] However, the links giving rise to non-oligopolistic collective dominance may be also an infringement of Article 101. Therefore, the

---

[36] ibid para 39.   [37] ibid paras 130, 134, and 136.

same evidence can be relevant under both Articles 101 and 102 but a competition authority or claimant cannot simply 'recycle' the evidence substantiating a finding of infringement under Article 101 in order to establish the existence of a collective dominance position. In *Italian Flat Glass*, the Court firmly rejected such an approach.[38] The Court, however, did not declare the evidence that is relevant under Article 101 inadmissible under Article 102. The injunction against the 'recycling' of the evidence relates to cases in which a competition authority or claimant relies exclusively on proof of an infringement of Article 101 to establish collective dominance under Article 102.[39] This was confirmed in *Compagnie Maritime Belge*, where the Court of Justice held that the mere fact that undertakings are linked by an agreement, a concerted practice, or a decision of an association of undertakings within the meaning of Article 101 is not 'a sufficient basis' for a finding of collective dominance.[40] However, explained the Court, the nature and terms of an agreement, concerted practice, or decision of association of undertakings and the way it is implemented may result in the undertakings concerned presenting themselves as a collective entity on the market.[41] On the facts, the Court held that a liner conference agreement whereby the participant undertakings coordinated their pricing policy gave rise to a collective dominant position.[42]

Compagnie Maritime Belge further illustrates what kind of links may give rise to a non-oligopolistic collective dominant position. Associated Central West Africa Lines (Cewal) was a liner conference operating between Zaire and Angola and the ports in the North Sea. It targeted its main competitor by insisting that an agreement concluded with the Zairean authorities and granting Cewal exclusive rights on the shipping routes between Zaire and Northern Europe be strictly complied with, by implementing a system of selective price cuts, and by loyalty contracts and anti-competitive rebates.[43] Before the Court of First Instance, the members of the conference disputed that they held a collective dominant position. Liner conferences were, at that time, exempted from the application of Article 101 TFEU. Regulation (EEC) 4056/86 defined liner conferences as follows:[44]

… a group of two or more vessel-operating carriers which provides international liner services for the carriage of cargo on a particular route or routes within specified geographical limits and which has an agreement or arrangement, whatever its nature, within the framework of which they operate under uniform or common freight rates and any other agreed conditions with respect to the provision of liner services.

In the light of the definition of liner conferences in EU law, three factors were considered relevant to the finding that Cewal was a collective entity. The first was structural: the members of the conference participated in a number of committees

---

[38] Joined Cases T-68/89, T-77/89, and T-78/89 *Italian Flat Glass*, para 360.   [39] ibid.

[40] Joined Cases C-395/96 P and C-396/96 P *Compagnie Maritime Belge*, para 43.

[41] ibid paras 44–45.   [42] ibid paras 46–48.

[43] Joined Cases T-24/93 to T-26/93 and T-28/93 *Compagnie Maritime Belge Transports SA v Commission* [1996] ECR II-1201 (*Compagnie Maritime Belge*) para 15, upheld in Joined Cases C-395/96 P and C-396/96 P *Compagnie Maritime Belge*.

[44] Council Regulation (EEC) 4056/86 of 22 December 1986 laying down detailed rules for the application of Articles 85 and 86 of the Treaty to maritime transport [1986] OJ L378/4, Art 1(3)(b).

in which they discussed their commercial policy. The second related to the absence of effective competition between the members of the conference: the purpose of the liner conference was 'to define and apply uniform freight rates and other common conditions of carriage'. The third was behavioural: the allegedly abusive conduct of the conference members demonstrated an 'intention to adopt together the same conduct on the market in order to react unilaterally to a change, deemed to be a threat, in the competitive situation on the market on which they operate'.[45]

The intention to adopt the same anti-competitive conduct is, however, not necessary for a finding of non-oligopolistic collective dominance. Structural or commercial links or direct or indirect contacts may suffice. In *Atlantic Container Line*, the Court of First Instance upheld the Commission's decision that the members of the Trans-Atlantic Conference Agreement were collectively dominant based on four factors: (a) the members applied a common or uniform tariff, which meant that they did not compete on price; (b) the conference agreement contained enforcement mechanisms and penalties to ensure compliance with the conference tariff; (c) the conference had a secretariat which represented the members vis-à-vis third parties; and (d) the conference members agreed and published annual business plans of the conference.[46]

Structural or commercial links or direct or indirect contacts must eliminate all effective competition among the undertakings concerned. Effective price competition between two or more undertakings is incompatible with a finding that they are a collective entity.[47] There is, however, no requirement that the parties of a collective entity must have eliminated all competition between them. Some marginal competition may survive as long as it does not result in effective competition.[48] When the elimination of effective price competition is proven, internal non-price competition rebuts a prima facie case that two or more undertakings are a collective entity only if it is of such intensity that it precludes reasonable reliance of the parties on their common price policy.[49]

Because all effective competition among the undertakings concerned must have been eliminated, the mere presence of structural links not amounting to control[50] is not sufficient to establish collective dominance or even to give rise to a presumption of collective dominance. In *Airtours*, the Court of First Instance clarified that the fact that the same institutional shareholders hold not insignificant

---

[45] Joined Cases T-24/93 to T-26/93 and T-28/93 *Compagnie Maritime Belge*, para 65. This analysis was upheld on appeal, Joined Cases C-395/96 P and C-396/96 P *Compagnie Maritime Belge*, paras 46–59. The quoted phrase is from para 65.

[46] Joined Cases T-191/98 and T-212/98 to T-214/98 *Atlantic Container Line AB v Commission* [2003] ECR II-3275, paras 592–629.

[47] ibid paras 650 and 695. The language used by the Court in para 695 strongly suggests that structural and commercial links and direct or indirect contacts may be sufficient evidence that the undertakings are a collective entity but the inference may be rebutted by evidence of effective price competition between them. This principle only applies to non-oligopolistic collective dominance.

[48] ibid para 654.

[49] Opinion of AG Fennelly in Joined Cases C-395/96 P and C-396/96 P *Compagnie Maritime Belge*, para 34; Joined Cases T-191/98 and T-212/98 to T-214/98 *Atlantic Container Line*, paras 714–715.

[50] In which case the different companies would be a single undertaking: see eg Case T-102/92 *Viho Europe BV v Commission* [1995] ECR II-17, paras 47–55, upheld on appeal in Case C-73/95 P *Viho Europe BV v Commission* [1996] ECR I-5457.

shareholdings (on the facts, between 30 and 40 per cent) in the major players on a concentrated market 'cannot be regarded as evidence that there is... a tendency to collective dominance in the industry'.[51]

(c) Dominance test

Once it is established that two or more undertakings act as a collective entity on the market, the dominance test is essentially the same as in single dominance. In *Compagnie Maritime Belge*, the Court of First Instance relied on the principle that 'in the absence of exceptional circumstances, extremely large market shares' are in themselves evidence of a dominant position.[52] Cewal's market share exceeded 90 per cent of the market during the relevant period.[53] A number of other factors were relevant to Cewal's dominant position: the difference between Cewal's market share and the market share of its main competition, an exclusivity arrangement with the Zairean authorities, the large size of Cewal's network, its capacity and frequencies, and its market experience.[54] The Court carried out the assessment of collective dominance in the same way as it would have examined single dominance. The Court of First Instance adopted the same approach in *Atlantic Container Line*, where the relevant factors sufficient to establish non-oligopolistic collective dominance were market shares, evidence of price discrimination, the limited ability of customers to switch to alternative suppliers, the weak position of competitors, and substantial barriers to entry.[55] In response to the argument that market shares had a different weight in the assessment of collective dominance, the Court held that an entity with a market share above 50 per cent is capable of behaving independently 'whether it is an individual entity or a single entity'.[56]

The approach to collective dominance adopted in *Compagnie Maritime Belge* and *Atlantic Container Line* is justified insofar as it applies to non-oligopolistic collective dominance only. The point can be clearly understood by contrasting *Compagnie Maritime Belge* and *Atlantic Container Line* with the analysis of oligopolistic collective dominance in *Kali and Salz*.[57] In that case, the Commission relied on two types of factor to prove that the merged entity and the other leading European undertaking in the market, Société Commerciale des Potasses et de

---

[51] Case T-342/99 *Airtours*, para 91.

[52] Joined Cases T-24/93 to T-26/93 and T-28/93 *Compagnie Maritime Belge*, para 76. This principle is well established in relation to single dominance: see Case 85/76 *Hoffmann-La Roche*, para 41; Case 322/81 *NV Nederlandsche Banden Industrie Michelin v Commission* [1983] ECR 3461(*Michelin I*), paras 32–61; Case 62/86 *AKZO Chemie BV v Commission* [1991] ECR I-3359, para 60; Case T-30/89 *Hilti AG v Commission* [1990] ECR II-163, paras 92–93, upheld in Case C-53/92 P *Hilti AG v Commission* [1994] ECR I-667; Case T-228/97 *Irish Sugar plc v Commission* [1999] ECR II-2969, paras 71–104; Case T-321/05 *AstraZeneca AB v Commission* [2010] OJ C221/33, paras 243–253, under appeal in Case C-457/10 P *AstraZeneca AB v Commission* [2010] OJ C301/18.

[53] Joined Cases T-24/93 to T-26/93 and T-28/93 *Compagnie Maritime Belge*, para 77.

[54] ibid para 78. The issue of dominance did not arise on the appeal: Joined Cases C-395/96 P and C-396/96 P *Compagnie Maritime Belge*, para 51.

[55] Joined Cases T-191/98 and T-212/98 to T-214/98 *Atlantic Container Line*, paras 903–942, 953–998, and 1009–1037. These factors correspond to the standard analysis of single dominance: see Mosso et al, 'Article 82', 320–335.

[56] Joined Cases T-191/98 and T-212/98 to T-214/98 *Atlantic Container Line*, para 932.

[57] Joined Cases C-68/94 P and C-30/95 P *French Republic v Commission* [1998] ECR I-1375 (*Kali and Salz*).

l'Azote (SCPA), would hold a collective dominant position after the merger. The first type of factor was in the nature of commercial and structural links. Kali and Salz and SCPA had a joint venture in Canada which was expected to start exporting to Europe in the future and was likely to be of key importance to SCPA.[58] Furthermore, Kali and Salz and SCPA participated in an export cartel relating to sales outside the European Union. There was evidence concerning the behaviour of another undertaking suggesting that the latter had only started competing with Kali and Salz and SCPA after it left the cartel.[59] Finally, Kali und Salz exported to France through SCPA and not through its own distribution network as it did elsewhere in the European Community.[60] The second type of factor was purely economic. The Commission found that the market was mature, transparent, and lacking innovation. The product was homogenous and the market shares of Kali and Salz and SCPA had remained stable over four years.[61] Furthermore, Kali and Salz and SCPA had been in a cartel in the past. After the termination of the cartel, and notwithstanding overproduction in Germany, where Kali and Salz was mainly active, most of the latter's sales in France were channelled through SCPA.[62] The Court of Justice annulled the Commission's decision. It held that, because of errors of assessment that led the Commission to overestimate their significance, the structural and commercial links between Kali and Salz and SCPA were not sufficient to establish a collective dominant position.[63] The purely economic factors relied on by the Commission could not 'be regarded as lending decisive support to the Commission's conclusion'. Of particular relevance was the defective analysis of the degree of competitive pressure that other undertakings were able to exercise on the duopolists. A foreign competitor imported 11 per cent of potash-salt based products in the European Union, while a Spanish undertaking had a 10 per cent market share and a spare capacity of 70 per cent.[64] These findings should also be read in conjunction with the principle that a duopoly with market shares of 23 per cent and 37 per cent cannot be found to be collectively dominant based on market shares alone.[65] In *Kali and Salz*, therefore, the Court established the important principle that when commercial or structural links or direct or indirect contacts are insufficient, in themselves, to establish than two or more undertakings act on the market as a single entity, it is necessary to carry out a systematic examination of oligopolist interdependence.

(2) Vertical non-oligopolistic collective dominance

Vertical non-oligopolistic collective dominance may arise when two undertakings at different levels of the supply or distribution chain act as a collective entity. In *Irish Sugar*, the Commission had found that Irish Sugar and its distributor Sugar Distributors Ltd (SDL) had a collective dominant position on the market for the retail of white granulated sugar in Ireland.[66] The abuse consisted in Irish Sugar

---

[58] *Kali—Salz/MdK/Treuhand* (Case IV/M.308) [1994] OJ L186/38, recitals 58–59.
[59] ibid recital 61. [60] ibid recital 61. [61] ibid recital 57.
[62] ibid recital 57.
[63] Joined Cases C-68/94 P and C-30/95 P *Kali and Salz*, paras 226–232.
[64] ibid paras 240–249. [65] ibid para 226.
[66] *Irish Sugar plc* [1997] OJ L258/1, recitals 99–113.

and SDL taking action to restrict imports of sugar from France and Northern Ireland.[67] SDL on its own had agreed with certain customers to swap Irish Sugar's products for a competitor's products[68] and had granted fidelity rebates to customers.[69] The rebates were funded by Irish Sugar.[70] The Court of First Instance upheld the Commission's finding of vertical collective dominance. The test for non-oligopolistic vertical collective dominance was the same as for non-oligopolistic collective dominance in general: whether structural or commercial links or direct or indirect contacts between two or more undertakings give them the ability to act on the market as a collective entity and, if so, whether such a collective entity was dominant.[71] On the facts, it was undisputed that Irish Sugar did not have management control of SDL and that, as a consequence, Irish Sugar and SDL were not a single undertaking even if Irish Sugar held 51 per cent of the shares in SDL's holding company.[72] The Court nevertheless ruled that the two undertakings were collectively dominant because of sufficient structural and commercial links and contacts between them that gave them the ability to adopt the same policy on the market. These links were:[73]

1. Irish Sugar's shareholding in SDL's holding company;
2. The fact that half of the members of the board of SDL's holding company were Irish Sugar's appointees;
3. Irish Sugar's representation on the board of SDL;
4. SDL's exclusive role, subject to availability of supply, as distributor of Irish Sugar's products;
5. Regular sharing of information relating to sales, marketing, and financial matters;
6. Monthly meetings to discuss key aspects of sugar trading; and
7. The fact that Irish Sugar financed all rebates and promotions to customers.

The Court held that the mere fact that Irish Sugar and SDL were in a vertical relationship was not incompatible with a collective dominant position. Had it been otherwise, there would have been a gap in Article 102. It is possible that undertakings in a vertical relationship are not so closely integrated as to constitute a single undertaking but have the ability and the incentive to behave as a single entity on the market. If they also have the ability and the incentive to harm competition, they would be allowed to do so if Article 102 did not apply to them.[74]

Commentators have puzzled at this concept of vertical collective dominance, stressing that the very premise of collective dominance is that undertakings are active on the same market, that Irish Sugar and SDL were probably a single undertaking, and that Article 101 would probably apply to most of the conduct under review in that case.[75] This confusion comes from the failure of the case law to

---

[67] ibid recitals 119–122 and 128–135.　　[68] ibid recitals 124–126.
[69] ibid recital 127.　　[70] ibid.　　[71] Case T-228/97 *Irish Sugar*, paras 45–47.
[72] ibid para 49 and *Irish Sugar*, recital 111, where the Commission appears to have conceded the point.
[73] Case T-228/97 *Irish Sugar*, paras 51–59.　　[74] ibid para 63.
[75] O'Donoghue and Padilla, *The Law and Economics of Article 82 EC*, 163–164.

articulate clearly the distinction between oligopolistic and non-oligopolistic collective dominance. There is no doubt that oligopolistic collective dominance presupposes that the oligopolists are active on the same market. Multi-market contacts may be relevant if, for instance, they facilitate the exchange of information or make retaliation more credible but undertakings that are not active on the same market have no ability or incentive to coordinate their behaviour through repeated market interactions. However, vertical collective dominance is a form of non-oligopolistic collective dominance. There are circumstances in which undertakings in a vertical relationship are closely connected but are not a single undertaking. In *Irish Sugar*, the upstream undertaking held, albeit indirectly, 51 per cent of the shares in the distributor but did not have management control over the latter. Still, the links between the two undertakings were such that they acted as a collective entity on the market. Nor are the structural and commercial links or direct or indirect contacts that give rise to a vertical collective dominant position necessarily prohibited under Article 101. Article 101 may not apply to structural links at all unless such links are enshrined in an agreement between undertakings. Even when they are, in principle holding a significant shareholding in a company at a different level of the supply chain is unobjectionable. Nor are exchanges of information between a supplier and its distributor unlawful under Article 101. Nevertheless a combination of these factors may align the incentives of vertically-related undertakings in such as way that they act as a collective entity. Furthermore, even if two undertakings in a vertical relationship act as a collective entity, this is still not sufficient to hold that they are dominant. In non-oligopolistic collective dominance, dominance must be separately proved. Finally, even holding a collective dominance position is unobjectionable. Only the abuse of a dominant position is prohibited. It seems, therefore, that while cases of vertical non-oligopolistic collective dominance may well be rare, they cannot be ruled out and *Irish Sugar* provides a sound legal basis for assessing them, providing for sufficient safeguards against the risk of false convictions and over-deterrence.

D. Oligopolistic collective dominance

(1) Structure of the test

Oligopolistic collective dominance arises when two or more undertakings have the ability and incentive to harm competition, provided that such an ability and incentive result, to a decisive extent, from the undertakings' repeated interactions on the market and not from structural or commercial links or direct or indirect contacts between them. Structural or commercial links or direct or indirect contacts may facilitate tacit coordination but must not be sufficient for tacit coordination to be sustainable. If they are, the case is one of non-oligopolistic collective dominance. The difference is an important one. Proof of non-oligopolistic collective dominance does not require an analysis of oligopolistic interaction. Once it has been established that two or more undertakings are a collective entity, the analysis of dominance is the same as for single dominance. On the other hand, if structural or commercial links or direct or indirect contacts are not sufficient to hold that two or more independent undertakings act as a collective entity on the market, it is necessary to examine whether they have the ability and incentive to harm competition as a result of oligopolistic interaction. If they do, they are also dominant. The members of a collectively dominant oligopoly cannot act as a collective entity and yet not be dominant.

The concept of oligopolistic collective dominance is heavily reliant on the economics of tacit oligopolistic coordination.[76] The complexity of the economic theories in this field[77] has meant that the EU courts have struggled to articulate a clear test, at least until the Court of Justice judgment in *Impala*.[78]

[76] Case C-413/06 P *Bertelsmann and Sony Corporation of America v Independent Music Publishers and Labels Association (Impala)* [2008] ECR I-495 (*Impala*), para 123 and Case T-342/99 *Airtours*, para 62.

[77] The references to economic theory or theories in the text distil the key principles from a vast literature: see JS Bain, 'Output Quotas in Imperfect Cartels' (1948) 62 Quarterly Journal of Economics 617; GJ Stigler, 'A Theory of Oligopoly', 44–61; J Friedman, 'A Non-Cooperative Equilibrium for Supergames' (1971) 38 Rev Econ Stud 1; R Porter, 'A Study of Cartel Stability: The Joint Executive Committee, 1880–1886' (1983) 14 Bell Journal of Economics 301; C Davidson and R Deneckere, 'Horizontal Mergers and Collusive Behavior' (1984) 2 Intl J Ind Org 117; EJ Green and RH Porter, 'Non-Cooperative Collusion under Imperfect Price Information' (1984) 52 Econometrica 87; WA Brock and J Scheinkman, 'Price Setting Supergames with Capacity Constraints' (1985) 52 Rev Econ Stud 371; MK Perry and RH Porter, 'Oligopoly and the Incentive for Horizontal Merger' (1985) 75 American Economic Rev 219; D Abreu, 'Extremal Equilibria of Oligopolistic Supergames' (1986) 39 Journal of Economic Theory 191; D Abreu, D Pearce, and E Stachetti, 'Optimal Cartel Equilibria with Imperfect Monitoring' (1986) 39 Journal of Economic Theory 251; D Fudenberg and E Maskin, 'The Folk Theorem in Repeated Games with Discounting or with Incomplete Information' (1986) 54 Econometrica 533; M Osborne and C Pitchik, 'Price Competition in a Capacity-Constrained Duopoly' (1986) 38 Journal of Economic Theory 238; J Rotemberg and G Saloner, 'A Supergame-Theoretic Model of Price Wars during Booms' (1986) 76 American Economic Rev 390; R Gilbert and M Lieberman, 'Investment and Coordination in Oligopolistic Industries' (1987) 18 RAND Journal of Economics 17; VE Lambson, 'Optimal Penal Codes in Price-Setting Supergames with Capacity Constraints' (1987) 54 Rev Econ Stud 385; R Schmalensee, 'Competitive Advantage and Collusive Optima' (1987) 5 Intl J Ind Org 351; J Harrington, 'Collusion Among Asymmetric Firms: The Case of Different Discount Factors' (1989) 7 Intl J Ind Org 289; BD Bernheim and MD Whinston, 'Multimarket Contact and Collusive Behavior' (1990) 21 RAND Journal of Economics 1; C Davidson and R Deneckere, 'Excess Capacity and Collusion' (1990) 31 International Economic Review 521; DL Booth et al, 'An Empirical Model of Capacity Expansion and Pricing in an Oligopoly with Barometric Price Leadership: A Case Study of the Newsprint Industry in North America' (1991) 39 Journal of Industrial Economics 255; J Haltiwanger and J Harrington, 'The Impact of Cyclical Demand Movements on Collusive Behavior' (1991) 22 RAND Journal of Economics 89; TW Ross, 'Cartel Stability and Product Differentiation' (1992) 10 Intl J Ind Org 1; RW Staiger and FA Wolak, 'Collusive Pricing with Capacity Constraints in the Presence of Demand Uncertainty' (1992) 23 RAND Journal of Economics 203; S Martin, 'Endogenous Firm Efficiency in a Cournot Principal-Agent Model' (1993) 59 Journal of Economic Theory 445; WN Evans and IN Kessides, 'Living by the "Golden Rule": Multimarket Contact in the US Airline Industry' (1994) 109 Quarterly Journal of Economics 341; VE Lambson, 'Some Results on Optimal Penal Codes in Asymmetric Bertrand Supergames' (1994) 62 Journal of Economic Theory 444; S Martin, 'R&D Joint Ventures and Tacit Product Market Collusion' (1996) 11 European Journal of Political Economy 733; LR Christensen and R Caves, 'Cheap Talk and Investment Rivalry in the Pulp and Paper Industry' (1997) 45 Journal of Industrial Economics 47; M Armstrong, 'Network Interconnection in Telecommunications' (1998) 108 Economic Journal 545; JJ Laffont, P Rey, and J Tirole, 'Network Competition: I. Overview and Nondiscriminatory Pricing' (1998) 29 RAND Journal of Economics 1; KU Kühn, C Matutes, and B Moldovanu, 'Fighting Collusion by Regulating Communication Between Firms' (2001) 32 Economic Policy 169; O Compte, F Jenny, and P Rey, 'Capacity Constraints, Mergers and Collusion' (2002) 46 European Economic Review 1; I Marc et al, 'The Economics of Tacit Collusion' Final Report to DG Competition, European Commission (Toulouse, March 2003).

[78] Case C-413/06 P *Impala*, para 123.

An economic test of tacit coordination would be structured around three elements: the ability of the oligopolists to coordinate, their incentive to do so, and the absence of incentives to deviate from the terms of coordination.

For tacit coordination to arise, firms must have the ability to coordinate their behaviour. The structural conditions for firms to be able to reach a tacit understanding of the terms of coordination are market transparency, a stable and inelastic demand, and an inelastic supply. Because oligopolistic collective dominance is defined as the ability of firms to coordinate their competitive behaviour based on repeated interactions on the market and not, or at least not to a decisive extent, because of structural or commercial links or direct or indirect contacts, the required level of market transparency must be reasonably high. A cartel may work at lower levels of market transparency than tacit coordination because competitors agree on prices or output directly or exchange, directly or indirectly, key information on price and output. In oligopolistic dominance, coordination must be feasible based mainly or exclusively on the observation of the relevant competitive parameters on the market. As regards the characteristics of demand, demand volatility or high elasticity makes tacit coordination unfeasible. If demand is volatile, firms must change their output frequently and would have to reach new terms of coordination each time. Equally, if the elasticity of the demand of the coordinating firms is high because customers are able to switch to other suppliers, coordination is unfeasible for the simple reason that the oligopolists lack sufficient market power so that they are unable to raise prices and restrict output or reduce investments. The same applies if supply is elastic because a contraction of output attracts new entry or leads firms outside the coordinating oligopoly to increase output. In practical terms, this means that three conditions must be met. First, the market share of the oligopolists on the relevant market must be very high and firms outside the coordinating oligopoly must be capacity constrained or supply inferior substitutes. Secondly, there must be no 'maverick' firm. A maverick firm is a firm which, being indifferent or almost indifferent between coordination and competitive behaviour, has a history or reputation for output-expansive conduct even in the face of price increases on the part of other market players.[79] Thirdly, there must be substantial barriers to entry to the market.

The ability to reach terms of coordination is not sufficient for oligopolistic dominance to arise. Firms must also have the incentive to coordinate their behaviour. This is inherent in the very definition of oligopolistic collective dominance, which provides that the members of a tight oligopoly must be 'strongly encouraged to align their conduct on the market in such a way as to maximise their joint profits by increasing prices, reducing output, the choice or quality of goods and services,

---

[79] There is, of course, no legal definition of a 'maverick' firm. However, the Guidelines on the assessment of horizontal mergers under the Council Regulation on the control of concentrations between undertakings [2004] OJ C31/5 ('Guidelines on Horizontal Mergers') refer to maverick firms twice: at para 20(d) as a 'firm with a high likelihood of disrupting coordinated conduct' and at para 42 as a 'firm that has a history of preventing or disrupting coordination, for example by failing to follow price increases by its competitors, or has characteristics that give it an incentive to favour different strategic choices than its coordinating competitors would prefer'.

diminishing innovation or otherwise influencing parameters of competition'.[80] For firms to have the incentive to engage in tacit coordination, they must have either a direct interest in each other's profitability through cross-ownership or cross-shareholdings or must have sufficiently symmetrical cost and demand functions. Cross-ownership and cross-shareholdings effectively internalize the externalities of the competitive process. However, in oligopolistic collective dominance, cross-ownership and cross-shareholdings cannot be the decisive factor that gives the undertakings in question the ability and incentive to behave as a single entity on the market. Otherwise, the case would be one of non-oligopolistic collective dominance. The role of structural links, if any, must be limited to facilitating the functioning of tacit coordination. Also relevant is the symmetry in the oligopolists' cost functions. Symmetrical cost functions mean that the terms of coordination, for instance a given level of output or price, will have the same effect for all firms. A misalignment of incentives resulting from different profit levels for different firms at the same industry output makes coordination less likely.[81] The same applies to different demand functions facing different firms, which may be reflected in the asymmetry of market shares or product differentiation. Demand prospects as well as actual demand are relevant.

In an oligopoly where firms have the ability and incentive to coordinate, each firm nevertheless has the incentive to lower its price and make a profit at the expense of the other oligopolists. This conduct is likely to be profitable if the other firms maintain their supra-competitive prices. If, however, they also lower their prices and they do so to the extent that the cheating firm's behaviour yields no profits, deviation is not rational. Therefore, for coordination to be sustainable, there must be a sufficiently deterrent punishment mechanism that the oligopolists have the ability and the incentive to impose on a deviating firm. Three conditions must be fulfilled for a punishment mechanism to exist and be a sufficient deterrent: (a) a monitoring condition; (b) a credibility condition; and (c) a deterrence condition. As regards monitoring, the market must be sufficiently transparent and concentrated for any significant deviation to be likely to be detected. These conditions are essentially the same as the concentration and transparency conditions relating to the ability to coordinate. As regards the credibility and the deterrent effect of the punishment, the other oligopolists must have the ability and incentive to punish the cheating firm so as to neutralize any benefits that the latter may derive from the deviation.

The test of oligopolistic collective dominance developed by the case law is in line with the economic theories of tacit coordination. In *Impala*, the Court of Justice held that for two or more undertakings to be collectively dominant based on oligopolistic interaction, they must have the ability to reach terms of coordination

---

[80] Case C-413/06 P *Impala*, para 121.
[81] A Jaquemin and ME Slade, 'Cartels, Collusion and Horizontal Merger' in R Schmalensee and RD Willig (eds), *Handbook of Industrial Organisation* (Amsterdam, North Holland 1989) 418; J Harrington, 'The Determination of Price and Output Quotas in a Heterogeneous Cartel' (1991) 32 Intl Economic Rev 767; R Rothschild, 'Cartel Stability when Costs are Heterogeneous' (1999) 17 Intl J Ind Org 717.

that negatively affect the parameters of competition, they must have the incentive to do so, and they must have no incentive to deviate from the tacit coordination.[82] At paragraph 123, the Court then set out four conditions that are relevant to the test:[83]

1. Coordination is more likely to arise if the oligopolists can easily arrive at a shared understanding of the terms of coordination and of the focal point of such coordination.

2. Because each oligopolist has an incentive to deviate from the common policy so as to increase its profits by increasing its market share, coordination must be sustainable over time. To this end, the oligopolists must be able to monitor to a sufficient degree whether the terms of coordination are being adhered to. This requires that the market be sufficiently transparent for each undertaking concerned to be aware, sufficiently, precisely and quickly, of the way in which the market conduct of each of the other participants is evolving.

3. There must be a credible deterrent mechanism, which can be used if deviation is detected.

4. The reactions of outsiders, ie actual or potential competitors and customers, should not be able to jeopardize the results expected from the coordination.

The Court in *Impala* was at pains to clarify that a mechanical approach to the factors that may be conducive to tacit coordination is to be avoided. What matters is the proof of the overall economic mechanism of tacit coordination rather than the proof of each criterion in isolation.[84] It is in this perspective that the relationship between the test in *Impala* and the conditions in paragraph 62 of *Airtours* must be understood. In *Airtours*, the Court of First Instance set out three conditions that must be met for collective dominance to be established:[85]

1. Each member of the dominant oligopoly must have the ability to monitor whether the others are implementing the terms of coordination. This means that the market must be sufficiently transparent for all the members of the oligopoly to become aware, sufficiently, precisely and quickly, of the others' conduct.

2. Tacit coordination must be sustainable over time. There must be an incentive not to depart from the terms of coordination. Retaliation is inherent in this condition. Each member of the oligopoly must be aware that its departure from the terms of coordination to gain market share will trigger identical action by the others. As a consequence, the former would derive no benefit from departing from the terms of coordination.

3. The foreseeable reaction of current and future competitors and customers must not be such as to jeopardize the results expected from the coordination.

---

[82] This test can be derived from an integrated analysis of paras 120–124 of the judgment: Case C-413/06 P *Impala*, paras 120–124.

[83] ibid para 123.   [84] ibid para 125.   [85] Case T-342/99 *Airtours*, para 62.

The Court of Justice in *Impala* said that the conditions set out in paragraph 62 of *Airtours* are not incompatible with the criteria laid down by the Court of Justice itself in paragraph 123 of *Impala*.[86] Therefore, the significance of the judgment of the Court of Justice is not to overrule *Airtours* but to clarify that it would be wrong to decide cases simply by verifying whether the three conditions set out in paragraph 62 of *Airtours* or indeed the four conditions set out in paragraph 123 of *Impala* are met by looking at each factor in isolation. It is necessary to identify a plausible hypothesis of oligopolistic collective dominance and to prove it on the facts of the individual case. In *Impala*, the lack of a comprehensive analysis of market transparency 'having regard to a postulated monitoring mechanism forming part of a plausible theory of tacit coordination' meant that the Court of First Instance had committed an error of law.[87] Such an error consisted in the analysis of market transparency in isolation and not as an element of the assessment of the ability and incentive of the oligopolists to harm competition on the particular facts of the case.

(2) Integrated analysis of structural and behavioural factors

(a) *The* Impala *approach*

Given the different but compatible formulations of the oligopolistic collective dominance test in *Airtours* and *Impala* and the fluidity of structural and behavioural factors[88] that are relevant to the analysis, a systematic and integrated assessment of the market is always required before oligopolistic collective dominance may be established. Following the approach mandated by the Court of Justice in *Impala*, the relevant factors must be examined not in isolation but in relation to the three elements of the legal test: the ability to coordinate, the incentive to coordinate, and the absence of incentives to deviate. In any oligopolistic collective dominance scenario, what ultimately matters is the proof of the overall coordination mechanism rather than the presence of a number of factors that, in theory, are conducive to tacit coordination.

(b) *Ability to coordinate*

(i) Concentration and stability of market shares

In oligopolistic collective dominance, the case law repeatedly relies on the concept of a 'tight' oligopoly.[89] It is, therefore, not sufficient that the market has an oligopolistic structure. The oligopoly must be particularly concentrated or, in the rather imprecise language of the case law, 'tight'. Two factors are relevant to the definition of a 'tight' oligopoly: the collective market share of the oligopolists

---

[86] Case C-413/06 P *Impala*, para 124.   [87] ibid paras 130–133.

[88] For an analysis of some of these factors, see I Kokkoris, 'Assessment of Mergers Inducing Coordinated Effects in the Presence of Explicit Collusion' (2008) 31 World Competition 499, 501–507.

[89] Case C-413/06 P *Impala*, para 121; Case T-342/99 *Airtours*, para 60; Case T-102/96 *Gencor*, para 276.

and the number of oligopolists. There are no clear rules on these two issues. Guidance may be derived from the case law and the decisional practice of the Commission.

The case law and decisional practice suggests that the collective market share of the oligopoly must be significantly above the 40 per cent market share that constitutes a safe harbour for single dominance,[90] and even above the 50 per cent market share that may give rise to a presumption of dominance.[91] In *Airtours*, the post-merger market share of the oligopoly would have been 80 per cent.[92] In *Impala*, post-merger, the four major recorded music suppliers would have held market shares ranging between 72 and 93 per cent on most relevant markets.[93] In *Gencor*, the post-merger market share of the duopoly was between 60 and 70 per cent but it would have been 'in all likelihood' 80 per cent within two years of the decision because of the exit of a significant competitor.[94] In *Kali and Salz*, the Court of Justice held that the duopolists's post-merger market shares of 23 per cent and 37 per cent could not, because of their size and the way in which they were distributed, 'point conclusively to the existence of a collective dominant position'.[95] However, the Court also said that the presence of competitors with market shares of 11 per cent and 10 per cent was prima facie evidence of effective competitive pressure on the duopoly.[96] In the *E.ON* commitments decision, the three oligopolists had a joint market share between 75 and 67 per cent during the relevant period.[97] The Commission merger control practice is to investigate coordinated effects at market shares of well above 70 per cent.[98] A higher market share requirement than in single dominance is consistent with the observation that, at market shares towards the lower bounds of single dominance (between 40 and 60 per cent),[99] outsiders are more likely to be able to grow and benefit from demand-related efficiencies on the market and exert competitive pressure on the oligopolists.

As far as concentration is concerned, the key observation is that, as the number of oligopolists increases, the number of competitive interactions that

---

[90] Guidance on Art 102, para 14.

[91] Case 85/76 *Hoffmann-La Roche*, para 41; Case 322/81 *Michelin I*, paras 32–61; Case C-62/86 *AKZO*, para 60; Case T-30/89 *Hilti*, paras 92–93; Case T-228/97 *Irish Sugar*, paras 71–104; Case T-321/05 *AstraZeneca*, paras 243–253.

[92] Case T-342/99 *Airtours*, para 67.

[93] *Sony/BMG* (Case COMP/M.3333) (19 July 2004) [2005] OJ L62/30, recital 47.

[94] Case T-102/96 *Gencor*, para 207.

[95] Joined Cases C-68/94 P and C-30/95 P *Kali and Salz*, para 226.　　　[96] ibid paras 242–248.

[97] *German Electricity Wholesale Market* [2009] OJ C36/8 (*E.ON*) recital 14, table 1.

[98] *Nestlé/Perrier* (Case IV/M.190) [1992] OJ L356/1, recital 42 (collective dominance found at 82%); *Syniverse/BSG* (Case COMP/M.4662) [2008] OJ C101/25, recital 104 (further investigation was warranted on markets where the oligopolists had joint market shares between 70 and 90% or 90 and 100% depending on the geographical market definition, with symmetrical individual market shares); *Pilkington-Techint/SIV* (Case IV/M.358) recitals 25–27 (joint market share of the two leading producers of over 50% did not warrant investigation of collective dominance as there was clearly sufficient competitive pressure from outsiders but joint market share of the five main players of over 96% did).

[99] Guidance on Art 102, para 14; Case C-62/86 *AKZO*, para 60; Case T-219/99 *British Airways plc v Commission* [2003] ECR II-5917, paras 211–226.

must be taken into account and monitored increases. However, the number of oligopolists is only one of the factors relevant to the ability to coordinate. The more transparent the market, the more undertakings would be able to coordinate because the increased difficulty in monitoring competitive interactions may be compensated by the ease of monitoring the terms of coordination. While the case law and the decisional practice of the Commission suggest that in a purely oligopolistic setting with no structural or commercial links or direct or indirect contacts between undertakings a finding of collective dominance is unlikely if the oligopolists are more than five,[100] it is impossible, and would be completely arbitrary as a matter of law, to extrapolate a clear-cut rule from the case law or economic theory.

Finally, stability of market shares makes coordination easier because it provides a historical focal point for future output decisions.[101] When the size of an undertaking is a relevant parameter of competition, growth by acquisition must be taken into account when assessing the stability of market shares.[102]

(ii) Market transparency

In order to be able to coordinate, the oligopolists must be able to reach an understanding of the terms of coordination. This requires that the market be sufficiently transparent.[103] Transparency, however, is not the same as the availability at all times of costless and perfect information about prices or the other relevant parameters of competition.[104] The sufficient degree of transparency must be assessed in relation to the form of coordination and the retaliatory mechanisms that are postulated on the facts of the case. Between the case of markets where prices are formed on public exchanges and output statistics are regularly published[105] and markets where prices are negotiated on a confidential basis with each customer,[106] there is a considerable grey area.

In *Airtours*, the Commission had found that the UK market for short-haul foreign package holidays was sufficiently transparent. Tour operators planned capacity in advance. They did so based on previous years' offerings that were

---

[100] eg in the following cases the number of the oligopolists was held to be in principle compatible with a collective dominant position even if some of these cases resulted in a finding that such a position was not proved: Case T-342/99 *Airtours*, paras 66–67 (four players before the merger and three players after the merger); *Sony/BMG* (Case COMP/M.3333) (19 July 2004), recital 156 (5 players before the merger and 4 players after the merger); *E.ON*, recital 13 (3 players); Case T-102/96 *Gencor*, para 207 (3 players before the merger and 2 players after the merger). In *Price Waterhouse/Coopers & Lybrand* (Case IV/M.1016) [1999] OJ L50/27, recital 103, the Commission stated that 'collective dominance involving more than three or four suppliers is unlikely simply because of the complexity of the interrelationships involved and consequent temptation to deviate: such a situation is unstable and untenable in the long term'.

[101] Case T-342/99 *Airtours*, para 111.   [102] ibid paras 113–118.

[103] Case C-413/06 P *Impala*, para 126; Case T-342/99 *Airtours*, para 156; Case T-102/96 *Gencor*, para 276; *E.ON*, recital 19; Guidelines on Horizontal Mergers, para 47.

[104] Case T-464/04 *Independent Music Publishers and Labels Association (Impala) v Commission* [2006] II-2289 (*Impala*) para 440, set aside on appeal in Case C-413/06 P *Impala*.

[105] See Case T-102/96 *Gencor*, para 228 and *E.ON*, recital 19.

[106] *Sony/BMG* (Case COMP/M.3333) (3 October 2007) [2008] OJ C94/19, recital 118 (in relation to the market for recorded music in digital formats).

known to the other operators. Changes in capacity would be known to the other oligopolists, because they all used the same hotels and each other's airline companies and because major capacity expansions were public, for instance as they required the long-term lease of additional aircraft.[107] The Court of First Instance disagreed. The planning decisions of tour operators were not simply a 'renewal' of past offerings but involved a year-by-year assessment of the factors that determine demand for short-haul foreign holidays.[108] Furthermore, aggregate capacity was the result of a myriad decisions relating to individual destinations, dates, airports of departure, accommodation, length of stay, and price. In order to forecast the planned capacity of other market players, each oligopolist would have to know and aggregate these decisions taken at the micro level.[109] Nor could the oligopolists monitor each other's overall capacity. It was not feasible to obtain accurate information on the capacity of other market players through hotels because of their large number and their preference to let their rooms to at least two tour operators.[110] Discussions between the tour operators on seat requirements on each other's airlines took place after capacity had been set and were too limited in scope to result in a sufficient degree of market transparency at the time when capacity decisions were taken.[111]

In *Impala*, the question of whether the market was transparent gave rise to some considerable difficulties. The major recorded music suppliers operated a system of published prices to dealers (PPDs) available in the suppliers' catalogues. There were generally more than 100 PPDs but most discs were sold at the top 5 PPDs. The Commission took the view that PPDs could be the focal point of coordination and that net prices were closely aligned with gross prices. However, the major suppliers granted customers campaign discounts, which varied from album to album and from customer to customer. There was evidence that hit charts increased transparency because they allowed the parties to indentify the titles that generated the most sales and that the major suppliers had close relationships with their customers. However, these factors were not such as to overcome the opacity of campaign discounts.[112] The Court of First Instance annulled the Commission's decisions on two grounds. First, it found that the Commission had failed to provide adequate reasons for the conclusion that campaign discounts made the market opaque. The Commission should have examined the nature of the campaign discounts, their size, the circumstances in which they were granted, and their impact on price transparency.[113] Secondly, the Court held that the Commission's decision was vitiated by a manifest error of assessment. The Court identified the following factors that were conducive to market transparency: (a) the public nature of gross prices; (b) the limited number of reference prices; (c) the limited number of albums to be monitored; (d) the publication of weekly charts; (e) the long-term relationships between suppliers and customers; (f) monitoring of the market; and (g) the small number of

---

[107] Case T-342/99 *Airtours*, paras 149–150.   [108] ibid para 164.
[109] ibid paras 166–168.   [110] ibid paras 173–174.   [111] ibid paras 173–180.
[112] *Sony/BMG* (Case COMP/M.3333) (19 July 2004) recitals 74–80 (dealing with the UK market—the position in the other markets was not materially different) and 111–112.
[113] Case T-464/04 P *Impala*, para 289.

players on the market.[114] The only element of opacity was the campaign discounts. However, the Court held that, while the campaign discounts varied by customer, by album, and over time, they could be based on a set of rules that would not be excessively difficult for a 'market professional' to understand.[115] Transparency must be sufficient to make coordination possible and to give rise to a serious risk that deviation from the terms of coordination would be detected.[116] The Commission had, instead, considered that all price components had to be transparent, including the list price and discounts. This was a 'high level of transparency'.[117] On appeal, the Court of Justice held that the Court of First Instance had committed an error of law by misconstruing the criteria for the assessment of market transparency. The Court of Justice defined transparency as a relative concept. There is no level of transparency that is sufficient as such. Transparency must be sufficient in relation to 'a postulated monitoring mechanism forming part of a plausible theory of tacit coordination'. The reference by the Court of First Instance to a set of rules that might be comprehensible to an industry professional was not sufficient. Those hypothetical rules should have been identified and the degree of market transparency tested against that benchmark.[118]

The Court of Justice ruling in *Impala* brings welcome discipline to the analysis of market transparency by requiring that a plausible theory of tacit coordination must be identified on the facts of each individual case. It goes without saying that such plausible theory of tacit coordination need not be consistent with a model published in the economic literature or constructed ad hoc to suit the facts of the case. However, it must be consistent with the evidence, including any economic evidence. *Airtours* and *Impala* provide two instructive examples. In *Airtours*, the theory of coordination related to the setting of capacity. Market transparency in relation to the prices of packaged holidays was, therefore, irrelevant. Transparency had to relate to capacity at the time when the planning decisions were taken. In *Impala*, the theory of coordination related to prices. However, actual prices were not transparent. A plausible theory of coordination should have explained how the oligopolists could learn each other's actual prices in the absence of a direct exchange of information, given that only list prices were published.

Finally, market transparency also depends on product homogeneity. Differentiated products are valued differently by consumers and, by definition, prices reflect these different valuations. Therefore, coordination is more difficult because it must focus on a number of different prices. This does not mean that any product differentiation automatically rules out tacit coordination. In *Impala*, discs were a highly differentiated product reflecting the very different and well defined preferences of consumers. However, the pricing structure was relatively standardized with the vast majority of high selling albums been sold at the top five published list prices. This pricing structure was held in principle to be capable of giving rise to

---

[114] ibid paras 347–352.   [115] ibid para 429.
[116] ibid para 440.   [117] ibid para 441.   [118] Case C-413/06 P *Impala*, paras 129–134.

tacit coordination.[119] Before the EU courts, the issue of market transparency was highly controversial but it was accepted that, if actual prices had been transparent, they could have been the focal point of tacit coordination.[120]

(iii) Price parallelism

Because Article 102 applies to past or present conduct, tacit coordination must have occurred or be occurring on the market. There is no doubt, therefore, that actual price parallelism is relevant evidence of oligopolistic collective dominance. It is, however, not sufficient evidence, as undertakings with similar cost structures on a homogeneous market may well be charging the same prices as a result of effective competition between them. Parallel prices in themselves are not, therefore, evidence of oligopolistic collective dominance. The case law allows undertakings to adapt themselves intelligently to market conditions, including by taking into account the current or expected conduct of their competitors.[121] In *Hoffmann-La Roche*, the Court distinguished dominance from 'parallel courses of conduct which are peculiar to oligopolies in that in an oligopoly the courses of conduct interact'.[122] This broad definition of oligopolies that are outside the concept of dominance under Article 102 is no longer an accurate statement of the law but does indicate that not all oligopolies are collectively dominant. The key is in the Court of Justice's definition of collective dominance in *Impala* as oligopolistic interaction that increases prices and reduces output or diminishes innovation.[123] The emphasis on negative effects on price, output, or investment is important. In the case of Bertrand competition with homogeneous products, the oligopolists still interact with each other and make their output decisions based on the expected decisions of the other market players. The result is, however, a price that equals MC.[124] This form of oligopolistic interaction does not fall under the definition of oligopolistic collective dominance.

If mere price parallelism is, in itself, not sufficient evidence of oligopolistic collective dominance, price parallelism carries more weight if corroborated by other evidence. For instance, if prices increase in parallel in a way that is not related to either cost or demand, this may be evidence of tacit coordination. Another example may be a situation in which there are significant and temporary price reductions that are neither related to costs nor to demand in an environment where prices have been stable or increasing for a significant period of time before and after the price reductions. This structural break in a stable price environment may indicate a deviation from the terms of coordination that triggered an industry-wide output expansion as a retaliatory measure inducing the parties to revert to coordinated conduct. This analysis is relevant evidence of oligopolistic collective

---

[119] *Sony/BMG* (Case COMP/M.3333) (19 July 2004) recital 76.

[120] See the discussion of transparency in Case T-464/04 *Impala*, paras 278–461, set aside on appeal in Case C-413/06 P *Impala*, paras 117–134.

[121] The case law under Art 101 is well established: Case 48/69 *Imperial Chemical Industries v Commission* [1972] ECR 619, para 64; Joined Cases 40/73 to 48/78, 50/73, 54/73 to 56/73, 111/73, 113/73, and 114/73 *Coöperatieve Vereniging 'Suiker Unie' UA v Commission* [1975] ECR 1663 (*Suiker Unie*), para 174.

[122] Case 85/76 *Hoffmann-La Roche*, para 39.   [123] Case C-413/06 P *Impala*, para 121.

[124] J Tirole, *The Theory of Industrial Organization* (Cambridge Mass, MIT Press 1988) 209–211.

dominance, although it will not be sufficient evidence thereof unless there is no other plausible explanation for the structural break.[125]

(iv) Reaction of customers and analysis of demand

Tacit coordination is not feasible if the demand faced by the oligopolists is elastic. A price increase would lead consumers to look for substitutes, making the price increase unprofitable. In *Airtours*, the reaction of consumers who could switch to smaller tour operators or to different holiday packages outside the relevant market was deemed capable of counteracting an oligopolistic restriction of output.[126] *Airtours* also clarifies that elasticity of demand is not the same as countervailing buyer power.[127] A fragmented demand can still be sufficiently elastic to deny the oligopolists the ability to raise prices and restrict output to the detriment of long-term social welfare. *A fortiori*, the presence of a few large customers capable of exercising countervailing buyer power is incompatible with oligopolistic collective dominance. In *SNECMA/TI*, a merger in the landing gear sector, the Commission held that oligopolistic collective dominance was unlikely, given 'the considerable buying power of the major customers'.[128] In *Sony/BMG*, the Commission found that the concentrated supply of the recorded digital music market with only four major suppliers would be counterbalanced by the concentrated structure of demand where iTunes and the other large digital music service providers had sufficient buyer power to 'react to potential coordination among the majors'.[129] A volatile demand makes coordination more difficult because price and output must change frequently in response to unpredictable changes in demand.[130] For the same reason, slow growth or stability in demand facilitates tacit coordination.[131] The Court of Justice in *Kali and Salz* said that a falling market is also generally considered to promote competition rather than coordination.[132]

(v) Reaction of actual and potential competitors

As with single dominance, for oligopolistic collective dominance to arise, actual and potential competitors must be unable to exercise an effective competitive constraint on the oligopolists. Substantial barriers to entry and expansion are a necessary condition of tacit oligopolistic coordination. In *Airtours*, smaller tour

---

[125] See, by analogy, Joined Cases C-204/00 P, C-205/00 P, C-211/00 P, C-213/00 P, C-217/00 P, and C-219/00 P *Aalborg Portland A/S v Commission* [2004] ECR I-123, para 57: 'In most cases, the existence of an anti-competitive practice or agreement must be inferred from a number of coincidences and indicia which, taken together, may, in the absence of another plausible explanation, constitute evidence of an infringement of the competition rules.'

[126] Case T-342/99 *Airtours*, paras 270–276.   [127] ibid para 274.

[128] *SNECMA/TI* (Case IV/M.368) [1993] OJ C42/12, recitals 37–38.

[129] *Sony/BMG* (Case COMP/M.3333) (3 October 2007), recital 146.

[130] Case T-342/99 *Airtours*, paras 134–147, where the Court addressed the issue from the perspective of the ability to detect deviations. Demand volatility, however, is also relevant to the ability to coordinate in the first place.

[131] ibid para 133, where the Court of First Instance set aside the Commission's finding that the market was characterized by slow growth and, therefore, conducive to oligopolistic coordination.

[132] Joined Cases C-68/94 P and C-30/95 P *Kali and Salz*, para 238; *Sony/BMG* (Case COMP/M.3333) (3 October 2007), recital 442.

operators in the United Kingdom were held to be able to respond to a restriction of output by the oligopolists by increasing their capacity.[133] In *Kali and Salz*, competitors with market shares of 11 per cent and 10 per cent, the latter with considerable excess capacity, were held to be prima facie capable of exercising effective competitive pressure on a duopoly with a joint market share of 60 per cent.[134] In *Syniverse/BSG*, a duopoly on the market for GSM roaming data clearing services to mobile network operators was held to be unable to coordinate because the likely entry of competitors would make coordination unprofitable.[135] Furthermore, customers would have the ability and incentive to sponsor new entry.[136] In *Gencor*, the Court of First Instance held that the slow growth of the market would not have encouraged new entry or aggressive competition by existing competitors.[137] On the contrary, a fast growing market is conducive to entry because post-entry output is expected to be larger than in a stable market where the entrant must capture a share of the existing demand.

(vi) Innovation

Markets characterized by a high rate of innovation are incompatible with tacit coordination. In *Kali and Salz*, the Court of Justice quoted without criticism the Commission's finding that the potash market was characterized by a lack of technological innovation.[138] Tacit coordination is generally incompatible with a dynamic and unstable market. In *Syniverse/BSG*, the Commission found that 'significant modifications to the industry' were expected 'as a result of ongoing technological change'. This would 'reduce the ability of market participants to reach and sustain' tacit coordination.[139] In addition, technological changes could trigger new entry from undertakings already operating neighbouring technologies.[140]

(c) Incentive to coordinate

For tacit coordination to arise, the oligopolists' incentives must be sufficiently aligned. This means that the parameters of supply and demand of each oligopolist must be similar. Undertakings with significantly different demand or cost structures would not have the incentive to coordinate because their respective profit-maximizing prices and output would be significantly different. In *Gencor*, the Court of First Instance considered two parameters: the allocation of market shares, including the shares of reserves, and the cost structures of the duopolists. Given the similarity in these parameters, the Court concluded that the duopolists' interests 'would have coincided to a higher degree and that this alignment of

---

[133] Case T-342/99 *Airtours*, paras 211–269.
[134] Joined Cases C-68/94 P and C-30/95 P *Kali and Salz*, para 242–248.
[135] *Syniverse/BSG* (Case COMP/M.4662) recital 109.
[136] ibid recital 110.   [137] Case T-102/96 *Gencor*, para 237.
[138] Joined Cases C-68/94 P and C-30/95 P *Kali and Salz*, para 240.
[139] *Syniverse/BSG* (Case COMP/M.4662) recital 106.
[140] ibid recital 106. For a description of the technological changes in question, see recitals 62–68.

interests would have increased the likelihood of anti-competitive parallel behaviour, for example restrictions of output'.[141]

Certain factors that are relevant to the ability to coordinate are also relevant to the incentive to do so. A fast-growing demand might make coordination more difficult but, in addition, enhances the oligopolists' incentives to coordinate because the future gains from coordination are higher. Differentiated products make coordination more difficult and, at the same time, misalign the incentives of the oligopolists as each of them faces a differently sloped demand.

(d) No incentive to deviate

For coordination to be sustainable, the oligopolists must have no incentive to deviate. For instance, a large and powerful buyer can induce an oligopolist to deviate by offering to buy at a lower price. Such an inducement would be strong because the buyer's requirements are large and may destabilize oligopolistic coordination.[142]

The condition of the absence of incentives to deviate requires that a credible deterrent mechanism be available.[143] A credible deterrent mechanism means that the oligopolists must have the ability and incentive to punish the deviator. The ability to punish the deviator depends on whether the oligopolists can obtain information about each other's conduct 'sufficiently precisely and quickly'.[144] Market transparency is a necessary condition. Following the judgment of the Court of Justice in *Impala*, it is now clear that it is not sufficient to prove that the market is transparent in the abstract but transparency must be assessed in relation to a plausible monitoring mechanism.[145] Generally, the degree of transparency necessary for the oligopolists to have the ability to coordinate will be the same as the degree of transparency necessary for the oligopolists to have the ability to detect deviations. A factor that makes detection of deviations more difficult is demand volatility. If demand is volatile, it is difficult for the oligopolists to distinguish deviations from capacity adjustment responding to changes in demand.[146] *Airtours* appears to establish a presumption, based on economic theory, that volatile demand is incompatible with oligopolistic collective dominance, unless the contrary is proved on the facts of an individual case.[147]

As well as being able to detect deviations, the oligopolists must have the ability to punish the deviator. The most obvious form of punishment is an increase in output that makes the deviation unprofitable. This form of retaliation has been an element of the definition of oligopolistic collective dominance since the early case law. In *Gencor*, the Court of First Instance said that in oligopolistic collective dominance each undertaking 'is aware that highly competitive action on its part designed to increase its market share . . . would provoke identical actions by others, so that it would derive no benefit from its initiative'.[148] The oligopolists must be able to increase output to the extent that it makes deviation unprofitable. This

---

[141] Case T-102/96 *Gencor*, para 222.
[142] *Sony/BMG* (Case COMP/M.3333) (3 October 2007), recital 146.
[143] Case C-413/06 P *Impala*, para 123. [144] ibid. [145] ibid para 130.
[146] Case T-342/99 *Airtours*, para 139. [147] ibid para 147.
[148] Case T-102/96 *Gencor*, para 276.

would not be possible if, for instance, they are capacity constrained[149] or they sell a differentiated product. Equally, if the market is characterized by few large buyers and lumpy orders or long-term contracts, timely retaliation would be difficult because of the need to wait for the next bidding round or to renegotiate existing contracts. The time lag between the deviation and the punishment may result in the punishment being interpreted as competitive behaviour.

Output expansion is not the only available retaliatory mechanism. In *Impala*, a potential retaliatory mechanism was the exclusion of the deviator from compilations. The major recorded music suppliers derived a significant part of their revenues from compilations but compilations were generally only attractive to consumers if they included artists from different suppliers. Therefore, suppliers licensed each other their repertoire or entered into compilation joint ventures. An oligopolist excluded from compilations would suffer a significant reduction of revenue that could have offset the benefits resulting from the deviation.[150] Punishment need not take place in the same market where the deviation occurs. In *Gencor*, the Court of First Instance held that multi-market contacts multiplied the risks of retaliation as punishment could also take place in other markets.[151] Multi-market contacts can take place between the same legal entities or between companies belonging to the same group.

The mere existence of a credible deterrent mechanism is sufficient for a finding of oligopolistic dominance. The retaliatory mechanism need not have been used in practice. Proof that the postulated retaliatory mechanism has never been used can rebut a prima facie case of oligopolistic collective dominance if two cumulative conditions are met: (a) it is established that one oligopolist deviated from the terms of coordination; and (b) it is established that the postulated retaliatory mechanism was not implemented.[152]

For a retaliatory mechanism to be credible and, thus, sufficiently deterrent, the oligopolists must have the incentive to implement it. As with all business decisions, this means that the benefits of carrying out the retaliation must outweigh its costs. In *Airtours*, one of the potential retaliatory mechanisms was directional selling at the distribution level. Tour operators were vertically integrated. As well as selling their own products, they also sold each others' package holidays, earning a commission. Retaliation could be in the form of conduct aimed at lowering the sales of the deviator's products. However, the Court found that 'such retaliation would entail economic loss for its perpetrators'. As a result, this form of retaliation was not credible.[153] The incentive to implement lower prices for retaliatory purposes is also reduced when customers are few and powerful and make lumpy orders or negotiate long-term contracts. In these circumstances, it is less likely that the oligopolists will be able to revert to tacit coordination and higher prices.[154]

---

[149] Case T-342/99 *Airtours*, para 203, where the Court said that the oligopolists would be able to add capacity during the same season only to a limited extent so that the retaliation would not be effective.
[150] Case T-464/04 *Impala*, paras 463–474. [151] Case T-102/96 *Gencor*, para 281.
[152] Case T-464/04 *Impala*, para 469. [153] Case T-342/99 *Airtours*, para 206.
[154] *Sony/BMG* (Case COMP/M.3333) (3 October 2007), recital 139.

E. Abuse of collective dominance

Article 102 prohibits the abuse of a collective dominant position. In *Irish Sugar* the Court of First Instance held that 'the abuse does not necessarily have to be the action of all the undertakings in question. It only has to be capable of being identified as one of the manifestations of such a joint dominant position being held'.[155] This means that the conduct of one or more undertakings holding a collective dominant position can be abusive only if the undertakings in question would not have the incentive to engage in the behaviour under review but for the collective dominant position. The language of the Court in *Irish Sugar* leaves room for little doubt in this respect. Furthermore, any other interpretation would give rise to a disproportionate risk that normal competitive behaviour by an oligopolist could be characterized as an abuse of a collective dominant position.

Joint abuses of a collective dominant position occur when some or all the collectively dominant undertakings engage in abusive conduct in concert. Generally, this form of abuse occurs in the case of non-oligopolistic collective dominance when undertakings communicate directly with each other or have established stable structural links. In *Compagnie Maritime Belge*, the members of a dominant liner conference engaged in exclusionary conduct jointly and under the coordination and supervision of the conference committees.[156] *Atlantic Container Line* shows that joint abuses may also consist in practices aimed at limiting or eliminating competition between the members of a collective entity[157] or in the provision of incentives by the collective entity to potential competitors to enter the market only as members of the collective entity.[158] This latter form of abuse is problematic as it could be interpreted to include all activities by a dominant collective entity aimed at increasing its membership. However, *Atlantic Container Line* must be read in conjunction with the *Irish Sugar* principle that the abuse must be a manifestation of the collective dominant position. Activities aimed at increasing the membership of a collective entity can only be abusive if the collective entity would not have any incentive to carry out the activities in question but for its collective dominant position. This could be the case, as was alleged, but ultimately not proved, in *Atlantic Container Line*, if the members of the collective entity were prepared to forgo significant revenues in order to induce a competitor to join the collective entity only because of the market power rents that they would have lost if the competitor had become an effective competitive constraint.[159]

---

[155] Case T-228/97 *Irish Sugar*, para 66.

[156] Joined Cases T-24/93 to T-26/93 and T-28/93 *Compagnie Maritime Belge*, para 105 (referring to action by 'the members of Cewal'), paras 139 and 151 (although the judgment is not explicit on this point, the loyalty contracts were drawn up by the conference: *Cewal, Cowac and Ukwal* [1993] OJ L34/20, recital 28), and paras 182–186.

[157] Joined Cases T-191/98 and T-212/98 to T-214/98 *Atlantic Container Line*, paras 1106 and 1190.

[158] ibid paras 1255–1367. The Court set aside the decision of the Commission on the evidence but accepted that the behaviour in question could constitute an abuse as a matter of law.

[159] ibid paras 1349–1367.

A single abuse of a collective dominant position was found in *Irish Sugar*, where the jointly dominant supplier and distributor of white granulated sugar in Ireland engaged in a number of abusive practices individually.[160] Even when the parties carried out the same type of practice on the same market, there was no requirement that the abuse had to be jointly planned or agreed.[161] Furthermore, certain practices were carried out by the distributor alone and still found abusive.[162] In *E.ON*, the Commission was concerned that E.ON, one of the three collective dominant undertakings on the German wholesale electricity market, could have deterred competitors' investment in the generation market by entering into long-term supply contracts and offering competitors a participation in an E.ON generation plant. In this way, E.ON could have been able to maintain high prices in the long-term.[163] There was no suggestion in the decision that the other two oligopolists could have engaged in similar practices. However, it appears that E.ON's alleged abuse was a manifestation of the collective dominant position because it would have been unprofitable if there had been effective competition instead of tacit coordination among the three main German electricity suppliers.

A potential abuse of oligopolistic collective dominance is the adoption of facilitating practices. Certain practices may facilitate an oligopolistic collective dominant position while not being sufficient on their own to give rise to it. For instance, any behaviour that enhances market transparency is clearly capable of making it easier to reach an understanding on the terms of coordination and to monitor deviations. An example would be the widespread use of most favoured nation clauses, which oblige the supplier to grant a customer the best terms it grants to any other customers. Most favoured nation clauses make deviation less profitable because the deviating firm must lower the price to all its customers and not only to the additional customers targeted by the price decrease.[164]

Finally, collectively dominant undertakings may commit exploitative as well as exclusionary abuses. In *E.ON*, the Commission took the view that E.ON could have abused its collectively dominant position by withholding available generation capacity that would have been profitable to sell in order to raise overall prices. The price of electricity is determined by the price of the short-term MC of the marginal plant. The marginal plant is also the most expensive to run as electricity suppliers use the cheaper plants first (for instance, hydroelectric and nuclear plants) before using the more expensive gas and oil plants. E.ON had substantial capacity in cheaper energy. Withholding capacity resulted in substantial profits on the energy generated by the more efficient plants. This had severe effects for consumers and long-term effects on the price of energy because of the impact of short-term prices

---

[160] *Irish Sugar*, recital 117.

[161] Case T-228/97 *Irish Sugar*, paras 173–193 (concerning border rebates granted by either Irish Sugar or SDL).

[162] ibid paras 226–234 (concerning product swaps agreed with one wholesaler and one retailer).

[163] *E.ON*, recitals 41–44.

[164] G Monti, 'The Scope of Collective Dominance under Article 82 EC' (2001) 38 CML Rev 131, 146–149.

on the forward markets.[165] The commitments decision does not discuss the position of the other two oligopolists. The practice could have been more profitable for E.ON than for the others if E.ON had a larger share of more efficient energy on which it would earn a higher margin. However, the profitability of E.ON's conduct could have been dependent on the other oligopolists not increasing capacity. If this was actually the case, the test that the abuse must be a manifestation of the collective dominant position would have been met.

F. Conclusion

Collective dominance arises when two or more undertakings acting together have the ability to harm competition. So far, collective dominance has been analysed as a unitary concept. This has hindered the development of robust legal tests. A closer analysis of the case law and its economic foundations shows that there are two distinct types of collective dominance that are governed by different legal tests.

Non-oligopolistic collective dominance arises when structural or commercial links or direct or indirect contacts are sufficient for two or more undertakings to act on the market as a collective entity. The analysis of the links or contacts that justify a finding that two or more undertakings are a collective entity is, however, only the first step in the test. The second step is to apply the test of dominance based on the same analytical structure that applies to single dominance. The same principles apply to undertakings in a vertical relationship.

Oligopolistic collective dominance is inherently different from non-oligopolistic collective dominance. Oligopolistic collective dominance arises when undertakings in a tight oligopoly have the ability and incentive to coordinate their behaviour by raising prices, restricting output, or reducing investment through repeated market interactions. Structural or commercial links or direct or indirect contacts may contribute to oligopolistic collective dominance but must not be sufficient. Otherwise, the non-oligopolistic collective dominance test applies. The oligopolistic collective dominance test in the case law provides that for two or more undertakings to be collectively dominant based on oligopolistic interaction, they must have the ability to coordinate, they must have the incentive to do so, and they must have no incentive to deviate. This test is consistent with economic theory and ensures that Article 102 can apply to address harm to long-term social welfare arising from anti-competitive conduct by the members of a collusive oligopoly.

Abuse of a collective dominant position can take various forms. It may be a joint abuse or an individual abuse. It may be exclusionary or exploitative. Or it may consist in facilitating practices that appreciably contribute to the maintenance of the collective dominant position. The guiding principle must always be that conduct is only capable of being a manifestation of the collective dominant position if, in the absence of such a position, the undertakings or undertaking in question would not

---

[165] *E.ON*, recitals 28–40.

have the incentive to carry out the conduct under review. There must, therefore, be a causal link between dominance and abuse.

Overall, the law on collective dominance is consistent with the objective of Article 102 and strikes the right balance between the risk of false convictions and over-deterrence and the need to ensure the effectiveness of Article 102 in addressing competitive harm caused by two or more undertakings which are jointly dominant. The law should, however, be clearer in distinguishing between non-oligopolistic and oligopolistic collective dominance as two different forms of dominance subject to different legal tests and in requiring a causal link between dominance and abuse, especially in cases of abuse of a collective dominant position by one undertaking only.

PART V

THE ANALYTICAL FRAMEWORK OF ARTICLE 102

12

General Conclusion

A. Introduction

The normative and legal analysis in the previous chapters is inevitably complex. Each chapter sets out its main conclusions in a comprehensive way. This chapter performs three tasks. Section B retraces the main thread of the reasoning in this book, from the identification of the normative foundations of competition law to the discussion of the objective of EU competition law and Article 102 and the design of the tests to determine whether conduct is abusive and whether one or more undertakings are dominant. A clear understanding of this overall analytical structure is important because it provides the tools to draw the boundaries between lawful and unlawful behaviour with reference to novel forms of conduct, in new markets, or in changing economic conditions. No jurisprudence or academic endeavour can ever provide comprehensive answers to all possible questions that the application of competition law may raise. But a coherent analytical structure allows new answers to new problems to be based on ascertainable principles and transparent reasoning in accordance with the rule of law rather than on opaque 'policy' preferences or arbitrary 'political' choices. Section C is the natural development of the analytical structure traced in Section B: the analytical structure is the fabric which yields operational results. Such operations results are set out in thirty-four propositions that summarize the law on Article 102 as clarified, developed, or proposed in the previous chapters. The propositions set out in Section C do not always reflect the case law of the EU courts or enforcement practice of the Commission. Section D highlights the main areas where the current case law or enforcement practice is in need of being reviewed in the light of the conclusions of this book.

B. Towards a coherent analytical framework for the application of Article 102

The lack of clarity in the application of Article 102, the criticism of the case law and the Commission enforcement practice, and the divergence in the approaches advocated in the literature, have a common root: the uncertainty regarding the objective of the prohibition of abuse of a dominant position. The solution to the problem of the objective of the prohibition is the necessary foundation for the development of a coherent analytical framework for the application of Article 102. Two steps can be distinguished in this analysis: one normative and one doctrinal. From a normative view point, the objective of competition law must be identified as the maximization of long-term social welfare construed as including not only a monetary measure of surplus but the values and preferences of society. Market integration, economic freedom, and fairness or equality of opportunities are social norms that can and should be interpreted consistently with the long-term social welfare objective. There is no justification for adopting consumer welfare as such as an objective of competition law, although consumer harm may, in certain circumstances, perform the function of an optimal test that maximizes the achievement of long-term social welfare. Besides the consumer harm test, two further tests are well suited to achieving the long-term social welfare objective of competition law: the intent test (which comprises a number of different tests) and the as efficient competitor test. However, no single test performs optimally in relation to all types of potentially abusive conduct. Furthermore, the tests in question may apply cumulatively to guard against the risk of false convictions and over-deterrence when such a risk would otherwise reach such a level that it would jeopardize the long-term social welfare objective of competition law. Finally, these tests should always be subject to the appropriate weight being given to the benefits of the conduct that are consistent with the long-term social welfare objective of competition law, including allocative, productive, and dynamic efficiency and qualitative social welfare benefits, such as environmental benefits.

The legal hermeneutics of the objective of the EU competition rules, and Article 102 in particular, lead to the conclusion that their objective is coincident with the normative objective of competition law: the maximization of long-term social welfare. This objective is also to be achieved by the application of legal norms protecting market integration, economic freedom, and fairness or equality of opportunities, with the important caveat that these legal norms are not freestanding objectives but must be construed consistently with the long-term social welfare objective of the EU competition rules. Consumer welfare as such has no role to play as an objective of the EU competition rules and, as a consequence, of Article 102. The Treaties and the case law of the Court of Justice point unequivocally towards this conclusion, which is not only legally correct but also normatively optimal.

Given the long-term social welfare objective of Article 102, the next problem is to determine the tests which apply to distinguish anti-competitive conduct from harmless or pro-competitive business behaviour. The analytical structure of the tests is based on the principle of proportionality. The test is bifurcated: first, it is necessary to prove that the conduct under review is prima facie harmful to long-term social welfare and, if so, it is then necessary to verify whether it nevertheless pursues a legitimate objective in a proportionate way. To determine whether conduct is prima facie abusive, the case law applies tests of intent, the as efficient competitor test, and the consumer harm test, or a combination thereof. In the application of the tests, the EU courts and the European Commission are not always consistent and often end up acting so as to jeopardize rather than give effect to the objective of Article 102. Those areas of the case law and the enforcement practice that need to be reviewed are discussed in section D. However, it is one of the main conclusions of this book that, in developing the abuse tests under Article 102, the EU courts have correctly grasped the fundamental relationship between the tests and the objective of Article 102 and have set out tests that are normatively suited to achieving the objective that the Treaties assign to Article 102. This is also true as regards defences and, in particular, with reference to proportionality defences and objective justification, which allow for a structured consideration of the legitimate aims and the benefits of conduct that is potentially prima facie anti-competitive.

Article 102 only applies to dominant undertakings. The teleological interpretation of Article 102 leads to the conclusion that dominance is the ability of one or more undertakings to harm long-term social welfare by engaging in unilateral conduct that restricts competition, exploits customers, or distorts the efficiency of the upstream or downstream industry. Synthetically, dominance can be defined as the ability to harm competition. Accepting a definition of dominance as the ability to harm competition implies a requirement for substantial and durable market power to guard against the disproportionate risk of false convictions and over-deterrence that the application of Article 102 to all firms that might be able to harm competition unilaterally would entail. However, dominance is a dynamic, not a structural concept. This means that dominance is part and parcel of the analysis of the abuse not a threshold requirement to be met in order to trigger the application of separate conduct tests. It is only for reasons of expediency and judicial economy that dominance is analysed before the assessment of conduct: if an undertaking lacks the ability to harm competition, there is no point in inquiring further into its conduct to verify whether an infringement of Article 102 has occurred. These principles apply to dominance in general. Contrary to what is normally believed, dominance is, however, a category that includes three different legal concepts: single dominance, non-oligopolistic collective dominance, and oligopolistic collective dominance. The ability of one or more undertakings to harm competition is different in each case and so is the analysis of the abuse.

C. Objectives, principles, and tests clarified

The objectives, principles, and tests that constitute the legal fabric of Article 102 can be summarized in the following propositions.

(1) Objectives and general principles

1. **Long-term social welfare objective.** The maximization of long-term social welfare is the objective of Article 102. Social welfare is the sum of the surplus of suppliers and consumers reflecting the values and preferences of the model of society envisaged in the Treaties.

2. **Market integration.** Free trade increases long-term social welfare. Therefore, a prima facie prohibition of conduct that impairs free trade is consistent with the objective of Article 102. This is always subject to any defence that the dominant undertaking may plead, in particular proportionality defences and objective justification. Like any other prima facie abusive conduct, a restriction of free trade may, therefore, escape the prohibition of Article 102.

3. **Fairness and equality of opportunities.** Fairness and equality of opportunities are not an objective of Article 102 but a legal norm which must be interpreted consistently with the objective of maximizing long-term social welfare. Fairness and equality of opportunities under Article 102 mean that all equally efficient firms must be able to compete on an equal footing without being prejudiced as a result of the ability of dominant firms to exclude them for reasons other than superior efficiency.

4. **No protection of less efficient undertakings under Article 102.** The principle of fairness and equality of opportunities has the important consequence that, under Article 102, a less efficient competitor must not be protected unless: (a) the competitor is likely to become as efficient as the dominant undertaking within a reasonable period of time; and (b) conduct by the dominant undertaking is preventing the competitor from becoming at least as efficient as the dominant undertaking.

5. **Economic freedom.** Economic freedom is the individualization of the objective purpose of competition law. The economic freedom which EU competition law protects is, therefore, the freedom of economic agents not to be limited in their economic activity by any behaviour of firms that reduces market rivalry, exploits customers, or distorts the efficiency of the upstream or downstream industry so as to harm social welfare in the long term.

6. **Effective competition.** Article 102 protects effective competition. Effective competition is the degree of competition that ensures that, on a given market, long-term social welfare is maximized. Market power and prices above MC are consistent with effective competition when they increase social welfare in the long term, for instance because they are necessary for the ability and incentive of firms to invest in new productive technologies or in the development of new products.

7. **Proportionality framework.** The analytical structure of the tests under Article 102 can be described as a proportionality framework stated as follows: (a) does the conduct under review prima facie cause competitive harm? The reasonable and proportional pursuit of a legitimate commercial objective is incapable of being even a prima facie abuse; (b) if the conduct prima facie causes competitive harm, it is relevant to determine whether: (b.1) it produces efficiencies or other benefits consistent with the maximization of long-term social welfare; (b.2) it is suitable to achieving the efficiencies or benefits in question; (b.3) it is the least restrictive means of achieving them; (b.4) the efficiencies or other benefits of the conduct, for both producers and consumers, outweigh the potential competitive harm; and (b.5) the conduct benefits consumers.

8. Causal link between dominance and abuse and multi-market abuses. Article 102 requires a causal link between dominance and competitive harm or, which is the same, anti-competitive effects. Proof of the causal link between dominance and anti-competitive effects is particularly important in multi-market abuses where it is necessary to prove that dominance gives the undertaking in question either the ability or the incentive to harm competition by engaging in abusive conduct or causing anti-competitive effects on markets on which it is not dominant.

(2) Assessment of conduct

9. Prima facie abuse tests. The tests that apply to determine whether conduct is prima facie abusive are: (a) the naked abuse test; (b) other intent tests (c) the as efficient competitor test, including in its dynamic application when the conduct under review excludes competitors that would be capable of becoming as efficient as the dominant undertaking but for the alleged abuse; and (d) the consumer harm test.

These tests may apply by themselves or in combination, depending on the enforcement risks and costs associated with the conduct under review.

10. Naked abuse test. The naked abuse test provides that conduct that has the sole or overwhelmingly predominant purpose of harming competition, has no conceivable redeeming virtue either by way of efficiencies or otherwise, and is reasonably capable of causing consumer harm is prima facie abusive.

11. Naked abuse test and market integration. The naked abuse test also applies to conduct that is detrimental to the internal market: conduct that has the sole or overwhelmingly predominant purpose of hindering free trade within the European Union is prima facie abusive.

12. Predation. Prices below the measure of cost that determines the temporary shut-down decisions in the relevant industry are prima facie abusive. Intent is presumed. Prices below the measure of cost that determines the market exit decision in the relevant industry are prima facie abusive if applied with the intent of causing competitive harm. Recoupment is relevant as anti-competitive motive or incentive but is not a necessary element of the test.

13. Conditional rebates. Conditional rebates that exclude an equally efficient competitor are prima facie abusive. Conditional rebates that exclude a competitor who would be capable of becoming as efficient as the dominant undertaking within a reasonable time frame but for the conditional rebates are prima facie abusive, provided that the actual exclusion of potentially equally efficient competitors is proved.

14. Exclusivity. Exclusive purchasing arrangements that exclude an equally efficient competitor are prima facie abusive. Exclusive purchasing arrangements that exclude a competitor who would be capable of becoming as efficient as the dominant undertaking within a reasonable time frame but for the exclusive purchasing arrangements are prima facie abusive, provided that the actual exclusion of potentially equally efficient competitors is proved.

15. Unconditional rebates. Unconditional rebates are prohibited if they reinforce another anti-competitive practice or if they are applied by a monopolist or quasi-monopolist as part of an exclusionary strategy with the effect of eliminating all residual competition on the part of potentially as efficient competitors, which in turn results in the maintenance or strengthening of the dominant position.

16. Tying. Tying is abusive if the dominant undertaking forecloses competition on the tied market with the intent of protecting, strengthening, or acquiring market power on the tied market, the tying market, or a related emerging market. Proof of anti-competitive intent dispenses with proof that competitors on the tied market are prevented by the tying from becoming as efficient as the dominant undertaking on the tied market because, if it were not so, the dominant undertaking would have no incentive to tie to protect, strengthen, or acquire market power on the tied market, the tying market, or a related emerging market.

17. Mixed bundling. Mixed bundling arrangements that exclude an equally efficient competitor are prima facie abusive. Mixed bundling arrangements that exclude a competitor who would be capable of becoming as efficient as the dominant undertaking within a reasonable time frame but for the exclusive purchasing arrangements are prima facie abusive, provided that the actual exclusion of potentially equally efficient competitors is proved. Mixed bundling arrangements that foreclose competition on an affected market and are applied by a dominant undertaking with the intent of protecting, strengthening, or acquiring market power on the tied market, the tying market, or a related emerging market are prima facie abusive, provided that competitors of the dominant undertaking cannot be reasonably expected to enter all relevant markets simultaneously.

18. Market-distorting discrimination. Discrimination under Article 102(c) is abusive if, and only if, it produces significant distortions of upstream or downstream competition. This means that the following elements must be established: (a) the discrimination must affect significantly the revenues or costs of the upstream or downstream undertakings; and either (b) these significant differences in revenues or costs affect the parameters of competition, including price, output, or innovation; or (c) there is a negative effect on the productive or dynamic efficiency of certain undertakings compared to others.

19. Vertical foreclosure. Vertical refusal to supply an indispensable input is prima facie abusive only if it eliminates all effective downstream competition and causes consumer harm. Vertical refusal to license an indispensable IP right is prima facie abusive only if it eliminates all effective downstream competition and causes consumer harm in the form of the prevention of the emergence of new or differentiated products or reduced innovation. Margin squeeze is prima facie abusive only if a refusal to supply the input by the dominant undertaking would be abusive and the spread between the upstream and downstream price forecloses as efficient downstream competitors.

20. Exploitative abuses. Exploitative abuses are examined under a test of actual consumer harm. However, because dominance is not prohibited in itself, a finding of abuse requires more that a mere finding that a dominant undertaking is charging its profit-maximizing price. Four alternative tests apply as limiting principles in this area: (a) the naked abuse test, which applies to actual exploitation having the sole or overwhelmingly predominant purpose of harming competition and having no redeeming virtue by way of efficiencies or other benefits; (b) an enhanced dominance test under which exploitative practices may be prohibited if committed by monopolists or quasi-monopolists or the holders of special or exclusive rights within the meaning of Article 106 and entry on a sufficient scale to counteract the abuse is unlikely in the long term; (c) an enhanced consumer harm test under which an exploitative abuse may be prohibited when the conduct causes consumer harm distinct from, and additional to, the mere charging of prices or application of trading terms persistently and significantly higher or more onerous than the prices or terms that would prevail under conditions of effective competition; (d) a post-exclusionary exploitation test under which exploitative conduct may be prohibited when it is the result of anti-competitive exclusion.

21. Default test. For business practices that are incapable of being subsumed under one of the tests set out above either directly or by analogy, consumer harm applies as a default test.

22. Burden of proof. Under Article 102 the dominant undertaking does not bear the burden of proof. The burden of proof rests on the competition authority or claimant which bears the ultimate risk of lack of proof of any material fact. However, when a prima facie case of abuse has been established, the dominant undertaking acquires the burden of adducing sufficient evidence to substantiate a defence. It is then for the competition authority or claimant to disprove the defence. If, at the end of the case and on the whole of the evidence, the competition authority or court is not persuaded to the required standard as to whether a defence is established, there is no abuse.

23. Anti-competitive effects tests. Conduct is prima facie abusive under Article 102 as soon as it runs counter to its objective. The application of this principle leads to three anti-competitive effect standards under Article 102: (a) a test of reasonable capability of the conduct to produce anti-competitive effects; (b) a test of the likelihood of anti-competitive effects; and (c) a test of actual effects. The reasonable capability test applies whenever the conduct is examined under a test of intent. The actual effects test applies whenever Article 102 protects potentially equally efficient competitors or protects customers or suppliers of the dominant undertaking from exploitation. The likelihood test applies in all other cases.

24. Taxonomy of defences. Defences under Article 102 are divided into mere defences and objective justification. Mere defences do not plead a new primary fact but are limited to challenging the weight or significance of the evidence adduced by the competition authority or claimant. Objective justification pleads a new primary fact consisting in benefits that contribute to long-term social welfare maximization.

25. Mere defences of proportionality. Proportionality defences are a sub-category of mere defences which deserves special consideration. A dominant undertaking is entitled to pursue a commercial interest consistent with the profit-maximizing conduct of a non-dominant undertaking provided it does so in a reasonable and proportionate way. The conduct must thus pursue a legitimate objective, must be suited to achieving the objective, and must be the least restrictive way of doing so. A proportionality defence never requires the balancing of the benefits of the conduct against its alleged competitive harm because mere defences do not introduce a new primary fact. Therefore, there are no benefits to be balanced against the harm. If a proportionality defence is established, the conduct under review is competition on the merits and there is no competitive harm.

26. The proportionality defence of meeting competition. The meeting competition defence is a proportionality defence. The meeting competition defence is not available as a matter of law in predation and margin squeeze cases. In cases relating to above-cost unconditional price cuts, the defence is also unavailable but for the reason that the abuse test in such cases is construed as a very narrow exception to the general principle that the dominant undertaking is entitled to respond to competition by unconditional above-cost discounts. As regards conditional above-cost rebates, meeting competition is an absolute defence whenever the rebates are examined under the as efficient competitor test, including in its dynamic dimension. Meeting competition is also an absolute defence, without qualification, to a prima facie case of market-distorting discrimination.

27. Objective justification test. Objective justification is a defence that pleads a new primary fact consisting in benefits that contribute to long-term social welfare maximization. The objective justification test has four limbs: (a) the conduct must pursue a legitimate objective; (b) it must be suited to achieving the objective being pursued; (c) it must not go beyond what is necessary to achieve the objective in question; and (d) the benefits of the conduct must counterbalance or outweigh the disadvantages and must benefit consumers. The fourth limb of the test is a qualitative balancing exercise which asks whether the competitive harm of the conduct is disproportionate to its benefits.

28. Taxonomy of objective justification. Objective justification can be divided into two categories: efficiency defences and social welfare defences.

29. Efficiency defences. Efficiency defences plead that the conduct under review increases allocative, productive, or dynamic efficiency. All three types of efficiency may be pleaded as a defence against all prima facie abuses.

30. Social welfare defences. Social welfare defences plead that the conduct under review increases long-term social welfare, broadly construed as the well-being of the European Union, including the values and the positive and negative preferences of society. Therefore, the benefits in question include environmental and social benefits. The objective justification test is no more difficult to apply to social welfare defences than it is to efficiency defences. More importantly, the ultimate objective of the efficiency defences and the social welfare defences is the same: to ensure that conduct that may be beneficial to long-term social welfare is not prohibited even if a prima facie abuse test is established.

(3) Assessment of dominance

31. Single dominance. Single dominance is the ability of a single undertaking to harm competition to the detriment of long-term social welfare. Its constitutive elements are: (a) substantial and durable market power; (b) the presence of dynamic barriers to entry; and (c) the absence of countervailing buyer power.

32. Non-oligopolistic collective dominance. Non-oligopolistic collective dominance is the ability to harm competition on the part of two or more undertakings acting as a collective entity because of structural or commercial links or direct or indirect contacts. The test has two limbs: first, it must be established that the relevant links justify a finding that two or more undertakings are a collective entity and, secondly, it must be established that the collective entity is dominant under the single dominance test. The same principles apply to undertakings in a vertical relationship.

33. Oligopolistic collective dominance. Oligopolistic collective dominance arises when undertakings in a tight oligopoly have the ability and incentive to coordinate their behaviour by raising prices, restricting output, or reducing investment through repeated market interactions. For two or more undertakings to be collectively dominant based on oligopolistic interaction, they must have the ability to coordinate, they must have the incentive to do so, and they must have no incentive to deviate from the terms of coordination.

34. Abuse of collective dominance. An abuse of a collective dominant position may be committed by all the undertakings concerned or by some of them only. However, the causal link between dominance and abuse must be the object of specific proof. This means that a competition authority or claimant must establish that the undertakings or undertaking in question would not have the incentive to carry out the conduct but for the collective dominant position.

D. Addressing the main shortcomings of the current case law and enforcement practice

The case law and the enforcement practice of the Commission are not always consistent with the objectives, principles, and tests outlined above. Throughout this book, uncertainties, ambiguities, and inconsistencies have been highlighted and explained and the way forward has been articulated and argued. It is worth recalling here the major areas that need to be reviewed in order to bring the current case law and practice into line with the objective, principles, and overall analytical framework of Article 102.

As a general proposition, the Guidance on Article 102[1] is not consistent with the overall analytical framework that the EU courts have developed in order to give effect to Article 102. The application of a consumer harm test to all abuses is wrong in law and misguided in policy. A careful reading of the Guidance on Article 102 reveals, however, that the consumer harm test put forward by the Commission is little more than a prediction of consumer harm based on structural indicators that are already relevant to the finding of dominance or to the assessment of the foreclosure effect of the conduct. As a consequence, the Guidance, while bringing unnecessary confusion to the application of Article 102 and generating an unwelcome divergence between the Commission's enforcement policy and the case law, may perhaps be saved as a prioritization exercise.

An area in need of urgent reform is the law on conditional rebates. The case law on conditional rebates is fundamentally out of line with the objective of Article 102 and with the overall analytical framework that the EU courts themselves have developed to give effect to that objective. As a result, the current application of Article 102 to conditional rebates may result in the protection of inefficient competitors, which runs counter to the purpose of Article 102. The principles developed by the case law on predation and margin squeeze and the enforcement practice of the Commission, including the Guidance on Article 102 and the *Intel* decision, show the way forward. Conditional rebates are only prima facie abusive in three sets of circumstances. First, under the naked abuse test, they may be prima facie abusive if they have the sole or overwhelmingly predominant purpose of harming competition, have no benefits either by way of efficiencies or other social welfare benefits, and are reasonably capable of causing competitive harm. Secondly, under the as efficient competitor test, they may be prima facie abusive if they are likely to foreclose equally efficient competitors. Thirdly, under the dynamic as efficient competitor test, they may be prima facie abusive if they have the actual effect of preventing competitors from becoming as efficient as the dominant undertaking.

Refusal to supply is another area where confusion reigns. The case law sets out several tests of foreclosure and consumer harm and distinguishes between refusal to supply an input in general and refusal to license an IP right. The Guidance on Article 102 adopts a unified approach by putting forward a single consumer harm test as a negative effect on prices, output, or innovation. This book demonstrates that proof of consumer harm is required in all vertical refusal to supply cases, and not only, as the case law appears to suggest, when the refusal to supply relates to IP rights. The reason for this is that to impose on a dominant undertaking an active duty to assist its competitors may have a significant negative effect on market-wide investment incentives. Because under the long-term social welfare objective of

---

[1] Communication from the Commission—Guidance on the Commission's enforcement priorities in applying Article 82 of the EC Treaty to abusive exclusionary conduct by dominant undertakings [2009] OJ C45/7 ('Guidance on Art 102').

Article 102 dynamic efficiency is particularly important, an enhanced intervention threshold is needed. Consumer harm plays the role of safeguarding against the risk of false convictions and over-deterrence is this area. Therefore, the principles developed by the case law on refusal to license IP rights, requiring proof of consumer harm, should be applied to refusal to supply any input. However, when a refusal to supply relates to IP rights, consumer harm must be in the shape of the prevention of the emergence of new or differentiated products or reduced innovation. This is because of the need to protect the very subject-matter of the IP right, which is the power to prevent anybody from reproducing the invention, mark, creative work, or information without the consent of the holder of the IP right. As a consequence, a mere decrease in output or higher prices are not sufficient proof of consumer harm if the undertaking requesting a licence intends to limit itself to reproducing the products of the dominant undertaking. The Guidance on Article 102 states the law correctly when it adopts a unified approach to all refusals to supply. However, in failing to draw a distinction between IP rights and other inputs, the Guidance does not recognize the need to protect the subject-matter of IP rights. Even as a prioritization exercise, this is problematic because it could draw unwarranted attention to refusals to license that pose no risk to competition. The case law and the Commission should, moreover, clarify that refusal to supply an existing customer should be treated in the same way as any other refusal to supply and that the effect of raising rivals' costs is not sufficient for a finding of abusive refusal to supply.

A related problem concerns margin squeeze. Margin squeeze is a form of vertical foreclosure. A duty to supply the upstream input is a necessary element of the abuse. The Court of Justice's misunderstanding of the test in *TeliaSonera* expands the scope of the margin squeeze abuse beyond what is permitted by Article 102.

Tying continues to be a controversial abuse. This book demonstrates that, contrary to what is often believed, the case law and enforcement practice of the Commission require a finding of foreclosure as a necessary element of tying. The problem lies with the requirement of consumer harm. The case law appears to exclude such a requirement. The Guidance on Article 102 applies the test of consumer harm on the tying market, the tied market, or both. This approach is unsatisfactory. Tying runs counter to the objective of Article 102 if, as well as having a foreclosure effect on the tied market, it is part of a strategy to acquire, maintain, or strengthen market power on the tied, the tying, or a third related market. This test would be in line with the post-Chicago analysis of tying but also with the Commission enforcement practice in *Tetra Pak II*, *Hilti*, and the two *Microsoft* cases. More importantly, this approach would be consistent with the case law of the Court of Justice in predation cases, which requires proof of an exclusionary strategy when prices are capable of excluding equally efficient competitors but may also be competition on the merits. The analogy with tying which forecloses competitors on the tied market is strong: tying may well be anti-competitive but may also be competition on the merits. Therefore, proof of foreclosure is not sufficient to distinguish pro-competitive from anti-competitive tying. Proof of the strategy of the dominant undertaking should be required to determine whether tying runs counter to the objective of Article 102 or is pro-competitive.

Discrimination is an area where the law and the enforcement practice are spectacularly out of line with the objective and overall analytical framework of Article 102. This book demonstrates that discrimination under Article 102(c) is abusive if, and only if, it produces significant distortions of upstream or downstream competition. This means that the following elements must be established: (a) the discrimination must affect significantly the revenues or costs of the upstream or downstream undertakings; and either (b) these significant differences in revenues or costs affect the parameters of competition, including price, output, or innovation; or (c) there is a negative effect on the productive or dynamic efficiency of certain undertakings compared to others.

Exploitative abuses remain a nebulous area of EU competition law. The problem is not so much that the case law and the enforcement practice are fundamentally wrong but that they are fundamentally unclear. This book puts forward a coherent and exhaustive framework for the analysis of exploitative abuses which is set out in Section C at point 20 above. It is of the utmost importance, especially in the context of the current decentralized application of EU competition law, that the EU courts and the Commission clarify the circumstances in which exploitation may be prima facie abusive.

Defences play an important role under Article 102: they recalibrate the balance of enforcement risks that is biased in favour of false convictions and over-deterrence once a prima facie case of abuse is established. An overly restrictive approach to defences is, therefore, contrary to the purpose of Article 102. The problem lies not so much in the admissibility of the defences as a matter of law but in the high evidential requirements that the Commission and the case law appear to place on dominant undertakings. The solutions to this problem are two: first, the clarification of the evidential nature of the burden on the dominant undertaking and, secondly, an increased relative weight to be given to efficiencies and other social welfare objectives pleaded under objective justification compared to the competitive harm established under a prima facie abuse test.

Objective justification is a defence that pleads a new primary fact consisting of benefits that contribute to long-term social welfare maximization. The objective justification test is set out in Section C at point 27 above. The Guidance on Article 102 departs from this test in two respects: by requiring that the net effect of the conduct must be at least neutral for consumers and by requiring that effective competition must not be eliminated. Instead, the objective justification test only requires that some benefits accrue to consumers and does not include a limb relating to the non-elimination of effective competition. These conditions, and particularly the latter, would make the objective justification defence inapplicable in practice in the vast majority of cases and are contrary to the overall scheme of Article 102, which considers favourably conduct that may benefit long-term social welfare, particularly because of dynamic efficiency. The test set out in Section C at point 27 above, instead, is consistent with the case law and strikes the optimal balance between the requirement to preserve the effective enforcement of Article 102 and the need to minimize the risk of false convictions and over-deterrence.

The analysis in this book highlights major areas of the case law and enforcement practice that are out of line with the objective of Article 102 and its overall analytical framework. The task of addressing these shortcomings must not be underestimated. However, this task must be accomplished not by importing into EU law this or that economic theory and even less by transplanting into EU law legal doctrines rooted in different legal, economic, and political contexts but by developing and refining the application of Article 102 in line with the core values that it enshrines as a key element of the economic and social model enacted by the Treaties for the sustainable long-term well-being of the European polity.

Bibliography

Abreu, D, 'Extremal Equilibria of Oligopolistic Supergames' (1986) 39 Journal of Economic Theory 191

Abreu, D, Pearce, D, and Stachetti, E, 'Optimal Cartel Equilibria with Imperfect Monitoring' (1986) 39 Journal of Economic Theory 251

Aghion, P and Bolton, P, 'Contracts as a Barrier to Entry' (1987) 77 American Economic Rev 388

Agnew, JH, *Competition Law* (London, Allen & Unwin 1985)

Ahlborn, C and Bailey, D, 'Discounts, Rebates and Selective Pricing by Dominant Firms: A Trans-Atlantic Comparison' (2006) 2 European Competition Journal 101

Ahlborn, C, Evans, DS, and Padilla, JA, 'The Antitrust Economics of Tying: A Farewell to Per Se Illegality' (2004) 49 Antitrust Bull 297

Ahlborn, C and Grave, C, 'Walter Eucken and Ordoliberalism: An Introduction from a Consumer Welfare Perspective' (2006) 2 Competition Policy International 197

Ahlborn, C and Padilla, AJ, 'From Fairness to Welfare: Implications for the Assessment of Unilateral Conduct under EC Competition law' in Ehlermann, C-D and Marquis, M (eds), *European Competition Law Annual 2007: A Reformed Approach to Article 82 EC* (Oxford, Hart Publishing 2008)

Aiginger, K, Mueller, D, and Weiss, C, 'Objectives, Topics and Methods in Industrial Organization during the Nineties: Results from a Survey' (1998) 16 Intl J Ind Org 799

Akman, P, 'Searching for the Long-Lost Soul of Article 82 EC' (2009) 29 OJLS 267

Alvarez-Labrador, MF, 'Margin Squeeze in the Telecommunications Sector: An Economic Overview' (2006) 29 World Competition 247

Amato, G, *Antitrust and the Bounds of Power* (Oxford, Hart Publishing 1997)

Amit, R and Livnat, J, 'Efficient Corporate Diversification: Methods and Implications' (1989) 35 Management Science 879

Anderman, SD, 'Does the Microsoft Case offer a New Paradigm for the 'Exceptional Circumstances' Test and Compulsory Copyright Licenses under EC Competition Law?' (2004) 1(2) Competition L Rev 7

Anderman, SD and Schmidt, H, *EU Competition Law and Intellectual Property Rights: The Regulation of Innovation* (2nd edn Oxford, OUP 2011)

Andreangeli, A, 'The Impact of the Modernisation Regulation on the Guarantees of Due Process in Competition Proceedings' (2006) 31 EL Rev 342

—— 'The Enforcement of Article 81 EC Treaty Before National Courts After the House of Lords' Decision in Inntrepreneur Pub Co Ltd v Crehan' (2007) 32 EL Rev 260

—— 'Interoperability as an "Essential Facility" in the Microsoft Case—Encouraging Competition or Stifling innovation?' (2009) 34 E L Rev 584

Areeda, P, 'Essential Facilities: An Epithet in Need of Limiting Principles' (1990) 58 Antitrust LJ 841

Areeda, P and Turner, DF, 'Predatory Pricing and Related Practices under Section 2 of the Sherman Act' (1975) 88 Harv L Rev 697

Areeda, P and Hovenkamp, H, *Antitrust Law: An Analysis of Antitrust Principles and Their Application* (2nd edn New York, Aspen Law & Business 2010)

Arezzo, E, 'Is There a Role for Market Definition and Dominance in an Effects-based Approach?' in Mackenrodt, M, Conde Gallego, B, and Enchelmaier, S (eds), *Abuse of Dominant Position: New Interpretation, New Enforcement Mechanisms?* (Berlin, Springer 2008) 21

Armour, L, 'Is Economic Justice Possible' (1994) 21(10) International Journal of Social Economics 32

Armstrong, M, 'Network Interconnection in Telecommunications' (1998) 108 Economic Journal 545

Armstrong, M and Vickers, J, 'Competitive Price Discrimination' (2001) 32 RAND Journal of Economics 579

Arnull, A, 'Gambling with Competition in Europe's Internal Market' (2009) 30 ECLR 440

Arnull, A, et al, *Wyatt & Dashwood's European Union Law* (5th edn London, Sweet & Maxwell 2006)

Arrow, KJ, 'Economic Welfare and the Allocation of Resources for Invention' in The National Bureau of Economic Research, *The Rate and Direction of Inventive Activity: Economic and Social Factors* (Princeton, Princeton University Press 1962, reprint 1975) 609

Art, J-Y and McCurdy, GS, 'The European Commission's Media Player Remedy in its Microsoft Decision: Compulsory Code Removal Despite the Absence of Tying or Foreclosure' (2004) 25 ECLR 694

Atkinson, AB and Bourguignon, D (eds), *Handbook of Income Distribution* (Amsterdam, Elsevier 2000)

Atkinson, SE and Kerkvliet, J, 'Dual Measures of Monopoly and Monopsony Power: An Application to Regulated Electric Utilities' (1989) 71 Rev Econ & Stat 250

Averitt, NW and Lande, RH, 'Using the "Consumer Choice" Approach to Antitrust Law (2007) 74 Antitrust LJ 175

Bacon, K, *European Community Law of State Aid* (Oxford, OUP 2009)

Bain, JS, 'Output Quotas in Imperfect Cartels' (1948) 62 Quarterly Journal of Economics 617

—— *Industrial Organization* (2nd edn New York, John Wiley and Sons 1968)

—— *Barriers to New Competition: Their Character and Consequences in Manufacturing Industries* (reprinted Fairfield NJ, Augustus M Kelley Publishers 1993)

Baldwin, WL, *Market Power, Competition and Antitrust Policy* (Homewood Illinois, Irwin 1987)

Barnard, C, 'Restricting Restrictions: Lessons for the EU from the US?' (2009) 68 CLJ 575

—— *The Substantive Law of the EU* (3rd edn Oxford, OUP 2010)

Barry, N, 'The Social Market Economy' (1993) 10 Social Philosophy and Policy 1

Basedow, J, *Von der deutschen zur europäischen Wirtschaftsverfassung* (Tübingen, JCB Mohr 1992) 24

Baumol, WJ, 'Quasi-Permanence of Price Reductions: A Policy for Prevention of Predatory Pricing' (1979) 89 Yale LJ 1

Beale, HG, Bishop, W, and Furmston, MP, *Contract: Cases and Materials* (5th edn Oxford, OUP 2008)

Beckner III, CF and Salop, SC, 'Decision Theory and Antitrust Rules (1999) 67 Antitrust LJ 41

Beggs, A and Klemperer, P, 'Multi-Period Competition with Switching Costs' (1992) 60 Econometrica 651

Bernard, KS, 'Private Antitrust Litigation in the European Union—Why Does the EC Want to Embrace What the US FTC is Trying to Avoid?' (2010) 3 Global Competition Litigation Rev 69

Bernheim, BD and Whinston, MD, 'Multimarket Contact and Collusive Behavior' (1990) 21 RAND Journal of Economics 1

Bertola, G, Foellmi, R, and Zweimüller, J, *Income Distribution in Macroeconomic Models* (Princeton, Princeton University Press 2005)

Besanko, D and Spulber, DF, 'Antitrust Enforcement Under Asymmetric Information' (1989) 99 Economic Journal 408

—— 'Contested Mergers and Equilibrium in Antitrust Policy' (1993) JL Econ & Org 1

Besanko, D et al, *Economics of Strategy* (5th edn Hoboken NJ, Wiley 2010)

Bhaskar, V and To, T, 'Is Perfect Price Discrimination Really Efficient? An Analysis of Free Entry' (2004) 35 RAND Journal of Economics 762

Binmore, K, Rubinstein, A, and Wolinsky, A, 'The Nash Bargaining Solution in Economic Modelling' (1986) 14 RAND Journal of Economics 176

Biondi, A, Eeckhout, P, and Flynn, J, *The Law of State Aid in the European Union* (Oxford, OUP 2004)

Bishop, SB, 'Power and Responsibility: The ECJ's Kali-Salz Judgment' (1999) 20 ECLR 37

Bishop, SB and Walker, M, *The Economics of EC Competition Law* (3rd edn London, Sweet & Maxwell 2010)

Black, O, 'Per Se Rules and the Rule of Reason: What are they?' (1997) 18 ECLR 145–61

—— 'Collusion and Co-ordination in EC Merger Control' (2003) 24 ECLR 408

—— 'Communication, Concerted Practices and the Oligopoly Problem' (2005) 1 European Competition Journal 341

Blair, RD, Kaserman, DL, and Romano, RE, 'A Pedagogical Treatment of Bilateral Monopoly' (1989) 55 Southern Economic Journal 831

Boge, U, 'Public and Private Enforcement: Harmony or Discord?' (2006) 5 Comp Law 114

Böhm, F, 'Das Problem der privaten Macht: Ein Beitrag zur Monopolfrage' (1928) 3 Die Justiz 324–45

—— 'Demokratie und ökonomische Macht', in Institut für ausländisches und internationals Wirtschaftsrecht (ed), *Kartelle und Monopole im modernen Recht: Band l* (Karlsruhe, CF Müller 1961)

—— 'Freiheit und Ordnung in der Marktwirtschaft' (1971) 22 ORDO 11–27

Bolton, P, Brodley, JF, and Riordan, MH, 'Predatory Pricing: Strategic Theory and Legal Policy' (2000) 88 Georgetown LJ 2239

Bolton, P and Whinston, MD, 'Incomplete Contracts, Vertical Integration, and Supply Assurance' (1993) 60 Rev Econ Stud 121

Booth, DL et al, 'An Empirical Model of Capacity Expansion and Pricing in an Oligopoly with Barometric Price Leadership: A Case Study of the Newsprint Industry in North America' (1991) 39(3) Journal of Industrial Economics 255

Bork, H, *The Antitrust Paradox* (New York, Basic Books 1978)

—— *The Antitrust Paradox: A Policy at War with Itself* (New York, The Free Press 1993)

Bourgeois, JHJ, 'EC Competition Law and Member State Courts' in Hawk, BE (ed), *International Antitrust in a Global Economy: Fordham Corporate Law 1993* (New York, Kluwer Law and Taxation 1994)

Bowley, AL, 'Bilateral Monopoly' (1928) 38 Economic Journal 651

Braun, JD and Kuhling, J, 'Article 87 EC and the Community courts: From revolution to evolution' (2008) 45 CML Rev 465

Brealey, M, 'The Burden of Proof before the European Court' (1985) 10 EL Rev 250

Brehm, W, 'Beweisrecht in Deutschland' in Lebre de Freitas, JM (ed), *The Law of Evidence in the European Union* (The Hague, Kluwer Law International 2004) 179

Brock, WA and Scheinkman, J, 'Price Setting Supergames with Capacity Constraints' (1985) 52 Rev Econ Stud 371

Brodley, JF, 'The Economic Goals of Antitrust: Efficiency, Consumer Welfare and Technological Progress' (1987) 63 NYU L Rev 1020

Brown-Collier, EK, 'Self-Interest, Economic Efficiency and the General Welfare' in O'Boyle, EJ (ed), *Social Economics: Premises, Findings and Policies* (London and New York, Routledge 1996)

Buckley, R, 'Breach of Statutory Duty' in Dugdale, A and Jones, M (eds), *Clerk & Lindsell on Torts* (20th edn London, Sweet & Maxwell 2010) 565

Buendia Sierra, JL, *Exclusive Rights and State Monopolies under EC Law: Article 86 (former Article 90) of the EC Treaty* (Oxford, OUP 1999)

—— 'Article 86: Exclusive Rights and Other Anti-Competitive State Measures' in Faull, J and Nikpay, A (eds), *The EC Law of Competition* (2nd edn Oxford, OUP 2007)

de Búrca, G, 'The Principle of Proportionality and its Application in EC Law' (1993) 13 YEL 105

Burnham, TA, Frels, JK, and Mahajan, V, 'Consumer Switching Costs: A Typology, Antecedents, and Consequences' (2003) 31 Journal of the Academy of Marketing Science 109

Caillaud, B, Jullien, B, and Picard, P, 'Competing Vertical Structures: Precommitment and Renegotiation' (1995) 63 Econometrica 621

Calvani, T and Fingleton, J, 'Dominance: A Comparative Economic and Legal Analysis' in Collins, WD (ed), *Issues in Competition Law and Policy* (Chicago, ABA Press 2008) 845

Campano, F and Salvatore, D, *Income Distribution* (Oxford, OUP 2006)

Capobianco, A, 'The Essential Facility Doctrine: Similarities and Differences between the American and European Approaches (2001) 26 EL Rev 548

Caprice, S, 'Incentive to Encourage Downstream Competition under Bilateral Oligopoly' (2005) 12(9) Economics Bulletin 1

Carlton, DW, 'A General Analysis of Exclusionary Conduct and Refusal to Deal—Why *Aspen* and *Kodak* are Misguided' (2001) 68 Antitrust LJ 659

—— 'Should "Price Squeeze" be a Recognized Form of Anticompetitive Conduct?' (2008) 4 J Comp L & Econ 271

Carlton, DW and Perloff, JM, *Modern Industrial Organization* (4th edn Boston, Pearson/Addison Wesley 2005)

Carlton, DW and Waldman, M, 'The Strategic Use of Tying to Preserve and Create Market Power in Evolving Industries' (2002) 33 RAND Journal of Economics 194

—— 'Competition, Monopoly and Aftermarkets' (2010) 26 JL Econ & Org 54

Cass, RA and Hylton, KN, 'Preserving Competition: Economic Analysis, Legal Standards and Microsoft' (1999) 8 Geo Mason L Rev 1

—— 'Antitrust Intent' Boston University School of Law, Working Paper Series, Law and Economics, Working Paper No 00-02 (Boston, 2000)

Cavallo, V, *La Libertà Umana Nella Filosofia Contemporanea* (Napoli-Città di Castello, F Perrella 1933).

Chamberlain, EH, *The Theory of Monopolistic Competition* (Oxford, OUP 1966)

Che, YK and Gale, I, 'Buyer Alliances and Managed Competition' (1997) 6 Journal of Economics and Management Strategy 175

Chemla, G, 'Downstream Competition, Foreclosure and Vertical Integration', (2003) 12 Journal of Economics and Management Strategy 261

Chen, Z and Ross, TW, 'Refusals to Deal, Price Discrimination and Independent Service Organizations' (1993) 2 Journal of Economics and Management Strategy 593

—— 'Refusal to Deal and Orders to Supply in Competitive Markets' (1999) 17 Intl J Ind Org 399

Chiang, R and Spatt, CS, 'Imperfect Price Discrimination and Welfare' (1982) 49 Rev Econ Stud 155

Chipty, T, 'Horizontal Integration for Bargaining Power: Evidence from the Cable Television Industry' (1995) 4 Journal of Economics and Management Strategy 375

—— 'Vertical Integration, Market Foreclosure, and Consumer Welfare in the Cable Television Industry' (2001) American Economic Rev 428

Choi, JP and Sang-Seung, Y, 'Vertical Foreclosure with the Choice of Input Specifications' (2000) 30 RAND Journal of Economics 717

Choi, JP and Stefanidis, C, 'Tying, Investment, and the Dynamic Leverage Theory' (2001) 32 RAND Journal of Economics 52

Christensen, LR and Caves, R, 'Cheap Talk and Investment Rivalry in the Pulp and Paper Industry' (1997) Journal of Industrial Economics 47

Christiansen, A and Kerber, W, 'Competition Policy with Optimally Differentiated Rules Instead of "Per Se Rules v Rules of Reason"' (2006) 2 J Comp L & Econ 215

Christoffersen, J, *Fair Balance: Proportionality, Subsidiarity and Primarity in the European Convention on Human Rights* (The Hague, Martinus Nijhoff Publishers 2009)

Church, J and Ware, R, *Industrial Organization: A Strategic Approach* (Boston, McGraw-Hill 2000)

Clarke, JM, 'Toward a Concept of Workable Competition' (1940) 30 American Economic Rev 241

Coate, MB, 'Alive and Kicking: Collusion Theories in Merger Analysis at the Federal Trade Commission' (2008) 4 Competition Policy International 145

Coate, MB and Fischer, JH, 'A Practical Guide to the Hypothetical Monopolist Test for Market Definition' (2008) 4 J Comp L & Econ 1031

Coke, R, *Treatises of the Nature of Man* (London, J Cotteral & F Collins 1696)

Colley, L and Burnside, S, 'Margin Squeeze Abuse' (2006) 2 European Competition Journal 185

Comanor, WS and Rey, P, 'Vertical Restraints and the Market Power of Large Distributors' (2000) 17(2) Rev Ind Org 135

Comoglio, LP, *Le Prove Civili* (Torino, UTET 2004)

Compte, O, Jenny, F, and Rey, P, 'Capacity Constraints, Mergers and Collusion' (2002) 46 European Economic Rev 1

Connor, JM, Rogers, R, and Bhagavan, V, 'Concentration Change and Countervailing Power in the US Food Manufacturing Industries' (1996) 11 Rev Ind Org 473

Connor, T, 'Accentuating the Positive: The "Selling Arrangement", the first Decade, and Beyond' (2005) 54 ICLQ 127

Craig, P, 'Once Upon a Time in the West: Direct Effect and Federalization of EEC Law' (1992) 12 OJLS 453

—— *EU Administrative Law* (Oxford, OUP 2006)

Craig, P and de Búrca, G, *EU Law: Text, Cases and Materials* (4th edn Oxford, OUP 2007)

Crane, A et al (eds), *Oxford Handbook on Corporate Social Responsibility* (Oxford OUP 2008)

Crane, DA, 'Mixed Bundling, Profit Sacrifice, and Consumer Welfare' (2006) 55 Emory LJ 423

Creighton, SA et al, 'Cheap Exclusion' (2005) 72 Antitrust LJ 975

Crocioni, P, 'Price Squeeze and Imputation Test: Recent Developments' (2005) 26 ECLR 558

Danov, M, 'Awarding Exemplary (or Punitive) Antitrust Damages in EC Competition Cases with an International Element—the Rome II Regulation and the Commission's White Paper on Damages' (2008) 29 ECLR 430

Davidson, C and Deneckere, R, 'Horizontal Mergers and Collusive Behavior' (1984) 2 Intl J Ind Org 117

—— 'Excess Capacity and Collusion' (1990) 31 Intl Economic Rev 521

Davidson, JS, 'Actions for Damages in the English Courts for Breach of EEC Competition Law' (1985) 34 ICLQ 178

Debroux, M and Tricot, E, 'Competition—EU Competition Law Enforcement: Towards a US Style Private Antitrust Action?' (2006) 27 Business L Rev 256

DeGraba, P, 'Input Market Price Discrimination and the Choice of Technology' (1990) 80 American Economic Rev 1246

Demesetz, H, 'Two Systems of Belief About Monopoly' in Goldschmidt, H et al (eds), *Industrial Concentration: The New Learning* (Boston, Little Brown 1974) 164

Desogus, C, 'Parallel Trade and Pharmaceutical R&D: The Pitfalls of the Rule of Reason' (2008) 29 ECLR 649

Dethmers, F and Dodoo, N, 'The Abuse of Hoffmann-La Roche: The Meaning of Dominance under EC Competition Law' (2006) 27 ECLR 537

Devlin, A, 'The Stochastic Relationship Between Patents and Antitrust' (2008) 5 J Comp L & Econ 75

Diamond, DW, 'Financial Intermediation and Delegated Monitoring' (1984) 51 Rev Econ Stud 393

Diaz, FEG and Garcia, AL, 'Tying and Bundling under EU Competition Law: Future Prospects' (2007) 3 Competition Law International 13

Dobson, PW and Waterson, M, 'Countervailing Power and Consumer Prices' (1997) 107 Economic Journal 418

Dobson, PW, Waterson, M, and Chu, A, 'The Welfare Consequences of the Exercise of Buyer Power', OFT Research Paper 16 (September 1998)

Doherty, B, 'Just What Are Essential Facilities?' (2001) 38 CML Rev 397

Dolmans, M and Graf, T, 'Analysis of Tying Under Article 82 EC: The European Commission's Microsoft Decision in Perspective' (2004) 27 World Competition 225

Douglas-Scott, S, *Constitutional Law of the European Union* (2nd edn London, Thomson Sweet & Maxwell 2004)

Doyle, C and Inderst, R, 'Some Economics on the Treatment of Buyer Power in Antitrust' (2007) 28 ECLR 210

DTI, 'Liberalisation and Globalisation: Maximising the Benefits of International Trade and Investment' DTI Economics Paper No 10 (July 2004)

Duncan, FF, 'No Margin for Error: The Challenges of Assessing Margin Squeeze in Practice' (2010) 9 Comp Law 124

Easterbrook, FH, 'The Limits of Antitrust' (1984) 63 Texas L Rev 1

—— 'When Is It Worthwhile to Use Courts to Search for Exclusionary Conduct?' (2003) Columbia Business L Rev 345

Economides, N and Lianos, I, 'The Elusive Antitrust Standard on Bundling in Europe and in the United States in the Aftermath of the Microsoft case' (2009) 76 Antitrust LJ 483

Ehlermann, C-D, 'The Modernization of EC Antitrust Policy: A Legal and Cultural Revolution' (2000) 37 CML Rev 537

Eilmansberger, T, 'How to Distinguish Good from Bad Competition under Article 82: In Search of Clearer and More Coherent Standards for Anti-Competitive Abuses' (2005) 42 CML Rev 129

Elhauge, E, 'Defining Better Monopolisation Standards' (2003) 56 Stan L Rev 253

—— 'Why Above-Cost Price Cuts to Drive out Entrants Are Not Predatory: and the Implications for Defining Costs and Market Power' (2003) 112 Yale LJ 681

Elliott, GP, 'The *Gencor* Judgment: Collective Dominance, Remedies and Extraterritoriality under the Merger Regulation' (1999) 24 EL Rev 638

Emiliou, N, *The Principle of Proportionality in European Law: A Comparative Study* (London, Kluwer Law International 1996)

Epstein, RA, 'Monopoly Dominance or Level Playing Field? The New Antitrust Paradox' (2005) 72 U Chi L Rev 49

Eucken, W, 'Die Wettbewerbsordnung und ihre Verwrklichung' (1949) 2 ORDO 1

—— *Die Grundlagen der Nationalökonomie* (9th edn Berlin, Springer 1989)

—— *Grundsätze der Wirtschaftpolitik* (6th edn Tübingen, JCB Mohr 1990)

European Commission, 'The European Commission Accepts an Undertaking from Digital Concerning its Supply and Pricing Practices in the Field of Computer Maintenance Services' Press Release of 10 October 1997 IP/97/868

—— DG Comp, 'DG Competition discussion paper on the application of Article 82 of the Treaty to exclusionary abuses' (Brussels, December 2005)

—— 'Antitrust: Commission accepts Microsoft commitments to give users browser choice' Press Release of 16 December 2009 IP/09/1941

Evans, DS and Padilla, AJ, 'Excessive Prices: Using Economics to Define Administrable Legal Rules' (2005) 1 J Comp L & Econ 97

——, Padilla, AJ, and Salinger, MA, 'A Pragmatic Approach to Identifying and Analysing Legitimate Tying Cases' in Ehlermann, CD and Atanasiu, I (eds), *European Competition Law Annual 2003: What Is an Abuse of a Dominant Position?* (Oxford, Hart Publishing 2006)

Evans, WN and Kessides, IN, 'Living by the "Golden Rule": Multimarket Contact in the US Airline Industry' (1994) 109 Quarterly Journal of Economics 341

Ezrachi, A, 'From *Courage v Crehan* to the White Paper—the Changing Landscape of European Private Enforcement and the Possible Implications for Article 82 EC Litigation' in Mackenrodt, M-O, Conde Gallego, B, and Enchelmaier, S (eds), *Abuse of Dominant Position: New Interpretation, New Enforcement Mechanisms?* (Berlin, Springer 2008) 117

Ezrachi, A and Gilo, D, 'Are Excessive Prices Really Self-Correcting?' (2009) 5 J Comp L & Econ 249

Farrell, J and Gallini, NT, 'Second-Sourcing as a Commitment: Monopoly Incentives to Attract Competition' (1988) 103 Quarterly Journal of Economics 673

Farrell, J and Katz, ML, 'The Economics of Welfare Standards in Antitrust', Competition Policy Center, Institute of Business and Economic Research, UC Berkeley 20 July 2006

Farrell, J and Shapiro, C, 'Dynamic Competition with Switching Costs' (1988) 19 RAND Journal of Economics 123

Farrell, J et al, 'Standard Setting, Patents, and Hold-Up' (2007) 74 Antitrust LJ 603

Federico, G, 'When Are Rebates Exclusionary?' (2005) 26 ECLR 477

Fellner, W, *Competition Among the Few* (London, Frank Cass & Co 1965)

Fenwick, H, *Civil Liberties and Human Rights* (4th edn New York, Routledge-Cavendish 2007)

Fernandez, PM, 'Increasing Powers and Increasing Uncertainty: Collective Dominance and Pricing Abuses' (2000) 25 EL Rev 645

Filippelli, M, 'Collective Dominance in the Italian Mobile Telecommunications Market' (2010) 31 ECLR 81

Fisher, FM, 'Diagnosing Monopoly' (1979) 19 Quarterly Review of Economics and Business 7

Fontenay, CC de and Gans, JS, 'Vertical Integration in the Presence of Upstream Competition' (2005) 36 RAND Journal of Economics 544

Forrester, IS, 'Article 82: Remedies in Search of Theories?' (2005) 28 Fordham Intl LJ 919

Fox, EM, 'What is Harm to Competition? Exclusionary Practices and Anti-competitive Effect' (2002) 70 Antitrust LJ 371

—— 'We Protect Competition, You Protect Competitors' (2003) 26 World Competition 149

Friedman, J, 'A Non-Cooperative Equilibrium for Supergames' (1971) 38 Rev Econ Stud 1

Friedman, M, *Free to Choose: A Personal Statement* (London, Pan 1990)

Fudenberg, D and Maskin, E, 'The Folk Theorem in Repeated Games with Discounting or with Incomplete Information' (1986) 54 Econometrica 533

Fudenberg, D and Tirole, J, 'A "Signal-Jamming" Theory of Predation' (1986) 17 RAND Journal of Economics 366

Furse, M, 'Monopoly Price Discrimination, Article 82 and the Competition Act' (2001) 22 ECLR 149

—— 'Caught Napping: DGFT and Napp Pharmaceutical Holdings Ltd' (2001) 22 ECLR 477

Gal, MS, 'Below-Cost Price Alignment: Meeting or Beating Competition? The France Télécom Case' (2007) 28 ECLR 382

Galbraith, JK, *American Capitalism: The Concept of Countervailing Power* (New York, Houghton Mifflin 1952)

Gale, D and Hellwig, M, 'Incentive Compatible Debt Contracts: The One-Period Problem (1985) 52 Rev Econ Stud 647

Gaudet, G and Long, N, 'Vertical Integration, Foreclosure and Profits in the Presence of Double Marginalisation' (1996) 5 Journal of Economics and Management Strategy 409

Gavil, AI, 'Exclusionary Distribution Strategies by Dominant Firms: Striking a Better Balance' (2004) 72 Antitrust LJ 3

Genin-Meric, R, 'Droit de la preuve: l'example français' in Lebre de Freitas, JM (ed), *The Law of Evidence in the European Union* (The Hague, Kluwer Law International 2004)

Geradin, D, 'A Proposed Test for Separating Pro-Competitive Conditional Rebates from Anti-Competitive Ones' (2009) 32 World Competition 41

Geradin, D and O'Donoghue, R, 'The Concurrent Application of Competition Law and Regulation: The Case of Margin Squeeze Abuses in the Telecommunications Sector' (2005) 1 J Comp L & Econ 355

Geradin, D and Petit, N, 'Price Discrimination under EC Competition Law: Another Antitrust Doctrine in Search of Limiting Principles?' (2006) 2 J Comp L & Econ 479

Gerber, DJ, *Law and Competition in Twentieth Century Europe* (Oxford, OUP 2001)

Gerber, DJ and Cassinis, P, 'The "Modernization" of European Community Competition Law: Achieving Consistency in Enforcement: Part 1' (2006) 27 ECLR 10

—— 'The "Modernization" of European Community Competition Law: Achieving Consistency in Enforcement: Part 2' (2006) 27 ECLR 51

Ghidini, G, *Intellectual Property and Competition Law* (Cheltenham, Edward Elgar 2006)

Gilbert, R and Lieberman, M, 'Investment and Coordination in Oligopolistic Industries' (1987) 18 RAND Journal of Economics 17

Glynn, D, 'Article 82 and Price Discrimination in Patented Pharmaceuticals: The Economics' (2005) 26 ECLR 135

Good, D, 'Eurotort with Europrocedure?' in Hutchings, M and Andenas, M, *Competition Law Yearbook 2002* (London, British Institute of International and Comparative Law 2003) 345

Gordon, C and R Richardson, R, 'Collective Dominance: The Third Way?' (2001) 22 ECLR 416

Gormsen, LL, 'The European Commission's Priority Guidelines on Article 82 EC' (2009) 14 Communications Law 83

—— *A Principled Approach to Abuse of Dominance in European Competition Law* (Cambridge, CUP 2010)

—— 'Why the European Commission's Enforcement Priorities on Article 82 EC Should be Withdrawn' (2010) ECLR 45

Goyder, D, *Goyder's EC Competition Law* (5th edn Oxford, OUP 2009)

Gravengaard, MA, 'The Meeting Competition Defence Principle—A Defence for Price Discrimination and Predatory Pricing?' (2006) 27 ECLR 658

Gravengaard, MA and Kjaersgaard, N, 'The EU Commission Guidance on Exclusionary Abuse of Dominance—and Its Consequences in Practice' (2010) 31 ECLR 285

Green, EJ and Porter, RH, 'Non-Cooperative Collusion under Imperfect Price Information' (1984) 52 Econometrica 87

Guth, LA, Schwartz, RA, and Whitcombe, DK, 'Buyer Concentration Ratios' (1977) 25 Journal of Industrial Economics 241

Gyselen, L, 'Rebates: Competition on the Merits or Exclusionary Practice?' in Ehlermann, C-D and Atanasiu, I (eds), *European Competition Law Annual 2003: What Is an Abuse of a Dominant Position?* (Oxford, Hart Publishing 2006) 287

Haltiwanger, J and Harrington, J, 'The Impact of Cyclical Demand Movements on Collusive Behavior' (1991) 22 RAND Journal of Economics 89

Harbo, T-I, 'The Function of the Proportionality Principle in EU Law' (2010) 16 ELJ 158

Harrington, J, 'Collusion Among Asymmetric Firms: The Case of Different Discount Factors' (1989) 7 Intl J Ind Org 289

—— 'The Determination of Price and Output Quotas in a Heterogeneous Cartel' (1991) 32 Intl Economic Rev 767

Hart, O and Tirole, J, 'Vertical Integration and Market Foreclosure' (1990) Brookings Papers on Economic Activity (Microeconomics) 205

Hartley, TC, *The Foundations of European Community Law* (6th edn Oxford, OUP 2007)

Hausman, D, *The Inexact and Separate Science of Economics* (Cambridge, CUP 1992)

Hawk, BE, 'The American (Anti-trust) Revolution—Lessons for the EEC?' (1988) 9 ECLR 53

—— *United States Common Market and International Antitrust, Volume II* (2nd edn New Jersey, Prentice Hall Law & Business 1990)

—— 'Antitrust in the EEC—The First Decade' (1992) 41 Fordham L Rev 229

—— 'The Current Debate About Section 2 of the Sherman Act: Judicial Certainty Versus Rule of Reason' (paper delivered at the II Lisbon Conference on Competition Law and Economics, 15 and 16 November 2007)

Hays, T, *Parallel Importation under European Union Law* (London, Sweet & Maxwell 2004)

Heidegger, M, *Being and Time* (Macquarrie, J and Robinson, E (trs), Malden, Mass, Blackwell Publishing 2010)

Heimler, A, 'Below-Cost Pricing and Loyalty-Inducing Discounts: Are They Restrictive and, If So, When?' (2005) 1 Competition Policy International 149

Hewitt Pate, R, 'The Common Law Approach and Improving Standards for Analyzing Single Firm Conduct', address before the Thirteenth Annual Conference on International Antitrust Law and Policy, Fordham Corporate Law Institute (New York, 23 October 2003)

Hicks, JR, 'The Foundations of Welfare Economics' (1939) 49 Economic Journal 696

Hildebrand, D, 'The European School in EC Competition Law' (2002) 25 World Competition 3

—— *The Role of Economic Analysis in the EC Competition Rules* (3rd edn Alphen aan den Rijn, Kluwer Law International 2009)

Hilgenfeld, M, 'Private Antitrust Enforcement: Towards a Harmonised European Model or a "Patchwork" of Various Member States' Rules?' (2008) 14 International Trade Law & Regulation 39

Horn, H and Wolinsky, A, 'Bilateral Monopolies and Incentives for Merger' (1988) 19 RAND Journal of Economics 408

Hovenkamp, H, 'The Monopolization Offense' (2000) 61 Ohio State LJ 1035, 103

—— *The Antitrust Enterprise: Principle and Execution* (Cambridge, Mass, Harvard University Press 2005)

—— 'Exclusion and the Sherman Act' (2005) 72 U Chi L Rev 147

—— *Federal Antitrust Policy: The Law of Competition and its Practice* (St Paul, Thompson/ West Publishing 2005)

Hovenkamp, H, Janis, MD, and Lemley, MA, 'Unilateral Refusals to License' (2006) 2 J Comp L & Econ 1

Hylton, KN and Salinger, M, 'Tying Law and Policy: A Decision-Theoretic Approach' (2001) 69 Antitrust LJ 469

Incardona, R, 'Modernisation of Article 82 EC and Refusal to Supply: Any Real Change in Sight?' (2006) 2 European Competition Journal 337

International Competition Network, 'Objectives of Unilateral Conduct Laws, Assessment of Dominance/Substantial Market Power, and State-Created Monopolies', ICN Reports (2007)

Jacobs, F, 'Damages for Breach of Article 86 EEC' (1983) 8 EL Rev 353

—— 'Civil Enforcement of EEC Antitrust Law' (1984) 82 Mich L Rev 1364

—— 'Recent Devlopments in the Principle of Proportionality in European Community Law' in Ellis, E (ed), *The Principle of Proportionality in the Laws of Europe* (Oxford, Hart Publishing 1999) 1

Jans, JH, 'Proportionality Revisited' (2000) 27 LIEI 239

Jaquemin, A and Slade, ME, 'Cartels, Collusion and Horizontal Merger' in Schmalensee, R and Willig, RD (eds), *Handbook of Industrial Organisation: Vol 1* (Amsterdam, North Holland, 1989) 418

Jebsen, P and Stevens, R, 'Assumptions, Goals and Dominant Undertakings: The Regulation of Competition under Article 86 of the European Union' (1996) 64 Antitrust LJ 443

Jephcott, M and Withers, C, 'Where to Go Now for EC Oligopoly Control?' (2001) 22 ECLR 295

Jones, A and Sufrin, B, *EU Competition Law: Text, Cases, and Materials* (4th edn Oxford, OUP 2011)

Jones, CA, 'Private Antitrust Enforcement in Europe: A Policy Analysis and Reality Check' (2004) 27 World Competition 13

Jones, DL, 'Article 6 ECHR and Immunities Arising in Public International Law' (2003) 52 ICLQ 463

Joshua, JM, 'Proof in Contested EEC Competition Cases: A Comparison with the Rules of Evidence in Common Law' (1987) 12 EL Rev 315

Joskow, PL and Klevorick, AK, 'A Framework for Analyzing Predatory Pricing Policy' (1979) 89 Yale LJ 213

Kaldor, N, 'Welfare Propositions In Economics and Inter-Personal Comparisons Of Utility' (1939) 49 Economic Journal 549

Kallaugher, J and Sher, B, 'Rebates Revisited: Anti-Competitive Effects and Exclusionary Abuse under Article 82' (2004) 25 ECLR 263

Kamann, H-G and Bergmann, E, 'The Granting of Rebates by Market Dominant Undertakings under Article 82 of the EC Treaty' (2005) 26 ECLR 83

Kamien, MI and Schwartz, NL, 'Potential Rivalry, Monopoly Profits and the Pace of Inventive Activity' (1978) 45 Rev Econ Stud 547

Kanter, D, 'IP and Compulsory Licensing on Both Sides of the Atlantic—An Appropriate Antitrust Remedy or a Cutback on Innovation?' (2006) 27 ECLR 351

Kaplow, L and Shavell, S, *Fairness versus Welfare* (Cambridge, Mass, and London, England, Harvard University Press 2002)

Katsoulacos, YS, 'Optimal Legal Standards for Refusals to License Intellectual Property: A Welfare-Based Analysis' (2008) 5 J Comp L & Econ 269

Katz, ML, 'Non-Uniform Pricing, Output and Welfare under Monopoly' (1983) 50 Rev Econ Stud 37

—— 'The Welfare Effects of Third-Degree Price Discrimination in Intermediate Good Markets' (1987) 77 American Economic Rev 154

Katz, ML and Shapiro, C, 'On the Licensing of Innovations' (1985) 16 RAND Journal of Economics 504

Kauper, TE, 'Article 86, Excessive Prices, and Refusals to Deal' (1990) 59 Antitrust LJ 441

Kavanagh, J, 'Assessing Margin Squeeze under Competition Law' (2004) 3 Comp Law 187

Kazazi, M, *Burden of Proof and Related Issues: A Study on Evidence before International Tribunals* (The Hague, Kluwer Law International 1996)

Keeling, DT, *Intellectual Property Rights in EU Law: Vol 1* (Oxford, OUP 2003)

Kellerbauer, M, 'The Commission's New Enforcement Priorities in Applying Article 82 EC to Dominant Companies' Exclusionary Conduct: A Shift Towards a More Economic Approach?' (2010) 31 ECLR 175

Kerr, M, Janda, R, and Pitts, C, *Corporate Social Responsibility: A Legal Analysis* (Toronto, LexisNexis 2009)

Killick, J, '*IMS* and *Microsoft* Judged in the Cold Light of IMS' (2004) 1(2) Competition L Rev 23

Kjølbye, L, 'Article 82 EC as Remedy to Patent System Imperfections: Fighting Fire with Fire?' (2009) 32 World Competition 163

—— 'Rebates under Article 82 EC: Navigating Uncertain Waters' (2010) 31 ECLR 66

Klein, B and Wiley Jr, JS, 'Competitive Price Discrimination as an Antitrust Justification for Intellectual Property Refusals to Deal' (2002) 70 Antitrust LJ 599

Klemperer, P, 'Markets with Consumer Switching Costs' (1987) 102 Quarterly Journal of Economics 375

—— 'Competition When Consumers Have Switching Costs: An Overview With Applications to Industrial Organization, Macroeconomics, and International Trade' (1995) 62 Rev Econ Stud 515

Kloosterhuis, E, 'Joint Dominance and the Interaction Between Firms' (2000) 21 ECLR 79

Koelman, KJ, 'An Exceptio Standardis: Do We Need an IP Exemption for Standards?' (2006) 37 Intl Rev IP & Comp L 823

Kokkoris, I, 'Buyer Power Assessment in Competition Law: A Boon or a Menace?' (2006) 29 World Competition 139

—— 'Assessment of Mergers Inducing Coordinated Effects in the Presence of Explicit Collusion' (2008) 31 World Competition 499

Kokott, J, *The Burden of Proof in Comparative and International Human Rights Law: Civil and Common Law Approaches with Special Reference to the American and German Legal Systems* (The Hague, Kluwer Law International 1998)

Komninos, AP, 'Non-Competition Concerns: Resolution of Conflicts in the Integrated Article 81 EC', The University of Oxford Centre for Competition Law and Policy Working Paper (L) 08/05 (30 June 2005)

—— 'Modernisation and Decentralisation: Retrospective and Prospective' in G Amato, G and Ehlermann, C-D (eds), *EC Competition Law: A Critical Assessment* (Oxford, Hart Publishing 2007) 629

—— *EC Private Antitrust Enforcement: Decentralised Application of EC Competition Law by National Courts* (Oxford, Hart Publishing 2008)

Korah, V, 'EEC Competition Policy—Legal Form or Economic Efficiency' (1986) 39 CLP 85

—— '*Gencor v Commission*: Collective Dominance' (1999) 20 ECLR 337

—— 'Access to Essential Facilities under the Commerce Act in Light of Experience in Australia, the European Union and the United States (2000) 31 Victoria University of Wellington L Rev 231

—— 'The Interface Between Intellectual Property and Antitrust: The European Experience' (2001) 69 Antitrust LJ 801

—— *An Introductory Guide to EC Competition Law and Practice* (9th edn Oxford, Hart Publishing 2007)

Koslowski, P, *The Social Market Economy: Theory and Ethics of the Economic Order* (Berlin, Springer Verlag 1998)

Kreps, DM and Wilson, R, 'Reputation and Imperfect Information' (1982) 27 Journal of Economic Theory 253

Kroes, N, 'Delivering Better Markets and Better Choices' Speech at the European Consumer and Competition Day, London, SPEECH/05/512 (15 September 2005)

—— 'Preliminary Thoughts on Policy Review of Article 82' Speech at the Fordham Corporate Law Institute, New York (23 September 2005)

—— Opening address at conference: 'Competition and Consumers in the 21st Century', Brussels SPEECH/09/486 (21 October 2009)

Kühn, K-U, Stillman, R, and Caffarra, C, 'Economic Theories of Bundling and Their Policy Implications in Abuse Cases: An Assessment in Light of the Microsoft Case' (2005) 1 European Competition Journal 85

Kühn, K-U, Matutes, C, and Moldovanu, B, 'Fighting Collusion by Regulating Communication Between Firms' (2001) 32 Economic Policy 169

Laffont, JJ, Rey, P, and Tirole, J, 'Network Competition: I. Overview and Nondiscriminatory Pricing' (1998) 29 RAND Journal of Economics 1

Lambert, TA, 'Evaluating Bundled Discounts' (2005) 89 Minn L Rev 1688

Lambson, VE, 'Optimal Penal Codes in Price-Setting Supergames with Capacity Constraints' (1987) 54 Rev Econ Stud 385

—— 'Some Results on Optimal Penal Codes in Asymmetric Bertrand Supergames' (1994) 62 Journal of Economic Theory 444

Langer, J, *Tying and Bundling as a Leveraging Concern under EC Competition Law* (Alphen aan den Rijn, Kluwer Law International 2007)

Lao, M, 'Reclaiming a Role for Intent Evidence in Monopolization Analysis' (2004) 54 American University L Rev 151

—— 'Defining Exclusionary Conduct Under Section 2: The Case for Non-Universal Standards' in Hawk, BE (ed), *International Antitrust Law & Policy: Fordham Competition Law 2006* (New York, Juris Publishing 2007) 433

Layne-Farrar, A, Padilla, AJ, and R Schmalensee, R, 'Pricing Patents for Licensing in Standard-Setting Organizations: Making Sense of Fraud Commitments' (2007) 74 Antitrust LJ 707

Lemley, MA, 'Intellectual Property Rights and Standard-Setting Organizations' (2002) 90 California L Rev 1889

Lenaerts, K, and van Nuffel, P, *Constitutional Law of the European Union* (2nd edn London, Sweet & Maxwell 2005) 109–14

Levine, ME 'Price Discrimination Without Market Power' (2002) 19 Yale J on Regulation 1

Lewis, TR and Yao, DA, 'Some Reflections on the Antitrust Treatment of Intellectual Property' (1995) 63 Antitrust LJ 603

Lianos, I, 'Categorical Thinking in Competition Law and the "Effects-based" Approach in Article 82 EC' in Ezrachi, A (ed), *Article 82 EC: Reflections on Its Recent Evolution* (Oxford: Hart Publishing 2009) 19

—— 'The Price/Non Price Exclusionary Dichotomy: A Critical Appraisal' (2009) 2 Concurrences 34

Lorenz, M, Lübbig, M, and Russel, A, 'Price Discrimination, a Tender Story' (2005) 26 ECLR 355

Lowe, P, 'The Design of Competition Policy Institutions for the 21st Century—the Experience of the European Commission and DG Competition' (2008) 3 European Commission Competition Policy Newsletter 1

Lücking, J and Simon, S, 'Definition of the Relevant Market' in Drauz, G and Jones, CW (eds), *EU Competition Law: Volume II—Mergers and Acquisitions* (Leuven, Claeys & Casteels 2006) 151

Lustgarten, SH, 'The Impact of Buyer Concentration in Manufacturing Industries' (1975) 47 Rev Econ & Stat 125

Lyons, B, 'Could Politicians Be More Rights than Economists? A Theory of Merger Standards' Revised Centre for Competition and Regulation (CCR) Working Paper 02-1 (European University Institute, 2003)

Ma, C-TA, 'Option Contracts and Vertical Foreclosure' (1997) 6 Journal of Economics and Management Strategy 725

Mahoney, P, 'Right to a Fair Trial in Criminal Matters under Article 6 E.C.H.R' (2004) 4 Judicial Studies Institute Journal 107

Maitland-Walker, J, 'A Step Closer to a Definitive Ruling on a Right in Damages for Breach of EC Competition Rules' (1992) 13 ECLR 3

Manne, GA and Wright, JD, 'Innovation and the Limits of Antitrust' (2010) 6 J Comp L & Econ 153

Manzini, P, 'The European Rule of Reason-Crossing the Sea of Doubt' (2002) 23 ECLR 392

Marc, I et al, 'The Economics of Tacit Collusion' Final Report to DG Competition, European Commission (Toulouse, March 2003)

Mares, R, *The Dynamics of Corporate Social Responsibilities* (Boston, Martinus Nijhoff Publishers 2008)

Marsden, P and Whelan, P, ' "Consumer Detriment" in the EC and UK Competition Law' (2006) 27 ECLR 569

Martin, S, 'Endogenous Firm Efficiency in a Cournot Principal-Agent Model' (1993) 59 Journal of Economic Theory 445

—— *Industrial Economics: Economic Analysis and Public Policy* (2nd edn New York, Macmillan 1994)

—— 'R&D Joint Ventures and Tacit Product Market Collusion' (1996) 11 European Journal of Political Economy 733

Martin, S, Normann, H-T, and Snyder, CM, 'Vertical Foreclosure in Experimental Markets' (2001) 32 RAND Journal of Economics 466

Mason, ES, 'Monopoly in Law and Economics' (1937) 47 Yale LJ 34

—— 'Price and Production Policies of Large-Scale Enterprise' (1939) 29 American Economic Rev 61

Mastromanolis, EP, 'Predatory Pricing Strategies in the European Union: A Case for Legal Reform' (1998) 19 ECLR 211

Mathewson, GF and Winter, RA, 'Buyer Groups' (1997) 15 Intl J Ind Org 137

McBarnet, DJ, Voiculescu, A, and Campbell, T (eds), *The New Corporate Accountability: CSR and the Law* (Cambridge, CUP 2007)

McEldowney, JF, *Public Law* (3rd edn London, Sweet & Maxwell 2002)

McGee, JS, 'Predatory Price Cutting: The Standard Oil (NJ) Case' (1958) 1 Journal of Law and Economics 137

McGucken, R and Chen, H, 'Interactions Between Buyer and Seller Concentration and Industry Price-Cost Margins' (1976) 4 Ind Org Rev 123

McMichael, S and Kemp, B, 'Private Enforcement' 6 Competition Law Insight (8 May 2007) 14

McSorley, C, Padilla, AJ, and Williams, M, 'Switching Costs' DTI Economic Discussion Paper 5 (15 April 2003) 1

Meese, AJ, 'Property, *Aspen*, and Refusals to Deal' (2005) 73 Antitrust LJ 81

Melamed, AD, 'Exclusionary Conduct Under the Antitrust Laws: Balancing, Sacrifice, and Refusals to Deal' (2005) 20 Berkeley Technology LJ 1247

—— 'Exclusive Dealing Agreements and Other Exclusionary Conduct—Are There Unifying Principles?' (2006) 73 Antitrust LJ 375

Mestmäcker, EJ, 'Meinungsfreiheit und Medienwettbewerb' (1994) 28 Sandai L Rev 293

Mezzanotte, FE, 'Tacit Collusion as Economic Links in Article 82 EC Revisited' (2009) 30 ECLR 137

—— 'Using Abuse of Collective Dominance in Article 102 TFEU to Fight Tacit Collusion: The Problem of Proof and Inferential Error' (2010) 33 World Competition 77

Miksch, L, *Wettbewerb als Aufgabe: Grundsätze einer Wettbewerbsordnung* (2nd edn Godesberg, Helmut Küpper 1947)

Milgrom, P and Roberts, J, 'Predation, Reputation and Entry Deterrence' (1982) 27 Journal of Economic Theory 280

Montagnani, ML, 'Predatory and Exclusionary Innovation: Which Legal Standard for Software Integration in the Context of the Competition Versus Intellectual Property Rights Clash?' (2006) 37 Intl Rev IP & Comp L 304

Monti, G, 'The Scope of Collective Dominance under Article 82 EC' (2001) 38 CML Rev 131

—— 'Article 81 EC and Public Policy' (2002) 39 CML Rev 1057

—— 'The Concept of Dominance in Article 82' (2006) 2 European Competition Journal 31

—— *EC Competition Law* (Cambridge, CUP 2007)

—— 'Article 82 EC: What Future for the Effects-Based Approach?' (2010) 1 Journal of European Competition Law & Practice 2

Morgan, EJ, 'The Treatment of Oligopoly under the European Merger Control Regulation' (1996) 41 Antitrust Bull 203

Morgan, JN, 'Bilateral Monopoly and the Competitive Output' (1949) 63 Quarterly Journal of Economics 371

Möschel, W, 'Competition Policy From An Ordo Point of View' in Peacock, A and Willgerodt, H, (eds), *German Neo-Liberals and The Social Market Economy* (London, MacMillan 1989)

—— 'Competition as a Basic Element of the Social Market Economy' (2001) 2 EBOR 713

Mosso, CE et al, 'Article 82' in Faull, J and Nikpay, A (eds), *The EC Law of Competition* (2nd edn Oxford, OUP 2007) 313

Motta, M, *Competition Policy, Theory and Practice* (Cambridge, CUP 2004)

—— 'The European Commission's Guidance Communication on Article 82' (2009) 30 ECLR 593

—— 'Michelin II—The Treatment of Rebates' in Lyons, B (ed), *Cases in European Competition Policy: the Economic Analysis* (Cambridge, CUP 2009)

Motta, M and de Streel, A, 'Excessive Pricing and Price Squeeze under EU Law' in Ehlermann, CD and Atanasiu, I (eds), *European Competition Law Annual 2003: What Is an Abuse of a Dominant Position?* (Oxford, Hart Publishing 2006) 91

Motulsky, H, *Principes d'une réalisation méthodique du droit privé: la théorie des éléments générateurs des droits subjectifs* (reprinted Paris, Dalloz 2002)

Moura e Silva, M, 'Predatory Pricing under Article 82 and the Recoupment Test: Do Not Go Gentle Into That Good Night' (2009) 30 ECLR 61

Mowbray, A, 'A Study of the Principle of Fair Balance in the Jurisprudence of the European Court of Human Rights' (2010) 10 Human Rights L Rev 289

Muller, U and Rodenhausen, A, 'The Rise and Fall of the Essential Facility Doctrine' (2008) 29 ECLR 310

Muysert, P, 'Price Discrimination—An Unreliable Indicator of Market Power' (2004) 25 ECLR 350

Nagy, CI, 'Refusal to Deal and the Doctrine of Essential Facilities in US and EC Competition Law: A Comparative Perspective and a Proposal for a Workable Analytical Framework' (2007) 32 EL Rev 664

Nalebuff, BJ, 'Bundling, Tying, and Portfolio Effects: Part 1—Conceptual Issues', DTI Economics Paper No 1 (February 2003)

—— 'Bundling as a Way to Leverage Monopoly' 1 Yale School of Management Working Paper No ES-36 (1 September 2004)

—— 'Bundling as an Entry Barrier' (2004) 119 Quarterly Journal of Economics 159

Naughton, MC and Wolfram, R, 'The Antitrust Risks of Unilateral Conduct in Standard Setting, in the Light of the FTC's case against Rambus Inc' (2004) 49 Antitrust Bull 69

Nazzini, R, 'Article 81 EC Between Time Present and Time Past: A Normative Critique of "Restriction of Competition" in EU law' (2006) 43 CML Rev 497

—— 'The Wood Began to Move: An Essay on Consumer Welfare, Evidence and Burden of Proof in Article 82 Cases' (2006) 31 EL Rev 518

—— 'Potency and Act of the Principle of Effectiveness: The Development of Competition Law Remedies in Community Law' in Barnard, C and Odudu, O (eds), *The Outer Limits of European Union Law* (Oxford, Hart Publishing 2009)

—— 'Welfare Objective and Enforcement Standard in Competition Law', in Bernitz, U and Ezrachi, A (eds), *Private Labels, Brands and Competition Policy* (Oxford, OUP 2009)

Nebbia, P, 'Damages Actions for the Infringement of EC Competition Law: Compensation or Deterrence?' (2008) 33 EL Rev 23

Neven, D, Papandropoulos, P, and Seabright, P, *Trawling for Minnows* (London, Centre for Economic Policy Research 1998)

Neven, D and Röller, L-H, 'Consumer Surplus vs Welfare Standard in a Political Economy Model of Merger Control' (2005) 23 Intl J Ind Org 829

Newmark, CM, 'Administrative Control, Buyer Concentration, and Price-Cost Margins' (1989) 71 Rev Econ & Stat 74

Nguyen, TT, 'Price Squeezing: Linkline in the United States—No Link to the European Union' (2010) 41 Intl Rev IP & Comp L 316

Niels, G, 'Collective Dominance: More than Just Oligopolistic Interdependence' (2001) 22 ECLR 168

Niels, G and Jenkins, H, 'Reform of Article 82: Where the Link between Dominance and Effects Breaks Down' (2005) 26 ECLR 605

Nilssen, T, 'Two Kinds of Consumer Switching Costs' (1992) 23 RAND Journal of Economics 579

Nordemann, JB, 'Buying Power and Sophisticated Buyers in Merger Control Law: The Need for a More Sophisticated Approach' (1995) 16 ECLR 270

Nozick, R, *Anarchy, State, and Utopia* (New York, Basic Books 1974)

O'Brien, DP and Shaffer, G, 'The Welfare Effects of Forbidding Discriminatory Discounts: A Secondary Line Analysis of Robinson-Patman' (1994) 10 JL Econ & Org 296

O'Donoghue, R and Padilla, AJ, *The Law and Economics of Article 82 EC* (Oxford, Hart Publishing 2006)

Odudu, O, 'Interpreting Article 81(1) Demonstrating restrictive effect' (2001) 26 EL Rev 261

—— 'The Role of Specific Intent in Section 1 of the Sherman Act' (2002) 25 World Competition 463

—— *The Boundaries of EC Competition Law: The Scope of Article 81* (Oxford, OUP 2006)

OECD, 'Barriers to Entry', Best Practice Policy Roundtables on Competition Policy (2005)

—— 'Monopsony and Buyer Power', Best Practice Roundtables on Competition Policy (2008)

OFT, *Assessment of Conduct: Draft Competition Law Guideline for Consultation* (OFT414a, 2004)

Ohana, G, Hansen, M, and Shah, O, 'Disclosure and Negotiation of Licensing Terms Prior to Adoption of Industry Standards: Preventing Another Patent Ambush?' (2003) 24 ECLR 644

Ordover, JA and Panzar, JC, 'On the Nonlinear Pricing of Inputs' (1982) 23 Intl Economic Rev 659

Ordover, JA and Willig, RD, 'An Economic Definition of Predation: Pricing and Product Innovation' (1981) 91 Yale LJ 8

Osborne, M and Pitchik, C, 'Price Competition in a Capacity-Constrained Duopoly' (1986) 38 Journal of Economic Theory 238

Overd, A, 'Buyer Power' (2001) 22 ECLR 249

OXERA, 'Assessing Profitability in Competition Policy Analysis' OFT Economic Discussion Paper 6 (OFT657, July 2003)

Page, WH, 'Microsoft and the Limits of Antitrust' (2010) 6 J Comp L & Econ 33

Park, JH, *Patents and Industry Standards* (Cheltenman, Edward Elgar Publishing 2010)

Parker, D, 'A Screening Device for Tacit Collusion Concerns' (2006) 27 ECLR 424

Parker, H, *Of a Free Trade* (London, Fr Neile for Robert Bostock, dwelling in Pauls Church-yard at the Signe of the King's Head 1648)

Parkin, M, Powell, M, and Matthews, K, *Economics* (5th edn Harlow, Pearson Education Ltd 2003)

Pauly, MV, 'Monopsony Power in Health Insurance: Thinking Straight While Standing on Your Head' (1987) 6 Journal of Health Economics 73

—— 'Market Power, Monopsony, and Health Insurance Markets' (1988) 7 Journal of Health Economics 111

Pepperkorn, L, 'IP Licences and Competition Rules: Striking the Right Balance' (2003) 26 World Competition 527

Perry, MK, 'Vertical Integration: Determinants and Effects' in Schmalensee, R and Willig, RD (eds), *Handbook of Industrial Organization: Vol I* (Amsterdam, North Holland 1989)

Perry, MK and Porter, RH, 'Oligopoly and the Incentive for Horizontal Merger' (1985) 75 American Economic Rev 219

Petritsi, EG, 'The Case of Unilateral Patent Ambush under EC Competition Rules' (2005) 28 World Competition 25

Pheasant, J, 'Damages Actions for Breach of the EC Antitrust Rules: the European Commission's Green Paper' (2006) 27 ECLR 365

Phillips, A, 'A Critique of Empirical Studies of Relations between Market Structure and Profitability' (1976) 24 Journal of Industrial Economics 241

Pigou, AC, *The Economics of Welfare* (4th edn London, MacMillan 1932)

Pinder, J, *The Building of the European Union* (3rd edn Oxford, OUP 1998)

Pitofsky, R, Patterson, D, and Hooks, J, 'The Essential Facilities Doctrine under US Antitrust Law' (2002) 70 Antitrust LJ 443

Pittman, R, 'Consumer Surplus as the Appropriate Standard for Antitrust Enforcement' (2007) 3 Competition Policy International 205

Polinsky, AM and Shavell, S, 'Legal Error, Litigation, and the Incentive to Obey the Law' (1989) JL Econ & Org 99

Polo, M, 'Price Squeeze: Lessons from the Telecom Italia Case' (2007) 2 J Comp L & Econ 453

Popofsky, MS, 'Defining Exclusionary Conduct: Section 2, the Rule of Reason, and the Unifying Principle Underlying Antitrust Rules' (2006) 73 Antitrust LJ 435

Porter, ME, *The Competitive Advantage of Nations* (New York, The Free Press 1990)

Porter, R, 'A Study of Cartel Stability: The Joint Executive Committee, 1880–1886' (1983) 14 Bell Journal of Economics 301

Posner, RA, *Antitrust Law: An Economic Perspective* (2nd edn Chicago, University of Chicago Press 2001)

—— 'Vertical Restraints and Antitrust Policy' (2005) 72 U Chi L Rev 229

Quigley, C, *European State Aid Law and Policy* (2nd edn Oxford, Hart Publishing 2009)

Rahnasto, I, *Intellectual Property Rights, External Effects and Antitrust Law* (Oxford, OUP 2005)

Ramsey, FP, 'A Contribution to the Theory of Taxation' (1927) 37 Economic Journal 47

Rawls, J, *A Theory of Justice* (rev edn Harvard, Harvard University Press 1999).

Reich, N, 'Some Reflections on Rethinking Community Consumer Law' in The International Academy of Commercial and Consumer Law, *New Developments in International Commercial and Consumer Law* (Oxford, Hart Publishing 1998)

Rey P, and Tirole, J, 'A Primer on Forelcosure' in Armstrong, M and Porter, R (eds), *Handbook of Industrial Organisation: Vol III* (Amsterdam, North Holland, 2007) 418

Ricardo, D, *On the Principles of Political Economy and Taxation* (London, Empiricus Books 2002)

Ridyard, D, 'Essential Facilities and the Obligation to Supply Competitors under UK and EC Competition Law' (1996) 17 ECLR 438

—— 'Exclusionary Pricing and Price Discrimination Abuses under Article 82—An Economic Analysis' (2002) 23 ECLR 286

—— 'Tying and Bundling—Cause for Complaint?' (2005) 26 ECLR 316

Riley, A, 'EC Antitrust Modernisation: The Commission Does Very Nicely—Thank You! Part One: Regulation 1 and the Notification Burden' (2003) 24 ECLR 604

—— 'EC Antitrust Modernisation: The Commission Does Very Nicely—Thank You! Part Two: Between the Idea and the Reality: Decentralisation under Regulation 1' (2003) 24 ECLR 657

Riordan, MH, 'Anticompetitive Vertical Integration by a Dominant Firm' (1998) 88 American Economic Rev 1232

Ritter, C, 'Does the Law of Predatory Pricing and Cross-Subsidisation Need a Radical Rethink?' (2004) 27 World Competition 613

—— 'Refusal to Deal and "Essential Facilities": Does Intellectual Property Require Special Deference Compared to Tangible Property?' (2005) 28 World Competition 281

Rivas, J and Horspool, M (eds), Modernisation and Decentralisation of EC Competition Law (The Hague, Kluwer Law International 2000)

Rizzuto, F, 'The Private Enforcement of European Union Competition Law: What Next?' (2010) 3 Global Competition Litigation Rev 57

Roberts, J, 'A Signalling Model of Predatory Pricing' (1986) 38 Oxford Economic Papers (supplement) 75

Roberts, KWS, 'Welfare Considerations of Nonlinear Pricing' (1979) 89 Economic Journal 66

Robinson, J, *The Economics of Imperfect Competition* (London, MacMillan 1933) 206

Rodgers, BJ, 'Oligopolistic Market Failure: Collective Dominance Versus Complex Monopoly' (1995) 16 ECLR 21

Röpke, W, *Civitas Humana* (Erlenbach-Zürich, Eugen Rentsch 1946)

Rosenbluth, G, 'Measures of Concentration' in National Bureau of Economic Research, *Business Concentration and Price Policy,* (Princeton New Jersey, Princeton University Press 1955)

Ross, TW, 'Cartel Stability and Product Differentiation' (1992) 10 Intl J Ind Org 1

Rotemberg, J and Saloner, G, 'A Supergame-Theoretic Model of Price Wars during Booms' (1986) 76 American Economic Rev 390

Roth, P and Rose, V (eds), *Bellamy & Child European Community Law of Competition* (6th edn Oxford, OUP 2008)

Rothschild, R, 'Cartel Stability when Costs are Heterogeneous' (1999) 17 Intl J Ind Org 717

Roughton, A, 'Intellectual Property Rights' in Roth, P and Rose, V (eds), *Bellamy & Child European Community Law of Competition* (6th edn Oxford, OUP 2008)

Rousseva, E, 'Modernizing by Eradicating: How the Commission's New Approach to Article 81 EC Dispenses With the Need to Apply Article 82 EC to Vertical Restraints' (2005) 42 CML Rev 587

—— *Rethinking Exclusionary Abuses in EU Competition Law* (Oxford, Hart Publishing 2010)

Ruffert, M, 'Rights and Remedies in European Community law: A Comparative View' (1997) 34 CML Rev 307

Salinger, MA, 'Vertical Mergers and Market Foreclosure' (1988) 103 Quarterly Journal of Economics 345

Saloner, G, 'Predation, Mergers and Incomplete Information' (1987) 18 RAND Journal of Economics 165

Salop, SC, 'Question: What is the Real and Proper Antitrust Welfare Standard? Answer: The True Consumer Welfare Standard', presented to the Antitrust Modernization Commission (4 November 2005)

—— 'Exclusionary Conduct, Effect on Consumers, and the Flawed Profit Sacrifice Standard' (2006) 73 Antitrust LJ 311

—— 'The Controversy over the Proper Antitrust Standard for Anticompetitive Exclusionary Conduct' in Hawk, BE (ed), *International Antitrust Law & Policy: Fordham Competition Law Institute 2006* (New York, Juris Publishing 2007) 477

Salop, SC and Romaine, RC, 'Preserving Monopoly: Economic Analysis, Legal Standards, and Microsoft' (1999) 7 Geo Mason L Rev 617

Samuels, D, 'Is Modernisation Working?' (2005) 8 Global Competition Rev 17

Scherer, FM, 'Predatory Pricing and the Sherman Act: A Comment' (1976) 89 Harv L Rev 869

—— 'Some Last Words on Predatory Pricing' (1976) 89 Harv L Rev 901

Scherer, FM and Ross, D, *Industrial Market Structure and Economic Performance* (3rd edn Boston, Houghton Mifflin 1990)

Schmalensee, R, 'A Note on the Theory of Vertical Integration' (1973) 81 Journal of Political Economy 442

—— 'Output and Welfare Implications of Monopolistic Third-Degree Price Discrimination' (1981) 71 American Economic Rev 242

—— 'Product Differentiation Advantages of Pioneering Brands' (1983) 73 American Economic Rev 250

—— 'Competitive Advantage and Collusive Optima' (1987) 5 Intl J Ind Org 351

Schmidt, I, *Wettbewerbspolitik und Kartellrect: Eine Einführung* (4th revised edn New Jersey, G Fischer 1993)

Schmidt, HKS, 'Private Enforcement—Is Article 82 EC Special?' in Mackenrodt, M, Conde Gallego, B, and Enchelmaier, S (eds), *Abuse of Dominant Position: New Interpretation, New Enforcement Mechanisms?* (Berlin, Springer 2008) 137

Schopenhauer, A, *The World as Will and Representation*, vol 1 (Norman, J, Welchman, A, and Janaway, C (eds and trs), Cambridge, CUP 2010)

Schumacher, U, 'Buyer Structure and Seller Performance in US Manufacturing Industries' (1991) 73 Rev Econ & Stat 277

Schuman Declaration, The, Declaration by Robert Schuman French Foreign Minister 9 May 1950

Schumpeter, JA, *Capitalism, Socialism and Democracy* (6th edn London, Unwin Paperbacks 1987)

Schwartz, B, *The Paradox of Choice: Why More is Less* (New York, HarperCollins 2005)

Schwartz, M, 'Third-Degree Price Discrimination and Output: Generalising a Welfare Result' (1990) American Economic Rev 80 1259

Schweitzer, H, 'The History, Interpretation and Underlying Principles of Section 2 Sherman Act and Article 82 EC' in Ehlermann, C-D and Marquis, M (eds), *European Competition Law Annual 2007: A Reformed Approach to Article 82 EC* (Oxford, Hart Publishing 2008)

Serra Dominguez, M, 'La preuve dans le procès civil espagnol' in Lebre de Freitas, JM (ed), *The Law of Evidence in the European Union* (The Hague, Kluwer Law International 2004) 381

Sharfstein, D, 'A Policy to Prevent Rational Test-Market Predation' (1984) 2 RAND Journal of Economics 229

Sheperd, WG, *The Economics of Industrial Organization* (2nd edn New Jersey, Prentice-Hall 1985)

—— 'The Twilight of Antitrust' (1986) 18 Antitrust Law and Economics Rev 21

Sher, B, 'Price Discounts and Michelin II: What Goes Around, Comes Around' (2002) 24 ECLR 482

Sibony, A-L, *Le Juge et le raisonnement économique en droit de la concurrence* (Paris, LGDJ 2008)

Sidak, JG, 'Patent Hold-up and Oligopsonistic Collusion in Standard-Setting Organizations' (2009) 5 J Comp L & Econ 123

Smith, A, *An Inquiry into the Nature and Causes of Wealth of Nations* 2 Vols (London, Methuen 1904)

Snell, J, 'The Notion of Market Access, A Notion or a Slogan?' (2010) 47 CML Rev 437

Snyder, CM, 'A Dynamic Theory of Countervailing Power' (1996) 27 RAND Journal of Economics 747

Soames, T, 'An Analysis of the Principles of Concerted Practice and Collective Dominance: a Distinction without a Difference' (1996) 17 ECLR 24

Spector, D, 'Loyalty Rebates: An Assessment of Competition Concerns and a Proposed Structured Rule of Reason' (2005) 1 Competition Policy International 89

Spence, M, 'Product Selection, Fixed Costs, and Monopolistic Competition' (1976) 43 Rev Econ Stud 217

Springer, U, ' "Meeting Competition": Justification of Price Discrimination under EC and US Antitrust Law' (1997) 18 ECLR 251

Staiger, RW, and Wolak, FA, 'Collusive Pricing with Capacity Constraints in the Presence of Demand Uncertainty' (1992) 23 RAND Journal of Economics 203

Stefanadis, C, 'Downstream Vertical Foreclosure and Upstream Innovation' (1997) 45 Journal of Industrial Economics 445

Steiner, J, 'How to Make the Action Suit the Case: Domestic Remedies for Breach of EEC Law' (1987) 12 EL Rev 102

Steiner, J, Woods, L, and Twigg-Flesner, C, *EU Law* (9th edn Oxford, OUP 2006)

Stigler, GJ, '*United States v Loew's Inc*: A Note on Block Booking' (1963) Sup Ct Rev 152

—— 'Barriers to Entry, Economies of Scale, and Firm Size' in Stigler, GJ, *The Organization of Industry* (reprinted Chicago, University of Chicago Press 1983) 67

—— 'Imperfections in the Capital Market' in GJ Stigler, *The Organization of Industry* (reprinted Chicago, The University of Chicago Press 1983) 113

Stone Sweet, A and Mathews, J, 'Proportionality Balancing and Global Constitutionalism' (2008) 47 Columbia Journal of Transnational Law 73

—— 'Proportionality, Judicial Review and Global Constitutionalism' in Bongiovanni, G, Sartor, G, and Valentini, C (eds), *Reasonableness and Law* (London, Springer 2009)

Stothers, C, 'Refusal to Supply as Abuse of a Dominant Position: Essential Facilities in the European Union' (2001) 22 ECLR 256

Stratakis, A, 'Comparative Analysis of the US and EU Approach and Enforcement of the Essential Facilities Doctrine' (2006) 27 ECLR 434

Stroux, S, 'Article 82—Dominance and Oligopolies' in Amato, G and Ehlermann, C-D, *EC Competition Law: A Critical Assessment* (Oxford, Hart Publishing 2007) 209

Stucke, ME, 'How Do (and Should) Competition Authorities Treat a Dominant Firm's Deception?' (2010) 63 SMU L Rev 1069

Stuyck, J, 'EC Competition Law After Modernisation: More than Ever in the Interest of Consumers' (2005) 28 Journal of Consumer Policy 1

Subramanian, S, 'Patent Trolls in Thickets: Who is Fishing under the Bridge?' (2008) 30 EIPR 182

Swanson, DG and Baumol, WJ, 'Reasonable and Non-Discriminatory (RAND) Royalties, Standards Selection, and Control of Market Power' (2005) 73 Antitrust LJ 1

Taylor, M, *International Competition Law: A New Dimension for the WTO* (Cambridge, CUP 2009)

Telser, LG, 'Cutthroat Competition and the Long Purse' (1966) 9 Journal of Law and Economics 259

Temple Lang, J, 'Community Antitrust Law: Compliance and Enforcement' (1981) 18 CML Rev 335

—— 'EEC Competition Actions in Member States: Claims for Damages, Declarations and Injunctions for Breach of Community Antitrust Law' in Hawk, BE (ed), *Annual Proceedings of the Fordham Corporate Law Institute: Antitrust and Trade Policies of the European Economic Community* (New York, Matthew Bender 1984) 219

—— 'Defining Legitimate Competition: Companies' Duties to Supply Competitors and Access to Essential Facilities' (1994) 18 Fordham Intl LJ 437

Temple Lang, J and O'Donoghue, R, 'Defining Legitimate Competition: How to Clarify Pricing Abuses under Article 82 EC' (2002) 26 Fordham Intl LJ 83

Thayer, JB, *A Preliminary Treatise on Evidence at the Common Law* (London, Sweet & Maxwell 1898)

Thompson, R and O'Flaherty, J, 'Article 82' in Roth, P and Rose, V (eds), *Bellamy & Child European Community Law of Competition* (6th edn Oxford, OUP 2008)

Tiley, J, *Revenue Law* (5th edn Oxford, Hart Publishing 2005)

Tirole, J, *The Theory of Industrial Organization* (Cambridge, Mass, MIT Press 1988) 379

Townley, C, *Article 81 and Public Policy* (Oxford, Hart Publishing 2009)

Townsend, RM, 'Optimal Contracts and Competitive Markets with Costly State Verification' (1979) 21 Journal of Economic Theory 265

Tridimas, T, 'Proportionality in Community Law: Searching for the Appropriate Standard of Scrutiny' in Ellis, E (ed), *The Principle of Proportionality in the Laws of Europe* (Oxford, Hart Publishing 1999) 65

—— *The General Principles of EC Law* (2nd edn Oxford, OUP 2006)

Tryfonidou, A, 'Further Steps on the Road to Convergence among the Market Freedoms' (2010) 35 EL Rev 36

UK Competition Commission, *Store Cards Market Investigation* (Competition Commission, 7 March 2006)

—— *Market Investigation into Supply of Bulk Liquefied Petroleum Gas for Domestic Use* (Competition Commission, 29 June 2006)

Valimaki, M, 'A flexible Approach to RAND Licensing' (2008) 29 ECLR 686

Van Bael, I and Bellis, J-F, *Competition Law of the European Community* (5th edn Alphen aan den Rijn, Kluwer Law International 2010)

Van den Bergh, RJ, 'The Difficult Reception of Economic Analysis in European Competition Law' in Cucinotta, P, Pardolesi, R, and Van den Bergh, R (eds), *Post-Chicago Developments in Antitrust Law* (Cheltenham, Edward Elgar 2002)

Van den Bergh, RJ and Camesasca, PD, *European Competition Law and Economics: A Comparative Perspective* (2nd edn London, Sweet & Maxwell 2006)

Varian, HR, 'Price Discrimination and Social Welfare' (1985) 75 American Economic Rev 870

Veljanovski, C, 'Markets Without Substitutes: Substitution Versus Constraints as the Key to Market Definition' (2010) 31 ECLR 122

Venit, JS, 'Two Steps Forward and No Steps Back: Economic Analysis and Oligopolistic Dominance after Kali & Salz' (1998) 35 CML Rev 1101

—— 'Article 82: The Last Frontier—Fighting Fire With Fire?' (2005) 28 Fordham Intl LJ 1157

Vernon, JM and Graham, DA, 'Profitability of Monopolization by Vertical Integration' (1971) 79 Journal of Political Economy 924

Vickers, J, 'Competition and Regulation in Vertically Related Markets' (1995) 62 Rev Econ Stud 1

—— 'Abuse of Market Power' (2005) 115 Economic Journal 244

—— 'Market Power in Competition Cases' (2006) 2 European Competition Journal 3

—— 'Some Economics of Abuse of Dominance', Department of Economics, University of Oxford, Discussion Paper 376 (November 2007)

Vogelaar, FOW, 'The Compulsory Licence of Intellectual Property Rights under the EC Competition Rules: An Analysis of the Exception to the General Rule of Ownership Immunity from Competition Rules' (2009) 6 Competition L Rev 117

von Ungern-Sternberg, T, 'Countervailing power revisited' (1996) 14 Intl J Ind Org 507

von Weizsäcker, CC, 'A Welfare Analysis of Barriers to Entry' (1980) 11 Bell Journal of Economics 399

Wade, HWR and Forsyth, CF, *Administrative Law* (10th edn Oxford, OUP 2009)

Waelbroeck, D, 'Private Enforcement of Competition Rules and its Limits' in Hutchings, M and Andenas, M, *Competition Law Yearbook 2002* (London, British Institute of International and Comparative Law 2003) 369

—— '*Michelin II*: A Per Se Rule Against Rebates By Dominant Companies?' (2005) 1 J Comp L & Econ 149

Waelbroeck, W, 'Meeting Competition: Is This a Valid Defence for a Firm in a Dominant Position?' in *Studi in onore di Francesco Capotorti: Divenire sociale e adeguamento del diritto* (Milan, Giuffrè 1999) Vol 2, 481

Warren-Boulton, FL, 'Vertical Control with Variable Proportions' (1974) 82 Journal of Political Economy 783

Werden, GJ, 'Economic Evidence on the Existence of Collusion: Reconciling Antitrust Law with Oligopoly Theory' (2004) 71 Antitrust LJ 719

—— 'Competition Policy on Exclusionary Conduct: Towards an Effects-Based Analysis' (2006) 2 European Competition Journal 53

—— 'Identifying Exclusionary Conduct Under Section 2: The "No Economic Sense" Test' (2006) 73 Antitrust LJ 413

—— 'Identifying Single-Firm Exclusionary Conduct: From Vague Concepts to Administrable Rules' in Hawk, BE (ed), *International Antitrust Law & Policy: Fordham Competition Law 2006* (New York, Juris Publishing 2007)

Wesseling, R, *The Modernisation EC Antitrust Law* (Oxford, Hart Publishing 2000)

Whinston, MD, 'Tying, Foreclosure, and Exclusion' (1990) 80 American Economic Rev 837

Whish, R, 'The Enforcement of EC Competition Law in the Domestic Courts of Member States' (1994) 15 ECLR 60

—— *Competition Law* (6th edn Oxford, OUP 2008)

Williamson, OE, 'Predatory Pricing: A Strategic and Welfare Analysis' (1977) 87 Yale LJ 284

—— 'Williamson on Predatory Pricing II' (1979) 88 Yale LJ 1183

Wils, WPJ, 'Should Private Enforcement Be Encouraged in Europe?' (2003) 26 World Competition 473

—— 'The Relationship between Public Antitrust Enforcement and Private Actions for Damages' (2009) 32 World Competition 3

—— 'Discretion and Prioritisation in Public Antitrust Enforcement, in Particular EU Antitrust Enforcement' (2011) 34 World Competition (forthcoming)

Wilson, JO, 'The "Junk Bond King" of Wall Street: A Discourse on Business Ethics' in Coughlin, RM (ed), *Morality and Efficiency: New Perspectives on Socio-Economics* (New York, ME Sharpe 1991)

—— 'Economy, Society and Ethics' in Ekins, P and Max-Neef, MA (eds), *Real Life Economics: Understanding Wealth Creation* (London and New York, Routledge 1992)

Witt, AC, 'The Commission's Guidance Paper on Abusive Exclusionary Conduct—More Radical Than it Appears?' (2010) 35 EL Rev 214

Wolff, N, *Poverty and Income Distribution* (2nd edn Hoboken, Wiley-Blackwell 2009)

WTO, '10 Benefits of the WTO Trading System' The World Trade Organization Pamphlets (2008)

Wurmnest, W, *Marktmacht under Verdrängungsmissbrauch: Eine rechtsvergleichende Neubestimmung des Verhältnisses von Recht und Ökonomik in der Missbrauchsaufsicht über marktbeherrschende Unternehmen* (Tübingen, Mohr Siebeck 2010)

Yoshida, Y, 'Third-Degree Price Discrimination in Input Markets: Output and Welfare' (2000) 90 American Economic Rev 240

Zhang, L, 'Refusal to License Intellectual Property Rights under Article 82 EC in Light of Standardisation Context' (2010) 32 EIPR 402

Index

Printed and bound by CPI Group (UK) Ltd, Croydon, CR0 4YY